SEVEN WORKS OF VASUBANDHU

RELIGIONS OF ASIA SERIES

Number 4

SEVEN WORKS OF VASUBANDHU

The Buddhist Psychological Doctor

STEFAN ANACKER

MOTILAL BANARSIDASS
Delhi Varanasi Patna Madras

First Published 1984, Reprint 1986

MOTILAL BANARSIDASS
Bungalow Road, Jawahar Nagar, Delhi 110 007
Branches
Chowk, Varanasi 221 001
Ashok Rajpath, Patna 800 004
6 Appar Swamy Koil Street, Mylapore, Madras 600 004

ISBN: 81–208–0203–9

PRINTED IN INDIA
BY JAINENDRA PRAKASH JAIN AT SHRI JAINENDRA PRESS, A-45 NARAINA INDUSTRIAL AREA, PHASE I, NEW DELHI 110 028 AND PUBLISHED BY NARENDRA PRAKASH JAIN FOR MOTILAL BANARSIDASS, DELHI 110 007

TABLE OF CONTENTS

ABBREVIATIONS FOR JOURNALS, ETC.

ASR	*Archaeological Survey of India—Reports*
BARB	*Bulletin de l'Académie Royale de Belgique*
BEFEO	*Bulletin de l'École Française d'Extrême-Orient*
BSOAS	*Bulletin of the London School of Oriental and African Studies*
EA	*Études Asiatiques*
HJAS	*Harvard Journal of Asian Studies*
IA	*Indian Antiquary*
IBK	*Indogaku Bukkyo Kenko*
IHQ	*Indian Historical Quarterly*
ISCRL	*Indian Studies in Honor of Charles R. Lanman*
IsMeo	Istituto per studie del medie e estremo oriente
JA	*Journal Asiatique*
JAOS	*Journal of the American Oriental Society*
JPTS	*Journal of the Pali Text Society*
JRAS	*Journal of the Royal Asiatic Society*
MCB	*Mélanges Chinois et Bouddhiques*
RO	*Rocznik Orientalistczy*
WZKM	*Wiener Zeitschrift für die Kunde des Morgenlandes*
WZKSOA	*Wiener Zeitschrift für die Kunde Süd-und Ostasiens*

PREFACE

The purpose of this book is to present a Buddhist philosopher, who, though among the most famous, cannot really be said to be well-known. The thought of Vasubandhu has usually been presented in an overly schematic and perhaps misleading way which does not do justice to this many-sided genius. The writings of Vasubandhu are also very relevant to the present time.

In these translations, it has been the goal to avoid the practise usually followed with Indian philosophical studies, where translated texts are encumbered with the original Sanskrit expressions in parentheses. This was done to make the texts as free-flowing as they are in the original, as has been done, for instance, in previous translations of Greek philosophers. Where the original Sanskrit texts exist, these have also been given here, and for key terms and their translations the reader is referred to the trilingual glossary. Professional Indologists may in fact prefer reading the glossary first, so that they know from the outset the original Sanskrit of technical terms. Logicians, on the other hand, will be most attracted to the first treatise presented here, and spiritual seekers certainly most to the sixth.

The work on this book has taken place over a period of many years, and on three different continents. As there is always room for critical re-appraisal in such studies, it is true that some few things I would do differently at this moment, if I were beginning these translations now. On the "prides", for instance, it is probably better to follow the translation of La Vallée Poussin in *Kośa* V (cf. *Discussion of the Five Aggregates*, p. 68), though mine has the advantage of avoiding the concepts of "superior" and "inferior" which Vasubandhu warns us against. It is also well to remember that the ethical categories "beneficial" (*kuśala*), "unbeneficial" (*akuśala*), and "indeterminate" (*avyākṛta*) refer not only to their effect of alleviation or infliction of suffering for others, but also to the "karmic" results for the "agent" "himself". Unless this is kept in mind, the statement that beneficial and unbeneficial acts cannot take place without conscious discrimination and volition (p. 62) may be misunderstood, as there may be totally unintentional actions harming to others for which the "agent" bears no karmic responsibility according to Vasubandu. As regards the list of "motivating dispositions" (*saṃskāra*), which have always been a source of controversy (even in the third century B.C.!), it is certain that some scholars would translate several of these items differently. But my translations are in conformity with Vasubandhu's own definitions, and on the whole I am quite happy with them.

Like the wandering youth Sudhana in the *Gaṇḍavyūha-sūtra*, I can honestly say that I have learned something from everyone I have ever met. To give complete acknowledgements is thus impossible. However, the following people who have been particularly helpful to me at various stages of this work can be mentioned: the venerable Gyaltrul Rimpoche, for some direct insights into Samantabhadra; Geshe Sopa (bZod-pa), for the meanings of certain technical turns of phrases in the *Karma-siddhi-prakaraṇa*; Jinamitra and all the other previous scholars who have worked on these texts; the eminent Prof. Gadjin Nagao, of the University of Kyoto, for this edition and index of the *Madhyānta-vibhāga-bhāṣya*; Professor T.V. Venkatachala Shastri, of the University of Mysore, for insight, through Old Kannada literature, into the Jaina point of view; P.K. Raja, of Pāḍuwārahaḷḷi, Mysore City, for modern Hindu applications of Mahāyāna Buddhist ethical thought; Prof. Jacques May, of the University of Lausanne, for his readiness to lend out volumes of his Tibetan Canon; the late Prof. Richard Robinson, for founding the Buddhist studies department at the University of Wisconsin, without which I would never have learned about these things at all; Prof. Alex Wayman, now of Columbia University, for introducing me to written Tibetan; Prof. Douglas D. Daye, now of Bowling Green University (Ohio), for many ideas on Indian logic and for the translations of the names of the members of the Indian inference-schema; the editors and printers at Motilal Banarsidass, for bringing out this book; and my father, the late Robert H. Anacker, who taught me so much about European cultural history that I had to turn to India to find something new.

STEFAN ANACKER

GENERAL INTRODUCTION

VASUBANDHU is one of the most prominent figures in the development of Mahāyāna Buddhism in India. His name can be found in any history of Buddhism or of India in the Gupta period. However, though many of his numerous works have been translated from the original Sanskrit into Chinese and Tibetan, and much later at least a few into French, hardly any have up to now appeared in English. The seven treatises presented here, though only a minuscule portion of what he wrote, are complete works with a most varied range of topics, and can serve at least as an introduction to his thought. Aside from the enormous influence he has had on almost the entire range of subsequent Buddhist writing, Vasubandhu makes particularly interesting reading because of the great scope of his interests, the flexibility, originality, and openness of his thought, and his motivation to alleviate suffering, particularly that unnecessary suffering that comes from constricted and constructed mental activity. He has used a great variety of therapeutic methods for this purpose, and, as a result, his name has a place in the lineages of teachers of practises as diverse as Pure Land[1] and Zen.[2] His works are in intensely diverse literary formats, including religious poetry[3], ethical animal fables[4], commentaries on sūtras[5] and treatises, and independent treatises in both prose and verse. His range of interests is also correspondingly vast, and his mental consciousness is equally penetrating when dealing with logic[6], psychology[7], the history of the Buddhist Canon[8], medicine[9], the most practical instructions for meditation[10], and the signless melting of all mental borders.[11] He demonstrates a fertility, flexibility, range, and profundity of thought that quite overwhelms : by any standards, he is one of the greatest of philosophic and therapeutic writers.

To Vasubandhu, dogmatic reliance on any one method never exists, and there may be even within one work multiple and constantly unfolding outlooks on a particular range of problems. This is why it is easy to misunderstand the purpose of his writings if only some works are considered. There has been a great deal of misrepresentation of what Vasubandhu's Mahāyāna methods are attempting to do, simply because certain few works were given a pre-eminent position at the expense of others, and even these weren't always understood. A young man much interested in Nāgārjuna and the *Prajñā-pāramitā-sūtras* once termed Vasubandhu a "reifier", since it is not generally said, but obvious when one reads widely in his works that anything he "reifies" he also dissolves. And then there is the standard discussion of Vasubandhu as an "idealist" philosopher, which rests mainly on the interpretations of Hsüan-tsang, who seems to have been most impressed by the preliminary portions of works, rather than their conclusions. Even Vasubandhu's most conscientious commentators, such as Sthiramati, seem often to become bogged down in what is least essential—sometimes even making distinctions never made by the master himself.[12] Vasubandhu uses such a wide variety of means with such skill that it is easy to see how this might happen. The Tibetan historian Bu-ston makes a suggestive statement when he says, "The teacher Sthiramati was even more learned than his teacher Vasubandhu in Abhidharma; the venerable Dignāga proved greater than his teacher Vasubandhu in the field of logic, and the saint Vimuktisena excelled his teacher Vasubandhu in the knowledge of *Prajñā-pāramitā*."[13] Though these gentlemen may have surpassed Vasubandhu in the mastery of one particular method, the open-endedness and multiplicity of therapeutic skills displayed by him is not fully continued by any one of them.

More recently, Vasubandhu has been split into two.[14] Those who assert that there were two great Vasubandhus are put in the quandary of having to state which works are which Vasubandhu's. Neither tradition nor internal evidence support their view. The effect of Vasubandhu's conversion to Mahāyāna among his former colleagues is well-documented.[15] For Vasubandhu is not only a great Mahāyāna philosopher; he is also a great Abhidharmika, and it is as an Abhiharmika that he began his writing career. Abhidharma is the ancient Buddhist phenomenology of moment-events, and the reduction of psychological processes to such moments. The combination of Abhidharma and Mahāyāna is one of the salient features of many of Vasubandhu's treatises. Vasubandhu perhaps found the wholesale denial of causality in Nāgārjuna's stricter works contrary to the spirit of *upāya*, "Skill in means" taken for the alleviation of suffering. But ultimately, that is, from the point of view of *prajñā*, or non-dualistic insight, Vasubandhu cannot really assert anything, either. The constructed "own-being", that range of events constructed by the mental consciousness, is recognized as exactly that, and is observed by Vasubandhu to have a constricting suffering-inducing effect if it is fixedly believed. It is true that present-day Tibetan classifications of Buddhist philosophy regard Nāgārjuna and Vasubandhu as disagreeing. But these are really the disagreements of sixth-century followers of Nāgārjuna and Vasubandhu. They belong to a time when Buddhism had become an academic subject at places such as the University of Nālandā. They may have disagreed because they were academics fighting for posts and recognition.[16]

Vasubandhu, on the other hand, seems interested in introducing concepts only for the dissolving of previously-held ones, and these new concepts remove themselves later. They are provisional : once they have had their alleviating effect, they can be discarded, just as the *Diamond Sūtra* recommends we do with all Buddhist formulations.[17]

They are makeshift rafts, and once they have taken us across a turbulent stream, we do not need to carry them on our backs. It is a "revolution at the basis" (*āśraya-parāvṛtti*) which Vasubandhu's works point towards—a state of consciousness where all previous modes of thought are abandoned.

The seven treatises presented here are arranged in a "progressive" fashion. The first work deals with the recognition of faulty logic in human statements; the second concerns types of moment-events and their delineations; the third, through the scholastic objection-and-reply method, fills up holes in the classical Abhidharma psychological theory; the fourth and fifth apply the new theory to startling conclusions; the sixth delineates a path to "revolution at the basis", and the seventh points to the deepest insights of a therapeutic method rooted in meditation (*yoga-ācāra*) and compassion. It is likely that some people will find certain works more interesting than others : the logician will be most attracted to the first, the ethical thinker or spiritual seeker most to the sixth, for instance.

The motivating hope behind this work of translation is that alleviating clarity may be found by those who suffer, that old cruel and stupid boundaries may vanish, and that the living world may find more harmony and bliss.

NOTES

1. The Pure Land schools of China and Japan strive for the attainment of the Western Paradise of the Buddha Amitābha by meditating on his name. There *is* a treatise dealing with this method ascribed to Vasubandhu. It is the *Sukhāvatīvyūhopadeśa*, and is extant in a Chinese translation by Bodhiruci. (Taishō no. 1514). It has recently been translated into English by Minoru Kiyota (in *Mahāyāna Buddhist Meditation : Theory and Practise*, University Press of Hawaii, Honolulu, 1978, pp 249-290).

2. There is a lot of "Zen" in Vasubandhu. Of the treatises presented here, the last two are replete with the same kind of insights Zen loves. But Vasubandhu is particularly known in Zen circles for his *Commentary on the Diamond Sūtra.* (For the later Zen master Han Shan's discussion of this work, see Charles Luk, *Ch'an and Zen Teachings*, series one, pp 159-200.)

3. The *Triratnastotra*

4. At least one survives, the *Pañcakāmopalambhanirdeśa*, Peking/Tokyo Tibetan Tripiṭaka, volume 29, pp 234 ff.

5. In a Buddhist context "sūtras" are those texts in which the Buddha is himself a speaker, or (as in the case of the *Avataṃsaka*), where he is present as the main inspiration.

6. See the *Vāda-vidhi, A Method for Argumentation*, presented in this volume.

7. This term would perhaps fit the bulk of Vasubandhu's output. Among the works presented here, see particularly *A Discussion of the Five Aggregates*, and *A Discussion for the Demonstration of Action.*

8. The *Vyākhyā-yukti*, Peking/Tokyo Tibetan Tripiṭaka, volume 113, pp 241-291.

9. See the description of obstetrics at *Kośa* III, ad 19.

10. See chapter four of *The Commentary on the Separation of the Middle from Extremes*, presented in this volume.

11. See the fifth chapter of the same work, and *The Teaching of the Three Own-Beings* presented here.

12. For instance, Sthiramati attempts to make a distinction between "empty" and "without own-being", which is consistent with neither Nāgārjuna nor Vasubandhu. (*Madhyānta-vibhāga-ṭīkā*, Yamaguchi ed., p 119, 11-17.)

13. Bu-ston, *Chos 'byung*, p 147, 149, 155.

14. In Frauwallner's *On the Date of the Buddhist Master of the Law Vasubandu.* This theory of two Vasubandhus has been widely followed,

though all evidence points to one thinker. In fact, the evolving thought of a philosopher is rarely seen more strikingly than in the case of Vasubandhu. Some of the statements made by Frauwallner reveal a peculiar misunderstanding of history, as when he says that a person living at the time of Frederick the Great could easily be confused by someone with the same name living at the time of Napoleon. Actually, one person could have been living in both those times. For instance, my putative ancestor, General Quosdanovič, when a young man, was defeated by Frederick the Great; when very old, was defeated by Napoleon.

15. See Jaini's collection of anti-Vasubandhu passages in the *Abhidharmadīpa*, given in his article "On the Theory of the Two Vasubandhus", *BSOAS* 21, 1958, pp 48-53. See also Saṅghabhadra's denunciations of Vasubandhu, in his *Abhidharma-nyāyānusāra*, chapt. 50-51, translated by La Vallée Poussin in *Mélanges Chinois et Bouddhiques* v p 2.

16. We may count Bhāvaviveka, Candrakīrti, Sthiramati, and Dharmapāla among the most famous of such academic Buddhists. They seem to love arguing among themselves.

17. *Vajracchedikā-prajñā-pāramitā*, Müller ed. p. 23, Vaidya ed. p. 77.

VASUBANDHU, HIS LIFE AND TIMES

So much controversy has surrounded the person and the time of Vasubandhu that it may appear to the casual observer that arriving at any definite conclusion regarding these matters must be an impossibility. Actually, however, we are comparatively well informed as regards the great philosopher, and a determination of his date, which will contradict neither what Sanskrit, Chinese, Tibetan, or Arabic sources have to say about his times, is manifestly possible. A brief résumé of the problems is however in order.

One of Frauwallner's main reasons for assuming two Vasubandhus, other than his own distrust of flexibility of thought, is the apparent discrepancies of the Chinese datings of the master. These had already been resolved by Péri[1], and have subsequently been thoroughly explained by Le Manh That[2], as resting on different calculations for the date of the Buddha's Nirvāṇa accepted at various times by Chinese tradition. By following all that is contained in Chinese tradition regarding the matter, both Péri and Le Manh That arrive at the fourth century A.D. for Vasubandhu's approximate time. Their conclusion seems obvious when one considers that Kumārajīva (344-413) knew and translated works by Vasubandhu, which fact has in turn been the subject of vast and thoroughly sterile investigations as to the authenticity of these ascriptions, whether the "K'ai-che Vasu" given by Kumārajīva as the author of the *Śataśāstrabhāṣya* can in fact be taken as "Vasubandhu", and so on. Actually, as Péri has already shown, this work in one portion has the complete name, and "K'ai-che Vasu" is also the only name given to the great master Vasubandhu in the colophon of the *Mahāyānasaṅgrahabhāṣya*, as well as elsewhere in Chinese sources. From the Chinese side, we also find that Kumārajīva is said to have written a biography of Vasubandhu (unfortunately lost today) in the year 409[3], and that Hui-yüan (344-416) quotes a verse of Vasubandhu's *Viṃśatikā*[4]. It should also be noted that the *Bodhisattva-bhūmi* of Vasubandhu's older brother Asaṅga was already translated into Chinese in the years 414-421.[5]

It has been said that the Indian tradition regarding Vasubandhu, as found in his biographer Paramārtha and several scattered literary notes in Sanskrit, contradicts the possibility of the fourth century as Vasubandhu's approximate time. Paramārtha calls Vasubandhu the subject of Kings Vikramāditya and Bālāditya. These have been assumed to be the Gupta emperors Skandagupta Vikramāditya (455-467) and Narasiṃhagupta Bālāditya I (467-473), respectively. However, there is evidence from Vāmana that the Bālāditya who became a pupil of Vasubandhu was in fact a son of Candragupta II, the most famous bearer of the *biruda* "Vikramāditya" (375-415).* No son of Candragupta II is specifically mentioned in inscriptions as having the cognomen "Bālāditya". Le Manh That suggests that the curious title "Bālāditya" ("Young Sun") may have been used by Gupta princes in their minority.[6] Thus "Bālāditya" may have been a title of Candragupta's son Kumāragupta I before ascending the throne. But it is more likely, in view of the fact that he is known to have functioned as "Young King" (*yuvarāja*) during the life-time of his father, that this "Bālāditya" was Govindagupta, who seems to have been the oldest son of Candragupta II. However, it is argued, Govindagupta is not known to have ascended the throne, which both Vāmana and Paramārtha claim for Vasubandhu's pupil, and the death of Candragupta II, in 415, would bring us to too late a date for Vasubandhu, who is known to have lived eighty years, and to have seen the accession of Bālāditya, but yet influenced Kumārajīva with Mahāyāna treatises as early as 360, and must have been dead by 409, the date of his earliest biography. Le Manh That has taken the rather radical course of doubting the very dates of the Gupta kings, which rest on the testimony of the

*The passage, in Vāmana's *Kāvyālaṅkārasūtravṛtti*, reads :

> "Soyaṃ samprati-Candragupta-nayaś candra-prakāśo yuvā /
> jāto bhūpatir āśrayaḥ kṛta-dhiyāṃ diṣṭyā kṛtārthaśramaḥ //

Āśrayaḥ kṛta-dhiyāṃ ity asya Vasubandhu-sācivyopakṣepa-paratvāt sābhiprāyatvam."

"This very son of Candragupta, young, shining like the moon, a patron of eminent men of letters, has now become lord deserving congratulations on the success of his efforts.

The words 'patron of eminent men of letters' contains an allusion to the tutorship of Vasubandhu." (Vanavilasam Press edition, p 86).

Arabic writer al-Bīrūnī. But there is another "way out" which is far more satisfying. It rests on what little we know about Govindagupta.

Govindagupta was the son of Candragupta II, by his first queen Dhruvadevī. According to several traditional Indian accounts[7], Dhruvadevī was originally the wife of Candragupta II's elder brother Rāmagupta, who had ascended the throne at the death of his father, the great conqueror Samudragupta. A Śaka ruler, most likely the Satrap of Gujarat and Malwa, Rudrasena IV, took a threatening stance against Rāmagupta, and was appeased only by Rāmagupta's offer to give Dhruvadevī to him. Thereupon, Candragupta and several companions disguised themselves as women, entered the Śaka satrap's camp as Dhruvadevī and her attendants, and killed him. Acclaimed as a hero, Candragupta shortly after overthrew his brother, and Dhruvadevī in gratitude for his protecting heroism took him as her husband. If these events occurred at all (and some modern scholars have tended to doubt it, because there is no epigraphical evidence[8]), they transpired around 375, initial regnal date for Candragupta II. Now Govindagupta himself is known in contemporary sources only from a series of clay seals found and issued at Vaiśālī (Besarh).[9] Some of them he issued jointly with his mother; some of them with ministers under his charge. They all bear texts along this order : "Mahārājādhirāja-Śrī-Candragupta-patnī- mahārāja - Śrī-Govindagupta-mātā-mahādevī-Śrī-Dhruvasvāminī, Śrī-yuvarāja-bhaṭṭāraka-padīya-kumārāmātyādhikaraṇasya", "Mahārāja-Govindagupta yuvarāja-bhaṭṭāraka-padīya-balādhikaraṇasya", etc.[10] ("The great Queen Śrī Dhruva, wife of Śrī Candragupta, Emperor, and mother of the great king Govindagupta, (issues this) from the office of the prince-minister to His Highness, the Young King", "The great king Govindagupta (issues this) from the Military Office of his Highness the Young King".) These in-inscriptions were issued while Candragupta II was still alive, yet Govindagupta had "ascended the throne", i.e. as *Yuva-rāja*, "Young King". What we know about Govindagupta thus dispels all controversy. Neither Paramārtha or Vāmana say anything about the death of Vikramāditya or Candragupta; they only say that his son ascended the throne during the life-time of Vasubandhu. As we know from ample other sources,[11] it was common in the Gupta age for Kings to consecrate their own sons as "Young Kings" long before their own death. This was a full-fledged anointing ceremony, in every way comparable to the total ascension to the throne, and usually involved subsequent adiministration of given provinces by the newly-consecrated "young king". It was both a method of giving the prince training in ruling, as well as a more Kauṭilyan expedient of assuring the continuance of the dynasty. We find parallel instances in the European Middle Ages, such as when the Holy Roman Emperor Frederick II appointed his son Henry King in Germany. In classical India, however, these appointments of "Young Kings" seem to have been the general rule. Thus the Pallava king defeated by Samudragupta was Viṣṇugopavarman, second son of the reigning King Skandavarman II, and "Young King" of Kāñcī. The practice seems to have been ancient in India, for in the *Mahābhārata*, Duryodhana is called "king" during the life-time of his father Dhṛtarāṣṭra.

The usual age at which the prince acceded as "Young King" was sixteen years. In the case of Govindagupta, this seems to have been c. 391, and the particular province given him was the central Gangetic valley, including the towns of Ayodhyā and Vaiśālī. As c. 390 is the beginning date of Candragupta II's campaign against the Śaka Satrap Rudrasiṃha III of Gujarat and Malwa, it seems probable that Govindagupta was made Governor of the ancestral realm in order to give the people a royal symbol during Candragupta's extended absences from home. It is in fact known that Candragupta II during his campaigns for a time had Ujjain as his capital.[12] At the end of these campaigns, he apparently re-established his capital at Pāṭaliputra, as it is called the capital by Fa-hsien (in India 399-414).

Thus there is no necessity for going against any tradition whatever. Taking into account the possibility that Vasubandhu may have lived beyond his pupil Govindagupta's consecration as "Young King", we may arrive at an arbitrary but plausible date, 316-396, for Vasubandhu. This should be taken as no more than a hypothesis, but it is at least one which will please all lovers of traditional history.[13] It also places Vasubandhu in one of the most brilliant ages in Indian history, and associates him with one of her most brilliant courts. Among countless other eminent men who may be mentioned as his contemporaries, the great poet Kālidāsa, the lexicographer Amarasiṃha, and the Mīmāṃsā philosopher Śabara were in all probability at the same court that invited Vasubandhu to his most famous debates, and to his most famous tutoring position. Whether his pupil Govindagupta ever fully ascended the throne is doubtful, though there are allusions in Subandhu[14] to troublesome times after the death of Candragupta II, so perhaps a struggle between Govindagupta and his brother Kumāragupta I, in which the latter emerged victorious, is to be assumed. On the other hand, Govindagupta may have pre-deceased his father. At present we have no way of knowing.

The details of Vasubandhu's life are known from several biographies in Chinese and Tibetan, the earliest of which is the Chinese rendering of the life of Vasubandhu by Paramārtha (499-569), who composed it while in China.[15] There was, as mentioned, apparently a previous account by Kumārajīva, which has not survived. The earliest Tibetan biography available to me is a good deal later—it is that of Bu-ston (1290-1364). In addition, there are several references to Vasubandhu in the works of Hsüan-tsang, Bāṇa-bhaṭṭa, Vāmana, and other writers. We shall attempt to reconstruct the main outlines of Vasubandhu's life, relying most heavily on Paramārtha, and supplying dates for the main events, so that the dating of Vasubandhu presented here can be put to the test. Some of this material is no doubt legendary, but nonetheless interesting as a light on how Vasubandhu was viewed by later generations.

Vasubandhu was born in Puruṣapura, present-day Peshawar, in what was then the Kingdom of Gāndhāra, around the year 316 A.D. According to Paramārtha, his father was a Brāhmaṇa of the Kauśika *gotra*, and his mother was named Viriñcī. The couple already had a previous son, later called Asaṅga, and a third, nicknamed Viriñcivatsa, was to follow.[16] Vasubandhu's father was a court priest, and, according to the later Tibetan historian Tāranātha, was very learned in the *Vedas*.[17] In all probability, he officiated at the court of the Śaka princes of the Śīlada clan, who at that time ruled from Puruṣapura.[18] According to the Tibetan historians, Asaṅga and Vasubandhu were half-brothers, Asaṅga's father being a Kṣatriya, and Vasubandhu's a Brāhmaṇa.[19] According to them, the mother of Asaṅga and Vasubandhu was named Prasannaśīlā.[20]

Gāndhāra was no longer at that time the heart of a great empire, as it had been under the last Kushan Emperors a century before; it had become a border land in the midst of small kingdoms, and perhaps the amazing decline in its population, which Hsüan-tsang was to notice, was already taking place at that time. It was, however, a very fertile area, and those who were willing to stay in a backwater country suffered no lack of prosperity. Though its ancient artistic tradition was dead by this time, this birthplace of the Sarvāstivāda masters Dharmaśrī and the Bhadanta Dharmatrāta, kept up its old tradition of scholastic Buddhist learning. It was known as the seat of the "Western masters"(Pāścatīyas) of Abhidharma. The Sarvāstivādins, "the asserters that everything exists", believed in the reality of external objects of consciousness, and further maintained that future and past events have existence. The main Sarvāstivāda movement in force in Gāndhāra was that of the Vaibhāṣikas, those who took the *Mahā-Vibhāṣā* ("Great Book of Options") as their authoritative text. This *Vibhāṣā* is a great scholastic edifice attempting to systematize everything importanւ n Buddhist theory and practise, and is the result of a great team effort of the noted North Indian Buddhist masters gathered in a conference called by the Emperor Kaniṣka two centuries before the time of Vasubandhu. Masters known to have taken part in the debates, and whose views are quoted in the book, are the Bhadanta Vasumitra, the Bhadanta Dharmatrāta, Ghoṣaka, and Buddhadeva. This tremendous work often reads like a committee report, with widely varying opinions being offered, but very often it is the opinion of the Bhadanta Vasumitra which prevails. For instance, on explanations of how events "in the three times" differ, the *Vibhāṣā* accepts the theory of the Bhadanta Vasumitra, which states that the difference between present, past, and future events lie in the state of their efficacy. In its full efficacy of engendering a consciousness proper to it, an event is obviously present and momentary. However, it can be remembered or anticipated : the only difference lies in the fact that as a past or future event, only a mental consciousness can apprehend it.[21] Many of the views of the *Vibhāṣā* are quite advanced. For instance, it maintains that "time", a real category to the Vaiśeṣikas (and to some people today who still speak of "time" as a "dimension"), is only a name for the flow of conditioned events.[22] At the time of Vasubandhu's youth, a certain dogmatism, certainly not apparent among the masters of the *Vibhāṣā* itself, was becoming evident within the Vaibhāṣika schools.

According to Tāranātha,[23] Vasubandhu was born one year after his older brother Asaṅga became a Buddhist monk. From the internal evidence of his works[24], Asaṅga seems to have studied mainly with scholars of the Mahīśāsaka school, which denied the Sarvāstivāda existence of the past and future[25], and which posited a great number of "uncompounded events"[26]

In his youth, Vasubandhu may have received from his father much of the Brāhmaṇical lore so obviously at his command, and it may be from him also that he was introduced to the axioms of classical Nyāya and Vaiśeṣika, both of which influenced his logical thought.

The name "Vasubandhu", which he never changed even upon entering the Buddhist priesthood, may perhaps tell us something about the character of its bearer. It means "the Kinsman of Abundance", in particular the abundance of the Earth, and his retention of this name, in view of his genuine concern for the well-being of others, as well as his love of metaphors from teeming plant-life, rushing streams, and rippling lakes, is probably not entirely coincidental.

While learning with the Mahīśāsakas, Asaṅga came into contact with the *Prajñā-pāramitā-sūtras* of Mahāyāna Buddhism, which was completely overturning the older monastic Buddhist ideal in favour of a life of active compassion to be crowned by complete enlightenment. Not being able to understand them, and not gaining any insight into them from his teachers, he undertook lonely forest-meditations. But after twelve years of meditation, he felt he had gained nothing. So he decided to give up seeking enlightement. Just at that moment, a miserable dog dragged itself across Asaṅga's path. Its wounds were filled with squirming maggots. Asaṅga, filled with compassion, decided to remove the maggots from the dog with his tongue (as he was afraid his fingers would hurt them), and to cut off a piece of his own flesh for them to live in. At that moment, the dog disappeared, and the Bodhisattva Maitreya stood before him. Maitreya told Asaṅga to show him to the people, but none could see him in his total form. (One old woman is said to have seen Asaṅga carrying a puppy, and to have become very wealthy thereafter.)

Maitreya dictated five works to Asaṅga, which are usually considered to be the *Abhisamayālaṅkāra*, the *Mahāyānasūtrālaṅkāra*, the *Madhyāntavibhāga* (of which an English translation is included in this volume), the *Dharmadharmatāvibhāga*, and the *Ratnagotravibhāga*. He also introduced him to the *Daśabhūmika-sūtra*, which details the path of a Mahāyānist.

The interpretations of this Maitreya story are varied. Was this Maitreya a private vision of Asaṅga's? Was he a hermit-philosopher whose works Asaṅga published? Is he a pious fiction? Some modern scholars wish to dismiss the Maitreya story altogether as a later fabrication.[27] But it is interesting that Vasubandhu himself distinguishes the author of the *Madhyāntavibhāga*, Maitreya(nātha), from its "expounder to us and others", Asaṅga.[28] Furthermore, the style of the works ascribed to Maitreyanātha and those all admit to be by Asaṅga, is very different. The first are compact often to a cryptic point; the latter are very wordy but also very clear. In this book, Maitreyanātha and Asaṅga will be distinguished from one another on the basis of the suggestion of these facts. At any rate, Asaṅga became the first main disseminator of the Yogācāra method of practising Mahāyāna. The name "Yogācāra", "practise of Yoga", indicates the primary importance of meditation for this method.

In the meantime, Vasubandhu had entered the Sarvāstivāda order, and was studying primarily the scholastic system of the Vaibhāṣikas. Apparently he remained impressed with this all-encompassing structure for some time. He in turn amazed his teachers with the brilliance and quickness of his mind. His main teacher seems to have been a certain Buddhamitra.

In time, however, grave doubts about the validity and relevance of Vaibhāṣika metaphysics began to arise in Vasubandhu. At this time, perhaps through the brilliant teacher Manoratha, he came into contact with the theories of the Sautrāntikas, that group of Buddhists who wished to reject everything that was not the express word of the Buddha, and who held the elaborate constructions of the *Vibhāṣā* up to ridicule. That there was a strong Sautrāntika tradition in Puruṣapura is likely in view of the fact that it was the birthplace of that maverick philosopher of the second century, the Bhadanta Dharmatrāta. In fact, the most orthodox Vaibhāṣika seat of learning was not in Gāndhāra, but in Kashmir, whose masters looked down their noses at the Gāndhārans as quasi-heretics. According to Hsüan-tsang's pupil P'u-k'uang, Vasubandhu finally decided to go to Kashmir to investigate the Vaibhāṣika teachings more exactly.[29] Fearing that the Kashmirian scholars might distrust his intentions if they knew he was a Gāndhāran, he entered Kashmir under a false name.[30] P'u-k'uang's account does not explain, however, how he could cross the border. The later Tibetan tradition does this by stating that Vasubandhu entered Kashmir under the guise of a "lunatic".[31] This story is told by Paramārtha in reference to an earlier Abhidharmika, Vasubhadra,[32] but it is so suggestive for Vasubandhu's activities that it will be interesting to tell it here. For unlike nowadays, at least in the West, where the so-called "insane" are quickly incarcerated, in India they were and often still are free to roam about at will. Posing as one would mean that Vasubandhu would have no doors barred to him. It is very interesting that Vasubandhu, who is so adamant on the point that there is no difference between a so-called hallucination and what is conventionally termed "reality", could have convincingly taken on a "schizophrenic" manner of relating to his environment. "He was always in the great assembly hearing the Dharma, but his manner was strange and incongruous, and his speech and laughter were ill-assorted. Now he would discuss in the assembly the principles of the *Vibhāṣā*, then he would inquire about the story of the *Rāmāyaṇa*. The people thought lightly of him, and though hearing him talk, disregarded him."[33]

Bu-ston says that Vasubandhu in Kashmir entered the school of Saṅghabhadra.[34] But it is unlikely that this intellectually acute and cantankerous individual assumed the professorship at that time, for, from what both Paramārtha and Hsüan-tsang tell us[35], Vasubandhu and Saṅghabhadra seem to have been about the same age. It is, however, more than likely that it was the school Saṅghabhadra was himself attending as a student, and this is in fact attested by P'u-k'uang.[36] He says that the main master there was the teacher of Saṅghabhadra, whose name is given in Chinese transcription as Sai-chien-ti-lo or Sai-chien-t'o-lo. This name has been variously interpreted as

"Skandhila" or "Sugandhara", though P'u-k'uang's translation, 悟 入 fits neither of these reconstructions. Sại-chien-ti-lo, whatever his Sanskrit name may have been, is known as the author of the brief but incisive *Abhidharmāvatāra*, an orthodox Vaibhāṣika treatise preserved both in Chinese[37] and Tibetan[38] translations.

Vasubandhu studied in Kashmir for four years, probably from about 342 to 346. He was however no docile student, but rather in his increasing frustration with the over-intellectual and category-ridden dogmatics of the Kashmirian masters, frequently voiced his own refutations of many of their points.[39] The master Sai-chien-ti-lo, disturbed by the obstreperous student, went into deep meditation, by the powers of which he discovered Vasubandhu's true origin. He then told Vasubandhu privately that he should return to Gāndhāra before his "uncultured students", among whom one can well imagine the sharp-tongued Saṅghabhadra, found out and attempted to harm him. Vasubandhu, doubly convinced that the Vaibhāṣika system did not reflect true Buddhism, decided to go home. But when he reached the border of Kashmir, the guards (who supposedly had supernormal insights and hence are called "yakṣas" in the story) said that a great scholar of the Abhidharma was about to leave the country. The people remembered Vasubandhu as a "lunatic", but decided to have him questioned by some scholars, anyway. But Vasubandhu's speech became free-associative, jumping from topic to topic, and the scholars did not understand him. They let him go. The guards a second time sent him back. He was re-examined, with the same result. Finally, on his fourth attempt, he was allowed to cross the border, the scholars being convinced that he was a "lunatic", and hence should not be disturbed.[40]

Vasubandhu returned to Puruṣapura. He began to prepare for an enormous project that had been in his mind for some time. He was at this time unattached to any particular order, and lived in a small private house in the middle of Puruṣapura. (Hsüan-tsang three centuries later saw this house, which was marked with a commemorative tablet.[41]) According to Paramārtha, Vasubandhu supported himself by lecturing on Buddhism before the general public, which presumably remunerated him with gifts. Such was the customary income for Buddhist public lecturers even in the days of the *Aṣṭasāhasrikā-prajñā-pāramitā*.[42] At the close of each day's lecture on the Vaibhāṣika system, Vasubandhu composed a verse which summed up his exposition for the day.[43] Paramārtha says, "Each verse was engraved on a copper plate. This he hung on the head of an intoxicated elephant, and, beating a drum made the following proclamation : 'Is there anyone who can refute the principles set forth in this treatise? Let him who is competent to do so come forth!' "[44] So in time he composed over six hundred verses, which gave an extensive outline of the entire Vaibhāṣika system. These constitute the *Abhidharma-kośa*.* Vasubandhu sent it, along with fifty pounds of gold, to his old teachers in Kashmir. Though Sai-chien-tī-lo himself cautioned them, all the others at the Kashmir school exulted that Vasubandhu had come over to their side, and had composed such a brilliant epitome of Vaibhāṣika doctrine besides. They were disturbed only because Vasubandhu in his treatise so often used terms such as "*kila*" ("it is claimed") and "*ity āhuḥ*" ("so they say").

As a matter of fact, during this entire time, Vasubandhu was working on his real project, his autocommentary on the *Kośa*, which contains a thoroughgoing critique of Vaibhāṣika dogmatics from a Sautrāntika viewpoint. He found a chance to publish this *Kośa-bhāṣya* when several of the Kashmirian scholars, puzzled by the abstruseness of many of the verses in the *Kośa*, sent his fifty pounds of gold back with an additional fifty, and asked him to write a commentary. Vasubandhu sent them his *Kośa-bhāṣya*, by this time completed. For the subsequent furious indignation of the orthodox Vaibhāṣikas, we need not rely on traditional accounts only—it is amply attested by the relentless invective employed by contemporary Vaibhāṣika writers such as Saṅghabhadra and the Dīpakāra. Vasubandhu was to the latter "that apostate", "that subscriber to theories that please only fools"[45], and the sharp-tongued Saṅghabhadra

*The *Pudgala-pratiṣedha-prakaraṇa*, "A Discussion for the Refutation of Personality", may be the only extant work by Vasubandhu written prior to the *Kośa*. This seems likely in view of the fact that its arguments and solutions are less developed. It was originally an independent treatise, but was finally attached by Vasubandhu to the *Kośa* as its last chapter. In this book, it will be referred to as "*Kośa* IX".

could hardly find words harsh enough to vent his spleen : "that man whose theories have the coherence of the cries of a mad deaf-mute in a fever-dream."[46]

Vasubandhu had thus at a fairly early age achieved a certain notoriety. His book was to become the standard Abhidharma work for the unorthodox in India[47], and, due no doubt in part to his subsequent fame as a Mahāyāna master, in China, Japan, Tibet, and Indonesia, as well.

In the years directly following the composition of the *Kośa*, Vasubandhu seems to have spent much time in travelling from place to place. It is certain that he stayed for a time at Śākala, the modern Sialkot.[48] This town was at this time the capital of the Mādraka Republic. Around 350, Samudragupta completed his lightning-quick conquest of North India, and the fate of Bhāratavarṣa was sealed. The elected executive council of the Mādraka Republic, along with so many other frightened rulers of the frontiers, rendered its personal obeisance to the Emperor.[49]

It was, in all probability, subsequent to that event that Vasubandhu, as well as his teachers Buddhamitra and Manoratha, decided to move to Ayodhyā.[50] Ayodhyā, the ancient city of Rāma, had become one of the main metropolises of the new Gupta Empire. Vasubandhu took residence in the old Saṅghārāma of the city[51], and Hsüan-tsang later saw the hall in Ayodhyā where Vasubandhu preached to "kings and many eminent men".[52]

Vasubandhu had, up to this time, but little regard for the Yogācāra treatises of his elder brother. He had perhaps seen the voluminous *Yogācārabhūmi* compiled by Asaṅga, which may have simply repelled him by its bulk. At any rate, he is reported to have said : "Alas, Asaṅga, residing in the forest, has practised meditation for twelve years. Without having attained anything by this meditation, he has founded a system, so difficult and burdensome, that it can be carried only by an elephant."[53] Asaṅga heard about this attitude of his brother, and decided to attempt to open him up to the Mahāyāna. He sent two of his students with Mahāyāna texts to Vasubandhu. The evening they arrived, they recited the *Akṣayamati-nirdeśa-sūtra*. In this sūtra, a figure from outer space teaches the terrestrial denizens about the absence of own-being, the absence of existing and ceasing, and the absence of any detriment or excellence, in all events and "personalities".[54] This sūtra seems to have greatly appealed to the critical mind of Vasubandhu. He told Asaṅga's students that he thought the logical principles of Mahāyāna were well-founded, but that it seemed to have no practice. The next morning, Asaṅga's students recited the *Daśabhūmika-sūtra*, which relates to the path of the Bodhisattva, who remains active in the world for the removal of suffering. Hearing this text, Vasubandhu saw that the Mahāyāna had a well-founded practice, too.[55] He so regretted his former disregard for it that he wanted to cut off his own tongue.[56] Asaṅga's students quickly intervened, urging him instead to visit his brother. So Vasubandhu went to visit Asaṅga in Puruṣapura. In the discussions on Mahāyāna, which the two brothers held, Vasubandhu grasped the meanings immediately, whereas Asaṅga always took some time to make his replies. Asaṅga urged Vasubandhu to use his superior mental consciousness to study, spread, and interpret the Mahāyāna.

Vasubandhu seems to have been quite overwhelmed by Mahāyāna literature. His desire to read the enormous *Śatasāhasrikāprajñā-pāramitā-sūtra* led him to read it all the way through without stopping, which took him fifteen days and nights, which he spent in a tub of sesame-oil.[57] The study of that huge work he regarded as of utmost importance. In that immense meditation, entities of a most diverse kind are brought up and made devoid of own-nature and "empty".

In view of the fact that they were the texts that converted him to Mahāyāna, Vasubandhu's commentaries on the *Akṣayamatinirdeśa-sūtra*[58] and the *Daśa-bhūmika* may[59] be his earliest Mahāyāna works. These were followed by a series of commentaries on other Mahāyāna sūtras and treatises. According to the Tibetans, his favorite sūtra was either the *Śatasānasrikāprajñā-pāramitā*, or the *Aṣṭasāhasrikā*.[60] That these texts should have pleased a man who so loved argument, and who in addition had such a great sense of humour, is hardly surprising, as they reveal the most profound insights through mind-boggling dialogues that are never far from laughter.

Since the output of Vasubandhu's Mahāyāna works is prodigious, he was probably writing new treatises every year. So he could have been a very famous Mahāyāna master by the year 360, the approximate date in which Kumārajīva took instruction from Bandhudatta in Kucha. By this time, Vasubandhu could easily have written those works which Bandhudatta transmitted to his brilliant pupil. Actually only one is specifically known to have been studied by Kumārajīva in his youth : this was a commentary on the *Saddharmapuṇḍarīka-sūtra*, which by its very nature is likely to have been an early Mahāyāna work of Vasubandhu.[61]

The year 376 brings Candragupta II, Vikramāditya, to the throne of the Gupta Empire. As famous for his liberal patronage of learning and the arts, as for his successful maintenance of the Empire, his reign marks one of the high points in the classical Indian period. And Ayodhyā, where Vasubandhu again took up his abode, became for a while the Emperor's capital-in-residence. It may have been shortly after this date that a great debate occurred, which was to stick in the minds of the Buddhist biographers.

Philosophical debating was in classical India often a spectator-sport, much as contests of poetry-improvisation were in Germany in its High Middle Ages, and as they still are in the Telugu country today. The King himself was often the judge at these debates, and loss to an opponent could have serious consequences. To take an atrociously extreme example, when the Tamil Śaivite Ñānasambandar Nāyanār defeated the Jain ācāryas in Madurai before the Pāṇḍya King Māṟavarman Avaniśūḻāmani (620-645) this debate is said to have resulted in the impalement of 8000 Jains, an event still celebrated in the Mīnākṣī Temple of Madurai today. Usually, the results were not so drastic : they could mean formal recognition by the defeated side of the superiority of the winning party, forced conversions, or, as in the case of the Council of Lhasa, which was conducted by Indians, banishment of the losers. One of the most stirring descriptions of such a debate is found in the account of Paramārtha, where he describes how the Sāṅkhya philosopher Vindhyavāsin challenged the Buddhist masters of Ayodhyā, in the presence of Emperor Candragupta II himself. At that time both Vasubandhu and Manoratha were absent from Ayodhyā, "travelling to other countries"(Vasubandhu seems really to have enjoyed a peripatetic existence), and only the old Buddhamitra was left to defend the Dharma. Buddhamitra was defeated, and had to undergo the humiliating and painful punishment of being beaten on the back by the Sāṅkhya master in front of the entire assembly. When Vasubandhu later returned, he was enraged when he heard of the incident. He subsequently succeeded in trouncing the Sāṅkhyas, both in debate and in a treatise, *Paramārthasaptati*. Candragupta II rewarded him with 300,000 pieces of gold for his victory over the Sāṅkhyas.[62] These Vasubandhu employed for building three monasteries, one for the Mahāyānists, another for his old colleagues the Sarvāstivādins, and a third for the nuns. Refutations of Vaiśeṣika and Sāṅkhya theories had been presented by Vasubandhu already in the *Kośa*, but it was perhaps from this point onward that Vasubandhu was regarded as a philosopher whose views could not be lightly challenged.

The meditative career of Vasubandhu is of course less easy to trace than his writing activity. In the Zen lineages[63], Vasubandhu is called the pupil of a certain Jayata. Whoever this Jayata was, he seems to have introduced Vasubandhu to the method of "meditating without props". Many of Vasubandhu's works, including *The Commentary on the Separation of the Middle from Extremes* presented here, show his great interest in the techniques of meditation. Hsüan-tsang says: "Vasubandhu Bodhisattva was attempting to explain that which is beyond the power of words to convey, and which came to him by the mysterious way of profound meditation."[64]

Around the year 383, at his eighth birthday[65], the crown prince Govindagupta Bālāditya was placed by the Emperor under the tutelage of Vasubandhu. The Empress Dhruvadevī also went to Vasubandhu to receive instruction.[66] This indicates that Candragupta II must have been secure in his image as a just ruler, for the Yogācārin is potentially a political activist, if compassion demands it. In Asaṅga's *Bodhisattva-bhūmi* it is stated that though non-harming is usually to be strictly observed, a Bodhisattva may be compelled to kill a king if this is the only way one can stop him from committing atrocities.[67] It is tempting to speculate on the effect of Vasubandhu's tutorship on his royal students. He may have done much to alleviate the conditions of the thousands subject to the Guptas. He is known to have founded many hospitals, rest-houses, and schools. That his compassion was not theoretical but practical can also be seen by the accounts which tell us of his helping quench the great fire that broke out in Rājagṛha, and his doing the utmost to help stop an epidemic in Janāntapura.[68]

In some Tibetan accounts, Vasubandhu is associated with the University of Nālandā.[69] This may or may not be an anachronism. He is known to have passed his technique of no-prop meditation on to his old associate Manoratha. His most famous pupil, according to tradition, was Dignāga.[70]

In his old age, Vasubandhu seems to have taken up the wandering life again. Some of his last works are known to have been written in Śākala and in Kauśāmbī.[71] Kauśāmbī, for instance, is the place where he wrote his *Twenty* and *Thirty Verses*, and Hsüan-tsang saw the old brick tower there, near the ancient Saṅghārāma of Ghoṣira, where these famous expositions of Yogācāra thought were written.

Around the year 391, the consecration of Govindagupta as "Young King" took place. He and his mother begged Vasubandhu to settle down in Ayodhyā and accept life-long royal support. Vasubandhu accepted the offer. The master was creative even at his advanced age, and more than a match for Vasurāta, the Young King's grammarian brother-in-law, in his favorite sport of debate. With the sums of money he received as remuneration for his debating victories, he built several rest-houses, monasteries, and hospitals in Ayodhyā, Gāndhāra, and Kashmir. But primarily, as Hsüan-tsang tells us, Vasubandhu was going farther and farther with his contemplative exercises.[72] Debate was to him mainly *upāya* : if it could lead to no one's interest in Mahāyāna, he would not engage in it. Thus, when Saṅghabhadra, who had written his two great treatises, one of which is a furious denunciation of the *Kośa Bhāṣya*, challenged Vasubandhu to defend the *Kośa's* statements, and was invited to come to court and debate by the jealous Vasurāta, Vasubandhu told his pupils that he could see no good reason for such a debate, but diplomatically sent the official answer that Saṅghabhadra would indeed be hard to defeat. He probably knew from his student days that Saṅghabhadra would not be convinced by anything, and, besides, the *Kośa* itself was probably no longer very important to him at the time. Thus, the debate never took place, but we can almost see the forms it might have taken, by comparing the *Kośa*, the *Abhidharma-*

nyāyānusāra of Saṅghabhadra, and the *Discussion for the Demonstration of Action* included here. Saṅghabhadra in fact died shortly after. At first, Vasubandhu had only this to say about his refusal to take on the Kashmirian : "Though the lion retires far off before the pig, nonetheless the wise will know which of the two is best in strength."[73] A little later, he seems to have made a more generous appraisal of his greatest rival in the field of Vaibhāṣika scholastics. "Saṅghabhadra was a clever and ingenious scholar," he is reported to have said; "His intellective powers were not deep, but his dialectics were always to the point."[74] No utterance attributed to Vasubandhu could more clearly demonstrate the difference he felt between mere intellectual acumen and true profundity.

Vasubandhu did not long survive Saṅghabhadra. In the eightieth year of his life, c. 396, he died. Tradition is unanimous in saying that he died at eighty, but there are various versions as to the place of his death. Paramārtha says that he died in Ayodhyā[75], but Bu-ston may be correct when he says that he died in the northern frontier countries, which he calls "Nepal".[76] For Hsüan-tsang corroborates the information that Vasubandhu was in the northern frontier at the time of Saṅghabhadra's challenge to debate, which according to all traditions was one of the last events in Vasubandhu's life. He says that Vasubandhu was at that time in Śākala, where the *Teaching of the Three Own-Beings*, possibly Vasubandhu's last work, was written.[77] Bu-ston gives an interesting detail about this last journey of the master. He says that while Vasubandhu was in the north, he went to visit a monk named Handu. Handu was inebriated, and carrying an immense pot of wine on his shoulder. Vasubandhu upon seeing this cried, "Alas! The Doctrine will go to ruin", recited the *Uṣṇīṣa-vijaya-dhāraṇī* in reverse order, and died.[78] According to Tāranātha, however, Vasubandhu was prompted to recite the *dhāraṇī* in reverse order when he saw a monk ploughing in his monastic robes.[79] Such is the account of his life, filled with prodigious activity, which can be reconstructed from the copious data of his biographers.

The "personality" of Vasubandhu which emerges from his works and his biographies shows him as a man filled with great compassion for the mental afflictions of others, and with a concern for their physical well-being, as well. The monetary rewards which he received for his teaching and his debating victories he did not keep (in contrast to Manoratha, who according to Hsüan-tsang amassed quite a fortune[80]), but utilized to build monasteries, hospitals, rest-houses, and schools. His familiarity with the classical Indian medical art of Caraka indicates a similar concern. One of his most passionate passages describes the delivery of a baby. It is filled with compassion verging on horror, for the suffering mother and the new-born child.[81] That passion, when tempered by compassion and insight, was for him no danger can be seen in the *Commentary on the Separation of the Middle from Extremes.* His ironic and subtle sense of humor will be much in evidence in the works presented here. Both Indians and Chinese recognized him as a Bodhisattva, and perhaps this tells us as much about him as we need to know.

NOTES

1. Péri, "À propos de la date de Vasubandhu", *BEFEO* XI, pp 355 ff.
2. Le Manh That, "Dũa vào viêc khào cú'u triêt Vasubandhu", typescript.
3. Hsüan-tsang, *Records* I p 168, n.
4. Le Manh That Op. Cit.
5. Introduction to Wogihara's edition of *Bodhisattva-bhūmi*, p 13.
6. Le Manh That, Op. Cit.
7. The drama *Devīcandraguptam* by Viśākhadatta; the Samjan plates of Rāṣṭrakūṭa Emperor Amoghavarṣa I. (871 A.D.)
8. Bharatiya Vidya Bhavan's *History and Culture of the Indian People*, volume III, *The Classical Age*, pp 17-18.
9. He is also mentioned in a later inscription at Mandasor of 467/68 A.D., as a son of Candragupta II. See Majumdar and Altekar, *The Vakataka-Gupta Age*, p 180.
10. *ASR* 1903-4, p 107.
11. Collected by Saletore, *Life in the Gupta Age*, pp 171-176.
12. Ibid, p 84.
13. Two additional problems which have sometimes been raised to give credence to the existence of two Vasubandhus rest on textual misinterpretation. It has been said that Yaśomitra, the famous commentator of Vasubandhu's *Kośa*, himself believes in two Vasubandhus, as there are references to a "Vṛddhācārya Vasubandhu" whose views are combated by the author of the *Kośa*. An investigation of the text does not bear this out. "Vṛddhācārya Vasubandhu", or "Sthavira Vasubandhu", is named only three times in Yaśomitra, at *Vyākhyā* ad I 13-14 c; ad III 27; and ad IV,

2b-3b. The first of these passages says that it is the Vṛddhācārya Vasubandhu's opinion regarding unmanifest action, that it be called "material" because it depends on the material elements of the body. (cf. *A Discussion for the Demonstration of Action*, note 3). This is, as a matter of fact, the opinion adopted by the *Kośa* itself. The second has been mistranslated by La Vallée Poussin (*Kośa* III, p 70, n) who makes it say that Sthavira Vasubandhu, the master of Manoratha, upheld the theory that ignorance comes from improper mental attention. This is again a view strongly upheld by the *Kośa* against the orthodox Vaibhāṣikas. But what Yaśomitra actually says is "*Apara iti Sthavira-Vasubandhor ācāryo Manorathôpādhyāya evam āha*". "The phrase 'an additional (theorist says that ignorance comes from improper mental attention)' refers to Manoratha, the teacher of the Sthavira Vasubandhu, who spoke of this matter in this way." Thus the theory of two Vasubandhus, one the teacher, the other a pupil of Manoratha, seems ruled out. Manoratha is always called the teacher of Vasubandhu. The third passage states that the Sthavira Vasubandhu and others believe that a flame is destroyed by an absence of a cause of stability. This is again clearly the position of the great Vasubandhu, as is amply demonstrated in *Kośa* IV and the *Discussion for the Demonstration of Action*. The objection "An absence cannot be a cause" belongs to the Vaiśeṣika. In each of these cases, the opinion attributed to "Vṛddhācārya Vasubandhu" or "Sthavira Vasubandhu" is in fact the one adopted by the author of the *Kośa*, and one of them does not refer primarily to the opinion of Vasubandhu at all, but to that of Manoratha. It may seem strange that Yaśomitra only on these occasions names Vasubandhu, whom he usually calls simply "the Master". But in each of these passages, there are several alternative opinions listed, so some ambiguity might have resulted from saying simply "the Master". "Vṛddha" in "Vṛddhācārya" does not necessarily mean "old"; it may simply mean "eminent" (Apte, p 1491). Similarly, much has been made of the fact that Yaśomitra calls Asaṅga a *pūrvācārya*, "ancient master". Since Yaśomitra lived several centuries after Asaṅga, this should not be surprising. But, besides, the expression may mean simply "previous master", i.e. a master prior to Vasubandhu. La Vallée Poussin has also used a passage from the Chinese translation of the *Saṃyuktābhidharmasāra* of Dharmatrāta, which speaks of a Vasu who wrote an Abhidharma commentary in 6000 ślokas, to support the idea of an older Vasubandhu. ("Vasubandhu l'Ancien", *BARB* 16, 1930, pp 15-39.) But this passage was inserted as a kind of foot-note by the translator Saṅghavarman in the year 434, and it may in fact refer to our Vasubandhu, whose *Kośa* has 600 verses, easily exaggerated to 6000. Besides, this "Vasu" could be "Vasumitra" or "Vasubhadra", names of known Abhidharmikas preceding Vasubandhu.

The second problem rests on the manner in which Paramārtha organizes his data in his life of Vasubandhu. It has been assumed that events are told in chronologial order. This has given rise to problems, because Vasubandhu's conversion by Asaṅga is mentioned only late in the text. But as a matter of fact, Paramārtha does not necessarily mention prior events first. Attention must be paid to the temporal particles in Paramārtha—

when he says "first" (as on page 287), this usually refers to a happening which occurred prior to the event being discussed directly before. Paramārtha's digressions on the founding of Puruṣapura and the compilation of the *Vibhāṣā* also clearly show that he is not writing in the historical order of the occurrences.

14. *Vāsavadattā*, v. 7.
15. translated by Takakusu in *T'oung Pao* 1904, pp 269-296.
16. According to Paramārtha, all three brothers originally had the name "Vasubandhu".
17. Tāranātha, *History of Buddhism in India* (tr. Anton Schiefner), p 118.
18. *The Classical Age*, p 53.
19. Bu-ston, *Chos' byung* II, p 137; Tāranātha, p 118.
20. Bu-ston, II, p 137; Tāranātha, p 107.
21. *Vibhāṣā* (selections) translated by La Vallée Poussin, *Mélanges Chinois et Bouddhiques* 1, pp 34 ff, pp 229 ff.
22. Ibid, p 8.
23. Tāranātha, p 107.
24. cf. Introduction to *A Discussion of the Five Aggregates*, p 81
25. Bareau, *Les sectes bouddhiques du Petit Véhicule*, p 183, thesis no. 1.
26. Ibid, thesis no. 19, p 185.
27. Paul Demiéville, "Le Yogācārabhūmi de Sangharakṣa", *BEFEO* XLIV, p 381, n. 4.
28. *Commentary on the Separation of the Middle from Extremes I*, invocatory verse.
29. P'u-k'uang, *Kośa Commentary*, quoted by Sakurabe in "*Abhidharmāvatāra* by an unidentified author", *Nava Nalanda Mahavihara Research Institute*, volume II, 1960, p 363.
30. Ibid.
31. See Tarthang Tulku, *Crystal Mirror* V., p 72.
32. Paramārtha, p 279.
33. Ibid. He is of course relating this in relation to Vasubhadra.
34. Bu-ston II, p 142.
35. Paramārtha, p 289; Hsüan-tsang *Records* I, pp 194-195.
36. Sakurabe, Op. Cit., p 363.
37. Taishō no. 1554.
38. Peking/Tokyo Tibetan Tripiṭaka volume 119, pp 43 ff.
39. P'u-k'uang, Sakurabe, p 363.
40. Paramārtha, pp 279-80, tells this story again in reference to Vasubhadra.
41. Hsüan-tsang, *Records* I, p. 105.
42. c. first century B.C. See the story of Sadāprarudita and Dharmodgata in the *Aṣṭasāhasrikā-prajñā-pāramitā*, chapter XXX (Rajendralal Mitra ed. p 438, Vaidya ed. p 241).
43. Paramārtha, p 287.
44. Ibid.
45. See Jaini's collection of anti-Vasubandhu Passages in the *Abhidharmadipa*, given in his article "On the Theory of the Two Vasubandhus", *BSOAS* 46, 1958, pp 48-53.

46. from Saṅghabnadra's *Abhidharma-nyāyānusāra*, as translated by La Vallée Poussin, *Mélanges Chinois Bouddhiques* 2, pp 25-180.

47. cf. Bāṇa's *Harṣa-carita*, VIII, p 317 (Bombay Sanskrit Series edition), where even the parrots of the Buddhist community can recite portions of the *Kośa*.

48. Hsüan-tsang, *Records* I, p 172.

49. Allahabad praśasti of Samudragupta, cf. *Classical Age*, p 9.

50. Nonetheless, Vasubandhu seems to have had fond memories of Śākala, as he returned there towards theend of his life (Hsüan-tsang, *Records* I, p 196).

51. Hsüan-tsang, *Records* I, p 325.

52. Ibid.

53. Bu-ston II, p 143.

54. *Akṣayamati-nirdeśa-sūtra*, Tibetan translation in Peking/Tokyo Tibetan Tripiṭaka, volume 35, pp 2-74.

55. For the account of Asaṅga's students bringing the *Akṣayamati-nirdeśa-sūtra* and the *Daśa-bhūmika*, see Bu-ston II, p 143.

56. Paramārtha, p 292; Bu-ston II, p 143; Hsüan-tsang *Records* I, p 228.

57. Tāranātha, p. 122.

58. *Akṣayamati-nirdeśa-ṭīkā*, Tokyo/Peking Tibetan Tripiṭaka, volume 104.

59. *Daśabhūmi-vyākhyāna*, Tokyo/Peking Tripiṭaka, v. 104, pp 54-136.

60. Bu-ston, II, p 145, says *Śata*, but Tāranātha, p 122, says *Aṣṭa*.

61. This is either the *Saddharmapuṇḍarīkopadeśa*, Taishō 1519-1520, or, as Wayman supposes, Taishō 1524. *Analysis*, p 22.

62. Hsüan-tsang's account of the debate (I, pp 97-109) differs somewhat, though it agrees in the important detail that the Emperor Vikramāditya was present, and that Vasubandhu was not at hand to defend the Dharma. Hsüan-tsang says that the debate was in part due to a personal vendetta of the Emperor against Manoratha. That master, not Buddhamitra, is designated by Hsüan-tsang as the victim of the Sāṅkhya's attack. He also gives the site of the debate as Śrāvastī.

63. Zen lineages in D.T. Suzuki, *Zen Buddhism*, p 60.

64. Hsüan-tsang I, - 192.

65. The traditional age for the beginning of a prince's instruction.

66. Paramārtha, p 288.

67. *Bodhisattva-bhūmi* (Nalinaksa Dutt edition), p 114.

68. Tāranātha, p 124.

69. Ibid p. 122.

70. Some scholars have tended to doubt that Dignāga was a direct pupil of Vasubandhu. It is true that Dignāga in his *Pramāṇasamuccaya*, is in doubt whether *A Method for Argumentation* is a work by Vasubandhu, but this may be, as Stcherbatsky has said, a polite way for Dignāga to express his fundamental disagreement with his teacher. At any rate, Dignāga wrote a small work on Abhidharma called the *Marmapradīpa*, which is nothing more than notes on the *Kośa*. If Kālidāsa in *Meghadūta* verse 14 is in fact making an allusion to the heaviness of Dignāga's philosophy, this would tend to support the latter's tutelage under Vasubandhu.

71. Hsüan-tsang, *Records* I, p 172, p 236.
72. Ibid, I, p 192, p 195.
73. Ibid, I, p 196.
74. Ibid, I, p 195.
75. Paramārtha, p 293.
76. Bu-ston II, p 145.
77. Hsüan-tsang, *Records* I, p 196, p 172.
78. Bu-ston II, p 145.
79. Tāranātha, p 125
80. Hsüan-tsang, *Records* I, p 108
81. *Kośa* III, ad 19.

A METHOD FOR ARGUMENTATION
(VĀDAVIDHI)

INTRODUCTION

A Method for Argumentation (*Vāda-vidhi*) is the only work on logic by Vasubandhu which has to any extent survived. It is the earliest of the treatises known to have been written by him on the subject.[1] This is all the more interesting because the *Vāda-vidhi* marks the dawn of Indian formal logic. The title, "Method for Argumentation", indicates that Vasubandhu's concern with logic was primarily motivated by the wish to mould formally flawless arguments, and is thus a result of his interest in philosophic debate. Topics previously discussed in works such as the *Nyāya-sūtra* of Gautama (c. 3rd century B.C. ?), the *Nyāya-bhāṣya* of Vātsyāyana (3rd-4th century A.D.), Asaṅga's "Rules of Debate",* and the Buddhistic *Tarka-śāstra*** are also discussed here. But what distinguishes the *Vāda-vidhi* from these works is that its discussions of inference contain complete criteria for determining the logical validity of an argument.

In all of these earlier texts, inferences were formulated in a five-membered schema, which is indicated by the following example :

(topic)

1. This mountain is fire-possessing (Demonstrandum)
2. because it is smoke-possessing (Justification)
3. as a kitchen (Parallel Positive Example) and unlike a lake (Parallel Negative Example)
4. and this is so (that the mountain is smoke-possessing)
5. therefore that is so (that the mountain is fire-possessing).

The redundancy of members 4 and 5 was seen by Vasubandhu, who drops them from his schema.*** But there is also something *missing* from this formulation, says Vasubandhu.**** For,

*, ** See Tucci, "Buddhist Logic Before Dignāga", *JRAS* 1929, 151-88, corrections 870-1.

****Vāda-vidhi* 5. That this is an innovation of Vasubandhu's is almost certain, since Asaṅga's work and the *Tarka-śāstra*, which can antedate him only by a little, still retain the five-membered schema.

*****Vāda-vidhi* 5.

in an argument, any event could be interconnected with any other event, as Vasubandhu's examples of spurious arguments show.* In other words, it is not clear what the necessary relationship between members 1 and 2 is. The *Nyāya-sūtra* assumes a "logical pervasion" (*vyāpti*): in this case, the logical pervasion of "smoke-possessing-ness" by "fire-possessing-ness." But this "logical pervasion" is not precisely defined in the *Nyāya-sūtra*, nor is a statement regarding it introduced into the schema itself. Vasubandhu says that the only way in which something can be validly demonstrated in an argument is if there is a specific indication of the "logical pervasion",** and it is also he who gives the first more exact definition of what this term might mean.*** Earlier definitions had focused on "regular co-existence" (*sāhacarya*), i.e. "Whenever Y is absent, X must be absent", but this definition is not strong enough to handle the principle of implication. Vasubandhu, however, defines it as an "invariable concomitance"(*avinābhāva*) between two events, meaning that the known event (e.g. "smoke-possessing-ness") can occur only if the deduced event ("fire-possessing-ness") occurs.[2] He also insists that a statement of the invariable concomitance between the perceived and deduced events is necessary to a valid inference-schema.

Using Vasubandhu's methods for formalizing an inference, the "fire-smoke" argument can be re-phrased as follows :

(topic)

1. Thesis : This mountain is fire-possessing (Demonstrandum)
2. Justification : because of its state-of-possessing-smoke and wherever there is a state-of-possessing-smoke, a state-of-possessing-fire must occur
3. Exemplification : as in a kitchen (Parallel Positive Example) and unlike in a lake (Parallel Negative Example).

From what has been said above, it is clear that Vasubandhu's logic operates from a different premise than Aristotle's. The focus of Indian logic in general is always on individuals, rather

***Vāda-vidhi* 14 ff.

****Vāda-vidhi* 5.

*****Vāda-vidhi* 4.

than their "classes".* Even where "classes" are referred to, they must always be made up of existing known particulars. Vasubandhu describes the process of inference as a particular event's being directly observed, and another invariably concomitant event's being remembered.** Vasubandhu's logic, as is Indian logic after him, is thus rather "intensional" than "extensional", with an emphasis on the properties of individuals.[3] This focus explains the insistence on the exemplification, without which no inference-schema is held to be valid. It ensures that the property discussed in the thesis is non-empty and relates to actual particulars. The positive parallel example guarantees that there are yet other particulars which follow the same invariable concomitance pattern as does the event referred to by the "topic", and the negative parallel example makes sure that these are contrasted with others not following the same invariable concomitance pattern. The *pakṣa*, or topic of discussion, must be either an existing particular, or a property of an existing particular. "Fire-possessing-ness" refers to a property of a particular. Vasubandhu adopts these abstract nouns from the *Nyāya-sūtra*, but for him they do not imply the existence of real universals, as they might to a Naiyāyika.[4] For Vasubandhu especially (even if not for all Indian logicians following him), logic must be based on particulars, and even, to follow his tentative theory***, particulars which are always-changing moment-events. But there will still be certain moment-events that exist only if others do, thus invariable concomitance is still a possibility.

Another original contribution of Vasubandhu's is the reduction of spurious argument-types, of which no less than twenty-four are mentioned in the *Nyāya-sūtra*****, to three basic flaws in arguments. These spurious arguments are all either "reversed", "incorrect", or "contradictory". The schemas called by Vasubandhu "reversed" are those which rest on confusions of the proper functions of the members of the schema, and always

*Aristotle's logic, and Western logic after him, is primarily class-oriented; see the method in *Prior Analytics* I, II-III ff.

***Vāda-vidhi* 10.

***see *A Discussion for the Demonstration of Action* 8, c.

*****Nyāya-sūtra* V, 1, 1 and ff.

involve the absence of a true invariable concomitance.* The "incorrect" or "unreal" are those where the event indicated in the thesis itself is not observed, or is in conflict with what is directly observed. The "contradictory" is where events expressed in the justification cannot co-exist with those adduced in the thesis.**.

Thus, several innovations in Indian logic previously ascribed to Dignāga are found in this treatise of his teacher Vasubandhu. These include the definition of "logical pervasion" as "invariable concomitance", the insistence on the necessary inclusion of a statement of invariable concomitance in the inference-schema, the reduction of the earlier five-membered schema to one of three members, and the reduction of pseudo-justification-types. Vasubandhu's criteria for a valid inference-schema are concise and precise, and there is nothing essential omitted. Dignāga's "wheel of justifications' (*hetu-cakra*), sometimes held to be the first complete Indian formulation of what constitutes the validity and invalidity of an argument[5], is in fact nothing of the kind : it is a pedagogic device mapping out in detail what Vasubandhu's criteria already presuppose.

On first sight, the subject matter of *A Method for Argumentation* might seem remote to those not specifically interested in logical forms. But Vasubandhu is possibly even in his logical work interested in the alleviation of suffering. Vasubandhu takes his examples of arguments to be rejected because of the lack of a true invariable concomitance primarily from the Mīmāṃsakas.*** This group of philosophers maintained that liberation can be reached only by strict observance of the Vedic rituals, and they asserted "the eternality of sounds of speech" because of their insistence that the Vedic mantras have eternal power.[6] But the beauty of Vasubandhu's criteria is that they can see through all spurious reasoning, and of suffering-promoting spurious reasoning, the human life-streams of the twentieth century have certainly had their fill. To give only some examples of current suffering-inducing spurious arguments which could be deftly destroyed by Vasubandhu's method, there are the following :

**Vāda-vidhi* 11, 13-18.

***Vāda-vidhi* 11.

***In this, he follows Gautama; see *Nyāya-sūtra* V, 1, 1 ff.

"Nation So-and-So is prosperous
because of its state-of-having-prosperous-rich-people
(meaning : they have more different kinds of stuff)".

"Nation So-and-So is happy
because of its state-of-having-many-types-of-industry-made-goods."

Or, we may hear the potentate of a great empire say :

"The poor in this country cannot be helped by the Government
because to do so would be monetarily inflationary"

and

"There must be more weapons of destruction produced at all costs, because if the Government cannot reach the potential for destroying all vertebrate life-forms on this planet fifteen times over rather than fourteen, we are in danger."

Following the criteria of *A Method for Argumentation*, the first argument is flawed on several grounds. For one, its topic, "Nation So-and-So", is not a real entity, as can be shown by the parallel example in the inference given in *A Discussion for the Demonstration of Action*, 3 :

topic *demonstrandum*

Thesis : " 'Configuration' is not a single entity
Justification : because of its state-of-consisting-of-totally-divided-parts
Statement of Invariable Concomitance :
for whatever consists of totally divided parts is not unity-possessing
Exemplification : just as an "army", a "forest", etc, (Positive Parallel Example)
and unlike a moment-event.
(Negative Parallel Example)."

Secondly, even admitting the somewhat tenuous definition of "prosperity", the justification is clearly "reversed". Since the perceived events should occur ONLY if the deduced events do, in this "inference", the demonstrandum-event is not properly related to the event referred to in the thesis : the state of having prosperous rich people is not invariably concomitant with the prosperity of all inhabitants of a "nation". The second "inference" would be rejected by Vasubandhu as "incorrect", since the thesis itself is a mere unobserved supposition. The third and fourth, if enunciated together, are grossly contradictory. So logic is not irrelevant to the alleviation of suffering.

In order to understand *A Method for Argumentation* properly, the equivalence of various terms used in regard to members of the inference-schema, and the reasons for there being such various expressions, must be kept in mind. The pair "demonstrandum/demonstrator" is essentially the same as the pair "demonstrandum/justification". The term "demonstrator" emphasizes the purpose of the justification. The terms "event" (*dharma*) and "event-associate"(*dharmin*) refer to the justification and demonstrandum, too, or rather to the events which they discuss. The "event" is always the observed or known "event", the "event-associate" is that which can be related to the "event" through invariable concomitance. In the inference-schema "This mountain is fire-possessing, because it is smoke-possessing", etc., the "event" is the directly perceived state-of-possessing-smoke, and the "event-associate" is the inferred state-of-possessing-fire. Where the terms "event" and "event-associate" are contrasted in this treatise, the "event" always refers to the event expressed in the justification; the "event-associate" always to the inferred object expressed in the demonstrandum.

Concerning the Text :

A Method for Argumentation has not survived as an integral text in any language, and the subsequent fame of Dignāga's logical treatises has made it relatively unknown. But it has been frequently quoted in Dignāga's *Pramāṇasamuccayavṛtti* and Jinendrabuddhi's *Pramāṇasamuccayaṭīkā*, both of which are extant in Tibetan translations. (Peking/Tokyo Tibetan Tripiṭaka, Gtan-tshigs rig-pa section Ce, 9 b ff.) All available fragments of *A Method for Argumentation* quoted in those texts have been collected and arranged through the painstaking efforts of Professor Frauwallner ("Vasubandhu's Vādavidhiḥ", *Wiener Zeitschrift für die Kunde Süd-und Ost-Asiens* 1, 1957, 104 ff).

This translation follows that edition, but not the interpretations of the text that accompany it there.

NOTES

1. The *Vāda-vidhāna* of Vasubandhu, also dealing with logic, is probably later than our text, but very little of it has survived. Dignāga also tells us that Vasubandhu later rejected opinions expressed in *A Method for Argumentation.* (*Pramāṇasamuccaya* I, ad I)

2. It was later found that Vasubandhu's definition did not cover several instances of valid "logical pervasions", and an exact definition of the term became one of the main concerns of the Navya-Naiyāyikas, the late formal logicians of India. (cf. Mathurānātha's *Vyāptipañcarahasya,* in Ingalls, *Materials for the Study of Navya-Nyāya Logic,* pp 90 ff.)

3. cf. Matilal, "The Intensional Character of Lakṣaṇa and Saṁkara in Navya-Nyāya", *Indo-Iranian Journal* VIII, 1964, pp 88 ff; Barlingay, *A Modern Introduction to Indian Logic,* p 57. Potter speaks of the possibility of calling Indian logic "property-extensional", that is, emphasizing classes made up of properties of individuals. ("Astitva, jñeyatva, and abhidheyatva" *Frauwallner Festschrift*).

4. Naiyāyika : a follower of the school of thought founded upon the *Nyāya-sūtra.* This school does recognize the existence of real classes, and each of these abstract terms corresponds to one of them. The translation of these abstract nouns has been a problem. They all end in "*tva*", which correspounds to the English "ty" or "ness". This does very well when the English equivalent is natural to the language, as in the "audibility" and "fireability" of *Vāda-vidhi,* 13. In the case of "*prayatnānantarīyakatva*", the literal equivalent would be "arising-immediately-upon-an-effort-ness". This is awkward, and in the context of Vasubandhu's logic, perhaps misleading. So a hyphenated equivalent, "state-of-arising-immediately-upon-an-effort", has been adopted for this term, as this is actually what it is referring to (again : a property of a particular). Any term ending in "ty" or "ness", as well as any hyphenated phrase beginning with "state-of", represent these "*tva*" expressions in these translations.

5. Frauwallner, "Vasubandhu's Vādavidhiḥ", p 131.

6. One of the Mīmāṃsaka phiosophers, Śabara, author of the great commentary on Jaimini's Mīmāṃsā-sūtra may have been a contemporary of Vasubandhu's, as he is associated with the court of Vikramāditya.

A METHOD FOR ARGUMENTATION

1. The topic (*pakṣa*) is the object of sense or understanding[1] one wishes to investigate.

2, 3. The characteristic of a thesis is the statement of a demonstrandum, i.e. something which one attempts to demonstrate. It cannot exist without the statement of a demonstrandum, i.e. one or another among the various events which could be demonstrated. That is, an event with inferability is accepted only because there is a statement of an example with inferability, such as fire, a seed, or the non-eternality (of sounds of speech) (in various stock examples of events with inferability : a fire is inferable where there is smoke, a previously-existing seed is inferable where there is a fruit, and the non-eternality of sounds of speech is inferable from their state-of-arising-immediately-upon-an-effort). There is no assertion which demonstrates in an argument if another (event) which can be demonstrated, among the many which could be demonstrated, is argued for, because a specified event-associate has not been asserted as having demonstrability through an event which can be demonstrated (i.e. the event-associate "fire" is related to the event "smoke" which can be demonstrated, since smoke is always concomitant with fire, but water is not, as water is not an event-associate of the event "smoke").

4. A justification is an indication of the invariable concomitance of an event with something of such-and-such-a-kind. i.e. an event's not arising if something of such-and-such-a-kind does not exist. Something of such-and-such-a-kind in a demonstrandum is, for example, non-eternality, etc., in reference to an object like sounds of speech. There must thus be an indication of some event which does not exist unless concomitant with another, i.e. if there is a cessation of one, the other cannot exist. A justification exists only when there is an indication of an invariable concomitance of an event-associate with something of such-and-such-a-kind, for example, the invariable concomitance of a state-of-arising-due-to-an-effort with non-eternality, or of smoke with fire. If it is a statement of such a kind, "because of a state-of-arising-immediately-upon-an-effort", it is

a justification (i.e. in the argument "Sounds of speech are non-eternal, because of their state-of-arising-immediately-upon-an-effort", "because of their state-of-arising-immediately-upon-an-effort" is a justification, because of the invariable concomitance of a state-of-arising-immediately-upon-an-effort with non-eternality). There is no justification where there is no such indication of an invariable concomitance, for instance, when one says, "Sound is non-eternal, because of its perceptibility by the eye".

5. The exemplification is the specific indication of the connection of the two (event and event-associate) when one is attempting to demonstrate something. The "connection" is the invariable concomitance of the demonstrandum and the demonstrator, that is, the non-arising of the demonstrator when the demonstrandum does not exist. That through which the connection, i.e. invariable concomitance, of the two is specifically mentioned, is called "the exemplification". It must take the form of a specific parallel example, plus the statement of an invariable concomitance. Thus, in the inference regarding sounds of speech, a specific parallel example would be "like a pot" ("Sounds of speech are non-eternal, because of their state-of-arising-due-to-an-effort, *like a pot*"), and the statement of the invariable concomitance would be "Whatever has come about through an effort is not eternal."

6, 7. Among pseudo-justifications, there are (1) those which are not demonstrated, (2) those which are not sufficiently certain, and (3) those which incur a self-contradiction. Among these, those which are not demonstrated are those where the characteristics stated in the exemplification do not exist. For example, if it is said, "Sound is non-eternal, because it is perceived by the eye", this is an argument which is not demonstrated; if it is said, "It is eternal, because it is without a body", this is an argument which is not sufficiently certain. An example of one which incurs self-contradiction for a Vaiśeṣika is : "It is not eternal, because it is perceived through the senses"; for a Sāṅkhya : "The effect is contained in the cause, because it comes to be (through the cause)."[2]

8. There is a flaw in the exemplification if it exists with an undemonstrated object, for instance, if it is stated that "Sound is eternal, because of its non-tangibility, like a cognition, not

like a pot." The object which is to be demonstrated, and the demonstrator, is not demonstrated by stating the negative parallel example "like a pot".

9. A direct perception is a consciousness through the object itself only. When a consciousness arises only on account of the object-of-sense after which it is designated, and not through anything else, then this cognition is direct perception, for example, cognitions of visibles, etc., or cognitions of pleasure, etc. With this definition, false cognitions are rejected, for example the cognition of mother-of-pearl as silver. For this cognition is designated by "silver" as a "silver-cognition", but does not arise on account of silver, but rather is evoked through mother-of-pearl. A conventional cognition is also rejected by this definition. For such a cognition is designated as "a cognition of pots" etc., but does not arise on account of pots which are really existing, but rather only through juxtapositions of visibles, etc., which are interpreted as "pots",[3] Pots themselves can in no way give rise to this cognition, because of their conventionality, and their thus not being in a state-of-being-a-cause. Finally, cognition through inference is also rejected by this definition, because such a cognition occurs, for instance, through the cognition of smoke and the memory of its invariable concomitance with fire, but not through the fire itself. That through which exclusively the cognition arises, and does not exist unless it arises, is regarded as an "object"in this passage.[4]

10. Knowledge which arises when an invariably concomitant object is observed, is inference. "Invariable concomitance" means that one object cannot arise unless the other one exists, as for example, fire and smoke. The non-observation of a possibility of one's arising without the other is inference, and it is through this invariable concomitance that something may be inferred. Accordingly, the cognition of an object which may be inferred is the result of an inference. By this definition, false cognitions are rejected. Knowledge through inference can be specified as an observation coming when the means-of-evidence is directly observed, and the invariable concomitance between it and what can be inferred is remembered. One (the event in the demonstrandum) does not occur unless something else (the means-of-evidence) is directly known. Otherwise, there is no inference.

11. Flaws exist in a rejoinder when it is reversed, incorrect, or contradictory. A rejoinder is reversed when in the anterior thesis[5], the formulation of the argument is separate from the characteristic of a true justification. An incorrect rejoinder is any that is false, i.e. when the object does not exist in the manner in which the thesis states that it does. A contradictory rejoinder in one that cannot co-exist with its own thesis.

12. Among these, the reversed etc., include spurious replies based on identity of the objects, complete unrelatedness of the objects, various alternatives, non-differentiation, lack of a justification, excess, reduction, direct apprehension (irrelevant to the inference), doubts, non-utterance, difference of effect, etc., (types of spurious replies as categorized by the *Nyāya-sūtra*)*.

13. Among these, four** are reversed, because there is an uncertain similarity adduced in what is to be inferred through a justification which is certain. Just as the reversed is uncertain as regards that which should be certain, so the contradictory is impossible because the objects in the argument cannot co-exist. It is possible to show that a rejoinder based on various alternatives is really one which is incorrect, because something is stated to be uncertain through something that is really certain and true.

14. (When one argues through unrelatedness where relatedness occurs, this is a case where, to follow the older categorization***, one is arguing from unrelatedness of objects.) Assuming that the thesis is as follows : "Sound of speech is not eternal, because of its state-of-arising-immediately-upon-an-effort, like a pot", the maker of such a spurious reply may say the following : "Though in this case, the relatedness alleged by you exists, yet of these two, only a pot is fireable and perceptible by the eye, whereas sound is not. Therefore the pot is non-eternal because of its perceptibility by the eye, and its fireability, whereas the same is not the case with sounds of speech. On the

***Nyāya-sūtra* V, 1, 1.

**Spurious replies based on complete unrelatedness of objects, direct apprehension irrelevent to the inference, non-utterance, and non-differentiation.

****Nyāya-bhāṣya*, ad V, 1, 2.

other hand, of these two only sound is eternal on account of non-perceptibility by the eye, etc., whereas the pot is not."

Such a rejoinder is reversed. For fireability is of insufficient strength to demonstrate non-eternality. One does not observe a state-of-arising-immediately-upon-an-effort without non-eternality; thus the inference is demonstrated in the same way as that relating to fire and smoke. Where fireability does not exist, as in the case of wind produced by a fan, etc., there still does not exist an object without observable non-eternality. Therefore, this reply is reversed. Even with audibility, sounds of speech are observed where a state-of-arising-immediately-upon-an-effort is also observed to occur. Thus this inference based on non-audibility is absurd, as it is refuted by the power of observation. It can be observed that a state-of-arising-immediately-upon-an-effort invariably exists with non-eternality, so through what power is the inference for sound's non-eternality refuted? It simply isn't. Therefore, this reply is reversed.

The opponent is arguing with two-fold uncertainty. This follows from our explanation of the occurrence of his justification together with an unrelated *topic*, though he is arguing from a relatedness of the objects, or, secondly, from our indication that if a demonstrandum is refuted because of unrelatedness of objects, the justification adduced by us is without a refutation. If one argues from a relatedness with fireability, which is certain, towards an uncertainty, though it is true that the relatedness alleged occurs, yet there is no connection in the anterior thesis' rejoinder when it is stated that as without fireability, etc., non-eternality is not observed, it does not exist in the case of sounds of speech. The statement proceeds from a relatedness of objects which does not exist. Because it has been indicated that the statement of the opponent for the eternality of sound because of its non-fireability, etc., is without a justification, and thus without a true demonstrandum, this reply is uncertain, as non-fireability is not concurrent with the demonstrandum eternality, since even where fireability does not occur, eternality still does not necessarily exist. Thus this reply is insufficiently cartain. When one is attempting to infer eternality from a total unrelatedness of objects to a relatedness, as when eternality is argued solely through audibility, one may reply that it is certainly not observed that non-audibility occurs necessarily with non-eternality. Thus this reply is reversed..... (Discussion of spurious replies based on non-differentiation, i.e. where a differentiation which should be taken note of is simply ignored in order to adduce a thesis.* The lost portion probably had as its aim the inclusion of this spurious type within the "reversed" category.)....

15. A reply proceeding from excess and reduction** is reversed. For example, when a justification is brought up with its exemplification, and one says, for example, "Sounds of speech are not eternal, because they have arisen due to an effort", and the reply is given, for example, in this manner: "If the justification demonstrates that the demonstrandum is associated with a certain event, then it follows that it is not different from the demonstrandum, like the water of a stream which has entered the ocean. An association with an event is not possible if the object associated with it is not obtained. But if the demonstrandum is obtained, what purpose can the justification possibly have? On the other hand, if it is not associated with the event of the demonstrandum, then it is not different from those objects which are not justifications, and thus is not a justification itself."

To this anterior thesis, it may be replied as follows : The opponent is speaking of a cause-as-condition-for-a-cognition. But instead of recognizing this, he speaks of it as if it were a material cause, and attempts to refute the inference in this way.[6] He is thus making a vain assertion, because he is attempting to argue against something other than a cause-as-condition-for-a-cognition. Thus this reply is reversed.

16. A justification through a direct apprehension (irrelevant to the inference)*** in the opponent's demonstrandum, is a spurious reply based on direct apprehension. For instance, in the

Nyāya-sūtra V, 1, 23; *Nyāya-bhāṣya* ad V, 1, 23; *Nyāya-kośa*, p 95. Example : "If sounds of speech are non-eternal because of their state-of-arising-due-to-an-effort, and this non-eternality of sounds of speech is argued through their similarity with non-eternal pots, etc., then, because of their inferability, all objects would be non-eternal." (*Nyāya-kośa's* example from the *Nīlakaṇṭhī*, 9, 44.)

***Nyāya-bhāṣya*, ad V, 1, 4.

****Nyāya-sūtra* V, 1, 27.

case already given, where the non-eternality of sounds of speech is inferred through their state-of-arising-immediately-upon-an-effort, the adversary may reply : "This is no justification for non-eternality, because in the case of a flash of lightning, etc., non-eternality is demonstrated through other means-of-cognition, such as direct perception, etc., (and there is no state-of-arising-immediately-upon-an-effort involved). There is no justification where one object exists even where the other (supposedly invariably concomitant one) doesn't." Others formulate this in a different manner : "There is no justification for non-eternality here, because there is no logical pervasion, just as in the case of the necessity of conscious activity for trees because of their sleeping at night, which occurs only for *śirīṣa-trees*."[7]

To this it may be replied as follows : In reply to the statement that non-eternality is demonstrated through a state-of-arising-immediately-upon-an-effort itself only, the opponent is saying : "There is no justification for non-eternality, and there is no logical pervasion, either, so we are made happy." But this reply is reversed. Because it is a vain assertion resting on the assumption that we are claiming that something is non-eternal only because of a state-of-arising-immediately-upon-an-effort, whereas what we are claiming is that something is non-eternal because of a state-of-arising-immediately-upon-an-effort itself only. Thus this reply is reversed.

....(discussion of reversal through doubt, where the means-of-evidence is itself doubtful)* ....

17. When one assumes that since a justification does not exist before its utterance, the demonstrandum also must not exist, this is a case of a reply based on non-utterance.** For example, the maker of such a spurious reply may say to this same argument that sounds of speech are non-eternal because they arise due to an effort : "Since the justification does not exist prior to its apprehension and utterance, it follows that the demonstrandum also does not exist. Thus, since sounds of speech are said to be non-eternal because they have arisen due to an

*cf. *Nyāya-sūtra* V, 1, 14.

** This is similar to the spurious argument based on not-having-arisen (*anutpatti-sama*) in the *Nyāya-sūtra* and *Nyāya-bhāṣya*. (See *Nyāya-sūtra* and *bhāṣya* V, 1, 12, and *Vāda-vidhi* 23.)

effort, it follows that, because the justification does not exist prior to its utterance, the sound is not yet non-eternal. Thus it must be eternal prior to the utterance of the justification. But once it is eternal, how can it become non-eternal?"

To this it may be replied as follows : This reply is reversed. We adduce the justification as something which brings about a cognition, but not as something which brings about a cessation. This maker of a spurious reply is however attempting to refute us on the grounds that the justification itself is supposed to bring about a cessation. Thus this reply is reversed.

18. When one attempts to show that the demonstrandum is not demonstrated on account of a minimal difference in effect*, this is a reply based on difference of effect. When for example the thesis has been set up as follows : "Sounds of speech are non-eternal, because they are an effect, like a pot", the adversary may reply as follows : "The pot is non-eternal because of being an effect of a different sort, so how does this apply to sounds of speech?"

To this it may be replied as follows : We are claiming that every effect in general is non-eternal, so the difference from the state-of-effect of a pot is irrelevant. Thus this reply is reversed.

19. The incorrect includes spurious replies based on unwarranted overextension of principles** and on mere conjecture.***

20. When it is said that sounds of speech are non-eternal because of their state-of-possessing-a-cause-by-obvious-means-of-evidence, just like a pot, a maker of a spurious reply might say, "What is your justification for stating that the pot itself is non-eternal?"

To this it may be replied as follows : Why is there no justification simply because it has not been related to the demonstrandum, when the object in the parallel example can be directly observed to be concomitant with the event in the demonstrandum? For it can be directly observed by you yourselves, too, that the arising of a pot occurs with the means-of-evidence of a cause. Thus this reply is unreal.

**Nyāya-sūtra, Nyāya-bhāṣya,* V, 1, 37.
**Ibid V, 1, 9-10.
***Ibid V, 1, 21.

21. (Spurious replies based on conjecture* may be reduced to unreal replies, also.) For instance, when it is argued that the self does not exist, because it cannot be apprehended, just like the son of a barren woman, the maker of such a spurious reply may respond as follows : "Then the self-evident supposition is incurred, that everything which is directly perceived must exist. But there are objects which though they are directly perceived do not exist, such as the circle which is seen when a torch is hurled in an arc."

To this it may be replied : It is being assumed that there is existence for everything that is directly perceived, which is a vain assertion. (What is being argued here is that that which is not directly perceived, and which cannot be inferred, does not exist.) Thus this reply is unreal.

22. The contradictory includes spurious replies based on not-having-arisen, on eternality, etc.

23. A reply made on the grounds of not-having-arisen** occurs when one assumes that before its coming into existence, the justification cannot have existed, and consequently the demonstrandum also cannot exist. For example, when it is being argued that sounds of speech are non-eternal because they have arisen through an effort, the maker of such a spurious reply might say : "If it is non-eternal, because it has arisen due to an effort, then prior to its arising it has not arisen due to an effort, and consequently it is eternal."

To this it may be replied : Before its arising, the sound does not exist. And to maintain that it does not exist and is eternal, is a contradiction, because non-existence and eternality cannot co-exist. Thus this reply is contradictory.

The same reply is also reversed on grounds of resting on a conjecture. For the adversary is saying : "Since before the arising of the sound its state-of-arising-immediately-upon-an-effort does not exist, it follows that it has not arisen due to an effort, and thus is eternal, because of its state-of-not-arising-immediately-upon-an-effort."

To this it may be replied as follows : There is no certainty that something is eternal because of its state-of-not-arising-

Nyāya-sūtra, Nyāya-bhāṣya V, 1, 21.
**Ibid. V, 1, 12.

immediately-upon-an-effort. For there are three possibilities here : Some things are eternal, like space, etc. And some things are non-eternal, such as flashes of lightning, etc. And some other things do not exist, like a sky-flower, etc. Thus this reply is reversed.

24. When one argues from an object's invariable association with non-eternality to eternality, then we have a spurious reply based on eternality.* In this case the adversary replies to the assertion that sounds of speech are non-eternal as follows : "In that case, sounds of speech are eternal, because they are eternally connected with non-eternality, and its unchanging nature is thus eternal."

To this it may be replied as follows : This is a contradiction. And why is this? Because something non-eternal is being called "eternal". Thus this reply is contradictory.

**Nyāya-sūtra* and *Nyāya-bhāṣya*, V, 1, 32.

NOTES

1. Throughout this translation, "object" means "an object of sense or understanding".

2. According to the Vaiśeiṣkas, simple entities are eternal, though they may be perceived by the senses. According to Sāṅkhya, effects pre-exist in their causes, and they are not a new creation, but only an explicit manifestation of that which is implicitly contained in the material cause. So the Sāṅkhya may assert the first half of the statement given, but not the second, since the effect strictly speaking does not come about because of the cause. Inconsistency with one's own unstated theses is not an extralogical ground for rejecting an argument in Vasubandhu's method.

3. According to the provisional theory most beloved to Vasubandhu, what we normally perceive as entities are in no way really entities; so, for instance, "pots" is a mere conventional expression for an interdependent complex with no unifying entity entering in.

4. The object is that without which a cognition cannot arise. This definition does not say anything about the ontological status of the "object": it only says that without that which is designated as an "object", there is no cognition.

5. "Anterior thesis" is the usual Indian scholastic term for an opponent's thesis, since this is always presented first.

6. Vasubandhu makes a clear contrast between those events which serve as conditions for a consciousness-moment inasmuch as they are its objects-of-consciousness, and those which are its truly generative conditions. (cf. *Kośa* V, ad 27),

7. The *śirīṣa* tree, Acacia speciosa Willd., or Acacia sirissa Buch., has leaves which close at night. Thus it is said to "sleep". The objector is saying that just as one cannot infer the necessity of conscious activity for trees from the sole example of the *śirīṣa's* sleeping, one cannot infer the non-eternality of sounds of speech from their state-of-arising-immediately-upon-an-effort, because a flash of lightning is non-eternal and there is no effort involved.

A DISCUSSION OF THE FIVE AGGREGATES
(PAÑCASKANDHAKA-PRAKARAṆA)

INTRODUCTION

This work is an analysis of those aggregations of events that constitute a living organism. The method for describing "personality" as aggregates of events of five different basic types goes back to the Buddha himself.* According to this analysis, what is called an "individual" or "personality" is a complex array of always-changing interdependent events. The analysis (and the meditation in which it is rooted) focuses on complex successions of aggregates of particular momentary phenomena, and, while treating them genetically, refuses to comprise them into hypothetical wholes. That is, an "individual" is really all of the changing states "which make him up", and there is no central entity underlying the organism. It is only the close interdependence of aggregations of moment-events which makes for their relationship.

The basic types of aggregates are : materialities, feelings, cognitions, motivating dispositions, and consciousnesses. Unlike the earlier Upaniṣadic view**, and the at least somewhat anterior Sāṅkhya and Jain theories***, the Buddha recognizes the body as a basic part of "individuality", and physiological differences as "personality" differences. But unlike Western physiological psychology, which attempts to reduce all personality factors to physiological causes, the Buddha sees other factors in "personality" which are not identical with physiological functions. Feelings are the mood-tones of the moment : these may have purely "psychological" causes apart from physiological ones. "Cognitions" are the mental seizings of characteristics

*cf. *Majjhima* I, 140-141, 145, 185, etc.

**cf. *Bṛhad-āraṇyaka-Upaniṣad* II, 1, where the subtle "self-body" is distinguished from the material body, and "the seven hostile kinsmen" are the organs of the body, which hinder the perception of the inner self. *Kaṭha-Upaniṣad* I, 3, 3, where the self is lord of the chariot and the body is the chariot.

***In Sāṅkhya, *prakṛti* (primal material nature) and *puruṣa* (the soul) are divided; in Jainism *pudgala* (matter) impinges on the separate personality-soul (*ātma*).

or "signs" : each aggregate-complex will have its own way of cognizing. "Motivational dispositions" are all the various events that impel the "organism" : these include various emotions, intellectual views, etc. "A person with anger" is not the same "individual" as "a person with tranquility" several moments later : too much in the entire psychophysical complex has changed. That views should be part of a "personality" is also not surprising, since they can totally color experience. Consciousnesses, finally, are the complex of sense and mental awarenesses.

Beginning about 380 B.C., Buddhist meditators/theorists began isolating, listing, defining, and treating genetically all those basic "personality" event-aggregate types talked about by the Buddha, in books now collected in the various *Abhidharma-Piṭakas* of the Canon.* This is a new very stark unadorned way of writing, which admits only those elements which have meditational provisional existence. Only successions of particular moment-phenomena are admitted, and their causal connections with succeeding moments are discussed. Since there are no hypothetical wholes, but only streams of constantly-changing interrelated moments, concepts such as "self", "individual", or "personality" have no validity. Neither do expressions such as "mind", since what is so designated is a complex array of always changing moment-events.

To give some idea of the methodology of early Abhidharma works, it may be useful to quote from the beginning of the *Dhammasaṅgaṇi*, first book of the Theravāda Abhidhamma (c. 380 B.C.). It begins as follows : "Which events are beneficial? At the time when a beneficial consciousness-moment belonging to the realm of desires† arises, connected with satisfaction, joined with knowledge, with a visible as its object-of-consciousness, a sound as its object-of-consciousness, a smell as its object-of-consciousness, a taste as its object-of-consciousness, a tactile

*Two survive in their entirety : the Theravāda *Abhidhamma*, in Pāli, which has been entirely translated into English, and the Sarvāstivāda *Abhidharma*, now extant only in Chinese translation, from which translations of some portions only have been made into French. (See the bibliography.)

†i.e. ordinary sensory realm outside of meditational states, see note 12 to text.

sensation as its object-of-consciousness, a mentally cognizable as its object-of-consciousness, or any other event that there might be as its object-of-consciousness, at that time there is a contact, there is a feeling, there is a cognition, there is a volition, there is a consciousness-moment, there is a mental application, there is a joy, there is a pleasure, there is a one-pointedness of consciousness, there is a faculty for faith, a faculty for energy, a faculty for memory, a faculty for meditational concentration, a faculty for insight, a mental faculty, a faculty of satisfaction, a faculty for life-continuance, a right view, a right intention, a right effort, a right undertaking, a right mindfulness, a right concentration, a power of faith, a power of energy, a power of mindfulness, a power of meditational concentration, a power of insight, a power of shame, a power of dread of blame, a lack of greed, a lack of hostility, a lack of confusion, a lack of harmful thinking, a tranquility of body, a tranquility of consciousness-moment, a lightness in body, a lightness of consciousness-moment, a pleasantness in body, a pleasantness in consciousness-moment, a fitness in body, a fitness in consciousness-moment, a recognition, a calm, an insight, a grasp, an absence of distraction; these and all the other events which have arisen dependent on conditions at that time—all these events are beneficial."*

Then follow definitions of every type of event enumerated above, but these "definitions" are often linguistic variants of the key term : "What at that time is contact? Whatever at that time is a contacting, a contacting-together, a state-of-having-contacted-together, that at that time is contact. What at that time is feeling? Whatever at that time is a perceived agreeableness arising from contact from a consciousness, an agreeable perceived pleasure, an agreeable pleasure arising from contact with consciousness, that at that time is called feeling."** Thus, each of these enumerated events, plus others which occur at the same time, arise in one moment along with a beneficial consciousness. The list is open-ended : the phrase "and all the other events which have arisen dependent on conditions at

***Dhammasaṅgaṇi* 1. The translations are "mine".

****Dhammasaṅgaṇi* 2-3.

that time" suggests that any enumeration is incomplete. Later Abhidharma lists tend to be closed-ended, and to imply that the enumerated events, and those enumerated events only, have existence in a moment. On the other hand, later Abhidharma works mark an improvement in definitions : in the treatment of a second-century Abhidharma master such as Ghoṣaka, they become more clearly true definitions, rather than, as is often the case in the *Dhammasaṅgaṇi*, lists of nearly equivalent terms derived from the same linguistic root. Thus Ghoṣaka defines "feelings" as follows in his *Abhidharmāmṛta* : "What are feelings? They are experiences, arising from contact with any of the six consciousnesses."*

But throughout its long and varied development, Abhidharma is true to the spirit of the *Dhammasaṅgaṇi* in admitting only particular moment-events. As such it is markedly different from Occidental theoretical psychology of the twentieth century, which always seems to deal with hypothetical wholes and categories. Abhidharma is perhaps more akin to twentieth-century physics. It of course experiments "internally" rather than "externally", as a good deal of it is concerned with investigating which moment-types remain in different meditational states.

Occidental theoretical psychology, on the other hand, usually does not arrive at anything which twentieth-century physics, or fourth-century B.C. Abhidharma, would consider elemental. There is a proliferation of categories and hypothetical wholes unrelated to any experienced moments. In some subtle way, this may be a legacy of Aristotle's *On the Soul*, the *a priori* constructions of which would have been totally rejected by the contemporaneous *Dhammasaṅgaṇi*.** Twentieth-century Occidental psychology, in spite of its attempts to be empirically experimental, often falls into similar traps, by inventing words ("Temperament type", "defense mechanism", etc.) which are at most hypostatized from existing psychophysiological moments, and are sometimes metaphors of dubious validity. The very

*Ghoṣaka, *Abhidharmāmṛta* 5, 3.

**On the contrast between the psychology of the *Dhammasaṅgaṇi* and Aristotle, Carolyn Rhys-Davids has already written an admirable essay, in her introduction to *A Buddhist Manual of Psychological Ethics*, p XXXVII .

Occidental psychological emphasis on "tendencies" would be impossible in Abhidharma, since the psychophysical complex in Abhidharma is always changing. To demonstrate to what an extent this category-invention can go in Occidental psychology, two sentences from a standard text are given : "A person with a high degree of cerebropenia might be expected to show delinquent or manic-depressive tendencies, since he would lack the control and inhibition that normally keep such tendencies in check. The somatopenic individual, on the other hand, would be susceptible to hebephrenia, because he lacked the drive and energy necessary to carry on a normal life."* These two sentences bristle with hypothetical assumptions and categories which the *Dhammasaṅgaṇi* would never admit to have any real existence, i.e. existence as experienced moments, and also suggest that Occidental psychology is much interested in straight-jacketing "individuals" into set pre-conceived patterns. From an Abhidharma point of view, they do not even indicate a very great familiarity with causal processes. For instance, is there really a "lack" in an "individual" categorized as "hebephrenic", or are there not rather visions "lacking" in others? In India, an "individual categorized hebephrenic" by Occidental psychological terminology, might be called a saint.

Buddhist psychology, on the other hand, is most interested in which psychological moments give rise to suffering, which to the cessation of suffering, and which to neither. Moment-events giving rise to suffering are termed "unbeneficial" (*akuśala*), those giving rise to the cessation of suffering are called "beneficial"(*Kuśala*), and those which give rise to neither suffering nor the cessation of suffering are called "indeterminate" (*avyākṛta*). In the quest for the alleviation of suffering, certain extraordinary mental states were recognized as beneficial; thus there is the enumeration of "right meditational concentration" in the *Dhammasaṅgaṇi* passage quoted above. This as well as "the faculty for meditational concentration" and "one-pointedness of consciousness-moment", is defined as follows : "Whatever at that time is a stabilizing of consciousness-moment, a settling, a balance, an absence of distractedness, an

*Leona E. Tyler, *The Psychology of Human Differences.*

unperturbed state of consciousness-moment, and a right meditational concentration, that at that time is a right meditational concentration."*

The first experiences of meditational concentration are described as the four meditations (*jhāna, dhyāna*), and these already take the consciousness-complex outside of "normal" ratiocinative functioning. In the first meditation, consciousness is still ratiocinative, with mental application and discursive thought, and filled with joy and pleasure. In the second, which is an inward tranquilization, mental application and discursive thought have ceased (thus there is no more ratiocination), and joy and pleasure still exist. In the third meditational state, the experience of joy fades out. In the fourth, finally, pleasure fades, and there is only "that utterly pure lucidity and indifference of consciousness, wherein there is neither happiness nor unhappiness."**

Additional meditational practices are enumerated as "the imageless attainments", which are described by the Buddha as follows : "When one has attained the stage of infinite space, the cognition of objects has ceased. When one has attained the stage of infinite consciousness, the cognition of the stage of infinite space has ceased. When one has attained the stage of nothing whatever, the cognition of the stage of infinite consciousness has ceased. When one has attained the stage which is neither cognitional nor non-cognitional, the cognition of the stage of nothing whatever has ceased. But cognition and feeling have ceased when one has attained the cessation of cognition and feeling."*** The deeper workings of consciousnesses, and their potentials for shattering previous constrictions totally, are thus recognized throughout Buddhism (as well as in non-Buddhist meditational systems such as Yoga). Thus Buddhist therapeutic techniques use only categories relating to experienced moment-events, and antidotes are applied to those of them which are seen to be unbeneficial, through meditational methods by which previous ways of cognizing are suspended or entirely discarded. This is the root of the Buddhist sceptical

***Dhammasaṅgaṇi* 24, cf. 15, 11.

**as described in *Saṃyutta* II, 210 ff.

****Saṃyutta* IV, 217.

attitude towards "normal consciousness"—an attitude which is to play a profound role in Mahāyāna.

Particular methods of doing Abhidharma evolved as Buddhist communities bacame isolated from one another with Buddhism's spread : these differences are reflected in the Abhidharma books of the Theravādins and those of the Sarvāstivādins. The second century A.D. saw a great resurgence of Abhidharma writing : it is the time of the *Vibhāṣā**, and of writers such as the Bhadanta Vasumitra, his uncle Dharmatrāta, Ghoṣaka, the Bhadanta Dharmatrāta, and Buddhadeva—all espousing quite different theories on points left unclear by the old Abhidharma manuals. The strongest divergences came on the subject of the "motivating dispositions". This is not surprising, inasmuch as these include what Western psychology would call "emotions", though the Abhidharma category is much more inclusive. It's not surprising that there should be sharply divergent views as to how many different types of motivating dispositions there are, which may arise together, which are unbeneficial, beneficial, and indeterminate. Buddhadeva, who perhaps gives the most radical theory on the subject, denied that they existed at all as definitely recognizable events, and said that all such "motivating dispositions" are really consciousness-moments.** The Bhadanta Dharmatrāta, on the other hand, asserted that all consciousness-moments and motivating-disposition-moments are only forms of volition-moments.*** On the question as to which motivating dispositions are themselves afflictions, there was much debate, and it will be seen that Vasubandhu himself changes his mind on this subject.†

To turn to our text itself, at first sight it appears to be another of the numerous definitional Abhidharma works that have been written since the *Dhammasaṅgaṇi*. But Vasubandhu's approach

*see page 12.

**cf. *Kośa* I, 35, n. 2; II, p 150, n. 2 (La Vallée Poussin), Lin Li-Kuang, *L'Aide-Mémoire de la Vraie Loi*, p 47.

***Lin Li-kuang, pp 47-48.

†In this work, Vasubandhu has six basic afflictions, which are reduced to three in the *Thirty Verses*. *The Commentary on the Separation of the Middle from Extremes*, ad II 2-3a, also shows considerable change of emphasis.

to Abhidharma is always iconoclastic*, and this work was clearly written after his conversion to Mahāyāna. The invocation to the Bodhisattva Mañjuśrī, who with his sword of awareness cuts through all mental discriminations, affirms this—so does the therapeutic concern for "antidotes" that so often marks Vasubandhu's Mahāyāna writing, so does the introduction of the Yogācāra store-consciousness, so does the surprise ending.

The particular Abhidharma scheme adopted and criticized here seems to be most kin to that of the Mahīśāsakas.** The Mahīśāsakas adopted a list of nine uncompounded events (*asaṃskṛta-dharma*).*** *A Discussion of the Five Aggregates* has only four, which is however more than most Abhidharmikas list, and includes some of the Mahīśāsaka elements. The reason for adopting a Mahīśāsaka-like framework for elucidation and criticism comes from the fact that *A Discussion of the Five Aggregates* is a re-working of Asaṅga's *Abhidharmasamuccaya*. Asaṅga, having been originally trained by the Mahīśāsakas, retains many features of their approach to Abhidharma.

In Vasubandhu's work, the lists of the *Abhidharmasamuccaya* are subjected to close scrutiny. The entire list of "motivating dispositions disassociated from consciousness" is called here mere designations for situations in the other aggregates. The Mahīśāsaka-like list of "uncompounded events" is also reduced to events explainable through the other aggregates. Vasubandhu had already in his *Kośa-bhāṣya* subjected Vaibhāṣika Abhidharma to sharp attack, in which many Vaibhāṣika "entities" were discarded. He is doing a similar thing here with Mahīśāsaka categories. He also reduces the somewhat prolix definitions of Asaṅga, by looking at the fundamental feature of the moment-event-type, and by never wasting a word.

In this translation, some terms have been translated differently than is usual. One of these is "*rūpa*". It is used both for the first aggregate and for the object of the first consciousness. As the object of the first consciousness, "*rūpa*" is defined as a "visible". But when treated as an aggregate the definitions focus on its dimensionality in a special locus, and its physical

*or, more exactly, "categoriaclastic".

**cf. Bareau, *Les sectes bouddhiques du Petit Véhicule*, pp 180-189.

***Ibid, p 185, Mahīśāsaka thesis no. 19

resistance (i.e. the space occupied by one *rūpa* cannot be simultaneously occupied by another).* Already in the *Dhammasaṅgaṇi*, it is stated that not all *rūpa* is visible.** As an aggregate, *rūpa* need not belong to the field of any one consciousness, and different aspects of it are perceived by consciousnesses I-V. In fact, according to the *Yamaka*, an early book of the Theravāda Abhidhamma, the *rūpa*-aggregate and the *rūpa* seen as "attractive", etc., are mutually exclusive.*** Presumably this is said because the primary characteristics of the *rūpa*-aggregate are perceived by a tactile consciousness. Good translations of "*rūpa*" as an aggregate are "matter", "materiality", "material forms", whereas as an object of the first consciousness, it must be rendered simply as "visible". The Chinese often translate "*rūpa*" as the object of the visual consciousness by "color", but in the Vaibhāṣika system at least, color is only one aspect of the visible. The reason for the somewhat clumsy "materiality" adopted here for "*rūpa*" as an aggregate, rests on a wish to avoid a radical mind/matter duality. There are in Abhidharma terminology compounds such as "*nāma-rūpa*", which seem to divide the "individual" into material and non-material aggregates, but, similarly, there is the category "*kāyaka*", "bodily", which includes all the aggregates except consciousness.† The researches of Maryla Falk have revealed that the aggregates subsumed under "*nāma*" also have spatial existence. She also says that the dimensionality of *rūpa* does not rule against its genetic connection with *nāma*.†† Besides, "*nāma*" and "*rūpa*" almost always occur together in a compound, which indicates a psychophysical complex not clearly divisible into the two aspects.

Some key terms in this treatise have also been left untranslated here. Of these the most important is "*citta*". This term has usually been rendered as "thought". This seems very

*cf. Asaṅga, *Abhidharmasamuccaya*, p 2, p 12.

**"Atthi rūpaṃ cakkhuviññāṇassa vatthu; atthi rūpaṃ cakkhuviññāṇassa na vatthu." *Dhammasaṅgaṇi* 585.

***"Piyarūpaṃ sātārūpaṃ rūpaṁ, na rūpakkhando." *Yamaka* II, 1, 4, 26.

†cf. Carolyn Rhys-Davids' *Dhammasaṅgaṇi* introduction, *A Manual of Buddhist Psychological Ethics*, p LXXV.

††Maryla Falk, *Nāmarūpa and dharmarūpa*, passim.

inadequate, inasmuch as the connotation of "thought" in English is ratiocinative, whereas *citta* exists in all the four meditatational stages mentioned above. *Citta* is in fact the basic consciousness-moment. In order to demonstrate the inadequacy of the translation "thought", it may be useful to turn to the discussion of "*citta*" by two of the foremost second-century Abhidharmikas, the Bhadanta Vasumitra and Ghoṣaka.

According to the Bhadanta Vasumitra, the meditational experience of states where there are neither cognitions nor feelings can be reduced to *cittas.** But according to Ghoṣaka, this is impossible, as *citta* always involves certain concomitant events, two of which are invariably cognitions and feelings.** Being thus according to Ghoṣaka always imbued with at least a basic intellective and emotive side, and according to the Bhadanta Vasumitra separable from both, "*citta*" is not rendered very well by "thought" in either case. What the Westerner is most apt to designate by that term are really streams of those moments subsumed in this treatise under the general heading "initial mental application" and "subsequent discursive thought". Both of these types of mental activity are eliminated fairly early in meditation, and in fact the second meditational concentration is already free of both of them.*** When meditation manuals speak of "watching the flow of *cittas*", they mean something much more fundamental than witnessing an internal discursiveness : they are talking about unattached observation of consciousness-moments of whatever sort that may arise. Similarly, when Padmasambhava speaks of "Eka-Citta"†, it is One Moment of Consciousness that includes them all, and renderings like "One Thought" or "One Mind" may be quite misleading.

Another term which has been left untranslated is "*manas*". It is employed for any consciousness which serves as a direct condition for a consciousness of the sixth, or "mental", variety. As such, it can be used for any occurrence of any of the six varieties of consciousness-moments which help give rise to an

*cf. *Discussion for the Demonstration of Action*, 34.

**Ghoṣaka, *Abhidharmāmṛta* 66, 12, cf. *Kośa* II, ad 44 c.

****Dīgha* I, 73 ff; *Majjhima* I 276 ff, 336 ff, 454 ff; *Vibhanga* 257 ff.

†cf. *The Tibetan Book of the Great Liberation*.

immediately subsequent mental consciousness-moment. "Consciousness", "*citta*", and "*Manas*" are regarded as synonyms in ancient Buddhism*, and Vasubandhu frequently makes mention of their fundamental equivalence.** However, strictly speaking, some instances of *citta* or consciousness-moments are not *manas*, since they don't give rise to a mental consciousness.

The writings of Asaṅga introduce a new meaning for "*manas*", which is sometimes used by Vasubandhu also.*** The term is there employed for a seventh type of consciousness, a witness-stream of moment-events responsible for the sense of ego****. It is basically an afflicted object-of-consciousness of the underlying store-consciousness, and can be eliminated fairly early in a Buddhist path†.

Residual impressions from past aggregate-moments in the present consciousness-moment have been given the metaphorical designation "seeds". The metaphor is in some ways a very apt one. A "seed" is actually a constantly changing series of interrelated energy-events which gradually, if conditions allow††, will give rise to a sprout. Similarly, a "latent impression" is a constantly changing series of moment-events which will gradually, if conditions allow, give rise to a memory, or a "reverberation" in the consciousness-series. In some ways, however, the metaphor is not so good, inasmuch as that series of moment-events called "a plant seed" only goes through the entire sequence once, whereas that series of moment-events called "a latent impression" may give rise to repeated transformations in the consciousness-series. The relationship between consciousness-moments and "seeds" is symmetrical, since each consciousness-moment leaves an impression in the consciousness-series, and this "seed"-series colors all future consciousnesses. This is true at least until consciousness undergoes

*cf. *Saṃyutta* II, 54.

***Kośa* I, ad 16 c-d; II 34 a-b; *Twenty Verses*, Introduction.

****Discussion of Five Aggregates*, end; *Thirty Verses* 5-6.

****Asaṅga, *Mahāyānasaṅgraha* I, 7. (Lamotte, p 18).

†*Thirty Verses*, 5.

††The Buddhist scheme of causality, dependent origination, assumes that there are always plural causes and conditions for any moment-situation, cf. *Commentary on the Separation of the Middle from Extremes*, I, 10, 11 a.

that enlightening transformation called in Yogācāra texts "revolution at the basis", where past "seeds" lose their influence, and a completely unfiltered perception results.

The Mahāyāna *Sandhinirmocana* and *Laṅkāvatāra* sūtras speak of a "store" or "root" consciousness which is the conditional ground for all the other, "evolving" consciousnesses. Asaṅga and Vasubandhu introduce it into their consciousness-systems partially to meet objections which will be given in the treatise following this one, partially to hint at constriction and liberation in the consciousness-series. The store-consciousness is a stream of moment-events which underlies all the other consciousness-moments : It is the "store-house" or "support" of the "seeds". In Vasubandhu's most category-cutting moments, it is seen to be totally equivalent to the consciousness-"seeds" themselves.*

Though having some affinities with the "unconscious" of post-Freudian Occidental theorists, particularly Jung's "collective unconscious" which includes all the "archetypes" of experience, the store-consciousness is in Vasubandhu's writings the only reason for a feeling of identity or continuity in the consciousness-series, though it is "itself" not an entity at all. The dualistic divisions that Freud and even Jung make for the unconscious can have no place in Vasubandhu's theories. It is recognized by Vasubandhu that a mental consciousness' attempted determinations in reference to that which is basically subconscious are nothing more than a type of mental-consciousness construction which cannot be a real description of that which is fundamentally indeterminate. It seems from a Yogācāra perspective a tragic error that Western psychological theorists have pushed "good-and-evil" dualisms down into the depths of the subconscious, thereby introducing an element of deterministic despair. To Vasubandhu, there is beneficiality and unbeneficiality of events only where there has been a conscious discrimination, and a volition.**

Certain omissions in those groupings of events called "motivating dispositions" may be on first sight puzzling. For instance, where is fear? Fear may usually result from a misunderstanding,

*cf. *A Discussion for the Demonstration of Action*, 32.
**Kośa IX (Pradhan, p. 477, 1-2, CVP, p. 274, 294.)

but so do any of the afflictions. No Abhidharma list seems to include it, though something is said about it in Vasubandhu's Mahāyāna works.*

The particular definitions Vasubandhu here gives are often deeply illuminating. There is in fact an entire Mahāyāna Buddhist way of experiencing and transmuting emotional energies inherent in this book. Particularly penetrating is the definition of "pride". It is seen there that a gloating about "one's superiority" and a brooding over "one's inferiority" both stem from a similar exaggerated and erroneous viewpoint.** Deeply interesting also is the definition of "meditational concentration". It is defined as any complete attention of a *citta*, or series of *cittas*, on any range of events. Thus, being completely absorbed in the sensations of the toes is as much meditational concentration as is a totally formless meditational experience. As the Bodhisattva Vimalakīrti said, "The way you are sitting here is not necessarily the only way of meditating."*** Any type of consciousness-moment may be meditationally concentrated. This also explains how all types of consciousness-moments "conform to understanding", since consciousnesses of any type may be non-dual experiences.

Since Abhidharma regards "personalities" as complexes of ever-changing interdependent streams of moment-events, therapeutic methods based on it are going to be very different from those usually adopted in the West. Western psychology and psychiatry usually operates from categorizations of the "individual". An entire ever-changing psychophysical complex may be boxed into an arbitrary category, and then equally arbitrarily "treated". More often than not this is done without any curiosity, awareness, or tolerance for what the psychophysical complex is actually experiencing. Instead, there is a proliferation of categories like "psychotic", "neurotic", etc. It is indeed unfortunate that the deeper workings of consciousness and "its" own potentials to shatter previous constrictions totally, do not seem to have been noticed : the self-styled observers

*See *Commentary on the Separation of the Middle from Extremes*, ad II, 9.

**This insight is traceable to some of the earliest Abhidharma books, see *Dhammasaṅgaṇi* 1116.

****Vimalakīrti-nirdeśa-sūtra*, III, beginning.

of consciousness in the West often seem extremely constricted by their own excluding categories. This is why in psychiatric institutions, the "patients" often see that their jailers—and this is what it amounts to—are stuck in much more confused levels of consciousness than they are themselves, for it takes a certain openness and deep sensitivity to arrive at those special states of perception called "psychotic", and "someone" who is stuck in categories of a most dualistic kind is not likely to be nearly as tolerant or understanding. Much incredible suffering has been inflicted by Western psychiatric categorizations of people : there have been sad epics of lobotomies, electroshock, poison drugs, ruined lives—even breaking the bones of "retarded" children may be defended as "behavior modification" !

What if instead the troubled "individuals" were treated in a manner of which Vasubandhu would approve, with the only categories used relating to psychophysical moment-events, and antidotes being applied to *those*, in such a way that all forms of perception and communication are equally valid and invalid, and where everyone's innate Buddha-nature is recognized?

Concerning the Text :

A Discussion of the Five Aggregates is lost in the original Sanskrit. The rendering into English which follows is based on the Tibetan translation of Jinamitra, Śīlendrabodhi, Dānaśīla, and Yeśes-sde. (Peking/Tokyo Tibetan Canon, vol. 113, pp 231-239.)

A DISCUSSION OF THE FIVE AGGREGATES
(PAÑÇASKANDHAKA-PRAKARAṆA)

Homage to Mañjuśrī-kumāra-bhūta[1]

1. The five aggregates are the aggregate of materialities, the aggregate of feelings, the aggregate of cognitions, the aggregate of motivational dispositions, and the aggregate of consciousnesses.

What is *materiality*? Materiality is whatever has dimensionality, and consists of all of the four great elements, and everything that is derived from the four great elements. And what are the four great elements? The earth-element, water-element, fire-element, and wind-element. Among these, what is the earth-element ? It is solidity. What is the water-element ? It is liquidity. What is the fire-element? It is heat. What is the wind-element? It is gaseousness.[2] What is derived from them ? The sense-organ of the eye, the sense-organ of the ear, the sense-organ of the nose, the sense-organ of the tongue, the sense-organ of the body, visibles, sounds, smells, tastes, everything that can be subsumed under tactile sensations, and unmanifest action.[3] And among these, what is the sense-organ of the eye ? It is sentient materiality which has color as its sense-object. What is the sense-organ of the ear? It is sentient materiality which has sounds as its sense-object. What is the sense-organ of the nose ? It is sentient materiality which has smells as its sense-object. What is the sense-organ of the tongue ? It is sentient materiality which has tastes as its sense-object. What is the sense-organ of the body ? It is sentient materiality which has tactile sensations as its sense-object. And what are visibles ? They are the sense-objects of the eye : color, configuration, and manifest action.[4] And what are sounds? They are the sense-objects of the ear, having as their causes great elements appropriated by the body, or great elements unappropriated. And what are smells? They are the sense-objects of the nose : pleasant smells, unpleasant smells, and those which are neither. And what are tastes ? They are the sense-objects of the tongue : sweet, sour, salty, sharp, bitter, and astringent. What is everything that can be subsumed under tactile sensations ? They are the sense-objects of the body : the great elements themselves, softness, hardness, heaviness, lightness, coldness, hunger, and thirst. What is unmanifest action? It is materiality which has arisen from manifest action or meditational concentration : it is invisible and exercises no resistance.[5]

2. And what are *feelings* ? They are experiences, and are of three kinds : pleasure, suffering, and that which is neither pleasure nor suffering. Pleasure is whatever there arises a desire to be connected with again, once it has stopped. Suffering is whatever there arises a desire to be separated from, once it has arisen. That which is neither pleasure nor suffering is whatever towards which neither desire arises, once it has arisen.

3. And what are *cognitions* ? They are the grasping of signs in a sense-object.[6] They are of three kinds : indefinite, definite, and inmeasurable.

4. And what are *motivational dispositions* ? They are events associated with cittas,[7] other than feelings and cognitions, and those that are disassociated from cittas. Among these, what are the events associated with cittas ? They are whatever events are associated with cittas. And what are they ? They are contact, mental attention, feelings, cognitions, volitions, zest, confidence, memory or mindfulness, meditational concentration, insight, faith, inner shame, dread of blame, the root-of-the-beneficial of lack of greed, the root-of-the-beneficial of lack of hostility, the root-of-the-beneficial of lack of confusion, vigor, tranquility, carefulness, equanimity, attitude of non-harming, attachment, aversion, pride, ignorance, views, doubt, anger, malice, hypocrisy, maliciousness, envy, selfishness, deceitfulness, guile, mischievous exuberance, desire to harm, lack of shame, lack of dread of blame, mental fogginess, excitedness, lack of faith, sloth, carelessness, loss of mindfulness, distractedness, lack of recognition, regret, torpor, initial mental application, and subsequent discursive thought.

Among these, the first five occur in every citta. The next five are certain only with specific objects-of-sense. The next eleven are beneficial. The next six are afflictions. The rest are secondary afflictions. The last four also become different (i.e. they are capable of being either afflictions or beneficial).

And what is *contact* ? It is the distinguishing which comes after the three (sense-organ, object-of-sense, and corresponding consciousness) have met together. And what is *mental attention* ? It is the entering into done by a citta. What is *volition* ? It is mental action, which impels a citta towards good qualities, flaws, and that which is neither. And what is *zest* ? It is desire towards a range of events of which there is consciousness. And what is *confidence* ? It is holding to certainty in regard to a range of events of which there is certainty. What is *memory*? It is the non-forgetting of a range of events towards which there is acquaintance, and is a certain kind of discourse of citta. What is *meditational concentration* ? It is one-pointedness of citta towards an examined range of events.[8] What is *insight* ? It is discernment as regards the same, and is either understanding, that which has arisen from not having understood, or that which is different from these two. What is *faith* ? It is firm conviction, desire, and serenity of citta towards action, its results, the beneficial, and the Gems.[9] What is *inner shame*? It is a shame coming about through a committed offense, in which the self, or rather the (psychological) event responsible, is predominant. And what is *dread of blame* ? It is that shame towards others that comes about through a committed offense, in which the outer world is predominant. What is *lack of greed* ? It is the antidote to greed, a non-attachment to that which is arising in *manas*.[10] What is *lack of hostility*? It is the antidote to hostility, and is loving kindness. What is *lack of confusion* ? It is the antidote to confusion, and is right recognition. And what is *vigor*? It is the antidote to sloth, and is enthusiasm of citta towards the beneficial. And what is *tranquility* ? It is the antidote to a situation of susceptibility to harm, and is a skill in bodily and mental action. And what is *carefulness*? It is the antidote to carelessness, a cultivation of those beneficial events which are antidotes, and abandoning unbeneficial events through continuing in those beneficial factors : lack of greed, up to vigor. What is *equanimity*? It is whatever evenness of citta, remaining in a tranquil state of citta, total tranquility in citta continuing in those factors-lack of greed up to vigor, through which there is continuity in a state without afflictions through the clearing away of afflicted events. And what is an *attitude of non-harming* ? It is the antidote to an attitude of harming, and is compassion. And what is *attachment*? It is adherence to any fixed intent in appropriating aggregates.[11] And what is *aversion*? It is a tormented volition towards sentient beings. And what is *pride*? There are seven kinds of pride : basic pride, greater pride, the pride that is more than pride, the pride of thinking "I am", conceit, the pride of thinking deficiency, and false pride. Basic pride is any inflation of citta which considers, through a smallness, either "I am greater", or "I am equal". What is greater pride ? Greater pride is any inflation of citta which considers, through an equality, that "I am greater" or "I am endowed with greatness." And what is pride that is more than pride? It is any inflation of citta which considers, through a greatness, that "I am great". And what is the pride of thinking "I am"? It is any inflation of citta which is connected with the view of either "I am" or "mine" in regard to appropriating aggergates. And what is conceit ? It is any inflation of citta which considers, in regard to an excellence which was previously obtained in another moment, but is no longer, "I've attained it." And what is the pride of thinking deficiency? It is any inflation of citta which considers, "I am only a little bit inferior to those of greatly excellent qualities." And what is false pride? It is any inflation of citta which considers "I am endowed with good qualities" when good qualities have not been acquired. And what is *ignorance* ? It is lack of knowledge regarding action, results of action, the Truths, and the Gems, and also the mentally constructed that rises together with it. In the realm of desires[12], there are three roots-of-the-unbeneficial : attachment, aversion, and ignorance, and these are the same as the roots-of-the-unbeneficial greed, hostility, and confusion. And what are *views* ? These views are generally of five kinds : the view of a fixed self in the body, views regarding the permanence or impermanence of the elements constituting personality, false views, adherence to particular views, and adherence to mere rule and ritual. And what is the view of a fixed self in the body? It is an afflicted udgment viewing either an "I" or "mine" in the appropriating aggregates. And what are views regarding the permanence or the impermanence of the elements constituting personality ? They relate to these same elements (the appropriating aggregates), and are afflicted judgments viewing them as either lasting or discontinuous. And what are false views? They are any afflicted judgments which involve fear towards the elements of existence, and which cast aspersions on the efficacy of cause and effect. What is adherence to particular views? It is any afflicted judgment viewing these same three views, and the aggregates which continue in them, as being the best, the most excellent, attained, and most exalted. And what is attachment to mere rules and rituals? It is any afflicted judgment seeing in rules and rituals, and in the aggregates continuing in them, purity, liberation, and a leading to Nirvāṇa. And what is *doubt*? It is any two-mindedness as regards the Truths, etc. The latter three of those afflicted views mentioned above, and doubt, are the basic mentally constructed. The rest of these views are the mentally constructed that often arise together with those.[13] What is *anger*? It is any tormented volition of citta which all of a sudden becomes intent on doing harm. What is *malice*? It is taking hold of a hostility. What is *hypocrisy*? It is unwillingness to recognize one's own faults. What is *maliciousness*. It is being enslaved by unpleasant speech. What is *envy*? It is an agitation of citta at the attainments of another. What is *selfishness*? It is a holding fast to a citta which is not in accord with giving. What is *deceitfulness*? It is attempting to show forth to another an unreal object through an action of decoying. What is *guile*? It is a deceitfulness of citta which seizes an opportunity for making secret one's own flaws. What is *mischievous exuberance*? It is holding fast to a delighted citta unconnected with internal good qualities. What is an *attitude of harming*? It is an intention unbeneficial towards sentient beings. And what is *lack of shame*? It is a lack of internal shame at offences one has committed. And what is *lack of dread of blame*? It is a lack of dread towards others at offences one has committed. What is *mental fogginess*? It is a lack of skill in mental action, and is thickheadedness. What is *excitedness*? It is lack of calm in citta. What is *lack of faith*? It is a lack of trust in a citta, which is not in accord with faith, towards action and its results, the Truths and the Gems. What is *sloth*? It is a lack of enthusiasm towards the beneficial in a citta, and is that which is not in accord with vigor. What is *carelessness*? It is any non-guarding of citta from afflictions, and non-cultivation of the beneficial, which comes about by being linked with greed, hostility, confusion, or sloth. What is *loss of mindfulness*? It is an afflicted mindfulness, an unclarity as to the beneficial. What is *distractedness*? It is any diffusion of citta, which partakes of greed, hostility, or confusion on the five sense-qualities of the realm of desires. What is *lack of recognition*? It is a judgment connected with afflictions, by which there is entry into not knowing what has been done by body, voice, or manas. What is *regret*? It is remorse, a piercing sensation in manas. What is *torpor*? It is a contraction of citta which is without capacity for entering down into anything. What is *initial mental application*? A discourse of inquiry by manas, a certain kind of volition and discernment, which can be characterized as an indistinct state of citta. What is (*subsequent*) *discursive thought*? A discourse of examination by manas, which in the same way can be characterized as a more precise state of citta.[14]

And what are the *motivating dispositions disassociated from cittas*? These are pure designations for situations in materialities, cittas, and events associated with cittas, and are designations only for these, and not for anything else.[15] And what are they? *Prāpti*, the attainment without cognitions, the attainment of the cessation of cognitions and feelings, any non-meditative state without cognitions, life-force, taking part in an organism, birth, decrepitude, continuity, lack of duration, the collection of words, the collection of phrases, the collection of syllables, the state of being separate from Dharma, and other factors like these.

Among these, what is *prāpti*? It is becoming connected with something attained.[16] Actually, it is a "seed"[17], a capacity, an approachment, and an adjustment to circumstances.[18] And what is an *attainment free from cognitions*? It is any cessation of non-stable events: cittas and events associated with cittas, which is totally clear and separate from attainments, and which comes about through a mental attention dispensing with cognitions about to arise, where former cognitions do not exist. And what is the *attainment of the cessation of cognitions and feelings*? It is any cessation of non-stable and more stable events, cittas and events associated with cittas, which comes about through a mental attention dispensing with cognitions, continuing in which comes after the summits of existence have been practised, and which is separate even from those attainments present in the stage-of-nothing-whatever.[19] And what is a *non-meditative state without cognitions*? It is the cessation of non-stable events: cittas and events associated with cittas, which takes place, for instance, within those groups of gods which are sentient, but do not have cognitions. What is *life-force*? It is, as regards any events taking part in an organism, any continuity, for a certain time, of motivating dispositions which have been projected by past action. And what is *taking part in an organism*? It is any close interrelationship of bodily parts as regards sentient beings.[20] What is *birth*? It is any arising of a stream of motivating dispositions which has not already arisen, as regards any collection of events taking part in an orgnism. And what is *decrepitude*? It is an alteration in the stream of those like that (i.e. events taking part in an organism). What is *continuity*? It is the serial propagation in the stream of those like that. What is *lack of duration*? It is the discontinuity in the stream of those like that. What is the *collection of words*? It is denotations for the own-beings of events. What is the *collection of phrases*? It is denotations for the particularities of events.[21] What is the *collection of syllables*? They are the syllables of actual sound through which the other two are disclosed. Though these all refer to speech, meanings are communicated dependent on words and phrases. For the same syllable does not arise with another synonym.[22] And what is the *state of being separate from Dharma*? It is the non-attainment of noble psychological events.

These all are called "the aggregate of motivational dispositions".

5. And what is *consciousness*? It is awareness of an object-of-consciousness, visibles, etc. "Citta" and "manas" are the same as consciousness. They are so designated because of their variety, and because of their providing a mental basis, respectively.[23] Actually, the store consciousness is also citta, as it accumulates the seeds for all motivating dispositions.[24] Its objects-of-consciousness and aspects are undiscerned.[25] It joins an assemblage pertaining to an organism into a felt relationship, and continues as a series of moment-events. Thus, though there is awareness of a sense-object immediately upon emerging from the attainment of cessation of cognitions and

feelings, the attainment free from cognitions, or a non-meditative state without cognitions, it arises as the consciousness of the attainments themselves; it is the state of evolvement into another aspect once there has been perception dependent upon any object-of-consciousness; it is the state of citta's arising again even after the consciousness-stream has been severed; it is entry into Saṃsāra* and transmigration in it.[26] This same store-consciousness is the support of all the seeds, the basis and causality for the body, and the state of continuance in a body. It is also called "the appropriating consciousness", because it appropriates a body. Used in the sense of a specific entity, *manas* is an object-of-consciousness, within the store-consciousness, a consciousness always connected with confusion of self, the view of a self, pride of self, love of self, etc. It also joins an assemblage pertaining to an organism into a felt relationship, and continues as a series of moment-events, but does not exist in a saint, the Noble Path, or at the time of the attainment of cessation.

Why are the aggregates thus designated ? It is through their collectivity, i.e. various kinds of materialities, etc., being heaped up together that "times", "series", "aspects", "developments", and "sense-objects" seem to occur.[27]

The twelve *sense-fields* are the sense-field of the eye and the sense-field of visibles, the sense-field of the ear and the sense-field of sounds, the sense-field of the nose and the sense-field of smells, the sense-field of the tongue and the sense-field of tastes, the sense-field of the body and the sense-field of tactile sensations, the sense-field of *manas* and the sense-field of mentally cognizables. The eye, visibles, the ear, sounds, the nose, smells, the tongue, tastes have all been discussed previously. The sense-field of the tactile is the four great elements and everything (all the incredibly numerous various sensations) which can be subsumed under tactile sensations. The sense-field of *manas* is any aggregate of consciousness. The sense-field of mentally cognizables is feelings, cognitions, motivating dispositions, unmanifest action, and the uncompounded. And what is the uncompounded ? Space, the cessation not through contemplation, the cessation through contemplation, and Such-

*The world of change.

ness. Among these, what is *space* ? It is any interval separating materialities.[28] What is a *cessation not through contemplation* ? It is any non-separation from cessation without antidotes to afflictions figuring in.[29] And what is *cessation through contemlation* ? It is any non-separation from cessation, any constant non-arising of aggregates through antidotes to afflictions. What is *Suchness* ? It is the "inherent nature (*dharmatā*) of any event", and is the selflessness of events.[30]

Why are these called "sense-fields" ? Because they are the doors to the rising of consciousness. The eighteen *sensory domains* are the domain of the eye, the domain of the visible, the domain of the visual consciousness; the domain of the ear, the domain of sounds, the domain of audial consciousness; the domain of the nose, the domain of smells, the domain of olfactory consciousness; the domain of the tongue, the domain of tastes, the domain of gustatory consciousness; the domain of the body, the domain of the tactile, the domain of tactile consciousness, the domain of the *manas*, the domain of mentally cognizables, and the domain of the mental consciousness. The domains of the eye, etc., and the domains of visibles, etc., are the same as the sense-fields. The domains of the six consciousnesses are awarenesses with objects-of-consciousness in visibles, etc., and which are dependent on the eye, etc. The domain of *manas* is any of these consciousness-moments which are past immediately afterwards, because of the continuity of the sixth consciousness.[31] In this way, the sensory domains have been determined as eighteen.

Ten of those sense-fields and domains (the sensory organs and their objects) and that part of the sense-field of mentally cognizables which may be subsumed under it (unmanifest action) constitute whatever is the aggregate of materiality. The sense-field of *manas* and the seven domains of citta (the visual, olfactory, gustatory, tactile, and mental consciousnesses, and the domain of mentally cognizables) constitute whatever is the aggregate of consciousness. The sense-fields and domains of mentally cognizables also constitute whatever are the other three aggregates (feelings, cognitions, and motivating dispositions), one part of the aggregate of materiality which may be subsumed under it (unmanifest action), and the uncompounded. Why are these called "domains" ? Because they grasp an "own-characteristic", though without a "doer".[32] As to why they are called "aggregates", etc., this serves as an antidote to the three kinds of grasping after self, in order. The three kinds of grasping after self are grasping for one central entity, grasping for an "enjoyer", and grasping for a "doer".

Among these eighteen sensory domains, which contain materiality ? Whatever has the own-being of the aggregate of materiality. Which do not contain materiality ? The rest of them. Which can be seen ? Only the sensory domain of visibles is an object-of-sense which can be seen.[33] Which are invisible ? The rest of them. Which exercise resistance ? The ten which contain materiality, which exercise resistance on each other. Which do not exercise resistance ? The rest of them. Which are liable to be connected with afflictions ?[34] Fifteen (i.e. the sensory domains of the eye to tactile consciousness), and part of the last three (*manas*, mentally cognizables, and mental consciousness). Which are unliable to be connected with afflictions ? Part of the last three. Those because of having a scope allowing for the direct perception of the arising of afflictions.[35] Which are without afflicitions ? Part of the last three. Which occur in the realm of desires ? All of them. Which occur in the realm of simple images ? Fourteen : all of them except smells, tastes, olfactory-consciousness, and gustatory-consciousness. Which occur in the imageless sphere? Part of the last three. Which are included within the aggregates ? All of them except the uncompounded. Which are included within the appropriating aggregates ? Those constituting a "personality". Which are beneficial, which unbeneficial, and which indeterminate ? Ten may belong to any of the three categories : the seven sensory domains of citta, and the sensory domains of visibles, sounds and mentally cognizables. The rest of them are all indeterminate. Which are "internal" ? Twelve of them : all of them except visibles, sounds, smells, tastes, tactile sensations and mentally cognizables. Which are "external" ? Six of them : those not included in the preceding. Which have an object-of-consciousness ? The seven sensory domains of citta, and one part of the sensory domain of mentally cognizables, namely, whatever events are associated with cittas. Which are without an object-of-consciousness ? The ten others and most of the sensory domains of mentally cognizables. Which contain discrimination? The sensory domains of *manas*, mental consciousness, and mentally cognizables. Which do not contain discrimination? The rest of them* Which are appropriated? Five of the "internal" (organs I-V) and part of the "external" (i.e. part of visibles, sounds, smells, tastes, and tactile sensations). Which are unappropriated? Part of the four (all visibles, smells, tastes and tactile sensations not integral parts of the sensory organism).[36] Which are similar in what they show? The five internal material ones (organs I-V), their respective consciousnesses and sensory domains, inasmuch as they have something in common. What is their similarity? These are all, by means of their respective consciousnesses, empty, because of a conformity of each to understanding.[37]

NOTES

*This seems in contradiction with note 14, but Yaśomitra explains: Though the sensory consciousnesses do have basic discrimination, they lack the discrimination of definition (abhinirūpaṇa-vikalpa), i.e. "This is this, that is that", and hence are called non-discriminatory. (Abhidharmakośavyākhyā, ad I 33).

1. On the Bodhisattva Mañjuśrī "who has become a prince", see Introduction to this text, p 58.

2. *The great elements.*

The great material elements accepted by the *Vibhāṣā* are earth, water, fire and wind. It has been held (cf. Jaini, *Abhidharma-dīpa*, Introduction, p 90) that the theory of these elements may have been inspired by the Vaiśeṣikas, who enumerate earth, water, fire, wind, space, time, place, soul and *manas* as *dravyas* (Kaṇāda, *Vaiśeṣika-sūtra* I, I, 5). But their adoption in Buddhism may actually antedate Kaṇāda, as it is in evidence in the *Dhammasaṅgaṇi* (648). It is possible that both Buddhist Abhidharma and Vaiśeṣika may derive their elements via the *Upaniṣads* (cf. *Praśna-Upaniṣad* IV, 8) from the cosmogenic categories of the *Brāhmaṇas*. The *Śatapatha-Brāhmaṇa*, XI, I, 6, 16-24, states that water, breath (wind), speech, and fire were created at the first full-moon and new-moon rites performed by Prajāpati and Parameṣṭhin; at the second rite, the sky (space), earth and water were created.

Already in the *Prakaraṇapāda* of Vasumitra (Chinese translations Taisho 1541 and 1542), a text held in canonical esteem by the *Vibhāṣā*, these elements are not the common things usually designated by the names "earth", etc., but rather represent more abstract principles to be found in materiality. Earth is the solid principle that holds things in place, water the wet principle which has cohesion as its special quality, fire the hot principle that cooks and transforms, and wind the mobile principle that expands and displaces (*Prakaraṇapāda* 13 a, quoted La Vallée Poussin, *Kośa* I, p 22). Vasumitra says further that these elements are directly perceptible only by the fifth, or tactile, consciousness.

3. A detailed discussion of the Vaibhāṣika concept of "unmanifest action" occurs in *A Discussion for the Demonstration of Action*, 14 and in note 3.

4. A discussion of these divisions of the visible (all of which except color are rejected by Vasubandhu) is given in *A Discussion for the Demonstration of Action*, 1-5. On "configuration", see note 5 to that text.

5. Though an "unmanifest action" is a residual force which has as its locus the material elements of the body, it does not share the usual characteristics of materiality, since it is not directly perceptible, and exercises no resistance. This latter phrase means that the locus of one materiality can not be occupied by another, so that if two instances of materiality collide, one will displace the other.

6. A cognition is a particularization of perception, and may accompany any type of consciousness-moment. Certain "signs" or salient features are taken hold of : thus there may be "the cognition of the smell of a jasmine flower", "the cognition of the taste of rice", or "the cognition that everything is impermanent" accompanying instances of smell-consciousness, taste-consciousness, and mental consciousness, respectively.

7. On cittas, see introduction to this text, p 59-60.

8. "One-pointedness" is a metaphor for complete concentration. Any range of events may serve as a focus for meditational concentration. See introduction, p 63. A totally formless meditation is still "one-pointedness of citta towards an examined range of events", since formless experiences are still included in a definite range of events.

9. This is a Buddhistic definition of "faith", which focuses on those few "articles of faith" accepted by Buddhism : that actions all have retributory effects for their "performers", that there is a beneficial course of action which is not conducive to the arising of suffering, and that the "Gems" (the Buddha, the Dharma and the Buddhist community) are worthy of respect because they indicate beneficial courses of action.

10. On *manas*, see introduction, pp 60-61. This definition of "greed" suggests that greed (or attachment, which is seen to be the same) can arise only in regard to mentally constructed events.

11. "The appropriating aggregates" are those collections of aggregates that constitute a definite life-stream : they "appropriate" their interrelationship.

12. The three realms of experience are "the realm of desires", "the realm of simple images" and "the imageless realm". Any state where all the sense-consciousnesses are operative, and where all passions and aversions have their full opportunity to develop, is subsumed under "the realm of desires". Thus, all non-meditationally concentrated states are included there. "The realm of simple images" comprises the four first meditational stages, where certain senses, such as smell and taste, are not operative. "The imageless realm" comprises any state where all senses except the mental consciousness are suspended. It is "imageless", then, in the sense that the first five consciousnesses no longer perceive their objects. These states are the ex-

treme meditational concentrations, the four "imageless attainments", which culminate in the attainment of the cessation of all cognitions and feelings.

The conception of these "realms" in Buddhism shows an amalgamation of cosmological needs with the result of meditational experimentation. In the earliest Buddhist conception, there were apparently only two "realms": a "realm of images" and an "imageless realm". (cf. *Sutta-nipāta* 755-756, *Itivuttaka* 51, 73.) Przyluski noted that the contrast between the 'realm of desires" and the "realm of images" was added later ("Bouddhisme et Upanishad", *Bulletin de l'Ecole Française de l'Extrême Orient*, 1932). Falk supplies an explanation for this when she says that the assumption of a three-"realm" division was made necessary by increasing experimentation with the imageless attainments (*Nāmarūpa*, p 98). Originally, these meditations were not very important in Buddhism, though they were practised and held central by several religious orders, including that of Udraka, the second religious teacher of the Buddha. In *Dīgha* III, 131, ff, it is stated that the four simpler meditations are all that are needed to attain the fruits of sainthood, and it is also significant that directly before his death, the Buddha went into those meditational concentrations only (*Dīgha* II, 156). Increasing experimentation with the sense-suspending attainments made it necessary to distinguish "realm-wise" between them and the simpler meditational stages.

13. It is primarily doubt as regards the clearly perceived, false views, adherence to any particular view, and adherence to mere rule and ritual, that gives rise to mental constructions—those focuses of mental consciousness that have no reality outside of the constructions of that consciousness. Other particular views which have an unbeneficial effect rest on those four types of confusion.

14. "Initial mental application" and "subsequent discursive thought" are two kinds of flows of discrimination—in fact the first of them is to Vasubandhu *svabhāva-vikalpa*, "basic discrimination", the kind that makes all other kinds possible. Both of these are regarded as existing together within the sensory consciousnesses by the *Vibhāṣā*, and by orthodox Vaibhāṣikas such as Saṅghabhadra and the Dīpakāra. But in the face of Vasubandhu's attacks, which state that these two are not genetically different, but only different stages in the same "series", and thus can't be situated together within one moment of consciousness, both Saṅghabhadra and the Dīpakāra are forced to admit that the second of these can be present in the first five types of consciousness only "in an unmanifest state", cf. *Abhidharmadīpa* ad II, 123, p 83; Yaśomitra's citation of Saṅghabhadra's *Abhidharmanyāyānusāra*, ad II 33, Law ed II, p 57. (See also Jaini's discussion, *Abhidharmadīpa*, introduction, pp 83-88.) To Vasubandhu, "initial mental application" is not really a separate event, but represents a certain kind of volition and constructing discernment existing, as he says, even in sensory consciousnesses, as long as these are not meditationally concentrated, (cf. Yaśomitra's discussion, *Vyākhyā*, ad I 33, Law I, p 74) whereas according to older definitions, such as the *Vibhāṣā's* and Asaṅga's, it and discursive thought rest on volition and discernment, rather than being strictly identifiable

with them (*Abhidharmasamuccaya*, p 10; Yaśomitra *Vyākhyā*, ad II 33, Law II, p 57). Following Vasubandhu initial mental application is volition or discernment inasmuch as it does or does not involve deduction (cf. Yaśomitra, ad I 33, Law I, p 74 : "Anabhyūhāvasthāyāṃ cetanā abhyūhāvasthāyāṃ prajñeti vyavasthāpyate)". The discussion of Schmidthausen in his article "Sautrāntika-Voraussetzungen in *Viṃśatikā* und *Triṃśikā*" which attempts to uphold some kind of a fundamental distinction between sensory and non-sensory consciousnesses in Vasubandhu's psychology, is confused to some extent by a misquotation from Yaśomitra in Jaini's edition of the *Abhidharmadīpa*. Initial mental application is certainly not for Vasubandhu "only an impulse", as Schmidthausen claims. Jaini's quotation from Yaśomitra is "Cetanāviśeṣa eva vitarka iti" (p 19, n 4), "He says that initial mental application is only a certain kind of volition", but the text clearly reads "Cetanā*prajñā*viśeṣa", "a certain kind of volition or discernment" (Yaśomitra, ad I 33, Law I, p 74). Vasubandhu does not place too much emphasis on the distinctness aspects of these mental streams, as he considers such descriptions quite relative (cf. *Kośa* II, ad 33a-b, La Vallée Poussin, pp 173-174). Sthiramati explains that the "indistinctness" of initial mental application when compared to subsequent discursive thought consists in the fact that initial mental application considers only the object of sense or understanding, without further connections being made. These are made by subsequent discursive thought. (*Triṃśikavijñaptibhāṣya*, p 32). (See also *Dhammasaṅgaṇi* 7-8, and Carolyn Rhys-Davids' comments on Buddhaghosa's *Atthasālinī* 114, 115, where "initial mental application" is described as "a distinctively mental procedure at the inception of a train of thought, a deliberate movement of voluntary attention" and "subsequent discursive thought" as "the movement and maintenance of a voluntary thought-continuum, as distinguished from the initial grappling with the subject of reflection.", *Dhammasaṅgaṇi* translation, p 10, note 1; p 11, note 2.)

It is interesting that Vasubandhu will characterize these mental flows which make for discriminations as being potentially afflictions. These flows tend to result in holding fast to views, etc., and thus give rise to afflictions. They are both eliminated fairly early in meditational concentration streams.

15. Vasubandhu is here eliminating the entire category of "motivating dispositions disassociated from citta", and proceeds to explain how each of these "moment-events" thus categorized really represents a particular condition in materialities, cittas, and events associated with cittas.

16. "Attained" is here being used in its most bland scientific sense, to mean "becoming intimately associated for a time".

17. See Introduction, pp 61-62. Here, what the Vaibhāṣika and Mahīśāsaka accept as a special entity *prāpti* is equated to residues in consciousness effected by latent impressions.

18. When one says, conventionally, that "X has Y", the Mahīśāsaka and Vaibhāṣika explain this as moment-event A subsumed in "series X" connected by a *prāpti* to moment-event B subsumed in "series Y". A *prā-*

pti is recognized by them as a special kind of entity that links diverse but related elements. As such it plays a role not unlike the inherence-category (*samavāya-padārtha*) of the Vaiśeṣikas, except that the latter, at least in the earlier theory, is single, whereas there is a *prāpti* for each connecting relationship between two events. Vasubandhu regards the concept of *prāpti* as bogus. What is thus designated may be a "seed", as when one says "X has such and such a view". This means that, within the aggregate-series designated as "X", there are consciousness-moments accompanied by latent impressions from past moments ("seeds"), making for a view. It may be a capacity, as when one says, "X has great bodily strength." This means that, within the aggregate-series designated as "X", there is the capacity for doing heavy bodily actions. It may be an "approachment", a growing physical proximity of two events, as when one says "X is eating food". It may be simply an "adjustment according to circumstances", as when one says, "X has a feeling of pain" (explained by the Mahīśāsakas and Vaibhāṣikas as a consciousness-series designated "X" linked to an aggregate of suffering-feeling by a *prāpti*). According to Vasubandhu, this is simply an alteration from one citta to the next because of a circumstance of pain in the feeling-aggregate interrelated to the consciousness-aggregate.

19. The attainment of the cessation of feelings and cognitions, last of the "imageless meditations", is reached only after the consciousness-sertes has passed through the other four imageless attainments, which are also designated as "the summits of existence". These latter are the meditational attainments focused on infinite space, on infinite consciousness, on nothing whatever, and the state which is neither cognitional nor non-cognitional. For the attainment of cessation of feelings and cognitions to be reached, even those events present in the stage which is neither cognitional nor non-cognitional must no longer be present. Vasubandhu says that the attainment of cessation of feelings and cognitions must be separate from the subtle attachments present even in the stage of nothing whatever, but actually he "should" say in addition that this attainment is separate even from the dim cognitions of the stage which is neither cognitional nor non-cognitional, as well.

20. The factor here translated as "taking part in an organism" has usually been rendered "generic similarity". This however is clearly not what is involved, as can be seen from Vasubandhu's definition.

21. A word may indicate the "own-being" or "nature" of a moment-event, e.g. "blue", but a complete meaning dealing with particulars of events can only be expressed by a phrase.

22. Syllables themselves are not the conveyors of meaning, otherwise each synonym would consist of the same syllables.

23. "Cittas" are so called because of their variety (*citratva*), and all instances of "*manas*" are so called becasue of providıng a mental basis (*manāśraya*). The first of these etymological explanations is used by Vasubandhu again in *A Discussion for the Demonstration of Action*, 31, and in *The Teaching of the Three Own-Beings*, 7.

24. This is the second etymological explanation of "citta", by the root

ci, cinoti, "to accumulate". This again occurs in *KSP* 31 and *TSN* 7. The six consciousnesses are variegated, thus fit with the first etymology; the store-consciousness accumulates "seeds", thus fits with the second.

25. According to Mahīśāsaka and Vaibhāṣika theory, each consciousness must have an object-of-consciousness and also an aspect, that is, some special characteristic by which it can be recognized. Since the store-consciousness underlies the six discerning consciousnesses which have definite objects-of-consciousness and aspects, it cannot be discerned by any of them. Thus its object-of-consciousness and aspect must be undiscerned. It is known only by inference, as Sumatiśīla says in *Karmasiddhiṭīkā*, ad 36. Though this may be an embarrassing admission to make in the face of Vaibhāṣika charges that a consciousness should be directly experienced, it at least has the value of consistency. Vasubandhu's admission that the object-of-consciousness and aspect of the store-consciousness are undiscerned is better than the approach of Occidental "depth-psychologists", who posit a "subconscious" and then try to fix its contents, which is tantamount to saying that the "subconscious" can be consciously discerned.

26. Here, Vasubandhu has compactly given the inferential justifications for assuming a store-consciousness within his definition of it. The meditational attainment of the cessation of cognitions and feelings must itself be accompanied by consciousness-moments, otherwise the consciousness-series could never resume once the attainment ceases. This is one of the main arguments for the existence of the store-consciousness in *A Discussion for the Demonstration of Action.* A consciousness-series changes permanently after it has been impressed by an object-of-consciousness : again this is impossible without some substratum. Entry into Saṃsāra, i.e. consciousness' becoming linked with an organism, is again impossible without some consciousness preceding temporally the six discerning consciousnesses, as these do not yet exist at the inception of an embryo's existence. Transmigration in Saṃsāra, or, more properly, the residue of the aggregate-complex from one life to the next, is again impossible unless there is a substratum where the residue exists. Some of these arguments were already used by Asaṅga. (The argument of a consciousness' being necessary in the attainment of the cessation of feelings and cognitions is raised by Asaṅga in *Mahāyānasaṅgraha*, I, 31., the change in aspects in consciousness implying a substratum in I, 32., no possibility of the carry-over of impressions from one moment to the next without an underlying consciousness, in I, 33-34., and the impossibility of there being a residue of one consciousness-complex from one moment to the next without a store-consciousness in I, 38.)

27. The aggregates are first of all so designated because they are not simple moment-events, but are moment-events "heaped together". For instance, "materiality", though one kind of aggregate, consists in one moment "in one organism" of a huge number of moment-events, in fact all the events which twentieth century physiological chemistry is attempting to define. Furthermore, they are not only "aggregated" in one moment, but the events in one aggregation-moment help give rise to the next. Time, a real category to ancient and modern Vaiśeṣikas, is recognized already in the *Vibhāṣā* as being only a name for the flow of compounded events (see

Vibhāṣā selections translated by La Vallée Poussin, *Mélanges* 1936-37, p. 8). Thus "time" exists only because moment-events are followed by subsequent moment-events. A "series", similarly, is only a metaphor for the phenomenon of one aggregate-moment's arising when the other has ceased, and being causally linked to the previous one. An "aspect", defined as a distinguishing characteristic for a moment-event, is really not anything of the sort, either, since "it" is abstracted from the many events arising in one moment. A "development", again, does not really occur, since there is not anything which can undergo change : rather each moment is distinct from the previous one. It is conventionally said that "A visible is a sense-object of an eye", but this statement comes only from the visual consciousness-aggregate arising in a compounded and cognitional form.

28. "Space", recognized as a definite kind of entity in Vaiśeṣika philosophy, is also accepted by many Abhidharmika systems, including that of the Mahīśāsakas (Bareau, Mahīśāsaka thesis no. 19, *Les sectes*, p. 185). If it is accepted, it must clearly be uncompounded, i.e. not consisting of conditioned moment-events. Vasubandhu however denies that space is an entity at all. He says that it is simply an interval between materialities, and is thus an absence of impinging materiality.

29. "Cessation not through contemplation" is the Abhidharmika term for a cessation of the psychophysical complex which has not come about through the specifically Buddhist contemplations of the truth of suffering, the truth of the arising of suffering, the truth of the cessation of suffering, and the truth of a path leading to the cessation of suffering. Passages which in detail discuss "cessation not through contemplation" indicate that any cessation of "an aggregate-series" can be designated in this way, as long as the cessation has not come from a contemplation of the Four Noble Truths, nor by the inherent destruction of each moment-event. (This latter type of cessation, which refers to moment-events rather than to "series", is called by the *Vibhāṣā* "cessation due to non-eternality" (*Vibhāṣā*, 31, translated by La Vallée Poussin, *BEFEO* XXX, p. 1 ff). Thus, a non-Buddhist yogi who through meditations is able to annihilate factors of suffering, has achieved this through "a cessation not through contemplation", because the knowledge of the Noble Truths was not involved. A series of blue visual consciousnesses ceases when the stimulus giving rise to blue visual consciousnesses ceases: this would also be, and far more obviously so, "a cessation not through contemplation". The nature of this cessation was however the subject of much dispute among Abhidharmikas (cf. *Vibhāṣā* 31, 32, translated by La Vallée Poussin, BEFEO XXX, pp. 1-28; Vasubandhu, *Kośa* I, ad 5-6; Saṅghabhadra, *Nyāyānusāra*, I, 32, translated by La Vallée Poussin, BEFEO XXX, pp 259-60, cf. pp 263-298). "Cessation through contemplation" is essentially an Abhidharmika synonym for "Nirvāṇa" (*Vibhāṣā* 31, synonym no. 1, La Vallée Poussin, p. 10).

It is interesting that Vasubandhu here reduces the cause of "cessation through contemplation" from a realization of the Four Noble Truths to antidotes to afflictions. Presumably, for him, a non-Buddhist not recognizing the Four Noble Truths could still give rise to cessation through contemplation, if antidotes to afflictions were applied.

30. In other words, the only inherent nature in all events is that they have none! Suchness is the equivalent of Emptiness, by which all events have no graspable nature. Vasubandhu has thus eliminated the entire Mahīśāsaka list of uncompounded events, for all of them, by his definitions, are mere absences.

31. The sixth consciousness, or mental consciousness, includes in its "domain" residues of consciousnesses of all six varieties. For example, an audial consciousness may arise in one moment, the mental consciousness "That note was flat", referring to the previous audial consciousness, may arise in the next moment. The domain of *manas*, i.e. any of the consciousnesses preceding a sixth-consciousness-moment, is itself "past immediately afterwards", i.e. it is momentary. But a reflection on this *manas* by a succeeding sixth-consciousness-moment, is possible. Thus, a kind of continuity in succeeding sixth-consciousness-moments is possible, because previous consciousness-moments of all six varieties affect succeeding sixth-consciousness-moments. In the example above, the sound itself is an audial consciousness, and lasts for a moment. The mental-consciousness-moment "That note was flat", which depended on the previous second-consciousness-moment can itself give rise to a "series" of new sixth-consciousness-moments, such as "The singer might have been under some strain at that moment", "This composition requires great skill in executing musical ornaments," etc., etc., all of which are continuous upon one another and derive in part from the audial consciousness-moment which has long passed.

32. There are only the efficacies of these particular domains, without there being any central "doer". This is of course a necessary recognition in realizing "the selflessness of personalities".

33. This should seem obvious, but the implications of this statement may not be. Thus, wherever visual "models" are made in regard to that which isn't visible, what is being made is a distortion. It is as futile as attempting to explain the visible in terms of smell.

34. See *A Discussion for the Demonstration of Action*, note 43. The term "connected with distress" (*sāsrava*) has been rendered by "liable to be connected with afflictions", which is what the prior term really means.

35. The mental-consciousness-aggregates have the possibility of recognizing the arising of afflictions; for instance, when they are meditationally concentrated in certain ways. Thus they may be either liable to be connected with afflictions, or not.

36. "Unappropriated" from the point of view of a particular aggregate "series", see note 11.

37. A consciousness-moment of any type may recognize its impermanence, signlessness (in the sense that any signs seized by cognitions are distortions) and emptiness (by which it is not amenable to any kind of categorization). Thus, any of them may conform to understanding when they are experienced non-dually. But by the same token, all of these types of consciousness-moments and sensory-domain-moments are empty, since the distinctions between them are actually void.

A DISCUSSION FOR THE DEMONSTRATION OF ACTION

(*Karma-siddhi-prakaraṇa*)

INTRODUCTION

The Buddhist academic Sumatiśīla, who in the late eighth century wrote a meticulous commentary on this text, perhaps not fully realized its revolutionary content when he allowed an objector the statement that this is one of those treatises that try to count the teeth of crows.* It *is* a highly scholastic work, in the style of the *Kośa*, and uses the technique of expressing the author's views as objections to opponents' theses. It is in fact a frontal assault on Vaibhāṣika theories, and answers many of the objections that Vaibhāṣika masters had raised towards earlier formulations by Vasubandhu.

It is not a "Hīnayāna"** treatise. It uses the store-consciousness to account for psychic continuity, quotes the Mahāyāna *Sandhinirmocana-sūtra* as authoritative scripture, and ends very Mahāyānistically with the transference of all merit gained to all sentient beings. But it is *directed* at "Hīnayānists", and, by filling up holes in earlier theories, is attempting to lure Vaibhāṣikas to become involved with the further implications of Yogācāra theory, which are not alluded to here deliberately "to ease the shock".

"Action" is "karma", that kind of activity which has an ethical charge, and which must give rise to a retributionary "reverberation" at a later time. If suffering is inflicted, the inflicting aggregate-complex "series" will feel future suffering as a retribution for it. But the "time interval" between the two events is a problem for a theory maintaining momentariness. This treatise thus becomes absorbed in the problem of psychophysical continuity.

In what is probably Vasubandhu's earliest theory, in *Kośa* IX, memory is explained by a sensory or mental impression remaining latent in the consciousness-"series" and subsequently, when the proper conditions are present, emerging to a conscious

*Sumatiśīla, *Karmasiddhiṭīkā*, Peking/Tokyo ed. Tibetan Canon no. 5572, volume 114, p 204, 1, 2.

**"Hīnayāna" (Lesser Vehicle) is the somewhat pejorative term given by Mahāyānists to Buddhists not following the Great Vehicle.

level. As we have seen, these latent impressions are often given the metaphoric designation "seed". Thus, volitions of beneficial and unbeneficial actions leave such "seeds" within "the series", which ripen as retribution. In the case of the experience of the attainment of the cessation of feelings and cognitions, this explanation runs into difficulties. For in this state all the normal functions of consciousness are suspended, and yet, after some time, "the practitioner" emerges from the meditational concentration with memories and retributions that continue exactly where the last moment of full consciousness left off. During the time of attainment, where can these "seeds" exist ? The theory as stated is inadequate to account for this.

The Vaibhāṣikas had evolved a solution to this problem. Following the time-theory of the Bhadanta Vasumitra* they could say that the experience of the attainment of cessation of feelings and cognitions and re-emergence from it could be explained by the last moment of the consciousness-"series" losing its full efficacy, that is, becoming past, and the next future moment of the "series" becoming fully activated, that is, present, after a lapse has removed the obstacles to such a development.

Vasubandhu, in *Kośa* II, ad 44 ff, admits that the Vaibhāṣikas can solve the problem of psychic continuity in this way. But the entire edifice of purely hypothetical entities which is being used by the Vaibhāṣikas goes completely against his grain. To speak of the existence of the past and future is nonsense to him, since the past is that which no longer exists and the future is that which does not exist yet. At *Kośa* V, ad 27, and again in this treatise, 16-17, Vasubandhu subjects the Vaibhāṣika theory to a series of sharp attacks. It cannot account for distortion in memories or for disappointments in anticipations. If an existent past entity accounted for every instance of memory, it is difficult to see why memory should become distorted, or why "one" shouldn't "have" all memories of all past events at any given moment. The disappointment in anticipations makes for an even more potent argument, since events may be anticipated which never become existent as present entities.

*See page 12

Orthodox Vaibhāṣika masters were not lacking in replies to these objections. The Dīpakāra, for instance, defends the existence of the past and future by stating that it is mentioned in the sūtras, that there could be no production of a retributional effect without an abiding past deed, and that each consciousness-moment must have an existent object.* A causal relation is possible, he says in reply to Vasubandhu's distinction between conditions-as-objects-of-consciousness (which need not exist outside of consciousness) and truly generative conditions (which must have real existence outside of the particular consciousness-moment), only between two existing entities.** So no event of purely designatory reality can exist without some reference to an ultimately real event. The Dīpakāra rounds off his arguments with the statement that the author of the *Kośa*, "that apostate from the Sarvāstivāda", has fallen straight into the precipice of the emptiness theory of the Mahāyānists, and that he is now affirming all kinds of utter nonsense, such as three different kinds of "own-beings" in reality.***

Saṅghabhadra in turn has only one criterion for regarding something as existent : it must give rise to at least one consciousness-moment as its object-of-consciousness.† He reduces all error to wrong connective combinations occurring after the impression of the existent has been perceived. There is really no such thing as an object-of-consciousness which has reference to a non-existent object. Even in the case of dreams, all objects-of-consciousness refer to things that have been experienced, or will be experienced, combined with present experience in a confused manner.†† The distortion of memory and the disappointment of anticipations can be explained in the same way. "If the manner of seeing a present object is infinitely variable", Saṅghabhadra says, "why cannot the same be true in regard to a future object ?"†††

**Abhidharmadīpa* V, ad 302, pp. 259-60.
**Ibid, V, ad 319, p. 279.
***Ibid, ad 324, p. 282.
†*Abhidharmanyāyānusāra*, 50, *Mélanges* 5:28.
††Ibid., p. 40
†††Ibid, p. 73.

Saṅghabhadra not only defends the existence of the past and future : he also takes the offensive against the transformation-of-the-series theory raised by Vasubandhu in *Kośa* IX. An action can't be considered as the beginning point for a gradual transformation of a consciousness-series, because the act and the citta may be totally different in nature and in their manner of conditioning what follows. According to Vasubandhu, in a karmic "series", a beneficial action is followed by a series of cittas of which the last (which can itself be unbeneficial) is supposed to have the force projected by the long past act to produce an agreeable sensation. The seed metaphor used by Vasubandhu for this process is inadequate, says Saṅghabhadra, since in the case of the series flower-fruit, there is always a constant relationship between the seed and the final fruit, that is, a certain seed always eventually gives rise to a fruit of the same nature.* On the other hand, each action must have an effect distinct from cittas following as a result of cittas, otherwise, the sudden arising of an unbeneficial citta after a beneficial one could never exist.

Vasubandhu in this treatise addresses himself to the insistence of Saṅghabhadra and the Dīpakāra, that an objectively real event must be posited for each object-of-conscionsness. He says that it is really *present* causes and anticipations that allow us to think of something in the future, and *present* effects and memories which allow us to think of the past. In addition, he makes much of the point that certain moments never project a complete efficacy, and can thus according to the Vaibhāṣikas never be "present", though they are perceived as such.** Furthermore, what kind of force is an event exercising when it is past, and how or why should there be a sudden occurrence of a new type of event once it gives its effect of memory, arising from the attainment of cessation, or karmic retribution ?†

On the other hand, Vasubandhu in this treatise is aware of the potency of Saṅghabhadra's arguments, and realizes that the scheme given in *Kośa* IX is seriously flawed. It does no good

**Abhidharmanyāyānusāra*, 51, *Mélanges* 5:80 ff.

***A Discussion for the Demonstration of Action*, 16-17.

†Ibid., 16-17, end.

to speak of the citta which attains the cessation of feelings and cognitions as a directly antecedent cause for the emerging citta, since the continuity of the "series" has obviously been interrupted within the meditational attainment. Several alternative theories are considered : The first of these says that the citta emerging from the attainment of cessation need not rest on the citta preceding that attainment, but can arise from the re-awakened body supplied with sense-organs. This is a coherent and parsimonious theory, and it does not appear that it has been full justice by either Vasubandhu or Sumatiśīla. Then there is the theory of the Bhadanta Vasumitra, that the attainment of the cessation of feelings and cognitions must itself be citta. But Ghoṣaka would object that citta without concomitant feelings and cognitions simply does not exist. Ghoṣaka himself proposes that the attainment of cessation itself constitutes an efficacious entity, which can be seen by the fact that it keeps the consciousness-series from renewing itself for some time. But Vasubandhu can attack Ghoṣaka's thesis by demonstrating that it is obviously not the attainment of cessation which has this function, but the consciousness-moment directly antecedent to attaining the meditation. The attainment of cessation is to Vasubandhu no more than the absence of full functioning consciousnesses.

The solution of this treatise is to introduce the concept of store-consciousness. In the attainment of cessation, the six consciousnesses are arrested by a powerful volition associated with the last conscious moment previous to this state, and all psychic processes remain latently "within the store-consciousness", which continues to function in a steady stream during the entire time of immersement in the meditation. Continuity is maintained because each moment-seed influences the next. Saṅghabhadra's objections are met because the citta-series is no longer one-tiered, but rather involves now a separate series underlying the six consciousnesses. The retribution of a past act may be explained by the volition of that act influencing the store-consciousness, and after the maturation of the seed there, its penetrating to a fully conscious level in the form of a pleasurable or unpleasurable result. The fact that the citta antecedent or concomitant to this result may be beneficial whereas the result itself is painful, no longer disturbs, for the pain can be traced back to the unbeneficiality of the seed previously deposited within the store-consciousness. With the reciprocality of the relationship of the store-consciousness and the six consciousnesses, memory can also be explained. A perception leaves an impression in the store-consciousness, which colors future cognitions, but, in addition, under special circumstances and in connection with special stimuli, the seed of that perception may suddenly evolve, penetrating the sixth consciousness in the form of a memory.

In this treatise, there are also arguments against theories of the Ārya-Sāmmitīyas, Buddhists not completely dedicated to the theory of momentariness, who admit a more-or-less unchanging personality-entity.* Vasubandhu argues against any entity "self". He also argues against the Sāmmitīya thesis that manifest action represents a "motion", "a progression of the same thing to another locus". Vasubandhu subjects all of the Sāmmitīya arguments for the existence of "motion" to sharp criticism. Just because a thing is perceived to be the same from one moment to the next does not mean that the thing at moment 1 and the thing at moment 2, may not be really different, because of subtle differences not directly perceived. The implication of Vasubandhu's arguments is that if things are not changing in every moment, they could never change at all.

Vasubandhu in this treatise reduces actions having karmic retribution to volitions. This is a point of ethics in which Vasubandhu is at great odds with the Jains. The Jains would say that any action which causes suffering, whether intentional or not, must have a retribution of suffering, since to the suffering being, it is irrelevant whether the action was intentionally committed or not. The unintentional suffering caused to others by eating is still the eater's responsibility : thus the Jain way out is *sallekhanā*, final self-starvation. But Vasubandhu must, to be consistent, focus on the intentions of the "agent". The Jain path of absolute non-action, so as to avoid unintended infliction of suffering, cannot appeal to Vasubandhu, since as a Mahāyānist he is committed to the active alleviation of suffering.

Many other problems are incidentally treated in this work, and many Abhidharmika categories subjected to criticism.

*See *Sāmmitīya-nikāya-śāstra*, cf. Bareau, pp 123 ff.

Concerning the Text :

A Discussion for the Demonstration of Action does not survive in its original Sanskrit form. This translation is based mainly on the Tibetan rendering of Viśuddhisiṃha, Devendrarakṣita, and dPal-brtsegs (Peking/Tokyo ed. Tibetan Canon, Vol. 113, pp. 295 ff), with some references to the Chinese translation by Hsüan-tsang (Taisho 1608-1609). Identifications of opponents have been supplied from the commentary of Sumatiśīla (*Karma-siddhitīkā*, Peking/Tokyo ed. Tibetan Canon, vol. 114, pp. 203-223). Because of the difficulty of the subject matter, phrases omitted in the somewhat conversational treatment of Vasubandhu have been supplied from this commentary also. It will be seen that this translation differs greatly from the only previous translation into an Occidental language, which is that of Lamotte ("Le Traité de l'Acte de Vasubandhu", *Mélanges Chinois et Bouddhiques* 4 : 151 ff). There are even differences in the two translations as to which statements are Vasubandhu's, and which the opponent's ! The translation presented here can safely claim to be the more accurate, inasmuch as it is based mainly on the Tibetan rather than the inflated Chinese, and it follows the break-up of dialogue as it is presented in Sumati-śīla. It should also be noted that though not all the arguments in the treatise proceed with the full criteria of inference-schema as demanded by *A Method for Argumentation*, Sumatiśīla, who is a master logician, provides us in each case with a full-blown inference complete with the necessary statements of invariable concomitance.

A DISCUSSION FOR THE DEMONSTRATION OF ACTION (KARMASIDDHI-PRAKARAṆA)

Homage to Ārya Mañjuśrī-kumāra-bhūta[1]

1. It is said in the sūtras : "There are three kinds of acts : bodily acts, verbal acts, and mental acts."[2] On this point

2. certain people (the Vaibhāṣikas) say : "The acts which are committed by the body are 'bodily acts'; speech itself is 'verbal action', and both of these singly constitute 'manifest and unmanifest action'.[3] Acts which are associated with *manas*[4] are 'mental actions', and they are equivalent to volitions." But this matter has to be investigated at this point.

What is this event which is called "manifest action" ?

Vaibhāṣika : To begin with, a "manifest action of the body" is a configuration[5] which has arisen from a citta[6] which has an object-of-consciousness referring to it.

V : Of what is it a configuration ?

Vaibhāṣika : It is a configuration of the body.

V. If it is a configuration of the body, how can one call it an act which has been committed by the body ? It is, after all, said to be an act committed by it.

Vaibhāṣika : Since such an act (i.e. a bodily act) has reference to one part of the body in general, it is called "a configuration of the body", (i.e. a configuration of one part of the body, e.g. "a gesture of the hand"), and since it arises dependent upon the great elements[7] of the body in general, it is called "an act committed by the body". Verbal expressions which refer to things in general often also refer to their particular parts, as for instance when it is said "He lives in the village" or "He lives in the forest" (when what is meant is : "He lives in a house in the village" and "He lives under a tree in the forest").

V : What is the purpose of saying that it "has arisen from a citta which has an object-of-consciousness referring to it" ?

Vaibhāṣika : Even though in speaking, there may arise a configuration of the lips, etc., this description is not appropriate for such a configuration, because it has not arisen from a citta which has an object-of-consciousness referring to it, but rather has arisen from a citta which has an object-of-consciousness referring to words. And though there may be a configuration which has arisen from the citta of a former aspiration, this description is not appropriate for such a configuration, either, because it has not arisen from a citta which has an object-of-consciousness referring to it, but rather has also arisen from another citta, which is a retributory cause.[8]

V : Why is it called "manifest action" ?

Vaibhāṣika : Because it informs one of (or : manifests to one) a citta which is instigating action in another.

> "By the transformations of external motions,
> one is shown the intentions in living beings' hearts,
> As one is shown a fish living hidden in a lake,
> through the transformations of the waves."

V : Well then, what is this which you call "configuration" ?

Vaibhāṣika : It is this : "length", etc.

V : But what is "length", etc. ?

Vaibhāṣika : It is that by virtue of which cognitions such as "This is long ! This is short !" arise.

V : To which sense-field does it belong ?

Vaibhāsika : To the sense-field of visibles.

3. V : Now is configuration to be regarded as a special kind of atom, like color[9], as some special aggregation of atoms, or as some single entity pervading the aggregations of color-atoms, etc. ? If it were a special kind of atom, "long", "short", etc., would have to be comprised separately in each part of the aggregate to which it belongs, just as color is. If, on the other hand, it were some special aggregation of atoms, what would be the difference between it and a special aggregation of color-atoms ? It could be due to a special aggregation of these colors that "long", "short", etc., arise as cognitions. Moreover, if it were a single entity pervading the aggregation of color-atoms, then, because it would be single, and because it would pervade, it would have to be perceived separately in each part of the aggregation, because it would have to be in all of the parts at one time. Or else it would not be a single entity, because it would be constituted with various parts.[10] Furthermore, your

basic doctrine which states that the first ten sense-fields are aggregations of atoms, would be invalidated by this view. And it would strengthen the doctrine of the school of Kanāda, which states that composites exist as entities which penetrate their components.[11]

4. [12]When an aggregation of color appears in one direction in great quantity, it evokes the idea of "long". If it appears thus in only a small quantity, it evokes the idea of "short". When it appears equal in each of four sides, it evokes the idea of "square". If there is an equal distance everywhere from its circumference to its center, it evokes the idea of "circular". When a greater quantity of color appears amassed at its central portion, it evokes the idea of "convex", and when a smaller quantity appears there, it evokes the idea of "concave". When it appears to go along in one direction, it evokes the idea of "even", and when it appears to go along in various directions, it evokes the idea of "uneven".

*Though ideas of various configurations may arise when a variegated quilt appears in such a manner, yet following your theory these various kinds of configuration cannot logically be situated within one locus, just as, for example, various colors cannot. But if they could, the idea of every configuration could arise in reference to every locus, and this is also not the case. (On the other hand, *one* configuration for each locus is ruled out because one can construe various configurations in one section of an embroidered quilt.) This being so, there is no separate entity "configuration". We form ideas of "long", etc., when color, and nothing else, is situated in special loci. As for example we form ideas of new "entities" with regard to arrays of trees, birds, ants, etc. There seems to be no flaw in this reasoning.

5. Vaibhāṣika : If this is so, how is it that something is discernible at a long distance through an object-of-consciousness of its configuration, while it is not discernible through an object-of-consciousness of its color-aggregations? **

V : Well, how is it that some things are discernible through an object-of-consciousness of the configurations of the arrays

*cf. *Kośa* IV ad 3 c (LVP p. 10, 2nd arg.).

**Ibid, though the *Kośa* argument is not quite identical.

or groups to which they belong, while they are not discernible through an object-of-consciousness of their main own configuration ? There is no further entity involved here. As a matter of fact, when we are confronted with something at a long distance, or in a dark cave, the object is undiscernible through objects-of-consciousness referring to either color or configuration, and we say, "What is this ? I can only perceive it dimly. What are we seeing here ?" Since this is so, it should be recognized that at this time, its color is not being clearly perceived, nothing more.* (i.e. when its color is not clearly perceived, its "configuration" isn't, either.) For this reason, manifest action consisting of "configuration" cannot be demonstrated.

6. Certain other people (the Ārya-Sāmmitīyas) say : "Manifest action is a movement which has arisen from a citta which has an object-of-consciousness referring to it."

V : What is the purpose of saying that it arises from a citta which has an object-of-consciousness referring to it ?

Ārya-Sāmmitīya : To exclude the movement of the lips, etc., which takes place in speaking.

V : What is this which you call "movement" ?

Ārya-Sāmmitīya : It is the progression (of a thing) to another locus.

V : To which sense-field does it belong ?

Ārya-Sāmmitīya : To the sense-field of visibles.

7. V : How do you know that there exists such a progression of the same thing to another locus ?

Ārya-Sāmmitīya : Because there is no special differentiating characteristic which can be ascertained for the thing (i.e. any special characteristic which would distinguish the thing at locus *A* from the thing subsequently at locus *B*).

V : But even though there is no special characteristic which can be ascertained for a product arising in a dyeing-process when it is removed immediately after conjoining with the conditions allowing it to arise in the process, i.e. fire, the sun, ice, plants, etc.,[13] yet this does not mean that the product is not something else than what has existed before. And though there

***Kośa* IV ad 3 c (LVP p. 11) develops the counter-argument in a slightly different manner.

is no special characteristic ascertained for different flames in contact with similar sections of tall grasses about to be burned, this does not mean that they are not different. Now if the sequence of products arising in the dyeing-process did not begin to arise immediately upon the conjoining of the thing being dyed with the conditions for dyeing, then it could not begin later, either, because there is no special characteristic changing within the conditions. And furthermore, if other flames did not also arise in some other sections of what is about to be burned, then, because of the special charcteristics in the *one* section involved, there would not be any new special characteristic in the flame's extent, glare, or heat. For these reasons it is not logical to say that something must be the same thing that existed before, simply because no new special characteristic can be ascertained for it.

8. Ārya-Sāmmitīya : Well, but there *is* such a progression, because there is no cause for the destruction (of the thing previously at locus *A*).

V : What is the cause of destruction for things that are certainly momentary : cittas, events associated with cittas, sounds, etc., and flames ? (These things have no causes for their destruction.) Similarly there may not be one for other things, either.*

Ārya-Sāmmitīya : But these things do have a cause for their destruction : their own innate lack of duration.

V : Why don't you similarly accept such a cause for other things, as well ? Just as there is no other cause for these things, in the same way, there need be no other cause for these other things, either.

Ārya-Sāmmitīya : If there were none, then the materiality of wood, etc., would not be perceived even before its contact with fire, etc., just as it isn't after it. Or else, afterwards, it would be just as it was before.

V : *a.* Now this is similar to the case where the flame of a lamp and the sound of a bell are both perceived before they are in contact with a gust of wind or a hand, respectively, but afterwards are not. Those two are not, however, destroyed

*cf. *Kośa* IV ad 2b-3b(LVP p. 6, 4) : "If one needed a cause for destruction, one would need one for every destruction."

because of these two (because different phases in the flame and the sound constantly displace each other, anyway, and finally lead to their own destruction even without the intervention of a gust of wind or a hand).*

b. If the materiality of wood, etc., were no longer perceived because it is destroyed by fire, etc., itself, then it would be destroyed even when removed immediately after its simple contact with fire.[14]

c. Though the external conditions for the products which arise in a dyeing-process remain undifferentiated, these various products arise through a gradual succession of causes first causing them to take on a special characteristic, then intensifying this special characteristic, then intensifying this special characteristic to a great degree. However, through what does the destruction of the previous characteristic come about ? For it is not logical that something only through which a thing comes to be, also be the cause of the thing's not being there later. It is commonly known that the causes of two contradictory results cannot be one.[15] This being so, we must conclude that these previous characteristics are destroyed without a specific cause of destruction.** That "something" is perceived or no longer perceived in the manner in which "it" was before, should be known as being due to the continuation of a series of momentary events without the intervention of any extraordinary special characteristics, and to the transformation of this series, respectively.

d. If these things that are destroyed become destroyed possessed of a specific cause of destruction, then no cittas, events associated with cittas, etc., would become destroyed without such a cause, either. Just as, for example, they depend on a specific cause for their arising. On the other hand, an innate lack of duration in any way different from the events themselves cannot be demonstrated.

e. There would be a special characteristic for it stemming from each of these special causes (if a special cause of destruction were necessary). Just as there are diverse products which arise in a dyeing-process from fire, the sun, ice, grasses, etc., respectively.

*cf. *Kośa* IV 2b-3d (LVP pp. 5-6).
**Ibid, IV ad 2b-3b, LVP p. 8.

f. Destruction would also be possessed of a cause, as are material substances. (An infinite regress would result.) This being so, there can be no special cause of destruction.

9. Ārya-Sāmmitīya : Well, (the thing at locus *B*) is ascertained to be the same because there is no cause for the arising of anything else in this manner.

V : But since there could be a cause for the arising of this subsequent thing, namely the preceding thing, there could be such a cause of arising. This would be like the cases where another citta arises from a citta, a different product in dyeing arises from a previous product, curds arise from milk, wine arises from the juice of grapes, and vinegar arises from wine.[16] If this were so, there would be nothing which could be called a true movement which has the characteristic of a progression of the same thing to another locus.

10. Moreover, when a thing is stable, it has no movement. And if it has no movement, it is constantly stable. (On the other hand, if it is not stable, it also has no movement*.)

Ārya-Sāmmitīya : If this is really so, what is it that appears in another locus (in those cases we construe as being movement of the same thing) ?

V : The same thing doesn't appear.

Ārya-Sāmmitīya : Well then what does ?

V : It is similar to the case where grass-fires or shadows appear in each locus as something new and something new again. The same shadow never appears in another locus. For (1) while that which is connected with it remains stationary, it appears to arise, to be obscured, and to change, because the sunlight is far away, near at hand, or changing; (2) as soon as a bright area is darkened in another place, a shadow appears.

Our opponent may well object : "Though, if someone says that there is a progression consisting of the same thing moving to another locus, it may be argued, 'How do you arrive at this ?'; if someone says that it is not the same thing moving to another locus, one can equally argue, 'How do you arrive at this ?'"

The basis for this assumption is the very argument already given : "Moreover, when a thing is stable, it has no movement",

*cf. *Kośa* IV ad 2b-3b, LVP pp. 4-5, on the second part of this argument.

etc. And there is this additional basis that even when the external conditions for products arising in dyeing are without variation, these products become something else from each moment to the next, a fact which can be ascertained through their subsequent special characteristics. Again, if you imagine a stable entity because there is no basis for its becoming something else, why not accept the theory that it does become something else, because there is also no basis for its being a stable entity ? This being so, as it follows that nothing can be resolved regarding either alternative, all that has been shown here is that a progression cannot be demonstrated.

11. The Sauryodayikas* say that though it is true that compounded events are without progression to another locus, because they are destroyed by their own-natures, yet there arises, in a hand, etc., a special event as a cause for something's arising in another locus immediately subsequent to a previous thing at the first locus, which event has a certain citta as its cause. It is (conventionally) called both "motion" and "manifest action".

V : To which sense-field does it belong ?

Sauryodayika : To the sense-field of visibles.

V : In that case, why isn't it seen by the eye, as color is ? And if it isn't seen, how can it be a manifest action which informs others ?

Sauryodayika : If it does not exist in this manner, how can a body arise in another locus ?

V : It is through the wind-element which has arisen from a certain citta (that something arises in another locus immediately subsequent to a previous thing in the first locus).

Sauryodayika : If this is so, what exactly is the cause for something's arising in another locus ?

V : It is the gaseousness of this same wind-element.

Sauryodayika : How can it be the cause of this immediately subsequent arising in another locus in the case of grass and leaves ?

V : (In this case, "motion" occurs) because of wind-element, which causes a distrubance, causes a thrust, and which has

*These are a group of Sautrāntikas basing their theories on the treatise *Sūryodaya* of Kumāralāta.

conjoined with the grasses, etc. And furthermore, if it is admitted that it is the same thing from which motion is held to arise that causes something to arise in another locus immediately subsequent to a previous thing at the first locus, what use is there for an examination of a principle of motion which cannot be revealed by any possible object-of-consciousness ?[17]

II

12. Sauryodayika : In that case, is it that same special wind-element which has arisen from a special citta, and which is the cause for a body's arising in another locus, which is manifest action ?

V : How can something which does not have the capacity for informing others be manifest action ? To hold that the sense-field of tactile sensations is either beneficial or unbeneficial is not the doctrine of the sons of Śākya.*[17a]

Sauryodayika : In that case, is the body which arises in another locus through the special citta itself manifest action ?

V : If this were so, manifest action would be purely mentally constructed, and would not be a true entity, since there is no constituency as one entity as regards the body. And also, manifest action would become non-informing, because there is no informing of others of the intentions of living beings through the smell, etc., connected with a body. Furthermore, to hold that the sense-field of smell, etc., is beneficial or unbeneficial is not the doctrine of the sons of Śākya.

Sauryodayika : In that case, is the color which arises from a special citta itself manifest action ?[18]

V : It does not arise from a special citta.

Sauryodayika : In that case, how does it arise ?

V : It arises from its own seed, and from a special wind-element. To hold that color is beneficial or unbeneficial is also not the doctrine of the sons of Śākya.

13. Sauryodayika : If it is correct that color is not manifest action, is its arising in another locus manifest action ?

V : Beloved of the gods![19] Though it can be seen that you are making efforts to the best of your abilities, what is the point

*cf. *Kośa* I, ad 29 c-d. "Sons of Śākya", i.e. sons and daughters of Śākya-muni, are the Buddhists.

in making an effort towards things that can't be demonstrated by any effort whatsoever ? Since this new supposed manifest action isn't seen, as visibles are, and as its force is also not an object which is seen, unlike in the case of an eye, etc.,[20] how is it possible to demonstrate its existence as something separate ? It has already been stated that if it is not seen, it must be explained how it can be manifest action. If color could be beneficial and unbeneficial, then its arising could be so, too, but it has already been explained that color is not like this. This being so, it appears that there is no manifest action which could be bodily action.

14. Vaibhāṣika : Then is bodily action only an unmanifest action ?

V : What is this which you call "unmanifest action" ?

Vaibhāṣika : It is materiality belonging to the sense-field of mentally cognizables, consisting of restraint, etc.*

V : Then an unmanifest action taking place in the realm of desires would arise without there being a previous manifest action.

Vaibhāṣika : If this is so, what is entailed ?

V : Unmanifest action would be subordinated to citta, as it is, for example, in the realm of simple images.[21] Accordingly, there could be neither restraint nor non-restraint in those who are joined with a different citta (i.e. a citta which itself had nothing to do with producing the unmanifest action), or in those who are without a citta (i.e. in an unconscious state).

Vaibhāṣika : This is not so, because it is projected from a determined time by a previous manifest action.

V : But how could there be a lie when there is no talk during a *Prātimokṣa* recital ? (At the confessional during the recital of the *Prātimokṣa* of the monastic rules, if a monk remains silent and does not confess the misdeeds he has done, this constitutes a lie, a kind of unbeneficial action, even though in this case there has been no manifest action, either previously or at the time of the recital.) Now because unmanifest action is only of two kinds, it can never be indeterminate, and because unmanifest action is dependent, it cannot arise as a bodily act which is both beneficial and unbeneficial at the same moment.[22]

*cf. note 3.

15. V : Though it is possible to imagine that bodily and verbal actions are material, their beneficiality and unbeneficiality is not demonstrated. And why is this ? When the body has released the action, how can it be demonstrated as having a pleasant or unpleasant result at a later time, since it itself has entirely come to an end by that time ?

Certain people (the Vaibhāṣikas) say that a past act, through which a pleasant or unpleasant result comes about at some later time, also exists at that later time, so how can one say that an act's beneficiality and unbeneficiality is not demonstrated ?[23]

V : To say that a past act exists is a pustule arising on top of a boil.[24] The expression "past" designates something that having existed in a former time, is subsequently no longer existing.

Vaibhāṣika : In that case, how could it have been said by the Exalted One,

> "Even after hundreds of aeons,
> acts do not perish.
> Obtaining their needed complex of conditions, and their needed time,
> their effects ripen for living beings."*

V : But what is the meaning of "do not perish" ? It means that they are not without effects, as is shown by the latter half of the verse. It is not being stated here that acts also exist for a long time along with their effects. What is to be investigated is how they give their effects : whether this is through a special transformation of the series, as is the case with a seed of a rice-plant, or whether it is through a situation in their own-characteristic. If only a situation in their own-characteristic can give their effects, then it must be explained how they give their effects through not having been destroyed.

Vaibhāṣika : It is not because of their non-existence as far as their own-characteristic is concerned, that they are said to be destroyed.

V : On account of what is it then ?

Vaibhāṣika : On account of the fact that they do not exercise their full efficacy.[25] And how don't they exercise it ?

*cf. *Divyāvadāna* II, 19; X, 1; XI, 7; XXI, 3, etc.

They don't project an effect.

V : Why don't they project it ?

Vaibhāṣika : Because they have already completed projecting it, they are unable to project it again. Just as what has arisen does not arise again.

16-17. V : Why doesn't it project another effect similar to it ?[26] As far as that goes, how does it project its effect at all ?

Vaibhāṣika : Because it prepares it for its arising.

V : But the last state of one who has destroyed all distress does not project an effect,[27] and there is also the stoppage of an effect through any cessation not through contemplation.[28] Since from the beginning these cases do not exercise an efficacy, how can they later be destroyed ? (i.e. Never exercising their efficacy, i.e. never projecting an effect, the last stage of one who has destroyed all distress and the last stage of an event-series before it undergoes cessation not through contemplation, are never really "present", given the Vaibhāṣikas' definition, and can thus never become "past".) Thus, the projecting of an effect for something with such a nature cannot be demonstrated.

Vaibhāṣika : In that case, how is an effect projected ?

V : An effect is projected through the obtainment and development of the effect's "seed".[29] As according to your theory, a future thing also exists as an entity just as a past thing does, why doesn't it project an effect ? If there were a constant existence for all entities, and nothing would cease to be because destroyed, would an effect ripen only if it obtained the necessary complex of conditions, as the verse says ? At this point it should be demonstrated through what it is determined that the effect exists, and also what the force is which is operating in this case. (If an act ceases to project its effect as soon as it becomes past, but yet continues to exercise some sort of force, the problem lies with the determination of this force, as well as its final giving of a retributional effect). Thus, the existence of a past act which causes an effect to arise at a future time is not demonstrated.*

18. Opponent : In that case, it must be that a certain other

*cf. *Kośa* V, ad 27.

event disassociated from citta arises in the aggregate-series, assosiated with beneficial and unbeneficial bodily and verbal acts. Some people (the Mahāsāṅghikas) call it "the accumulation", others again (the Ārya-Sāmmitīyas) call is "the imperishable". It is that through which a pleasant or unpleasant effect is brought about at a future time. (This event must be posited also for mental acts.) If this other event did not arise in the citta-series, how could a mental act which has already disappeared, as another citta has arisen, bring about an effect ? Without a doubt, this event must be accepted.[30]

19. V : In that case, when one has studied a text, and after a long time has elapsed, a memory still arises regarding it, and memories arise in regard to other objects that have been seen, etc., what is the event through which this memory later arises for (this object) which has been studied or seen, etc. ? And at what moment does it actually arise ?[31]

Also, as regards the citta which attains the attainment of the cessation of feelings and cognitions, through what does the citta which emerges from this state later arise ?[32]

When a lemon flower is penetrated by the red of liquid lac, and it perishes along with it, what is the event through which there is later produced, within its fruit also, a red within its inner core ?[33]

20. Thus, as there is no arising of this other event, which seems to be purely mentally constructed,[34] it should be known that, because a special force is produced within the citta-series by a volition, an effect arises at a later time through a special transformation within the series which has been penetrated (influenced) by this volition. Just as, for example, in the case of the lemon flower, it is through the whole series from flower to fruit being penetrated by the liquid lac that the inner core of the fruit arises as red.[35]

21. Vaibhāṣika : In this case, why is it that, as regards the citta-series, it is not accepted that it is penetrated (influenced) by bodily and verbal acts, also ?

Sautrāntika : They become beneficial and unbeneficial in this way dependent upon cittas. Though it is logical that when something is rendered beneficial or unbeneficial by something, there be the force necessary for the same event to give a pleasant or unpleasant effect in the series with which it is associated, the series itself is not capable of doing so. (i.e. Though it is logical that when a bodily and verbal action is rendered beneficial or unbeneficial by a beneficial or unbeneficial volition, there be the force necessary for the bodily or verbal action to give a pleasant or unpleasant effect within the citta-series, the citta-series is of itself not capable of giving a pleasant or unpleasant result, and thus is not to be regarded as necessarily beneficial or unbeneficial.)

In that case, if an effect arises at a later time because of a citta-series which has been penetrated (influenced) by an act endowed with this force, how is it that the effect of a former action arises for those who have interrupted the citta-series in the two meditational attainments that are without citta (the attainment free from cognitions and the attainment of the cessation of feelings and cognitions), or in a non-meditative state without cognitions ?

22. Certain people (among the Sautrāntikas) say that it is through the citta-series, which has been influenced by it, retaking its course at this very time.

V : But how does it retake its course ?

Reply : It retakes its course because there is the citta which attains the meditational attainment, which serves as a directly antecedent condition.[36]

V : But since a long time has elapsed since this citta has come to an end, how can it be a directly antecedent condition ? There has already been the rebuttal that an effect does not arise from that which is past. So from where does that other citta (that emerges from the meditational attainment) arise ?

23. Certain people (among the Sautrāntikas) say that it is from its seeds which rest upon the material organs that this citta arises after the meditational attainment has been completed. The seeds of the cittas and events associated with cittas rest upon the citta-series or on the series of the material organs, or on both, depending on the case.*

V : But isn't it said** that mental consciousness arises dependent upon *manas* and a mentally cognizable ? When there is no *manas*, how can it arise ?[37]

*cf. *Kośa* II ad 44 d (LVP, p. 212).
**cf. *Saṃyutta* II, 72; IV, 33.

These "certain people" (among the Sautrāntikas): It should be known that sometimes there is a metaphor of an effect for a cause. (i.e. the expression designating something's effect is employed metaphorically in place of the expression designating the cause.) So that one says "*manas*" for *manas*' seeds. (In this case, when "*manas*" is said, what is meant is the seeds that give rise to *manas*, which in our opinion rest upon the material organs during the attainment of the cessation of feelings and cognitions.) Just as, for example, one says "hunger" and "thirst" for a certain kind of tactile sensation (when really this tactile sensation is the effect of hunger and thirst).

V : In that case, there would be two separate series of seeds for cittas and events associated with cittas, but this situation is not observed in things that naturally have seeds : sprouts, etc.[38] Though conditions for something may not be single, this is not the case with its seed. Furthermore, with this theory there omy remains the flaw as to how the former actions of those who have interrupted the citta-series in the two meditational attainments without citta,[38a] or in a non-meditative state without cognitions, give their effects at a later time.[39]

24. Opponent : That flaw lies within the theory itself.

V : In what theory ?

Opponent : In the view of those who say that these situations are without citta. Certain people accept the idea that these situations are endowed with citta. For instance, it is said by the Bhadanta Vasumitra in his *Paripṛcchā*[40]: "There is a flaw in the view of those who say that the attainment of cessation is without citta. In my view, the attainment of cessation is endowed with citta."* And there is also a basis for this view in a sūtra, which says : "For him who has entered the attainment of cessation, bodily motivational dispositions are stopped, but the sense-organs are not and continue to function, and consciousness is not separated from the body."**

25. V : What consciousness is held to exist for them at that time ?

*cf. *Kośa* II ad 44d (LVP, p. 212).

**cf. *Majjhima* I. 296. Motivational dispositions of the body : inhalation and exhalation. Motivational dispositions of speech : initial mental application and subsequent discursive thought. Motivational dispositions of *manas* : volition, cognitions, etc.

Certain people say that it is a mental consciousness.

V : *But hasn't it been said by the Exalted One that a mental consciousness arises dependent upon *manas* and mentally cognizables, and that at the same time there must exist a contact consisting of the conjunction of the three, along with simultaneously arising feelings, cognitions, and volitions ?** And how can there be a conjunction of the three without contact ? And how can there be contact without feelings and cognitions ? And this in a state which is called "the attainment of the cessation of cognitions and feelings".[41]

Certain people say that though the Exalted One said that craving is conditioned by feelings, yet not all feelings are conditions for craving. So in the same way, contact is not always a condition for feelings.[42]

V : But these have been clearly differentiated by the Exalted One in other passages, for he says : "Craving arises dependent upon the feelings that arise from a contact accompanied by ignorance."*** But contacts themselves have not been differentiated anywhere. Thus, because there is no such special differentiation within contacts, what is said by you is no rebuttal.

26. The adversaries say that when the meeting (of *manas*, mentally cognizable, and mental consciousness) is endowed with a special force giving rise to contact, then it is called a "conjunction". At this time, however, the meeting of the three is without any force, as this force has been forfeited because of the attainment (of the cessation of feelings and cognitions). For this reason, as there is no contact at this time, how could there be cognitions and feelings ? For this reason, only a mental consciousness remains in this state. (i.e. The attainment of cessation is a state where there exists a mental consciousness without the force to enter into real contact with mentally cognizables, and thus powerless to help give rise to feelings and cognitions.)

V : In that case, of what sort is it ? Is it beneficial, or afflicted, or unobstructed-indeterminate ?[43]

*cf. *Kośa* II ad 44 d (LVP, pp. 212-213).

***Saṃyutta* II 2; 13, 14.

***Ibid. III, 96.

Opponet : What is implied by this ?

27. V : If it is beneficial, how can it be beneficial without being conjoined with the roots of the beneficial : lack of greed, etc. ? When there is lack of greed, etc., can it be that there is no contact ?[44]

Opponent : What if it is beneficial because it has been projected by a directly antecedent condition, which is beneficial ?*

V : But this is not sufficient to guarantee the beneficiality of anything, because immediately subsequent to something beneficial, there may arise cittas of all three kinds (beneficial, unbeneficial, indeterminate), and because when there is a citta which has beneficiality, which has been projected by the power of the roots of the beneficial, it is not appropriate that there be a cause for these roots to be removed, (thus it cannot be beneficial), and its being unbeneficial leads similarly to an absurdity. The attainment of cessation is beneficial in the same way that final cessation is.[44a]

If it were afflicted, how could it be afflicted without being conjoined with afflictions ? When there are afflictions, how can it be that there is no conatct ? Thus it was said by the Exalted One in the *Sūtra of the Ten Questions* :[45] "Any possible aggregate of feelings, aggregate of cognitions, or aggregate of motivating dispositions, arises dependent upon contact."[46] Furthermore, if it is not accepted that the meditational attainment free from cognitions is afflicted, how much the more so in the case of the attainment of cessation.[47]

Now as to its being unobstructed-indeterminate, is it the result of retribution, or is it related to bodily postures, related to artistic activity, or to magical creations ?[48]

Opponent : What is entailed by this ?

28. V : If it is supposed that it is the result of retribution, how could a retributional citta, which is necessarily of the realm of desires, become manifest immediately after a citta which has entered into the attainment of the summit of existence (i.e. the meditational state which is neither cognitional nor non-cognitional), as such a citta has already been severed for eight successive other meditational stages ?[49] How would the absurdity

*cf. *Kośa* II ad 43 a (LVP, p. 203); *Mahāyānasaṅgrahabhāṣya* ad I, 54, (Tokyo vol. 112, p 282, 2-4)

not ensue that the attainment of cessation also belongs to the realm of desires ? And how could a citta of utter non-agitation, etc., be manifest immediately after this attainment ?[50] Thus it has been said in the *Mahākauṣṭhila-sūtra** : "When one has emerged from the attainment of cessation, the contacts which one reaches are three, Mahākauṣṭhila : they are contact with utter non-agitation, with nothing whatever, and with the signless."

Supposing that this mental consciousness were a retributional citta projected by former actions, what is the reasoning here which would ensure that for those who have entered the attainment of cessation, it would not have been transcended at the period of emergence, as it was engendered by a former volition ?

Indeed, how is it that when the citta of the attainment of the summit of existence, which has cessation as its object-of-consciousness, has come to an end, there should be obtained, because it is demonstrated as being present in the following attainment of cessation, the continuation of a retributional citta, which has latent impressions of the past, and belongs to the realm of desires, when such a citta has not been arising for a long time previously ?

And, indeed, why would a retributional citta retake its course when retributional materiality, being severed there, does not retake its course ? (Afflicted retributional materiality is gotten rid of by these highest meditations**; it follows that a retributional citta which is susceptible to being connected with afflictions, would also be severed at this time.)

29. Now as to the theory that it could be related to bodily postures, etc., can there be a citta at this time which has as its object-of-consciousness a bodily posture, etc. ? How can such a citta be formed, when there is no contact ?

Because it is held that the nine attainments of successive stages and the eight deliverances[51] are beneficial, it is not logical that there be an afflicted, or indeterminate, citta at hand at this time.[52]

The attainment of the cessation of cognitions and feelings occurs dependent upon the attainment of the summit of existence,

*cf. *Dīgha* III, 217; *Saṃyutta* II, 82; *Majjhima* II, 254, 262.
**cf. *Dīgha* III, 211; *Saṃyutta* IV, 201.

where there has been a mental attention, associated with tranquility, directed at such cessation. Thus it is said in the *Mahākauṣṭhila-sūtra* in reference to the attainment of cessation : "The causes and conditions for a signless attainment are two, Mahākauṣṭhila : an absence of mental attention to any signs, and a mental attention to the signless."

V : If there is a mental consciousness for those who have attained the cessation of cognitions and feelings, what is its object-of-consciousness, and what is its aspect ?

Opponent : What if it had cessation as its object-of-consciousness, and tranquility as its aspect ?

V : In that case, wouldn't it be beneficial ? And being beneficial wouldn't it be conjoined with lack of greed, etc. ? And if it were thus conjoined, wouldn't there be scope for the condition for contact ?

Opponent : What if it had some other object-of-consciousness and aspect ?

V : How would it be logical that the citta immediately after the citta which attains the attainment of cessation, be distracted ? Because of these same two previously given arguments, this other additional indeterminate kind of citta constructed by the opponents themselves, is also contrary to fact. Accordingly, since you dialecticians[52a] do not understand things according to the intent of the scriptures, your understanding that there is a citta which is a mental consciousness within the states of the attainment of cessation, etc., is thought out in unheeding rashness.

III

30. Opponent : In that case, how is it to be held that the attainment of cessation is endowed with citta ?

V : In the manner in which certain Sautrāntikas hold it.

Opponent : In what manner do these certain Sautrāntikas hold it ?

V : (There is a special retributory consciousness.) As this retributory consciousness, which contains all the seeds coloring future perceptions, etc., continues in a stream, once it has arisen after conception in the womb, and takes on various forms because of various retributory causes, without any interruption until the limit of Nirvāṇa, this consciousness is not severed at this time. On this account, this state is called "endowed with citta". But the group of remaining six consciousnesses does not continue there, because their seeds have been impaired for a short time by force of the citta which enters the attainment of cessation, etc. On this account, this state is called "without citta."[53]

31. Citta has two aspects: the first accumulates (*cinoti*) seeds; the second is manifold (*citra*) on account of having various objects-of-consciousness, aspects, and special differentiating characteristics.* The state is said to be without citta because there is a deficiency of the second kind there, just as, for example, one calls a chair that has only one leg, "legless".

32. The state which impairs the seeds gradually becomes weak, weaker, and even more weak, in the same manner as there is a gradual diminution of boiling water, or in the velocity of a projected arrow, and because of this, when at the time of the emergence from the attainment, the conclusion of the projection is reached, due to a special transformation in the retributory consciousness from one moment to the next, and through the resumption of the seeds, the mental consciousness, and subsequently the other consciousnesses, also, arise as their conditions have renewed themselves. The retributory consciousness, which is only the various kinds of seeds themselves, is influenced by the other beneficial and unbeneficial events arising together with the consciousnesses different from it, by means of their augmentation of these seeds, according to circumstances. In accordance with the force of this special transformation of the series, the process of impression resumes, and desired and undesired effects are brought about.[54] In reference to this, it has been said :

> "This citta which has limitless seeds continues in a stream,
> and when, for this citta, there arise its proper conditions,
> it and its seeds become augmented.
> Augmented by them and resuming its course,
> it is able to give its effects in time,

*on the etymologies, cf. *Teaching of the Three Own-Beings*, v. 7; *Discussion of the Five Aggregates*, p. 71.

just as for the dyed lemon flower,
the color appears in the core of its fruit."[55]

Regarding this also, it was said by the Exalted One in the Mahāyāna sūtra named *Sandhinirmocana* :

"The appropriating consciousness, profound and subtle,
moves with all its seeds like the current of a stream.
It has not been taught by me to fools,
so that they might not imagine it to be a self."*[56]

33. It is also called "the appropriating consciousness", because it appropriates a body for the factors at the time of conception in the womb during the time of re-birth.** Because it becomes the support of the seeds of all experienced events, it is called "the store-consciousness". Because it is the retribution for former acts, it is called "the retributory consciousness".

34. Furthermore, if it is not accepted, then by what consciousness is the body appropriated ? There is no other consciousness apart from it which does not leave the body for life's duration, or which remains pervading it. And where do the residues of afflictions reside when they are removed by their antidotes ? If it is said that it is within the same citta which is their antidote, how could it be appropriate that it be the antidote, since it would be conjoined with the residues of afflictions ?[57]

For those who, born into the imageless realm, possess a citta-series which is afflicted, beneficial, or not liable to affliction, though their bodies consist of certain retributional entities collected by their particular life-course (i.e. being born in the imageless realm), their life-course itself would not be retribution nor connected with retribution if there were no special retributory consciousness.

When Non-returners[58], at the summit of existence, are engaged in putting an end to all distress, and they manifest a citta without distress which belongs to the stage of nothing whatever, through what is it that they don't fall away to death ? Taking part in an organism and life-force (which are employed by the Vaibhāṣikas to explain the absence of death in these highest meditational states) are not entities which are apart, because

Sandhinirmocana-sūtra, verse 7.

**cf. *Mahāyānasaṅgraha* I, 5, pp 14-15; I, 35, p. 5.

they are only metaphors for the similarity and parpetuation of retributory aggregates.* Just as there are no separate entities of similarity and continuity in the case of the similarity and continuity of seedlings of fruit, etc. Accordingly, without a doubt, another consciousness of the type that has been described, must be accepted.

35. The honorable Tāmraparṇīyas[59] recognize this same consciousness, calling it the consciousness which is the requisite for existence.[60] Others again (the Mahāsāṅghikas) call it the "root-consciousness".

36. Opponent : In that case, what is its object-of-consciousness, and what is its aspect ?

V : Its object-of-consciousness and aspect are undiscerned.

Opponent : How can it be a consciousness and be like this ?

V : The adversaries who claim that there exists a consciousness in the states of the attainment of cessation, etc., will have to agree to this, too.

Opponent : In that case, in what appropriating aggregate is it included ?

V : Following the literal meaning of the term, it would be included within the appropriating aggregate of consciousness.

37. Opponent : In that case, how can one explain the statement of the sūtra which says : "What is the appropriating aggregate of consciousness ? It is the collection of six consciousnesses"**, and "In the statement 'The psycho-physical complex comes about through the condition consciousness', what is consciousness ? It is the collection of six consciousnesses."***?

V : It must be recognized that these passages have an intention. Just as, in the passage "What is the aggregate of motivating dispositions ? It is the six classes of volition", this is not to say that other events are also not included there.†

Opponent : What is the intention in this ?

V : Now this has been stated by the Exalted One himself in the *Sandhinirmocana-sūtra* :

> "It has not been taught by me to fools,
> so that they might not imagine it to be a self."

*cf. *A Discussion of the Five Aggregates*, pp. 70-71.
**cf. *Majjhima* I, 53.
****Saṃyutta* III, 60.
†cf. *Kośa* I ad 15a-b.

Opponent : Why would they imagine it to be such ?

V : Because its aspect is without fundamental changes as long as Saṃsāra lasts. The intention there was to indicate only those consciousnesses which are less subtle, on account of their substrata, objects-of-consciousness, aspects, and special differentiating characteristcs being easily delimited, in which the processes of affliction and alleviation are determined, on account of their being connected with both afflictions and their antidotes, and through which, being its effects, the consciousness relating to their seeds can be inferred, but not to indicate the cause-consciousness, because it is opposite from those other consciousnesses as regards these features.[61] In regard to this matter, it can be replied that the consciousness which is the requisite of existence can be indicated suitably as being the collection of six consciousnesses itself.

It has also been demonstrated in the *Vyākhyāyukti* that nowadays not all sūtras are extant. Thus even if in the extant sūtras it is not mentioned explicitly, this does not mean that the store-consciousness is not to be accepted.[62]

38. Opponent : Now if it is thus as you say, then there would be two consciousness-series simultaneously : the retributional consciousness-series, and the other.

V : If this is so, what flaw is incurred ?

Opponent : A body which has two consciousness-series must be regarded as two sentient beings existing separately simulaneously, as, for instance, a second consciousness-series in another body is.

V : This is not so, because of the admission that the two are not different as regards the being of their cause and effect, and because the retributional consciousness is influenced by the other consciousnesses. In the case of two consciousness-series belonging to different bodies, this state of affairs does not exist. Accordingly, this flaw does not occur.[63]

39. Opponent : Isn't there sometimes a difference to be seen between the series of the seed and the series which has the seed ? (At the time when the result of the seed can be seen, i.e. the fruit, the original seed is no longer seen.)

V : In the case of a blue lotus, etc., the roots and the things possessed of the roots can both be seen simultaneously.[64] Thus, if it is seen, it is appropriate, and if it is not seen, it is also appropriate. If it is not accepted in the way that we describe it, then the absurdities ensue as we have described them. Thus, without a doubt, the store-consciousness must be accepted.

40. Opponent : In that case, why not accept a self with existence as an entity, as the substratum of the six consciousnesses ?[65]

V : In what way is a self accepted ? If it presents itself only as a series of moment-events, and transforms itself constantly through conditions, then what is the difference between it and that store-consciousness ?

Opponent : But it is single and constantly devoid of transformations.

V : In that case, how can it be demonstrated that it is also influenced by the latent impressions left in it by the consciousnesses, etc. ? It is the latent impressions which produce the special forces which make the consciousness-series continue, just as a lemon flower is penetrated by liquid lac. If there is no special characteristic which undergoes transformation, how, as there are no impressions possible in such a case, do there arise in time special memories, recognitions, passions, etc., from special familiar former experiences, cognitions, and passions, etc. ? As this self would exist in those states that are without citta, through what would it be that a mental consciousness later arises at the culmination of the state, as there are no special characteristics undergoing transformations within the self ? In what way are the consciousnesses subject to it, through which it could be understood that the self is their substratum ? If the arising of the consciousnesses is subject to the self, why do they arise gradually, as there are "no special transformations within the self" ? If it is that they are dependent upon other auxiliary causes, why should these causes be acknowledged at all, since the force for making these consciousnesses arise lies according to you in something quite apart from them ?

Now it may be claimed that their stability is subject to it. But what sort of stability is there for things that cease to abide as soon as they have arisen, and which cannot be attained ? Accordingly, such an entity (which is stable, unchanging, etc.) cannot be accepted as their substratum. And in this way (i.e. if the theory of a self were upheld), there would be a violation of scriptural authority, as it is said : "All events are without a self".* Accordingly, the conception that there exists a lasting independent entity "self", is a poor one. Thus, these effects seem to arise at a later time by the store consciousness being influenced by certain volitions. But thus it can also be demonstrated that bodily and verbal actions are not possessed of the characteristics which have been described for them.

41. Opponent : If bodily and verbal actions are not accepted in that manner (i.e. in the Vaibhāṣika manner, where a bodily act is defined as an act committed by the body, etc.), is it possible to deny the statement of the sūtra, which states that there are three kinds of acts ?

V : It is not possible. But it is possible to explain all this in such a manner that no flaw exists.

Opponent : How will there not be a flaw ?

V : It is our purpose to explain why it has been taught that there are three kinds of acts, what a body is, what an act is, in what sense one can speak of "body" and "action" and "bodily action". Similarly, it is our purpose to state this also in regard to verbal and mental acts, and as to why only bodily acts, etc., have been spoken of, and not acts of the eye, etc.

42. To begin with, why has this been taught in this manner ? In order to summarise the ten paths of action (the taking of life, taking what has not been given, offenses of lust, abandonment of the taking of life, abandonment of taking what has not been given; false speech, slander, harsh speech, idle talk, the abandonment of false speech, the abandonment of slander, the abandonment of harsh speech, and the abandonment of idle talk; covetousness, malice, wrong views, the abandonment of covetousness, the abandonment of malice, the abandonment of wrong views) with three kinds of action for those who would become frightened by the many things to be done, just as the three trainings were taught to Vṛjiputraka**.[65a]

Certain people (the Tīrthaṅkaras)[66] say that only the actions committed by the body truly exist, and that verbal and mental acts both do not exist, because they are only discriminations, and it was also to explain to them that those two are also action that the three kinds of acts were taught in this manner.

*cf. *Majjhima* I, 138 II, 263 etc, etc.
***Aṅguttara* I, 130.

43. The body is a special collection of great material elements and events derived from the great material elements, a corporeal mass associated with sense faculties. Action is a special volition. (Thus bodily action is actually a volition directed towards the body.)

44. A body exists in the sense that an accumulation exists, for it is an accumulation of atoms of great material elements, and atoms of that which is derived from the great material elements. Certain people say that it exists only in the sense of an accumulation of defilements, because the body is a well of unclear elements. But following the view of these people, there could be, for example, no bodies for gods.

45. An act is an intentional impulse in an "agent's" *manas*.

46. An act which sets the body into agitation is called a "bodily act". There are three kinds of volitions: those which prepare, those which decide, and those which "set into agitation". Those that "set into agitation" are those which are called "bodily action", as it is they through which there is brought about the motile element (wind, gaseousness) which is the cause for the arising in another locus on the part of the series which is associated with it. It is called "bodily action" because the middle phrase has been omitted, just as one speaks of "medicinal *balā-oil*"[67], or of a "dust wind" (when what is really meant is "the medicinal oil prepared from the *balā*-plant" and "a wind which raises dust").

Opponent: But as three divisions of the paths of action, namely: the taking of life, the taking of what has not been given, and offenses of lust, are admitted to be bodily action, how can this term refer to a volition?

V: Because this killing and taking and offenses take place because of it. That which has been committed by a bodily series engendered by it is said to be committed by it (i.e. that which is committed by a bodily series impelled by a volition, is said to be committed by that volition). Just as one says "a village burned by thieves" and "rice cooked with grass" (for a village which has been burned by a fire kindled by thieves, and for rice which has been cooked by fire arising from grass).

Opponent: How can a volition be called a path of action?

V: Though it is also simply action, it is also a path of action as it is the path which leads to the two kinds of courses:

favorable and unfavorable. Or, if you will, the path of action is the agitation of the body, since the three kinds of action we have called "volition" evolve dependent upon it.

47. It is as a favor to worldlings that these are also described as bodily action. Though there is nothing beneficial or unbeneficial within them, they are thus designated metaphorically, because by that means the world will undertake resorting to, and abandoning, certain volitions.

Opponent : If only volition is beneficial and unbeneficial action, how is it that it is said in the sūtras* : "There is a threefold action which when committed by the body after having been intended, is accumulated as unbeneficial, giving rise to suffering, and having suffering as its retribution." ?*

V : The intention was to speak of volition's medium, substratum, and object-of-consciousness. The volition which is different from those volitions having a medium, substratum, and object-of-consciousness in the body or voice, is called "mental action", because it is associated with *manas*, and because it does not incite the body or voice.

Opponent : If this is so, how is it that the Exalted One has spoken of "volition" and "the act which is committed after having willed" ?**

V : Among the three kinds of volition which we have indicated previously, it is the third which is called "act committed after having willed", since the body, etc., is incited by it after this has been willed by the first two kinds of volitions.

48. "Speech" means "words", i.e. those special vocal emissions which communicate meanings. Verbal action is that volition which brings forth these utterances. Something is speech because it is certain sorts of syllables, or inasmuch as it expresses a desired meaning.† Just as before, the action is the action which originates speech, because, just as before, the middle phrase has been omitted.

*cf. *Aṅguttara* V, 297 ff; *Madhyamāgama* Taisho 1, p 437 b 25-438 a 23; *Karmaprajñapti* Tokyo vol. 115, pp 85 : (the very beginning of the *Karmprajñapti*), which quotes this sūtra.

**Ibid.

†cf. *Kośa* II, ad 47, (LVP, p. 238)

49. Consciousness is *manas.* It is *manas* because it produces a sense of "mine", and because it becomes intent on other "births" and objects-of-sense. The rest is to be explained just as before.

Opponent : If only volition is bodily action, how can there be either restraint, or absence of restraint in those who are of distracted citta, or without citta, as there is no volition in these states ?

V : Because the impressions left by special volitions have not been suppressed, both restraint and the absence of restraint may exist in these states. The term "special" refers to that special volition which can be examined as originating the unmanifest action "restraint" and "absence of restraint".

Opponent : What is the suppression of these impressions ?

V : As has been acknowledged, this suppression is the being of any cause for a volition of either abandonment or non-abandonment of the unbeneficial paths of action.

Opponent : Through what does this suppression occur ?

V : It occurs through whatever volition can be examined as originating a manifest action which is the cause for the abandoning of restraint and its non-arising, and through any other causes of abandoning different from that.

50. Actions of the eye, etc., are not spoken of in the sūtras by the Exalted One, because he wanted to speak only of those acts connected with an effort, and not simple acts of performance.[68]

Opponent : What is an act connected with an effort ?

V : Anything which motivates "the agent's" *manas.*

Opponent : What is a simple act of performance ?

V : Wherever there is simply the distinct energy of the eye, etc., there is a simple act of performance.

Having explained the three kinds of acts which were spoken of by the Exalted One,
completely demonstrating them in a manner in which they have not been explained before,
with these solemnly declared demonstrations of actions,
may the beings in all life-courses, through whatever merit I have gained,
obtain the perfect clarities of Buddhas !

NOTES

1. See p. 58.
2. *Action and its threefold division*

The threefold division of action into bodily, verbal, and mental act occurs in fully-developed form already in various suttas of the Pāli *Nikāyas* (notably *Dīgha* III, 191, 245, and 279; *Majjhima* I 415-420; *Aṅguttara* I 32, 104, and 201). The germs for such a division can be seen in some of the earliest Buddhist writings, where the monk is implored to guard himself in body, speech, and mental activity (*Sutta-nipāta* 330, 365; *Dhammapada* 231-234, 281, 361, 391). Sometimes in the suttas there are mentioned only two kinds of activity, e.g. at various passages where guarding body and speech are referred to only (*Majjhima* I, 461; *Saṃyutta* I, 182). But the triple division is taken for granted in both early Theravāda and Sarvāstivāda Abhidharma (*Dhammasaṅgaṇi* 981; Bareau, *Sectes*—Sarvāstivāda thesis no. 117, p. 150) as well as in other Abhidharma traditions (e.g. the Mahīśāsaka (?) *Śāriputrābhidharmaśāstra,* Taisho 1548, cf. Bareau, p. 198, thesis no. 42). It is a natural enough division for a school of thought that holds that intentions themselves determine the ethical nature of an act, though the specific interpretation of what it includes differs radically among Buddhist ethical theorists.

It must be kept in mind that when Vasubandhu, and his Vaibhāṣika opponents, speak of "action" (*karma*), they mean an activity which can be subsumed under one or another of the retributional categories : unbeneficial (*akuśala*), beneficial (*kuśala*), and indeterminate (*avyākṛta*).* That is, they either have, for the "agent", a consequence of suffering, or freedom from suffering, or are volitional but devoid of a definite consequence. By no means all activity (Sumatiśīla's "*karaṇa*") is action in this technical sense.

3. *Vijñapti and avijñapti : Manifest and unmanifest action*

A "*vijñapti*" (lit. "an announcement", "communication", "intimation", but also in Vasubandhu's later usage "a perception") is an act which is manifestly perceptible to others besides the agent. A "manifest action" of the body is thus any action which can be seen by another, such as a gesture, etc.; a "manifest action" of speech is the actual closing and opening of the lips perceptible by the visual consciousness, and the result of which is perceived by the audial consciousness.

"*Avijñapti*", on the other hand, is a peculiarly Vaibhāṣika term involving some difficulties. An *avijñapti* is always preceded by a manifest action (see *Kośa* I, ad 13-14c), and represents a subtle continuation which the action proper, the manifest action, has initiated. It may arise even when the agent is not conscious. Initially dependent on a conscious manifest action or a mental action, it represents a residual force which has as its locus the material elements of the agent's organism. It is itself regarded as material for this reason (*Kośa* I, ad 13-14, LVP, p. 20), though it is exempt from the usual characteristics of materiality, inasmuch as it is not directly perceptible, and does not exercise physical resistance.

*see page 55.

To clarify this somewhat difficult concept, one may take recourse to an example employed by both La Vallée Poussin (*Kośa* IV, p 3, n. 2, 2) and Gokhale ("What is avijñapti-rūpa ?", *New Indian Antiquary* I, 1938, p 69) in their explanations of the term : A man orders another man to commit a murder, and in so doing commits a manifest verbal action. The assassin in turn, at the time of the murder, commits a manifest bodily action. When the murder is committed, the instigator himself becomes guilty of the crime, though he may not be committing any manifest action at the time, and may in fact be asleep. To the Vaibhāṣika, there must be a real entity present to account for his acquiring the retribution of a murderer, and this is supplied by positing an "unmanifest action", which arises as soon as the crime is committed, but which can be traced back to the verbal action and volition which instigated it. Unmanifest actions are divided into three general types : those which can be characterized as "restraint"(*saṃvara*), as "lack of restraint"(*asaṃvara*), and as neither one nor the other (*Kośa* IV, ad 13a-b, LVP, p. 43). Our murder would belong actually to the third type, which is described as any unbeneficial or beneficial act which can be comprised neither within manifest action, mental action, nor within the restraint of disciplinary rules, meditation, and the holy man's path, nor within their reversal (*Kośa* IV, ad 37c-d, LVP, pp. 93-94). According to the Vaibhāṣikas, the beneficiality of the higher meditational states, where there is no more possibility of manifest action or volition, is due to the *avijñapti* of restraint resulting from the initial act of entering into meditation. A monk's keeping silent at the confession of misdeeds during the recital of the *Prātimokṣa* would similarly be an unmanifest action of lack of restraint, if he has committed misdeeds, as again no manifest or mental action may be present during his silence. "*Avijñapti*", by the way, is not really analogous to the psychoanalytic concept of "unconscious act", since a conscious act must always precede its emergence. Nor should it be considered the mechanism of any retribution, as this is taken care of in other ways by the Vaibhāṣika, and *avijñapti* arises only as a result of certain acts, not all. (On this, see the article by Yamada, "On the idea of avijñapti-karma", *IBK* 10, 1962, pp. 51-55.)

Vasubandhu defined unmanifest action (*Kośa* I, 11) only to subsequently refute it as a real entity (*Kośa* IV, ad 3d). His definition came under the attack of Saṅghabhadra in his *Abhidharmasamayapradīpikā*, and resulted in Vasubandhu's revision of his definition in *A Discussion of the Five Aggregates*. (On this, see the notes of La Vallée Poussin and Gokhale.) Arguments against unmanifest action are found also in this treatise.

4. On *manas*, see pp. 60-61.

5. *Saṃsthāna*, "*configuration*".

To the Vaibhāṣika, the visible is divided into two aspects : color and "*saṃsthāna*". (See *Kośa* I, ad 10a.) These two are considered distinct sense-impressions, and are thus for the Vaibhāṣikas two separate sorts of real entities (*dravya*, see note 5a). "*Saṃsthāna*" is usually divided into eight general categories : "long", "short", "quadrangular", "circular", "convex", "concave", "even" or "straight", and "uneven" or "crooked".

(On the translations of these terms, see note 12.) The omission of triangles may rest on the fact that they can be derived from quadrangulars.

"*Saṃsthāna*" can thus be rendered as "shape". The only reason the translation "configuration" is employed here is because "*saṃsthāna*" is either a shape that appears stable to the visual consciousness, or one which is undergoing changes. It is to this second kind of "*saṃsthāna*" that the Vaibhāṣika reduces manifest bodily actions. For example, we say that we see a man moving his arm, but what we actually see, the Vaibhāṣika says, is certain combinations of visual shapes undergoing changes. Apparently manifest bodily actions, to be truly manifest, have to be seen, since they can only be *inferred* by a blind man. Of course, one's own bodily actions are directly manifest to oneself, but the defining characteristic of manifest action is that it should be manifest *to another*. As it is being used here, the word "configuration" means both a shape and any combination of shapes, changing or unchanging.

5a. *Dravya*

The Vaibhāṣika criteria for considering something a real entity, or *dravya*, are :

(1) its characteristic must be distinguished as special by at least one consciousness (*Kośa* I, ad 10d) (a characteristic of this sort is called a "*svalakṣaṇa*", "own-characteristic");

(2) it must not be susceptible to further division (Ibid, and *Kośa* VI, 4). True entities would thus to the Vaibhāṣika be only the moment-atoms of materiality and the momentary flashes of feelings, motivating dispositions, cognitions, and consciousness-perceptions. A body, a flame, and, for that matter, a consciousness-series, can thus not really be considered a *dravya*. (cf. *Vibhāṣā, MCB* V, pp 128-129; Saṅghabhadra's *Abhidharmanyāyānusāra* chapt. 51, tr. LVP, *MCB* V, p. 106.)

A *dravya* has a specific manner of being, or nature (its "own-being", *svabhāva*) which is apprehended by one or another of the consciousnesses, or a combination of several, as an "own-characteristic". A change in characteristics is always a change in things : there are in fact no underlying entities which *have* characteristics—there is only whatever is presented to the consciousnesses themselves.

In this connection, the *Vibhāṣā* makes much of its distinction between two levels of reality. First, there is common-sense reality, convemtional reality (*saṃvṛti-satya*), sometimes called "truth of designation" (*prajñapti-satya*), which speaks of "people" as people, "jars" as jars, and, even more remotely from any true dravyas, "nations" as nations, "armies" as armies, etc. Then there is ulimate truth (*paramārtha-satya*), which has as its object the true *svalakṣaṇas* of true dravyas. Actually, one could very well say* that the *Vibhāṣā* really distinguishes three levels, because it categorizes all events into 75 basic types of dravyas, constituents which even in the last analysis work in a certain way. This is not quite the same as *paramārtha-satya*, since it subsumes true dravyas, the momentary entities, into various broader categories. We might for convenience's sake call this level "*dra-*

*Vasubandhu in fact does something of the sort at *Kośa* II, ad 22.

vyasatya", though this term is usually used by the *Vibhāṣā* as a synonym for "*paramārthasatya*'. At least one of the philosophers held in great esteem by the *Vibhāṣā*, namely the Bhadanta Vasumitra, had come to an interesting conclusion regarding *paramārthasatya*. He held that *all* designations are only prajñaptisat, but that underlying each designation there is some complex of moments which are paramārthasat but in their true state hopelessly elusive to those who rely on discursive thought alone, and characterizable only by the most general of designations (such as "being in the state of having causes and conditions") (*Vibhāṣā*, quoting the Bhadanta Vasumitra, *MCB* V, pp 166-167). And the *Vibhāṣā* itself, in one of its "options", went so far as to say that it was possible to hold that there is only one theory reagarding conditioned events which can be ultimately true, i.e. "All things are empty and devoid of self." (*Vibhāṣā*, *MCB* V, p. 164). This is, of course, the opinion of Nāgārjuna as well as, ultimately, the opinion of Vasubandhu himself (See the *Commentary on the Separation from Extremes*, and the *Teaching of the Three Own-Beings* included in this volume). Later Vaibhāṣikas seem to have lost sight of the Bhadanta Vasumitra's word of caution. Evidence for this is to be found not only in Vasubandhu's critiques of their theories (which after all may have been hardened into more rigid shape by Vasubandhu himself, in order to make his polemic more convincing*), but also in the treatises of Saṅghabhadra and the Dīpakāra themselves.

To return to the question of "dravyas", the Vaibhāṣikas consider the sense-fields such true entities, though strictly speaking they meet neither of the criteria given above. A sense-field is really a *collection* of dravyas, grouped together because of certain common distinctive general characteristics (*sāmānyaviśeṣalakṣaṇa*)—they are thus (in our usage) "dravyasat", but not paramārthasat. Vasubandhu attacked the Vaibhāṣikas for calling such a collection a "dravya", and said that their use of the term was inconsistent and capricious (*Kośa* II, ad 22). As a matter of fact, for the Vaibhāṣika to remain consistent, a "sense-field" can have only "truth of designation", since they are collections of atoms (cf. *Kośa* I, ad 44a-b), and the individual atoms themselves, according to the Vaibhāṣika, are not perceptible, and thus cannot be sense-fields(*Kośa* I, ad 20a-b). Similarly, an aggregate making up "personality" cannot be a real entity, since it is a series of momentary events (Ibid). It had been usual for a long time within Abhidharma to subsume all the basic constituents of experience under at least one aggregate, and one of the sense-fields (See the methodology of *Dhātukathā* I). This again cannot be an ultimately real way of looking at things, particularly if atomism is adhered to. On the other hand, an object-of-consciousness has to be a real entity, because what isn't real has no faculty for producing a cognition, according to the Vaibhāṣika. The Vaibhāṣikas' atom has no such faculty, and "aggregations of atoms", which are said

*It is at least the opinion of G. Sasaki that Vasubandhu may have deliberately made the *Vibhāṣā* sound more dogmatic than it is (*A study of Abhidharma Philosophy*, Introduction, p 3 ff).

to have it, have no unity, and thus can't be entities, following the Vaibhāṣikas' other criterion. Vasubandhu, on this and other grounds (see *Kośa* I ad 10; I ad 13; I ad 44; II ad 22; I ad 43c-d, III ad 100a-b), dispenses with atomism, and, while maintaining the two criteria, regards as dravya that which is *perceived* as one, thus ruling out the Vaibhāṣika atom as well as collections such as "a body", "an army", etc. (Dignāga, following Vasubandhu, also criticized the Vaibhāṣika atom on the grounds mentioned above, cf. *Pramāṇasamuccaya* I, II, ad 2c-d, Hattori, pp. 33-34; *Ālambanaparīkṣā*, and cf. Hattori, n.2, 17, p. 118. Similar arguments are to be found in the Jain logician Mallavādī, cf. *Dvādaśāraṇyacakra*, ed, Muni Jambuvijaya, p. 96).

Saṅghabhadra himself drops the *Vibhāṣā's* criteria, and the character of a dravya is for him simply that it can give rise to a citta, when this citta arises without having to depend on anything but the one thing perceived (*Nyāyānusāra*, chapt. 50, *MCB* V, pp. 28-29). According to Saṅghabhadra, a dravya may differ in *bhāvas*, specific types, but its general manner of being, its *svabhāva*, is of one sort. This would seem to be some sort of a distinction between essential and secondary characteristics, which the *Vibhāṣā* itself, in spite of some resulting difficulties, does not make. In fact it considers this distinction a major flaw in the theories of the Bhadanta Dharmatrāta (*Vibhāṣā, MCB* V, p 24). It is certainly anathema to Vasubandhu, who holds that criteria for the determination of primary, as against secondary, characteristics cannot be found (*A Discussion for the Demonstration of Action*, 15-17).

6. *Ālambana*

This term is here translated as "object-of-consciousness" in order to bring out the distinction between it and *viṣaya*. The latter is usually defined as the object of the sense-organ itself, whereas the former is the object of the corresponding consciousness. The *viṣaya* is properly the "thing out there" as the organ comes "into contact" with it; the *ālambana* is one's impression of it. (See *Kośa* I, ad 29b-c.) On "citta", see pp. 59-60.

7. See *A Discussion of the Five Aggregates*, p. 65.

8. *Vipākahetu*, "Retributory cause" or "maturational cause".

A retributory cause is any volitional act with an ethical "charge" strong enough to give the result either of suffering or of freedom from suffering for the "series" which instigated it (cf. *Kośa* II, 54c-d). Presumably, what is intended here by "a configuration which has arisen from former aspiration" is any change in shape, size, etc. which was longed for in the past, and which has finally been attained due to beneficial past actions. Sumatiśīla's example, "May I have lips as red as a bimba-fruit" (*Karmasiddhiṭīkā* p. 204, 4, 8) is perhaps not completely adequate, as this would not necessarily entail a change of configuration for the Vaibhāṣika. But it is a humorous example of the kinds of rather frivolous motivations which often lay behind Buddhist acts of piety. As an example of such an aspiration which includes the Vaibhāṣikas' "configuration", and yet echoes the spirit of Sumatiśīla's example, there is the following inscription of the Burmese Queen Caw, from the 8th-9th centuries, marking the dedication of a monastery at Pagān : "Meantime, before I reach Nirvana, by virtue of the great work of merit I have done, may I prosper as a man and be more happy than all other men. Or as a spirit, may I be full of color, dazzling brightness, and victorious beauty. But more especially I would like to have a long life, freedom from disease, a lovely complexion, a pleasant voice, and a beautiful figure. I would like to be the loved and honored darling of every man and spirit. Gold, silver, rubies, coral, pearls, and other lifeless treasure—elephants, horses, and other living treasure—may I have lots of them. By virtue of my power and glory I would be triumphant with pomp and retinue, with fame and splendor. Wherever I am born, may I be filled with noble graces, and not know one speck of misery, and after I have tasted and enjoyed the happiness of men and the happiness of spirits, may I at last attain the peaceful bliss of Nirvana." (*Archeological Survey of Burma*, inscription no. 334, quoted Niharranjan Ray, *Theravāda Buddhism in Burma*, p. 165.)

9. *The Vaibhāṣika Atomic Theory*

The atomic theory evolved by the Vaibhāṣika philosophers is found neither in the *Jñānaprasthāna*, the ancient work on which the *Vibhāṣā* is ostensibly a commentary, nor in any of the other "padas" of the Sarvāstivāda Abhidharma (see McGovern, *Manual of Buddhist Philosophy*, p. 125). One of the earliest texts to give the theory is apparently the *Abhidharmasāra* of Dharmaśrī, which was translated into Chinese (Taisho 1550) in 250 A.D. McGovern thinks that Dharmaśrī borrowed the theory from Kaṇāda, and that the Jain atomic theory may have a similar source. But Dharmaśrī's atomism is quite different in nature from Kaṇāda's, and the Jain theory, which may actually antedate Kaṇāda, differs radically from them both. (cf. Schubring, *Doctrine of the Jainas*, pp. 131 ff). An important difference between Dharmaśrī's and Kaṇāda's atomism is that for Kaṇāda, atoms are eternal, whereas for Dharmaśrī, they are momentary, though they may form "series". Another difference lies in the fact that Dharmaśrī maintains fourteen different kinds of atoms : Besides the atoms of the four great elements (see p. 75), each sense-object and sense-organ has within it a special kind of atom to which its particular qualities are due (*Abhidharmasāra* 1, quoted McGovern, p. 126). This is, as McGovern says, similar to the conception of late 19th century chemistry, where each of the ninety odd elements was held to have a special kind of atom. Though perhaps the seed for Dharmaśrī's atomism may be seen in his familiarity with the Vaiśeṣika and Jain theories, to speak of outright borrowing, as McGovern does, is somewhat strong in the light of the fact that Dharmaśrī's theory is really quite unique, and moulded to Buddhist sentiments of impermanence. Dharmaśrī's theory is considered standard by the *Vibhāṣā*, which makes frequent use of it. Through this highly influential text it found its way not only into the crystallizations of its system in the philosophies of the "Neo-Vaibhāṣikas" : Saṅghabhadra, the Dīpakāra, and, in fundamental opposition, Vasubandhu, but even into the Theravāda theories of Buddhaghosa (in the *Atthasālinī*) and Anuruddha (*Compendium*, p. 164 ff). (The question of the extent of Vaibhāṣika influence on 5th century Theravāda has as yet not been much investigated : There is a possibility that Buddhaghosa derived many of his specific theories from the *Vibhāṣā*. Certainly Anuruddha's atomism, at any rate, is identical with the *Vibhāṣā's*. On a probable influence of Vasubandhu's Yogācāra on 5th century Theravāda, see S. Sarathcandra, "The Abhidhamma Psychology of Perception and the Yogācāra Theory of Mind," *U. of Ceylon Review* IV, 1956, pp. 49-57.)

There are thus, in standard Vaibhāṣika theory these fourteen different kinds of atoms : atoms of "earth", "fire", "water", and "wind", atoms of color, sound, smell, taste, and the tangible, eye-atoms, ear-atoms, nose-atoms, tongue-atoms, and body-atoms, for the specific parts of these organs that function as sense-fields for the consciousnesses (On the arrangement of these special atoms in the organs, see *Koṣa* I, ad 43c-44d). The atoms corresponding to the sense-fields own their origination and specific qualities to transformations and combinations within the elemental atoms—therefore they are called "derivative"(*upādāya*) or "secondary" (*bhautika*).

In the theories of Saṅghabhadra and the Vaibhāṣika as criticized by Vasubandhu, a minimum of eight kinds of atoms must join to form an aggregation or molecule (*saṅghāta*), for actual perceptibility in the realm of desires, i.e. the normal world outside of meditation(*Kośa* II, ad 22). These are the four kinds of elemental atoms and the four atoms of color, odor, taste, and secondary tangibility (i.e. smoothness, roughness, etc. Primary tangibility—liquidity, etc., is a mark of the four great elements themselves). Each atom of derivative materiality needs a set of four elemental atoms for itself, so that the actual number of atoms in the simplest molecule is sixteen. In the case of molecules which resound, there will in addition be present a sound-atom, so that there will be five derivative and twenty elemental atoms. The molecules of the simplest animate bodies will become even complex, since they must each contain an atom of the tactile sense, touch being in Vaibhāṣika biological theory, as in Aristotle's and Darwin's the most basic and primordial sense held by living beings. Molecules of the other sense-organs must have at least ten kinds of atoms, since each must contain not only the four elemental atoms, four sense-object atoms, and the atom of tactile sense, but also an additional kind of atom for the particular sense-organ in question. It can thus be seen that no matter what the number of atoms in a molecule may be, the four great elements always appear together, and in equal proportion. There is as much of the hot element, "fire", in wood, or in water, as there is in a flame. The difference lies only in the "intensity", which is not further explained (at least not in the *Kośa*, the *Dīpa*, and the *Abhidharmāvatāra*). Vasubandhu says that the presence of "water", the cohesive element, in a flame is proved by the flame's keeping a shape, and the presence of the solid element, "earth", in water, is shown by the fact that water can support a ship (*Kośa* II, ad 22).

Within this theory, an atom should strictly speaking be that portion of materiality so small that it cannot be subjected to further division, whether physically or by reasoning, just as the moment is the smallest extent of time. This is the manner in which Saṅghabhadra defines it (*Nyāyānusāra* 23, 3, cf. La Vallée Poussin, *Kośa* II, p. 144, note 3). But Vasubandhu notes that occasionally there is an inconsistency in the terminology of the Vaibhāṣikas, i.e. sometimes they say "atom" when they should say "aggregation of atoms" (*Kośa* II, ad 22). Saṅghabhadra himself is very careful to make the distinction (La Vallée Poussin, *Kośa* II, p. 145, note 3), but it seems somewhat botched in the discussion of the Dīpakāra(*Dīpa* II, 110-111, pp. 65-66). For the Dīpakāra, the atoms are the ultimate units of materiality which have the capacity for appearing in the world, i.e. they would correspond to what Vasubandhu and Saṅghabhadra designate as an "aggregation". When referring to the different elements making up this "atom", the Dīpakāra speaks only of "entities"(*dravya*). Furthermore, his discussion differs from Saṅghabhadra's and Vasubandhu's on the question of the minimum number of kinds of "entities" necessary for an atom's appearance in the realm of desires. He says seven, which presumably would be the four great elements, color, odor, and taste—the tangible being for him entirely included within the properties of the great elements.

10. See note 5a.

11. *The Vaiśeṣika Theory of Composite wholes*

This theory, which states that a composite exists as a new entity, a composite whole (*avayavin*) penetrating its component parts, is, as Vasubandhu tells us, a speciality of the Vaiśeṣikas. However, it is not found in the sūtras of Kaṇāda himself, but rather finds its first extant explicit mention in the *Nyāya-sūtras* of Gautama (*Nyāya-sūtra* II, I 31-37; IV, II 4-16). It is further elaborated by Praśastapāda and by Vātsyāyana, both of whom may have been older contemporaries of Vasubandhu (cf. *Praśastapāda-bhāṣyaṭīkāsaṅgraha*, Chowkhamba Sanskrit Series No. 255, pp. 169, 173; Vātsyāyana, *Nyāyabhāṣya*, ad II, I, 31-37; ad IV, II 4-16).

The reasons for the formulation of this theory are, in brief, the following : The Vaiśeṣika, like the Vaibhāṣika, subscribes to an atomic theory, though his atoms, unlike the moment-atoms of the Vaibhāṣika, are eternal. To both, discrete and detached minute entities form the basic stuff of the material universe. External reality as it presents itself to us however has unified realities, and the question emerges as to what the unifying agency is. To the Vaibhāṣika, as to Vasubandhu, and as later to Dignāga, these unities are constructed subjectively, but the Vaiśeṣika, being a "realist" (curiously in both the modern and medieval senses of the term), has to posit an objective reality as their basis. There is furthermore a problem because Vaiśeṣika atoms, like Vaibhāṣika ones, are imperceptible, and yet their compounds are perceived (cf. *Nyāya-sūtra* IV, II, 13-14). The Vaibhāṣika takes care of this problem by assuming that aggregations of atoms become perceptible, though atoms in isolation are imperceptible, just as one hair may not be visible at a distance, but a mass of hair will be. The Vaiśeṣika, however, assumes atoms to be *absolutely* imperceptible. Thus it is assumed by the Vaiśeṣika that a composite is an entity in itself, having a different set of qualities from its parts, though occupying the same locus. If the composite whole did not exist, Vātsyāyana says, one could only infer, and never directly perceive, objects like trees, since at any one time one has only a partial perception of parts of the tree. According to Vātsyāyana, the perception of the composite whole "tree" takes place simultaneously with the perception of certain parts of the tree (*Nyāyabhāṣya*, ad II, I, 30-

37). He adds that unitary conceptions, such as "tree", "jar", etc. must arise from something which is really one, and can't emerge from mere aggregations (*Nyāyabhāṣya*, ad II, I, 37).

The concept of the composite whole also plays a role in Nyāya-Vaiśeṣika causality. In a cause and effect sequence, a new substance, a composite whole (cloth) emerges from the material causes (threads), and the parts continue to exist within the composite whole, though, according to Vātsyāyana, the avayavin together with its parts make up only one entity. It was not until Uddyotakara that the parts were regarded as separate entities persisting along with the composite-whole entity. (See D.N. Shastri, *Critique of Indian Realism*, pp 262-271, on the differences between the earlier causal theory of Vātsyāyana, where the cause, as an entity, is destroyed before the emergence of the effect, and the later theory, hinted at by Uddyotakara, but not crystallized until Śrīdhara, where the causes continue to exist as entities within the composite whole.) Even to Vātsyāyana, atomic causality is an exception : the two atoms making up the composite whole of a dyad or double-atom (*dvyaṇuka*) continue to exist as entities. The fact that all further combinations of atoms are composite wholes having different qualities from their parts, will explain why a jar is perceptible, whereas its atoms are not.

Vasubandhu does not here bother to refute the composite whole alternative, since its mere mention would probably be enough to make a true Vaibhāṣika flinch. On a previous occasion, however, he has presented a refutation of the avayavin theory, a theory he considers "infantile"(*Kośa* III, ad 100a-b). His arguments there for the most part rest on the same sorts of epistemological reasons that Vātsyāyana raises in favor of the concept. They can be outlined as follows :

(1) When the organ of the visual or tactile consciousness is in contact with one thread, the cloth is not perceived. If the composite whole "cloth" exists in each thread, it would have to be perceived even if only one of its threads is (*Kośa* III, ad 100a-b, LVP, p 211).

(2) If the Vaiśeṣika says that the composite whole does not exist within each of its parts, how will it be demonstrated that it is anything but the collection of these parts ? (Ibid, p 212).

(3) If the Vaiśeṣika says that the composite whole does exist within each of its parts, but that the perception of one thread does not result in the perception of cloth because the perception of cloth presumes contact of the organ with several of the parts, then if one sees the border of a cloth, one would see the whole cloth.

(4) If the Vaiśeṣika says that the perception of the composite whole depends upon the perception of its central and other portions, one could never see a composite whole, since one can never see its central and end-parts simultaneously.

(5) If the Vaiśeṣika says that these parts are perceived in succession, then the perception of "cloth" does not differ from the perception of a "circle" that results from hurling a torch in a full arc. Objects-of-consciousness of such perceptions cannot be real entities in any way.

(6) When threads of different colors come together to form a cloth, how can this cloth be considered an entity ? (Ibid, pp 212-213). This argument depends on the fact that according to Vaiśeṣika metaphysics, qualities like color, etc. must pervade their substances wholly. Thus one substance can have only one quality of a type. So what does one do with a cloth of many colors ? Clearly it cannot be a substance-entity in the Vaiśeṣika sense. This last argument was quite terrifying to the Vaiśeṣikas, and prompted Uddyotakara to assume that "variegated color" must in this case be regarded as one color. This conclusion was rejected as absurd by the Navya-Naiyāyikas (cf. Shastri, p 256). Even admitting Uddyotakara's rather far-fetched solution, the question can be re-phrased in a manner which makes the problem remain : What does one do about a cloth which is variegated in color, but has a border of one color only ?

Other criticisms, some of which had already disturbed Vātsyāyana :

(1) If one thing exists at one place, it can't at the same time exist in another. According to Vātsyāyana, the dyad, being a composite whole, resides in its two parts. But its existence in one atom would necessarily exclude its existence in the other.

(2) Does the composite whole, which is one, pervade its parts in its entirety, or partially ? In the former case, the composite whole will be exhausted in one part, and the remaining parts will be without it. In the latter case, the composite whole must itself have further parts, by which it pervades its constituent parts.

(3) If the composite whole is a different entity from its parts, it should have a different weight.

(4) There seems to be no criterion for which combinations of entities give rise to a composite whole (not all do, e.g. a forest does not).

(5) Nor which objects should be regarded as ultimate composite wholes (i.e. those which cannot form further composite wholes).

(6) No composite whole can be formed out of parts based on different material elements, because there is no possibility of generality (*sāmānya*), which must inhere in every particular instance, according to the Vaiśeṣika. Thus neither a human body, which contains blood (water-element), as well as earth-elements, nor a tree (with its sap) can be a composite whole.

12. This passage is close to, but not identical with, *Kośa* IV, ad 2b-3b. Both the *Kośa* and the *Demonstration of Action* passages have been translated into French with some confusion (which cannot, of course, be usually said for translators as eminent as La Vallée Poussin and Lamotte). Actually, there is some confusion in the Tibetan translation of the *Kośa* passage as well, since "*vṛtta*", which definitely means "circle", has been translated as "*lham-pa*", "square' (Peking/Tokyo Tibetan Tripiṭaka, vol. 115, p 193, 1, 5 ff; cf. the Sanskrit original, ed. Pradhan, p 194). This error is probably the source of the *Mahāvyutpatti's* confusion where it gives words which unequivocally mean "circular" (*Vṛtta* 圓) and "quadrangular" (*lham-pa* 方) as synonyms (*Mahāvyutpatti* 1878-1886). In the definition of

"square" given in this treatise, the phrase "in each of four sides)" is supplied from Hsüan-tsang's translation (Taisho 1609, vol. 31, p. 781 b-c) :

見 四 面 等 便 起 方 覚

The Sanskrit original of the term "square" in this treatise may have been "*varga*". This is the term for "square" employed by Ārya-bhaṭa in both the senses of an "equiquadrangular" and "the product of two equal quantities". (*Āryabhaṭīya*, II v. 3 : "*Vargas sama-caturaśraḥ phalañ ca sadṛśa-dvayasya saṃvargaḥ.*" "Square' means 'an equiquadrangular'; 'the area (of such a quadrangular)', and 'the product of two equal quantities.")

The terms "*unnata*" and "*avanata*" have been rendered by both translators into French as "high" and "low", respectively. 高 and 下 are also the usual translations into Chinese (cf. *Mahāvyutpatti* 1884-1885). However, though "*unnata*" is a common word for "high", "*avanata*" does not usually mean "low". Besides, the inclusion of "high" and "low" in a list that has already included "long" and "short", seems somewhat strange. Add to this the fact that Vasubandhu's definitions of the terms "*unnata*" and "*avanata*" make little sense if they are supposed to refer to "high" and "low". They in fact define the terms "convex" and "concave". The translation of "*unnata*" by "convex", and "*avanata*" by "concave", is unproblematical as far as the Sanskrit is concerned. "*Unnata*" means not only "raised, elevated", etc. but also, as Apte's dictionary provocatively puts it, "projecting, plump, full (as breasts)" (p. 435). And though we may not want to translate "*unnata*" as "convex" when we are translating Kālidāsa ("*nibaḍônnata-stanam*" : "full, projecting breasts", *Mālavikāgnimitra*, Act II, v. 3), this translation fits well with the less passionate and more analytic point of view of a fellow Gupta protégé, Vasubandhu. Mālavikā's shapely breasts must certainly be appreciated by Vasubandhu at least as ideal examples of convex configurations. As for "*avanata*", it never seems to mean "low" in classical Sanskrit, but rather "bent down", "stooped", "crouched", "bowed". All these are concave configurations.

Further light on the terms was provided by "Sai-chien-ti-lo's" *Abhidharmāvatāra.* In its list of the various kinds of configuration, the usual terms "*mthon-po*" and "*dma'-ba*" are omitted, and in their place we have "*sgang*" and "*gshong*"(Tokyo Peking Tibetan Tripiṭaka vol. 119, p 44, 1, 1). "*Sgang*" means "a hill-spur, the ridge or top of a hill" (Sarat Candra Das, p 320), and seems to be cognate to the verb "*sgang-ba*", "to grow" or "become full", specifically used in the "becoming full" of a nubile girl (Jäschke, p 114). "*Gshong*" can also be a "mountain-ridge", and it seems to be cognate to the verb *shong-ba,* "to have room or space in" and "to remove and carry away." A mountain-spur can be either convex or concave, depending on what part one is looking at, but the term *sgang* emphasizes the projection, a convexity, whereas *gshong* emphasizes the cavity, a concavity. A "valley" is indeed "low" in comparison to a mountain, but even more it too is a concavity.

The terms "*śāta*" and "*viśāta*", finally, have been translated by both Lamotte and La Vallée Poussin as "*égal*" and "*inégal*". But it makes little sense to speak of a configuration "equal", since "equal" expresses a relationship. The trouble may lie in the fact that Vasubandhu defines "*śāta*" as "*sama-sthāna*", and "*viśāta*" as "*viṣama-sthāna*" (*Kośa* I ad 10a, Pradhan, p 9). This is the old Vaibhāṣika definition, as can be seen by the *Abhidharmāvatāra's* definitions "*mnyam-pa*" and "*mi mnyam-pa*" : "*sama*" and "*viṣama*" (Tib vol. 119, p. 44, 1, 2). Now "*sama*" may mean "equal", but that is by no means the only meaning of the term. It also means "even, level, straight, plain, easy, pleasant, convenient". "*Viṣama*" correspondingly may mean "uneven, not level, rough, painful, troublesome". Besides, "*śāta*" never means "equal", anyway. Its meaning is "sharpened, whetted, polished, smoothed, made even, thin, pleasant". It is clear that as configurations, "*śāta*" and "*viśāta*" must mean something like "even" and "uneven", or "straight" and "crooked". Vasubandhu's definitions seem to bear this out. (*Sama* and *viṣama* occur again at *Kośa* I, ad 10c, Pradhan, p 7; La Vallée Poussin, p 18, in reference to smells. Here, La Vallée Poussin's translation "excessives" and "non-excessives" are very good. This is the "pleasant" and "rough" aspect of *sama* and *viṣama*.)

It is intersesting that Vasubandhu here concentrates solely on the visual aspect of "configuration", which becomes reduced to color. And as far as visual configuration is concerned, this reduction seems unassailable, particularly if one remembers that the ancient Indians, unconfined by the definitions of modern optics, regarded any shades of light and dark as colors. The Vaibhāṣikas in their color-lists included, of the colors recognized by ordinary language, only white and the primary colors blue, yellow, and red. Green, etc. were correctly recognized as compound colors, and thus unworthy of entry into a list of elements. Aside from these four, the Vaibhāṣikas listed as colors cloudy (*abhram*), smoky (*dhūmaḥ*), dusty (*rajaḥ*), misty (*mahikā*), shadowy (*chāyā*), bright or hot light (*ātāpa*), dimmer or reflected light (*āloka*), and darkness (*andhakāra*) (cf. *Kośa* I, ad 10a, Pradhan, p 6, La Vallée Poussin, p 16), which seem to be different gradations and mixtures of light and dark.

In contrast to his exclusive focus on visual configuration in this treatise, Vasubandhu in the *Kośa* (IV, ad 3c) had made a powerful argument against configuration's being an entity on the grounds that configuration is equally an object of the fifth, or tactile consciousness, as of the first or visual. In fact, the convexity of Mālavikā's breasts can perhaps be most fully appreciated by means of the fifth, not the first, consciousness! The Vaibhāṣika objection that the tactile consciousness does not properly apprehend configurations, but only construes them on the apprehension of certain arrangements of the soft, hard, etc. is brilliantly converted by Vasubandhu into the statement that the visual consciousness does not apprehend them either, but similarly construes them on the apprehension of certain arrangements of colors. "Configuration" is thus not a distinct object-of-consciousness which could be allotted definitely to one sense-field, and as such is not a real entity, at all. Why Vasubandhu chose to omit this beautiful argument from this treatise is puzzling. Perhaps he thought he had enough refutations, already.

**The geometry of Vasubandhu and Āryabhaṭa*

Āryabhaṭa's geometry is particularly interesting to a student of the *Demonstration of Action,* as this great mathematician is not too distant from Vasubandhu in both time and place. Āryabhaṭa, who is the earliest extant exponent of the mathematics and astronomy of the school of Pāṭaliputra, gives his own birth-date as 476, and the date of the composition of his treatise as 499 (*Āryabhaṭīya* III, v. 10). This is assuming that he used the date 3102 B.C. for the beginning of the Kali-yuga, which is almost certain, as in fact he may be one of the foremost exponents of this date (cf. Fleet, "The Kaliyuga Era of B.C. 3102", *JRAS* 1911, pp 480 ff). The Sanskrit reads :

> "Ṣaṣṭy abdānāṁ ṣaṣṭir yadā vyatītās trayaś ca yugapādāḥ,
> try-adhika viṁśatir abdās tadêha mama janmano 'tītāḥ."
> "Now, when three yugapādas and sixty times sixty years have elapsed, twenty-three years of my life have passed." (N.B. The end of the third yugapāda marks the beginning of the Kali-yuga.)

He specifies Kusumapura, i.e. Pāṭaliputra, as the seat of his activity, or at least as the place where his work was appreciated. (II, v. 1 : "Āryabhaṭas tviha nigadati Kusumapure 'bhyarcitaṃ jñānaṃ.") He may thus also have been a subject of the Guptas, presumably of Budhagupta and his successors.

He is most famous for his contributions to astronomy, arithmetic, and algebra. He was apparently the first Indian astronomer to hold that the earth is a sphere and rotated on an exis (IV 2, 6, 7, 9), for which he was criticized by Brahmagupta and other later astronomers. His arithmetic and algebra is quite advanced. And though his solid geometry often leaves something to be desired (cf. II, 6b and 7b), his plane geometry is quite impressive. For instance, he arrives at a usable value for π, 3. 1416 (II, 10). Unfortunately, the *Āryabhaṭīya* is not a complete text of mathematics, and many definitions are taken for granted.

However, there are certain definitions of shapes in Āryabhaṭa, and these contrast with Vasubandhu's in several interesting, though to some extent predictable, ways. Āryabhaṭa defines "square" quite rigorously from a mathematical point of view : "Vargas sama-caturaśraḥ" (II, v. 3) : "'Square' means 'equiquadrangular' " i.e. a plane figure which has only four angles, all of them equal. His term for "equiquadrilateral", a quadrilateral whose sides, but not necessarily whose angles, are equal, would be "*samacaturbhuja*" (cf. II, 11). Following this definition, Vasubandhu's is geometrically inexact, as he is defining the seeing of an equiquadrilateral only. (There might be the temptation to accuse Āryabhaṭa's commentator Parameśvara of a similar slip in his gloss on "equiquadrangular". He says, "Yasya caturaśrasya kṣetrasya catvāro bāhavaḥ parasparaṃ samās syuḥ karṇadvayañ ca parasparaṃ samaṃ bhavet tat kṣetraṃ samacaturaśram ity ucyates." "Any quadrangular plane figure of which plane figure all sides are equal to each other, and of which both diagonals are equal to each other, is called an 'equiquadrangular'." But *karṇa*, "diagonal", is actually a very special sort of diagonal, meaning only one which conjoins with a right angle. Thus it is used for the hypotenuse of a right triangle and the diagonal of a square or rectangle. Thus Parameśvara's definition holds.)

Āryabhaṭa's definition, on the other hand, is useless for Vasubandhu's purposes, i.e. as an aid for discovering what is occurring physio-psychologically when we speak of "seeing a square". It does not include anything that Vasubandhu could recognize as being fundamentally, i.e. psychologically, existent. It must however be noted that what we see as "square" is actually not always, as Vasubandhu says, a "color-aggregation which appears equal in each of four sides." This may be how we geometrically determine that it is a square or equiquadrilateral rhombus, but if we take into account what the visual consciousness presents to us, whenever we speak of a "square", an equal appearance of each of the four sides is not always involved. At present there is a "square" piece of paper on "my" desk—but what the visual consciousness is actually presenting to "me" is a kind of rhomboid with unequal sides. Vasubandhu may leave himself a way out with his verb "appear", which could include interpretations immediately put on the object of visual consciousness. Thus, while Āryabhaṭa's is a precise mathematician's definition, Vasubandhu's may be almost as good a one for telling us what underlies it psychologically. In fact, it is in dealing with plane figures that Vasubandhu's reduction of shape to color is most convincing.

Āryabhaṭa, though he gives us several methods for determining whether a figure is a circle (II, 7; II, 3) unfortunately gives us no complete definition. Vasubandhu's definition is an impeccable one, which even Āryabhaṭa could have appreciated.

13. The causes and conditions for dyeing an object here enumerated may refer to different types of dyeing, any deliberate changing of an object's color being referred to in this way. Fire, as Sumatiśīla's explanations show*, refers perhaps primarily to the firing of pottery. But the other three examples, like Sumatiśīla's additional example of "chemical dyes"**, seem to refer to the dyeing of garments. Fire also being an auxiliary condition in cloth-dyeing (the boiling of water containing colorific plants and chemical dyestuffs), perhaps all the examples actually refer to the dyeing of garments. Bleaching also being regarded as a dyeing process, the inclusion of "the sun" and "ice" becomes clear to one who is familiar with the ancient bleaching processes employed in Kashmir and Gāndhāra. Freshly-dyed garments were often bleached by long exposure to the sun, and encasing a garment in ice had a similar effect. On some of the dyeing techniques employed in ancient India, see *Jātaka* no. 38; Asaṅga, *Mahāyānasaṅgraha* I, 18, pp 36-37.

**Karmasiddhiṭīkā*, p 206, 3, 4.

**Ibid, p 206, 3, 2.

14. In reply to a similar Sāmmitīya argument in favor of external causes of destruction, Vasubandhu had already previously engaged in a rigorous investigation of combustion (*Kośa* IV, ad 2-3)—an investigation which, like so many of Vasubandhu's regarding natural phenomena, leaves us with the most un-rigid conclusion ("Whatever you may say about it may be right, but isn't necessarily so"). The Sāmmitīya supposes his argument, that in the case of combustion, fire is the external cause for the destruction of the wood, to be self-evident, i.e. "demonstrable through the means-of-cognition of direct perception". Vasubandhu however counters that actually there is nothing like "a direct perception" of the destruction of wood, just as there is no direct perception of motion. When we suppose that wood is being destroyed because of its relation with fire, it is simply because we no longer see the wood intact after such a relation. To go from the direct perception of the disappearance of the wood to the assumption that fire is the external cause of the wood's destruction, involves an inference, and what's more, an inference which is not entirely fool-proof. Actually, Vasubandhu says, the fact that we no longer see the wood after its relation with fire is susceptible to two interpretations : either the wood is destroyed on account of the relationship, as the Sāmmitīyas claim, or the wood is constantly changing within itself, and maintaining a certain continuity because of other factors within itself, which factors are transformed in proximity with fire. Vasubandhu accuses the Sāmmitīya of inconsistency, for the Sāmmitīya does admit that flames are destroyed spontaneously, and yet a gust of wind, conventionally speaking, may "put out a flame". To the Sāmmitīya, this means only that the wind has served as a catalyst for hastening a process which would at any rate have come about. Vasubandhu says that analogously, the flame may only be a similar catalyst in regard to wood. He thinks that this alternative is not only just as possible as the other, but even more likely, since the wood is not destroyed immediately when brought into contact with fire.

Relating the same argumentation to the dyeing example, Vasubandhu would argue that there is a constant series of modifications in the products resulting from contact with fire, rather than the fire itself changing the product. We may symbolize the reactions as follows :

WIND AND FLAME

Interpretation :

$\underline{W}$ & $\underline{F}$/ W, $\dfrac{F}{X}$/ $\qquad$ $\underline{W}$ & $\underline{F}$/ $\underline{W}$ & $\underline{F''}$/ $\underline{F}$/ $\dfrac{F''}{X}$

There are an infinite number of conditions that may give rise to $\dfrac{F}{X}$, and some of them are clearly not dependent on anything external, but rather to changes within the fire itself. Wind is not necessarily the cause for a flame's destruction, as the following may equally well happen :

$\underline{W}$ & $\underline{F}$/ $\underline{W''}$ & $\underline{F}$/ $\underline{W''}$ & $\underline{F}$/ F

and

$\underline{F}$/ $\underline{F''}$/ F″/ F
X

WOOD AND FIRE, DYEING-PROCESS

$\underline{F}$ & $\underline{S}$/ $\underline{F}$, S
X

Interpretation :

$\underline{F}$ & $\underline{S}$/ $\underline{F}$ & $\underline{S''}$/ S″/ S
X

but sometimes :

$\underline{F}$ & $\underline{S}$/ $\underline{F}$ & $\underline{S''}$/ $\underline{S}$, F
X

Key :

F : fire-moment

W : wind-moment

S : solid-moment

— : Power to renew "series"

: loss of power to renew "series"

X : in decrease to annihilation

The idea that any one reaction (or intervention of a substance) should be held an inevitable cause for any given other substance, or its annihilation, seems to be ruled out in Vasubandhu's framework.

15. The cause of *a* cannot at the same time be the cause for the destruction of *a*. This axiom is traceable to the *Vaiśeṣika-sūtras* of Kaṇāda, where it occurs as follows : "A substance is not destroyed either by its effect or by its cause" (*Na dravyaṃ kāryaṃ kāraṇaṃ ca bādhati.*", *VS* I, I, 12). This axiom seems to have been accepted at large among Indian philosophic circles. Kaṇāda himself of course restricted it to substances, which are only one kind of entity within his system. He in fact supplies an answer to Vasubandhu's contention here (8a), that sounds need no external cause of destruction, by assuming that attributes like sound *are* destroyed by their effects, as well as by their causes. The first sound in a series of sounds is destroyed by its effect, i.e. the succeeding sound, but the last is destroyed by its cause, for the last sound but one destroys the last (the axiom "*Ubhayathā guṇāḥ*", *VS* I, I, 13). Vasubandhu presented a refutation of *Vaiśeṣika-sūtra* I, I, 13 at *Kośa* IV, ad 2-3, LVP, p 6, bottom, and is thus able to extend the axiom of *VS* I, I, 12 over the whole range of Vaiśeṣika categories. In the case cited in this treatise, the destruction of a characteristic cannot occur on account of the same causes which are responsible for its intensification.

16. These are examples of what are termed "homogeneous causes" (*sabhāgahetu*) in Vaibhāṣika philosophy. This type of cause was fully accepted by Vasubandhu (*Kośa* II, 52a-c). When a substance gradually gives rise

to another substance, in such a manner that one can speak of a "transformation of the original substance", and no other external substance can be recruited to serve as an external cause for this transformation, Vasubandhu and the *Vibhāṣā* speak of the original substance's being a "homogeneous cause" for the latter substance. The concept of "homogeneous cause" served to fill many gaps in causality which we nowadays explain by chemical decomposition, or the intrusion of microbes. As regards the latter example, Vasubandhu has perhaps the last card, since the growth of an organism itself is termed by him an instance of homogeneous causation. The advantage of employing the concept of homogeneous causality in this instance lies in the fact that the continuity between the event at locus *A* and the new event at locus *B* could be accounted for.

17. The element wind being properly the mobile principle which expands and displaces, its role as the principle of motion is recognized by both Vasubandhu and the Sauryodayika. Vasubandhu, who, as regards motion, carries a Heraclitean stand to a Parmenidean conclusion in this treatise, 10, must of course modify the traditional viewpoint considerably. For him, calling the element wind the mobile principle can mean only that it is responsible for making a new event arise in another locus immediately subsequently to a previous event which is related to the new event by being its homogeneous cause.

Again we see that "mental" phenomena such as *citta*, and "material" elements such as "wind", are genetically related in such a manner as to make a dichotomy untenable. In *Kośa* IX (LVP, p 294, Pradhan, p 477, 1-2), Vasubandhu enumerates the processes taking place to give rise to a "manifest bodily action", as follows : A drive or impulse (*chandas*) is followed by an initial mental application (*vitarka*) towards an effort, which effort produces a wind-series which in turn sets the body "into motion ".

17a. "beneficial": *kuśala*, "unbeneficial": *akuśala*. Sometimes translated as "good" and "bad". These are not very good translations, because the ultimate good of Buddhism is the eradication of suffering. *Kuśala* actions are those which have results and retributions conducive to the eradication of suffering, *akuśala* those which have results and retributions of suffering. Thus, *kuśala* actions are *productive* of good, i.e. the alleviation of suffering. The caused good itself is always retributionally indeterminate. Thus Nirvāṇa itself is so categorized. (cf. *Dhammasaṅgaṇi* 983, 989; C. Rhys-Davids *Buddh. Psych.*, p 139.) The *Karmaprajñapti-śāstra* extends this principle even further, stating that though volitions in meditation where one is not fully concentrated are *kuśala*, volitions where one is completely collected and tranquil, are indeterminate. (*Karmaprajñapti*, Peking/Tokyo vol. 115, p 87, 2, 406: "gzhan yang yongs su zin pa ma yin pas bstam gtan bzhi dang gzugs med pa bzhi bsgom pa'i, sems pa gang yin pa nas sems mngon par du byed pa dang yid kyi las kyi bar du sbyar te 'di ni dge ba'i sems pa zhes bya'o—". p 87, 5, 3-5: "yongs su zin pa'i sems kyis bsam gtan bzhi dang gzugs med pa bzhi—'di ni lung du ma bstan pa'i sems pa zhes bya'o//" "Furthermore, any volition—impelling of citta, and mental action of one who is cultivating the four meditations and the four imageless attainments with *cittas* which are not completely collected, is designated as a beneficial volition. Any volition—impelling of citta, and mental action, of one who is cultivating the four meditations, etc. with *cittas* completely collected, is designated as indeterminate.")

18. Configuration having been refuted as an entity, is manifest action to be accounted for simply by the remaining visible quality, the "moving" color combinations which we see when we say "I see him doing that"? Vasubandhu seems to be playing here, and relishing a series of totally absurd alternatives. A given color can clearly intrinsically be neither beneficial nor unbeneficial, as all meteriality is basically indeterminate (cf. *Kośa* I, ad 29c-d, *Kathāvatthu* VIII, 9).

19. On the gradual shift of this term from being the honored epithet of the Emperor Aśoka, to meaning something like "simple fool", see S. Lévi, *Journal Asiatique* 1891, p 549, and *Bull. Ac. Roy. de Belgique*, 1923, p 35 ff. The usage is common in Vasubandhu (cf. *Kośa* II, ad 26a-c), and also in Śaṅkara (*Brahmasūtrabhāṣya* ad I, 2, 8; ad II 4, 5).

20. The eye proper, i.e. the actual seeing part of the eye, is itself inferred, not seen, since according to the Vaibhāṣika theory accepted by Vasubandhu it consists of an invisible sentient materiality covering what is conventionally called "the eye". It is inferred through its force or efficacy of presenting visibles to our *citta*-series (cf. *Kośa* I, ad 9). On this sentient materiality, see also *Dhammasaṅgaṇi* 616, 628, and *Vibhaṅga* 122.

21. According to the *Vibhāṣā*, the arising of an unmanifest action is not the same in the three "realms"(see *Discussion of the Five Aggregates*, note 12). In the realm of desires, restraint or absence of restraint is always originated by a manifest bodily or verbal action. In the states subsumed under "the realm of images", discipline is subordinated directly to *citta*. This cannot be true in the realm of desires, since unmanifest action develops even when cittas are absent in sleep. Vasubandhu, in denying the real existence of manifest actions, i.e. bodily and verbal actions which themselves carry an ethical and retributional nature, must also deny "unmanifest action" in the realm of desires. As a matter of fact, Vasubandhu had already lambasted the entire Vaibhāṣika concept of "unmanifest action"(*Kośa* IV, ad 3c).

22. A bodily action may have a double ethical charge, which results in its being indeterminate only inasmuch as its beneficiality and unbeneficiality are roughly equal. Because unmanifest action according to the Vaibhāṣikas is always either clearly beneficial or unbeneficial, it could never occur in connection with such a manifest action.

According to Vasubandhu unmanifest action is also ruled out as an explanation of the unbeneficiality of an impure monk's remaining silent during the *Prātimokṣa* confessional, since for the Vaibhāṣika to be consistent, he must here also assume a prior manifest action, which simply does not seem to occur in this case. Saṅghabhadra attempts to defend the Vaibhāṣika position by noting that the very sitting down in an assembly hall for the recital constitutes a previous manifest action (cf. *Kośa* IV, LVP, pp 163-164, n 5). This argumentation is feeble, because, as has been shown, unmanifest action cannot arise from actions which are indeterminate.

Vasubandhu would of course explain the unbeneficiality of the monk's silence simply by the unbeneficiality of his volition to remain silent. If he remains silent without such a motivation, e.g. if he has suddenly been struck dumb, there can be for Vasubandhu no question of a misdeed. Vasubandhu succeeds here in giving a viable explanation for what determines the ethical nature of a "sin of omission", where Saṅghabhadra, in his attempt to buttress the traditional Vaibhāṣika structure, seems to singularly fail.

23. The existence of past and future events is the cardinal doctrine of the old Sarvāstivāda school, from which the Vaibhāṣika is derived. It is criticized already by the *Kathāvatthu* (I, 6-7), and defended against these criticisms by the snarling polemic of Devaśarman, author of the *Vijñānakāya* (*Vijñānakāya*. tr. La Vallée Poussin, *Etudes Asiatiques* 1925, pp 343 ff). The *Vibhāṣā* adopts the theory (*Vibhāṣā* 76, p 393b, tr. La Vallée Poussin, *MCB* V, pp 5 ff), and the genius of the "Great Four Masters" of the *Vibhāṣā* was enlisted to explain it. These philosophers are the Bhadanta Vasumitra, the Bhadanta Dharmatrāta, Ghoṣaka, and Buddhadeva. All their theories are rejected by Vasubandhu (*Kośa* ad V 25-28). The doctrine was again defended against Vasubandhu by orthodox Vaibhāṣikas such as Saṅghabhadra (*Abhidharmanyāyānusāra* 50-52, *MCB* V, pp 75 ff) and the Dīpakāra (*Abhidharmadīpa* V, 289-324, Jaini, pp 245 ff). The whole controversy was finally summarized by Śāntarakṣita, *Tattvasaṅgraha* 1793-1806.

24. The expression "pustule arising on top of a boil" was a common Sanskrit idiom at the time of Vasubandhu. It is found also in Kālidāsa, *Śākuntala* Act II, opening speech of the Vidūṣaka : "*Tato gaṇḍasyōpari piṇḍakaḥ saṃvṛttaḥ.*" The idiom is used to express the idea of additional troubles where troubles enough already abide. In this case, the troubles are the poor Vaibhāṣika's.

25. The process for the retribution of an act can be reduced, Vasubandhu says, either to a special transformation within the series of momentary events making up the aggregates of the "personality", or to a change in the state (*avasthā*) of the act itself. The Bhadanta Vasumitra had reduced the differences among events in the three times to differences in their states, or modes of being (*cf. Vibhāṣā* 76, 11: *Mélanges* 5: 1 ff). That is to say, a present event has a full efficacy range, and is able to give rise to visual, etc. objects-of-consciousness, whereas a past event, though existent, can only be remembered, and a future event only anticipated. As the *Vibhāṣā* itself had a clear preference for Vasumitra's explanation of the doctrine, the Vaibhāṣikas, who took it as their cardinal text, followed suit. The retribution of an act, following Vasumitra, would be explained by assuming that an act, though it loses its full efficacy-range as soon as it is past, continues to exist, and finally undergoes an additional change in its state, which allows it to give its retributional effect.

The Vaibhāṣika vocabulary employed here involves some technicalities: An act "projects" an effect as long as it is present, but it "gives" its retributional effect when it is already past. The connection of the act with the aggregate-series is explained by the Vaibhāṣikas through *prāptis*—see *Discussion of the Five Aggregates*, p. 70 note 16.

Vasubandhu says that the Vaibhāṣika explanation, violates *Aggregates*, note 16. :

Vasubandhu says that the Vaibhāṣika explanation, alternative 2, violates the principle of the momentariness of all events. This principle, is curiously enough, accepted by the Vaibhāṣika as much as it is by the Sautrāntika. Vasubandhu's argument is however not a valid criticism of the Vaibhāṣika, given the Vaibhāṣika's framework. Vasubandhu is quick to recognize this himself, as he has the Vaibhāṣika reply with the proper Vaibhāṣika view of momentariness. Though in its "own-characteristics" an event exists in the past as well as the future (since it can be remembered or anticipated with all its characteristics), it no longer has the power to "project" its full effect, as it cannot be perceived by consciousnesses I-V. And it is this power, marking the event as a present phenomenon, which is momentary. When it ceases, we say that the event ceases, i.e. it has entered upon another state of being.

26. If the act is still around, what is it that keeps it from continuing effects similar to the effects it projected in its moment as a present event ? In what sort of "cold storage" are we to assume the act to be ?

27. The last moment of "one" who has eradicated all the root-afflictions does not project an effect. That is, once "such a person" dies, her or his physio-psychic series is not resumed within another existence : in other words, "she or he goes into Nirvāṇa".

28. See *Discussion of the Five Aggregates*, note 29.

29. "The obtainment and development of an effect's seed" is a metaphorical expression employed by Vasubandhu for the existence of latent impressions within the series which may produce a new effect. The concept of "seeds" developing within a physio-psychic series is used to illustrate the continuity of the series. "*Prāpti*" serves much the same function for orthodox Vaibhāṣika philosophers (see *Discussion of the Five Aggregates*, note 18). But whereas Saṅghabhadra and the Dīpakāra insist that *prāpti* is a real entity apart from the series itself, it is recognized by Vasubandhu that his "seed" is only a metaphor for a force within entities constituting a "series" which allows them to gradually undergo transformations (*Kośa* II, ad 36c-d). More exactly, "a seed for an event" means simply the psychophysical complex itself, when it is capable of producing this effect, either immediately or mediately, through a transformation in "its own" "series".

By this botanical analogy, Vasubandhu is able to maintain an organic, dynamically changing universe.

30. The view that a special event disassociated from citta is responsible for an act's retribution is, as Sumatiśīla tells us*, a speciality of the Sāmmitīyas and Mahāsāṅghikas. The *Kathāvatthu*, which already discusses and criticizes the theory, attributes it to the Sāmmitīyas and the Andhakas (the Mahāsāṅghikas of Andhra). There it is stated that according to the Sāmmitīyas and Andhakas, an event must be posited for the continuation of retributional results even in those cases where the citta-series is interrupted.

**Karmasiddhiṭīkā*, p 212, 5, 1.

Thus the citta-series itself cannot be responsible for retribution. The *Kathāvatthu* counters that when mental processes are interrupted, the karmic process must by rights be broken off as well (*Kathāvatthu* XV, 11).

31. Vasubandhu asks how the theory of "the accumulation" or "the imperishable" can explain memory. The problem of the retribution of acts is only an aspect of the larger problem of the continuity of the psycho-physical series. Thus any theory which explains retributions, but which cannot explain this continuity in broader terms, must be rejected as inadequate. One of the main problems regarding the continuity of the physio-psychical series is the question of memory. As Sumatiśīla tells us*, the theory of "the accumulation" or "the imperishable", cannot serve to account for memory, since an "accumulation", or "the imperishable", arises only, according to the Sāmmitīyas and Mahāsāṅghikas, with acts that are clearly beneficial or unbeneficial. The studying of a text, and the intitial perception of an object-of-sense, which serve as root-causes for future memory regarding the text or object, are however completely indeterminate acts. Thus, an "accumulation" or "the imperishable" cannot arise in those cases. Even if it could, there would still remain the problem as to which moment produces the "accumulation". Is it the moment of the initial perception of the object, the moment in which the memory arises, or yet some other moment? Clearly none of these alternatives can explain the phenomenon.

It is interesting to note that with all our so-called scientific knowledge, the factors of memory are still not really understood, though they have been the subject of psychological research since Hermann Ebbinghaus. The largely metaphorical solutions with which modern psychology has emerged, such as "changes in the synapse taking place with vivid impressions", "increase in the size of synaptic knobs following such impressions", though supportable by electro-stimulatory experimentation, are no more adequate or inadequate than Vasubandhu's admittedly metaphorical solution of an impression-storing consciousness-substratum. (cf. Rosvold's "Memory", *McGraw-Hill Encyclopedia of Science and Technology*, 1960, vol. 8, pp 216-223.)

32. The question of what goes on in the highest meditation, "the attainment of the cessation of feelings and cognitions", is one of the crucial problems in the psychology of the Northern Abhidharma theorists. This will become apparent later in this treatise. Here the problem more specifically is that the theory of "accumulation", or "the imperishable", cannot account for the re-emergence of the citta-series, since obviously no particular beneficial or unbeneficial action directly precedes this emergence.

33. This is an argument by analogy. The idea seems to be that the continuity of redness from flower to fruit does not depend on a special entity, so similarly the transformation from seed to retribution needs no special entity either. This sort of Occam's Razor principle is employed often by Vasubandhu against the Vaibhāṣika categories in the *Kośa*. In addition, some amount of botanical experimentation seems to have been done in an

*Ibid, p 213, 1.

attempt to discover possible principles of continuity. Nonetheless, this argument against "accumulation", or " the imperishable", seems to be the weakest of the three.

34. The "(mentally) constructed" is the lowest of three kinds of reality in Vasubandhu's later philosophy (*Commentary on the Separation of the Middle from Extremes*, ad III 3b, *Teaching of the Three Own-Beings*, 1). It has sometimes been rendered as "the imaginary", but both its etymology and its characterizations by Vasubandhu (*Commentary on the Separation of the Middle from Extremes*, ad III 12a; *Teaching of the Three Own-Beings*, 4-5) do not support such a translation, though the ontological status of "the imaginary" in ordinary language may be close to that of the *parikalpita*. The "*parikalpita*" is literally "the thoroughly constructed", which constricts consciousness into ever narrower grooves, and includes most notions of "common-sense" reality. It is thus the result not so much of the "imagination" condemned by some Western philosophers (e.g. Hobbes, or the Renaissance philosopher Gianfrancesco Pico della Mirandola in his *On the Imagination*), but rather on the very mental consciousness so praised by these gentlemen, i.e. the mental consciousness in its capacity for fabricating abstract constructions of its own, which are subsequently taken far too seriously. Less abstract categorizations, in fact delimiting anything at all with strict separations, fall also within the scope of the constructed (See *Commentary of the Separation of the Middle from Extremes*, ad III 12a). Mental consciousness in its colorful image-building fantasizing aspect is not in itself a danger to Vasubandhu, as it is to Gianfrancesco Pico della Mirandola, otherwise Vasubandhu could hardly have been the great lover of Mahāyāna sūtras he apparently was.

35. The previous example of the dyed lemon flower's resulting in a dyed lemon-core is here being used to illustrate the theory of the transformation of the psycho-physical series without the intervention of an entity external to it. In fact, Vasubandhu uses a vocabulary which completely parallels his example, but which is difficult to carry over adequately into English. He uses the verb 'penetrate' (*paribhāvayati*) in order to express the volition's lasting influence on the psycho-physical series, on the analogy of the liquid lac's penetrating the entire series of the lemon plant. This penetration, or influence, of the volition, results in a special force (he could as well have said "seed"), an alteration in the series which leads eventually to its own transformation. For Vasubandhu, the only real retribution lies within the psycho-physical series itself, and this is borne out by his famous arguments in *The Twenty Verses* demonstrating the irrationality of assuming external hells (*Twenty Verses* ad 3, 4).

The transformation of the series theory perhaps does not really explain anything (how many schemata of modern physics, not to speak of modern psychology, might be accused of the same thing ?), but it does present a plausible way to patch the holes in the Buddhist karma theory acutely felt by the North Indian scholasticists. In the last analysis, Vasubandhu will abandon it anyway, since it is obviously a constructed structure (*Teaching of the Three Own-Beings*, 3-4).

36. A directly antecedent condition (*samanantara-pratyaya*) is any condition which helps give rise to an event which is similar to it, and which follows on it immediately (*Kośa* II, ad 62a-b). The motivating dispositions which arise immediately previous to a consciousness are by necessity its directly antecedent conditions, since they not only help give rise to the consciousness, but its very nature, whereas the eye, for a visual consciousness, is only its substratum, since it does not condition the emotional nature of the consciousness. As regards a mental consciousness, its substrata are always directly antecedent conditions, though again there may be directly antecedent conditions which are not its substrata, namely the immediately preceding motivating dispositions (*Kośa* I, ad 44c-d). The term "directly antecedent condition" is usually reserved for cittas and motivating dispositions only, though the Bhadanta Vasumitra was of the opinion that materiality-moments could also serve as such conditions (*Kośa* II, ad 62a-b, La Vallée Poussin, p 301).

37. A mental consciousness cannot possibly arise where the material organs exist, but where their function does not give rise to a sensory citta. Here is a passage which demonstrates just how misleading the translation "mind" for "*manas*" is. By "*manas*", Vasubandhu means here primarily a sensory consciousness which serves as a directly antecedent condition for a mental consciousness. During the attainment of cessation, such sensory consciousnesses are by necessity absent, since they are always concomitant with feelings.

38. If in states with both citta and materiality there is a seed for a *manas* resting on the material organs, and another resting upon the citta-series, then *manas* in these states results from two separate series of seed-moments. Yet two separate series of seed-moments are never found to exist for plants which have natural seeds. A given plant always results from one seed, not two.

It might be argued that Vasubandhu is here making too much of the metaphor "seed". But the positing of a capacity for producing an identical result in two different kinds of entities, is actually somewhat puzzling. The position might be saved by assuming that the capacity for engendering a citta is relegated to the series of the material organs during the attainment of cessation and is transferred back to the citta-series once the capacity is actualized. This would be a principle of "vicarious functioning", which is accepted in similar contexts by modern physiological psychology (cf. D. C. Debb, *Physiological Psychology*, p 210).

38a. See *Discussion of the Five Aggregates*, p 70. The attainment of the absence of cognitions is characterized already by Vasumitra in his *Prakaraṇapāda* (*Kośa* II, La Vallée Poussin, p 200, note 2) as a meditation special to non-Buddhist schools, and it is in fact mentioned in the *Yogasūtras* of Patañjali.

39. Contrary to what Vasubandhu says, and contrary to Sumatiśīla's best efforts to support his assertion*, it seems that this theory can explain the re-

**Karmasiddhi-ṭīkā*, p 214, 1.

emergence of the citta-series. The position is unacceptable to Vasubandhu as to Saṅghabhadra, mainly because of their squeamishness toward accepting a basically non-sensate cause for a sensate result (for the materiality-series must certainly be non-sensate when there are no co-existent cittas). This is an example of the axiom discussed by Robinson in connection with conceptions of causality in Īśvarakṛṣṇa, Nāgārjuna, and Śaṅkara : "The cause must be like its effects". ("Classical Indian Axiomatic", *Philosophy East and West* XVII, 1967, axiom 6, p 150). But the interrelationship of material and psychic entities has been recognized in Buddhist psychology since the *Dhammasaṅgaṇi* and the *Jñānaprasthāna*, and is in several instances admitted by Vasubandhu himself (see note 17). If a sensate citta with volition can give rise to a non-sensate wind, as Vasubandhu says in *Kośa* IX, it is difficult to see why the process in reverse should be unacceptable to him.

40. In the Chinese translation of Hsüan-tsang, this citta supposed by the Bhadanta Vasumitra to exist within the attainment of cessation is qualified as a "subtle citta". The theory of a subtle citta existing within this attainment is alluded to also by Asaṅga (*Mahāyānasaṅgraha* I, 53). Vasubandhu gives the same passage from the Bhadanta Vasumitra's *Paripṛcchā* at *Kośa* II, ad 44d.

The *Paripṛcchā* itself is unfortunately lost. As the Great Master Vasumitra of the *Vibhāṣā* is most often referred to as "the Bhadanta Vasumitra" (cf. Saṅghabhadra, *Nyāyānusāra*, *MCB* V, p 91; *Vibhāṣā*, Ibid, pp 166-167), it is most likely that he is identical with the author of the *Paripṛcchā*. La Vallée Poussin (*Kośa* Introduction, pp XLIV-XLV) and Lamotte ("Traité de l'Acte", n. 11) assume otherwise, but their reasoning does not seem to be based on certain grounds. On the other hand, Lin Li Kuang's thesis that there is only one ancient master Vasumitra, and that he was responsible for the theory of "*mahābhūmikas*", motivating dispositions accompanying every citta, seems insupportable by the internal evidence of the texts involved. (*L'Aide-Mémoire de la Vraie Loi*, pp 48-49).

The following texts are attributed to a Vasumitra : the *Prakaraṇapāda* (Taisho 1541, 1542), the *Dhātukāya* (Taisho 1540), both among the six basic texts of Sarvāstivāda Abhidharma; the *Saṅgītiśāstra* (Taisho 1549), the *Pañcavastuka* (Taisho 1556 and 1557), the lost *Paripṛcchā*, and the *Samayabhedoparacanacakra* (Taisho 2031, 2032; Peking-Otani 5639, tr. A. Bareau, *Journal Asiatique* 1954, pp 229 ff). There is in addition a commentary on Vasubandhu's *Kośa* of an obviously later date. Now it is true that the *Prakaraṇapāda* and the *Dhātukāya* contain the earliest-known mention of the "mahābhūmikas", and the *Saṅgītiśāstra* is apparently also in consonance with the theory (cf. La Vallée Poussin, *Kośa* Introduction, p XLIV). But the motivating disposition list of the *Pañcavastuka* is conspicuous by its absence of any arrangement which would fit the mahābhūmika-pattern. In the first set of motivating dispositions given in the *Pañcavastuka*, there are listed many of the moment-events which are considered mahābhūmikas by the *Prakaraṇapāda*. Yet within this same set there is "carelessness" (*pramāda*) and "absence of carelessness" (*apramāda*), which are difficult to imagine as being concomitant in *any* citta, not to speak of *every* citta (Taisho 1556, vol. 28, p 995, 3, 10-11). The term "mahābhūmika,' itself nowhere occurs in the *Pañcavastuka*. It occurs only in the *Pañcavastuka-vibhāṣā*, a commentary on the text by Dharmatrāta (Taisho 1555, vol. 28, p 994, 2, 3-4), who seems to be inspired in his ordering of the motivating dispositions primarily by Ghoṣaka (cf. *Abhidharmāmṛta*, p 66, 12). The whole question of whether there are motivating dispositions separable from cittas, and the problem of whether there are mahābhūmikas, were two issues on which there was much individual disagreement, as might be expected from the very nature of such an emotional topic ! It is highly unlikely that the probable originator of the mahābhūmika-theory in the *Prakaraṇapāda* would have so completely ignored the entire concept while discussing the motivating dispositions in the *Pañcavastuka*. The theory of one Vasumitra is also contradicted by the fact that the *Saṅgītiśāstra*, though discussing the existence of past and future events, explains it in a manner quite different from the Bhadanta Vasumitra's famous theory of "states" discussed in the *Vibhāṣā* (*Saṅgītiśāstra*, chapt. 13, cf. La Vallée Poussin, *Kośa* Introduction, p XLIV), and that one Vasumitra quoted in the *Vibhāṣā* (152, 1, Ibid) (not necessarily the Bhadanta Vasumitra as assumed by La Vallée Poussin), clearly denies the existence of cittas in the attainment of cessation, which roundly contradicts the *Paripṛcchā*. Tradition is also uniform in distinguishing three Vasumitras: the author of the *Prakaraṇapāda* and *Dhātukāya*, the Bhadanta Vasumitra of the *Vibhāṣā*, and the author of the *Samayabhedoparacanacakra*, who is identical with the *Kośa* commentator, and said to be a contemporary of Candrakīrti (sixth century, Tāranātha I, p 68, p 174). Yaśomitra also gives some valuable information. He says that the Bhadanta Vasumitra wrote not only the *Paripṛcchā*, but also the *Pañcavastuka* and other treatises. (Yaśomitra, *Vyākhyā*, ad II 44). This seems plausible, as the *Pañcavastuka's* ordering of the motivating dispositions and the *Paripṛcchā's* theory of a subtle citta both have at least this in common: they are inimical to the mahābhūmika-theory of the *Prakaraṇapāda*, *Dhātukāya*, and *Saṅgītiśāstra*.

The quasi-canonical character of the *Prakaraṇapāda* and the *Dhātukāya* for the *Vibhāṣā* indicates that these are in all probability works of an earlier era. The statements of the Bhadanta Vasumitra, on the other hand, though usually highly respected by the *Vibhāṣā*, have hardly this kind of status there. Following the internal evidence and the traditional accounts, we thus arrive at three Vasumitras: (1) the old Vasumitra, author of the *Prakaraṇapāda*, of the *Dhātukāya*, and, in all probability, of the *Saṅgītiśāstra*, the probable originator of the mahābhūmika-theory; (2) the Bhadanta Vasumitra, author of the *Paripṛcchā* and the *Pañcavastuka*, opposed to the mahābhūmika-theory, upholder of a subtle citta, forger of the most accepted theory regarding past and future events, cautioner of dogmatists, one of the "Great Masters" of the *Vibhāṣā*, and, from all we can tell, a truly great philosopher; (3) the later Vasumitra, author of a commentary on the *Kośa* and the *Samayabhedoparacanacakra*.

According to traditional accounts, the four great masters Ghoṣaka, Buddhadeva, the Bhadanta Vasumitra, and the Bhadanta Dharmatrāta were contemporaries, and all had a hand in the rough draft of that tremendous team-work compilation, the *Vibhāṣā*, at the council of the Emperor Kaniṣka. In spite of their philosophical differences (which become quite apparent in this treatise), Ghoṣaka and the Bhadanta Vasumitra apparently remained on good terms, and after the death of Kaniṣka, went together to live in the country of Aśmāparāntaka, at the invitation of the king of that country (*Kośa*, La Vallée Poussin, introduction, p XLIV; *Abhidharmāmṛta* introduction, p 1).

By the way, the Dharmatrāta who commented on the *Pañcavastuka* was apparently an uncle of the Bhadanta Vasumitra's. He was a strict Sarvāstivādin attempting a harmonization between the theories of Ghoṣaka and his nephew, and was also responsible for the *Saṃyuktābhidharmasāra* (Taisho 1552), an elaboration of the work of Dharmaśrī. He is to be distinguished from that great maverick, the Bhadanta Dharmatrāta, whom in fact he criticizes by name in the *Saṃyuktābhidharmasāra*. (On this point, and on the philosophies of the two Dharmatrātas, Lin Li Kuang is quite convincing, cf. *L'Aide-Mémoire*, pp 315-342.)

41. This is identical to the rebuttal to the Bhadanta Vasumitra's thesis given in *Kośa* II, ad 44d, which is there attributed to the great Ghoṣaka. The necessary connection of a mental consciousness with contact, feelings, and cognitions is of course an irreversible axiom to this upholder of the mahābhūmikas. At *Abhidharmāmṛta* p 66, 12, Ghoṣaka says: "Feeling, cognition, contact, volition, mental attention, zest, mental application, memory, concentration, and discernment are the ten mahābhūmikas. And for what reason is this ? Because they arise together with every citta." ("Vedanā sañjñā sparśaś cetanā manaskāraḥ chandaḥ adhimuktiḥ smṛtiḥ samādhiḥ prajñā ity ete daśa mahābhūmikā dharmāḥ. Tat kasya hetoḥ ? Sarvacitta-sahôtpādāt."). For Ghoṣaka, the attainment of cessation cannot be reduced to a citta of any kind, since the cessation is that of cognitions and feelings.

42. This argument is again attributed to the Bhadanta Vasumitra in the *Kośa* (II, ad 44 d).

43. Western translators of Buddhist texts have not usually given much attention to the various characterizations of mental and physical states traditional in abhidharma. This is unfortunate, for the whole basis of Buddhist ethical theory has been misunderstood thereby, and as a result there have been many erroneous conceptions of Buddhism: that it is anti-sensual, that it is necessarily anti-passion, that it basically considers all mundane existence evil, and so forth. Actually, a careful examination of the employment of terms used in Abhidharma ethical theory, as well as attention to their true etymological meaning, will destroy many of these misconceptions, which have arisen in part due to the incredibly arbitrary translations which have become "standard" among certain translators. As an example, "*kleśa*" has never meant, either in Sanskrit or for any people in direct contact with Indian masters, "defilemement", as it is usually translated. The Sanskrit root "*kliś*" means "to be afflicted, to be tormented, to suffer", and a *kleśa*

is accordingly "an affliction, pain, anguish, suffering". In Tibetan, the term "*kleśa*" has been rendered by "*nyon mongs pa*", which means "misery, trouble, distress" as well as "to be afflicted", as in the expression "*tsha bas nyon mongs te*/" "to be molested by the heat" (Sarat Candra Das, p 489). In Chinese, it is rendered by both Paramārtha and Hsüan-tsang by two characters which mean "to be troubled, vexed, grieved, irritated, distressed" (Matthews, characters no. 1789 and 4635), which together regularly mean "vexed", "vexation". Why therefore introduce into English a basically meaningless word such as "defilement," which in conjuring up all sorts of angry God, original sin, and "man is defiled" complexes, is not only etymologically indefensible, but also, for the twentieth century, rotten "means" (see Introduction to the *Commentary on the Separation of the Middle from Extremes*, p 194) ? There is a good word in English which is in consonance with basic life needs as well as, which goes without saying, the Four Noble Truths. Here "*kleśa*" is translated as "affliction", and the adjective "*kliṣṭa*" as "afflicted".

We have seen Vasubandhu's list of afflictions in the *Discussion of the Five Aggregates*, p 92, p 94. But there is considerable variation in what mental states are included within the afflictions among Abhidharma writers, and Vasubandhu himself changes "his" "mind" on what motivating dispositions to include there. At *Kośa* II, ad 26-28, Vasubandhu had accepted the *Vibhāṣā's* list of *kleśa-mahābhūmikas*, those which make all other afflictions possible. These are confusion, carelessness, sloth, lack of faith, slackness, and excitedness. In *The Commentary on the Separation of the Middle from Extremes*, Vasubandhu lists complacency, aversion, pride, ignorance, views, adherence to mere rules and rituals, doubt, envy, and selfishness as "obstructions which are afflictions" (ad II 2-3 a). Later he reduces the afflictions again to the six he had accepted in *A Discussion of the Five Aggregates* (Thirty Verses, 11). To show the extreme examples of the disagreement in Abhidharma concerning the afflictions, Dharmatrāta the Sarvāstivādin in his *Saṃyuktābhidharmasāra* has fifteen fundamental afflictions (Lin Li Kuang, p 49), whereas the Bhadanta Dharmatrāta says that all afflictions are nothing but unbeneficial volitions, and that there are in fact no "events associated with citta" apart from feelings, cognitions, and volitions (Lin Li Kuang, p 47).

To clarify some often confused concepts : Afflicted states are "bad", being suffering, but are not necessarily unbeneficial (i.e. "bad" in the sense of ethically reprehensible). There is an entire category of factors which are categorized as afflicted, but which are ethically beneficial (the *kuśalasāsravas*), and another which is similarly afflicted, but ethically indeterminate (the *nivṛtāvyākṛtas*, "obstructed but indeterminate events"). For instance, attachment may sometimes be beneficial, and doubts, remorse, and aversion, though afflicted, may have good results. Similarly, any afflicted state which has come about as a result of retribution is by necessity indeterminate ("obstructed but indeterminate"), since anything which is retribution itself carries no further retribution. (A very just credo which leaves everybody an opening for escape from suffering.) The term "afflicted" is somewhat broader than that of "affliction", since an affliction is that basic kind of mental suffering which involves adjunct sufferings. Thus, the "obstructed but indeterminate" events are afflicted, but not afflictions. An affliction itself must always arise from a volition, an impulse, and a discrimination(*Kośa* IX, LVP, p 294; Pradhan, p 477, 1-2). Furthermore, the terms "obstructed" and "afflicted", synonymous in older Abhidharma (though in Mahāyāna there are obstructions which are not afflictions, see *Commentary on the Separation of the Middle from Extremes*, ad II 1), are often equated to "connected with distress" (*sāsrava*). However, as Yaśomitra says, the last term is actually used in a much broader sense, to mean any state where basic afflictions *may* attach themselves. (*Vyākhyā* ad I, 4b). Further principles : Whatever arises from a mental construction is never indeterminate, and whatever arises from an impulse is never retribution. Combining the "ethically good and bad" (beneficial-unbeneficial) with the "instrinsically good and bad" (afflicted-unafflicted), we arrive at the following divisions :

afflicted	[entailing retribution]	1.	unbeneficial (*akuśala*) *U*
		2.	beneficial but connected with afflictions or liable to be so connected (*kuśalasāsrava*) *B*
	[free from retribution]	3.	obstructed but indeterminate (*nivṛtāvyākṛta*) *I*
unafflicted	[entailing retribution]	4.	first states free from affliction (*prathamānāsrava*) *B*
	[free from retribution]	5.	unobstructed but indeterminate (*anivṛtāvyākṛta*) *I*
		6.	last states free from afflictions *I* (*antānāsrava* or simply *anāsrava*)

B : beneficial; *U* : unbeneficial; *I* : indeterminate

The *Kośa's* (II, ad 7-19; II ad 30 a-b; II, ad 60-61; IV, ad 8; IV, ad 127) categorization of the twenty-two faculties into these groups will show the subtlety of the entire ethical structure :

1. Faculty of the Eye I S *r I*
2. Faculty of the Ear I S *r I*
3. Faculty of the Nose I S *r I*
4. Faculty of the Tongue I S *r I*
5. Faculty of the Tactile Body I S *r I*
6. Faculty of the Consciousnesses I E r @ (
7. Faculty of Masculinity I S *r I*
8. Faculty of Femininity I S *r I*
9. Faculty of Life-Force S R *r I*
10. Faculty of Pleasure (*R I*
11. Faculty of Suffering S (–R U
12. Faculty of Cheerfulness (*R* @
13. Faculty of Depression S ((or X)
14. Faculty of Equanimity E *R* @

15-16. Faculties of Faith and Vigor E X *B*

17-19. Faculties of Mindfulness,

Concentration, and Insight E, X *B*
20-22. Highest Faculties A X *B*

KEY:

I internal
S *sāsrava* (potentially linked to afflictions)
A *anāsrava* (never linked to afflictions)
r both in suffering and non-suffering states, retribution for acts
r retribution for beneficial act in non-suffering state, for unbeneficial in a suffering state
R always retribution
R always retribution for a beneficial act when retribution
–R always retribution for an unbeneficial act when retribution
U can be beneficial, unbeneficial, i or indeterminate
I always indeterminate
B always beneficial
@ can belong to any ethical category
(not retribution when beneficial, unbeneficial or unobstructed / indeterminate other than retribution.
E may be either linked to afflictions, or not
X never retribution

44. The three roots of the beneficial are, as we have seen in *A Discussion of the Five Aggregates* p 66, lack of greed, lack of hositility, and lack of confusion. (cf. also *Kośa* II, ad 25-26 c.) They are those motivating dispositions which make all other beneficial ones possible. By necessity, they involve contact with an object-of-consciousness, and consequently involve feelings and cognitions, as motivating dispositions depend on conscious volitions to be beneficial. In other words, "lack of greed" occurring in the attainment of cessation is not lack of greed as a root of the beneficial, because no choice can arise there, due to the absence of contact with a specific object-of-consciousness. In the absence of such choice, and in the absence of consciously-conceived roots of the beneficial, there can be no beneficial citta.

This same argument is employed by Vasubandhu in his *Mahāyānasaṅgrahabhāṣya* (ad I, 54, Peking/Tokyo Tibetan Tripiṭaka vol. 112, p 282, 2-4). It is an independent argument there, not found in any developed form in Asaṅga's *Mahāyānasaṅgraha* itself. The fact that most of these independent arguments in the first chapter of this commentary show such close affinities to this treatise seems to rule against Frauwallner's "last-ditch" effort to save his fabrication of "the two great Vasubandhus" (i.e. that the *Kośa*, the *Demonstration of Action*, and the *Thirty Verses* are indeed by one Vasubandhu, but that only the Mahāyāna commentaries are by Asaṅga's brother).

44a. Final cessation is actually indeterminate (since nothing results from it) and is beneficial only in the sense of a beneficial goal. (See note 17a.)

45. Analogous Pāli suttas : *Aṅguttara* II, 40; III, 388; IV, 167. I have not been able to find a sutta where the topic is subsumed under ten questions, as it apparently is in this *Daśaparipṛcchāsūtra* : "The Sūtra of the Ten Questions". The necessary dependence of cognitions, feelings, and motivating dispositions on contact with an object-of-consciousness is an axiom

accepted in all Abhidharma, as it is in fact one of the links of "dependent origination". (See *Commentary on the Separation of the Middle from Extremes*, ad I 10 and 11, and note 7 to that text.)

46. Afflictions presuppose the existence of feelings, cognitions, and certain other motivating dispositions, as they always arise from an impulse and a discrimination (*Kośa* IX, Pradhan, p 477, 1-2). Thus there can be no afflictions without contact with an object-of-consciousness.

47. Even the attainment of the absence of cognitions praised by Patañjali is beneficial, so one would think that the attainment of cessation practised by Buddhists is even more so.

48. Only these four types of citta are traditionally regarded as unobstructed-but-indeterminate by the *Vibhāṣā*-inspired philosophies. Anything born of retribution, as well as retribution itself, is by necessity indeterminate (cf. note 43), and cittas connected with artistic or professional activity, and with postures of the body such as sitting, lying, and standing, are of course also indeterminate and unafflicted. The last category is somewhat more problematical. It seems to refer to any citta which produces pure fantasies, which beholds a magical creation, or which deals with after-images in meditation. An artist's preconception of his creation, on the other hand, seems to belong to the category of "cittas related to artistic or professional activity" (cf. *Kośa* II, ad 71b-72).

Vasubandhu gives his argumentation a somewhat different twist in the *Mahāyānasaṅgrahabhāṣya*. He dismisses beneficial and unbeneficial cittas, and cittas related to postures, professional activity, and mental creations, in the same manner as here. But he leaves a possibility open for the "born of retribution" category. He says that it would be possible to call the attainment of cessation indeterminate *qua* "born of retribution", but that only the store-consciousness, of all consciousnesses, can be indeterminate in this sense (*Mahāyānasaṅgrahabhāṣya* ad I, 54, Peking/Tokyo Tibetan Tripiṭaka vol. 112, p 282, 4, 5). The arguments raised in this treatise against a retributional mental consciousness existing directly subsequent to the attainment of cessation would of course still hold.

49. The attainment of cessation is reached only after one has passed through the four basic meditations and the four other imageless attainments (See *Discussion of the Five Aggregates*, p 56, p 70). One of the objects of meditation being to sever afflicted cittas which are retributional, it is held that all mental retributional consciousness will be severed by the practise of these meditations.

50. The citta which occurs immediately after the attainment of cessation has been completed, must, be completely without agitation. "Utter non-agitation" is a mark of the fourth meditational state (cf. *Kośa* III, LVP, px 216; *Kośa* IV, ad 46; *Kośa* VIII, ad 26).

51. The nine attainments of successive stages are the four basic meditations and the five imageless meditational attainments. The eight deliverances are preparative stages to the imageless attainments, plus these attainments themselves. The preparatives are listed as :

"oneself containing visible forms, one sees visibles" (*rūpī rūpāṇi paśyati*)
"not being aware of inner visible forms, one focuses on outward visibles" (*adhyātman arūpa-saṃjñī bahirddhā rūpāṇi paśyati*)
"one becomes intent on what is lovely" (*śubham ity eva adhimukto bhavati*)

52. The *Karmaprajñapti's* solution is to make these completely concentrated meditational cittas indeterminate (cf. note 17 a). This is indeed another way out, which Vasubandhu, in spite of his apparent sympathies with the treatise, rejects here.

52a. In spite of his own great contributions to Indian logic, which are apparent in *A Method for Argumentation*, people who rely on dialectics only are not for Vasubandhu in a very exalted category. In his chapter on "realities" in the *Commentary on the Separation of the Middle from Extremes*, he recognizes arguments based on logical principles as belonging to a special kind of reality which has validity while playing a certain kind of dialecticians' game (ad III, 12). But here, as well as later in the *Twenty Verses*, actual insight into ultimate realities cannot be provided by any amount of reasoning alone. As a writer of treatises, Vasubandhu wishes his arguments to be based on logical principles, but he recognizes logic as more than inadequate when dealing with ultimate insights. He labels himself as a dialectician in *Twenty Verses*, ad 22a, and there clearly states that ultimate reality is not within the range of dialectics. Here in the *Discussion for the Demonstration of Action*, Vasubandhu uses the term "dialectician" almost as a jeer. This is reminiscent of the *Laṅkāvatāra-sūtra*, where dialecticians are constantly being lambasted. A bit of the same spirit can be found also in Asaṅga (*Mahāyānasaṅgraha* X, 3 end).

53. Some, like the Bhadanta Vasumitra, say the attainment of cessation is endowed with citta; others, like Ghoṣaka, say it is not. Yet they both apparently refer to the same state. Some way must be found to account for the discrepancy (cf. *Abhidharmadīpa* II, 126, p 149).

54. Impression: impregnation: augmentation of the seeds: the initial point of the transformation of the series, particularly that induced by past volitions and other experiences. Yaśomitra calls "impression" a synonym for "seed" (cf. Jaini, *Dīpa*, p 109), but, following Asaṅga, we may regard it as the process of everything in past experience entering the consciousness-stream to help in its transformation (Asaṅga, *Mahāyānasaṅgraha* I, 18).

55. This verse is ascribed to Aśvaghoṣa by Sumatiśīla, *Karmasiddhiṭīkā*, p 217, 2. So perhaps there is something to the Chinese tradition that Aśvaghoṣa was a proto-Yogācārin, and responsible for treatises like *The Awakening of the Mahāyāna Faith* !

56. The Sanskrit for this verse is given by Sthiramati in his *Triṃśikābhāṣya*, p. 34 :

"Ādāna-vijñāna gambhīra-sūkṣmo
ogho yathā vartati sarva-bījo/

bālāna eṣo mayi na prakāśī
mā haiva ātmā parikalpayeyuḥ //"

Vasubandhu's citation of the *Sandhinirmocana-sūtra* is of great interest for several reasons. For one thing, it clearly contradicts Lamotte's thesis that the *Discussion for the Demonstration of Action* was written at a time prior to Vasubandhu's conversion to Mahāyāna (as do also the closing verses of the treatise, with their beautiful Mahāyāna transferral of merit sentiments). It leaves little doubt that Vasubandhu has been holding back on Mahāyāna vocabulary with the intention of leading his old Vaibhāṣika opponents on as far as possible with arguments they more or less have to accept, in order to finally bombard them with the conclusion that only the Yogācāra conception of consciousness can completely fill the holes in the karma theory. We may regard this entire treatise as a preliminary to the more profound Yogācāra insights, which is directed at the Vaibhāṣikas and Sautrāntikas who could by this means be forced to a recognition of the innate worth of Yogācāra, and thus be lured to further writings of the school. In Asaṅga's *Mahāyānasaṅgraha*, the consciousness-theory is preliminary to the teaching of the three natures and their realization, the true heart of his and Vasubandhu's Yogācāra. (*Mahāyānasaṅgraha* I, II, and III, especially III, 9). In Vasubandhu's works, we find the same movement in the *Twenty Verses*, *Thirty Verses*, and the *Teaching of the Three Own-Beings* included here.

The *Sandhinirmocana* is of course not a sūtra which is accepted by the Vaibhāṣikas. But if the Vaibhāṣika can cry, "This is not authoritative scripture." Vasubandhu can counter that neither should the *Vibhāṣā* and its beloved Abhidharma "padas" be regarded as such, since they are clearly not thewords of the Buddha. Orthodox Vaibhāṣikas, such as the Dīpakāra, retort that the Abhidharma serves only to *interpret* the sūtras, and furthermore, that these Abhidharma interpretations must be taken as "higher" than any sūtras which comtradict them, since sūtras can be conventional (*aupacārika*), i.e. conditioned by the exigencies of expedient methods (*Dīpa* II, ad 138-139, pp 98-104; IV, ad 185, p 146; VIII, ad 548, p 410). The thesis that Abhidharma interpretations must be taken above sūtras in contradiction with them is "old hat" in Buddhist schools that evolved Abhidharma : already in the *Vibhaṅga*, there are interpretations conformable to the sūtras (*suttabhājanīya*) and interpretations conformable to the Abhidharma(*abhidhammabhājanīya*), and the latter always take precedence in case of any conflict between the two. A whole body of Buddhist teachers however objected : these are the "Sautrāntikas", "those who look to the sūtras as the final end of the Buddha's teaching." Vasubandhu of course belongs to this tradition at the inception of his writing career. Though his slashing at Vaibhāṣika categories is perhaps the most thoroughgoing one, he had predecessors in this field—certainly the Bhadanta Dharmatrāta, and presumably the "mūlācarya" of the Sautrāntikas, Kumāralāta.

The question of what is to be considered canonical was raised almost at the inception of Buddhism. Because of the absence of a sacerdotal hierarchy and an initial lack of codified collections of texts, and due to the fact that many of the farflung Buddhist communities became quite isolated from one another, divergences in doctrine naturally arose. The Buddha himself had already given means by which to test the authenticity of scripture. If a man came with something he claimed the Buddha had said, the community was to compare it to what stood in the sūtras and the *Vinaya* they had received, and if it did not conform to them, it was not to be accepted (*Dīgha* II, 124). In this analysis, it was the spirit rather than the letter which counted most. Thus the *Nettipakaraṇa* says of this passage: "With which sūtra should one confront these texts or untterances ? With the Four Noble Truths. With which *Vinaya* should one compare them ? With any *Vinaya* which leads one away from greed, hostility, and confusion. With which Dharma should one test them ? With dependent origination."("Katamasmiṁ sutte otāretabbāni ? Catūsu ariyasattesu. Katamasmiṁ vinaye samdassayitabbāni ? Rāgavinaye dosavinaye mohavinaye. Katamiyaṁ dhammatāyām upanikhipitabbāni ? Paṭiccasamuppāde." p 221.) Thus there came to be admitted into several ancient Canons sūtras which were recognized as being post-Buddha (e.g. *Majjhima* II, 83 ff; *Majjhima* II, 57; *Majjhima* III, 7, and *Aṅguttara* III, 57 ff, composed under King Muṇḍa). Collections of scriptures were accepted as sūtras in certain schools which never had this status in others (such as the *Dhammapada* and the *Jātakas*, challenged as late as the fifth century by teachers such as Sudinna Thera, cf. Buddhaghoṣa's *Sumaṅgalavilāsinī* II, p 566, and *Manorathapūraṇī* III, p 159).

The case for the Vaibhāṣikas is somewhat weakened by the fact that the *Vibhāṣā* itself admits that there are many valid sūtras which are not included in its Canon, "because they have been lost" (*Vibhāṣā* 16, p 79 b, quoted Lamotte, "La critique d'authenticité dans le Bouddhisme", *India Antiqua*, p 218). It also says that many "false sūtras", "false *Vinayas*" and "false Abhidharmas" have been incorporated into many Canon collections (185, p 925c. Ibid). The problem is further compounded by the *Vibhāṣā's* recognition that certain sūtras are to be taken literally (*nītārtha*), whereas others must be further interpreted (*neyārtha*) (cf. Lamotte, "La critique d'interpretation dans le Bouddhisme", *Annuaire de l'Institut de philologie et d'histoire orientales et slaves*, IX, 1949, p 349 ff). According to traditional accounts, the Second Buddhist Council, at Vaiśālī, had already upheld such a distinction in 383 B.C. (Ibid, p 351).

From the Mahāyāna side, reasons for accepting the Mahāyāna sūtras were given by several authors. A cardinal text supporting giving their revelations, or if you will their forgeries, the status of authoritative scripture was the *Adhyāśrayasaṃcodana-sūtra*, which said that everything which is well-spoken can be said to be the word of the Buddha (cf. Snellgrove, *BSOAS* XXI, 1958, pp 620-623, on this sūtra's re-interpretation of the famous saying of Aśoka : "E keci bhaṃte bhagavatā Buddhena bhāsite save se subhāsite vā.") A defense of the Mahāyāna sūtras is given by Śāntideva (*Śikṣāsamuccaya*, B, p 15, V, p 12) and Prajñākaramati (*Bodhicaryāvatārapañjikā* IX, 43-44, V, p 205) on the perhaps not unassailable grounds that their inspiration and root-purpose is the same as those of other sūtras. Prajñākaramati further says that in the face of so many dissensions even among the "Hīnayānists", it is difficult to see how any one transmission of sūtras can be regarded as Āgama. Haribhadra in his *Abhisamayālaṅkārāloka* goes one further, saying that anyone who attempts to do so must be regarded as a fool. (Tucci ed, pp 260-261; Wogihara ed, pp 400-401; Vaidya ed., p 402).

57. The residues (*anuśaya*) are traces left by past afflictions, and thus also "proclivities" towards further unbeneficial action. The Vaibhāṣika, with his theory of the existence of the past and future, regards "*anuśaya*" and "*Kleśa*" as synonymous, a view Vasubandhu had combatted already at *Kośa* V, ad 1 ff. (See also Jaini, "The Sautrāntika Theory of Bīja", and *Dīpa* introduction, pp 103-107, and *Kathāvatthu* XIV, 5.)

58. Any saint not liable to return to Saṃsāra, who may however, in contrast to the Arhat, be re-born into god-realms.

59. The Tāmraparṇīyas are the Theravādins of Ceylon. They are only sporadically mentioned in Vaibhāṣika and Mahāyāna works. "The island Tāmraparṇī" is a name for Ceylon at least since the days of King Ikṣvāku Vīrapuruṣadatta, whose Nāgārjunikoṇḍa inscription mentions it by that name (c. 200 A.D.). "The Tāmraparṇa" is however properly the Tinnevelly region of the Pāṇḍya Kingdom, which is incidentally also mentioned in the same inscription. However, at this time, Theravāda seems to have been one of the dominant sects of this area as well, as both Buddhaghoṣa and Buddhadatta claim it as their home (see Law, *Buddhaghosa*).

60. The *bhavāgravijñāna*, "consciousness which is the requisite of existence", is indeed a particularly Theravāda conception, which goes back to the *Paṭṭhāna* (1, 1, 3, B I, p 138; 6, 7, 81, 4, B, II, p 54; 7, 7, 23, B II, p. 121). It is a substratum underlying the six consciousnesses, which, though it is also a series of moment-events, does not undergo much change. It is not entirely subconscious, as it consists of cittas which may at times penetrate to the sixth consciousness. However, it may exist entirely without initial mental application and subsequent discursive thought, and exists in the highest meditational attainments, as well as in dreamless sleep. It may be said to be nothing but the six consciousnesses in an unactive state.

This substratum is accepted by Buddhaghoṣa, who assumes for it a material base (the "*hadayavatthu*", *Visuddhimagga* XIV, 458). Such a material base may itself be deduced from certain passages in the *Paṭṭhāna*, though it does not mention the term "*hadayavatthu*" itself. Yaśomitra (*Vyākhyā* ad I, 17) alludes to the full-blown theory of a substratum with a material basis, and also identifies it as a Tāmraparṇīya doctrine.

61. A similar argument, that it was the subtlety of the store-consciousness which prohibited the Buddha from teaching it to his early disciples, is found also in Asaṅga, *Mahāyānasaṅgraha* I, 10. As Sumatiśīla interprets it, the import of Vasubandhu's argument is however somewhat different. It is rather that the grouping together of events with such dissimilar characteristics would only serve to confuse the student of Buddhism. It was better

to leave the store-consciousness out of the scheme for beginners (*Karmasiddhiṭikā*, p 219, 1).

62. This is a typically Mahāyāna argument, which must however have some force for the followers of the *Vibhāṣā*, which also admits that many sūtras have been lost. Vasubandhu is here conceding that the Vaibhāṣikas need not recognize the *Sandhinirmocana* as an authentic sūtra. His intellectual honesty here stands in some contrast to the approach of Asaṅga, who attempts to make the Vaibhāṣikas admit the existence of the store-consciousness by claiming that it is mentioned in the Sarvāstivāda Canon. This he does by wringing a meaning out of an *Ekottarāgama* passage in a most arbitrary way (*Mahāyānasaṅgraha* I, 13). This procedure seems to have somewhat embarrassed Sthiramati, for though he mentions this argument of Asaṅga's, he doesn't go into any details, and refuses to identify the sūtra (*Triṃśikavijñaptibhāṣya*, p 13, bottom).

The *Vyākhyāyukti* is a work of Vasubandhu's dealing with the history of the formation of the Buddhist Canon.

63. The store-consciousness conditions the evolving consciousnesses I-VI by coloring all their perceptions through its seeds; the evolving consciousnesses in turn alter the store-consciousness through the process of "impression". Asaṅga says that this mutual conditioning is not only reciprocal, but simultaneous, just as in the case of the arising of a flame and the combustion of a wick (*Mahāyānasaṅgraha*, I, 17).

64. I do not understand how this statement of Vasubandhu's is very apposite, unless an identity "root" and "seed" is urged on the grounds that the incipient roots are the locus of the developing seeds. The Vaibhāṣika argument, which is Saṅghabhadra's, rests on the charge that "seed" is not a very good metaphor, since the original seed no longer exists when the fruit has developed. A seed, or even a seed-series, is not adequate to explain the sudden retribution occurring for beneficial and unbeneficial actions. The cittas which are present at the time of the moment of retribution may themselves be beneficial, where the retribution is one for an unbeneficial act. Thus the constant relation that exists in natural seeds, that such and such a seed results in such and such a fruit, does not seem to be in evidence either (*Abhidharmanyāyānusāra*, chapt. 51, tr. LVP, *MCB* 4-5).

65. The theory of self criticized here is probably that of the Vaiśeṣikas, against which Vasubandhu had already directed his supplement to the *Kośa* (*Kośa* IX). It is nonetheless interesting to compare his critique here with Śaṅkara's argumentation in favor of an unchanging self, which is directed against the Yogācārins (*Brahmasūtrabhāṣya* II, II 31). Śaṅkara says that the Yogācārins' store-consciousness cannot serve as a substratum for impressions, because it lacks fixity of nature, as it consists only of a series of momentary events. The store-consciousness is "stable", as Asaṅga tells us, only in the sense that it forms a continuous, never greatly altered series (*Mahāyānasaṅgraha* I, 23). Thus it cannot be an abiding locus for these impressions. Unless an abiding entity pervading the three times is assumed (or else some conditioning agent which is immutable and omniscient), the processes of impression and memory cannot be explained.

Here is an instance where it is difficult to say who has the better argument. Śaṅkara says that the lack of stability of the store-consciousness makes it inadequate as an explanation for our "sense of continuity". On the other hand, Vasubandhu's argument touches on one of the fundamental difficulties of Advaita-Vedānta: that it is impossible to relate an immutable entity to a world of phenomena constantly changing.

65a. Sumatiśīla tells the story as follows : "There was a man named Vṛjiputraka who, upon hearing the 251 rules*, abandoned them, not being able to accede to them. (The Exalted One addressed him as follows) : 'Vṛjiputraka, would you be able, Vṛjiputraka, could you exert yourself, to train yourself well in three trainings ?' He replied, 'I could exert myself, Exalted One, in three, Sugata. I could guard myself with three,' and the Exalted One replied, 'Then, Vṛjiputraka, discipline yourself from time to time in the training of higher ethics (*adhiśīla*), the training of higher cittas (*adhicitta*), and the training of higher insight (*adhiprajñā*)'. With this teaching of the three trainings of higher ethics, etc. he summarized the 251 rules of discipline with these three trainings."**

66. "Tīrthaṅkaras" is the name given by the Jains to their completely enlightened saints. Some of the Jain sūtras actually do state that mental acts and intentions are only "half-acts", and do not carry as great a retribution as actual physical acts (*Uvāsakadasao*, pp. 83, 165, 179). The *Sūtrakṛtāṅga* however clearly states that even an unfulfilled evil intention has its bad retribution (I, I, 2, 23-30). But it clearly mocks the ancient Buddhist focus on volition (which is again taken up by Vasubandhu after the Vaibhāṣikas had let the emphasis somewhat drop). For the Jains, any physical action, whether intentional or not, carries the same kind of retribution, and it is chiefly physical action which receives their full attention. The *Sūtrakṛtāṅga* has a Buddhist say : "If one thrusts a spear through the side of a granary, mistaking it for a man, or through a gourd, mistaking it for a baby, and roasts it, one will be guilty of murder according to our views. If one puts a man on a spit and roasts him, mistaking him for a fragment of the granary, or a baby, mistaking him for a gourd, he will not be guilty of murder according to our views. If anybody thrusts a spear through a man or a baby, mistaking him for a fragment of the granary, puts him on the fire, and roasts him, that will be a meal fit for the Buddhas to breakfast upon" (II, VI, 26-29, Jacobi's translation).

67. *Balā* was a plant commonly used in ancient Indian medicine in the preparation of oil-baths. Avinash Chunder Kaviratna, Ayurvedic physician and translator of Caraka, identifies it with *Sida cordifolia* (p. 281).

68. Obviously these simple acts of performance (Sumatiśīla's "activity which is not action") cannot be action in the Buddhist sense, i.e. action carrying retribution. As we have seen in note 43, the activity of the physical organs themselves must be completely indeterminate.

*of the *Prātimokṣa*. In the Pāli *Pātimokkha* there are only 227.

***Karma-siddhi-ṭīkā*, p. 220, 5. For the original sūtra, see *Aṅguttara* I, 230.

THE TWENTY VERSES AND THEIR COMMENTARY

(VIṂŚATIKĀ-KĀRIKĀ [VṚTTI])

INTRODUCTION

This famous work may well be one of the last three Vasubandhu wrote. It, *The Thirty Verses*, and *The Teaching of the Three Own-Beings* seem to belong together : the implications of one lead to the revelations of the next.

Perhaps no work of Vasubandhu's has been more consistently misunderstood than *The Twenty Verses*. It has frequently been used as an authoritative source for opinions that are in fact not even there. The main point here is not that consciousness unilaterally creates all forms in the universe, as has been supposed by Dharmapāla and Hsüan-tsang, but rather that an object-of-consciousness is "internal", and the "external" stimuli are only inferrable.* What is observed directly are always only perceptions, colored by particular consciousness-"seeds". The very fact that these "seeds" are spoken of at all indicates a double influence. On one hand, every consciousness-moment deposits a "seed"; on the other, each "seed" influences every subsequent consciousness-moment, until a "revolution at the basis" of consciousness is achieved.

In its entirety, this work is very free-wheeling, and directed at a wide variety of philosophical and generally human problems. Its ingenious refutation of atomism could stop even a twentieth-century particle physicist thinking.

Most interesting is the approach in this work towards "realities". Since experienced realities are all equally without a perceptible externally existing reference point, the difference between illusion and reality falls away. That is, all "realities" involve an amount of "illusion". Even where there is a unanimous concensus among aggregate-"series" regarding experienced events, this does not mean that their view is illusion-free reality. An aggregate complex "undergoing hallucinations"

*Vasubandhu admits the possibility of the necessity of external stimuli in his *Mahāyānasaṅgrahabhāṣya*, where he says, "A visual consciousness arises dependent on a visible and the eye, together with the store-consciousness." ["de la (kun gzhi) rnam par shes pa dang bcas pa'i mig dang gzugs rnams la brten nas mig gi rnam par shes pa 'byung ste /"], *Mahāyānasaṅgrahabhāṣya*, Peking/Tokyo ed. Tibetan Canon, vol. 112, p. 275, 4, 3.

(in conventional parlance) is experiencing as much "reality" as those which are not.

Since it is admitted that entire "realities" may be mentally created, Vasubandhu can dispense with a feature of Buddhist dogmatics that does not seem to him logical. Traditional Buddhist exegeses sometimes speak of "hells" as places of temporary retributional suffering for those "series" that committed acts of suffering. Vasubandhu says that these hell-states must be totally "internal", since assuming "an approved place for the infliction of suffering" is to him abhorrent. These hell-states arise in the psychophysical complex, and it is there where the working out from them is done.

Concerning the Text :

The Twenty Verses, and their commentary, which is also by Vasubandhu, exist in their original Sanskrit form. They were edited by Sylvain Lévi in *Bibliothèque de l'École des Hautes Études*, sciences historiques et philologiques, Librairie Ancienne Honoré Champion, Paris, 1925, volume 241-245. This translation is based on that edition.

TWENTY VERSES AND COMMENTARY (VIṂŚATIKĀ-KĀRIKĀ- [VṚTTI])

In the Great Vehicle, the three realms of existence[1] are determined as being perception-only. As it is said in the sūtra*, "The three realms of existence are citta-only." Citta, manas, consciousness, and perception are synonyms. By the word "citta", citta along with its associations is intended here. "Only" is said to rule out any (external) object of sense or understanding.

All this is perception-only, because of the appearance of
non-existent objects,
just as there may be the seeing of non-existent nets of hair
by someone afflicted with an optical disorder.1

Here it is objected :

"If perception occurs without an object,
any restriction as to place and time becomes illogical,
as does non-restriction as to moment-series[2]
and any activity which has been performed."2

What is being said ? If the perception of visibles, etc. arises without any object of visibles, etc. why is it that it arises only in certain places, and not everywhere, and even in those places, why is it that it arises only sometimes, and not all the time ? And why is it that it arises in the moment-series of all that are situated in that time and place, and not just in the moment-series of one, just as the appearance of hair, etc. arises in the moment-series of those afflicted by an optical disorder, and not in the moment-series of others ? Why is it that the hair, bees, etc. seen by those afflicted by an optical disorder don't perform the functions of hair, etc. while it is not the case that other hair, etc. don't perform them ? Food, drink, clothes, poison, weapons, etc. that are seen in a dream don't perform the functions of food, etc. while it is not the case that other food, etc. don't perform them. An illusory town does not

Avataṃsaka-sūtra: Daśa-bhūmika VI, p. 32 (R, p 49).

perform the functions of a town, because of its non-existence, while it is not the case that other towns don't perform them. Therefore, with the non-being of an object, any restriction as to place and time, any non-restriction as to moment-series, and any activity which has been performed, would be illogical.

Reply :

No, they are not illogical, because
Restriction as to place, etc. is demonstrated as in a dream. 3a

Now how is this ? In a dream, even without an (external) object of sense or understanding, only certain things are to be seen : bees, gardens, women, men, etc. and these only in certain places, and not everywhere. And even there in those places, they are to be seen only sometimes, and not all the time. In this way, even without an (external) object of sense or understanding, there may be restriction as to place and time.

And non-restriction as to moment-series
is like with the *pretas*.[3] 3b

The phrase "is demonstrated" continues to apply here (to make the verse read : "And non-restriction as to moment-series is demonstrated as with the *pretas*."). How is it demonstrated ?

In the seeing of pus-rivers, etc. by all of them 3c

all together. A "pus-river" is a river filled with pus. Just as one says "a ghee pot". For all the *pretas* who are in a similar situation due to a similar retribution for action, and not just one of them, see a river filled with pus. With the expression "etc." rivers full of urine and feces, guarded by men holding clubs or swords, and other such perceptions, are included also. Thus, non-restriction as to moment-series in regard to perceptions is demonstrated even with an (external) object of sense or understanding being non-existent.

And activity which has been performed
is just like being affected in a dream.[4a] 4a

A case of being affected in a dream is like where semen is released even without a couple's coming together. So, by these various examples, the four-fold restriction as to place and time, and so on, is demonstrated.

> And as in a hell-state,[4b]
> all of these 4b

are demonstrated. "In a hell-state" means "among those experiencing a hell-state". How are they demonstrated ?

> In the seeing of hell-guardians, etc.
> and in being tormented by them. 4c

Just as the seeing of hell-guardians, etc. by those experiencing a hell-state (and with the expression "etc." the seeing of dogs, crows, moving mountains, and so on, is included) is demonstrated with a restriction as to place and time for all of those experiencing a hell-state, and not just for one of them, and just as their torment inflicted by them is demonstrated through the sovereignty of the common retribution for their individual actions, even though the hell-guardians, and so on, are really non-existent. So the four-fold restriction as to place and time is to be known as demonstrated in yet another way.

Objection: But for what reason is the existence of hell-guardians, dogs, and crows (experienced in hell-states) not accepted ?

Reply :

Because they are illogical. For to assume that these kinds of hell-beings have an external existence is not logical. This is so because they don't feel the sufferings there themselves, or if they tormented each other mutually, there would be no difference in situation between those experiencing a hell-state and the hell-guardians, and if they mutually tormented each other having equal make-ups, sizes, and strengths, there would be no fear in those experiencing a hell-state, and since they couldn't stand the burning suffering of standing on a ground made of heated iron, how could they be tormenting others ? And how could there be an arising of those not experiencing a hell-state, together with those who are ?

Objection : How is this ? The arising of animals in a heaven-state may occur, so in the same way, there may be the arising of hell-guardians, etc. which have the distinct qualities of animals or *pretas*, in hell-states.

Reply :

There is no arising of animals in hell-states,
as there is in heaven-states,
nor is there any arising of *pretas*,
since they don't experience the sufferings that are engendered there. 5

Those animals which arise in heaven-states experience all the pleasure that is engendered there because of (past) actions bringing pleasure to their environment. But hell-guardians, etc. don't experience hellish suffering in the same way. So the arising of animals (in hell-states) is not logical, and neither is the arising of *pretas* there.

An opinion: Then it's because of the actions of those experiencing a hell-state, that special material elements arise, which have special qualities as to color, make-up, size, and strength, and are cognized as hell-guardians, etc. That's why they are constantly transforming in various ways, and appear to be shaking their hands, etc. in order to instill fear, just as mountains that look like sheep appear to be coming and going, and just as thorns in forests of iron silk-cotton trees, appear to be bowing down and rising up again. And yet it isn't that (these phenomena) aren't arising.[5]

Reply :

If the arising and transformation of material elements due to the actions of those is accepted,
why isn't (such arising and transformation) of a consciousness accepted ? 6

Why is a transformation of consciousness itself due to (past) actions not accepted, and why instead are material elements constructed ? And furthermore,

It's being constructed that the process of impressions from actions takes place elsewhere than does its effect,
and it is not being accepted that it exists there where the impressions take place : Now what is your reason for this ? 7

Because it is through their action that such an arising and transformation of material elements is constructed for those experiencing a hell-state, and inasmuch as impressions through actions enter together into their consciousness-series, and not anywhere else, why is it that that effect is not accepted as being such a transformation of consciousness taking place just where the impressions themselves do ?[6] What is the reason for an effect being constructed where there is no process of impression ?

(You may say) : By reason of scriptural authority. If consciousness were only the appearance of visibles, etc. and there were no (external) objects of visibles, etc. the existence of the sense-fields of visibles, etc. would not have been spoken of by the Exalted One.

Reply :

This is no reason, because
Speaking of sense-fields of visibles, etc.
was intended for those to be introduced to Dharma,
just as in the case of spontaneously-generated beings.[7] 8

It's just like in the case where spontaneously generated beings were discussed by the Exalted One. This was done with the intention of indicating the non-discontinuity of the citta-series in the future.[8] "There is neither a sentient being, or a self, but only events along with their causes", has been stated by the Exalted One.* Thus, statements were made by the Exalted One regarding the existence of the sense-fields of visibles, etc. with an intention directed at people to be introduced to the Dharma. And what was the intention there ?

Because their appearances continue as perceptions,
because of (consciousnesses') own seeds,
the Sage spoke in terms of states of two-fold sense-fields." 9

What was said ? The Exalted One spoke of sense-fields of the eye and of visibles in those cases where a perception with the appearance of visibles arises from the attainment of a special transformation (in the consciousness-series) through its own seeds, and when this seed and perception become manifest with this appearance, respectively.[9] In the same way, in those cases where a perception with the appearance of tactile sensations

**Majjhima* I, 138.

arises from the attainment of a special transformation (in the consciousness-series) through its own seeds, and when this seed and that appearance become manifest, the Exalted One spoke of sense-fields of the body and of tactile sensations, respectively. This is the intention.

What is the advantage of teaching with such an intention ?
In this way, there is entry into the selflessness of personality. 10a

If the sense-fields are taught in this way, people will enter into an understanding of the selflessness of personality. The group of six consciousnesses evolves because of duality. But when it is known that there is not any one seer, (any one hearer, any one smeller, any one taster, any one toucher), or any one thinker, those to be introduced to Dharma through the selflessness of personality will enter into an understanding of the selflessness of personality.

And in yet another way, this teaching is entry into the selflessness of events. 10b

"And in yet another way", etc. is in reference to how the teaching of perception-only is entry into the selflessness of events, when it becomes known that this perception-only makes an appearance of visibles, etc. arise, and that there is no exprienced event with the characteristics of visibles, etc. But if there isn't an event in any way, then perception-only also isn't, so how can it be demonstrated ? But it's not because there isn't an event in any way that there is entry into the selflessness of events. Rather, it's

in regard to a constructed self. 10 c

It is selflessness in reference to a constructed self, i.e. all those things that constitute the "own-being" believed in by fools, that is the constructed with its "objects apprehended" and "subjects apprehendors", etc. and not in reference to the ineffable Self, which is the scope of Buddhas.[10] In the same way, one penetrates the selflessness of perception-only itself in reference to a "self" constructed by another perception[11], and through this determination of perception-only, there is entry into the selflessness of all events, and not by a denial of their existence.[12] Otherwise, there would be an object for this other perception because of a perception itself (i.e. either "perception-only" or "the perception of self" would be a real object), there would be at least one perception which has an object consisting of another perception, and the state of perception-only wouldn't be demonstrated, because of the perception's state of having objects.[13]

But how is it to be understood that the existence of the sense-fields of visibles, etc. was spoken of by the Exalted One not because those things which singly become sense-objects of the perceptions of visibles, etc. really exist, but rather with a hidden intention ? Because

A sense-object is neither a single thing,
  nor several things,
from the atomic point of view,
nor can it be an aggregate (of atoms),
so atoms can't be demonstrated. 11

What is being said ? The sense-field of visibles, etc. which consists (in a moment) of a single sense-object of a perception of visibles, etc. is either a unity, like the composite whole constructed by the Vaiśeṣikas*, or it is several things, from the atomic point of view, or it is an aggregation of atoms. Now, the sense-object can't be a single thing, because one can nowhere apprehend a composite whole which is different from its component parts. Nor can it be plural, because of atoms, since they can't be apprehended singly.[14] Nor does an aggregation of atoms become a sense-object, because an atom as one entity can't be demonstrated, either.

How is it that it can't be demonstrated ? Because

Through the simultaneous conjunction of six elements,
  the atom has six parts. 12a

*cf. *Discussion for the Demonstration of Action*, note 11, and the entire discussion in that treatise in section 3.

If there is a simultaneous conjunction of six elements in six directions, the atom comes to have six parts.[15] For that which is the locus of one can't be the locus of another.

> If there were a common locus for the six,
> the agglomeration would only be one atom. 12b

It might be maintained that the locus for each single atom is the locus of all six elements. But then, because of the common locus for all of them, the agglomeration would be only one atom, because of the mutual exclusion of occupants of a locus. And then, no agglomeration would become visible.[16] Nor, for that matter, can atoms join together at all, because of their state of having no parts. The Vaibhāṣikas of Kashmir say, "We aren't arguing such an absurdity. It's just when they're in aggregation, that they can join together." But the question must be asked : Is then an aggregation of atoms not an object different from the atoms themselves ?

> When there is no conjunction of atoms,
> how can there be one for their aggregations ?
> Their conjunction is not demonstrated,
> for they also have no parts. 13

So the aggregations themselves can't mutually join together, either. For there is no conjunction of atoms, because of their state of having no parts. That is to say, such a thing can't be demonstrated. So even in the case of an aggregation, which does have parts, its conjunction becomes inadmissible (because there can be no aggregation of atoms unless individual atoms conjoin. And so the atoms as one entity can't be demonstrated. And whether the conjunction of atoms is accepted, or isn't

> (To assume) the singleness of that which has divisions
> as to directional dimensions, is illogical. 14a

For one atom, there may be the directional dimension of being "in front", for another, of being "on the bottom", and if there are such divisions as to directional dimensions, how can the

singleness of an atom, which partakes of such divisions, be logical ?

Or else, how could there be shade and blockage ? 14b

If there were no divisions as to directional dimensions in an atom, how could there be shade in one place, light in another, when the sun is rising ? For there could be no other location for the atom where there would be no light.[17] And how could there be an obstruction of one atom by another, if divisions as to directional dimensions are not accepted ? For there would be no other part for an atom, where, through the arrival of another atom, there would be a collision with this other atom. And if there is no collision, then the whole aggregation of all the atoms would have the dimensions of only one atom, because of their common locus, as has been stated previously.

It may be argued : Why can't it be accepted that shade and blockage refer to an agglomeration, and not to a single atom ?

Reply : But in that case, is it being admitted that an agglomeration is something other than the atoms themselves ? Objector : No, that can't be admitted.

If the agglomeration isn't something other,
then they can't refer to it. 14c

If it is not accepted that the agglomeration is something other than the atoms, then shade and blockage can't be demonstrated as occurring in reference to the agglomeration only. This is simply an attachment to mental construction. "Atoms" or "aggregations" : what's the point of worrying with those, if "their basic characteristics of being visibles, etc." are not refuted ?

What then is their characteristic ? That they are in a state of being sense-objects of the eye etc., in a state of being blue, etc. It is just this which should be investigated. If a sense-object for the eye, and so on, is accepted in the form of blue, yellow, etc. then are these one entity, or several ? Now what follows from this ? The flaw inherent in assuming their severalness has already been discussed (in relation to the arguments on atomic aggregation).

If their unity existed, one couldn't arrive at anything gradually,
there couldn't be apprehension and non-apprehension simultaneously,

there couldn't be separate, several, developments,
and there would be no reason for the non-seeing of the very subtle. 15

If one entity as a sense-object for the eye, with no separations, and no severalness, were constructed, then one couldn't arrive at anything gradually on the Earth : that is, there could be no act of going. For, even with placing down a foot once, one would go everywhere. There could be no apprehension of a nearer "part of something" and a non-apprehension of a more removed "part", simultaneously. For a concurrent apprehension and non-apprehension of the same thing isn't logical. There would be no special development for species that are separate, such as elephants, horses, etc. and since they would all be one in that case, how could their separation be accepted ? And how can they be accepted as single, anyway, since there is the apprehension of an empty space between two of them ? And there would be no reason for the non-seeing of subtle water-beings, since they would be visible in common with the more apparent.

An otherness in entities is constructed if there is a division of characteristics, and not otherwise, so when speaking from the atomic point of view, one must by necessity construct divisions, and it cannot be demonstrated that they (the atoms) are in any way of one kind. With their unity undemonstrated, visibles', etc.'s state of being sense-objects of the eye, etc. is also undemonstrated, and thus perception-only *is* demonstrated.

If the existence and non-existence of objects of sense or understanding are being investigated by force of the means-of-cognition (direct perception, inference, appeal to reliable authority), direct perception must be recognized as being the most weighty of all means-of-cognition. But with an object of sense or understanding not existing, how can there be any cognizing which can be termed "direct perception" ?

Cognizing by direct perception is like in a dream, etc. 16a

For it is without an object of sense or understanding, as has been made known previously.

And when it occurs, the object is already not seen,
so how can it be considered a state of direct perception ? 16b

When a cognition through direct perception arises in the form "This is my direct perception", the object itself is already not seen, since this distinguishing takes place only through a mental consciousness, and the visual consciousness has already ceased by that time, so how can its being a direct perception be accepted ? This is especially true for a sense-object, which is momentary, for that visible, or taste, etc. has already ceased by that time.[18] It may be said that nothing which hasn't been experienced (by other consciousnesses) is remembered by the mental consciousness, and that this takes place by necessity as it is brought about by the experience of an object of sense or understanding, and that those can be considered to be a state of direct perception of sense-objects, visibles, etc. in this way. But this remembering of an experienced object of sense or understanding is not demonstrated, either. Because

It has been stated how perception occurs with its appearance. 17a

It has already been stated how perceptions in the shape of eye-consciousnesses, etc. arise with the appearance of an object, even without there being any (external) object of sense or understanding.

And remembering takes place from that. 17b

"From that" means "from the perception". A mental perception arises with the discrimination of a visible, etc. when that appearance is linked with memory, so an experience of an (external) object can't be demonstrated through the arising of a memory.

Objection : If, even when one is awake, perception has sense-objects which weren't, like in a dream, then people would understand their non-being by themselves. But that isn't the case. So it's not that the apprehension of objects is like in a dream, and all perceptions are really without an (external) object.

Reply : This argument won't bring us to the cognition you wish, because

Somebody who isn't awake doesn't understand the non-being of the visual sense-objects in a dream. 17c

Just as people when they are asleep in a dream have their faculties concentrated on impressions of appearances of discriminations which appear differently than they do later, and, as long as they aren't awake, don't understand the non-being of objects of sense and understanding that weren't, just so when they become awakened by the attainment of a supermundane knowledge free from discriminations, which is the antidote to these (discriminations), then they truly understand the non-being of these sense-objects through meeting with a clear worldly subsequently attained knowledge.[19] So their situations are similar.

Objection : If, through a special transformation of "their own" moment-series, perceptions with the appearance of (external) objects of sense or understanding arise for beings, and not through special objects themselves, then how can any certainty as regards perceptions be demonstrated from association with bad or good friends, or from hearing about existent and non-existent events[20], since there can exist neither association with the good or bad, nor any real teaching ?

Reply :

The certainty of perceptions takes place mutually,
by the state of their sovereign effect on one another. 18a

For all beings there is certainty of perception through a mutual sovereign effect of perceptions on one another, according to circumstances[21]. "Mutually" means "each affecting the other". So one special perception arises within a moment-series through a special perception within the moment-series, and not because of a special object.

Objection : If a perception is without an (external) object, just like in a dream, even for those who are awake, why is it that in the practise of the beneficial and unbeneficial there won't be an equal result from desirable and undesirable efforts, for those who are asleep and those who aren't ?[22]

Reply : Because

Citta is affected by torpor in a dream,
so their results are different. 18b

This is the reason, not the existing being of an (external) object.

Objection : If all this is perception-only, there can't be body or speech for anybody. So how can the dying of sheep who have been attacked by shepherds, take place ? If their dying takes place without the shepherds having done anything, how can the shepherds be held responsible for the offense of taking life ?

Reply :

Dying may be a modification resulting from a special perception by another,
just like losses of memory, etc. may take place through the mental control of spirits, etc. 19

Just as there may be modifications in others, such as loss of memory, the seeing of dreams, or being taken possession of by spirits, by the mental control of psychic powers, as in the case of Sāraṇa's seeing dreams through Mahā-Kātyāyana's mental force, or, as in the case of the vanquishing of Vemacitra through mental harming coming from the forest-dwelling seers.[23] In the same way, through the force of a special perception of another, a certain modification of the aggregate-series, destroying its life-force, may arise, through which dying, which is to be known as a name for a discontinuity in the aggregate-series taking part in an organism*, takes place.

Or else, how was it that the Daṇḍaka Forest became empty because of the anger of seers ? 20a

If it isn't accepted that the dying of beings can occur through the force of a special perception in others, how is it that the Exalted One, in order to demonstrate that mental harm constitutes a great offense, questioned Upāli when he was still a householder, as follows : "Householder ! Through what agency were the Daṇḍaka, Mataṅga, and Kaliṅga Forests made empty and sacred, as has been reported ?", and Upāli replied, "I heard that it happened through the mental harming of seers, Gautama."**

If not, how could it be demonstrated that mental harm constitutes a great offense ? 20b

*cf. *Discussion of Five Aggregates*, p. 71.
***Majjhima* I, 37-38.

If this situation were constructed as not taking place through a mental harming, and it were to be said that those sentient beings that were living in that forest were destroyed by non-human spirits that had been propitiated as if they were seers, how could it be demonstrated by this passage that mental harm through mental action is a greater offense than bodily or verbal harm ?[24] This passage demonstrates that the dying of so many sentient beings came about only through a mental harming.

Objection : But if all this is perception-only, do those who understand the cittas of others really know the cittas of others, or don't they ?

Reply :

What about this ?

Objector : If they don't know them, how can they be "those who understand the cittas of others" ?

Reply : They know them.

> The knowledge of those who understand others' cittas is not like an object.
> And how is this ? As in the case of a knowledge of one's own citta. 21a

Objector : And how is *that* knowledge (of one's own citta) not like an object ?

Reply :

> Because of non-knowledge, as in the case of the scope of Buddhas. 21b

It's just like in the case of the scope of Buddhas, which comes about through the ineffable Self. Thus both of these knowledges, because of their inherent non-knowledge, are not like an object, because it is through the state of an appearance of something which appears differently than it does later that there is a state of non-abandonment of the discrimination between object apprehended and subject apprehendor.[25]

Though perception-only has unfathomable depth, and there are limitless kinds of ascertainments to be gained in it,

> I have written this demonstration of perception-only according to my abilities,

but in its entirety it is beyond the scope of citta. 22 a

It is impossible for people like me to consider it in all its aspects, because it is not in the range of dialetics. And in order to show by whom it is known entirely as a scope of insight, it is said to be

the scope of Buddhas. 22b

In all its modes, it is the scope of Buddhas, Exalted Ones, because of their lack of impediment to the knowledge of everything that can be known in all aspects.

NOTES

1. See *A Discussion of the Five Aggregates*, note 12.

2. "There would be no restriction as to place and time of objects perceived" means that any object of sense or understanding would arise anywhere and at any time if there were no definite external object to which it corresponded. "Nor would there be non-restriction as regards consciousness-'series' perceiving them" means that if there were no definite external object, it couldn't happen that all consciousness- 'series' in a given place and time see the same object. Of course Vasubandhu will deny that the latter is true at all, since there are always various ways of perceiving "the same sequence." And the restriction as to place and time for objects of sense and understanding does not depend on a definite external object, as it is a principle operating even in the perceptions taking place in dreams.

3. The *pretas* are "the hungry ghosts" of traditional Buddhist lore, who undergo special sufferings because of past unbeneficial actions. All of them will see the same pus-rivers, etc. even though others won't : another indication that experienced reality may be totally mentally created.

4a. The objector is saying that an external object of consciousness is proved by "action's being performed". This means, for instance, that food which is tasted while awake has the activity of nourishing, while "food" that is tasted in a dream is not really food, as it does not nourish the organism. Vasubandhu says that this argument is not fool-proof, because when a man has a sexual dream, the biological function of releasing semen is performed in this case.

4b. The hell-states will be reduced by Vasubandhu to afflicted events existing only in the consciousness-streams of those experiencing them.

5. Hallucinations exist as much as anything else does, since they are perceptions.

6. Residual impressions take place in consciousness. Retribution is a fruition or maturation of impressions, and thus should take place in the consciousness-series only.

7,8. "Spontaneously generated beings" are those that arise all at once, with all their organs neither lacking nor deficient. They do not have to undergo embryonic stages or any other development. Traditionally, gods, hell-beings, and the intermediate existences between one full life-"series" and the next (the *bardo* of the *Bardo-Thödol,* or *Tibetan Book of the Dead*) are considered to be "spontaneously generated beings" (cf. *Kośa* III 9 b-c). We have seen that Vasubandhu in *The Twenty Verses* denies the existence of special hell-beings, and "god-states" are for him again only special transformations of consciousness. As regards "intermediate existences" between lives, he says that they aren't really born yet, but only in the process of being born (*Kośa* III, ad 10, end). In the deeper perspective of Vasubandhu's *Explanation of Dependent Origination* and *The Tibetan Book of the Dead,* every life-stream consists of an alternating series of "life" and "death", i.e. there is a dying and being again in every moment. In that sense, every "dying moment" is an intermediate existence. But then it also no longer really had the traditional characteristic of a "spontaneously generated being". Vasubandhu here assumes that the category of "spontaneously generated beings" really doesn't exist, and that the Buddha spoke of them, and in particular of spontaneously generated intermediate existences, only to demonstrate the non-discontinuity of the citta-series. Without the assumption of a spontaneously generated intermediate existence, people might assume that there is a discontinuity in citta between one life and the next, including the one life, next one, next one, next one, next one, etc. that is going on in each successive moment.

9. As far as what we directly experience is concerned, a "seed" and perception become manifest in what we term "seeing a visible." "The visible seen" is really a reflection of the "seed", i.e. an impression in consciousness, the visual consciousness is a special transformation in the consciousness-series affected by that "seed".

10. The completely signless perception of Buddhas is here seen to be equivalent with the Universal Self of the *Upaniṣads.* The recognition of their fundamental oneness is rare in Buddhist writing. The selflessness of events and personalities does not of course refer to this Universal Self, which Vasubandhu might more usually call "Emptiness" or "the Ground of all events". It refers rather to any fixed particular individualizing force in particulars.

11. "One" sees the selflessness of perception-only when "one" has seen that the "self" previously constructed by another perception is void. Actually, the use of the pronoun "one" is inaccurate, and does not occur in Sanskrit, where verbs need have no subjects. It has been adopted here as the least pernicious pronoun, but should not be taken too literally. In other words, the phrase "one sees" really stands for "there is a new consciousness-moment of seeing in a psychophysical complex". "One", as used here and subsequently in these rtanslations, is not numerically "one".

12. This is an important difference. It is not that anything is being denied. It is just that any particular unchanging characters by which we could delimit events and personalities, don't exist.

13. If perception-only is not self-dissolving, "perception-only" would be an object of perception, and perception-only wouldn't be demonstrated. Obviously, "perception-only" is itself perception-only, and not a fixed object.

14. In Vaiśeṣika, atoms are absolutely imperceptible.

15. Any collision of one atom with another, any atom's being in a positional relation to another, implies that the atom has parts, and thus is not really an atom.

16. Since the atom is imperceptible, if the locus for an aggregation of atoms is common for all of them, then this aggregation, as taking up only the place of one atom, would only be one atom itself, and hence imperceptible.

17. The arising of shade is explainable only if there is blockage of one material complex by another. Now this becomes atomically impossible, since the mutual resistance of materialities is possible according to an atomic theory only where atoms collide. And the collision of atoms implies parts to atoms, cf. note 15.

18. A mental consciousness which becomes aware of a visible depends on a previous visual consciousness. But since all events are momentary, and the mental consciousness registers the visible after the visual consciousness has arisen, the visual consciousness is already past by that time, thus "cognizing a visible" is not strictly speaking "direct perception"

19. "A supermundane knowledge" is a perception free from mental marks and dualities, "pure perception". It is followed by "a clear worldly subsequently attained knowledge", where "objects" are again seen plurally, but are no longer conceptually clung to, since characteristics which would warrant dividing them off from one another are seen to be constructed.

20. If everything perceived is equally a transformation of consciousness, then what are the criteria by which one can distinguish the beneficial, unbeneficial, the existent and the non-existent ?

21. Here it is seen that each perception influences the next, and the only basis for certainty of perception is the consistency of these influences.

22. If all perception is without a clear external object, then why is it that beneficial and unbeneficial acts committed in a dream don't have the same retributory effect as those committed while awake ?

23. The objector is saying that if everything is perception-only, then only mental actions exist, and bodily and verbal actions have no reality. In that case, he says, when a shepherd kills a sheep, we can't really call him responsible for a death, because that bodily action wasn't real. Vasubandhu has already evolved an answer to this objection in *A Discussion for the Demonstration of Action,* where the ethical nature of an act is traced to the beneficiality or unbeneficiality of the "agent's" volition. The shepherd faces retribution for unbeneficial action as soon as the volition to kill arises. But then another volition, that "which sets into agitation", which puts the materiality-aggregate into action, must occur for there to be what is conventionally called "a bodily act" "A bodily act" is thus really, according to Vasu-

bandhu, "an act of volition affecting the body", and the killing of the sheep is strictly speaking a result of this volition. (See *A Discussion for the Demonstration of Action* 46, 47.)

Instead of reiterating this argument, Vasubandhu here focuses upon another point: that death may come about through special mental forces (i.e. perceptions) of "another". However, this does not seem to be an answer to the objector's question. The objector is asking how one can call the shepherd responsible for a bodily act if there is no bodily act; Vasubandhu is replying that death can result from a mental act, which seems besides the point. However, Vasubandhu's reply does emphasize again the organic interrelationship of the consciousness- and materiality- aggregates. (It is by the way not inconsistent to continue to speak of a materiality-aggregate in the context of "perception-only", since the materiality-aggregate are those events which are perceived primarily by the tactile consciousness. Here, one consciousness-aggregate is stated to have a radical effect on another psychophysical complex. Vasubandhu cites two canonical stories to back up his assertion. Sāraṇa, the son of King Udayana of Vatsa, became a pupil of Mahā-Kātyāyana, one of the Buddha's chief disciples. Mahā-Kāktyāyana and Sāraṇa together journeyed to Ujjain, in the Kingdom of Avanti. There, King Pradyota of Avanti suspected Sāraṇa of having relations with his wives. Though the charge was unfounded, Pradyota had Sāraṇa beaten until he was streaming with blood. When released, Sāraṇa asked Mahā-Kātyāyana to absolve him from his monastic vows. He wanted to go to his father and levy an army against Pradyota. (The hostility between the Kingdoms of Avanti and Vatsa under Pradyota and Udayana had some history behind it by that time. Udayana had already spent some time as a prisoner of Pradyota, and had only been released because of the love between Udayana and Vāsavadattā, the daughter of Pradyota. This is the theme of Bhāsa's famous drama, *Pratijñāyaugandharāyaṇa*. However, Sāraṇa apparently felt that his father's forces were equal to those of Pradyota in a fair fight, since on that previous occasion, Pradyota had captured Udayana by means of a ruse.) Mahā-Kātyāyana refused to release Sāraṇa from his vows, and instead preached to him about the unbeneficiality of violent action. When Sāraṇa remained obdurate, Mahā-Kātyāyana waited until he was asleep, and then affected his dreams by his own mental powers. He made Sāraṇa see in a dream a huge battle, in which Pradyota was victorious. Sāraṇa himself was led away for execution. On the way to death, he met Mahā-Kātyāyana, and begged him for forgiveness. In order to show him that this was only a dream, Mahā-Kātyāyana made rays of light come out of his right arm. This story is told in detail in Kumāralāta's *Kalpanāmaṇḍatikā*, XII, story no. 65. (This text used to be known as Aśvaghoṣa's *Sūtrālaṅkāra*, cf. Sylvain Lévi, "Aśvaghoṣa, le *Sūtrālaṅkāra* et ses sources", *Journal Asiatique*, 1908, II, pp 149 ff.) In the second story alluded to by Vasubandhu, Vemacitra, King of the Asuras, decided to pay no respect to a group of virtuous seers who were living together in leaf-huts in a great forest. He came to them with his shoes on, his sword hanging at one side, and his canopy of state held over him. After he left, the seers decided that danger might come to them from him, unless he was led to see the limitation of his powers in comparison with theirs. Using their special powers, those seers, "as quickly as a strong man might stretch out his bent arm, or bend his arm stretched out, vanished from their leaf-huts and appeared before Sambara".* They asked him for a safety-pledge, Vemacitra arrogantly refused, telling them, "Terror is all that I do give."** The seers then replied :

> "And dost thou only peril give
> to us who ask for safety-pledge ?
> Lo ! Then, accepting this from thee,
> May never-ending fear be thine !
> According to the seed that's sown,
> So is the fruit ye reap therefrom."***

Then they disappeared from his presence, and re-appeared in their forest huts. That night, Vemacitra was tormented by terrible nightmares three times. These came directly from the forest seers' mental powers. According to Buddhaghoṣa, he was afflicted by terrible dreams thereafter, and finally became constantly terrified even when awake. This story is told in the *Saṃyutta-Nikāya* (I, XI, 225-227), and expanded in Buddhaghoṣa's *Sārathappakāsinī* (Comment on I, XI).

24. A violent mental act towards another's mental series carries more weight than a physical or verbal violence. For physical or verbal violence can be borne with forbearance, but a deliberate alteration of the consciousness-series of another may make even equanimity impossible.

25. The non-dual awareness of enlightened ones, and the empathetic insight into another's citta, are not knowledges in the sense of apprehending "an object", but rather represent the free flow of consciousness. The apprehension of an "object" always implies the presence of an appearance which is abandoned in these two kinds of awareness. Thus, these "knowledges" are really non-knowledges, because a specific object is not known within them.

*i.e. Vemacitra. This is the verslon of Carolyn Rhys-Davids in her translation of *Saṃyutta* I, XI, 227 (10), p 292.

**Ibid.

***Ibid., 9. 293.

THE THIRTY VERSES

(TRIṂŚIKĀ-KĀRIKĀ)

INTRODUCTION

In this famous work, the reciprocal relationship between the store-consciousness and the evolving consciousness (one through six) is clearly outlined with all concomitant motivating dispositions for each evolvement being listed. It is stated that the store-consciousness, even in its subliminal state, has certain threshold-of-consciousness experiences which indicate the presence of contact, mental attention, feelings, cognitions, and volitions.

But it is possible to free consciousness from latent impressions. This is why Vasubandhu speaks of the de-volvment of the store-consciousness.

In the very first verse, Vasubandhu speaks of the "metaphors of 'self' and 'events'". The "self" has been regarded as a metaphor throughout Buddhism. But here the concept of "event", accepted in Abhidharma circles, is also called a metaphor. Just as the "self" is a metaphor for the constantly changing aggregate-series, just so, to follow the reasoning of the *Twenty Verses*, an "event" is a metaphor for a transformation in a consciousness-series. But it is well to remember, and in fact Vasubandhu reminds us of this in several other passages*, that the expressions "store-consciousness", "series" and "seeds" are themselves metaphorical, also.

The term "*manas*" is here used in Asaṅga's new sense of a seventh consciousness-type that projects a sense of ego.** Such projections are erroneous in the sense that there is no entity underlying them, and they can be totally removed from the consciousness-aggregate.*** The very sense of ego can be

**Thirty Verses*, 18; *A Discussion for the Demonstration of Action*, 32, on the "store-consciousness'" being only a metaphor for the "seeds"; on "seed's" being a metaphor for "a special force within the "consciousness-series" as a result of an impression, see *Mahāyānasaṅgrahabhāṣya* Tokyo/Peking Tibetan Tripitaka, vol. 112, p 277, 5, 1, on "series" being a metaphor for the genetic relation between aggregate-moments, see *Discussion of the Five Aggregates*, p 71

**Asaṅga, *Mahāyānasaṅgraha* I, 7.

****Thirty Verses*, 7.

discarded. And so can the idea of psychic continuity, once it is seen that every event is unique. And so can the concept of a defined "event", once it is seen that it is a perception without graspable or repeatable characteristics. This means in turn that there are no "own-beings" or "natures" which would warrant the positing of different "types" of "events". "The absence of own-beings" is equivalent to "Emptiness" as this term is used by Nāgārjuna.*

But unless consciousness undergoes "a revolution at the basis" in which Emptiness is realized, consciousness-moments will continue to present what are construed as "objects". This leads Vasubandhu to the conclusion that all non-meditational states (in the very broad sense as defined in *A Discussion of the Five Aggregates*) are constructed. That is, the consciousness-aggregate may statisize experience through the influence of latent impressions. Here we are introduced to the three states which are the heart of Yogācāra therapeutic theory.** These are called "own-beings", but are not ultimately accepted as such, inasmuch as "the fulfilled own-being" is really "the absence of any own-beings". These are rather provisional tools which show the possibility in consciousness-moments to discontinue latent impressions. These three are the "constructed", the "interdependent", and the "fulfilled". Actually, two of these, the "constructed" and the "fulfilled", are states of that basic interdependent reality, "which is without cessation, without arising, without discontinuity, without eternality, neither one object nor many, neither coming or going", as it has been stated by Nāgārjuna.*** The interdependent without the constructed is the fulfilled, i.e. continuance in perception-only is possible. This makes possible the removal of all afflictions, which have arisen only on account of the constructions of consciousness. This state is equated to "the Ground of all Events". It is also equated to the Dharma-body, which is a metaphor for the essence of the Buddha's teachings. As this state is without mental constructions (and as verbal activity is all mental construction), and as it is the "basic" state of consciousness (since all constructions arise only after the cycle of consciousness-

*Nagārjuna, *Vigrahavyāvartanī.*

***Thirty Verses*, 20-25.

***Nāgārjuna, *Mūla-madhyamaka-kārikā*, I 1-2.

latent impression has taken place), the "fulfilled" is ineffable. This is the fundamental point of contact between the philosophies of Nāgārjuna and Vasubandhu. Vasubandhu may be said to retain the Abhidharmika's interest in the moments of psychological processes, as he in general uses a greater number of provisional therapeutic tools. And here he indicates consciousness ability to utterly remove previously-occurring constructions and constrictions.

Concerning the Text :

The Thirty Verses are extant in the original Sanskrit. They were edited by Sylvain Lévi (*Bibliothèque de L'École des Hautes Études*, sciences historiques et philologiques, Librairie Ancienne Honoré Champion, Paris, 1925, volume 241-245). This translation is based on that edition.

THIRTY VERSES
(TRIṂŚIKĀ-KĀRIKĀ)

The metaphors of "self" and "events" which develop in so many different ways
take place in the transformation of consciousness : and this transformation is of three kinds : 1

Maturation, that called "always reflecting", and the perception of sense-objects.
Among these, "maturation" is that called "the store-consciousness" which has all the seeds. 2

Its appropriations, states, and perceptions are not fully conscious,
yet it is always endowed with contacts, mental attentions, feelings, cognitions, and volitions. 3

Its feelings are equaniminous : it is unobstructed and indeterminate.[1]
The same for its contacts, etc. It develops like the currents in a stream. 4

Its de-volvement[2] takes place in a saintly state : Dependent on it there develops
a consciousness called "manas", having it* as its object-of-consciousness,
and having the nature of always reflecting; 5

It is always conjoined with four afflictions, obstructed-but-indeterminate,
known as view of self, confusion of self, pride of self, and love of self. 6

And wherever it arises, so do contact and the others. But it doesn't exist in a saintly state,
or in the attainment of cessation[3], or even in a supermundane path. 7

This is the second transformation. The third is the apprehension

*The store-consciousness.

of sense-objects of six kinds : it is either beneficial,
or unbeneficial, or both. 8

It is always connected with *sarvatragas*[4], and sometimes with
factors that arise specifically,
with beneficial events associated with citta, afflictions, and
secondary afflictions : its feelings are of three kinds.[5] 9

The first* are contact, etc.; those arising specifically are
zest, confidence, memory, concentration, and insight; 10

The beneficial are faith, inner shame, dread of blame.
the three starting with lack of greed**, vigor, tranquility,
carefulness, and non-harming;
the afflictions are attachment, aversion, and confusion, 11

pride, views, and doubts.
The secondary afflictions are anger, malice, hypocrisy,
maliciousness, envy, selfishness, deceitfulness, 12

guile, mischievous exuberance, desire to harm, lack of shame,
lack of dread of blame, mental fogginess, excitedness,
lack of faith, sloth, carelessness, loss of mindfulness, 13

distractedness, lack of recognition, regret, and torpor,
initial mental application, and subsequent discursive
thought : the last two pairs are of two kinds[6]. 14

In the root-consciousness, the arising of the other five takes
place according to conditions,
either all together or not, just like waves in water.[7] 15

The co-arising of a mental consciousness takes place always
except in a non-cognitional state,
or in the two attainments[8], or in torpor, or fainting, or in a
state without citta. 16

This transformation of consciousness is a discrimination, and
as it is discriminated, it does not exist, and so everything
is perception-only.[9] 17

*The *sarvatragas*, see verse 3.
**lack of greed, lack of hostility, lack of confusion.

Consciousness is only all the seeds[10], and transformation
takes palce in such and such a way,
according to a reciprocal influence, by which such and
such a type of discrimination may arise. 18

The residual impressions of actions, along with the residual
impressions of a "dual" apprehension,
cause another maturation (of seeds) to occur,
where the former maturation has been
exhausted. 19

Whatever range of events is discriminated by whatever discrimination
is just the constructed own-being, and it isn't really to
be found.— 20

The interdependent own-being, on the other hand, is the
discrimination which arises from conditions,
and the fulfilled is its* state of being separated always
from the former.** 21

So it is to be spoken of as neither exactly different nor non-
different from the interdependent,
just like impermanence, etc.[11], for when one isn't seen, the
other is.[12] 22

The absence of own-being in all events has been taught with
a view towards
the three different kinds of absence of own-being in the
three different kinds of own-being. 23

The first is without own-being through its character itself,
but the second
because of its non-independence, and the third *is*
absence of own-being. 24

It is the ultimate truth of all events, and so it is "Suchness",
too,
since it is just so all the time, and it's just perception-only. 25

As long as consciousness is not situated within perception-
only,

*the interdependent's. **the constructed.

the residues of a "dual" apprehension will not come to an end. 26

And so even with the consciousness : "All this is perception only",
because this also involves an apprehension,
For whatever makes something stop in front of it isn't situated in "this-only".[13] 27

When consciousness does not apprehend any object-of-consciousness,
it's situated in "consciousness-only",
for with the non-being of an object apprehended, there is no apprehension of it. 28

It is without citta, without apprehension, and it is supermundane knowledge;
It is revolution at the basis[14], the ending of two kinds of susceptibility to harm.[15] 29

It is the inconceivable, beneficial, constant Ground, not liable to affliction,
bliss, and the liberation-body called the Dharma-body of the Sage. 30

NOTES

1. cf. *Discussion for the Demonstration of Action*, note 43.

2. "Revolution at the basis" is the undoing of the particular hold of latent impressions ("habit-energies")—thus it is the dis-evolvement of the store-consciousness, which is only a metaphor for these. This means that all colorations given by particular "seeds", and all "habit-energies", will be eliminated, and there's only an awareness of whatever the moment actually presents.

3. The attainment of the cessation of feelings and cognitions, cf. *Discussion of the Five Aggregates*, p. 70; and the discussions on this meditational state throughout the *Discussion for a Demonstration of Action.*

4. The "sarvatragas" are those motivating dispositions that occur in every citta, and thus equivalent to Ghoṣaka's "mahābhūmikas", cf. *Discussion for a Demonstration of Action,* note 41. The "sarvatragas" admitted by Vasubandhu are those motivating dispositions enumerated in verse 3: contacts, mental attentions, feelings, cognitions, and volitions. These exist even for states of the store-consciousness or latent impressions themselves.

5. Pleasure, suffering, and that which is neither pleasure nor suffering, for definitions, see *Discussion of the Five Aggregates*, p 66.

6. Regret, torpor, initial mental application, and subsequent discursive thought may be either afflicted, or not.

7. The multiplicity of waves in water depends on the force of the prior agitation in the water: in the same way the extent to which the evolving con-

sciousnesses occur depends on the force of prior agitation in the citta-series.

8. The attainment free from cognitions and the attainment of the cessation of feelings and cognitions, see *Discussion of the Five Aggregates*, p 70.

9. That is, any instance of the mental consciousness involves discrimination, and speaking of a "mental consciousness" rests on discrimination. From the point of view (or non-point of view) of "revolution at the basis", all discriminations are voided. Hence this transformation of consciousness ceases on two grounds : (1) since there are no more discriminations, "mental consciousness" isn't discriminated, (2) since there are no more discriminations, discriminating mental consciousness doesn't occur. Since this transformation really doesn't exist, then, from the point of view or non-point of view of "revolution at the basis", everything that exists is pure undiscriminated perception-only.

10. It is only the presence of seeds, or the absence of seeds, that makes for states of discrimination, or states of non-discrimination. Again it is said, as at *Discussion for the Demonstration of Action*, 32, that consciousness is really only aggregations of latent impressions or "seeds".

11. Impermanence is neither exactly the interdependent (which looked at "as a whole" may not be impermament), nor does it exist anywhere except in the interdependent. Actually, neither the constructed nor the fulfilled are exactly different or non-different from the interdependent, since the constructed is basically the interdependent constructed and constricted, and the fulfilled is basically the interdependent unconstructed and unconstricted.

12. The interdependent is "discrimination which arises from conditions" in the sense that though, for instance, the concept of the aggregate of consciousnesses is a construction, inasmuch as this discrimination rests on real interdependent conditions, it is of the interdependent nature. (cf. *Commentary on the Separation of the Middle from Extremes* ad, III, 16.) Now as long as even these interdependent discriminations persist, the fulfilled, revolution at the basis, has not yet occurred. When the fulfilled occurs, even those discriminations vanish. Of course, in a fulfilled state, there will not be any discrimination of "fulfilled", either.

13. As long as consciousness isn't flowing with perception-only, there will be residues of dualistic and constructing apprehension. But the consciousness "All this is perception-only" is also not to be indulged in, since it itself involves a dualistic apprehension. Any grasping at the flow is itself not immersement in the flow. Really being in perception-only means being in "this-only", whatever the present perception presents, without the tunications of past impressions, expectations, or the desire to make something stop still.

14. "Revolution at the basis" is where all constructions are shed, all mental borders are shattered, all past "habit-energies" re-directed. It is the same as the realization of Emptiness, where all boundaries between "one" and "the other" cease.

15. The two kinds of susceptibility to harm are susceptibility to harm through the afflictions themselves, and susceptibility to harm through the obstructions of the knowable. (See *Commentary on the Separation of the Middle from Extremes*, II.)

COMMENTARY ON THE SEPARATION OF THE MIDDLE FROM EXTREMES
(MADHYĀNTA-VIBHĀGA-BHĀṢYA)

INTRODUCTION

This is one of the several commentaries Vasubandhu wrote on texts ascribed to Maitreyanātha transmitted to him by Asaṅga. It is a gradual peeling-away of "illusions", a concrete indication of alleviating practises, and the dissolving of these also as discriminations not to be clung to : It is a most conscientious series of expedients for afflictions human beings are prone to fall into—and in this it is ever-widening, and directed at ever-widening levels of insight. So it is not surprising that some statements in this work seem on first sight inconsistent with one another, since they are expedients directed at different problems, at different stages of insight. For instance, at I. 4 b, it is said that the facts of affliction and alleviation cannot be denied; in the last chapter, these terms lose all true meaning.

The title of the treatise itself is interesting. The Buddha in his first sermon* said that his was a Middle Path, steering clear of the extremes of desire for life and desire for death. Six centuries later Nāgārjuna called his philosophy "that of the Middle" (Madhyamaka), as in it there is neither desire for Saṃsāra nor desire for Nirvāṇa, since both are indistinguishable.** And, here, two centuries later, in this work of Maitreyanātha and Vasubandhu, there is "the separation of the Middle from extremes". As Vasubandhu interprets Maitreyanātha's list of "extremes"***, an extreme turns out to be any rigid assertion. So Vasubandhu's "Middle" is not so different from Nāgārjuna's since both wish to rid consciousness of fixed views, which invariably lead to suffering. Nāgārjuna's method for doing this is to reduce all the possible alternatives regarding causality, etc. to absurdities, so that finally nothing can be asserted at all. Vasubandhu's method is much more gradual, since layers of therapeutic theories are expounded, each one dissolving the next, none of which retains a literal significance once they have attained their aim. Both Nāgārjuna's *Mūla-madhyamaka-kārikā*

* *Saṃyutta* V. 421-3.

** *Mūla-madhyamaka-kārikā*, XXV, 19.

*** *Commentary on the Separation of the Middle from Extremes*, ad V 23-26.

and Vasubandhu's *Madhyānta-vibhāga-bhāṣya* can be called "Śūnyavāda", for both finally assert nothing. But Vasubandhu's work is also "Yogācāra", in its fundamental sense of delineating a therapeutic course of action (*ācāra*) rooted in meditation (*yoga*). In this capacity, it is extremely succinct, telescoping methods for psychological transformation. It has been regarded in the Tibetan tradition as one of the chief sources for the description of a meditational practise.* It has thus also a phenomenological, or Abhidharmika, side, in wishing to present a therapeutic course in terms of moment-events. So there is a delicate balance here of the two main "ingredients" in Mahāyāna enlightenment : *upāya* (skill in expedient methods : "skill in means") and *prajñā* (fundamental insight in which all dualities vanish, and only ineffable "Suchness" remains). There is an intense interest here in realizing the ideal of the Bodhisattva, and also in being grounded nowhere**, in explaining the processes by which human beings become ensnared and the methods by which they can be alleviated, only to deny that such dualities fundamentally exist, and in outlining a spiritual path only to shatter the last dualities that lie behind the assumption of the possibility of one. Given Vasubandhu's relegation of all verbal formulations to the constructed "own-being", being such a series of therapeutic aids is the best thing a theory can be, since no theory is ultimately true, and all are finally abandoned. The state of realizing the Emptiness of all events is to Vasubandhu, as well as to Nāgārjuna, a state where all mental constructions dividing reality into discrete entities are absent, and there is a seeing of everything "as it really is". But this state by definition allows for no more statements.

Nāgārjuna posits only two kinds of truth, conventional and ultimate. It is here where Vasubandhu may argue. For a dual truth-scheme perhaps does not make the existence of confusion and suffering "real" enough. Vasubandhu's expedient of dividing reality into three, rather than two, fulfils this purpose. The constructed is that which is seemingly fixed, ordered,

* Ṅag-dbaṅ-dar-rgyas, *Lam-rim-man-ṅag* (transmitted and transcribed by Sherpa Tulku and Khamlung Tulku, translated by Alexander Berzin), typescript, p. 16.

** According to the *Aṣṭasāhasrikā-prajñā-pāramitā*, the two are the same.

and static. It exists only because of a propensity in the interdependent to become "a construction of that which was not" (*abhūta-parikalpa*). This term could also be rendered "a construction of the unreal", since the Sanskrit word "*abhūta*" comes to mean "unreal", and it is in fact so rendered by the Chinese and Tibetan translators.* But this translation ignores the peculiar manner in which this term is used in this treatise, and makes impossible puns which Vasubandhu himself makes on "*bhūta*" and "*abhūta*".** In fact, for Vasubandhu any duality "real/unreal" cannot exist. It would be "an extreme relating to being and non-being".*** What the construction of that which was not constructs is something which "was not" before it was mentally constructed, which "is" as long as it is believed, and which "isn't" as soon as it is dropped from consciousness. Reliance on these mentally constructed events, or any attempt to force experience to fit them, is bound to lead to all kinds of anguish. A state where their constricting hold is no longer felt is however possible, and so it is said that "the fulfilled is the interdependent without the constructed".****

The entire moment-event framework of such works as *A Discussion of the Five Aggregates* and *A Discussion for the Demonstration of Action* is employed here as a theoretical substratum for what is initially an art of mental alleviation. Suppose Vasubandhu meets an "individual" who is filled with all kinds of anxieties. Whatever they are, it is certain that they are linked with some sort of self-view. Occidental psychiatric practise would perhaps look for origins, and would attempt to categorize the "individual's" reactions symptomatically. "You are doing this, therefore you are in such-and-such a category, and this is what you should do"—no doubt take a drug—behind all such expressed and unexpressed notions, the roots of the "individual's" sufferings remain unchallenged. The "individual's" basic premise, that "he" is in fact an individual (clearly of one or another type), set within an environment in some way in opposition to "him", is never questioned. But all Vasu-

* 虛 妄 分 別 *yaṅ-dag-pa-ma-yin-pa'i-kun-tu-rtogs-pa*

** *Commentary on the Separation of the Middle from Extremes, ad* V 23-26.

*** *Separation of the Middle from Extremes,* V 25.

**** *Thirty Verses,* 21.

bandhu would be willing to admit, and even this he would admit only tentatively, is that here is a "stream" of suffering. And for the suffering to be alleviated, the entire outlook must be changed. Meditation will help, but not at the outset. "Reversals", meaning such mental habits that lead invariably to suffering, must first be removed, before the meditational course can be embarked on with any good results.*

Among these "reversals", the notion of "self", "ego", or "I" itself is one of the foremost, and means to destroy this view occupy Vasubandhu in large parts of chapter III. In the theory which Vasubandhu finds provisionally most therapeutically fruitful, what are called "individuals" are streams of psycho-physical moment-aggregations, and nothing is fixed or static. The anxieties caused by "self-categorization" rest on a colossal distortion, and it is the commonness of such distortions that makes Vasubandhu say, at least temporarily, that there is a force inherent in the world which accounts for them.

But it is not only the notion of "self", but the distinction between the perceiver and what is perceived, which gives rise to the constructed. So this text begins by saying that this distinction is itself constructed. None of the dualities from which it grows are anything more than "a construction of that which was not", and they can be removed completely from consciousness.

From here on it is already quite impossible to talk. A mental attention towards talk is always suffused with an implicit grasped/grasper dichotomy.** The emptiness of whatever object of consciousness a Bodhisattva might resort to is included in Vasubandhu's "emptiness of ultimate truth". And the attainment of an unafflicted Nirvāṇa/Saṃsāra is the only excuse for resorting to them.***

In spite of his thorough "commitment to Emptiness", Vasubandhu, unlike Nāgārjuna in his stricter works, is not reluctant to tell us his intentions. The mere removal of sufferings due to constructions may be enough for the anxiety-ridden "individual" who has visited Vasubandhu earlier. But for Vasubandhu himself, this results in a great transformation, which affects

* *Commentary on the Separation of the Middle from Extremes*, ad II, 9.
** ad V, 16.
*** ad I, 17.

all aspects of life. Vasubandhu wants to see as close an adherence to the Bodhisattva-ideal as is possible. The second chapter of this treatise, which deals with obstructions to the realization of this ideal, then naturally follows upon the first, where "mental constructions, fears, inactivity, and doubts have been brought to complete rest".

From a certain point of view, the new chapter may contain more constructed dichotomies than the first. Nonetheless, it is clear that a progression is intended, in fact the step from a "Path of Seeing", where the blatant confusions of the mental consciousness are removed, to a "Path of Cultivation", where afflictions are eliminated. Now concepts are brought up not because they are believed in, but because they correspond to practises effective in removing the obstructions of the knowable.

In the fulfilled life-stream, there is neither agitation nor complacency. Agitation does not allow for the calm necessary in face of the disagreeable and hostile, and complacency is clearly an obstacle to passion, compassion, and energy. The ancient list of "fetters" makes its appearance as kinds of obstructions, but with some changes. Significantly, excitedness, lust for sensuous pleasures, desire for experiences in the realm of images, and desire for experiences in the imageless sphere, have been dropped, and a much more explicit break-down of what was earlier simply called "ill-will"(*vyāpāda*) is given, in the form of envy, selfish greed, and basic aversion. The additional obstructions enumerated by Maitreyanātha, verses II 4-8, and further elucidated by Vasubandhu, show by their contrasts many of the characteristics of the ideal desired. But it is significant that Vasubandhu does not delimit a goal with strings of "should's"—this would be too much construction, and too much construction of dubious *upāya* value. Rather, he concentrates on a delimitation of obstructions, which are all given as motivating disposition-type events. In a Mahāyāna life-stream, there is confidence, satisfaction with very little, lack of concern with any type of gain, there is tremendous compassion, there is no lack of activity, there is the full taking up of Saṃsāra, sense-fields are used to an ultimate extent, there is enormous capacity to evolve, and skill in the Mahāyāna *upāyas* and meditations.

But what is the relation between this ideal and the fulfilled own-being ? The fulfilled own-being has been defined only as the absence of the constructed, and here we have a constructed set of transformations being recommended. But this path is presented only in relation to the removal of obstructions to the fulfilled : that is, the path is again a construction tentatively acted upon in order to effect the removal of constructions.

There is a hint of a further reason for the necessity of the cultivation of such attitudes in chapter three. Each of the three own-beings is connected with the Truth of Suffering. Suffering exists in the constructed, because of the clinging that comes through adherence to views of "personalities" and "events". Suffering exists in the interdependent, because of the basic characteristics of the world itself. But suffering exists also in the fulfilled, "because of connection with suffering".* This last phrase would seem to indicate a *voluntary* connection with the sufferings of Saṃsāra, even after the natures of the constructed and interdependent have been realized. So, even though the fulfilled is freed from any of those sufferings which arise unchecked with adherence to the constructed, it is still involved, and voluntarily so, in the suffering "of others". And in such a context, the necessity of renewing the steps of the path becomes evident. The obstructions to the full taking up of Saṃsāra might present themselves over and over again, no matter whether the "practitioner" has "gone through" the entire meditational program.

As a matter of fact, it is one thing to practise the applications of mindfulness with "one's own" body, feelings, consciousness-moments, and cognizables as the meditational objects—this is done by any "Hīnayāna" practitioner—but it is quite another thing to apply them to "others'" bodies, cittas, etc. And this is stated by Vasubandhu to be a salient feature of the Bodhisattva's practise.**So meditation cannot be something done exclusively or even mainly in isolation : One is to Mahāyānistically meditate in the marketplace, with everything that comes along seen for what it is. "One" is suffused with a one-pointed-

*ad III, 6.
**ad IV, 13 a

ness of consciousness, "outer" as well as "inner" directed, as "one" is walking down the street. With the absence of any felt distinction between perceived and perceiver, an extraordinary openness of consciousness results.

A certain more strictly meditational technique is needed. So Vasubandhu speaks of other obstructions which relate directly to the meditational process itself. One-pointedness of consciousness is at first most disturbed by slackness and excitedness. Concentration must be maintained, but on the other hand, any agitation or tenseness must be avoided.* When the applications of mindfulness, which stand at the basis of all further meditations here, have been practised, the four right efforts can be pursued for the arising of beneficial mental events and the removal of unbeneficial ones. Then, for complete mastery in meditational concentration, the four bases of psychic power—zest, vigor, consciousness, and exploration, are raised in relation to various flaws in meditation.**

Then the factors conducive to penetration may be tried.*** These are a special series of intellective meditations. One begins by "coming to heat", with meditating first on the impermanence of events, then upon the absence, in reality, of a rise and fall in those events, then upon the realization that all the "Truths" are only constructs. In the next stage, the "Summit", all mental marks vanish. Because the next state is suffused with forbearance, because all aversion-causing constructions have been shattered, it is called "forbearance". The "highest mundane events" which follow is a condition where all the personality-factors "of the practitioner", and everything "around her or him", have merged into meditational concentration, and "one" contemplates the non-arising of "own-beings" in any "inner" or "outer" events. At the end of this process, there is no more discrimination of any type within the meditational concentration.****

But eventually "one" has to come out of completely signless meditation, and then subtle agitations may present themselves

*ad IV, 4.
**ad IV, 5b-6a.
***ad IV, 8.
**** Maitreyanātha, *Abhisamayālaṅkāra*, I 25-34 ff.

again. Their delimitations, and their antidotes, are given by Vasubandhu with medical precision. Not everyone will have all the agitations he enumerates, as many of them depend on specific attitudes towards the meditational course itself. Thus "agitation due to mental marks" rests on a deliberate intention in "one's" meditation, which is a flaw. Vasubandhu simply enumerates different possibilities. And constructions to shatter constructions of this subtler kind are built, and immediately dismantled.* The Vajra Words, and the delimitation of "extremes" to be avoided, culminate this ever-widening shedding of prior ways of looking, until finally the very last dualities of all, such as those of "affliction" and "alleviation", "rightness" and "wrongness", "practise" and "non-practise" are totally discarded.

The factors conducive to penetration constitute a "Path of (Initial) Application" : it is preceded by "A Path of Preparation", which includes the "factors conducive to liberation" : faith in the validity of the basic direction of Buddhist practise, vigor, mindfulness, meditational concentration and insight in their first conscious occurrences. The factors conducive to penetration can be applied to the applications of mindfulness, those basic meditations on body, feelings, consciousness-moments, and all moment-events together. "The Path of Initial Application" is followed by "A Path of Seeing", involving the specifically Mahāyāna way of looking at phenomena. "The Path of Seeing", in turn, is followed by "The Path of Cultivation", where all afflictions are gradually removed. It corresponds to most of the stages in a Bodhisattva's career.

Since a knowledge of these "Paths" and "stages" is presupposed in the *Commentary on the Separation of the Middle from Extremes*, it might be good to give an outline of them here. They are part of a heritage Vasubandhu received. It should be noted, however, that in this treatise itself, these "paths" and "stages" are discussed, though in an extremely compressed form.

The Mahāyāna path begins with the arising of an enlightenment-citta, the first consciousness-moment directed at enlightenment. It is a desire for supreme enlightenment for the welfare

*ad V. 12-21.

of others.* From the very beginning, this is the emphasis of Mahāyāna : that enlightenment is of value only if it results in the alleviation of others' sufferings. The Mahāyānistic Bodhisattva is "one" who "does not go into Nirvāṇa", but rather "stays in Saṃsāra for the alleviation of the sufferings of others", motivated by a great compassion. Asaṅga describes the arising of the enlightenment-citta as occurring after four conditions have arisen. The first he describes as follows : "Here a son of the community or a daughter of the community sees the unthinkable and marvellous power of a Buddha or a Bodhisattva in drawing out (afflictions), or hears about it in the presence of one who has experienced it...He or she then becomes confident in regard to the possibility of becoming enlightened, and gives rise to a citta directed at the great enlightenment."** This citta is the first resolve of the Bodhisattva, to attain enlightenment no longer how difficult it may be, or how long it will take. The second condition is the arising of a citta where one has seen or heard of the depth of the Mahāyāna writings, a citta which is confident in, and resolves to attain, a Buddha's knowledge. Just as "enlightenment" is linked with "insight", "knowledge" can be linked with "skill in means", because what is meant here by "knowledge" are all the worldly expedients for alleviation, many of which are included in Mahāyāna literature. This citta is thus the second resolve of a Bodhisattva, to learn all Mahāyāna texts and expedient methods, no matter how innumerable they are. The "third condition" is the arising of a citta which considers that staying in the path of a Bodhisattva for a long time would help sentient beings remove their countless sufferings. This citta is the third resolve of a Bodhisattva, to help remove the sufferings of all sentient beings, however immeasurable they may be. The "fourth condition" is again a citta directed at the sufferings of sentient beings, where it is considered how they are tormented by the afflictions. One resolves to impart the same training one is undergoing to others, so that they too can rid themselves of afflictions and become enlightened.*** This is the fourth resolve of a Bodhisattva, to

* Maitreyanātha, *Abhisamayālaṅkāra*, I, 18-20.

** Asaṅga, *Bodhisattvabhūmi* II, p. 9 (Nalinaksha Dutt ed.)

*** Ibid, II, p. 10.

lead others to enlightenment, no matter how difficult this may be. The enlightenment-citta is thus the first citta directed at attaining enlightenment "oneself". It is accompanied by the first arising-together of the "factors conducive to liberation"*, and is also called "the Path of Preparation".

The Path of Initial Application" which follows is known as "the stage where confidence is cultivated"(*adhimukti-caryā-bhūmi*).** It is connected with the first arising of "the factors conducive to penetration", discussed above.*** The first of these meditative states "coming to heat", has in its weak state as its meditational object the impermanence of all events, without considering that separate events exist.**** In its medium state, it has as its meditational object the lack of an arising and perishing in the events of the aggregates, without considering them as either continuous or discontinuous.***** In its strong state, the truths of "impermanence", etc. are seen to be mere designations, and it is realized that they cannot be expressed in words.‡

In the weak state of the "Summits", the object is not to make a view of the aggregates, and also the absence of own-being in them. A common state of own-being for both the aggregates and the emptiness of all events is realized.‡‡ The medium state focuses on emptiness, where all notions of "own-being" cease.‡‡‡ The strong state, following immediately upon this, is that there is no more looking at signs, and there is "an investigation by insight into the absence of the apprehension of anything."‡‡‡‡

The state of "forbearance" means that there is an absence of anger or impatience towards events that are seemingly hostile, which forbearance is made possible by the realization that

*p. 202.

***Commentary on the Separation of the Middle from Extermes*, ad IV 14, ad V 3.

***Haribhadra, *Abhisamayālaṅkārāloka*, ad I, 19

****Maitreyanātha, *Abhisamayālaṅkāra*, I, 28.

*****Ibid., I 29a.

‡Ibid., I 29a.

‡‡Ibid., I 29 c-30a

‡‡‡Ibid., I 30b.

‡‡‡‡Paraphrase of Conze's translation of *Abhisamayālaṅkāra*, I 31b

since all events are empty of "own-being", they do not really arise and perish at all. The weak state has as its object of meditation the absence of own-being in the aggregates, the medium the absence of arising and perishing, and the strong the absence of signs.*

In the "highest mundane events", the meditative concentration following on the absence of apprehension of any signs, there is no longer an object of meditation, and the meditative state itself is not discriminated.** The series of the factors conducive to penetration is also called "the stage where confidence is cultivated", because when one experiences them, confidence in the possibility of attaining complete enlightenment is nurtured.

The "highest mundane events" are immediately*** followed by the meditational concentration which constitutes "the Path of Seeing". It consists of sixteen moments only, and is equivalent to the development of higher vision(*vipaśyanā*), i.e. insight (*prajñā*). The first moment is "the forbearance for the knowledge of a moment-event in suffering" (*duḥkhe dharma-jñāna-kṣānti*). It involves no perception of the separate existence of the moment-event, but rather the realization of the identity of the aggregates and Suchness (Emptiness).****The second moment, "Knowledge of a moment-event in suffering", focuses on the impossibility of there being any knowledge through mental discourse.*****The third moment, "forbearance for a subsequent knowledge in suffering", focuses on the measurelessness of events. The fourth, "subsequent knowledge in suffering", focuses on the absence of limitations in events. The fifth, "forbearance for the knowledge of a moment-event in the

**Abhisamayālaṅkāra*, I 32a-33a.

**Ibid, I 34a.

***Haribhadra, *Abhisamayālaṅkārāloka*, ad II 10 b : "*Sa* (darśana-mārga) ca samāsato laukikāgradharmasya samanantaram anupalambhaḥ samādhiḥ."

****This is found in the *Pañcaviṃśatisāhasrikā-prajñā-pāramitā* as the identity of the Suchness of the aggregates with the Buddha. But the *Hṛdayaprajñā-pāramitā's* equivalence of the aggregates to Emptiness is basically the same, and perhaps clearer.

*****This is the correct translation of Maitreyanātha's "paryāyeṇānanujñānam". II (III), 12. Conze's translation is faulty here.

origination of suffering", focuses on the absence of extremes in all events.* This "absence of extremes" is discussed in detail in this treatise.** The sixth moment of the Path of Seeing, "knowledge of a moment-event in the origination of suffering", involves an accurate determination of the aggregates, which finds in them all a basically unafflicted character.*** The seventh moment, "forbearance through a subsequent knowledge in the origination of suffering", involves the not taking up and the not abandoning of anything.**** In the eighth moment, the "subsequent knowledge in the origination of suffering", there is an intense focus on "the unlimited" : compassion, rejoicing at the joy of others, loving kindness, and equanimity.‡ In the ninth, "forbearahce for the knowledge of a moment-event in the cessation of suffering", emptiness is seen as the nature of all the aggregates. Hence their suffering is "adventitious", not arising inevitably with the events. The tenth moment, "knowledge of a moment-event in the cessation of suffering", leads "to the attainment of the state of a Buddha".‡‡ Maitreyanātha equates it to the moment when it is known that the aggregates do not bring about anything that was apprehended.‡‡‡ The eleventh, "forbearance for a subsequent knowledge in a cessation of suffering" is the taking hold of, or encompassing‡‡‡‡ of all alleviations, and is linked, in the "esoteric" explanation Maitreyanātha gives later in the *Abhisamayālaṅkāra*, with realization of the fundamental lack of afflictions in all the aggregates.‡‡‡‡‡ The twelfth moment, "a subsequent knowledge in a cessation of suffering", focuses on "the removal of all diseases and injuries"; "esoterically", again, it is the knowledge that no diseases and injuries arise for aggregates.‡‡‡‡‡‡ The thirteenth, "forbearance for the

**Abhisamayālaṅkāra* II (III). 13.
**ad V, 26.
***Ibid, II (III), 13.
****Ibid, II (III), 13, end.
‡Ibid, II (III), 13.
‡‡Ibid, II (III), 13.
‡‡‡"Nopalabdhakṛt", *Abhisamayālaṅkāra*, III (IX), 14.
‡‡‡‡This relates to the "encompassing" in this treatise, V, ad 3.
‡‡‡‡‡*Abhisamayālaṅkāra* III (IX), 14.
‡‡‡‡‡‡Ibid, II (III) 14; III (IX), 14.

knowledge of a moment-event in a path that leads to the cessation of suffering", any grasping after Nirvāṇa is brought to an end.* In the fourteenth, "knowledge of a moment-event in a path leading to the cessation of suffering", there is no discrimination about the realization of a fruition.** In the fifteenth, "forbearance through a subsequent knowledge in a path leading to the cessation of suffering", there is, founded on no more harming to any living being, a leading of sentient beings to the knowledge of all aspects***; esoterically, there is no connection with any cognitional signs.**** The sixteenth moment, "subsequent knowledge in the path" is the great transformation to put sentient beings into an alleviating path‡, and is, esoterially, the non-arising of knowledge itself.‡‡

When non-dual Emptiness is known in the Path of Seeing, it is possible to remove all obstructions gradually in a Path of Cultivation, which directs itself to "calm"(*śamatha*). These obstructions are discussed in detail by Vasubandhu‡‡‡, and their antidotes are also fully described.‡‡‡‡ The necessity of "reiterating" steps of the Path is given by Maitreyanātha, where he states that repeated reflections on emptiness, the factors conducive to penetration, and on the Path of Seeing, occur on the Path of Cultivation.‡‡‡‡‡

**Abhisamayālaṅkāra*, II (III), 15.
**Ibid, III (IX), 14.
***Ibid, II (III), 15.
****Ibid, III (IX), 15.
‡Ibid, II (III), 16.
‡‡Ibid, III (IX), 15.

The "exoteric" and "esoteric" explanations of the Path of Seeing, as given by Maitreyanātha are equivalent to looking at in both as a path involving successions of kinds of knowledge needed for alleviation, as well as an unfolding of the basic Emptiness, non-affliction, and ineffability of everything, which relates to insight (*prajñā*). Such a dual interpretation of a part of the Path is to be found already in two works by Aśvaghoṣa on the enlightenment-citta. In the "conventional" description, skill in means relating to motivational dispositions towards enlightenment are discussed; in the "ultimate", the emptiness of everything is revealed. (Aśvaghoṣa, *Saṃvṛtibodhicittabhāvanopadeśa-varṇasaṅgraha*, and *Paramārthabodhicittabhāvanākramavarṇasaṅgraha*, Peking/Tokyo Tibetan Tripitaka, volume 102, pp 18-19.

‡‡‡*Commentary on the Separation of the Middle from Extremes*, II
‡‡‡‡Ibid, IV.
‡‡‡‡‡*Abhisamayālaṅkāra* III (XVIII), 53.

After all obstructions have been removed, there is only "the Path of the Accomplished", those who have nothing further in which to train themselves. The Path of Cultivation is thus also equivalent to the second through the last stages of a Bodhisattva's career, the first stage being regarded as the last moment in the Path of Seeing.

These stages are the complete development of the *Pāramitās*, those events to be cultivated "to the utmost extent".* The first stage, that of giving to others "cultivated to its utmost extent", is called by Vasubandhu "the all-encompassing", because it involves an understanding of the fundamental sameness of "self" and "others",** In the Mahāyāna sūtra which most fully discusses these stages, it is called "filled with love in helping everyone",***

The second stage is directed at ethical conduct towards others "to the utmost extent". This means "no harming of any sentient being".‡ Asaṅga discusses this *pāramitā* in detail,‡‡ and shows how this "non-harming" may sometimes have to be suspended in the interests of compassion. For instance, if there is a king or minister who is continually torturing his subjects, it will be part of ethical conduct to topple the government, even through violent means if necessary.‡‡‡ Because non-action in this case will just mean that so much unnecessary suffering will just continue. In the latest version of the *Suvarṇa-prabhāsa-sūtra*, there is an interesting statement which says that the main hindrance on the second stage consists in the ignorance which lets different kinds of harmful acts arise without one's knowing it.‡‡‡‡

*cf. *Abhisamayālaṅkāra* I 49-71.

** *Commentary on the Sepration of the Middle from Extremes,* ad II, 14-16, see also the "sattveṣu samacittatā" of *Abhisamayālaṅkāra* I 49.

*** "Sarvopakaraṇasneha", *Daśabhūmika-sūtra,* I, Rahder, p 13, Vaidya p 9.

‡*Commentary on the Separation of the Middle from Extremes,* ad V 5

‡‡*Bodhisattvabhūmi,* X, pp 95-129.

‡‡‡Ibid, X, p 114: "Yathāpi tad-bodhisattvo bhavati rāja-mahāmātrā vā ye sattvā rājāno vā adhimātraraudrāḥ sattveṣu nirdayā ekānta-para-pīḍā-pravṛttāḥ. Tāṃ satyāṃ śaktau tasmād rājyaiśvaryādhipatyāc cyavayati yatra sthitās te tan-nidānaṃ bahu-puṇyaṃ prasavanti anukampā-citto hita-sukhāśayāḥ."

‡‡‡‡*Suvarṇaprabhāsa-sūtra,* (I-tsing translation), 4, VI.

The third stage is that of "forbearance to the utmost extent". This means, as Vasubandhu tells us, primarily the pardoning of any harm done to "one" by others.* The *Daśabhūmika-sūtra* gives practical instructions as to how this *pāramitā* can be used to lessen pain even when "one" is being tortured. For instead of getting angry and hateful towards the torturer, which would only increase the pain, "one" focuses on the susceptibility to harm of the bodily elements, on how the torturers themselves are mentally tormented, and how this is but a fraction of the suffering of the world.** "One" can also meditationally focus upon the rise and fall of the moments of suffering.***

The fourth is the stage of vigor, particularly that vigor directed towards "the increase of alleviating qualities".**** With deep psychological insight, Vasubandhu links it with "the aim of non-grasping, for here even the craving for Dharma is abandoned".***** The *Suvarṇa-prabhāsa,* in a similar vein, states that one of its main hindrances is the ignorance that makes one indulge in too-frequent enjoyment of meditation, which makes compassionate action impossible.****** In Vasubandhu's great *Commentary on the Daśabhūmika,* he states that a focus on antidotes to occurring situations of suffering is one of the main features of this stage.*******

The fifth is the stage of "meditation to an utmost extent". On the basic techniques of meditation, Vasubandhu has quite a bit to say in this work. The *Suvarṇa-prabhāsa* again has an interesting warning, that one of the main hindrances on this stage is the ignorance that makes one "turn one's back on Saṃsāra and strive for Nirvāna".********

The sixth stage is that of insight "to its utmost extent", the realization of Emptiness.********* The seventh is that of skill in

**Commentary on the Separation of the Middle from Extremes,* ad V, 6.

***Daśabhūmika-sūtra,* III, V. p 20 (R, p 33).

***Ibid, III, V., p 19 (R., p 31).

*****Commentary on the Separation of the Middle from Extremes,* ad V, 6.

*****Ibid, ad II 14-16.

*******Suvarṇaprabhāsa-sūtra,* 4, VI.

********Daśabhūmivyākhyāna*, Peking/Tokyo Tibetan Tripitaka, volume 104, p 97, 4.

*********Suvarṇa-prabhāsa-sūtra,* 4, VI.

**********Commentary on the Separation of the Middle from Extremes,* ad II, 14

means. Whereas the previous stage is linked with "a supermundane seeing", this one is connected with "a worldly supermundane subsequently attained seeing",* and involves all the expedient means necessary to be effective in the alleviation of suffering. An obstruction on this stage, Vasubandhu says, is an unafflicted ignorance "which counter-acts the aim of a lack of diversity, for there is a lack of dealing with any diversity of mental signs in the events spoken of in the sūtras, etc.,"** the sūtras and other writings being repositories of expedient methods. Interestingly enough, the *Suvarṇa-prabhāsa* makes its hindrance on this stage the ignorance that makes one rejoice in a mental state free from signs.*** For if there is only a continuous abiding in a *prajñā-state*, there would be no return to the cognitional world, a world "used" in the stage of expedient methods.

The eighth, ninth, and tenth stages all deal with the transformation to complete enlightenment. The eighth is the stage of having brought about the resolves of the Bodhisattva to their utmost extent.****It is linked by Vasubandhu to "potency in the absence of discriminations" and "potency in the total clearing of the Buddha-field."***** The ninth is the stage of the powers : power in faith, power in vigor, power in mindfulness, power in meditational concentration, and power in insight; in this work, all these are linked to "potency in knowledge". The tenth stage, that of knowledge itself, is "the state for the basis of a potency in action", and involves all mundane and supermundane knowledges for the alleviation of suffering, in short, complete enlightenment.******

It is admitted by Vasubandhu that any description of the fruitions of the Mahāyāna path is impossible, "for in their full extent they are immeasurable."******* The events described

**Commentary on the Separation of the Middle from Extremes*, ad IV, 9b-10a.

**Ibid, ad II 14-16.

****Suvarṇa-prabhāsa-sūtra*, 4, VI, 1.

****On the resolves, see this introduction, p 201.

******Commentary on the Separation of the Middle from Extremes*, ad II, 14-16, end.

*******Daśabhūmika-sūtra* X. "Knowledge" is linked to "skill in means", by Vasubandhu in *Daśabhūmivyākhyāna*, p 109, 3, line 6.

*******ad IV, 18.

in the Path are also beyond any discussion of them, for "these may occur in many different ways."* Descriptions of a Path are at best schematizations of a sequence of events always totally unique. Nor is there really any possibility of a path leading to enlightenment, since engagement in a practise would be being bound by a construction.** Insight arises spontaneously, and may do so in one moment.*** These descriptions are "skill in means" for the alleviation of suffering. "Aimlessness" does not mean a lack of desire to ease suffering, as Vasubandhu says elsewhere. And yet this desire is tempered by the absence of a cognition of "self" and "others", and this absence of cognition in turn by the absence of the very notions of "being" and "non-being".****

Any dualistic view is finally rejected, and this includes the duality afflicted/alleviated.***** There is no detriment in what is termed "affliction", no excellence in what is termed "alleviation". For all these terms are but mental constructions. To say that anything *was* is an extreme of superimposition regarding events; to say that anything *wasn't* is an extreme of denial. Thus, anyone's view of reality is equally real and equally unreal. Everything that is commonly designated as "real" has its admixture of confusion, and many events commonly designated "unreal" yet have their effects.

Vasubandhu is confident, however, that fundamentally afflictions are secondary and the result of mental construction, whereas the essential "Ground of all events" is basically pure and undisturbed.

Concerning the Text :

The Sanskrit original for *The Commentary on the Separation of the Middle from Extremes* is extant, and has been edited several times in recent years. The most scholarly edition is that of the eminent Gadjin Nagao (*Madhyāntavibhāga-bhāṣya*, Suzuki Research Foundation, Tokyo, 1964).

*ad IV, 14.

**ad V, 23-26, second example of the oil-lamp.

***Ibid, cf. ad III, 22a, and *Abhisamayālaṅkāra*, VII 1-5.

*****Daśabhūmivyākhyāna*, p 106, 3, 3-4, 1.

******Commentary on the Separation of the Middle from Extremes*, ad V 23-26.

Almost contemporaneous with it is the edition of Nathmal Tatia and Anantalal Thakur (*Madhyānta-vibhāga-bhāṣya*, Tibetan Sanskrit Works Series, published under the Patronage of the Government of Bihar, K.P. Jayaswal Research Institute, Patna, 1967), which also has its merits. This translation is based on both these editions, with reference being made also to the Tibetan translation of Śīlendrabodhi and Ye-śes-sde (Peking/Tokyo ed. Tibetan Canon vol. 112, pp 121-133), and to the several editions of the sub-commentary by Sthiramati (*Madhyānta-vibhāga-ṭīkā*, ed. V. Bhattacharya, G. Tucci, Luzac & Co., London, 1932, ed. Susumu Yamaguchi, Librairie Hajinkahu, Nagoya, 1934, ed. R. Pandeya, Motilal Banarsidass, Delhi, 1971).

COMMENTARY ON
THE SEPARATION OF THE MIDDLE FROM EXTREMES
(MADHYĀNTA-VIBHĀGA-BHĀṢYA)

I. Reverencing both this Treatise's author, the son of Sugata*—, and its expounder to us and others**, I will attempt to explain its meaning.

Here, at first, a framework for the Treatise has been arranged as follows :

> "Characteristics, obstructions, realities, the cultivation of antidotes, situations there, the attainment of fruition, and the supremacy of the Vehicle" I. la

That is to say that the following seven topics are dealt with in the Treatise : the main characteristics (of beings and the world), their obstructions, realities, the cultivation of antidotes to the obstructions, situations which may arise in this cultivation of antidotes, the attainment of fruition there, and a path to the attainment of fruition, a path having no superior.

Referring to the characteristics, the author says :

("he")
"There *is* the construction of that which was not;
duality is not found there;
("She")
But emptiness is found there;
And "he" is found in "Her", as well." I.1.

In this passage, "the construction of that which was not" is the discrimination between the object apprehended and the subject apprehendor. "Duality" is the object apprehended and the subject apprehendor. And "Emptiness" is the separation of the construction of that which was not from the being of object apprehended and subject apprehendor. "And 'he' is found

*Maitreyanātha, author of *The Separation of the Middle from Extremes*, to which this work by Vasubandhu is a commentary.

**Asaṅga, pupil of Maitreyanātha, and elder brother of Vasubandhu, through whom Vasubandhu was converted to the Great Vehicle.

in 'Her', as well" : i.e. the construction of that which was not (is found in Emptiness, as well). And if it (duality) is not there in that way, then, as a result, one sees "as it is", namely, that it is empty. Furthermore, one knows that that which remains (after duality vanishes) is what is (really) existent here, and the emptiness-characteristic is made to arise in an unreversed manner.[1]

> "Therefore, everything is taught as neither empty nor non-empty,
> because of *its* existence, *its* non-existence, and *its* existence,
> and *this* is the Middle Path." I.2.

It is not empty, either because of emptiness or the construction of that which was not. Neither is it non-empty, because of the duality, object apprehended and subject apprehendor, and thus it has been taught, that "Everything compounded is called 'the construction of that which was not'; everything uncompounded is called 'Emptiness' ", because of the existence of the construction of that which was not, because of the non-existence of duality, and the existence of emptiness in the construction of that which was not, and the existence of the construction of that which was not in emptiness. And *this* is the Middle Path : that everything is neither totally empty nor totally non-empty. And this is in accordance with passages in the *Prajñā-pāramitā-sūtras*, etc., which say : "All this is neither empty nor non-empty."*[2]

Having explained the existent character and the non-existent character of the construction of that which was not, he next explains its own-characteristic.

> "Consciousness arises as the appearance of objects of the senses and of understanding, and as the appearance of sentient beings, self, and perceptions. There is no (real) object for it, and in its non-being, it itself is not." I.3.

In this passage, the appearance of objects of senses and understanding is that which appears because of the being of

*cf. *Kauśika-prajñā-pāramitā-sūtra*

visibles, etc. The appearance of sentient beings is that which appears because of there being sense-faculties in "one's own" and "others'" life-streams. The appearance of self is afflicted *manas*, because of its association with confusion of self, etc. The appearance of perceptions is the taking shape of the six consciousnesses. "There is no (real) object for it", the author says, because of the lack of a fixed aspect in the appearance of objects and sentient beings, and because of the false appearance of the appearance of self and perceptions. "In its non-being, it itself is not", the author says; because of the non-being, in these four ways, of the object apprehended, i.e. visibles, etc., the five sense-faculties, *manas*, and the six consciousnesses which cognize, the apprehendor, consciousness, is also non-existent.[3]

> "Consciousness' character as the construction of that which was not is demonstrated by its being, because it is not in that way, and yet is not totally non-being." I.4.

Because its being is not as its appearance arises, but it is not totally a non-being, because of the arising of this much confusion! Furthermore, it couldn't be simply non-being, because,

> "Liberation through its extinction is accepted." I.4b

Otherwise, bondage and freedom would be contradicted, and this would incur the flaw of denying affliction and alleviation.

Having explained the own-characteristic of the construction of that which was not in this way, the author proceeds to explain its comprising characteristic. Even though this is only construction of that which was not, there comes to be a comprising of three own-beings in this way:

> "The constructed, the interdependent, and the fulfilled
> are indicated by objects of sense and understanding,
> the construction of that which was not,
> and the non-being of dualities." I.5.

"Objects of sense and understanding" are constructed own-being. The construction of that which was not is interdependent own-being. The non-being of object apprehended and subject apprehendor is fulfilled own-being.[4]

Next the author illuminates the characteristic within that construction of that which was not, allowing it to penetrate its own non-existent character.

> "A non-apprehension comes about dependent on apprehension,
> a non-apprehension comes about dependent on this non-apprehension". I. 6.

A non-apprehension of objects as separate objects of sense and understanding comes about dependent on the apprehension that everything is perception-only. Accordingly, a non-apprehension of "perception-only" comes about dependent on this non-apprehension of objects. And thus one enters into the non-existent character of object apprehended and subject apprehendor.

> "Thus it is demonstrated that this 'apprehension' has the nature of a non-apprehension". I.7a

because of the impossibility of a true apprehension with the non-being of a separate object for apprehension.

> "Because of this, it can be known that there is an identity between apprehension and non-apprehension." I.7b

Because of the inability to demonstrate an apprehension through its apprehenending anything. Nevertheless, it is called "apprehension" because of the appearance of objects of sense and understanding which were not previously, even though it really has the nature of a non-apprehension.

Next, the author explains the construction of that which was not's characteristic of being divided.

> "And the construction of that which was not is the cittas and caittas of the three realms." I.8a.

That is to say, it exists with the division of experience into the realm of desires, the realm of simple images, and the imageless realm.[5]

And then he explains the characteristics of its synonyms :

> "Observing an object there, is consciousness;
> observing it with special qualities, are the caittas."
> I. 8b

That is to say : Observing in terms of "a simple object" is a consciousness; observing in terms of special qualities "in the object", are the caittas (i.e. psychological events associated with consciousness), such as feelings, etc.

Then the author explains the construction of that which was not's characteristic of evolving :

> "One is the condition-consciousness,
> the second relates to experience;
> in the latter are the caittas that experience, distinguish,
> and impel." I. 9

Because the store-consciousness is the conditional ground for all the other consciousnesses, it is the "condition-consciousness". Conditioned by it, there are the evolving consciousnesses which relate to experience. Experiencing itself is basically feeling, distinguishing is cognition, and the impellers of consciousness are the motivating dispositions : volition, mental attention, etc.

Then the author proceeds to discuss the construction of that which was not's characteristic of having afflictions.

> "Because of concealment, planting, conducting, and holding fast; because of filling up, the triple distinguishing, experiencing, being pulled along; because of binding, confrontation, and the more palpable states causing suffering, the living world is afflicted." I. 10 and 11a.

In this passage, "concealment" means the obstruction to seeing as it is which arises through ignorance; "planting" means the setting up of latent karmic impressions in consciousness by the motivating dispositions, "conducting" means meeting with a situation for the further arising (of impressions) in consciousness, "holding fast" is the holding fast to a "self-being" through the psychophysical complex, "filling up" is the filling up (of experience) by the six sense-fields, the "triple distinguishing" is the triple determination (of sense-organ, object, and corresponding consciousness through contact), "experiencing" is feeling, "being pulled along" is craving, conducive to being-again,[6] projected by action, "binding" is being bound by desires, etc. which are conducive to the arising of consciousnesses through clingings; "confrontation" is the direction of a done act which gives retribution in a being-again, and the more palpable states causing suffering come about through birth, decrepitude, dying, etc. The living world is afflicted by all of these.

> "Threefold, twofold, and sevenfold affliction-together,
> because of the construction of that which was not." I. 11b

Affliction-together is threefold: the affliction-together of afflictions proper, the afflictions-together of action, and the afflictions-together of birth. Among these, ignorances, craving, and clinging are afflictions-together of afflictions proper, motivating dispositions and being are the afflictions-together of action, and the afflictions-together of birth are the rest of the limbs of dependent origination.[7]

Afflictions-together are twofold: causal and resultant. Among these, causal afflictions-together consist of those limbs of dependent origination which have the nature of affliction and action (i.e. the limbs ignorance, motivating dispositions, craving, clinging, and being); resultant afflictions-together consist of the rest of the limbs.

Afflictions-together are sevenfold: These are essentially causal afflictions-together in their seven modes: the cause of reversal, the cause of being thrown forth, the cause of conducting near, the cause of holding fast, the cause of experiencing, the cause of being pulled along, and the cause of agitation. Among these, ignorance is the cause of reversal, motivating dispositions are the cause of being thrown forth, consciousness is the cause of conducting near, the cause of holding fast is the psycho-physical complex and the six sense-fields, the cause of experiencing is contact and feeling, the cause of being pulled along is craving, clinging, and being, and the cause of agitation is birth, decrepitude, and dying. In every way, afflictions-together develop because of the construction of that which was not : this is the compact meaning. So the nine-fold characteristics of the construction of that which was not have been illuminated :

its character as existent, its character as non-existent, its own-character, its comprising character, its character allowing it to penetrate to its own non-existent character, its character of being divided, the character of its synonyms, its character of evolving, and its character of afflictions-together.

Having in this way explained the construction of that which was not, in order that emptiness can also be known, he says :

> "Emptiness' characteristics, synonyms, meanings, divisions, and its demonstration, should be concisely known." I. 12

How should its characteristics be known ?

> "The non-being of duality,
> and the being of this non-being,
> is the characteristic of emptiness." I. 13a

It is the non-being of duality, i.e. of the object apprehended and subject apprehendor. It is also the being of this non-being. In this way, emptiness' characteristicness of both non-being and own-being is illuminated.

As it is both non-being and own-being, it is

> "neither a being nor a non-being". I. 13b.

How is it not being ? Because of the non-being of duality. How is it not non-being ? Because of the being of the non-being of duality. And this is the characteristic of emptiness.[8] Thus it is

> "a characteristic neither the same nor different" I. 13c.

from the construction of that which was not. If it were different, the real nature of an event would be different from the event itself (since emptiness is the real nature of the construction of that which was not). To speak of emptiness and the construction of that which was not as being different would be as absurd as speaking of "impermanence" and "suffering" as being something different from impermanent and suffering beings themselves. If they were the same, then there would be no knowledge with alleviation *as its object, and their character would be totally common. With this, the characteristic of freedom from otherness in reality, becomes illuminated.

How are synonyms for emptiness to be recognized ?

> "Suchness, the reality-limit, the signless,
> the ultimate, the Gıound of all events, are, in brief,
> synonyms for emptiness." I. 14.

How are the meanings of these synonyms to be known ?

> "From being non-otherness,
> non-reversal, cessation
> the scope of the exalted,
> and the cause of exalted events,
> the meanings of the synonyms are understood in order." I. 15.

It is Suchness in the sense of non-otherness in the sense that it is just so, all the time. It is the reality-limit in the sense of there being no reversals there, because of the insubstantiality of reversals. (It is also the reality-limit in that it is the furthest point of awareness.) It is the signless in the sense of being the cessation of all signs, there being a total non-being of signs there.[9] Because it is the scope of exalted knowledge, it is called "the ultimate", and because it is the causal ground for exalted events, it is called "the Ground of all Events". For the meaning of "ground" is here the meaning of "cause".

How are the divisions of emptiness to be known ?

> "Both afflicted and cleared" I. 16a.

This is its division. In which situations is it afflicted and in which cleared ?

> "With flaws and without flaws" I. 16b.

When it exists with flaws, then it is afflicted. When it is freed from flaws, then it is cleared.

*"Clearing"

If, having been with flaws, it becomes freed from flaws, how is it that it is not impermanent, as it undergoes change ?

Because its

> "clarity is assented to, like the clarity of water, gold, and space" I. 16c.

No otherness of own-being occurs for it, because of the removal of adventitious flaws.[10]

There is yet a further division : the sixteen kinds of emptiness, which are : the emptiness of the internal, the emptiness of the external, the emptiness of the internal and external, the great emptiness, the emptiness of emptiness, the emptiness of ultimate truth, the emptiness of the compounded, the emptiness of the uncompounded, the very great emptiness, the emptiness of inferior and superior, the emptiness of non-rejection, the emptiness of Nature, the emptiness of characteristics, the emptiness of all events, the emptiness of non-being, and the emptiness of the own-being of non-being. These are to be known in brief as :

> "The emptiness of experiencer,
> of whatever is experienced,
> of the body, of the habitat,
> the emptiness through which those (emptinesses) are seen,
> and the emptiness of whatever is resorted to." I. 17.

Among these, emptiness of the experiencer refers to the internal sense-fields, and the emptiness of whatever is experienced refers to "external things". The body is the seat of experiencer and the experienced, that is, the physical body, and its emptiness is called the emptiness of the internal and external. The habitat is the world inhabited, and because of this world's extensiveness, its emptiness is called the great emptiness. The emptiness of emptiness is the emptiness of that emptiness through the knowledge of which it is seen that the internal events, sense-fields, etc. are empty. And the emptiness of ultimate truth is the emptiness of all that as it is seen under the aspect of "ultimate truth", and the emptiness of whatever object of understanding a Bodhisattva may resort to. For what reason, then, are they resorted to ?

> "for the attainment of a pure pair" I. 18a.

for the attainment of a beneficial compounded and uncompounded, and

> "continually for the welfare of all beings" I. 18b.

that is, for the welfare of limitless sentient beings, and

> "in order not to abandon Saṃsāra" I. 18c.

If one did not see the emptiness of Saṃsāra and the emptiness of any "inferior" and "superior", oppressed, one would abandon Saṃsāra.

> "and for the non-perishing of the beneficial" I. 18d.

Even in a "Nirvāṇa with no remainder", one does not reject, does not throw off, anything, and the emptiness of this is called the emptiness of non-rejection.

> "for the sake of clearing the lineage" I. 19a.

the lineage meaning one's nature, because of a state of own-being[11], and

> "in order to receive the characteristics and secondary marks of a great person, and for the clearing of Buddha-dharmas,
> the Bodhisattva has recourse to objects of understanding." I. 19b.

for the attainment of the powers, confidences, special Buddha-events[12], etc. The situations of these fourteen kinds of emptiness can be known in this way.

What again is emptiness here ?

> "The non-being of personalities and events is emptiness, and the existing being of this non-being in it is another emptiness." I. 20.

The non-being of "personality" and "events" is emptiness. And it is also the existing being of this non-being. "In it", he says, so that it is clear that this is not another emptiness from the emptiness of experiencer, etc. In order to explain a characteristic of emptiness in this way, he specifies emptiness as two-fold in relation to extremes[13], as the emptiness of non-being and the emptiness of the own-being of that non-being, in order to remove, the superimposition of "personalities" and "events", and the denial of this emptiness respectively. The division of emptiness can be known in this way.

How can its demonstration be known ?

> "If it did not become afflicted, then all beings would be liberated, if it were clear, then all effort would be fruitless." I. 21.

If the emptiness of events were not afflicted by adventitious secondary afflictions when their antidotes have not arisen, all sentient beings would be liberated even without any effort, because the afflictions-together would not come about. If, even when antidotes have arisen, it were not to become alleviated, then all effort made for the sake of freedom would be fruitless.

Thus

> "it is neither afflicted nor unafflicted, neither clear nor unclear" I. 22a.

How is it neither afflicted nor unclear ?

> "because of the luminousness of citta" I. 22b.

by nature.

How is it neither unafflicted, nor clear ?

> "because of the adventitiousness of afflictions in it." I. 22c.

Thus the division of emptiness, previously alluded to*, is demonstrated.

Now the compact meaning of emptiness can be known—from its character, and from its determination. From its character means from its character as non-being and being. Its character as being is both from its character as being freed from being

*at I, 16a.

again and from its character as being freed from all otherness in reality.[14] Its situations can be known from the determination implicit in its synonyms, etc.

Here, through this four-fold exposition, the own-characteristic of emptiness : its characteristic of action, its characteristic of affliction and alleviation, and its character of logical fitness, is caused to occur, bringing discriminations, fears, inactivity, and doubts to complete rest.

II. The Obstructions

Concerning obstructions, the author says :

> "The pervading and the limited ones,
> the excessive and the equal,
> accepting and abandoning,
> are called obstructions of the two." II. 1.

In this passage, "the pervading" is the obstructions consisting simply of afflictions, and the obstructions of the knowable, because both are obstuctions to those of the Bodhisattva-lineage. "The limited" is the obstruction to the Śrāvaka-lineages, which is affliction only (i.e. the sole goal of the Śrāvakas, that is the followers of the "Hīnayāna", is the eradication of their own afflictions). The "excessive" is the obstruction in those who act with attachment (hostility or confusion). The "equal" is that in those who make everything alike.[15] The obstruction of accepting or abandoning Saṃsāra is an obstruction to those of the Bodhisattva-lineage, because of being an obstruction to Nirvāṇa without a basis.[16] Thus, the obstructions of those of the Bodhisattva-lineage, those of the Śrāvaka-vehicle, and those of others, have been made known.

> "The characteristics of the obstructions that are simply affliction are nine-fold, being the fetters." II. 1b.

The nine fetters are the obstructions that are simply afflictions. To what are they obstructions ?

> "to excitement and to equanimity,
> and to the seeing of reality." II. 2a.

The fetter of complacency is an obstruction to excitement, and the fetter of aversion is an obstruction to equanimity. (Because of the former, there is no passion, compassion, or energy); because of the latter, one cannot stay calm in face of the disagreeable or hostile. The rest of the fetters are obstructions to the seeing of reality. How does this occur ?

> "Leading towards the view of self,
> obstructing insights regarding this and "external objects",
> regarding the cessation of suffering, the Path, the Gems,
> others' attainments, and regarding the knowledge of being satisfied with little." II. 2—II. 3a.

The fetters become specific obstructions. The fetter of pride becomes an obstacle leading to the view of self. This is because this view has not been cast off through proper practise in a time of clear understanding, working against the pride of thinking that "I exist" in what is internal or external. The fetter of ignorance is an obstacle to knowledge about external objects and also involves the view of a self. This is because it is a lack of knowledge concerning the appropriating aggregates. The fetter of holding fast to views is an obstruction to the knowledge of the truth of the cessation of suffering. This is because such holding fast goes against the possibility of the cessation of suffering, because of the various anxieties caused by the view of a self in the body, and views regarding the permanence or impermanence of the elements constituting personality. The fetter of adherence to mere rules and rituals is an obstruction to the knowledge of the truth of the Path, because of its adherence to the view that the highest clarity lies elsewhere than it really does. The fetter of doubt is an obstruction to the knowledge of the Three Gems (Buddha, Dharma, Saṅgha), because it involves a lack of faith in the good qualities of these three. The fetter of envy is an obstruction to satisfaction in others' attainment, because one wishes to see only others' flaws. The fetter of selfishness leads to a lack of knowledge of satisfaction with little, because of one's obsession with possession.[17]

> "Further obstructions stand in the way of welfare, etc. in ten ways." II. 3.

There are further obstructions that stand in the way of welfare, etc. in ten ways. What are these obstructions, and what is meant here by "welfare, *etc.*" ?

> "The lack of means to rouse "oneself" from inactivity,
> the lack of complete use of "one's" sense-fields,
> careless activity,
> non-arising of the beneficial,
> lack of mental attention to what lies around you,
> unfulfillment of the necessary preparation (to live in the Great Vehicle),
> separation from "one's" spiritual lineage, and separation from good friends,
> wearying distress and agitation of citta,
> lack of opportunity to practise the Great Vehicle,
> being forced to live with stupid or depraved people,
> susceptibility to harm, lack of control, and lack of maturation of insight because of the three,
> susceptibility to harm by nature, sloth, and carelessness,
> attachment to being, and longing for enjoyment,
> muddle-headedness,
> lack of confidence, lack of faith, deliberation according to words,
> lack of reverence for the Good Dharma,
> respect for gain,
> lack of compassion,
> casting away what one has heard,
> being ill-versed in what's been heard,
> and lack of engagement in meditation." II. 4-8.

These are the obstructions to welfare, etc. And what is welfare, etc. ?

> "Welfare, enlightenment, the full taking up of Saṃsāra,
> insight, lack of confusion, lack of obstructions,
> ability to evolve, fearlessness,
> lack of selfishness and potency." II. 9.

So that it can be known how many obstructions can arise to which of these factors : welfare, etc. he says,

"By threes, the obstructions of the knowable arise for these." II. 10a.

To each of these beneficial factors, three obstructions can arise. To welfare, arise the lack of means to rouse "oneself" from inactivity, the lack of complete use of "one's" sense-fields, and careless activity. To enlightenment, arise the non-arising of good caittas, lack of mental attention to what lies around you, and the unfulfillment of the necessary preparation. To the full taking up of Saṃsāra, which is the arising of the enlightenment-citta[18], arise separation from "one's" spiritual lineage, separation from good friends, and wearying distress and agitation of citta. To insight, which is the state of a Bodhisattva, arise the lack of opportunity to practise the Great Vehicle, and being forced to live with either stupid or depraved people. In this passage, "stupid people" are fools, and "depraved people" are frustrated, harmed people. To lack of confusion, arise susceptibility to harm through reversals, lack of potency because of the three kinds of obstructions : afflictions, etc. and lack of maturation in insight which matures confidence. As obstructions to the abandonment of obstructions, arise natural susceptibility to harm, sloth, and carelessness. To the ability to evolve, arise attachment to (rigid) being, longing for enjoyment, and muddle-headedness, through which citta evolves otherwise than towards supreme perfect enlightenment. To fearlessness, arise lack of confidence in the "personality", lack of trust in Dharma, and deliberations according to words. To lack of selfishness, arise lack of reverence for the Dharma, respect for the acquisition and worship of gain, and lack of compassion for sentient beings. To potency, arise three, because of which one can't attain (psychic) power, which are casting away what has been heard (regarding Dharma), because it brings about actions leading to the rejection of Dharma, being ill-versed in what's been heard, and lack of engagement in meditation.

Because these obstructions become ten kinds of causes in relation to welfare, etc. these ten kinds of causes are to be made known now, because of their bearing upon them. There is a cause as one thing's being the direct condition for the arising of another, such as when the eye gives rise to a visual consciousness. There is a cause as one thing's maintaining another's existence, such as the four foods maintaining sentient beings. (The four "foods" are : morsel-food maintaining the organism itself, contact giving stimuli to the living being, *manas* and volition motivating its activity, and consciousness.) There is a cause as one thing's sustaining another, in the sense of providing a support, as the inhabited world does for the world of sentient beings. There is a cause as one thing's manifesting another, as the action of looking does the visible. There is a cause as one thing's transforming another, as fire does that which is being cooked. There is a cause as one thing's disjoining another—such is the relation of a cutting instrument to that which is being cut. There is a cause as one thing's evolving another step by step, such as the action of a goldsmith, who works bracelets out of masses of gold. There is a cause as one thing's giving rise to the idea of another, such as the perception of smoke, etc. giving rise to the idea of fire, etc. There is a cause as one thing's causing us to form the idea of another, as a justification does for a thesis.* There is a cause as one thing's leading to the attainment of the other, as the Path leads to Nirvāṇa, etc.

Thus, an obstruction to the arising of alleviation is an obstruction to welfare, because of its causing it to arise. An obstruction to its maintenance is an obstruction to enlightenment (i.e. the enlightenment-citta), because of its resulting in an absence of anger and frustration. An obstruction to sustaining it is an obstruction to the full taking up of Saṃsāra, because this becomes the support for the enlightenment-citta. An obstruction to manifesting it to others is an obstruction to insightedness, because of its making it clear to others. An obstruction to its transformation is an obstruction to lack of confusion, because of its folding away all confusions obstructing alleviation. An obstruction to its disjunction is an obstruction to the lack of obstruction, because it causes separation from obstructions. An obstruction to its evolving gradually is an obstruction to citta's ability to evolve towards enlightenment. An obstruction to giving rise to the idea (of the Great Vehicle) is an obstruction to fearlessness, because this idea does not arise where there is any fear. An obstruction to causing the

*cf. *Method for Argumentation*, 4.

idea to arise in others is an obstruction to lack of selfishness, because it is the lack of selfishness in the Dharma that causes the idea (of the Great Vehicle) to arise in others. An obstruction to its attainment is an obstruction to potency, because it has the characteristic of the attainment of powers.

> Causes of ten kinds : for arising, maintaining, sustaining,
> manifesting, transforming, disjoining, evolving,
> causing the idea to arise, causing the idea to be formed in others,
> and attaining : for these the eye, foods, the earth,
> a lamp, a fire, are examples,
> and a cutting instrument, an artisan's skill,
> smoke, justifications, and the Path.

It is through the desire to obtain enlightenment that the roots of the beneficial are at first caused to arise. Then, through the power of the roots of the beneficial, enlightenment (the enlightenment-citta) can be attained. The enlightenment-citta is the basis for the arising of the roots of the beneficial. The Bodhisattva is the support of the enlightenment-citta. Again, with these roots of the beneficial attained through the enlightenment-citta which has been made to arise, reversals will be abandoned by the Bodhisattva, and a complete absence of reversals will be caused to arise. Thus, freed from reversals in the Path of Seeing, all obstructions are abandoned in the Path of Cultivation.[19] Again, the three roots of the beneficial, once obstructions have been gotten rid of, will become evolved to supreme complete enlightenment. Then, through the exercise of the power of this transformation, one will not be afraid of the various kinds of teachings in the deep extensive Dharma. Thus, through not being alarmed, seeing the various qualities in the events of the teachings, one can explain these events in detail to others. Thereafter, the Bodhisattva, having thus attained the exercise of these powers through these various qualities, quickly attains supreme complete enlightenment, and attains also potency in all events. This is the gradual sequence of welfare, etc.

> "Furthermore, there are other obstructions ;
> to the allies, pāramitās, and stages." II.10b

First of all, to the allies of enlightenment :[20]

> "Lack of skill as regards the meditational object,
> sloth, two defects in meditational concentration,
> lack of planting, weakness,
> being flawed by views and susceptibility to harm." II.11.

Lack of skill as regards the meditational object is an obstruction to the application of mindfulness.[21] Sloth is an obstruction to the right exertions.[22] Two defects in meditational concentration are a lack of completion of meditation due to a deficiency in either zest, vigor, citta, or exploration, and a lack of completion of meditation due to a deficiency in the secondary motivational dispositions necessary for efforts in meditating. These (lack of completions of meditation) are obstructions to the bases of psychic power.[23] To the faculties[24], non-planting of the factors conducive to liberation[25] is an obstruction. To the powers[26], weakness of these same faculties due to the interference of adverse factors is an obstruction. To the limbs of enlightenment[27], the flaw of views is an obstruction, due to their working against the Path of Seeing. To the limbs of the Path[28], the flaw of susceptibility to harm is an obstruction, because of its working against the Path of Cultivation.

Obstructions to the pāramitās :

> "Obstructions to having, happy states,
> to not forsaking sentient beings,
> to casting off and growth of flaws and virtues, to descent" II. 12.
> "to liberating, to inexhaustibility, to continuance in welfare,
> to making certain, to enjoyment and maturation of Dharma." II. 13.

Here it is explained which result of which among the ten pāramitās is liable to damage by which obstruction[29]. In this connection, an obstruction to having is an obstruction to (the effect of) the pāramitā of giving. An obstruction to a happy state is an obstruction to (the effect of) the pāramitā of good conduct towards others. An obstruction to the non-abandonment of sentient beings is an obstruction to (the effect of) the pāramitā of forbearance. An obstruction to the casting off of flaws and the growth of virtues is an obstruction to (the effect of) the pāramitā of vigor. An obstruction into descent into what is to be mastered is an obstruction to (the effect of) the pāramitā of meditation. An obstruction to the act of liberating ("self" and "others") is an obstruction to (the effect of) the pāramitā of insight. An obstruction to the inexhaustibility of giving, etc. is an obstruction to (the effect of) the pāramitā of skill in means, because of their inexhaustibility through the enlightenment-transformation. An obstruction to a beneficial uninterrupted continuance in all kinds of being again is an obstruction to (the effect of) the pāramitā of resolve, because it is through the power of the Bodhisattva's resolve that one takes on births which are favorable to this continuance in Saṃsāra. An obstruction to making the beneficial unfailing is an obstruction to (the effect of) the pāramitā of power, because it is through the two powers of contemplation and cultivation that adverse factors are overpowered. An obstruction to the enjoyment and maturation of Dharma in both "oneself" and "others" is an obstruction to (the effect of) the pāramitā of knowledge, because of one's not truly understanding the meaning of what one has heard.

And to the stages, there may be obstructions, in this order :

"In regard to the all-encompassing aim,
to the higher aim,
to the yet higher aim which flows from that,
to the aim of non-grasping,
to a lack of division in the series,
to the aim of neither affliction or alleviation,
to the aim of a lack of diversity,
to the aim that there is neither "inferior" nor "superior",
and to the four-fold basis of potency,
there is this ignorance in the Ground of Events,
a ten-fold non-afflicted obstructing,
by way of factors adverse to the Stages,
but the antidotes to them *are* the Stages!" II. 14-16.

An unafflicted ignorance which arises successively in the tenfold Ground of Events in relation to its all-encompassing, and other, aims, is an obstruction to the stages of enlightenment, because it is an adverse factor to them. That is, on the first, all-encompassing stage, it counter-acts the all-encompassing aim by which one understands the sameness of "self" and "others". On the second stage, it counter-acts a further aim (of the Great Vehicle), by which one decides that one should do practises (*yoga*) for the sake of bringing about a clearing of all aspects (in a total rooting-out of afflicting characteristics). On the third stage, it counter-acts a further aim which flows from that, by which one is able, after having realized the ultimate nature of what has been heard which flows from the Ground of Events, to hurl oneself into a fire-pit which has the extent of the whole Tri-Chiliocosm. On the fourth stage, it counter-acts the aim of non-grasping, for here even the craving for Dharma is abandoned. On the fifth stage, it counter-acts the aim of a lack of division in the citta-series, with its ten samenesses of citta and intention in total clearing (i.e. with the sameness of cittas and intentions in all ten stages). On the sixth stage, it counter-acts the aim where there is neither affliction nor alleviation, because of its counter-acting the realization that there is no event which is being afflicted or alleviated in dependent origination. On the seventh stage, it counter-acts the aim of that lack of true diversity, for here there is a lack of dealing with* any diversity of mental signs in the events spoken of in the sūtras, etc. On the eighth stage, it counter-acts the aim that there is neither "inferior" or "superior", because of the lack of observing any "lesser" or "greater" in any event of affliction and alleviation, because there is the forbearance (through realizing) the non-arising of "events". There is a four-fold potency : potency in absence of discriminations, potency in the total clearing of the Buddha-field[30], potency in knowledge, and potency in action. One penetrates the state for the basis of the first and second potencies in the Ground of Events on the eighth stage, one completely attains the state of a basis for potency in knowledge on the ninth stage, with the attainment of the particular knowledges, and the state of the basis for potency in action on the tenth stage, which is the state of being able to do actions for the sake of sentient beings through various transformations at will.

*"because of a lack of arising of"—Tib.

Again, in brief :

> "Those which are called the obstructions which are afflictions,
> and the obstructions of the knowable,
> are all obstructions,
> and liberation is sought through their extinction." II. 17.

Through extinction of these obstructions of two kinds, liberation from all obstructions is sought.

The compact meaning of the obstructions : the great obstruction, which is the same as "the pervading"; the narrow obstruction, which is the same as "the limited"; the obstruction through courses of action, which is the same as "the excessive"; the obstruction to attainment, which is the same as "the equal"[31]; the obstruction to special attainment, which is the same as "accepting or abandoning"[32]; the obstruction to right application, which are the nine-fold obstructions which are afflictions; the obstruction to the cause, which is the same as an obstruction to welfare, etc. because of its position as a ten-fold cause of obstruction; obstruction to entering into reality, which is the same as an obstruction to the allies of enlightenment; obstruction to supremacy in welfare, which is the same as obstructions to the pāramitās; an obstruction to special states, which is the same as an obstruction to the Stages. In brief, these obstructions may be comprised together as two-fold : afflictions and obstructions of the knowable.

III. Realities

Concerning reality, the author says :

> "Basic reality, characteristic reality, the reality that is non-reversal,
> the reality which consists of fruition and its cause,
> more subtle and more gross realities,
> the accepted, the range of clearing, comprising reality,
> the characteristic of differentiation,
> the ten-fold reality of skill (in means), antidotes of the view of self." III.1-2.

Ten-fold reality is enumerated here, namely : basic reality, the reality of the characteristics, the reality of non-reversal, the reality of fruition and its causes, reality as that which is accepted, more gross and more subtle realities, the reality of the scope of complete clearing, comprising reality, the reality of differentiation, and the reality of skill (in means). And the reality of skill (in means) is to be known as being a ten-fold antidote to the ten-fold grasping after self, namely as skill concerning the aggregates, skill concerning the sense-fields, skills concerning the sensory domains, skills concerning dependent origination, skills concerning states and non-states, skills concerning the twenty-two faculties[33], skills concerning the concept of time, skills concerning the Truths, skills concerning the Vehicles, and skills concerning the compounded and uncompounded.

What is here called "basic reality" is

> "the three-fold own-being", III. 3a

the constructed, the interdependent, and the fulfilled. They make possible all other realities.

What is meant here by "reality in three own-beings" ?

> "It's non-existent, and it is always;
> it exists and yet not really;
> it's really existent and non-existent :
> in this way three own-beings are assented to." III. 3b

The characteristic of the constructed is that it is always really non-existent, and thus there is reality in the constructed nature, because of its un-reversedness.[34] The characteristic of the interdependent is that it is existent, and yet not in a real way, because of its state of confusion, and thus there is reality in the interdependent.[34a] The characteristic of the fulfilled is that it is really both existent and non-existent, and thus there is reality in the fulfilled own-being.[35] As to what he means by "characteristic reality" or "the reality of the characteristics", the author says :

> The characteristic of reality here is that from the knowledge of which the seeing of superimposition and denial regarding events, and personalities, objects apprehended and subjects apprehendors, being and non-being, do not arise." III. 4.

The seeing of (false) superimposition and denial involved in assuming "personalities" or "events", through the knowledge of which it does not develop, is the characteristic of reality in the constructed own-being. The seeing of (false) superimposition and denial involved in assuming "objects apprehended" and "subjects apprehendors" through the knowledge of which it does not develop, is the characteristic of reality in the interdependent own-being. The seeing of (false) superimposition and denial involved in assuming "being" and "non-being", through the knowledge of which it does not develop, is the characteristic of reality in the fulfilled own-being.[36] This characteristic in basic reality is called its "unreversed characteristic".

Inasmuch as it is an antidote to reversed views of permanence, etc. the reality of non-reversal is the existence of impermanence, suffering, the empty, and the lack of a self. And how is one to know that this impermanence, etc. are a part of basic reality according to a certain order ?

> "Objects actually non-existent,
> objects impermanent,
> the characteristics of arising and ceasing,
> are all, in basic reality in order,
> along with being with flaws,
> and being without flaws." III. 5-6a

Basic reality is the three own-beings. In them there are, in order : objects of sense and understanding which are really non-existent, (in the constructed own-being); objects of sense and understanding which are impermanent and fluxional, and the characteristic of arising and ceasing, (in the interdependent own-being); and the being of affliction and alleviation, (fully realized in the fulfilled own-being)[37].

> "Moreover, suffering is seen to exist
> because of adherence, the characteristics, and connection." III. 6b

There is suffering in basic reality because of the following reasons, in order : because of clinging, that is to say, because of the clinging that comes through intentness upon views concerning "personalities" and "events"; because of the basic characteristics of the world itself; because of connection, with suffering. These three exist in basic reality in a certain order. (The adherence to views concerning "personalities" and "events" is adherence to the constructed; the basic characteristics of the world itself are the characteristics of the interdependent; connection with the sufferings of Saṃsāra, even after having realized the nature of the constructed and interdependent,[38] is the characteristic of the fulfilled.)

> "Basic reality is seen to be emptiness :
> as simple non-being,
> as non-being of this or that,
> and as the fundamental nature." III. 7a

Since the characteristic of the constructed is that it is not truly existent in any form, non-being is its emptiness. Since the characteristic of the interdependent is that it is not as it is constructed, but yet is not non-existent, it is empty inasmuch as it entails the non-being of this or that definite thing. Since the characteristic of the fulfilled is that it has the nature of emptiness itself, it is emptiness in its fundamental nature.

> "Selflessness (in fundamental reality)
> is expressed as 'no characteristic',
> 'characteristic apart from *that*'
> and 'own-characteristic'." III. 7b and 8a

Since the characteristics of the constructed own-being themselves do not exist, its selflessness is that it has "no characteristic". Since the characteristics of the interdependent exist, but not as they are constructed, its selflessness is that it has a "characteristic apart from *that*" (the focused, filtered construct). Since the fulfilled own-being is selflessness, its selflessness is its fundamental nature. Impermanence is illuminated as being triple in basic reality : impermanent in the sense of not being a true object at all (i.e. vanishing once its true nature is realized); impermanent in the sense of arising and decaying; and (impermanent as far as its characteristics are concerned) being first afflicted and then alleviated. Suffering is triple : the suffering of clinging, the suffering coming about through the basic characteristics of the world, and connection with this suffering. Emptiness is triple : the emptiness of non-being, the emptiness of non-being of *this* or *that*, and the emptiness of own-being. Thus selflessness is triple : the non-being of self of having no characteristics, the non-being of self of having a characteristic other than *this* or *that*, and the non-being of self through own-characteristic.

The reality of fruition and its causes is the truths of suffering, the origination of suffering, cessation of suffering, and a Path to the cessation of suffering, which exist in basic reality. How is this threefold basic reality to be considered "the truth of suffering", etc. ? Because of its having the characteristics of impermanence, suffering, emptiness, and absence of self (the last two being both the causes and the antidotes to the second. Causes when unrealized, antidotes when realized.).

> "The truth of suffering is considered (to arise) from these (characteristics)" III. 8b.

The truth of the origination of suffering is to be known in respect to a threefold origination, which threefold origination is

> "residual impressions, increase, and lack of separation." III. 8c.

There is the origination of suffering by means of the residual impressions that cause intentness on the constructed nature. The afflictions of action are the origination by means of increase, and the non-separation of Suchness from obstructions is the origination occurring "through lack of separation". (Connect this with the connection with suffering that marks a fulfilled nature.)

The truth of the cessation of suffering is to be known in respect to a threefold cessation, which cessation is

> "Non-arising by own-being, non-arising of duality, and the two : flaws and peace." III. 9a.

There is that which is non-arising by own-being, there is the non-arising of object apprehended and subject apprehendor as things apart, and there is the process from being flawed to peace, which process is called cessation through contemplation*

*See *Discussion of the Five Aggregates*, p 73 and note 29.

and Suchness. So this three-fold cessation may be called cessation through own-being, cessation of duality, and cessation by nature.

How is the truth of the Path arranged in three-fold basic reality ?

> "In full knowledge, in abandoning, in attaining and intuitively realizing, the Truth of the Path is fully explained." III. 9b-10a.

The arrangement of the truth of the Path in basic reality is to be known in full knowledge of the constructed (which leads to its dissolving as a major force), in the full knowledge of the interdependent and its abandonment (as far as it involves the processes of the arising of suffering), and in the full knowledge, attainment, and intuitive realization of the fulfilled. These may be known as the three-fold Truth of the Path, through full knowledge, abandonment, and realization.

Furthermore, "conventional" and "ultimate" truths are, respectively, more gross and more subtle realities. How are they to be known in basic reality ?

> "The gross exists in the form of designations,
> determinations, and words used in practise." III. 10b.

The conventional is here divided into three basic kinds : the conventionality of designations, the conventionality of determinations (as strained through various constricting caittas), and the conventionality of all words used in religious practise. (Designations belong to the constructed nature; perceptions of senses and understanding properly to the interdependent nature, but an interdependent nature often determined by constrictions, and practise, though this practise leads to the fulfilled nature, yet represents only conventional truth.)

> "Whereas the ultimate exists only in relation to the one". III.10c.

Ultimate truth is to be known as existing because of the one fulfilled own-being, only. In what way is it "ultimate" ?

> "It is ultimate in three ways :

> as regards object, attainment, and practise." III.11a.

It is ultimate as an object because Suchness is the object of ultimate knowledge (of the six consciousnesses taken to their ultimate point). It is ultimate as an attainment because its attainment is equal to Nirvāna, which is the ultimate aim. It is ultimate as practise, because it is the Path, which has the ultimate aim.

How can the fulfilled nature be called both compounded and uncompounded ?

> "It is both, inasmuch as it consummates
> a lack of transformation,
> and consummates a lack of reversal." III. 11b.

The fulfilled is uncompounded in the sense of consummating a lack of further transformation back into what was before, and it is compounded as those things that are comprised in the Truth of the Path, which are "fulfilled" in the sense that they consummate a lack of the reversed, and in all those things that are to be known, which are "fulfilled" because of their basic non-reversal. (The stages comprised in the Truth of the Path, and all those things that are to be known, are, of course, compounded.)

How is "accepted reality" determined in basic reality ? What is termed "accepted reality" or "reality as that which is accepted" is of two kinds : that accepted by the world at large, and that which is accepted by right reasoning. Among these two,

> "That which is accepted by the world at large is due to the one" III. 12a.

the constructed own-being, in which, regarding its range of events, there is a certain sameness of views among all worldly people because their intellects have adapted themselves with acquaintance to certain conventional symbols, e.g. "This is *earth*, not fire", "This is a *visible*, not a sound", etc.

> "Whereas that which is accepted by right reasoning is due to three factors." III. 12b.

It is any range of events accepted by "reasoning of conclusive substantiation", which must rely on the three means of cognition accepted by dialecticians who are experts in such matters of reasoning.[38a]

The reality of the scope of complete clearing is two-fold : that of the scope of knowledge that clears away the obstructions which are pure afflictions, and that of the scope of knowledge that clears away the obstructions of the knowable. Thus

> "The reality of the scope of complete clearing is two-fold,
> though it is well-known that it comes from only one"
> III. 12c.

the fulfilled own-being. The double scope of the knowledge of complete clearing is no other nature apart from that.

How is "comprising reality" to be known in basic reality ?

> "There are two kinds of comprising together :
> that of the sign and its discrimination,
> and that of naming." III. 13a.

There is the comprising done by apprehending objects of senses of the five varieties (visibles, sounds, smells, tastes, and tactile sensations), and the discrimination of their sensuous characteristics—this occurs through the interdependent own-being. Then there is the comprising done by naming, which occurs because of the constructed own-being.

> "And there is the comprising of the reality of right knowledge,
> through the one". III. 13b.

And there is a comprising of Suchness and right knowledge, through the fulfilled own-being.

And how is the reality of differentiation to be known in basic reality ? In seven different ways : as the reality of development, as the reality of characteristics, as the reality of perceptions, as the reality of settlement into them, as the reality of false practise, as the reality of complete clearing, and as the reality of right practise, which seven-fold Suchness was discussed in the *Sandhinirmocana-sūtra*. And there is a three-fold reality of evolution : Saṃsāra goes neither to "lower" or "higher", sentient beings are afflicted because of afflictions—together in the Suchness-citta, and thus everything is the truths of suffering, etc.[39]

Here

> "Development-reality is two-fold", III. 14a.

and is to be known as basic reality with the characteristics of the constructed and interdependent. And in the same way as development-reality evolves

> "There is settling into them, and becoming disturbed." III. 14b.

As the states of settling into them and false practise, basic reality is also two-fold : (constructed and interdependent).

> "*One* is the right attainment of the clearing away of the perception of characteristics." III. 14c.

The realities of characteristics, etc. are the Four Noble Truths, which are one in basic reality, as the fulfilled characteristic.

The reality of skill in means has been called an antidote to views. There is a ten-fold view of self related to the aggregates, etc. :

> "There is a view of self when there is the idea of one thing underlying the living being—oneness, one cause, one experiencer, one doer, one in power of all its movements,
> one possessor, one entity lasting through time,
> one substratum for affliction and alleviation,
> one entity in steady concentration,
> one entity that is either bound or liberated." III. 15-16a.

to which, by way of antidote, there is a ten-fold skill in means, involving the observing of grasping after oneness, grasping after causeness, grasping after experiencerness, grasping after doerness, grasping after independence, grasping after possessor-ness, grasping after affliction/clearingness, grasping after steady concentration, and grasping after being bound/or being liberated-ness. This ten-fold skill in means evolves with the concepts of aggregates, etc. How are these ten kinds of skill in means included in basic reality ? In such a way that the aggregates are included in the three own-beings,

> "as constructions, as objects of discrimination, and as objects of Dharmatā". III. 16b.

Inasmuch as the concept of the aggregate of materiality is a construction, it belongs to the constructed own-being. Inasmuch as this construction rests on an object of discrimination, the discrimination of materiality is effected, which rests upon the interdependent own-being. Inasmuch as materiality in this sense takes part in the realization of Dharmatā, it belongs to the fulfilled own-being. The same holds for the other aggregates : feelings, cognitions, motivating dispositions, and consciousnesses, and the domains, sense-fields, etc. This ten-fold skill in means regarding the view of a self becomes part of basic reality with the inclusion of the aggregates within the three own-beings. It has already been mentioned that skill in the concepts of aggregates, etc. works as an antidote to the ten kinds of view of self. But the meaning of the aggregates, etc. themselves, has not yet been mentioned.

> "In regard to the first (concept used in skill in means), it exists from the point of view of severalness,
> heaping together, and distinguishing." III. 17a.

First, (let us discuss) the aggregates. They can be known in three different ways. In the sense of separatedness, everything which is materiality, etc. (is separate) as past, future, present, and so on. In the sense of heaping them together, their total singleness may be heaped together. In the sense of distinguishing them, (they may be distinguished) through a distinguishing of their separateness, by their characteristic as materiality, etc.[39a] The meaning of "aggregate" is the same as that of "heap", and thus the meaning of "heap", in common usage, is seen to apply here.

> "Yet others are the objects of the seeds of the subject apprehendor,
> the objects apprehended, and their apprehension."
> III.17b.

"Yet others" are the sensory domains. They are the objects of the seeds of the subject apprehendor : the domains eye, etc.; the objects of the seeds of the objects apprehended : the domains visibles, etc.; and the objects of the seeds for their apprehension : the domains visual consciousnesses, etc.

> "Yet others exist from the point of view of being doors to experiences and object-distinguishing". III.18a

"Yet others" are the sense-fields. The six internal sense-fields exist in the sense of being doors to felt experiences. The six external sense-fields exist in the sense of being doors to the experience of the distinguishing of objects of sense and understanding.

The aim of dependent origination* is

> "in order to have non-superimposition and non-denial as regards cause, effect, and effort." III.18b.

The aim of dependent origination is the aim of non-superimposition and non-denial as regards cause, effect, and activity. Here, a superimposition regarding causality would be to construct a cause different from motivating dispositions, etc. A denial regarding causality would be to construct that nothing like causality takes place at all. A superimposition regarding effect would be to construct the development of motivating dispositions, with ignorance, etc. as conditions, with selves entering in. A denial regarding effect would be to construct that even when ignorance does not exist, ensnaring motivating dispositions would arise. A superimposition regarding activity would be to construct an effort apart from ignorance being necessary

*See note 7.

for the arising of motivating dispositions. A denial regarding activity would be to construct that even ignorance has no power to make the motivating dispositions arise. The non-being of these constructions can be known as an absence of superimposition and denial.

> "Interdependence with regard to what isn't wanted
> and to what is wanted,
> with regard to complete clearing, simultaneous arising,
> sovereignty, attainment, and proper practise,
> is the meaning of 'good and bad states'." III.19.

The so-called good and bad states can be known as referring to seven kinds of interdependence. Interdependence in regard to what isn't wanted can be explained as taking place through arrival in an unhappy state at which one arrives because of actions, undesirable to others, and interdependence in a desirable state can be explained as taking place through arrival at a happy state occurring because of beneficial actions. Then there is an interdependence regarding what is called complete clearing, since this cannot be attained without abandoning the five obstructions* and without practising the seven limbs of enlightenment putting an end to suffering (mindfulness, investigation of events, vigor, zest, tranquility, meditational concentration, and even-mindedness). Interdependence in regard to simultaneous arising means the impossibility of two Tathāgatas, or two world-emperors, arising at the same time in the same world-realm.[40] Interdependence regarding right practise means that those perceiving reality have little trouble in right practise, and naturally do not commit actions harming living beings. But people separate from Dharma may do so. For details in these matters, one should consult the *Bahudhātuka-sūtra.***

The twenty-two faculties are sovereign in six ways :

> "Apprehension, continuity, continuation, experience,
> and the two kinds of clearing." III.20a.

**Majjhima* CXV
**See II, 1, ad II. 1.

The twenty-two faculties are thus ascertained according to their sovereignty regarding six functions. The sovereignty of the six faculties beginning with the eye (eye, ear, tongue, nose, body, *manas*) refers to the apprehension of sense-objects such as visibles, etc. The vital faculty is sovereign with regard to prolonging continuous existence for one period of life. The female and male organs are sovereign in regard to continuing the species, because of sovereignty in bringing forth offspring. The faculties which are feelings (the faculty of suffering, the faculty of pleasure, the faculty of satisfaction, the faculty of dissatisfaction, and the faculty of equanimity) are sovereign in regard to experience, because of the experience of the effects of beneficial and unbeneficial actions. The five faculties of faith, etc. (faith, vigor, mindfulness, concentration, and insight) are sovereign with regard to mundane complete clearing. The faculties of coming to know what wasn't known, knowing, and having known, are sovereign in regard to supermundane ccmplete clearing.[41]

> "The completed efficacy of effect and cause which has already taken place or is yet to take place, refers to yet another (concept used in skill in means)." III. 20b.

And what is this "yet another" ? The three times. It should be known that the action of effect and cause which has already taken place or is yet to take place is, as the case demands, the distinguishing element marking what is called "the three times". The completed efficacy of both cause and effect is referred to as "something in past time". If neither the efficacy of the cause or effect has been completed, it is called "something in future time." And if the efficacy of the cause has been completed, but the efficacy of the effect has not yet been completed, it is called "something in present time".

> "Feeling and its preparatory causes,
> activity causing suffering,
> the bringing to rest of two,
> and the antidote,
> are accepted as yet others." III. 21.

"Yet others" are the Four Noble Truths. The Truth of

Suffering is here called equivalent to feeling when it has preparatory ensnaring factors constricting it : whatever is felt in such a way involves or will involve suffering. The preparatory causes for suffering can be known as all events which make for the continuity of feeling-again (in a similar mode as before). The Truth of the Origination of Suffering is here equivalent to the action of these preparatory factors which are causes for the Truth of Suffering. The Truth of the Cessation of Suffering is the bringing to rest of both these preparatory factors and the feelings conditioned by them. The Truth of the Path of the Cessation of Suffering can be known as whatever serves as antidotes to such feelings and their preparatory causes.

> "Emancipation relying on 'oneself' or others
> through the knowledge of good qualities and faults,
> and through knowledge free from discriminations,
> is to be known as the meaning of the vehicles." III. 22a.

If through hearing from others about the so-called merits of Nirvāṇa and the so-called flaws of Saṃsāra, there arises a knowledge into these so-called merits and flaws, and through this knowledge, emancipation from Saṃsāra is attained, this is the vehicle of the Śrāvakas. If one does not hear anything about the merits of Nirvāṇa and the flaws of Saṃsāra from others, but works towards emancipation "by oneself", then this is the vehicle of the Private Buddhas. If knowledge free from discriminations arises by itself, and through this knowledge there is emancipation, this can be known as the Great Vehicle.

> "The last one is explained through designation,
> cause, preparatory factors, putting to rest,
> and the objects contemplated in it." III. 22b.

The topic under discussion is the meaning of the concepts "compounded" and "uncompounded". The term "designation" means everything which goes into the function of naming, etc. "Cause" is the store-consciousness that takes up the seeds ("seeds" being a metaphor for latent potency in the residual impressions). "Preparatory factors" are the eavironment, body, and objects of experience, along with *manas*, apprehension, and discrimination included in the evolving consciousnesses. *Manas* is that consciousness (linked with the idea of "I", etc.) whose mode of existence is to be always reflecting. "Apprehension" is the five consciousnesses of seeing, hearing, smelling, tasting, and touching. "Discrimination" is the sixth consciousness, because it discriminates all these objects. Designations, causes, preparatory factors, and the events associated with the store-consciousness, *manas*, the five sensuous consciousnesses, and the sixth consciousness, are "the compounded".

The uncompounded, on the other hand, is a putting to rest, a cessation, and the object of this putting to rest. Here, putting to rest is both cessation and the Path (leading to cessation), because putting to rest takes place because of these two. The object of a putting to rest is Suchness, because there is no other object in a putting to rest, because of its state of being the object-of-consciousness for the Path. There is also a state of putting to rest in the Path, because the action of putting to rest takes place because of it.

It should be known that skill in these knowledges regarding the concepts "aggregates" up to "compounded" and "uncompounded" is all skill in means.[42]

The compact meaning of "reality" : In summarization, there are two kinds of reality : mirror-reality and the reality of that which is seen (in the mirror). Mirror-reality is primary three-fold basic reality (constructed, interdependent, and fulfilled), because it manifests all the others. The seen realities would then be the subsequent nine, because they are seen in primary basic reality. The nine seen realities are : (1) the reality seen in the absence of conceit; (2) the reality seen in antidotes to reversals; (3) the reality seen in the emancipation of the Śrāvaka-vehicle; (4) the realities seen in the emancipation of the Great Vehicle—more gross reality having the power of maturing sentient beings, and more subtle reality the power of liberating them; (5) the realities seen in the flaws of others' theories, seen in the flaws of their exemplifications and justifications; (6) the realities seen while revealing the Great Vehicle to others; (7) the reality seen when one penetrates what can be known in all its aspects; (8) the reality seen in revealing true reality : signless Suchness; and (9) the reality seen in penetrating the motives lying behind the different manners of grasping after "self".

IV. The Cultivation of Antidotes, Situations There, and The Attainment of Fruition.

The cultivation of antidotes is the cultivation of the allies of enlightenment. This is to be discussed just now. First of all,

> "The cultivation of the applications of mindfulness
> comes about through susceptibility to harm,
> the cause of craving, the state of being the sensory domain,
> and lack of confusion, in relation to the Four Truths."
> IV. 1.

Susceptibility to harm is displayed by the body. Because it has the characteristic of compounded events susceptible to harm, one enters into the Truth of Suffering by an examination of it. Susceptibility to harm is the suffering state of compounded events, through which those who know see that all is liable to afflictions because of suffering. The cause of cravings is feelings, and one enters into the Truth of the Origination of Suffering by an examination of them. But attachment to the idea of "self" is only citta, and one enters into the Truth of the Cessation of Suffering by an examination of it, because there is the disappearance of any fear of the cessation of self (when one has understood that the "continuity of self" is only cittas). Through an examination of moment-events, one enters into the Truth of the Path, through a lack of confusion as regards events which serve to afflict, and those which serve to alleviate. So, at first, the cultivation of the applications of mindfulness is determined in relation to entry into the Four Truths.

After these, there is the cultivation of the right exertions. Because

> "The adverse factors and antidotes being known in every way,
> there develops a four-fold vigor,
> for their removal and approach." IV. 2.

From the cultivation of the applications of mindfulness, where adverse factors and antidotes have been completely known in all their aspects, a four-fold vigor for the removal of adverse factors, and for the arising of antidotes, develops. For the abandoning of malignant and unbeneficial events which have arisen, and so forth (i.e. for the arising of beneficial events which have not yet arisen, for the non-arising of unbeneficial events which have not yet arisen, and for the maintenance, further development, and complete fulfillment of beneficial events which have arisen).

> "Skill in steadiness for the increase of all aims,
> following upon eight motivating factors of abandoning
> five flaws." IV. 3.

In this cultivation of vigor for the removal and approach of these factors, a skill in steadiness of citta is the four bases of psychic power, because they are the cause of an increase in all psychic aims. "Steadiness" here is to be known as steadiness in citta, i.e. meditational concentration. "Thus the bases of psychic power follow immediately upon the right exertions". This skill can be known as being associated with the cultivation of eight motivating factors for the abandonment of five flaws. To tell us what five flaws these are, he says :

> "Sloth, forgetting instructions, slackness, excitedness,
> lack of motivating factors, and motivating factors :
> these are considered to be the five flaws." IV.4.

Here, slackness and excitedness are made into a single flaw. A lack of motivating factors is a flaw at a time when slackness and excitedness are being put to rest. Motivating factors are a flaw when they have been put to rest.

And how are the eight motivating factors of abandonment, which work towards their abandonment, to be determined ? The four which are conducive to the abandonment of sloth are zest, effort, faith, and tranquility. These are further to be known, in order, as being

> "The basis, that which is based on it, its mark, and its result." IV. 5a.

Zest is the support of effort. Effort is that which is based on zest. The mark of this basis, zest, is faith, because of its longing for truth in firm confidence. The result of this exertion, which is thus based, is tranquility, because of the attainment of special meditational concentrations after vigor has been undertaken. The remaining four motivating factors of abandonment : mindfulness, the state of knowing, volition, and equanimity, are to be known as antidotes to the four flaws as they are enumerated.

Furthermore this mindfulness, etc. are to be known, respectively, as being

> "A lack of loss in the meditational object,
> a recognition of slackness and excitedness,
> motivating factors in their removal,
> and continuance in tranquility in a state of rest." IV. 5b.

Mindfulness is a lack of loss of image, etc. in the meditational object. The state of knowing is the recognition of slackness and excitedness, when a lack of loss of mindfulness has occurred. The motivational factor towards their removal when they have been recognized is volition, and equanimity of citta is continuance in tranquility once slackness and excitedness have been put to rest.

Immediately upon the bases of psychic power, arise the five faculties, faith, etc. And how are they to be determined ?

> "When the factors conducive to liberation have been planted,
> from their sovereignty in zest in application,
> from non-loss of the meditational object,
> non-gliding, and investigation." IV.6.

By their sovereignty. When the factors conducive to liberation, the roots of the beneficial, have been planted in a skilled citta with the bases of psychic power, the five faculties : faith, etc. are to be known by being sovereign in faith, by being sovereign in vigor in application, by being sovereign in non-loss of the meditational object, by being sovereign in the non-gliding-about of citta, and by being sovereign in the investigation of events, respectively. Each of these faculties :

faith, etc. is to be known as being related to one of these sovereignties, respectively.

When these same faculties : faith, etc. are powerful, they are called "the powers". And their state of having power follows

> "from the adverse factors being diminished" IV. 7a,

when these powers are not dissipated by adverse factors : lack of faith, etc.

And for what reason is there a successive enumeration of faith, etc. in this way ?

> "because the latter are the result of the former." IV. 7b.

Having taken hold of faith, one undertakes the result of this cause, vigor. Having undertaken vigor, mindfulness occurs, and through this mindfulness having occurred, citta is concentrated. When citta is concentrated, one knows "as it is". They are called the faculties of the fully planted factors conducive to liberation.

Since it has been explained that the factors conducive to liberation, once they are planted, are faculties, are the factors conducive to penetration[43] to be known as faculties, or as powers ?

> "Two each of the factors conducive to penetration are
> faculties and powers." IV. 8a.

Coming to heat and the summits are faculties; the forbearances and highest mundane events, are powers.

Immediately after the powers, the limbs of enlightenment occur. And what is their determination ?

> "The limb serving as a basis, the limb through own-being,
> the limb of emancipation as the third,
> the fourth is the limb which is of good effect to others,
> and the limb which causes an absence of affliction is
> three-fold." IV. 8b.

The limbs of enlightenment are the different parts but contributing to enlightenment on the Path of Seeing. And among these, the limb which is the basis of enlightenment is mindfulness. The limb which is enlightenment by its own-being is the discernment of events. The limb of emancipation is vigor. The limb which is of good effect to others is friendly love. The limb which causes an absence of affliction is three-fold, being tranquility, meditational concentration, and equanimity. But to what purpose has the limb which causes an absence of affliction been indicated as three-fold ?

> "It is indicated thus because of initial cause, support, and own-being." IV. 9a.

The initial cause of an absence of affliction is tranquility, because tranquility is an antidote to that affliction-together caused by susceptibility to harm. The support for an absence of affliction is meditational concentration. And, by own-being, absence of affliction is equanimity.

Immediately upon the limbs of enlightenment, the limbs of the Path occur. And how are they to be determined ?

> "The limbs of the Path are eight-fold, and are accurate distinguishing, attainment, three-fold for its cultivation by others,
> and antidotes to adverse factors." IV. 9b-10a.

On the Path of Cultivation, the limb which serves for its accurate distinguishing is right views, by which one determines one's own realization of a worldly supermundane subsequently attained seeing.[44] The limb which serves for its attainment by others is right intention and right speech, because by its development, it may be caused to be attained by others. The limb for its cultivation by others is three-fold : right speech, action, and livelihood.

> "It is accepted that the perception (of Dharma) by others comes about with one's good conduct and satisfaction with little, which can be directly observed."
> IV. 10b.

It is through right speech, i.e. the certainty of suggestions and discourses, that a cultivation of insight arises in others. It is through right action that one is established in good conduct, because one no longer does what is not to be done. It is through right livelihood that one is established in satisfaction with little, because one seeks only garments, etc. to the extent as is conformable to Dharma. The limbs which serve as antidotes to adverse factors are again three : right effort, right mindfulness, and right meditational concentration. In these there is, respectively,

> "The capacity to serve as antidotes to afflictions,
> secondary afflictions,
> and adverse factors to power." IV. 11a.

For adverse factors are of three kinds : afflictions which are to be abandoned by cultivation; secondary afflictions : slackness and excitedness; and adverse factors to power : hindrances to the bringing about of special qualities. Among these, right effort is an antidote to the first, because of the cultivation of the Path. Right mindfulness is the antidote to the second, because of the absence of slackness and excitedness in mindfulness which is well-established in the preparatory causes for calm etc. Right concentration is the antidote to the third, because of the bringing about of the qualities of super-knowledges, etc. by dwelling in meditation.

This cultivation of antidotes may be known in brief as threefold :

> "Favorable when reversed, flowing continually when unreversed,
> non-flowing continuously of reversals when unreversed."
> IV. 11b-12 a.

as favorable to lack of reversal when reversed, favorable to lack of reversals when unreversed, unfavorable to reversals when unreversed, in the situations of those separated from Dharma, learners, and accomplished ones, respectively.

For the Bodhisattvas, on the other hand,

> "There is a distinction as regards objects-of-consciousness,
> mental attention, and attainment." IV. 12b.

The Śrāvakas' and Private Buddhas' object of meditation is the bodies, etc. of their own life-streams. The Bodhisattvas' is the bodies, etc. of both their own and others' life-streams. The Śrāvakas and Private Buddhas are mentally attentive to their bodies, etc. in their aspects of non-eternality, etc. but Bodhisattvas with the method of non-apprehension. The Śrāvakas and Private Buddhas cultivate the applications of mindfulness, etc. for a lack of attachment to their bodies, etc. Bodhisattvas do it neither for lack of attachment, nor for non-lack of attachment, but for a Nirvāṇa without a basis.* The cultivation of antidotes has been discussed.

What are the different situations that arise in this cultivation of antidotes ?

> "The causal situation, called "descending";
> that known as the preparation and fruition,
> where there is something left to do, and where there
> isn't, the distinctive (situation),
> the "higher" and that "having no higher",
> entry, confidence, gaining certainty, prediction,
> fully relating and gaining potency,
> attaining it,
> being of good effect,
> and completion of all undertakings." IV. 13-14.

The causal situation is the situation of someone first standing on a Bodhisattva-path, which is the situation of descending into a Path by the arising of the enlightenment-citta.[45] The situation of becoming prepared is everything that happens after the arising of the enlightenment citta, before any fruition has been attained. The situation of fruition is when some (fruition) has been attained. The situation of having something left to do is that of the learner. The situation of having nothing left to do is that of the accomplished one (i.e. the one who has passed beyond having to learn specifics or practise anything specific). A distinctive situation is that of one who is endowed with the special qualities of the super-knowledges, etc. A "higher situation" is that of a Bodhisattva, who does not enter the stages of a Śrāvaka, etc. A "situation having no higher" is that of

*See note 16.

a Buddha, because there is no other situation beyond it. The situation of gaining confidence is the stage where confidence is cultivated.[46] The situation of entering occurs at the first stage.[47] Gaining certainty occurs in the next six stages. The situation of being predicted for full enlightenment occurs in the eighth stage. The situation of being able to relate totally occurs in the ninth stage. The situation of gaining full potency occurs in the tenth stage. The situation of attaining enlightenment is the dharma-body of the Buddhas.[48] The situation of being of good effect (to others) is the enjoyment-body. The situation of completing (beneficial) actions is the formation-body of the Buddhas. All of these various situations which occur in many different ways, are here made known in brief only.

> "Further, in the ground of all events, they are threefold :
> unclear, unclear and clear, and completely clear." IV. 15

In this passage, "the unclear situation" starts with the causal situation, and goes up through the entire Path of Application.[49] "The unclear and clear situation" is that of the learners, and "the completely clear situation" is that of the accomplished ones.

> "And from this the situations of persons (on the Path) is known as is fitting." IV. 16.

And from this division of situations the situation of persons (on the Path) is known as is fitting. It is in this way that one can know whether a person stands in the lineage, or whether one has descended down into the Path.

Situations have been talked about, but what is the attainment of fruition there ?

> "Becoming a receptacle, called 'maturation';
> the power that comes about through its capacity;
> delight; growing; becoming completely cleared:
> these, in order, are fruitions." IV. 17.

Becoming a receptacle is that maturation which is favorable to the beneficial.[50] Power is where the beneficial becomes intensely great, due to the capacity coming from becoming a receptacle. Delight is that delight in the beneficial which comes from previous continued practise. Growing is the nourishing of the roots of the beneficial which comes through the continued practise of beneficial events, once they have become present. Becoming completely cleared is the eradication of obstructions. This is the five-fold fruition, which can be known as occurring in this order : the fruition of maturation, the fruition of capacity, the fruition which flows out from that, the fruition which makes one a full person, and the fruition of disjunction (from obstructions).

> "Ever increasing, the beginning, that through
> continuous practise,
> through their attainment all together,
> through being favorable,
> through disjunction from adverse factors,
> through distinction,
> through becoming higher,
> and through having no higher,
> another set of fruitions is given in conciseness." IV. 18.

The ever-increasing fruition is to be known by the succession (of beneficial events) coming about through the lineage, beginning with the arising of the enlightenment-citta. The beginning fruition is the first attainment of supermundane events (where emptiness is first realized). The fruition of continual practise is going beyond that, in the situation of a learner. The fruition of their attainment all together is all the events occurring together in the situation of an accomplished one. The fruition of favorability can be known as the ever-increasing fruition as it is the cause of all further fruitions.[51] The beginning fruition is the path of disjunction from adverse factors, and can be considered to be the antidotes. The fruition of disjunction is the fruition which comes through continuous practise and the fruition of completing it, which is the path of the learners, and accomplished ones where one is disjoined from afflictions. The fruition of distinction is the distinction that comes through the qualities of the super-knowledges. The stages of the Bodhisattva are the higher fruition, because they are higher than any other vehicle. The fruition having no higher is the stage of a Buddha. These four constitute the division of the fruition of continual practise and the attainment of all beneficial factors together. Thus, these other fruitions are indicated in brief, for in their full extent they are immeasurable.

Now, the compact meaning of the cultivation of antidotes : the cultivation that awakens, the cultivation of restraint, the cultivation of applications, the cultivation of necessary prerequisites one after the other, the cultivation of sticking to it, which comes by sticking to the Path of Seeing,[52] the cultivation of becoming involved,[53] elevated cultivation, beginning cultivation, intermediate cultivation, concluding cultivation (these three referring to the Path of Cultivation, where afflictions are eradicated), the cultivation having a higher (referring to entry into the Bodhisattva-stages and the full enfoldment of the pāramitās), and the cultivation having no higher, where the object of consciousness, mental attention & attainment is (always) distinctive.[54]

The compact meaning of the situations (in the cultivation of antidotes) : the situation which is the chance for becoming situated in a lineage, the situation of beginning undertakings which begins with the arising of the enlightenment-citta and lasts through (the path of) Application, which is begun with the arising of the enlightenment-citta, (in which the factors conducive to penetration are cultivated), situations which are not yet clear, situations that are both unclear and clear, situations that are completely clear, situations that are adorned (with special qualities), the situation of pervading all, which comes through the pervasive power of the ten Stages, and the situation which has no higher.

The compact meaning of fruition : the fruition which comes from favoring others, the fruition which comes through special qualities, the fruition which comes through former continual practise, the fruition which comes through gradual drawing out (of all afflictions), the fruition through suggestion and mutual investigation (directed towards the afflictions "of others"), and the fruition through unfailing ascertainment and advice. The fruition that comes from favoring others are the five fruitions (becoming a receptacle, gaining strength, gaining delight, growing, becoming completely clear). The fruitions that come about through special qualities are the others (ever-increasing, beginning (of supermundane events), continuous practise as a learner, attainment of all beneficial factors as an accomplished one, the fruition of favorability, disjunction from adverse factors, distinction, becoming higher, and having no higher). That which comes about through former continual practise is the fruition of maturation. And that which comes about through the gradual drawing out of all afflictions are the other four fruitions (gaining strength, gaining delight, growing, becoming completely clear). The fruitions which come about through suggestion and mutual investigation are the four fruitions beginning with the ever-increasing one (ever-increasing fruition, beginning fruition, fruition from continual practise as a learner, and the fruition of attaining all beneficial factors together). The fruition through unfailing ascertainment and advice are the six fruitions beginning with the fruition of favorability (the fruition of favorability, the beginning fruition, the fruition of disjunction from afflictions, the fruition of distinction, the higher fruition, and the fruition having no higher), which come because these four have been clearly ascertained and taught (to others).

V. The Supremacy of the Vehicle

Now the supremacy of the Vehicle is to be discussed. The author introduces the topic thus :

> "Its supremacy is considered to lie in its practise,
> its support, and its full realization." V. 1a.

The three-fold supremacy of the Great Vehicle, through which it is a vehicle having no higher, is the supremacy of its practise, the supremacy of its support, and the supremacy of its full realization.

The supremacy of its practise is to be known as lying in the practise of the ten pāramitās. With these pāramitās

> "Practise, moreover, is sixfold." V. 1.
> "The highest, mental attention,
> 'after-Dharma',
> the avoidance of extremes,
> and distinct and indistinct practise." V. 2a.

This is the sixfold practise : practise developed to its highest, practise of mental attention, practise 'after-Dharma', practise of the avoidance of extremes, distinct practise, and indistinct practise.

Among these,

> "The highest form is twelvefold." V.2b.
> "Practise is considered to take its highest form
> with magnanimity, persistence, development,
> inexhaustibility, continuity, lack of trouble,
> power, an encompassing quality,
> its beginning undertakings,
> its attainment, its steady flow, and fulfillment." V.3.

Practise is considered to take on its highest form when it is characterized by the following twelve features : magnanimity, persistence, development, inexhaustibility, continuity, lack of trouble, power, an encompassing quality, beginning undertakings, attainment, steady flow, and fulfillment.

The highest form of practise through magnanimity comes through eminence in desirelessness for all those things that constitute "prosperity" in common parlance. The highest form of practise through persistence comes with the ability to cultivate it even for three uncountable aeons. The highest form of practise through development in effort comes through exertions towards the bringing about of all sentient beings' aims.[55] The highest form of practise through inexhaustibility is to be known as that complete lack of exhaustion which comes through a transformation one undergoes with the Great Enlightenment.[56] The highest form through continuity is to be known through fulfillment of all the pāramitās of giving, etc. towards all sentient beings without any interruption, the ability for which comes with the confidence that "self" and "others" are really the same. The highest form through lack of trouble comes through the fulfillment of the pāramitās, giving, etc. being accompanied only by great rejoicing. The highest form of practise through power means the fulfillment of the pāramitās of giving, etc. accompanied by the meditational concentration on the Treasury of the Sky[57] etc. The highest form of practise that comes through its encompassing quality means that it comes through the encompassment of the knowledge free from discriminations. The highest form of practise in beginning undertakings comes in the stage where confidence is cultivated, in an intensely great forbearance. The highest form of practise in its (first) attaining comes with the first stage, and the highest form of practise in its steady flow is characterized by continuing strong in later stages. The highest form of practise in its fulfillment means that it is climaxed in the tenth of Tathāgata stages with one's fulfillment as a Bodhisattva, or one's fulfillment as a Buddha.

> "Because of them, the pāramitās exist in an ultimate sense." V. 4.

The ten pāramitās exist, ultimately, only when practise has attained these highest forms, and such a practise is found in full practise of the pāramitās. As there may be a question as to what these ten are, their names are given at this point :

> "Giving, good conduct, forbearance, vigor, meditation,
> insight, means, resolve, power, and knowledge :
> these are the ten pāramitās." V. 5.

What is the action of each of these pāramitās separately ?

> "Favoring, not harming, forgiveness, increase of good qualities,
> ability in descent and liberating, inexhaustibility,
> constantly developing, enjoyment and maturing (of others)." V. 6.

Thus their actions are explained in order : The Bodhisattva favors sentient beings through giving. Because of good conduct, one does no harm to others. Because of forbearance, one pardons any harm done to one by others. One increases good qualities through vigor. Through meditation, one plunges down and sets things going with the supernormal faculties. Through insight, one is able to liberate others by giving them the right advice. Through the pāramitā of skill in means that comes with the transformation one undergoes with the Great Enlightenment, one is able to make one's giving, etc. inexhaustible. Through the pāramitā of resolve[58], because one is able to embrace all occurrences favorable to the pāramitās, one develops constantly in giving, etc. empassioned for the arising of Enlightenment in all sentient beings. Through the pāramitā of power, that is, the twin strengths of contemplation and cultivation, one is able to course constantly in giving, etc. because they do not allow adverse factors to arise. Through the pāramitā of knowledge, one experiences again the enjoyment of all events which are sovereign in giving, etc. because of the removal of confusion as regards these much-praised events, and brings sentient beings to maturity. Highest practise has been herewith described.

And what is the practise of mental attention ?

> "Mahāyāna mental attention towards events as they have been prescribed,
> comes about through insight of three kinds in the Bodhisattva continually." V. 7.

The practise of mental attention is a mental attention through insight consisting of repeatedly hearing about, reflecting upon, and meditating upon the events in the Great Vehicle which, according to the manner in which they are prescribed, make possible giving, etc. What good quality does this mental attention through three kinds of insight bring ?

> "For nurturing sensory domains, for entry, and for success in aims, it comes to be." V. 8a.

By being mentally attentive with the insight that consists of listening, there arises a nurturing of the sensory domains. With that which consists of reflection, one enters into the meaning of what one has heard. By meditation, finally, one attains success in aims, by completely clearing an entry into the Bodhisattva-stages.

> "And it is to be known as connected with ten acts of Dharma." V.8b.

The practise of mental attention is furthermore to be known as being comprised of ten acts of Dharma. And what ten acts of Dharma are these ?

> "Writing, reverencing, giving, hearing, saying, taking up, explaining, studying by 'oneself', reflecting and meditating." V.9.

The writing up of the Great Vehicle (i.e. the composition and copying of Mahāyāna works), reverencing the Great Vehicle, giving to others, listening to that which is said by others, saying things "oneself", taking up the Great Vehicle, explaining it to others, studying the meanings of the texts by "oneself", reflecting, and meditating.

> "This ten-fold action constitutes an immeasurable heap of merit". V. 10a.

Why is the great fruition of these ten acts of Dharma spoken about to a great degree only in the Great Vehicle, but not in the sūtras of the Śrāvaka-vehicle ?

> "Because of its distinctiveness and inexhaustibility." V. 10b.

What sort of "distinctiveness" is this ? And what sort of "inexhaustibility" ?

> "due to its favoring others, due to its lack of repose." V. 10c.

It has distinctiveness due to its favoring of others. Its inexhaustibility can be known as being due to its never stopping, because it does not rest even in complete Nirvāṇa, (but rather returns continually to Saṃsāra). The practise of mental attention has been explained.

What is practise "after-Dharma" ?

> "Practise 'after-Dharma' is development of lack of distractedness, and lack of reversal." V. 11.

This practise 'after-Dharma' is twofold, being the development of lack of distractedness, and lack of reversal.[59] Lack of distractedness comes through six-fold absence of distractedness, corresponding to the following six-fold distractedness : distractedness in the nature of things, distractedness towards the "external", distractedness towards the "internal", distractedness due to signs, distractedness due to susceptibility to harm, and distractedness due to mental attention. So that it can be known what character these have, he says:

> "Emergence, gliding to objects-of-sense, relishing,
> slackness and excitedness, deliberate intentions towards experience,
> a sense of 'I' in mental attention, and defective citta,
> are to be known by the wise as distractedness." V. 12.

At the time of emergence from meditational concentration, there is distractedness due to the nature of things, because of the collection of five consciousnesses; gliding to objects-of-sense is distractedness towards the "external"; relishing the meditational state, and slaekness or excitedness in regard to it, is distractedness towards the "internal"; deliberate intentions in meditation is distractedness due to mental signs, because of the attachment to certain mental signs (inherent in deliberate intentions); mental attention linked with a sense of "I" is distractedness due to susceptibility to harm, because it is through the force of susceptibility to harm that the pride of thinking "I am" arises;[60] distractedness of mental attention is a small-minded state of citta, which comes with mental attention to and practise of the Lesser Vehicle (and all those who would assert a fundamental duality).

The development of lack of reversal is to be known as lying in ten things, which are

> "Not gliding to a mental attention towards mental marks and meanings,
> avoiding the reversal of two characteristics,
> realizing the adventitiousness, lack of fear, lack of pride in susceptibility to harm and clearing;
> realizing that there is familiarity due to connection, and lack of familiarity with disjunction;
> the existence and non-existence of objects : this is lack of reversal towards mental marks." V. 12-15a.

> "Appearance through duality is non-existence as it appears;
> a lack of reversal towards objects is avoidance of (ideas of) existence and non-existence;

mental attention towards talk arises with a basis in talk,
and a realization of this is lack of reversal in a mental
attention where there is the appearance of a duality;
the object's existence and non-existence is like that of
a magical creation;
and so non-reversal is a non-gliding towards the ideas
of being and non-being." V. 15b-18a.

A lack of reversal in regards to mental marks can be known in this way : In connection (with a so-called object of a sense or understanding), it may be thought "This is its name !", because linguistic habits have not been severed; this has meaningfulness only because of past familiarity, meaninglessness because of basic reversal. (ad V, 13-14)

And how is there a lack of reversal in regard to "objects of a sense or understanding ?" A lack of reversal in regards to an "object" of sense or understanding is that observing which recognizes, in regard to the "object" of a sense or understanding, that it does not exist as it appears, since it appears with duality, i.e. the division of object apprehended and subject apprehendor, due to the arising of their semblance. This lack of reversal is avoidance of the idea of an object of a sense or understanding's existence, because of the non-being of object apprehended and subject apprehendor, and avoidance of the idea of its non-being, because of the existing being of the confusion in its appearances. (ad V, 15.)

A lack of reversal in regard to mental attention is the cognition that a mental attention towards talk, being suffused with talk which leads to the notion of object apprehended and subject apprehendor, is the only basis for the discrimination between object apprehended and subject apprehendor. As regards mental attention which is the cause for the semblance of object apprehended and subject apprehendor as things apart, this mental attention towards talk is itself to be known as the basis for the distinction between object apprehended and subject apprehendor, because it is suffused with cognitions of verbal specification. (ad V, 16.)

Immediately subsequently, the existence and non-existence of the "object" is discussed (i.e. in what way it can be said to have existence, and in what way it can be said to have no existence). It is to be regarded like a magical creation, etc. as follows : A magical creation does not exist with the true appearance of an elephant, etc. (being produced in spectators' vision in a magical show), and yet it doesn't not exist, because of the existence of the illusion itself only. In the same way, an "object" does not exist as it appears, with the state of having object apprehended and subject apprehendor aspects, but yet it doesn't not exist, because of the existence of the illusion itself. Because of looking at the "object" like a magical creation, etc. (and by the word "etc.", mirages, dreams, the moon in the water, and other examples are to be known), mental factors observe without gliding, and there is lack of reversal in this lack of gliding, and, on this account, also a lack of gliding of citta to the very conceptions of "being" and "non-being".[61] (ad V, 17.)

> "Lack of reversal in the own-characteristic is everything's being only a name,
> with all discriminations' non-evolving." V.18b-c.

"All this, from visibles seen by the eye, to mentally cognizables grasped by the *manas*, is only names" : this knowledge is lack of reversal in the own-characteristic, because of being an antidote to all discriminations. In which own-characteristic ?

> "In the own-characteristic of ultimate truth." V.18d.

For in conventional truth, it is not realized that all this is only names.

> "Being freed in the Ground of all Events, because no event is found there,
> a universal characteristic arises : this is a further lack of reversal." V.19.

Not a single event is found without the absence of self in all events, therefore this Ground of all Events (emptiness) is the universal characteristic of all events, and the knowledge of this in this manner is a lack of reversal in regard to the universal characteristic. The knowledge that the non-clarity of this Ground of all Events consists only in the non-abandonment of reversed mental attention, and that clarity is its abandonment, is non-reversal in regard to non-clarity and clarity, respectively. (ad V, 20)

> "Because of the Ground of all Events' clarity by nature,
> it is like the sky;
> there is a total adventitiousness of duality,
> and this is an additional lack of reversal." V. 21.

Because of the Ground of all Events being like space, it is clear by nature, and the duality "clear" and "unclear" is only adventitious, arising later. The knowledge of this in this way is a lack of reversal as regards the purely adventitious.

> "There is no affliction or thorough clearing either for
> events or persons, and, because of this non-existence,
> there can be neither fear nor pride,
> and this is an additional lack of reversal." V. 22.

Because there is neither a "person" nor "events", there can be neither afflictions-together or thorough clearing for them. So there is no afflictions-together or thorough clearing for anyone or anything at all. So there is no detriment on the part of affliction, and no excellence on the part of alleviation. So how can there be fear ? How can there be pride ? This is the non-reversal relating to lack of fear and pride.

These ten lacks of reversal may be connected to the ten Vajra-Words, in this order. The ten Vajra-Words : existing, non-existing, the non-reversed substrata, their likeness to a magical creation, lack of discrimination, luminousness of nature, affliction and alleviation, their likeness to space, lack of detriment, and lack of excellence. The setting-up of the essence of the Vajra-Words takes place through own-being, objects-of-consciousness, lack of discriminations, and the rebuttal to objections. "Through own-being" : through the three own-beings which are called the fulfilled, the constructed, and the interdependent : they relate to the first three Vajra-Words in order; and through objects-of-consciousness, and through lack of discrimination in regard to them, by which one does not discriminate, there is knowledge free from discriminations, and through it, that which one does not discriminate: luminousness of nature; through this luminousness one arrives at the determination of that which can be known, and of its knowledge, because of lack of discrimination as regards the three own-beings. The rebuttal to objections is as follows : To these remaining Vajra-Words, the objection may arise : "If these events which have the characteristics of the constructed and the interdependent are not to be found, how is it that they are apprehended ? And if they do exist, luminousness of nature is not logical." This objection is refuted by the likeness of magical creations, for that which is magically created is not to be found, and yet is apprehended. (The second objection) : "If there is luminousness of nature, how can there be affliction in events, and only subsequently alleviation ?" The refutation of this objection can be known as coming through the likeness of affliction and alleviation to space. For space, which is perfectly pure by nature, may yet be disturbed, and alleviated from disturbance. (The third objection) : "If the afflictions of limitless beings have gone to rest with the arising of limitless Buddhas, how is it that there has not been an eradication of Saṃsāra, and an increase of Nirvāṇa ?" The refutation to this comes through the lack of detriment and lack of excellence (in Saṃsāra and Nirvāṇa). And because of their very limitlessness, the realms of sentient beings belong to the alleviation-alternative.

The second setting-up of the essence of the Vajra-Words ;

> Where, which, and from which confusion;
> where and which lack of confusion;
> the two fruitions of confusion and lack of confusion;
> the termination of them both;
> lack of reversal in "existence" and "non-existence";
> likeness of the substrata to magical creations;
> lack of discriminations; luminousness by nature itself eternally;
> affliction and alleviation; their likeness to space;
> thus an absence of detriment and excellence:
> these are the ten Vajra-Words.

Practise "after-Dharma" has been spoken of. But what is practise in the avoidance of extremes ? This is what is taught in the *Ratnakūṭa-sūtra** as "the middle practise". Through the avoidance of which extremes is it to be known ?

> "The extremes of maintaining separateness and identity of the Jains and Śrāvakas,
> the twofold extremes of superimposition and denial, in regard to personality and events, V. 23
> the extreme of assuming adverse factors and their antidotes,
> cognitions of eternality and annihilation,
> object apprehended and subject apprehendor,
> affliction & alleviation in two ways, in three ways, V. 24
> the seven-fold extremes of discrimination :
> extremes relating to being and non-being,
> something which is to be brought to rest, putting to rest, & something which is to be feared, V. 25
> occupation with rightness and wrongness as regards objects apprehended and subjects apprehendors,
> and the extremes of discriminations as regards non-arising and simultaneity." V. 26

To say that there is a difference between materiality, etc. and the self, is an extreme, and to say that there is an identity between them, is also an extreme. In order to avoid these extremes, there is the middle path, by which there is no consideration of "self", and no consideration of "humanity". To say that as far as view of a self is concerned, there is no life-force except the body, and another life equals another body, becomes another view. In this case, the extreme of the Jains[62] is to say that this materiality is eternal, whereas the extreme of the Śrāvakas[63] is to say that it is not eternal. In order to avoid these extremes, there is the middle path, which does not regard materiality, etc. as either eternal or non-eternal. "There is a self" is the extreme of superimposing a fixed personality, and the extreme of denial is to say that "All is without a self". In order to avoid these extremes, there is the middle path which is a knowledge free from discriminations standing midway between maintaining self and maintaining non-self.[64] "A citta was" is an

**Kāśyapa-parivarta-sūtra* 52-71.

extreme of superimposition as regards events, and "It wasn't" is an extreme of denial. In order to avoid these extremes, there is the middle path, where there is neither "citta" nor "volition" nor "*manas*" nor "consciousness". The extreme of assuming adverse factors is to say that unbeneficial events, etc. are affliction-together; the extreme of assuming antidotes is to say that beneficial events are alleviation. In order to avoid these extremes, there is the middle path, which does not admit these two extremes, does not speak of them, and has nothing to do with them. The extreme of assuming eternality is to say, in regard to personalities and events, that they continue to exist; the extreme of assuming annihilation is to say of them that they do not continue to exist. In order to avoid these two extremes, there is the middle path, which stands in the middle as regards tnese two extremes. To suppose that objects apprehended and subjects apprehendors always imply ignorance, is another extreme. Thus the extreme which says that compounded factors and the uncompounded constitute understanding, and the extreme which says that (discriminating) objects apprehended and subjects apprehendors constitute the virtual cessation of the uncompounded, or that they in turn are made to cease by the Path, constitute extremes in regard to objects apprehended and subjects apprehendors in two ways, by making divisions into black and white fixed alternatives. In order to avoid these extremes, there is the middle path, which says that understanding and ignorance are not two, because of the non-being of the notions of understanding, ignorance, objects apprehended, subjects apprehendors, etc.

Afflictions-together are of three kinds : the afflictions-together of the afflictions, the afflictions-together of actions, and the afflictions-together of birth. Among these, the afflictions-together of the afflictions are three-fold : views, anything marked by attachment, hostility, and confusion, and aspiration for being-again, of which the antidotes are emptiness of knowledge, the signlessness of knowledge, and the aimlessness of knowledge. The afflictions-together of action are unafflicted and afflicted motivating dispositions, of which the antidote is the lack of motivating dispositions in knowledge. The afflictions-together of birth are the arising, in each moment, of cittas and events associated with cittas, which constitute a being bound to being-again, of which the antidote is lack of birth in knowledge, lack of arising in knowledge, and lack of an own-being in knowledge. The disappearance of these three kinds of affliction constitutes alleviation. In this connection, because of the emptiness of knowledge, etc. events are emptiness of the knowable, etc. and it is through this three-fold afflictions-together that they are temporarily not made emptinesses, for by nature there are only these emptinesses, etc. because of the lack of afflictions-together in the Ground of all Events by nature. So if there is the discrimination that something is being afflicted-together or thoroughly cleared, this is an extreme, because of the non-being of afflictions-together and thorough clearing in that which is unafflicted by nature. In order to avoid this extreme, there is a middle path, which does not make events empty because of an "emptiness", but yet sees all events as empty.

Furthermore, there may be seven kinds of discrimination which involve an extreme of duality. Discrimination even in regard to being is an extreme. A discrimination as to a non-being, e.g. that personality must exist because it is through its destruction that emptiness, an absence of self, exists, or that it doesn't—these are extremes—and as there may be such discrimination, there is a middle path which avoids these extremes discriminating a duality, which goes as follows : Emptiness doesn't occur because of the destruction of personality, rather, emptiness itself is already empty, by the emptiness of the extreme of assuming a "previous", the emptiness of the extreme of assuming a "subsequent", and the emptiness of the present.[65]

A discrimination as to "something which is to be brought to rest" is an extreme. A discrimination as to a state of putting to rest is another extreme. Because of a fear of emptiness that comes with discriminating "something to be abandoned" and "its abandonment".[66] For avoiding these extremes discriminating a duality, there is the example of space.* A discrimination as to "something that is to be feared" is an extreme, and a discrimination of fear that comes from assuming "something that is to be feared" is an extreme, because of the frightening aspect of suffering which comes from fear towards the aggregates of materilaity, etc. when constructed into a frightening aspect due

*cf. ad V., 22, comments on Vajra Words, reply to second objection

to suffering. In order to avoid this extreme of discriminating a duality, there is the example of the painter.[67] The former example of space is employed by Śrāvakas also, but this example only by Bodhisattvas.

A discrimination as to "an object apprehended" is an extreme; a discrimination as to "a subject apprehendor" is also an extreme. For avoiding these extremes discriminating a duality, there is the example of the magician.[68] Though there is no being of an object because of the knowledge of perception-only, through this knowledge that there is no object, "perception-only" is also refuted. When there is no being (of an object), perception is not possible, so these are alike in this way.

A discrimination as to "rightness" is also an extreme. A discrimination as to "wrongness" is also an extreme, because one discriminates from an investigation of what already was, as regards either "rightness" or "wrongness". For avoiding these extremes involving a duality, there is the example of two sticks of wood. Just as, from the friction of two sticks of wood, where there is no characteristic of fire present, a fire suddenly arises, and once arisen, burns up the sticks of wood, just so, it is in an examination of how events were which has a characteristic which does not partake of rightness, that the aim which has a characteristic of rightness, i.e. the faculty of insight, arises. And when it has arisen, it causes the same investigation of what was to disappear. So these are alike in this way. For there is no favoring of rightness except through a characteristic of non-rightness, i.e. an investigation of what already was, which has the characteristic of wrongness.[69]

A discrimination as to "practise" is also an extreme and discrimination as to "non-practise" is also an extreme, by which one discriminates either an activity which is preceded by enlightenment, or by a lack of capacity. For avoiding these extremes discriminating a duality, there is the example of the oil-lamp.[70]

A discrimination as to a "state of non-arising" is an extreme. A discrimination as to simultaneity is also an extreme. Such as when one discriminates the non-arising of antidotes, or the loug duration of the afflictions-together. For avoiding these extremes discriminating a duality, there is the second example of the oil-lamp.[71] And so the practise of abandoning extremes discriminating a duality, has been explained.

What is distinct and indistinct practise ?

> "Distinct and indistinct practise are to be known in reference to the Ten Stages." V. 27a.

The excellence in the pāramitās which relate to certain specific stages in the Bodhisattva's career is distinct practise. Indistinct practise is that which springs up everywhere (without any distinctions).

And what is the supremacy of its support ?

> "Determination, from that the Ground, what is to be brought about,
> bringing it about, sustension, reflection, preserverence, penetration, extensiveness, going forth (to meet others), remaining in a tranquil state, and its support in its pre-eminence." V. 27b-28.

the author says, referring to twelve kinds of support, which are : its support in determining designations for events, its support in the Ground of all Events, its support in what is to be brought about, its support in bringing it about, its support in sustension, its support in its reflection, its support in its preserverence, its support in its penetration, its support in its extensiveness, its support in its going forth (to meet others), its support in its remaining in a tranquil state, and its support in its pre-eminence. Among these, the first is those events, which relate to the pāramitās, etc. becoming determined. The second is Suchness. The third and fourth come about gradually through penetration of the Ground of all Events resulting from mastery in the events of the pāramitās, etc. The fifth is the support of the knowledge consisting in what has been heard. The sixth comes about through sustension after having understood that which consists of reflection.[72] The seventh comes about through sustension of that which consists of cultivation "each individually"[73]. The eighth comes about on the First Stage, on the Path of Seeing;[74] the ninth on the Path of Cultivation up to the Seventh Stage;[75] the tenth on the Seventh Stage through understanding events in the manner of a mundane-and-supermundane path;[76] the eleventh on the Eighth Stage,[77] and the twelfth in the ninth and tenth stages.[78] Just as for the first two, each of these obtains a name of a support in each of these situations, respectively. And that is why they are called "supports".

And what is its full realization?

> "Non-deficiency, non-turning-away,
> non-distractedness, fulfillment,
> arising, nurturing, skill,
> the state of no-basis,
> the state of no obstuctions,
> and not remaining tranquil in that (state of no obstructions) :
> that is full realization." V. 29-30.

Its full realization comes in seven ways : the non-deficiency of conditions (necessary to enter the Great Vehicle), which is the full realization of becoming situated in the lineage; not turning away from the Great Vehicle, which is the full realization of confidence; non-distractedness by a lesser vehicle, which is the full realization of the arising of the enlightenment-citta; fulfillment of the pāramitās, which is the full realization of practise; the arising of the Noble Path, which is the full realization of entering down into restraining (flaws); the state of having nurtured the roots of the beneficial, which is the full realization of maturing sentient beings through intimacy for a long time; a state of skill in citta, which is the full realization of clearing the field; being based in neither Saṃsāra nor Nirvāṇa, which is the full realization of the attainment of a prediction (to complete enlightenment) on the Irreversible Stage; the absence of obstructions, which is the full realization of the Buddha-stage; not remaining tranquil in that (complete enlightenment), which is the full realization of showing full enlightenment forth.[79]

> "This Treatise is the Separating Out, the
> Explanation of the Middle"

because of its explanation of the Middle Path by an explanation of the middle and two extremes, or by an explanation of the middle's avoiding these extremes,

"And it has as its import the deep essence"

because it is beyond the scope of dialectics, and because it is impenetrable by antagonists

"and is of great use"

both to "oneself" and "others".

"It has use for all"

because it relates to all three vehicles

"and is the pushing away of all unhappiness" V.31

because it brings one close to the abandonment of the obstructions which are afflictions and the obstructions of the knowable.

The compact meaning of "supremacy" : In brief, there are three kinds of "supremacy" : supremacy in practise, supremacy in the support of practise, and supremacy in fruition of practise. A practise is highest which is of such a kind by which there is "Mahāyāna mental attention towards events as they have been prescribed" (V. 7), etc. through which manner of operating there is both evolvement from distractedness through cultivation of calm, and evolvement into lack of reversals through the cultivation of higher vision, which is undertaken for emancipation by means of a middle path, and in which ,in ten stages, there is both distinct and indistinct practise (V.27a).

The compact meaning of "lack of reversals" : through lack of reversal in that which is manifested, one penetrates the aim of calm; and through lack of reversal towards "objects", one penetrates the aim of higher vision. Through lack of reversal in mental attention, one avoids the initial cause for the reversals, and through the lack of the reversal of "gliding" (cf. V. 11; V. 13; V. 17), one brings it about that these aims are well taken hold of. By lack of reversal in own-characterisucs, one practises the path without discriminations which serves as its antidote. And by lack of reversal in the common characteristic, one penetrates the nature of alleviation. Through lack of reversal of mental attention towards "uncleared" and "cleared", one comes to know the state that is both the abandonment and the non-abandonment of the obstructions, and by the non-reversal of realizing their adventitiousness, one comes to know affliction and alleviation as they truly are. Through the non-reversal which consists in being neither afraid or proud, one goes forth to freedom from all obstructions.

Herewith, the *Separation of the Middle from Extremes* is completed.

> If there is any merit in composing this commentary,
> may it be helpful for all beings' growth in merit and in
> knowledge.
> By this, may all the beings acquire before too long
> Great well-being and the three kinds of enlightenment.

NOTES

1. In this beginning passage of the *Commentary on the Separation of the Middle from Extremes*, we have an illustration of the striking difference between the methodologies of Nāgārjuna and Vasubandhu. Whereas Nāgārjuna emphasizes "the lack of own-being in events" to such a degree that he wishes to dialectically invalidate any statement that could be made, Vasubandhu is interested in the psychological processes which allow us to reach a state where "the lack of own-beings in events" is realized. Nāgārjuna has little to say on this, and in fact in upholding a radical distinction between conventional and ultimate truths, does not give us any path for bridging the two. Vasubandhu, however, as we have seen in *The Thirty Verses*, regards both affliction (the constructed) and alleviation (the fulfilled) as aspects of one constantly changing interdependent stream of events. His "fulfilled", being the absence of own-beings in any event, is the same as Nāgārjuna's "ultimate truth". But whereas Nāgārjuna wishes to demonstrate the inadequacy of all conventional statements (and all statements are, by necessity, conventional), Vasubandhu is interested in showing a path, conceived in conventional terms, which leads to the abandonment of all mental constructions. The provisional constructions used by Vasubandhu for this purpose are however self-dissolving, since, finally, for Vasubandhu as for Nāgārjuna, there can be only ineffable Emptiness.

In emphasizing the existence of the construction of that which was not, Maitreyanātha and Vasubandhu affirm that there is a force in interdependent events which gives rise to constructions and afflictions. Thus there is a reality given to suffering which does not arise with Nāgārjuna's dialectical denials of any existent contrasts or causalities.

To Vasubandhu, what is necessary in getting rid of all dualities, i.e. in realizing Emptiness, is the removal of the discrimination between objects apprehended and subjects apprehendors. Once this duality vanishes, it is assumed that all others do, too. There *is* a force which gives rise to the duality of object and subject, but when it is investigated, it is seen that the duality is untenable. Once the duality is no longer seen, Emptiness *is* seen, for "Emptiness is the separation of the construction of that which was not" i.e. the interdependent "from the being of object apprehended and subject apprehendor." So Emptiness can be realized in the construction of that which was not, and the construction of that which was not is found in Emptiness, as well, for it has no "own-being", either. The sentence "That which remains (after duality vanishes) is what is really existent here" indicates that after the dualities of constructions cease, whatever remains is what is really existent, and is Emptiness. What all this is must of course remain ineffable, because words are constructed on dualistic lines. (See the article by Nagao, "What remains in *Śūnyatā*", in *Mahāyāna Buddhist Meditation : Theory and Practise*, pp 66-82.)

2. There is a playing with words here which implies that "Emptiness" could equally well be called "Fullness". Because Emptiness and the construction of that which was not may both render everything non-empty—Emptiness because it is "itself" the flow of all events; the construction of that which was not because it constructs the flow into discrete entities. But everything *is* empty because there is the appearance of objects apprehended in the latter case, which constructions are seen to be empty. And the construction of that which was not itself is empty. Thus it is stated that "Everything is neither empty nor non-empty." If one simply said, "It is empty", this would be characterizing everything by a single characteristic (which would be a construction of that which was not); if one simply says, "It is non-empty", this would be denying the possibility of emptying out all constructions from the flow.

3. Here, Maitreyanātha and Vasubandhu address themselves to the phenomenology of the construction of that which was not. That is, how do those dualities, which may be utterly discarded, first arise ? Vasubandhu says that the appearance of objects of sense and understanding arises because there is the experience of visibles, etc. In other words, the experience of visibles in consciousness makes the belief in visible objects separate from consciousness, arise. Similarly the appearance of sentient beings arises because of sense-faculties directly experienced in "one's own" life-stream, and inferred in "others'" life-streams. The appearance of "self", an ego-sense, arises only with an afflicted *manas*, that term here being used in Asaṅga's new sense of a witness consciousness projecting the view of self. Finally, the appearance of perceptions is just the six consciousnesses themselves, constantly transforming. Maitreyanātha can say, "There is no real object for it", just as Vasubandhu is to say in *The Twenty Verses*. Vasubandhu here explains how this can be said. There is no fixed aspect in the appearances of objects of sense and understanding, and sentient beings, because these are constantly changing, and a so-called "object" will appear differently to one consciousness-stream than to another. The appearances of self and perceptions, on the other hand, are "false", because such a self does not exist, and because the perceptions usually appear with divisions. Thus,

there is non-being of visibles (as objects separate from consciousness), there is non-being of the five sense-faculties (because they are not characterizable), there is non-being of *manas* (which projects a false sense of ego), and there is non-being for the six consciousnesses (since their divisions do not exist). If all these have no own-being, then consciousness itself cannot exist, either.

4. As long as objects of sense or understanding are discriminated, it is the constructed "own-being". But the capacity for this construction lies in the interdependent. The annihilation of any duality between object apprehended and subject apprehendor is the fulfilled.

5. The *caittas* are the motivating dispositions associated with citta. (See *Discussion of the Five Aggregates*, p 66.) On the three "realms of existence", see *Discussion of the Five Aggregates*, note 12.

6. "Being again" is usually rendered as "re-birth" But since every new arising moment is a new birth according to Vasubandhu's *Explanation of Dependent Origination*, this term has reference mainly to what is happening "in one life-stream". It is craving which sets the series going in a certain "habit-energy" way of "being again"

7. The traditional formulation of dependent origination is : ignorance→motivating dispositions→consciousness→psychophysical complex→six sense-fields→contact→feelings and cognitions→craving→clinging→(rigid) being→decrepitude→dying. Ever since the *Paṭṭhāna*, this formulation has been interpreted both embryologically up to six sense-fields, after/birth up to dying, as well as "taking place in a single moment"

All of the limbs of dependent origination working together are called "the afflictions-together" in this work. But only three are simple afflictions by themselves. These are ignorance, craving, and clinging. The limbs of dependent origination which are action, i.e. retributive action, are motivating dispositions (quite naturally for Vasubandhu since he regards action which carries retribution as volitions, a kind of motivating disposition, in *A Discussion for the Demonstration of Action*) and "being" (which rigidification itself depends on volitions). The afflictions-together of birth, i.e. those suffering-linked events which come about simply by being born, are consciousness, the psychophysical complex, the six sense-fields, contact, feelings and cognitions, decrepitude, and dying, since these will occur simply by being born.

8. Bhāvaviveka in his *Madhyamakahṛdaya* disagrees with Vasubandhu's characterization of emptiness as "being of non-being", and states that "emptiness" has reference only to non-being (*Madhyamakahṛdaya*, V, 10-16, Peking/Tokyo Tibetan Tripiṭaka, volume 96, p 11). Sthiramati in his *Madhyāntavibhāgaṭīkā* in turn attacked Bhāvaviveka's criticism by stating that emptiness is not merely the non-being of duality, but has a characteristic of being (*bhava-lakṣaṇa*) as well (*Madhyāntavibhāgaṭīkā*, Yamaguchi ed, p 47, 1-12). It may be that both Bhāvaviveka and Sthiramati are missing Vasubandhu's point, which is that Emptiness is *neither* being nor non-being. If one says that it is only non-being, this is a dogmatic limitation on the Ineffable through a mental construction. If one says that it *is* being, the same is true. But Vasubandhu wishes to expel both notions of "being" and "non-being". Later in this treatise, he makes the point that it cannot be said of *anything* that it has "being" or "non-being" (ad V, 17).

Harping on the "being" or "non-being" of Emptiness must be considered a mistake from the perspective of earlier Mahāyāna. In the first of the many amusing and profound discussions in the *Aṣṭasāhasrikā-prajñā-pāramitā*, the worried Śāriputra is made to ask: "That citta which is no citta, is that something which is ?", and Subhūti replies, "Does there then exist, or can one apprehend, in this state of absence of citta either a 'there is' or 'there is not' ?" Śāriputra has to reply, "No, not that." Subhūti then says, "Was it a suitable question when the venerable Śāriputra asked whether that citta which is no citta is something that is ?" (*Aṣṭasāhasrikā-prajñā-pāramitā*, I, Rajendralal Mitra ed. pp 5-6, Vaidya ed., p 3). In another early Mahāyāna sūtra, the *Samādhi-rāja*, there is the statement, "Neither does everything exist, nor, again, does it not exist" (*Samādhi-rāja-sūtra*, XXVII, 17). In the *Vimalakīrti-nirdeśa-sūtra*, the heavenly girl tells Śāriputra that "everything is fundamentally neither existing nor non-existing" (*Vimalakīrti-nirdeśa-sūtra*, VII). So Vasubandhu is here totally in the spirit of earlier Mahāyāna. This can be seen more clearly later in this work, where he speaks of the seeing of a false superimposition and denial involved in assuming the "being" and "non-being" of anything (ad III, 4). Bhāvaviveka's interpretation of Emptiness was certainly not followed by the later Sahajīyavāda Buddhist writers, who are in agreement with Vasubandhu. Thus Saraha writes: "The own-being of the Natural is neither being nor non-being" (Saraha, *Dohakośa*, v. 22: "Sahaja-sahāba ṇa bhābâbhāba").

9. "Signs" : those discriminated characteristics from which discernments are made seized by cognitions (See *Discussion of the Five Aggregates*, p 66, and note 6). They all involve a large measure of arbitrary confusion, and are eliminated in the realization of Emptiness.

10. "Adventitious flaws": Flaws that come to Emptiness that are not of its fundamental nature. The removal of these, which were only secondarily there anyway, does not mean that Emptiness has in any way really been altered.

11. "Belonging to a lineage" means the capacity in a life-stream towards the goal of the Śrāvakas (Hīnayāna saint), the Private Buddhas (who are enlightened but do not teach others), and that of the Mahāyānistic Bodhisattva. There may also be those of "indeterminate lineage", and those which have no spiritual lineage at all. (See the discussion in Dutt's *Aspects of Mahāyāna and its Relation with Hīnayāna*, pp 84-87, and in Har Dayal's *The Bodhisattva Doctrine*, pp 51-53.) A "lineage" is thus properly a life-stream's spiritual capacities or predispositions. Though Vasubandhu here calls it a special state of "own-being", in light of the fact that he rejects "own-being" from the fulfilled point of view, it might have been better to characterize it in a different way. Yaśomitra does this by equating these predispositions to "seeds". According to him, when the Buddha recognized innate capacities in life-streams, as he did in the case of Śāriputra, (*Vinaya* I, p 55), this rested on his recognition of "seeds" within the consciousness-stream (*Abhidharmakośavyākhyā*, quoted Jaini, *Abhidharmadīpa*, introduction, p 116).

12. "The special Buddha-events" are : (1) unspecified unparticularized boundaryless giving, (2) unspecified unparticularized boundaryless good conduct to others, (3) boundaryless forbearance, (4) boundaryless energy,

(5) boundaryless meditation, (6) boundaryless insight, (7) being favorable to others through special ways of favoring them, (8) knowledge of transformations, (9) being able to show forth all *upāyas*, (10) not falling from Mahāyāna, (11) knowing the doors to the identity of Saṃsāra and Nirvāṇa, and being able to show them forth, (12) skill in both restraint and adjustment "to others" in order to draw them out, (13) development of being able to face all knowledges without any deficiencies because of being unaffected by the motivating dispositions of previous knowledges, (14) being engaged in beneficial bodily, verbal, and mental actions, (15) not abandoning the realms where sentient beings are suffering, (16) taking delight in all situations, (17) being of undistracted citta in knowledge of skills needed to help others, (18) continuance in being able to show forth and investigate all events needed for a holy life.

These are at least "the eighteen special events of the Bodhisattva" listed in *Mahāvyutpatti* 786 ff. "The eighteen special events of a Buddha" are more properly : (1) one never trips up, (2) one is not rash or noisy in speech, (3) one is never distracted from mindfulness, (4) one has no perception of difficulties, (5) one's cittas are never unconcentrated, (6) one's equanimity is not due to lack of consideration, (7) one's zest never fails, (8) one's vigor never fails, (9) one's memory never fails, (10) one's meditational concentration never fails, (11) one's insight never fails, (12) one's deliverance never fails, (13) all one's bodily actions are preceded by knowledge, and continue to conform to knowledge, (14) all one's verbal actions are preceded by knowledge, and continue to conform to knowledge, (15) all one's mental actions are preceded by knowledge, and continue to conform to knowledge, (16) one's cognition and vision proceed unobstructed and freely with regard to the past, (17) with regard to the future, and (18) with regard to the present. see *Mahāvyutpatti* 135 ff.

The ten powers of a Buddha are : (1) one knows with insight, as it is, what can be as what can be, and what can't be as what can't be, (2) one knows with insight as they really are, the karmic results of past, future, and present actions, (3) one knows with insight, as they really are, the various elements in the world, (4) one knows with insight, as they are, the various dispositions of other beings, (5) one knows with insight, as they are, practises and the processes of afflictions and alleviation, (6) one knows with insight as they are, the faculties of sentient beings, (7) one knows with insight, as it is, the Path that leads everywhere, (8) one recollects one's various previous lives, (9) one sees the decrease and rebirth of beings as it is, (10) one realizes the end of the all distress (cf. *Mahāvyutpatti,* 120-129).

The four confidences of a Buddha are : (1) confidence in knowing all events as they happen, (2) confidence in knowing the destruction of all distress, (3) confidence in having correctly described the impediments to liberation, and (4) confidence in having shown how one must enter on the Path that leads to liberation (cf. *Mahāvyutpatti* 131-134).

13. It would be an extreme to say that emptiness is being; it would equally be an extreme to say that emptiness is only non-being. So the emptiness of emptiness as non-being, and the emptiness of the own-being of that non-being, serve as antidotes to these extremes (see note 8).

14. Emptiness is just so, all the time, so it is free from any otherness in reality. It is a kind of being because it is free from any being-again which would involve an evolvement into something "other".

15. Sthiramati explains this term in a somewhat different manner, assuming that the "equalness" refers to those afflictions which are equal to Bodhisattvas and Śrāvakas, which means that afflictions arise for them in regard to sense-objects, but not to an excessive degree (*Madhyānta-vibhāga-ṭīkā*, Yamaguchi, p 67). In light of what follows in Vasubandhu's delimitation of "obstructions", it seems more likely that the "equal" are those who are governed by complacency and apathy, and who are indifferent to the sufferings of others.

16. "A Nirvāṇa without a basis" is the Bodhisattva's taking a stand nowhere, being grounded nowhere fixedly. (cf. *Aṣṭasāhasrikā-prajñā-pāra-mitā*, II, first dialogue with Śāriputra : "Nowhere did the Tathāgata stand.") It is clear that both abandoning Saṃsāra, or becoming completely involved in it, would be an obstruction to such a free-flowing attitude.

17. Here is Vasubandhu's famous new look at the fetters, see Intr, p 199.

18. On the enlightenment-citta, see Intr, pp 202-204.

19. On the Paths of Seeing and Cultivation, see Intr, pp 205-210.

20. "The allies of enlightenment" are the applications of mindfulness, (those basic meditations on the body feelings, consciousness-moments, and all mentally cognizables or all those events together), the right exertions (see note 22), the bases of psychic power (see note 23), the faculties (see note 24), the powers (see note 26), the limbs of enlightenment (see note 27), and the limbs of the Path (see note 28).

21. The applications of mindfulness are meditations on the flow of "one's own" and (in Vasubandhu's expansion of the term) "others'" bodies, feelings, consciousness-moments, and cognizables.

22. The right exertions are : zest in making unbeneficial events which have not yet arisen not arise, zest in abandoning unbeneficial factors that have already arisen, zest in making those beneficial factors which have not yet arisen arise, and zest in maintaining those beneficial factors which have already arisen.

23. The bases of psychic power are : zest towards meditational concentration, vigor in meditational concentration, well-honed consciousnesses, and exploration in meditation.

24. The faculties are : (1) the faculty of faith, (2) the faculty of vigor, (3) the faculty of mindfulness, (4) the faculty of meditational concentration, and (5) the faculty of insight. On their genetic arrangement (meaning that each is the cause of the next) see ad IV, 7b.

25. The factors conducive to liberation are : faith in the validity of the basic direction of Buddhist practise, vigor, mindfulness, meditational concentration, and insight.

26. The powers are : power in faith, power in vigor, power in mindfulness, power in meditational concentration, and power in insight.

27. The limbs of enlightenment are : mindfulness, the investigation of events vigor, friendly love, tranquility, meditational concentration, and equanimity.

28. The limbs of the Path are : right views, right intentions, right speech, right action, right livelihood, right effort, right mindfulness, and right meditational concentration.

29. This is what this sentence seems to mean. Sthiramati says also that these are not obstructions to the pāramitās themselves, but to their results (*Madhyānta-vibhāga-ṭīkā*, Yamaguchi, p 94). Accordingly, the phrases "the effect of" have been added in this translation.

30. A Buddha-field is that area which has been chosen by a Bodhisattva for her or his special attention in the removal of afflictions. Obviously, a single Bodhisattva cannot be attentive to the afflictions of everybody everywhere, and must focus upon those to which she or he has actual access.

31. The worst obstruction to attainment of psychic mastery comes with the complacency that "makes everything alike". Obviously, if "one" is completely complacent, there is no motivation for undertaking those practises which would result in attainments.

32. Full accepting or total rejecting of Saṃsāra is an obstruction to the further development of consciousness which makes "one" an effective Bodhisattva.

33. The twenty-two faculties are : (1) the faculty of the eye, (2) the faculty of the ear, (3) the faculty of the nose, (4) the faculty of the tongue, (5) the faculty of the sensate body, (6) the faculty of *manas*, meaning the collection of all the consciousnesses, (7) the faculty of masculinity, (8) the faculty of femininity, (9) the faculty of suffering, (10) the faculty of bliss, (11) the faculty of cheerfulness, (12) the faculty of depression, (13) the faculty of equanimity, (14) the faculty of faith, (15) the faculty of vigor, (16) the faculty of mindfulness, (17) the faculty of meditational concentration, (18) the faculty of insight, (19) the faculty of coming to know what has not been known, (20) the faculty of knowing, (21) the faculty of having come to know, and (22) the faculty of life-force.

34. That is, it does not change (because it is non-existent), so it cannot be "reversed". But this very feature indicates a reality. The non-existent has a reality, if it is so constructed. The constructed has an effect, though it is ultimately non-existent, i.e. it is removable. But as long as it has a reality, "there is the construction of that which was not". Vasubandhu here playfully takes the constructed's state of unreversedness, and says that this shows its "reality".

34a. "The interdependent exists, but not in a real way"—this implies that the interdependent, as long as the transformation to "fulfilled" has not been made, arises with appearing dualities, thus "a state of confusion". And this very state of confusion indicates a reality.

35. The fulfilled is existent as it is the removal of the "non-existent" constructed, but by the same token it is non-existent, since it is simply the non-existence of the constructed. When the fulfilled is realized, "the fulfilled" is non-existent, since the notion of "fulfilled" is constructed.

36. Any statement as to something's "being" or "non-being" involves a false superimposition and denial. That nothing can be dogmatically stated regarding something's "being" or "non-being" has been seen in *The Twenty*

Verses. The fulfilled means "revolution at the basis", where the constructed, and hence false superimposition and denial, is completely removed. So it has the characteristic of reality, since the bases of erroneous views, including the clinging to notions of anything's being or non-being, have been discarded.

37. States are not fully known until their contrasts are. Thus the full realization of affliction comes in the fulfilled nature, which has the character of alleviation.

38. There will be "connection with suffering" even in the fulfilled state, since that state is still a life-state, and thus susceptible to suffering (See note 7). Even in a state of non-constructed consciousness, there may be a feeling of pain, if the body is suffering in some way. There may also be an allusion here to the Bodhisattva's *voluntary* connection with suffering, in order to help sentient beings.

38a. The three means of cognition accepted by Vasubandhu are : (1) direct perception, (2) inference, and (3) reliance on reliable authority. Dignāga eliminates the last of these in his logical works, and it is significant that Vasubandhu too uses it only when arguing with those who would accept the same sources as being reliable authority. Thus he uses it frequently by appealing to ancient Tripiṭaka sūtras when he argues with Vaibhāṣikas in *A Discussion for the Demonstration of Action*, but only sparingly in a work of this kind, where commonly accepted authority has not yet been established.

39. The status of this sentence is somewhat in doubt as it exists neither in the Chinese nor the Tibetan translation, but does exist in the Sanskrit manuscript. But in any case it is consistent with this work, and in fact states beautifully two of its main points : the existence of suffering even in an enlightened citta, and the absence of any "lower" and "higher".

39a. Though the term "aggregate of materiality" is used in reference to past, future, or present events, only a present moment of materiality has the characteristics given for the aggregate. Every present materiality-moment is distinct from each past and future one, and each simultaneously occurring materiality-moment is different from all the rest. "Their total singleness" means that inasmuch as the aggregates are constantly interreacting, it is impossible to clearly divide them from one another. (This was already admitted by Śāriputra, where he says that feelings, cognitions, and consciousnesses are really the same, "and it is impossible to point out any difference among these events even after analyzing them again and again." *Majjhima* I, 293.) In distinguishing them, however, one looks at their distinctness, their distinct characteristics of materiality on one hand, feelings on the other, etc. There is a certain range of efficacy which however much the individual moments may differ, all moments of one aggregate-type have "in common" when present. Though Vasubandhu uses the concept of "aggregates", he is careful not to fall into the trap of the Vaibhāṣikas, who assume that they are true entities. The Vaibhāṣikas put their seventy-five types of entities into fixed lists because they assume that each type is distinct from the others by clearly-definable efficacies, and that these efficacies can be observed for past and future events so categorized as well as for present ones. Vasubandhu denies that it is strictly possible to do this at all, because past and future events do not have the efficacy of present events (and in fact do not exist at all), because different aggregates may have a single efficacy in a moment, and because each moment-event is different from each other one.

40. The passage dealing with "interdependence regarding sovereignty" and "interdependence regarding attainment" has been deliberately deleted from the main body of this translation as being poor skill in means for the post-Lakṣmīṅkarā age. (Lakṣmīṅkarā, one of the founders of the Buddhist sahajīyavāda movement, authoress of the *Advayasiddhi*, is a woman whose enlightenment can hardly be doubted. And there have been many more.) It was already not strictly true in the later days of Vasubandhu's life, where we find a woman, Prabhāvatīguptā, exercising all functions (if officially only as regent) of a "world-emperor" in the fourth century conception of that title (cf. Majumdar and Altekar, *The Vākāṭaka-Gupta Age*, p 106, p 111). The passage reads as follows : "Interdependence regarding sovereignty means the impossibility of women functioning as world-emperors, and 'interdependence regarding attainment' means the impossibility of their attaining either the Private Buddhas' or fully enlightened Buddhas' types of enlightenment." In spite of the statement's harshness to feminists (and its actual inaccuracy), there is a "democratic" element to it, for it states that the *only* interdependence regarding functioning as a world-emperor or becoming a Buddha is that one be male. With the emendations suggested by h torical events as connected with names such as Lakṣmīṅkarā and Makhatā, on one hand and Prabhāvatīguptā and Indira Gandhi, on the other, any female can, "do it" too. Royal birth is not necessary for a future "world-emperor", nor is caste a factor in Enlightenment. This leaves no room for categorizing human beings into the "worthy" and "unworthy", or any variations thereof.

In the *Vimalakīrti-nirdeśa-sūtra*, the heavenly girl lectures the sexist Śāriputra about non-dualistic enlightenment, and even has the power to turn him into a woman, so that he can see that it isn't so bad. Fundamentally, as she says, "All things are neither male nor female." (*Vimalakīrti-nirdeśa*, VII).

41. These then are the "faculties" that lead to non-dual clearing of consciousness, see faculties (20), (21), and (22) in the list in note 33.

42. It is interesting that Vasubandhu regards the basic Buddhist analysis of "personality" as being only a provisional expedient against the view of individual self. Similarly, he regards the concepts of dependent origination, so-called good and bad states, the times, the Four Noble Truths, the compounded and uncompounded, as being such provisional expedients against views that would cause suffering, also. They are not to be taken literally : they are only temporary antidotes to suffering-inducing conceptions, and must ultimately be abandoned themselves.

43. See Introduction, pp 201-202, 204-205.

44. "A supermundane seeing" is a total non-dual awareness. "A worldly supermundane subsequently attained seeing" is awareness which again makes use of the cognitions abandoned in "a supermundane seeing", for the purpose of being effective in the world, in such a way that cognitions

will not be clung to, but used only as long as they are effective in removing afflictions.

45. On the enlightenment-citta, see Introduction, pp 202-204.

46. See Introduction, pp 204 ff.

47. This stage corresponds to the last moment on the Path of Seeing, Introduction, p 207, 208. On the stages, see pp 208-210.

48. The Dharma-body represents the essence of the Buddha's teachings. According to Maitreyanātha, *Abhisamayālaṅkāra*, VIII (XXIX) 2-6, it consists of the allies of enlightenment (see note 20, discussed in this work at IV, 1 9-10a), the four unlimited (compassion, loving kindness, rejoicing at the joy of others, and equanimity), the eight deliverances (see *Discussion for the Demonstration of Action*, note 51), the ten *kasina* meditations (on blue, yellow, red, white, earth, water, fire, wind, space, consciousness, unlimited earth in all directions, unlimited water, fire, wind, blue, yellow, red, and white in all directions), the eight stages for overcoming obstructions (meditations on the golden visibles "within" and "without", blue visibles, yellow visibles, red visibles, white visibles, infinite space, and infinite consciousness), the meditational concentration bringing to rest afflictions in others, the great resolves, (See Introduction, pp. 202-204), the super-knowledges, the conventional knowledges needed for effectiveness in removing sufferings, freedom from obstructions, the confidences (See note 12), the uprooting of latent impressions leading to suffering, the great compassion, the special Buddha-events (see note 12), and the knowledge of everything in all aspects. According to this interpretation, "the Dharma-body" is the entire "body" of events that make for enlightenment.

The "enjoyment-body" is the vision of a Buddha that appears to meditators : it is fitted out with thirty-two special marks and eighty secondary characteristics, which are explained by Haribhadra (*Abhisamayālaṅkārāloka*, ad VIII (XXIX) 12-20), as each having a relationship to the Buddha's beneficient activity. Here Vasubandhu explains it being solely "the situation of being of good effect."

The "formation-body" is the material body of a teaching Buddha while present on earth. Maitreyanātha, *Abhisamayālaṅkāra* VIII (XXIX), 33-40, explains it in terms of the actual techniques used for teaching others, including the pāramitās. Again, Vasubandhu greatly compresses these explanations by speaking of the formation-body's being "the situation of completing (beneficial) actions".

49. On the Path of (Initial) Application, see Introduction, pp 204-205.

50. "Becoming a receptacle" means that "one" is open to everybody and their sufferings.

51. It is the capacity to favor others compassionately which stands at the basis of all further developments towards enlightenment.

52. On the Path of Seeing, see Introduction, pp 205-207.

53. Without involvement in the sufferings of others there is no Mahāyāna.

54. Distinctive by being either "supermundane seeing" or "worldly supermundane subsequently attained seeing", see note 44.

55. The alleviation of others' sufferings can be achieved only with inti-

macy with sentient beings and their aims. The type of giving, etc. which will be specifically needed depends on the need of the sentient being that is being faced : If someone is hungry, give them food; if someone is suffering because of confusions, get at the heart of these confusions, etc.

56. The Great Enlightenment results in a great transformation and intensification of energies.

"The Tibetan translators interpret this "transformation" as the "turning over" of all merits gained to other sentient beings (*yoṅs-su-bsṅos-pa*). This is indeed another technical meaning for the term "*pariṇāmanā*", and makes some sense in this context, since transferring merit to all sentient beings would make this practise "inexhaustible." It is not clear, however, that Vasubandhu had this particular "transformation" in "mind".

57. This "power" comes from the realization of limitlessness, which can be gained by meditating on the sky, i.e. space. In the Mahāyāna sūtra *Gagana-gañja-paripṛcchā* (Tokyo/Peking Tripiṭaka, vol. 33, pp 1-36), concentration on space is used in a great variety of ways : to see the essential purity and non-affliction of everything (p 2, 1,; 3-4), the basic sameness of all events (p 3, 3, 6), the selflessness of sentient beings (p 5, 3, 4), the limitlessness of sentient beings, the limitlessness of forbearance (p 6, 4), and the lack of characteristics for all events (p 28, 3). The sūtra thus links "meditational concentration on the Treasury of the Sky" with the true practise of the pāramitā of giving, which is to be done without any concept of a definite sentient being; with the true practise of the pāramitā of ethics, because everything is pervaded by loving kindness just as space pervades the sky, and with the true practise of the pāramitā of forbearance, which must be limitless like space. Vasubandhu says that the practise of *all* pāramitās becomes effective only with this meditational concentration on the Treasury of the Sky.

58. The pāramitā of resolve is the fulfilling to an utmost point the resolves of the Bodhisattva, (see Intr, pp 202-204).

59. Practise "after-Dharma" is all those actions which must be taken to avoid subtle afflictions which may arise immediately after coming out of meditational concentration.

60. Here is an interesting indication that "the pride of thinking 'I am'" comes primarily from the force of susceptibility to harm. If the aggregate-complex had no susceptibility to harm, "it" would cognize "itself" as properly plural. It is susceptibility to harm that is the most impelling force resulting in a sense of "I am". For the injury of a materiality-aggregate can become suffering for all the aggregates in the organism, and can even result in their collective "deaths". So a unity is posited where there is only an intense interdependence of events. The implication is that if there were only pleasures, they would all be perceived plurally, but since there is susceptibility to harm, there is a false superimposition of unity.

61. An illusion itself exists. So this is not the kind of arrogant "therapy" which dictates to others what is to be real and what is to be unreal. For finally, everything is equally real, or equally unreal. Objects of sense and understanding are like the magical creation in an Indian magician's show : It does not exist as it appears, and yet does not *not* exist, because

the apparition itself exists. There is then no more gliding of citta on the very terms "being" and "non-being".

62. The Jain philosopher Kundakunda says souls, *pudgala* (matter), *dharma* (medium of motion for souls and matter), *adharma* (medium of rest for souls and matter), and space, are all eternal (*Pañcāstikāya-samayasāra*, v. 4). The later Jain philosopher Umāsvāmi also says all five *dravyas* are eternal. (*Tattvārthasūtra*, V, 4).

63. In the earlier Buddhist view, all the aggregates are impermanent to the point of being momentary (See *Majjhima* I 140-141, I 185, etc). This is the viewpoint which Vasubandhu himself upholds against Sāṁmitīya "quasi-eternalism" in his *Discussion for the Demonstration of Action*, 7-10. Here Vasubandhu says that adherence to any fixed view can become a problem, and so "eternalism" and "non-eternalism" are both rejected.

64. To say that an individual self doesn't exist is finally as much of a "hang up" as saying that it does. All clinging to opinion must be abandoned.

65. Only the present moment exists, hence there is no "previous" or "subsequent". But the present moment itself is empty and ineffable. It is interesting that some post-quantum mechanics physicists have also come to the view that linear time is non-existent, cf. John A. Wheeler's *Geometrodynamics*.

66. The "Hīnayāna" Buddhist idea that there is "something to be abandoned or shunned" is here discarded because it only gives rise to fears and anxieties.

67. The example is that of a painter, who himself paints a picture of a demon, and then becomes afraid of what he has himself created. The discrimination of "something which is to be shunned" works in the same way: it is totally mentally constructed, and yet has the power to make fear rise in the "one" who has constructed it. This example is from the *Kāśyapa-parivarta-sūtra*, 67, as are all the others in this section.

68. The magician creates apparitional elephants which will vanish utterly as soon as he wants them to. In the same way, the discrimination between "an object apprehended" and "a subject apprehendor" has existence as long as the constructed is operative, but as soon as the constructed is cleared away, vanishes utterly, just like the magical creation (cf. *Kāśyapa-parivarta*, 68).

69. Whatever is being investigated is past by the time it is being observed by the mental consciousness, and hence does not really exist. This is true by the principle enunciated in *The Twenty Verses*, ad 16b, pp 172-173. But in a certain kind of wrongness, an investigation of what was, there suddenly arises a rightness : an insight which shatters all conceptions. It of course also dissolves the previous investigation. So the simile is most apt. It occurs at *Kāśyapa-parivarta-sūtra*, 69.

70. There is no practise leading to enlightenment or non-practise not leading to enlightenment. The simile of the lamp explains it as follows (*Kāśyapa-parivarta* 70, quoted by Sthiramati, *Madhyānta-vibhāga-ṭīkā*, Yamaguchi ed., p 249) : Just as an oil-lamp, as soon as it is lit, causes darkness to disappear, just so knowledge may suddenly arise in a consciousness-stream, and cause all non-knowledge to disappear. Because this knowledge

is non-discriminatory (*nirvikalpaka*), it has nothing to do with any effort. So there is not really anything to be done, any practise. The knowledge will arise suddenly of itself, and adverse factors will just as suddenly vanish.

71. The second simile of the oil-lamp is given at *Kāśyapa-parivarta*, 71 (quoted by Sthiramati, *Madhyānta-vibhāga-ṭikā*, Y., p 249 ff). The discrimination which is to be avoided is one where it is considered, "The antidotes aren't arising in the way that they should be", or "The afflictions-together have surely been going on for a long time." The simile goes as follows : There may be a house where none has lit an oil-lamp for a thousand years. And then suddenly, someone comes and lights one. In the same way, there may be afflictions of actions lasting a thousand years which disappear in one moment of investigation with careful mental attention.

72. This refers to the reflection on what has been heard, discussed at V, 8a. After that which has been reflected on is understood, there is the possibility of sustaining this understanding, hence the use of the expression "sustension".

73. Preserverence is possible only with cultivation of careful mental attention done by each "series" "individually". Yet this does not imply any special set of actions which could be recommended for every "series". (cf. note 70).

74. On Path of Seeing, see Intr, pp 205-207. For the first stage, see Intr, p 207, 208.

75. On the Path of Cultivation, see Intr, p 208-210.

76. Going forth to meet others in a true Mahāyāna fashion is possible only where there is an understanding of the moment-events that go into both worldly (discriminated, anxiety-filled, etc.) and supermundane (undiscriminated, tranquil, etc.) ways of living. Without understanding and empathising with the mundane problems of those stuck in discriminations, there is no effectiveness in relieving these problems; without knowledge of a "path" free from discriminations, the best antidote of all cannot be offered. The "Bodhisattva's" path is thus by necessity both mundane and supermundane, since "she" or "he" will take part in the joys and sufferings of those stuck in discriminations, without setting "herself" or "himself" apart and aloof, and yet "she" or "he" will offer those antidotes that are realized only upon non-discriminated awareness.

77. On the eighth stage, see Intr, p 210.

78. On the ninth and tenth stages, see Intr, p 210.

79. Remaining tranquil in a state of complete non-dual awareness would be egotistical, for the sufferings of others are not thereby reduced. So there is a re-entry into the mundane world, for the sake of showing that full enlightenment is possible.

Since there may still be some doubts as to what is involved in the type of path suggested by Maitreyanātha/Vasubandhu, the following passages have been taken from their *Ornament to the Mahāyāna Sūtras* (*Mahāyāna-sūtrālaṅkāra* of Maitreyanātha, *Mahāyānasūtrālaṅkārabhāṣya* of Vasubandhu):

Engaged in saving all sentient beings,
joined with skills in a knowledge path going everywhere,

with the same delight in going forth and staying calm,
the one of understanding can be known as going everywhere. II, 3.

She or he risks dangers for a long time. She or he quickly releases (others) from them. She or he is aware of even the smallest sufferings she or he comes in contact with. With an agitated spirit, full of compassion, she or he matures the sentient beings she or he comes into contact with.

ad III, 8

She or he should go at will, as unconfused
as the world is confused by special signs and marks,
Going at will, their going forth is unensnared
because of revolution at the basis. XI, 18.

THE TEACHING OF THE THREE OWN-BEINGS

(TRI-SVABHĀVA-NIRDEŚA)

INTRODUCTION

This may be Vasubandhu's last work. It is a startling one, playfully undermining the distinctions between the three "own-beings" which are such a part of Yogâcāra therapeutic theory, and at the same time demonstrating their successive unfoldment. The absence of any dualities in consciousness, the complete abandonment of the constructed, is the apprehension of the "Ground of all events", enlightenment. So all constructions including the raft just built, will be abandoned.

In spite of the fact that this little book contains the most profound self-dissolving revelations, it has remained fairly obscure, and there are no commentaries on it by any subsequent writer. This neglect has done much towards the misrepresentation of Vasubandhu's thought which is so often encountered.

The central simile used in *The Teaching of the Three Own-Beings* is that of a magical creation. To those unfamiliar with the dazzling feats of Indian magicians, it may need explanation. Some kinds of magicians in India operate with what might be described as a form of mass hypnosis. For instance, they may sit in front of a pot, and make a huge flower grow very rapidly from it. Anyone who walks into the middle of the performance will see the same thing all the other spectators are seeing. But if a photograph of the event is taken, all that appears is the magician sitting in front of an empty pot. In Vasubandhu's example, a magician of this type is sitting in front of pieces of wood. Suddenly, an elephant appears where the wood has been, and all the spectators can see it. But just as suddenly, the magician can make "this elephant" disappear. Vasubandhu's magician uses a mantra to make everyone see "the elephant". So the mantra is compared to the store-consciousness, Suchness or underlying non-dual Emptiness to the wood, discriminating discrete entities to the elephant's appearance, and duality to the elephant itself. In other words, duality can disappear from consciousness as suddenly as it arose.

This treatise is fundamentally Śūnyavāda, and yet, as so often in Vasubandhu, a dynamic process is being described.

Concerning the Text:

The Teaching of the Three Own-Beings exists in its original Sanskrit form, and has been edited by Louis de la Vallée Poussin in *Mélanges Chinois et Bouddhiques*, 2, 1932-1933, pp 147-161. This translation is based on that edition. That edition also includes the two Tibetan translations of the text, one of which erroneously ascribes the text to Nāgārjuna. In the glossary, both Tibetan versions are considered.

THE TEACHING OF THE THREE OWN-BEINGS (TRI-SVABHĀVA-NIRDEŚA)

The constructed, the interdependent, and the fulfilled :
these three own-beings are accepted as a most profound thing
to be known by the discerning. 1.

That which appears is the interdependent; "how it appears"
is the constructed,
through the former's state of developing subject to conditions,
through the latter's being construction-only. 2.

The constant state-of-not-being-found of "how it appears"
in that which appears,
can be known as the fulfilled own-being,
because of its state of non-otherness.[1] 3.

Among these, what is it that appears ?
A construction of the non-existent.
How is it that it appears ?
Through dualities.
What is its non-existence ?
It is, as regards it, a state of events of non-duality. 4.

What is a construction of the non-existent ?
A citta, by which it* becomes constructed
in such a way that the object which it constructs,
cannot be completely found in that way. 5.

This citta is accepted as being of two kinds, being either cause
or result :
the "store-consciousness" and "the evolving consciousness"
of seven kinds. 6.

"Citta" is so called because of its state of becoming accumulated (*citatvāt*)
through the seeds of the residual impressions of the afflictions-
together :

*the interdependent

This is the first kind of citta*; the second kind is so called
through evolvement of various (*citra*) aspects. 7.

This construction of that which was not is thought of in brief
to be three-fold :
as maturational, as having signs, and as flashing appearances. 8.

The first is the root-consciousness, because it consists of maturation;
the others are the evolving consciousnesses,
because of their evolving with cognitions of "seen" and
"seeing"[2]. 9.

The profundity of these own-beings comes from their non-difference in characteristics,
from existing-and-not-existing, from duality-and-unity,
and from afflictions-together and alleviation. 10.

The constructed own-being is perceived as existent,
yet it is complete non-being,
so it is thought of as having an existent-and-non-existent characteristic. 11.

The interdependent exists, but not in the way that it appears,
there being confusion there,
so it is thought of as having an existent-and-non-existent characteristic, too. 12.

The fulfilled own-being exists through non-duality,
but is simply the non-being of "two":
so it is thought of as having an existent-and-non-existent characteristic, too. 13.

Because of the dual state of the constructed object**,
and because of its being one through the non-existence of duality,
own-being as constructed by fools is thought of as consisting
of duality-and-unity. 14.

Because of its appearing with there being a duality,

*the store-consciousness.

**as implying the duality of object apprehended and subject apprehendor.

and because of its being one because this (duality) is only confusion,
the own-being called "interdependent" is thought of
as consisting of duality-and-unity, too. 15.

Because of its state as the own-being of the two beings,
and because of its being the *one* own-being of non-duality,
the fulfilled own-being is thought of
as consisting of duality-and-unity, too. 16.

The characteristic of the afflictions-together
can be known as the constructed and interdependent,
but the fulfilled is accepted as the characteristic of alleviation. 17.

Because of (one's) state as the own-being of a non-existent duality,
and because of (the other's) being the own-being of the non-being of that duality,
it can be known that the fulfilled is non-different in characteristic from the constructed. 18.

Because of (one's) state as the own-being of non-duality,
and because of (the other's) being the own-being of the non-being of duality,
it can be perceived that the constructed is non-different in characteristic from the fulfilled. 19.

Because of (one's) being non-existent as it appears,
and because of (the other's) being the own-being of that non-existence in that way,
the fulfilled is non-different in characteristic from the interdependent, too. 20.

Because of (one's) state as the own-being of a non-existent duality,
and because of (the other's) having no own-being as it appears,
it can be perceived that the interdependent is non-different in characteristic from the fulfilled. 21.

Still, as far as their arising is concerned,
a difference in the order of occurrence of these own-beings is taught,

from the point of view of conventional practise,
and from the point of view of entry into them.[3] 22.

The constructed consists of conventional practise,
that which consists of engaging in conventional practise is the other (the interdependent),
and the severance of conventional practise is accepted as yet another own-being (the fulfilled). 23.

At first, the interdependent, which consists of the non-being of duality, is entered,
then and there construction-only, non-existent duality, is entered, 24.

then and there the fulfilled, the non-being of duality, is entered,
thus it's said that it both exists and doesn't exist.[4] 25.

These three own-beings have characteristics which are surely non-dual and ungraspable,
because of (one's) simple non-being, (the other's) non-being like that (in the manner in which it appears),
and (the third's) being the own-being of that non-being. 26.

A magical creation produced by force of mantras may appear like an elephant,
but there is only an appearance there, and no elephant's there at all. 27.

The constructed own-being is the elephant,
the interdependent is its appearance,
and the fulfilled is the non-being of the elephant there. 28.

The construction of the non-existent appears in the same way
from the root-consciousness by nature of duality;
there is no duality there at all: there's only an appearance there. 29.

The root-consciousness is like the mantra;
Suchness is like the wood;
discrimination is like the elephant's appearance,
and duality is like the elephant itself.[5] 30.

In a penetration of the "reality of objects", there arises simultaneously in regard to the three own-beings
complete knowledge, abandonment, and attainment, in that order. 31.

The complete knowledge (of the constructed) is its non-apprehension,
the abandonment (of the interdependent as constructing) is its non-appearance,
the attainment, realization (of the fulfilled) is its signless apprehension. 32.

With the non-apprehension of duality, the appearance of duality vanishes,
and with this disappearance, the fulfilled, the non-being of duality, is understood. 33.

It's just like the non-apprehension of the elephant,
its appearance's disappearance,
and the apprehension of the wood,
take place simultaneously in a magical show. 34.

Because of the state of there being contradictory views in relation to the same moment,[6]
because of the intellect's seeing without a true object[7],
because of the different development of the three kinds of knowledge[8],
and because of the fact that without this,
the attainment of freedom would come without effort,[9] 35.

there is the apprehension of the knowable,
by the apprehension of its being citta-only,
and through this non-apprehension of a knowable "object",
there is the non-apprehension of çitta itself.[10] 36.

Through the non-apprehension of any duality,
there is the apprehension of the Ground of events,
because of the apprehension of the Ground of events,
there is the apprehension of psychic mastery. 37.

With psychic mastery apprehended, and through fulfilling both one's own and others' aims, the discerning attain that enlightenment which has no higher, and which consists of the three Buddha-bodies.[11] 38.

NOTES

1. Whenever it is considered "how something appears", there is a duality. But the constant absence of "how it appears" in that which appears is the absence of duality, i.e. the fulfilled. Unlike the constructed ("how it appears"), and the interdependent (that which appears), which occur in innumerable different ways, the fulfilled, being freed from duality, appears with no division of "one" and "the other". Since any moment of investigation into that which appears can give rise to the fulfilled, the fulfilled is "the *constant* state-of-not-being-found of 'how it appears' in that which appears."

2. The "evolving consciousnesses" are the first seven consciousnesses: the visual, audial, olfactory, gustatory, tactile, and mental consciousnesses, and the *manas*, or ego-consciousness. They evolve with cognitions of "seen" and "seeing" in the case of the visual consciousness, "heard" and "hearing" in the case of the audial, "smelled" and "smelling" in the case of the olfactory, "felt tactilely" and "feeling tactilely" in the case of the tactile, "thought" and "thinking" in the case of the mental consciousness, and "I" and "I am existing" in the case of the *manas*. That is, they usually have within them the cognitions of "object" and "subject". Because of these cognitions, they are called "having signs".

3. Though there is no essential difference between these so-called "own-beings", they are taught as three because of their respective relations to "conventional practise", and because they are "entered" serially. Conventional practise, i.e. any dealings from the point of view of conventional "reality", is based totally on the constructed. That which engages itself in such conventional practise is the interdependent, and the disappearance of conventional practise is the fulfilled. This leads us to the second reason for speaking of three own-beings: the fact that they arise at different times. The interdependent is prior, as it is the play of the phenomenal world itself. But at some point the constructing of dualities may begin, which results in the purely constructed. Once the constructed is present, the non-existent character of its dualities can be realized, and thus the fulfilled is attained. So there must be the interdependent before there can be the constructed. and there must have been the constructed before there can be the fulfilled,

4. The fulfilled exists inasmuch as it is the interdependent without the constructed; it does not exist inasmuch as it is only the non-being of any duality. This ties in with Vasubandhu's previous characterization of emptiness as being "neither being nor non-being". (*Commentary on the Separation of the Middle from Extremes*, ad I, 13).

5. The store-consciousness or "seeds" of residual impressions is like the mantra which sets the magical creation going, for it is only by power of latent impressions that dualities appear to arise. Discriminating, i.e. the constructing of dualities, is like the appearance of an apparitional elephant

in the magical show. The dualities which are held to are like the elephant, or, to put this another way, the belief in the elephant's existence. What underlies it, non-dual Suchness or Emptiness, is like the sticks of wood the magician has before him, which are transformed into the apparition in the spectators' eyes.

6. The same moment will be perceived in different ways by different consciousness-streams. This is one of the main points of *The Twenty Verses*.

7. The intellect can conceive of something without there being an object to correspond to it: another one of the main points of *The Twenty Verses*.

8. "The three kinds of knowledge" are interdependent knowledge, constructed knowledge, and fulfilled knowledge. On their "different development", see this treatise, 22-25.

9. Without the processes of the construction of that which was not, there could be no bondage or act of freedom for anyone. See *Commentary on the Separation of the Middle from Extremes*, ad I 4b.

10. Without the apprehension of a knowable "object", there is no citta, either. (Compare *Commentary on the Separation of the Middle from Extremes*, ad I 6-7.)

11. On the three Buddha-bodies, see *Commentary on the Separation of the Middle from Extremes*, note 48.

GLOSSARY AND INDEX OF KEY TERMS
ABBREVIATIONS

KSP *Discussion for the Demonstration of Action* (*Karma-siddhi-prakaraṇa*)
MVB *Commentary on the Separation of the Middle from Extremes* (*Madhyānta-vibhāga-bhāṣya*)
PSP *Discussion of the Five Aggregates* (*Pañcaskandhaka-prakaraṇa*)
TK *Thirty Verses* (*Triṃśikā-kārikā*)
TSN *Teaching of the Three Own-Beings* (*Tri-svabhāva-nirdeśa*)
V Tibetan text ascribed to Vasubandhu
N Tibetan text ascribed to Nāgārjuna
VK *Twenty Verses and Commentary* (*Viṃśatikā-kārikā*)
VV *Method for Argumentation* (*Vāda-vidhi*)

GLOSSARY AND INDEX OF KEY TERMS
(ENGLISH-SANSKRIT-TIBETAN)

A

abandoning, *abandonment*

prahāṇa, *spaṅ-ba*, *spoṅ-ba*, *vivarjana*, *spoṅ-ba*

MVB III II 1, ad II 1, ad II 17, 9 b-10 a, ad III 9 b-10 a, ad IV 2, IV 3, ad IV 3, ad IV 5a, ad IV 17 ("eradication"), ad IV, 18, ad V, 20, ad V 23-26, ad V 31. *vivarjana*, *spoṅ-ba* *MVB*, II 1, ad II 1, ad II 17

KSP 49.

TSN 31, 32 (*hāni*)

abandon(*ing*)

tyajana, *gtaṅ-ba*, *btaṅ-ba*, *gtoṅ-ba*

KSP 49.

MVB I, 18 c, ad I 18 c ("would abandon", *parityajeta*, *yoṅs-su-gtoṅ-ṅo*).

ability

sāmarthya, *nus*

MVB, V 6.

ability to cultivate

paribhāvanā, *yoṅs-su-bsgoms-pa*

MVB, ad V, 3.

ability to evolve

pariṇati, *sgyur-ba*

MVB II 9 (*nati*, *bsṅo-ba*), ad II 10 a

absence of affliction

niḥkleśa, *ñon-moṅs-med*

MVB IV 8 b, ad IV 8 b.

absence of anger

akopyatva, *mi-ḥkhrus-pa*

MVB ad II 10 a

absence of own-being

niḥsvabhāvatā, *ṅo-bo-*(*ñid*)*-med-pa-ñid*

TK 23, 24.

absence of reversals

aviparyāsa, *phyin-ci-ma-log-pa*

(See also "lack of reversal", "unreversed", "non-reversal")
MVB ad II 10 a

absence of self (see also "selflessness")
nairātmya, bdag-med-pa
MVB ad V 23-26,

absence of self in all events
dharma-nairātmya, chos-la-bdag-med-pa
MVB, ad V 19.

absurd, absurdity ensues
prasaṅga, prasajyate, thal-bar-ḥgyur
VV 14, *KSP* 10, 27, 28 a, 39 c, *VK*, ad 12 b, f.

accepted
iṣyate, ḥdod-pa
KSP 18, 23, 27, 34, 37, 39, 40, 41.
VK ad 4 c, 6, ad 6, 7, ad 7, ad 13, ad 14, ad 15, ad 16 b, ad 20 a.
MVB I, 4b, II, 17, ad II 17 ("sought")
TSN 1, 6, 17.

accepted reality
prasiddha-tattva, grags-pa-de-kho-na
MVB III 1-2, ad III 1-2, ad III 11 b, III 12 a, ad III 12 a, III 12 b.

accepting
ādāna, len-(pa)
MVB II 1, ad II 1, ad II 17, III 6 ("adherence")

accomplished ones
(literally, "non-learners", those who have no longer anything specific to learn) *aśaikṣa, mi-slob-pa*
MVB ad IV 11 b-12 a, ad IV 13-14, ad IV 15, ad IV 18.

according to a certain order—see "in order"

according to circumstances
yathāyogam, ci-rigs-su
PSP 4, p 70; *VK*, ad 10 18 a, *KSP* 32.

according to conditions
yathāpratyayam

according to the manner in which they are designated
yathāprajñapta, ji-ltar-btags-pa
MVB, ad V 7.

accumulates

cinoti, *bsags-pa*
PSP 5, p 71; *KSP* 47.

accumulation
saṁcaya, *bsags-pa*
KSP 44

accumulation (as Mahāsāṅghika technical term)
upacaya, *brtsegs*
KSP 18

accurate determination (see also "determination")
pariccheda, *yoṅs-su-gcod*
MVB IV 9 b-10 a, ad IV 9b-10 a.

acquaintance
saṃstava, *ḥdris-pa*
PSP 4, p 67; *MVB*, ad III 12 a.

act, *action*
karma, *las*
PSP 4, p 67; *KSP* 1, 2, 13, 14, 15, 16-17, 18, 21, 23, 28, 33, 40, 41, 42, 43, 45, 46, 47, 48, 49, 50
TK 19; *MVB* ad I 10-11 a, ad I 11 b, ad I 22 c, ad II 10 a, ad II 14-15, ad III 8, ad III 20 b, ad V 5, ad V 6, ad V 23-26

act associated with manas
manaḥsaṃprayuktakarma, *yid-daṅ-mtshuṅs-par-ldan-paḥi-las*
KSP 2.

act committed after having willed
cetayitvā-karma, *bsams-paḥi-las*
KSP 47

act committed by the body
kāya-kṛta-karma, *lus-kyis-byas-paḥi-las*
KSP 2.

act connected with an effort
prayogakarma, *rtsol-ba-can-gyi-las*
KSP 50.

act of Dharma
dharma-carita, *chos-spyod-pa*
MVB V 8 b, ad V 8 b, ad V 9.

act of performance
kāritra-karma, *byed-paḥi-las*
KSP 50.

activity
kriyā, byed-pa
VK 2, ad 2, 4 a; *MVB*, ad III 18 b.
adapted
anupraviṣṭa, rjes-su-žugs-pa
MVB, ad III 12 a.
adherence
abhyavasita, lhag-par-chags-pa
PSP 4, p 68.
adherence
ādāna, len
MVB, III 6 b.
adherence to mere rule and ritual
śīla-vrata-parāmarśa, tshul-khrims-daṅ-brtul-žugs-mchog-tu-ḥdzin-pa
PSP 4, p 68; *MVB* ad II 2-3 a (*parāmarśa* only).
adherence to particular views
dsṛṣṭi-parāmarśa, ḷta-ba-mchog-tu-ḥdzin-pa
PSP 4, p 68-69.
adjustment
samudānayana, sbyar
PSP 4, p 70.
adventitious
āgantuka, glo-bur(-yin-pa)
MVB ad I 16 c, ad I 21, ad V 21.
adventitiousness
āgantukatva, glo-bur
MVB I 22 c, V 13, V 21, ad V 31.
adverse factors
vipakṣa, mi-mthun-paḥi-phyogs
MVB ad II 11, ad II 13, II 14-16, ad II 14-16, IV 2, ad IV 2, IV 7 a, IV 9-10 a, ad IV 10 b, IV 11 a, ad IV 11 a, IV 18, ad IV 18, ad V 6, V 24, ad V 23-26.
advice
avavāda, gdams-pa (see also "instructions")
MVB, ad V, 6.
aeon
kalpa, bskal-pa
KSP 15, verse.; *MVB*, ad V 3.
afflicted

kliṣṭa, saṃkliṣṭa, ñon-moṅs, kun-nas-ñon-moṅs-pa-can

KSP 27, 29, 34; *MVB* ad I 3, I 21, ad I 21, I 22a, ad I 22 a, ad I 22 b, ad I 22 c, I 16 a, ad I 16a, ad I 16 b., ad III 7b-8 a.

affliction

kleśa, ñon-moṅs-pa

PSP 4, p 66; *KSP* 27, 34, 37, note 43; *TK* 6, 9, 11; *MVB* I 10-11 a (*kliśyate* "is afflicted"), ad I 21 (*parikliśyate*), ad II 1, II 1 b, ad II 1b, ad II 10 a, ad II 14-16, II 17, ad II 17, ad III 8, ad III 12, III 15, 16 a, ff, ad III 15-16 a, IV 8, ad IV 8, ad IV 9, IV 11 a, ad IV 11a, ad IV 18, V 24, ad V 24.

afflictions-together

saṃkleśa, kun-nas-ñon-moṅs-pa

MVB ad I 4 b, ad I 9, I 11, ad I 11, ad I 21, II 14-16, III 15-16 a, ad III 15-16 a, ad IV 9 a, ad II 14-16, V 22, ad V 22, V 23-26, ad V 23-26, ad V 31.

TSN 7, 10, 17.

afflictions-together of action

karma-saṃkleśa, las-kyi-kun-nas-ñon-moṅs-pa

MVB ad I 11b, ad V 23-25.

afflictions-together of affliction

kleśa-saṃkleśa, ñon-moṅs-paḥi-kun-nas-ñon-moṅs-pa

MVB ad I 11 b, ad V 23-25.

afflictions-together of birth

janma-saṃkleśa, skye-baḥi-kun-nas-ñon-moṅs-pa

MVB ad I 11 b, ad V 23-25.

"*after-Dharma*"

anudharma, rjes-mthun-chos

MVB V 2 a, ad V 2 a, ad V 10 b, V 11, ad V 11, ad V 22, end.

agglomeration

piṇḍa, gar-bu

VK 12 b, ad 12 b, ad 14 b, 14 c.

aggregate

skandha, phuṅ-pa

PSP 1 and throughout; *KSP* 18, 27, 34, 36, 37;
MVB ad III 1-2, ad III 14 c, ad III 15-16 a, ad III 16 b, ad III 17 a, ad III 22 b, ad V 23-26.

aggregation (of atoms)

(paramāṇu-)saṃghāta, (rdul-phra-rab-gyi-)ḥdus-pa

KSP 3, 4; *VK* 11 (*saṃhata*), ad 11, ad 12, 13a, ad 14b, ad 14c.

agitation(physical)

cala, gYo-bo

KSP 46.

agitation(psychological)

udvega, skyo-ba

MVB, ad I 11b.

agitation

vyāroṣa, khoṅ-nas-ḥkhregs-pa

PSP 4, p 69

aim

artha, don

MVB, II 14-16, ad II 14-16, ad III 11a, IV 3, ad IV 3, ad V 3, V 8, ad V 23-26, ad V 31.

aimlessness

apraṇihita, smon-pa-med-pa

MVB, ad V 23-26.

all-encompassing

sarvatraga, kun-tu-ḥgro-ba

MVB II 14-16, ad II 14-16.

alleviation

vyavadāna, rnam-par-byaṅ-ba

KSP 37; *MVB* ad I 4b, ad I 13, ad I 22c, II 14-16, ad II 14-16, III 15-16a, ad V 22, V 24, ad V 23-26, ad V 31

TSN 10, 17.

allies of enlightenment

bodhi-pakṣya, byaṅ-chub-kyi-phyogs

MVB ad II 10b, note 20, ad II 17, ad IV 1.

alteration

anyathātva, gẑan-du-ḥgyur-ba

PSP 4, p 71.

alternatives

vikalpa, rnam-par-rtog-pa

VV 12.

always

nitya, rtag-tu

MVB ad I 15, ad III 3b, ad III 22.

anger

krodha, khro-ba

PSP 4, p 66; definition, p 69

VK 20 a (*kopa*); *TK* 12.

annihilation

uccheda, *chad-pa*

MVB V 24, ad V 23-26.

anterior thesis

pūrva-pakṣa, *phyogs-sṅa-ma* and *sṅa-maḥi-phyogs*

VV 11, 14, 15, note 5.

antidote

pratipakṣa, *gñen-po*

PSP 4, p 67; p 73;

KSP 34, 37; *VK* ad 17 c

MVB I 1a, ad I 1a, ad I 21, II 14-16, ad II 14-16, III 1-3, ad III 1-3, ad III 4, ad III 14c, ad III 15-16a, ad III 16b, III 21, ad III 21, ad IV 1, IV 2, ad IV 2, ad IV 5a, IV 9b-10a, ad IV 9b-10a, ad IV 10b, IV 11a, ad IV 11a, ad IV 12b, ad IV 18, ad V 18b, ad·V 23-26, ad V 31.

anxiety

uttrāsa, *skrag-pa*

MVB ad II 2-3a.

appear

bhās, *pratibhās*, *snaṅ-ba*

KSP 4, 10; *MVB* ad I 3, ad V 15

khyā, *khyāti*

TSN 2, 3, 4, 12, 20, 21, 27, 29.

appearance

pratibhāsa, *ābhāsa*, *snaṅ-ba*

VK 1, ad 3, ad 7, 9, ad 9, 17a, ad 17a, ad 17c, ad 21a;

MVB I, 3, ad I 3, ad I 4a, V 15, ad V 15;

ākāra and *ākṛti*, *rdam-pa*

TSN 27, 28, 29, 33, 34.

appearing

prakhyāna, *snaṅ-ba*

TSN 15.

application

yoga, *sbyor-ba*

MVB IV, 6, ad IV 6 (*prayoga*)

applications of mindfulness

smṛtyupasthāna, *dran-pa-ñe-bar-gžag-pa*

MVB ad II 11, IV 1, ad IV 1, ad IV 12b.

apprehend

upalabhate, dmigs-par-gyur
TK 28; *MVB* ad V 22.

apprehension (perceptual)
grāha, grahaṇa, ḥdzin-pa
VK 15, ad 15; *TK* 19, 26, 28; *MVB* III 20, ad III 20, ad III 17b

apprehension, apprehended
upalabdhi, upalabdha, dmigs-pa
VV 16-21; *VK* ad 11, ad 17b, ad 17c; *TK* 8, 26, 27; *MVB* I 6, ad I 6, I 7, ad I 7, I 7b, ad I 7b; *TSN* 32, 34, 36, 37, 38.

approach
āya (Tib. tr. misunderstand it as ending of *apāya*)
MVB IV 2, ad IV 3.

approachment
ābhimukhya, mṅon-du-gyur-pa
PSP 4, p 70

appropriate (verb)
upādā, upādadāti, ñe-bar-len-pa
KSP 33, 34.

appropriate (adjective)
yogya, ruṅ-ba
KSP 2, 21, 27, 34, 38.

appropriated
upātta, zin-pa
PSP 1, p 65; 5, p 75.

appropriating aggregates
upādāna-skandha, ñe-bar-len-paḥi-phuṅ-po
PSP 4, p 67; 5, p 103; *KSP* 36, 37; *MVB* ad II 2-3a.

appropriating consciousness
upādāna-vijñāna or *ādāna-vijñāna, len-paḥi-rnam-par-śes-pa*
PSP 5, p 72; *KSP* 32, 33.

appropriation
upādi, len-pa
TK 3.

approved
prasiddha, grags-pa
MVB III 1-2, ad III 1-2, ad III 11b, III 12a, ad III 12a, ad III 12b (in last three cases, tr. as "accepted").

argument, argumentation

vāda, rtsod-pa
VV 2 and throughout; *KSP* 10 ("argued", *brtsad-pa*)

arise
(*utpad, jāyate; skye-ba, ḥbyuṅ-ba*)
(These terms are used interchangeably)
KSP 8, 9, 12, 15, 18, 19, 21, 22, 23, 32, 40, 46
VK ad 9, ad 17c; *TK* 18; *MVB* ad I 4, ad I 21, ad II 10a, ad III 18, I 3, I 6, ad I 6, ad V 23-26.

arising
saṃbhava, utpatti, udbhava, byuṅ-ba, skye-ba
VK ad 4 c, 5, ad 5, 6; *TK* 15; *KSP* 9, 11, 16-17, 20;
MVB ad II 10-11a, ad III 5, ad III 7b-8a ad III 19, ad IV 2, ad IV 13-14, ad V 6, ad V 22, ad V 24, V 29-30, ad V 29-30

arising of antidotes
pratipakṣopagama, gñen-po-bskyed-pa
MVB ad IV 2.

arranged
vyavasthāpyate, rnam-par-gžag-pa
MVB ad I 1, ad IV 1.

arrangement
vyavasthāna, rnam-par-gžag-pa
MVB ad III 9b-10a, ad III 17a.

array
paṅkti, dṅar-ka
KSP 5.

as it appears
yathākhyānam, ji-ltar-snaṅ, ji-bžin-snaṅ (21-N)
TSN 20, 21.

as it has been designated
yathāprajñaptitas, ji-ltar-btags-pa
MVB V 7b-8a, ad V 7b-8a.

as it is
yathābhūta, yaṅ-dag-pa-ji-lta-ba-bžin-du
MVB ad I 1, ad 10-11a, ad IV 7b, ad V 31 ("as they are")

as it is constructed
yathā parikalpyate, ji-ltar-kun-brtags-pa
MVB ad III 7a.

ascertained
avadhṛta, ṅes-par-zin-pa
KSP 7, 9.

ascertainment

viniścaya, rnam-par-ṅes-pa

VK, ad 21a

aspect

ākāra, rnam-pa

PSP 5, p 71; *KSP* 29, 31, 36, 37; *VK* ad 22a (*prakāra*), ad 22b;

MVB ad I 3, ad I 17, ad II 14-16, ad III 7a ("form" : *prakāra*),
ad III 22b ("mode of existence"); ad III 22b, ad IV 2, ad V 15 ("semblance"), ad V 28 ("in the manner of", *prakāratas*)

TSN 7

aspersions

abhyākhyāna, skur-ba-ḥdebs-pa

PSP 4, p 69.

aspiration

praṇidhāna, smon-pa (See also "resolve")

MVB ad V 23-26; *KSP* 2.

assented to

iṣyate, ḥdod-pa (see also "accepted", "sought")

MVB I 4b, I 16.

assertion

abhidhāna, brjod-pa

VV 2 and throughout

astringent

kaṣāya, bska-ba

PSP 1.

at will

yathecchas, ji-ltar-bẓed-pa-bẓin-du

MVB ad II 14-16.

atom

paramāṇu, rdul-phra-rab

KSP 3, note 9, 44; *VK* 11, ad 11, 12a, ad 12a, 13, ad 13, ad 14a, ad 14b, ad 14c.

attachment

rāga, ḥdod-chags

PSP 4, p 66; defined p 68; p 68, p 69, p 70, p 71.

TK 11

MVB ad II 1, ad V 23-26/

attachment to being
bhava-sakti, srid-pa-la-chags-pa
MVB II 2 4-8, ad II 10a.
attachment to the idea of "self"
ātmābhiniveśa, bdag-tu-mṅon-par-źen-pa
MVB ad IV 1
attained
pratilabdha, rñed-pa
PSP 4, p 70
(*first*) *attaining*
pratilambha, (*rab-tu-*)*thob-pa*
MVB ad IV 18, V 3, ad V 3.
attaining
samprāpti, ḥthob-pa
MVB IV 13-14
attainment
prāpti, thob-pa
MVB I 1a, ad I 1a, I 18a, ad I 18a, ad I 19a, ad II 10a, ad II 17, ad III 9b-10a, III 11a, ad III 11a, ad IV, 16, IV, 18, ad IV 18, IV 9b-10a (*samprāpti, go-byed*), ad IV 9b-10a, IV 12b, c, V 3, ad V 3; *TSN* 31, 32.
attainment (meditational)
samāpatti, sñoms-par-ḥjug-pa
KSP 21, 22, 23; *TK* 16.
attainment all together
samāpti, rtsogs-pa
MVB IV 18, ad IV 18.
attainment by others
para-samprāpaṇa, gźan-go-ba-byed-pa
MVB ad IV 9b-10a
attainment of freedom
mokṣāpatti, grol-bar-thal-ḥgyur (V) *thar-pa-thob* (N)
TSN 35
(*others'*) *attainments*
lābhasatkāra, rñed-pa-daṅ-bkur
MVB II 2-3a, ad II 2-3a, ad II 10a.
attainment of cessation (*of feelings and cognitions*)
nirodha-samāpatti, ḥgog-paḥi-sñoms-par-ḥjug-pa
PSP 4, p 70, defined 4, p 70-71.
KSP 19, 21, 24, 25, 27, 28, 29, 30, 36

TK 7

attainments of successive stages

anupūrvavihārasamāpatti mthar-gyis-gnas-paḥi-sñoms-par-ḥjug-pa

KSP 29.

attainment of supermundane events

lokottara-dharma-pratilambha, ḥjig-rten-las-ḥdas-paḥi-chos-thob-pa

MVB ad IV 18

attainment without cognitions

asaṃjñi-samāpatti, ḥdu-śes-med-paḥi-sñoms-par-ḥjug-pa

PSP, 4, p 71, defined 4, p 71; *KSP* 27

audial consciousness

śrotra-vijñāna, rna-saḥi-rnam-par-śes-pa

PSP, 5, p 73

attitude of non-harming

ahiṃsā, rnam-par-mi-tshe-ba

PSP 4, p 66; definition 4, p 66-67

TK 11

auxiliary cause

sahakāra-hetu, lhan-cig-byed-paḥi-rgyu

KSP 40

aversion

pratigha, khor-khro-ba

PSP 4, p 66; definition 4, p 68; *TK* 11; *MVB* ad II 2a.

augmented

vikāsita, rtas-par-hgyur

KSP 32

augmentation

vikāsana, rtas-par-byed-pa

KSP 32

avoidance

varjita, (rnam-par-)spaṅs-pa

MVB V 2a, ad V 2a, V 15, ad V 15.

avoiding

varjana, spaṅ(s)-pa

MVB, ad V 23-26, ad V 31.

awareness

vijñānanā, rnam-par-rig-pa

PSP 5, p 71, p 73

B

bad
asat, dam-pa-ma-yin-pa
VK, ad 17c.
bad and good friends
pāpa-kalyāṇa-mitra, sdig-paḥi grogs-po daṅ dge-baḥi-bśes-gñen
basic reality
mūla-tattva, rtsa-baḥi-de-kho-na
MVB III 1-2, ad III 1-2, ad III 4, ad III 5, ad III 6, III 7a, ad III 14a,b, ad III 22b.
bases of psychic power
ṛddhi-pāda, rdzun-ḥphrul-gyi-rkaṅ-pa
MVB ad II 11, ad IV 3, ad IV 5b, ad IV 6.
basis
āśraya, gnas (See also "support")
MVB IV 5a, IV 8a, ad IV 8a, V 15b-18a, ad V 16.
ālaya, kun-gẑi
PSP 5, p 72.
basis
mūla (?), *khuṅs*
KŚP 10, 24.
basis (mental)
nilamba, brten
PSP 5, p 71.
basis of potency
vaśitāśraya, dbaṅ-baḥi-gnas
MVB II 14-16, ad II 14-16.
becomes constructed
kalpyate, brtags-pa
TSN 5.
becomes intent on
nimnobhavati, gẑol-bar-byed-pa
KSP 49.
becomes something else
anyaṃ bhavati, gẑan-du-ḥgyur-ba
KSP 10
becoming a receptacle
bhājanatva, snod-(du)-gyur(-pa)

MVB IV 17, ad IV 17.

becoming disturbed

kupannatā, ṅan-par-źugs

MVB III 14b.

becoming enslaved by unpleasant speech

caṇḍavacodāsitā, tshig-brlaṅ-mos-źer-ḥdebs-pa-ñid

PSP 4, p 69.

becoming higher

uttara, bla-ma

MVB IV 18, ad IV 18.

becoming intensely great

adhimātratā, śas-cher-gyur-pa

MVB ad IV 17, ad IV 17.

beginning

ādya, thog-ma

MVB IV 18.

beginning fruition

ādi-phala, thog-maḥi-ḥbras-bu

MVB ad IV 18

beginning undertakings

ārambha, rtsom-pa

MVB V 3, ad V 3, ad IV 18.

being

bhāva, dṅos-po

KSP 38; *VK* ad 18b; *MVB* ad I 1, ad I 3, I 4, ad I 4, I 13a, ad I 13a, I 13b, ad I 13b, I 20, ad I 20, V 18a, ad V 15b-18a, V 25, ad V 23-26

TSN 15, 16

being (as link in dependent origination)

bhava, srid-pa

MVB ad I 11, ad II 10a.

being-again

punarbhava, yaṅ-srid-pa

MVB ad I 10-11a, ad I 22c, ad II 22c, ad II 12-13, ad V 23-26.

being comprised of

parigṛhīta, yoṅs-su-bzuṅ-ba

MVB ad V 8b.

being based in neither Saṃsāra nor Nirvāṇa

saṃsāra-nirvāṇâpratiṣṭhitā ḥkhor-ba-daṅ-mya-ṅan-las-ḥdas-pa-la-mi-gnas-pa

MVB ad V 29-30.
being diminished
saṃlekha, srab-pa
MVB IV 7a
being favorable, favorability, favoring
ānukūlya, rjes-su-mthun-pa
MVB IV 18, ad IV 18, ad V 26.
being flawed
duṣṭatā, skyon-chags
MVB II 11
being forced to live with stupid or depraved people
kuduṣṭajanavāsanā, skye-bo-ṅan-sdaṅ-ḥgrogs-pa
MVB II 4-8, ad II 10a.
being freed
vinirmukta, ma-gtogs-pa
MVB V 19.
being ill-versed in what's been heard
alpa-śrutatva, thos-pas-ñuṅ-ba
MVB II 4-8, ad II 10a.
being of good effect
anuśaṃsana, phan-yon
MVB IV 13-14, ad IV 13-14.
being pulled along
karṣaṇa, sdud-pa
MVB I 10-11a, ad I 10-11a.
being put to rest
praśamana, rab-tu-ži-bar-byed-pa
MVB ad IV 4.
beneficial
kuśala, dge-ba
PSP 4, p 66; 5, p 74;
KSP note 17a, 12, 13, 14, 18, 20, 21, 26, 27, 29, 32, 39, 47
VK ad 18c.; *TK* 8, 11, 30
MVB ad I 18a, I 18d, ad II 10a, ad II 12-13, ad II 14-16, ad III 19, ad III 20a, ad IV 13-14, ad IV 17, ad V 23-26
beneficiality
kuśalatva, dge-ba-ñid
KSP 15, 27.
beyond the scope of citta
acintya, bsam-par-mi-nus

VK, 22a.

binding

nibandhana, sbyor-ba

MVB I 10-11a, ad I 10-11a.

birth

jāti, skye-ba

PSP 4, p 70, p 71 (definition);

KSP 49; *MVB* ad I 10-11a, ad I 11b.

bitter

tikta, kha-ba

PSP, 1, p 65

blockage

āvṛti, sgrib-pa

VK 14b, ad 14b, ad 14c.

Bodhisattva

byaṅ-chub-sems-dpaḥ

MVB ad IV 11b-12a, ad IV 12b, ad V 3.

bodily act

kāya-karma, lus-kyi-las

KSP 1, 2, 13, 14, 15, 18, 21, 40, 41, 42, cf. 43, 46, 47, 49.

body

kāya, lus

PSP 1, p 65

KSP 2, 11, 12, 15, 24, 33, 34, 38, 41, 43, 44, 46, 47

VK ad 9, ad 18b; *MVB* ad IV 1, ad IV 12b, ad V 23-26 (*śarīra*) ad I 17 (*deha*)

bondage

bandha, bciṅs-pa

MVB ad I 4b.

bound

amukta, ma-grol-ba

MVB III 15-16a, ad III 15-16a.

bringing about

abhinirvṛt, sṅon-par-hgrub-pa

KSP 18

abhinirhāra, mṅon-par-bsgrub-pa

MVB ad II 14-16, ad IV 11a.

bringing about of all sentient beings' aims

sarva-sattvārthakriyā sems-can-thams-cad-gyi-don-bya-baḥi-ched

MVB ad V 3.

bringing it about

sādhanā, sgrub-pa

MVB V 27b-28a, ad V 27b-28a

bringing to rest

śama, ži-ba

MVB III 21, ad III 21 (III 22b, ad III 22b)

brings forth

utthāpayati, sloṅ-bar-byed-pa

KSP 48.

brings to maturity

paripācayati, yoṅs-su-smin-par-byed

MVB, ad V 6.

by necessity

avaśyam, ṅes-par

VK ad 16b.

C

caitta

sems-las-byuṅ-ba (See also "events associated with citta")

MVB I 8a, ad I 8b, I 9(*caitasa*), ad II 10a, ad V 23-26

called

ākhya, žes-bya (sometimes indicated by " ")

TK 2; *TSN* 6, 15, 20.

calm

śamatha, ži-gnas

MVB ad IV 11a, ad V 31.

can be demonstrated

sidhyate, ḥgrub-pa

VV 2, 3, 8; *VK* ad 17c, 20b, ad 20b; *KSP* 4c, 28.

can be perceived

(*vi*)*jñeya*), *śes-bya, śes-par-bya*

TSN 18, 19, 21

can be seen

sanidarśana, bstan-du-yod-pa

PSP 5, p 74

cannot be completely found in that way

tathātyantaṃ na vidyate de-ltar-śin-tu-med-pa(*V*) *de-bžin-śin-tu-yod-ma-yin*(*N*)

TSN 5
cannot be demonstrated
na sidhyati, mi-ḥgrub-pa
KSP 5, 8, 13, 15, 17; *VK* 11, ad 11, ad 13, ad 15, ad 17b.
capacity
vaśa, dbaṅ
PSP 4, p 70
capacity
ādhipatya, dbaṅ, dbaṅ-ḅyed-pa (see also "sovereignty)"
MVB IV 17, ad IV 17, ad V 23-26.
carefulness
apramāda, bag-yod-pa
PSP 4, p 66; definition 4, p 67.
careless activity
ayogavihitā, rnal-ḥbyor-min-pas-bskyed
MVB II 4-8
carelessness
pramāda, bag-med-pa
PSP 4, p 66; definition p 69; *TK* 13; *MVB* II 4-8, ad II 10a.
casting away what one has heard
śrutavyasana, thos-pas-phoṅs-pa
MVB II 4-8, ad II 10a.
casting off
hāni, ḥbri-ḅa
MVB II 12, ad II 12-13.
causal situation
hetvavasthā, rgyuḥi gnas
MVB IV 13-14, ad IV 13-14.
causality
hetutva, rgyu-ñid
PSP 5, p 72
causing the idea to arise
saṃpratyāyana, yid-ches-par-byed-pa
MVB, ad II 10a.
cause
hetu, rgyu
KSP 8, 9, 11, 27, 29, 30, 38, 49; *VK* ad 8
MVB I 15, ad I 15, ad II 10a, ad II 17, III 1-2, ad III 1-2, ad III 7b-8a, ad III 15-16a, IV 1 ad IV 1, ad IV 3, ad IV 7b

TSN 6
kāraṇa, rgyu, byed-rgyu
MVB ad II 10a, ad V 15b-18a
cause-as-condition-for-a-cognition
jñāpaka-hetu, śes-byed-gyi-rgyu
VV 15.
cause-consciousness
hetu-vijñāna, rgyuḥi-rnam-par-śes-pa
KSP 37.
cause of all further fruitions
upaniṣadbhava, rgyuḥi dṅos-po
MVB ad IV 18
cause of arising
utpatti-hetu, skye-baḥi-rgyu
KSP 9
cause of destruction
vināśa-hetu, ḥjig-paḥi rgyu
KSP 8
causeness
hetutva, rgyu
MVB III 15-16a, ad III 15-16a
cease
nirudh, zig-pa
KSP 16-17
VK, ad 16
ceasing
vyaya, ḥjig-pa
MVB III 5, ad III 5, ad III 7b-8a.
center portion
madhya, dbus
KSP 4.
certain
niyata, niścita, ṅes-pa
VV 6, 13, 23b, *VK* ad 17c, 18a, ad 18a
PSP 4, p 67
certainty, niyama, ṅes-pa
cessation
vyaya, ḥjig-pa
VV 17
nirodha, ḥgog-pa

PSP 4, p 70; *KSP* 27, 28;
MVB I 15, ad I 15, II 2-3a, ad II 2-3a, ad III 7b-8a, ad III 8b, ad III 9a, ad III 21, ad III 22b, ad IV 1, ad V 23-26

cessation not through contemplation
PSP, 4, p 73, note 29; *KSP* 16-17
apratisaṅkhyā-nirodha so-sor-brtags-pa-ma-yin-paḥi-ḥgog-pa

cessation of self
atmoccheda, bdag-chad-pa
MVB ad IV 1.

cessation of suffering
duḥkha-nirodha, sdug-bsṅal-gyi-ḥgog-pa
MVB II 2-3a, ad II 2-3a, ad III 1 7b-8a, ad III 21, ad IV 1

cessation through contemplation
pratisaṅkhyā-nirodha, so-sor-brtags-paḥi-ḥgog-pa
PSP 4, p 73; *MVB* ad III 9a.

change (see also "transformation")
vipariṇāma, ḥgyur-ba
KSP 37
"*as it undergoes change*", *vikāradharmitvāt, ḥgyur-baḥi-chos-can-yin-pas*
MVB ad I 16b.

characteristic
lakṣaṇa, mtshan-ñid
KSP 7, 8c, 8e, 9, 10, 40; *VV* 2; *VK* ad 10b, ad 14, ad 15; *TK* 24; *TSN* 10, 11, 12, 13, 17, 18, 19, 20, 21
MVB I 1a, ad I 1a, ad I 1b, ad I 2, ad I 4b, ad I 5, ad I 6, ad I 7b, ad I 8, ad I 9b, ad I 9, ad I 11b, I 12, ad I 12, ad I 13a, ad I 13a, I 14a, ad I 14a, ad I 16, ad I 20, ad I 22c, II 1b, III 1-2, ad III 1-2, ad III 3, III 4, ad III 4, III 5, ad III 5, ad III 7a, III 7b, ad III 7b, ad III 13b, ad III 14a, III 14b, ad III 14b, ad IV 1, V 19, ad V 19, ad V 26.

characteristic apart from that
tadvilakṣaṇa, de-daṅ-mi-mthun-mtshan-ñid
MVB III 7b-8a, ad III 7b-8a (also "characteristic apart from this or that").

characteristic of being divided
prabheda-lakṣaṇa, rab-tu-dbye-baḥi-mtshan-ñid
MVB ad I 7b, ad I 11.

characteristic of evolving

pravṛtti-lakṣaṇa, ḥjug-paḥi-mtshan-ñid
MVB ad I 8b, ad I 11.
characteristic of having afflictions
saṃkleśa-lakṣaṇa, kun-nas-ñon-moṅs-paḥi-mtshan-ñid
MVB ad I 9, ad I 11
circular
vṛtta, zlūm-po
KSP 4
circumference
samanta, khor-yug
KSP 4
citta
sems
PSP, Introduction, pp 60; *PSP*, p 66, 67, 68, 69, 70, 71, 73, 74, 75.
KSP 2, 6, 8, 9, 11, 12, 14, 18, 19, 20, 21, 22, 23, 24, 27, 28, 29, 30, 31, 32, 34, 40, 49
VK ad 1, ad 8, 18b, ad 20b, 21a, ad 21a, 22a
MVB I 8a, I 22b, II 4-8, ad II 10a, ad II 11, ad IV 1, ad IV 3, ad IV 5b, ad IV 6, ad IV 7b, ad IV 13-14, ad IV 18, V 12, ad V 12, ad V 23-26, ad V 29-30; *TSN* 5, 6, 7, 26.
citta of a former aspiration
pūrva-praṇidhāna-citta, sṅon-gyi-smon-lam-gyi-sems
KSP 2, note 8.
citta which is instigating action
(karma)-pravartaka-citta (las-)ḥjug-par-byed-paḥi-sems
KSP 2
clarity
śuddhi, viśuddhi, dag-pa, rnam-par-dag-pa
PSP 4, p 69; *MVB* I 16c, ad V 19, V 21(*viśuddhatva*)
KSP 50, verse.
cleared, clear
viśuddha, rnam-dag, rnam-par-dag-pa
MVB I 16a, ad I 16a, I 21, I 22a, IV 15, ad IV 15, ad II 14-16, ad IV 17, ad V 21, ad V 31.
clear understanding
abhisamaya, sṅon-par-rtogs-pa
MVB ad II 2-3a
clear worldly subsequently attained knowledge
pṛṣṭhalabdhaśuddhalaukikajñāna, rjes-las-thob-pa-dag-

pa-ḥjig-rten-paḥi-ye-śes
VK ad 17c.
clearing
viśuddhi, rnam-par-dag-pa
MVB ad I 13b, I 19a, I 19b, III 1-2, ad III 1-2, III 12b, ad III 13b, III 19, ad III 19, ad IV 17, ad VI 18 (śin-tu-dag-pa) V 22, ad V 22, ad V 23-26, ad V 29-30;
pariśodhana, yoṅs-su-sbyoṅ-ba
MVB ad II 14-16, ad V 8b.
clearly
vyaktam, gsal-bar
KSP 5
clinging
upādāna, ñe-bar-len-pa
MVB ad I 10-11a, ad I 11b, ad III 6b, ad III 7b-8a
close interrelationship
anukṛti, ḥdra-ba
PSP, 4, p 71
co-arising
sambhūti, lhan-skyes
TK 16
cognition
saṁjñā, ḥdu-śes
VV 9, 10; *PSP* 1, p 90; 3, p 92(definition); 4, p 92, p 98
KSP 25, 26, 27, 40
TK 3; *MVB* III 16b, ad V 16.
cognizing
buddhi, blo
VK ad 15, 16a, ad 16b.
(cognizing by)
cognition through direct perception
pratyakṣa-buddhi, mṅon-sum-gyis-blo
VK 16a, ad 16b.
coldness
śītatva, graṅ-ba-ñid
PSP 1, p 66
collection
vṛnda, gaṇa, or *samāja* ?, *ḥdus-pa*
KSP 43
collected

vicita ?, *bsdus-pa*
KSP 34
collection
? *tshogs*
KSP 37
collection of phrases
pada-kāya, tshig-gi-phyogs
PSP 4, p 70, p 71.
collection of syllables
vyañjana-kāya, yi-geḥi-tshogs
PSP 4, p 70, p 71.
collection of words
nāma-kāya, miṅ-gi-tshogs
PSP 4, p 70, p 71.
collision
pratighāta, thog-pa, thogs-pa
VK, ad 14b
color
varṇa, kha-dog
PSP 1, p 63; *KSP* 3, 4, 5, 11, 12, 13
come to an end
niruddha, ḥgags
KSP 22
chid, chinatti, ḥchad-pa
KSP 15, 28
coming to heat
uṣmagata, dro-bar-gyur-pa
MVB, Introduction; ad IV, 8a.
common, in common
samāna, sādhāraṇa, sāmānya, thun-moṅ-pa
PSP 5, p 75; *VK* ad 14 b; *MVB* ad I 18c (*spyi*)
commonly known
prasiddha, grags
KSP 8
communicate
pratipādayati, go-bar-byed-pa
KSP 48
compact meaning
piṇḍārtha, don-bsdus-pa
MVB ad I 11, ad I 22c, ad II 17, ad III 22b, ad IV 18, ad V 31.

compassion
karuṇā, *sñiṅ-rje*
PSP, 4, p 68
complacency
anunaya, *rjes-su-chags-pa*
MVB, ad II 2a
complete knowledge
parijñā, *yoṅs-(su-)śes*
TSN 31, 32
complete Nirvana
parinirvāṇa, *yoṅs-su-mya-ṅan-las-ḥdas-pa*
MVB ad V 10b.
completing fruition
sākṣātkriyā(phala), *sṅon-sum-du-byas-pa(ḥi-ḥbras-bu)*
MVB ad IV, 18
completing beneficial actions
kṛtyānuṣṭhāna, *kṛtyānuṣṭhā*, *bya-ba-sgrub-pa*
MVB IV 13-14, ad IV 13-14
complete non-being
atyantābhāva, śin-tu-med-pa(V), śin-tu-med-pa-ñid(N)
TSN 11
complete unrelatedness of the objects
vaidharmya, *chos-mimthun-pa*
VV 11
completed efficacy
upayoga, *spyad-zin-pa*
MVB III 20b, ad III 20b
complex
sāmagrī, *tshogs*
KSP 15, verse, 16-17
component
aṅga, *yan-lag*
KSP 3
composite
aṅgin, *yan-lag-can*
KSP 3
composite whole
avayavī, *cha-śas-can*
KSP, note 11; *VK*, ad 11
compounded

saṁskṛta, ḥdu-byas
KSP 11; *MVB* ad I 2, ad I 16, ad I 18a, ad III 1-2, ad III 11a, ad III 11b, ad III 23, ad V 23-26.

compounded events
saṁskāra, ḥdu-byed
MVB ad IV 1

comprised
upagṛhīta, gzuṅ-bar-gyur
KSP 3

"*obstruction which may be comprised together*", *saṁgrahāvaraṇa, bsdus-paḥi-sgrib-pa,*
MVB ad II 17

comprising
saṁgraha, bsdu-ba
MVB ad I 4, III 13, ad III 13, III 1-2, ad III 1-2

comprising characteristic
saṁgraha-lakṣaṇa, bsdu-baḥi mtshan-ñid
MVB ad I 4b, ad I 11

concave
avanata, dmaḥ-ba
KSP 4

concealment
chādana, sgrib-pa
MVB I 10-11a, ad I 10-11a

conceit
abhimāna, sṅon-paḥi-ṅa-rgyal
PSP 4, p 67-68; *MVB* ad III 22b (*ṅa-rgyal*)

conception (*in the womb*)
pratisandhi, ñiṅ-mtshuṅs-sbyor-ba
KSP 33

concisely
samāsatas, mdo-bsdu-na (see also "in brief")
MVB I 12, I 14, IV 18, ad IV 18

concluding cultivation
paryavasānabhāvanā, mthaḥi sgom-pa
MVB ad IV 18

concurrent
tadidānīṁ
VK, ad 15

condition (causal)

pratyaya, rkyen
KSP 7, 10, 14, 16-17, 22, 25, 27, 29, 32, 37, 40; *MVB* ad I 9, ad III k 8b, ad II 10a, ad V 29
TSN 2

conditional ground
pratyayatva, rkyen
MVB ad I 9

condition-consciousness
pratyaya-vijñāna, rkyen-gyi-rnam-par-śes-pa
MVB I 9, ad I 9

conducive
anukūla, rjes-su-mthun-pa
MVB ad I 10-11a, ad V 6

conducting
nayana, ḥkhrid-pa
MVB I 10-11a, ad I 10-11a, ad I 11b.

confidence
adhimokṣa, mos-pa
PSP 4, p 66; definition, p 67
TK 10; *MVB* IV 13-14 (*adhimukti*) ad IV 13-14, ad V 3, ad V 29-30

confidences (special)
vaiśāradya, mi-ḥjigs-pa
MVB ad I 19a

configuration saṁsthāna, dbyibs
PSP, 1, p 65;
KSP 2, 3, 4, 5, note 5,

conformity
sārūpya, mthun-pa
PSP 5, p 75

confrontation
ābhimukhya, mṅon-du
MVB I 10-11a, ad I 10-11a

confusion
moha, saṁmoha, rmoṅs-pa
PSP 4, p 68, 69, 70; *TK* 11; *MVB* ad V 6, ad V 23-26

confusion (in sense of perplexity)
bhrānti, ḥkhrul pa
MVB ad I 4, ad II 9, ad V 15b-18a, ad V 22, ad III 3b ("state of confusion" : *bhrantatva*)

TSN 12, 15
confusion of self
ātma-moha, bdag-tu-tmoṅs-pa
PSP 5, p 72; *TK* 6; *MVB* ad I 3.
conjecture
arthāpatti, don-gyi-go-ba
VV 19, 21
conjoined
sahita, ḥbrel-ba
TK 6, *KSP* 34
conjunction
saṁnipāta, yaṅ-dag-par-ḥdus-pa
KSP 25, 26
saṁyoga, phrad-pa
KSP 11, *VK* 13, ad 13, 12a, ad 12a; *MVB*, V 14
connected
saṁyukta, yaṅ-dag-ldan-pa
MVB V 8b.
connection
saṁbandha, ḥbrel-ba
VV 5, 10; *MVB* III 6b, ad III 6b, ad III 7b-8a, cf. ad III 8b.
connected with
saṁprayukta, mtshuṅs-par-ldan-pa
KSP 37
consciousness
vijñāna, rnam-par-śes-pa
VV 9, *PSP* 5 and 1 (5 includes definition),
TK 1, 17, 18, 26, 27, 28
KSP 24, 25, 32, 33, 34, 35, 36, 37, 38, 40, 49
VK ad 1, 6 ad 6, ad 7
MVB I 3, ad I 3, I 4, I 8, ad I 8, ad I 9, ad I 10-11a, ad I 11b, ad III 16b, ad III 23, ad V 12, ad V 23-26.
consciousness which is the requisite for existence
bhavāṅgavijñāna, srid-paḥi-yan-lag-gi-rnam-par-śes-pa
KSP 35, 37
consideration
pratyavekṣā, so-sor-rtog-pa
MVB ad C V 23-26.
considered
mata, ḥdod

VK 16b, ad 16b; *TSN* 8, 11, 12, 13, 14, 15, 16

consists of

ātmaka, bdag-ñid

TSN 9, 14, 15, 16, 23, 38

constant

dhruva, rtag

KSP 16-17; *TK* 30; *TSN* 3(*sadā, rtag-tup*

constantly

sadā, rtag-tu

MVB V 6, ad V 6.

constituency as one entity

dravyatva, rdzas-su-yod-pa

KSP 12

construct

kḷp, brtags-pa

VK ad 6, 7, ad 11, ad 15, ad 20b.

TSN 5

(*mentally*) *constructed*

parikalpita, kun-tu-brtags-pa

PSP, 4, p 68, p 69; *KSP* 12, 20, 20, *VK* 10c (*kalpita*), ad 10c;

TK 20; *MVB* I 5, ad I 5, ad III 3a, ad III 3b, ad III 4, ad III 5, ad III 6, ad III 7a, ad III 7b-8a, ad III 8b, ad III 9b-10a, ad III 12a, ad III 14a, ad III 16b, ad V, 22, ad V 23-26;

TSN and (*kalpita, brtags*(V), *kun-brtags*(N)) : 1, 2, 11, 14, 17, 18, 19, 28., 23(*kun-brtags* V and N)

construction

parikalpa, kun-tu-rtog-pa

VK, ad 14c; *MVB* III 16b; *TSN* 24 (*kalpa*, brtags (V), brtag-pa(N)).

construction of that which was not

abhūta-parikalpa, yaṅ-dag-pa-ma-yin-pa(ḥi)-kun-tu-rtog-pa, yaṅ-dag-ma-yin-kun-rtog

MVB I 1, ad I 1, ad I 2, I 4, ad I 4b, ad I 5, ad I 7, I 8a, ad I 8b, ad I 9, I 11, ad I 14a

TSN 8

construction of the non-existent

asat-kalpa, min-rtog-pa (N), *med-brtags*(V)

TSN 4, 5, 29 (*ma-yin-kun-rtog* (V), *mib-kun-rtog* (N))

contact

sparśa, reg-pa

PSP 4, p 66, definition, 4, p 67;

KSP 25, 26, 27, 29; *TK* 3, 4, 7, 10; *MVB* ad I 10-11a, ad I 11b.

containing materiality

rūpī, gzugs-can

PSP 5, p 74

contemplation

pratisaṅkhyāna, so-sor-brtags-pa, so-sor-rtog-pa

MVB ad II 13, ad V 5

continuance, continuity

nairantarya, rgyun-mi-ḥched-pa

MVB II 13, ad II 12-13, V 3, ad V 3.

continuance

vāhitā, ḥjug-pa

MVB IV 5b, ad IV 5b.

continuation

saṁghāta, rgyun-mi-ḥchad

MVB III 20a, ad III 20a

pravartana, ḥjug-pa

KSP 8cm, 32 ("continuous")

continued practise

abhyāsa, goms-(par-)byas-pa

MVB ad IV 17, IV 18, ad IV 18

continuity

sthiti, gnas-pa

PSP 4, p 70, p 71

98 99; *MVB* III 20a, ad III 20a(*sthāna*)

nivāsa, gnas-pa-ñid

PSP 4, p 67; p 71

contradicted

na pratisidhyet, mi ḥgrub

MVB, ad I 4b.

contradictory

savirodha, ḥgal-ba

VV 11, 13, 23, 24; *KSP* 8.

contrary to fact

nôpapadyate, mi ḥthad-do

KSP 29

contraction
āvarjana, sdud-pa
PSP 4, p 70
conventional
saṁvṛti, kun-rdzob-pa
VV 9; *MVB* ad III 9b-10a, ad III 10b, ad V 18a.
conventional practise
vyavahāra, tha-sñad
TSN 22, 23.
conventional symbol
saṁketa, brda
MVB, ad III 12a
convex
unnata, mthon-po
KSP 4
corporeal mass
kalevara, khog
KSP 43.
counter-acts
pratividhyati, rab-tu-rtogs-pa
MVB ad II 14-16
courses of action
prayoga, sbyor-ba
MVB ad II 17
craving
tṛṣṇā, sred-pa
KSP 25; *MVB* ad I 10-11a, ad I 11b, ad II 14-16, IV 1 (*tarṣa*), ad IV, 1.
cultivation
bhāvanā, sgom-pa, bsgom-pa
PSP 4, p 67
MVB I 1a, ad I 1a, ad II 11, ad II 12-13, ad IV 1, ad IV 2, ad IV 3, ad IV 9b-10a, ad IV 11a, ad IV 13a, ad IV 18, ad V 6, ad V 27-28, ad V 31
cultivation by others
para-saṁbhāvanā, gźan-yid-ches-bar-byed-pa
MVB IV 9b-10a, ad IV 9b-10a
cultivation having a higher
sôttarā bhāvanā, bla-ma-daṅ-bcas-paḥi-sgom-pa
MVB ad IV 18

cultivation having no higher
niruttarā bhāvanā, bla-ma-med-paḥi-sgom
MVB ad IV 18
cultivation of applications
parikarma-bhāvanā, yoṅs-su-sbyaṅ-ba-bya-baḥi-sgom-pa
MVB, ad IV 18
cultivation of becoming involved
praviṣṭa-bhāvanā, žugs-paḥi-sgom-pa
MVB, ad IV 18
cultivation of necessary prerequisites one after the other
uttarôttarasamārambhabhāvanā, goṅ-ma-yaṅ-dag-par-rtsom-paḥi-sgom-pa
MVB ad IV 18
cultivation of restraint
nirlekha-bhāvanā, bsrabs-paḥi-sgom-pa
cultivation of sticking to it
śliṣṭa-bhāvanā, ḥdre-bahi-sgom-pa
MVB ad IV 18
cultivation that awakens
vyutpatti-bhāvanā, byaṅ-bar-bya-baḥi-sgom-pa
MVB ad IV 18

D

decaying
bhaṅga, ḥjig-pa
MVB ad III 7b-8a
deceitfulness
māyā, sgyu
PSP, 4, p 66; definition, 4, p 69; *TK* 12
decrepitude
jarā, rga-ba
PSP 4, p 70; definition, p 71; *MVB* ad I 10-11a, ad I 11b.
defect
hīnatā, ñams-pa
MVB II 11, ad II 11
defective citta
hīna-citta, chuṅ-ṅuḥi-sems, dman-paḥi-sems
MVB V 12, ad V 12.
deficiency

vaikalya, ma-tshaṅ-ba
KSP 31; *MVB* ad II 11.
deliberate intention
abhisandhi, bsam-pa
MVB V 12, ad V 12.
deliberation according to words
yathā-ruta-vicāraṇa, sgra-ji-bžin-du-dpyod-pa
MVB II 4-8, ad II 10a
delight
ruci, ḥdod-pa
MVB IV, 17, ad IV 18
delimited
paricchinna, yoṅs-su-chad-pa
KSP 37
deliverances
vimokṣa, rnam-par-thar-pa
KSP 29
demonstrandum
sādhya, bsgrub-par-bya-ba
VV 2, 3, 5, 14, 15, 16, 17, 18, 20, 23
demonstration
siddhi, sgrub-pa
VV 2, *VK* 22a; *MVB* I 12, ad I 20 (*sādhanā*)
demonstrated
siddha, grub-pa
VK 3a, ad 3b, ad 4a,b,c, ad 15, ad 20b; *MVB* I 4, I 7a, ad I 7b, ad I 22c
VV 6, 7, 8, 15, 16, 18, *KSP* 50 (*sādhita*)
demonstrator
sādhaka, grub-byed
VV 5, 8
demonstrable
sādhya, bsgrub-par-bya-ba
VV 2, 3
denial
apavāda, skur-ba-ḥdebs-pa
VK, ad 10c.; *MVB* ad I 4b, ad I 20, ad II 2-3a, III 4, ad III 4, III 18b, ad III 18b, V 23, ad V 23-26.
denotation
adhivacana, tshig-brla-drags

PSP 4, p 71
dependent
anubaddha ?, *rjes-su-ḥbraṅ-ba*
KSP 14
dependent origination
pratītyasamutpāda, *rten-ciṅ-ḥbrel-bar-ḥbyuṅ-ba*
MVB ad I 11b, ad II 14-16, ad III 1-2, ad III 18a, ad III 18b.
dependent upon
āśritya, *brten-nas*, *rten-nas*
TK 5; *MVB* I 6 (*samāśrita*), ad I 6 (*niśritya*)
KSP 2, 21(*apekṣya*, *bltos-nas*), 23, 25, 27, 29, 30.
depth
gāmbhīrya, *zab-pa*
VK ad 21b.
descending
avatāra, *žugs-pa*
MVB IV 13-14, ad VI 13-14
descent
avatāraṇa, *ḥdzun-pa*
MVB II 12, ad II 12-13
avatāra, *ḥdzun*
MVB V, 6; ad IV 13-14 ("descending")
designation
prajñapti, *gdags-pa*, *btags-pa*
PSP 4, p 70; *MVB* III 10b, III 22b, ad III 22b, ad V 23-26, ad V 27-28a
designated (it is designated)
vyavahrīyate, *tha-sñad-bya-ba*
VV 9
desirable
iṣṭa, *ḥdod*
VK ad 18a
desire
kāma, *ḥdod-pa*
PSP 4, p 67, 68; *MVB* ad I 10-11a
desire to harm
vihiṁsā, *rnam-par-ḥtshe-ba*
PSP 4, p 67, definition, p 69; *TK* 13
desirelessness
anarthitva, *mi-ḥdod-pa*

MVB, ad V 3

destroyed, destruction

vinaṣṭa, vināśana, ḥjig-pa

KSP 8, 15, 16-17; *MVB* ad V 23-26.

determination

vyavasthāna, rnam-par-ḥjog-pa, rnam-par-gžag-pa

MVB ad IV 8a, ad IV 9a, ad I 22c, ad V 22, V 27b-28a, ad idem.

vyavasthāpana, rnam-par-bžag-pa

VK, ad 10c

determine

vyavasthāp, rnam-par-bžag-pa

PSP

determined

vyavasthāpyate, rnam-par-gža-pa or *bžag-pa*

MVB ad IV 1, ad IV 4, ad IV 5b; *KSP* 16-17, 37; *VK*, ad 1

parigṛhīta, yoṅs-su-gzuṅ-ba

KSP 14

develop

pravartate, vartate, saṁpravartate, ḥbyuṅ-ba

TK 1, 14; *MVB* ad I 11b, ad III 4, IV, 2m, ad IV 2, ad V 6.

development

pravṛtti, ḥgro-ba

PSP 5, p 72; *MVB* ad III 13b, III 14a, ad III 14a, ad III 18b, V 3, ad V 3, V 11

vṛtti, ḥiug

VK, 15, ad 15; *MVB*, V 6.

de-volvement

vyāvṛti ldog

TK 5

Dharma-body

dharma-kāya, chos-kyi-sku

TK 30, *MVB* ad IV 13-14.

dialectician

tārkika, rtog-ge-ba

KSP 29, *MVB* ad III 12b

dialectics

tarka, rtog-ge

VK, ad 22a; *MVB*, ad V 31.

difference

pṛthaktva, tha-dad-pa
MVB, ad V 23-26
viśeṣa, khyad-par
KSP 40
difference in the order of occurrence
krama-bheda, dbye-baḥi-go-rim (V) *rim-paḥi-raṅ-bžin-raṅ-bžin* (N)
TSN 22
different, nānā, tha-dad-pa
KSP 38, 39
different development of the three kinds of knowledge
jñānatrayānuvṛtti, ye-śes-gsum-gaḥi-rjes-ḥbraṅ (V) *ye--śes gsum-la-rjes-ḥjug* (N)
differentiation
bheda, dbye-ba
MVB III 1-2, ad III 1-2(*prabheda*)
differentiate
viśiṣyati, khyad-par-du-mdzad
KSP 25
diffusion
vigamana rnam-par-ḥgro-ba
PSP, 4, p 70.
direct preception
pratyakṣa, mṅon-sum
VV 9, 16; *VK* ad 15, 16a, 16b, ad 16b
direction
pradeśa, phyogs
KSP 4; *VK*, ad 12a (*dik*)
direction (intentional)
abhimukhīkaraṇa, mṅon-par-byed-pa
MVB ad I 10-11a
directional dimension
dig-bhāga, phyogs-cha
VK 14a, ad 14a, ad 14b
directly antecedent condition
samanantara-pratyaya, de-ma-thag-paḥi-rkyen
KSP 22, note 36, 37.
disagreeable
pratikūla, mi-mthun-pa
MVB ad II 2a

disappearance
apagama, *vigama*, *ḥbral-ba*
MVB ad V 23-26
TSN 33, 34 (*nub-par-ḥgyur*(V), *mi-dmigs pa* (N))
disappeared
apagata, *log-pa*
KSP 18
discernible
bhedya, *phyed-pa*
KSP 5
discerning
dhīra, *dhīmān*, *blo-ldan*, *blo-daṅ-ldan-pa*
TSN 1, 38
discernment
pravicaya, *rab-tu-rnam-par-ḥbyed-pa* *prajñā*, *prajñānana*, *śes-rab*
PSP 3, p 70
PSP, 4, p 67; *MVB* ad IV 8b (*vicaya* in MS, but Tib and *Ṭikā pra-v.*)
discontinuous, *discontinuity*
viccheda, *vicchinna*, *chad-pa*
PSP 4, p 69; 4, p 71; *VK* ad 19
discourse of manas
manojalpa, *yid-kyis-brjod-pa*
PSP 4, p 70
discriminate
vikḷp, *rnam-par-rtog*
TK 17, 20; *MVB* ad V 22
discrimination
vikalpa, *rnam-par-rtog-pa*
PSP 5, p 75; *KSP* 42; *VK* ad 17c, ad 21b; *TK* 17, 18, 20, 21
MVB ad I 1, ad I 22c, III 13, ad III 13, III 16b, ad III 16b, III 22 ad III 22, ad V 3, ad V 16, V 18 b-c, ad V 18b-c, ad V 22, V 25, ad V 23-26, ad V 31
TSN 30 ("discriminating")
discursive thought
vicāra, *dpyod-pa*
PSP, 4, p 66; 4, p 70 (definition), note 14
disjunction

visaṁyoga, bral-bar-bya-ba
MVB IV 18, ad IV 18, V 14 (*viyoga, ma-ḥbrel*)
dispensing with
?, *sṅon-du-btaṅ-ba*
PSP 4, p 70
dissipate
vyavakṛ, ḥdre-ba
MVB ad IV 7a
distinct
pṛthak, so-so
KSP 50
distinct (*practise*)
viśiṣṭa(*-pratipatti*), *khyad-par*(*-can*)*-gyi-sgrub-pa*
MVB V 2a, ad V 2a, ad V 23-26, V 27a, ad V 27a, ad V 31.
distinctive
viśiṣṭa, khyad-par-du-ḥbags-pa
MVB ad IV 18
distinctive situation
viśiṣṭâvasthā, khyad-par (*gnas-skabs**)
MVB IV 13-14, ad IV 13-14
distinction
viśiṣṭatā, khyad-par-du-ḥphags-pa
MVB, IV 12b.
distinction
viśeṣa, khyad-par
MVB IV 18, ad IV 18
distinctiveness,
viśeṣa, bye-brag
MVB V 10a, ad V 10a, ad V 10b
distinguishing
pariccheda, yoṅs-su-bcad-pa, yoṅs-su-gcod-pa
PSP 4, p 67; *VK* ad 16b; *MVB* I 9, ad I 9, I 10, ad I 10, III 17a, ad III 17a, III 18, ad III 18, ad IV 9a, IV 9b-10a
distracted
vikṣipta, rnam-par-gYens-pa
KSP 49, 29
distractedness
vikṣepa, rnam-par-gYeṅ-ba

PSP 4, p 66; definition, p 70; *TK* 14; *MVB* ad V 11, ad V 12, ad V 31.

distress

āsrava, zag-pa

KSP 16-17, 34

disturbance

calana, gYo-ba

KSP 11

division

bheda, tha-dad-pa

MVB ad I 7, ad I 8, I 12, ad I 15, ad I 16a, ad I 16c, ad I 20, ad I 22, II 14-16, ad II 14-16 (*prabheda also*)

VK 14a, ad 14a, ad 15

divisions into black and white fixed alternatives

kṛṣṇa-śukla-pakṣa-bheda, nag-po-daṅ dkar-poḥi phyogs-kyi bye-brag

MVB ad V 23-26.

do not allow to arise

anābhibhava, zil-gyis-mi-gnon-pa

MVB ad V 6.

doer

kartṛ, byed-pa

PSP, p 74, *MVB* III 15-16a, ad III 15-16a (*kartṛtva*, "doer-ness")

does not admit

anupagama, khras-mi-len

MVB ad V 23-26

does not speak of them

anudāhāra, mi-brjod

MVB ad V 23-26.

door

dvāra, sgo

PSP, 5, p 73; *MVB* III 18a, ad III 18a

doubt

vicikitsā, the-tshom

PSP 4, p 66; definition 4, p 63. *TK* 12, *MVB* ad I 22a, ad II 2-3a

dread of blame

apatrāpya, khrel-yod-pa

PSP 4, p 66, definition, 4, p 67; *TK* 11

E

VK, ad 7
MVB III 18b, ad III 18b, III 20b, ad III 20b, IV 13-14, ad IV 13-14

efficacy
kriyā, byed-ba, bya-ba
PSP 3, p 69; *KSP* 15, 16-17

effort
āyatya, āyāsa, ārambha, vyāyāma, rtsol-ba, rtsom-pa.
KSP 50; *VK* ad 18a; *MVB* I 21, ad I 21, ad IV 4, ad IV 5a

elevated cultivation
utkṛṣṭa-bhāvanā, mchog-gi sgom-pa
MVB, ad IV 18

emancipation
niryāṇa, ṅes-par-ḥdyuṅ-ba
MVB III 22a, ad III 22a, ad III 22b, IV 8b, ad IV 8b, V 31

embrace
parigraha, yoṅs-su-ḥdzin-pa
MVB, ad V 6

emergence from meditation
1 *vyutthāna, ldaṅs-pa*
KSP 19, 28, 32; *MVB* V 12, ad V 12.

eminence
utkṛṣṭatā, mchog
MVB, ad V 3

empassioned
ārāgaṇa, mñes-par-byed
MVB, ad V 6

emptiness
śūnyatā, stoṅ-pa-ñid
MVB I 1, ad I 1, ad I 11, I 12, I 13a, ad I 13a, ad I 13b, ad I 13c, I 14, ad I 15, ad I 16c, I 17, ad I 17, ad I 18c, ad I 18d, ad I 19b, I 20, ad I 20, ad I 21, ad I 22c, III 7a, ad III 7a, ad V 23-26.

emptiness of all events
sarva-dharma-śūnyatā, chos thams-cad stoṅ-pa-ñid
MVB, ad I 16c

emptiness of characteristics
lakṣaṇa-śūnyatā, (raṅ-gi)-mtshan-ñid-stoṅ-pa-ñid
MVB, ad I 16c

emptiness of emptiness

śūnyatā-śūnyatā, stoṅ-pa-ñid-stoṅ-pa-ñid
MVB ad I 16c, ad I 17
emptiness of inferior and superior
anavarâgra-śūnyatā, thog-ma daṅ tha-ma med-pa stoṅ-pa-ñid
MVB ad I 16c, ad I 18c
emptiness of own-being
svabhāva-śūnyatā, ṅo-be-ñid-kyis stoṅ-pa-ñid
MVB ad III 7b-8a
emptiness of the compounded
saṁskṛta-śūnyatā, ḥdus-byas-stoṅ-pa-ñid
MVB, ad I 16c
emptiness of the external
bahirdhā-śūnyatā, phyi-stoṅ-pa-ñ
MVB ad I 16c
emptiness of the internal
adhyātma-śūnyatā, naṅ-stoṅ-pa-ñid
MVB, ad I 16c
emptiness of the internal and external
adhyātma-bahirdhā-śūnyatā, phyi-naṅ-stoṅ-pa-ñid
MVB ad I 16c, ad I 17
emptiness of Nature
prakṛti-śūnyatā, raṅ-bžin-ston-pa-ñid
MVB, ad I 16c
emptiness of non-being
abhāva-śūnyatā, dṅos-po-med-pa-stoṅ-pa-ñid
MVB ad I 16c, ad I 20, ad III 1 7b-8a
emptiness of non-rejection
anavakāra-śūnyatā, dor-ba-med-pa-stoṅ-pa-ñid
MVB ad I 16c, ad I 18d
emptiness of the own-being of non-being
abhāva-svabhāva-śūnyatā, dṅos-po-med-paḥi-ṅo-bo-ñid-stoṅ-pa-ñid
MVB ad I 16c, ad I 20
emptiness of the uncompounded
asaṁskṛta-śūnyatā, ḥdus-ma-byas-stoṅ-pa-ñid
MVB ad I 16c
emptiness of ultimate truth
paramārtha-śūnyatā, dam-paḥi-don-stoṅ-pa-ñid
MVB ad I 16c, ad I 17

empty

śūnya, stoṅ-pa

PSP 5, p 75; *VK* ad 15, 20a, ad 20a; *MVB* ad I 1, I 2, ad I 2, ad I 17, ad III 4, ad V 23-26.

encompassment

parigṛhītatva, yoṅs-su-bzuṅ-ba

MVB, ad V 3

encompassing quality

parigraha, yoṅs-(su)gzuṅ(-ba)

MVB, V 3, ad V 3, see *MVB* Introduction, p 312

endowed with

anvita, samanvāgata, ldan-pa

PSP 4, p 66; *KSP* 24, 26; *TK* 3; *MVB* ad IV 13-14

energy

śakti, nus-pa

KSP 50

enjoyment

(saṁ-)bhoga, loṅs(-par)-spyod(-pa)

MVB II 13, ad II 12-13, ad IV 13-14(enjoyment-body), V 6, ad V 6.

enlightenment

bodhi, byaṅ-chub

MVB II 9, ad II 10a, ad II 10b, ad II 14-16, ad II 17, ad IV 1, ad IV 8b, ad IV 13-14, ad V 3, ad V 6, ad V 29-30, V end verse.

enlightenment-citta

bodhi-citta, bjaṅ-chab-kyi sems

MVB, Introduction, pp 307-308: ad II 10a, ad IV 13-14, ad IV 18, ad V 29-30

enlightenment-transformation

bodhi-pariṇāmanā, byaṅ-chub-tu-yoṅs-su-bsṅos-pa (see also "transformation undergone with great enlightenment")

MVB ad II 12-13

enlightenment which has no higher

anuttarā bodhi, byaṅ-chub-bla-med(N) *bla-med-paḥi-byaṅ-chub* (V)

TSN 38

entering into, entry into, entered into, etc

praveśa, praviṣṭa, praviśati, etc; *ḥjug-pa-zugs-pa*

PSP 4, p 67; *KSP* 24; *VK* 10a, ad 10a, 10b, ad 10b, ad 10c
MVB ad I 6, ad II 17, IV 13-14, ad IV 13-14,V 8a, ad V 8a
TSN 22, 24, 25
enthusiasm
abhyutsāha, mṅon-par-spro-ba
PSP, p 67, p 69
entity
dravya, rdzas
KSP 3, 4, 4, 12, 16-17, 34, 40; *VK* ad 13, ad 15
entity lasting through time
nityatva, rtag-pa
MVB, III 15-16a
envy
īrṣyā, phra-dog
PSP 4, p 66; definition, 4, p 69
TK 12; *MVB* ad II 2-3a
equal
tulya, sama, mñam-pa
KSP 4; *VK* ad 18a; *MVB* II 1, ad II 1, ad II 17
equanimity
upekṣā, btaṅ-sñoms
PSP 4, p 66, definition, 4, p 67
TK 4; *MVB* II 2a, ad II 2a, ad IV 5a, ad IV 5b, ad IV 8a, ad IV 8b, ad IV 9a
especially
viśeṣeṇa, khyad-par-du
VK ad 16b
eternal
nitya, rtag
VV 6-7, 8, 14, 15, 17, 23, 24
MVB ad V 23-26
eternality
nityatva, rtag-pa-ñid
VV 14, 24
śāśvatatā, rtag-pa
MVB V 24, ad V 23-26
ethics
śīla, tshul-ḥkhrims : see "good conduct towards others".
even
śāta, phya-le-ba

KSP 4

evenness of citta

citta-samatā, sems-sñam-pa-ñid

PSP 4, p 67

event

dharma, chos

VV 2, 3, 4, 5, 10, 15; *KSP* 2, 8, 11, 18, 19, 20, 37, 40
VK ad 8, ad 10b; *TK* 1, 23, 25
MVB I 20, ad I 20, ad II 14-16, III 4, ad III 4, ad IV 1, ad IV 6, ad IV 8b, ad IV 18, ad V 6, V 7, ad V 7, V 19, ad V 19, ad V 20, V 22, ad V 22, V 23, ad V 23-26, ad V 27b-28a
(see also "selflessness of events")

event-associate

dharmin, chos-can

VV 2, 3, 4, 5

events associated with cittas

citta-saṁprayukta-dharma, sems-daṅ-mtshuṅs-par-ldan-paḥi-chos

(equivalent term : *caitasika-dharma* : *sems-les-byuṅ-baḥi-chos*)
PSP 4, p 66; cf. pp 67-70.
KSP 8, 23; *TK* 9; *MVB* ad I 8a, ad I 8b, I 9, ad V 23-26.

events derived from the great material elements

bhautika(*-dharma*), *ḥbyuṅ-ba-las-gyur-ba*(*ḥi-chos*)

PSP 1, p 65; *KSP* 43, 44.

events disassociated from cittas

cittas-viprayukta-dharma sems-daṅ-ldan-pa-ma-yin-paḥi-chos

PSP 4, p 66; *KSP* 18

events which serve to afflict

sāṁkleśika-dharma, kun-nas-ñon-moṅs-paḥi-chos

MVB ad IV 1

events which serve to alleviate

vaiyavādanika-dharma, rnam-par-byaṅ-baḥi-chos

MVB ad IV 1

ever-increasing

uttarôttara, phyi-ma-phyi-ma

MVB IV 18, ad IV 18

everything that can be subsumed

ekapakṣa, phyogs-gcig

PSP 1, p 65, 5, p 72

evolvement
pariṇata, *gyur-ba*
MVB ad V 31
pravṛtti, *rab-tu-ḥjug* (V), *ḥjug* (N)
TSN 7
evolving consciousnesses
pravṛtti-vijñāna, *ḥjug-paḥi-rnam-par-śes-pa*
MVB ad I 9, ad III 22b; *TSN* 6, 9.
evolving with cognitions of "seen" and "seeing"
dṛṣya-dṛg-vitti-vṛtti, *blta-bya mthoṅ-byed rtog-pas ḥjug*(V)
mthoṅ mthoṅ-bya yan-lag-gñis-ḥjug(N)
TSN 9
exalted
ārya, *ḥphags-pa* (see also "noble")
MVB I 15, ad I 15
examination
pratyavekṣaṇa, *rtog-pa*
PSP 5, p 70
parīkṣā, *yoṅs-su-brtags-pa*
MVB ad IV 1
KSP 11
examined
anvīkṣita *brtags-pa*,
PSP 4, p 67: *KSP* 49
excellence
atiriktatarā, *śas-che-ba*
MVB ad V 27a
excess see "spurious argument based on excess"
excessive
udrikta *lhag-pa*, *lhag-ma*
MVB II 1, ad II 1, ad II 17
excitedness
auddhatya, *rgod-pa*
PSP 4, p 66, definition, p 69; *TK* 13; *MVB* IV 4, ad IV 4, ad IV 5b, ad IV 11a, V 12, ad V 12
excitement
udvega, *saṁvega*, *kun-tu-skyo-ba*, *skyo-ba*
MVB II 2a, ad II 2a
exemplification
dṛṣṭānta, *dpe*

VV 5; *MVB* ad III 22b, ad V 23-26 ("example")

exercise (efficacy)

karoti, byed-pa

KSP 15, 16-17

exercises no resistance

apratigha, thogs-pa-med

PSP 1, p 66

exercise resistance

sapratigha, thogs-pa-daṅ-bcas-pa

PSP, p 74

exhausted

kṣīṇa

TK 19

exist

asti, yod

KSP 15, 24; *TK* 17; *MVB* ad III 7b-8a, ad V 16; *TSN* 12, 13, 25

existence

astitva, satva, yod-pa

KSP 16-17(*yod-pa-ñid*); *VK* ad 10c, ad 15; *MVB* I 2, ad I 2, ad V 15, ad V 16, ad V 17

existing, existent

sat, yod-pa

VK ad 18b; *MVB* ad I 1, ad I 2, ad I 11, I 20, ad I 20, III 3, ad III 3, ad V 15, ad V 22; *TSN* 11

existing-and-not-existing

sad-asattva, yod daṅ med (V), *yod-med* (N)

TSN 10, 11, 12, 13

experience, experiencing, experienced

anubhū, anubhava, upabhoga, myoṅ-ba, ñe-bar-spyod-pa

PSP 2, p 66; *KSP* 40; *VK* ad 16b, ad 17b

MVB ad I 9, I 10-11a, ad I 10-11a, ad I 11b, III 18a, ad III 18a, III 20a, ad III 20a, V 12, ad V 12

relates to experience aupabhogika, ñe-bar-sphod-pa-can

MVB I 9, ad I 9

experiencer

bhoktṛ, za-ba

MVB ad I 17, ad III 15-16a

experiences again

pratyanubhavati, myoṅ-ba

MVB ad V 6

experts in matters of reasoning
yuktârthapaṇḍita, rigs-paḥi-don-la **mkhas-pa**
MVB ad III 12b
explained, explanation
prakāśana, prakāśita rab-tu-bstan
VV 14; *KSP* 15 (*bstan*)
explaining
prakāśana, ḥchad-pa
MVB V 9
explicitly
spaṣṭena, lhaṅs-por
KSP 37
exploration
mīmāṁsā, dpyod-pa
MVB ad II 11
express
vācayati, brjod-par-byed-pa
KSP 48
extensiveness
vistīrṇatva, rgya-che-ba
MVB ad I 17
prātanatā, rab-rgyas
MVB V 27b-28a, ad V 27b-28a
external
bahirdhā, phyi-rol
PSP 5, p 74-75; *KSP* 2, verse; *MVB* ad I 17, ad III 18a, ad V 11, 12
external condition
bāhya-pratyaya phyi-rol-gyi rkyen
KSP 8c, 10
extinction
kṣaya, zad
MVB I 4, II 17, ad II 17
extraordinary
adbhuta, rmad,
KSP 8c.
extreme
anta, mthaḥ
MVB ad I 20 (*tha-ma*), ad V 2, V 23-26, ad V 23-26, ad V 31 V 2

extremely great forbearance
adhimātrā kṣānti, bzod-pa-cher-gyur-pa
MVB ad V 3
eye
cakṣus, mig
PSP 1, p 65; 5, p 72, p 73; *KSP* 11, 50. *VK* ad 9, ad 14c, ad 15; *MVB* ad II 10a

F

factors conducive to liberation
mokṣa-bhāgīya, thar-paḥi cha-daṅ-mthun-pa
MVB ad II 11, IV 6, ad IV 6, ad IV 7
factors conducive to penetration
nirvedha-bhāgīya, ṅes(-par-)ḥbyed-(paḥi)-cha-(daṅ) mthun-pa
MVB Introduction, pp 309-310, ad IV 7b, IV 8a
faculty
indriya, dbaṅ-po
KSP 43; *VK* ad 17c.; *MVB* ad I 3, ad II 11, ad III 1-2, ad III 19, ad III 20a, ad IV 5b, ad IV 6, ad IV 7a,b, IV 8a, ad IV 8a, ad V 23-26
fainting
mūrchana
TK 16
faith
śraddhā, dad-pa
PSP 4, p 66, definition, p 67; *TK* 11; *MVB* ad IV 4, ad IV 5a and b.
false appearance
vitatha-pratibhāsa, logs-par-snaṅ-ba
MVB ad I 3
false cognition
mithyā-jñāna, ḥkhrul-paḥi śes-pa
VV 9
false pride
mithyā-māna, log-laḥi-ṅa-rgyal
PSP 4, p 67, p 68
false views
mithyā-dṛṣṭi, log-par-lta-ba

PSP 4, p 68, 69

familiarity

saṁstava, ḥdris-pa

MVB V 14, ad V 13-14

fault

avadya, kha-na-ma-thob

PSP 4, p 69

favorable

anukūla rjes-sn-mthun-pa

MVB ad II 12-13, IV 11b-12a, ad IV 11b-12a, ad IV 17, ad V 6

favorability, favoring, being favorable

ānukūlya, rjes-su-mthun-pa

MVB IV 18, ad IV 18, ad V 26

anugraha, rjes-su-ḥdzin-byed

MVB V 6, V 10, ad V 10

favors

anugṛhṇāti, rjes-su-ḥdzin

MVB ad V 6

fear

bhaya, ḥjig-pa

PSP 4, p 69; *MVB* ad IV 1, ad V 23-26

trāsa, skrag-pa

MVB ad I 22c, ad V 22, ad V 31 ("afraid")

fearlessness, lack of fear, not afraid

atrāsa, mi skrag-pa

MVB II 9, ad II 10a, V 12-15a, ad V 22, ad V 31

feeling again

punar-vedanā, yaṅ tshor-ba

MVB ad III 21

feelings

vedanā, tshor-ba

PSP 1, p 65; defined 2; 4, p 66; *KSP* 25, 26, 27; *TK* 3, 4, 9

MVB ad I 8b, ad I 10-11a, ad III 16b, ad III 20a, ad III 21, ad IV 1

felt

vedita, tshor

MVB ad III 18a

female organ

strīndriya, moḥi dbaṅ-po
MVB, ad III 20a
fetter
saṁyojana, kun-tu-sbyor-ba
MVB II 1b, ad II 1b, ad II 2a, ad II 2-3a
field, i.e. Buddha-field
kṣetra, źiṅ
MVB ad V 29-30
filling up
pūraṇa, rdzogs-byed
MVB I 10-11a, ad I 10-11a
fire-element
tejo-dhātu, meḥi khams
PSP 1, p 65; *MVB* ad III 12a
firm confidence
sampratyaya, yid-ches-pa
MVB ad IV 5a
firm conviction
abhisaṁpratyaya, mṅon-par-yid-ches-pa
PSP 4, p 67
fixed intent
abhiniveśa, mṅon-par-žen-pa
PSP 4, p 68
flashing appearances
prātibhāsika, so-sor-snaṅ-ba(N), *gžan-du-snaṅ-ba*(V)
TSN 8
flaw
doṣa, ñes
see *VV*; *KSP* 38, 23, 24, 41; *PSP*, p 93 (*žes-pa*)
MVB ad I 4b, ad II 2-3a, II 12, ad II 12-13, IV 3, ad IV 3, IV 4, ad IV 4, ad IV 5a
avadya, kha-na-ma-tho-ba
KSP 4; *VK* ad 18b
mala, dri-ma
MVB ad I 16c, III 9a, ad I 16b, ad I 16b, ad III 7b-8a (*samala* also)
flowing continuously
anubandham rjes-su-ḥbrel-ba
MVB IV 11b-12a
forbearance

kṣānti, bzod-pa
MVB ad II 12-13, ad II 14-16, ad IV 8a, ad V 3, V 5, ad V 6
forbearance through realizing the non-arising of events
anutpattika-dharma-kṣānti mi-skye-baḥi-chos-la bzod-pa
MVB ad II 14-16
force
śakti, sāmarthya, nus-pa
KSP 16-17, 20, 21, 26, 40
formation-body
nirmāṇa-kāya, sprul-paḥi sku
MVB ad IV 13-14
forsaking
tyāga gtoṅ
MVB II 12
free from discriminations
avikalpa, nirvikalpa, rnam-par-mi-rtog-pa, mi-rtog-pa
MVB III 22b, ad III 22b, ad V 3
freedom
mokṣa, thar-pa
MVB ad I 4b, ad I 21; *TSN* 35(*grol-ba* V)
freedom from otherness in reality
tattvānyatva-vinirmukta, de-ñid daṅ gžan-las rnam-par-grol-ba
MVB ad I 13c, ad I 22c
fruition
phala, ḥbras-bu
MVB ad I a, ad IV 13-14, 16, 17, 18; III 1-2, ad 1-2, ad 7b, ad V 9, ad V 22, ad V 31
fruition which flows from that
niṣyanda-phala, rgyu mthun-paḥi ḥbras-bu
MVB ad IV 17
fruition which makes one a full person
puruṣa-kāra-phala, skyes-bu byed-paḥi ḥbras-bu
MVB ad IV 17
fulfilled
pariniṣpanna, yoṅs-su-grub-pa
TK 21; *MVB* I 5, ad I 5, ad III 3a, ad III 4, ad III 5, ad III 6, ad III 7a, ad III 7b-8a, ad III 9b-10a, ad III 10c, ad III 11a, ad III 11b, ad III 12c, ad III 13b, ad III 14b, ad V 22

TSN 1, 3, 13, 16, 17, 18, 19, 20, 21, 25, 28

fulfilling both one's own and others, aims

sva-parârtha-prasiddhi, bdag gžan don-ni rab-grub-ḥgyur(V)

raṅ daṅ gžan-gi don ḥjug (N)

TSN 38

full knowledge

parijñā, yons-su-śes

MVB III 9b-10a, ad III 9b-10a

full realization

samudāgama, yaṅ-dag-par-ḥgrub-pa

MVB V 1a, ad V 1a, ad V 27b-28a, V 29-30, ad V 29-30

full taking up of Saṁsāra

samādāna, yaṅ-dag-par-ḥdzin-pa

MVB II 9, ad II 10a

fully relating

kathikatva, brjod-pa

MVB IV 13-14, ad IV 13-14

function

kriyā, bya-ba

VK, ad 2

G

gaseousness

laghu-samudīraṇatva, yaṅ-žiṅ-gYo-ba-ñid

PSP 1, p 65

giving

dāna, byin-pa

MVB ad I 10-11a ("which gives"), ad II 12-13m, ad V 3, V 5, ad V 6, V 9, ad V 9.

gliding

sāra, visāra, ḥjug-pa

MVB V 12, ad V 12

going forth

pragama,

rnam-par-rtog, rnam-par-khoṅ-du-chud-pa (neither of these seems to be a translation of the Sanskrit)

MVB V 27b-28a, ad V 27b-28a

good conduct towards others

śīla, tshul-ḥkhrims

MVB ad II 12-13, IV 10b, ad IV 10b, V 5, ad V 6
grasping after self
ātma-grāha, bdag-tu ḥdzin-pa
MVB ad III 1-3, ad III 23, end
grasping for a doer
kartā-grāha, kartṛ-grāha, byed-par ḥdzin-pa
PSP, p 74
grasping for an enjoyer
bhoktā-grāha, bhoktṛ-grāha, za-bar ḥdzin-pa
PSP, p 74
grasping for one central entity
ekākī-grāha, gcig-pur ḥdzin-pa
PSP, p 74
great elements
mahā-bhūta, ḥbyuṅ-ba-chen-po
PSP 1; *KSP* 2, 43, 44
Great Vehicle
Mahā-yāna, Tḥeg-po chen-po
KSP 30; *VK* ad 1; *MVB* ad III 22, ad V 1, V 7, ad V 9, ad V 29
greed
lobha chags-pa
PSP 4, p 66, p 67, p 68, p 70
Ground of all events
dharma-dhātu, chos-kyi dbyiṅs
MVB I 14, ad I 15, II 14-16, ad II 14-16, IV 15, V 19, ad V 19, V 21, ad V 21, ad V 23-26, V 27b-28a ("Ground"), ad V 27b-28a.
TSN 37
guile
śāṭhya, gYo
PSP, p 66, definition, p 69; *TK* 13
gustatory consciousness
jihvā-vijñāna, lceḥi rnam-par-śes-pa
PSP 5, p 73, p 74

H

hardness
karkaśatva, rtsu-ba-ñid

PSP, p 66
having signs
naimittika, mtshan-pa-can
TSN 8
having the nature of always reflecting
mananātmaka
TK 5
heat
tāpana, tsha-ba
PSP, p 65; *KSP* 7
heaviness
gurutva, lci-ba-ñid
PSP, p 66
hell-state
naraka, rdmyal-ba
VK 4b, ad 4b, 5, ad 5
higher aim
agrârtha, mchog-gi don
MVB II 14-16, ad II 14-16
higher situation
uttarâvasthā, bla-na-gnas-skabs
MVB IV 13-14, ad IV 13-14
highest clarity
agra-śuddhi, mchog-gi dag-pa
MVB ad II 2-3a
highest mundane events
laukikâgra-dharma, ḥjig-rten-paḥi chos-kyi mchog
MVB, ad IV 8a; described, Introduction, p 310.
highest practise
paramā (*pratipatti*), *dam-pa*(r)-(*bsgrub-pa*)
MVB V 2a, ad V 2a ("practise developed to the highest"), V 2b, ad V 2b.
hindrances to the bringing about of special qualities
vaiśeṣikaguṇâbhinirhāravibandha, yon-tan-khyad-par-can-myoṅ-par-bsgrub-paḥi-gegs-su-gyur-pa
MVB ad IV 11a
holding fast
samparigraha, kun-ḥdzin
MVB I 10-11a, ad I 10-11a, ad I 11b.
hostile

pratigha-vastu, *khoṅ-khro-baḥi gži*
MVB ad II 2a
hostility
dveṣa, *ze-sdaṅ*
PSP 4, p 68; p 69, p 70; *MVB* ad V 23-26
"*How it appears*"
yathā khyāti, *ji-(ltar)snaṅ*
TSN 2, 3, (*ji-bžin-snaṅ-ba* N), 4
humanity
mānava, *śes-bu*
MVB ad V 23-26
hunger
bubhūkṣā, *bkres-pa-ñid*
PSP, p 66; *KSP* 23.
hypocrisy
mrakṣa, *ḥchab-pa*
PSP, p 66, definition, p 69; *TK* 12

idea
mati, *blo*
KSP 4
identity
samatā, *ekatva*, *mñam-pa-ñid*, *gcig-pa*
MVB I 7b, ad II 14-16, V 23, ad V 23-26, ad I 13, ad III 15
identity of the objects
sādharmya, *chos-mthun-pa*
VV 11
ignorance
avidyā, *ma-rig-pa*
PSP 4, p 66, definition, p 68; *MVB* ad I 10-11a, ad I 11b, ad II 2-3a, ad II 14-16, ad III 18b, ad V 23-26
KSP 25
illogical
ayoga, *ma ruṅ-ba*
VK ad 4c, 4a
imageless realm
arūpya-dhātu, *arūpyāvacāra*, *gzugs-med-paḥi-khams*

MVB, ad V 3

in conciseness

samāsatas, mdor-bsdu-na

MVB IV 18

in every way

sarvathā, thams cad

MVB IV 1

in general

sāmānya, spyi

KSP 2

in its entirety

sarvathā, thams-cad-du

VK 22a

in many different ways

bahuvidha, rnam-pa-maṅ-po

MVB ad IV 13-14

in order

yathākramam, go-rims-bžin

PSP 5, p 74; *MVB* I 15, ad III 4, III 5, ad III 5, ad III 6b, ad IV 4, ad IV 5ə("as they are enumerated"), IV 17, ad IV 17, ad V 6; *TSN* 31.

in so many different ways

vividhaḥ, sna-tshogs-dag-ni

TK 1

in the manner as before

yathāpūrvaṁ, sṅa-ma-bžin-du

KSP 8c

in the way that it appears

yathākhyānaṁ, ji-ltar-snaṅ-bžin(V), *ji-ltar-snaṅ-ba*(N)

TSN 12

in their full extent

vyāsatas, rgyas-par-bya-ba

MVB ad IV 18

inactivity—see "sloth"

indication

upadeśa, ñe-bar-ston-pa

VV 4, 5

indistinct

sthūla, rtsiṅ-ba

PSP 4, p 70

indistinct (*practise*)
aviśiṣṭatā(*-pratipatti*), *khyad*(*-par*)*-med*(*-pa*) (*-sgrub-pa*)
MVB ad V 2a, V 2a, ad V 23-26, ad V 26b, V 27a, ad V 31
independence
svatantratva, *raṅ-dbaṅ*
MVB ad III 15-16a
independent
svatantra, *raṅ-dbaṅ-can*
KSP 40
indeterminate (ethically)
avyākṛta, *luṅ-du-ma-bstan-pa*
PSP 5, p 74; *KSP* 14, 29
inference
anumāna, *rjes-su-dpag-pa*
VV 3, 9, 10
inferred, is inferred, can be inferred
anumīyate, *rjes-su-dpag-par-bya-ba*
VV 10; *KSP* 37
inferior
hīna, *bri*
MVB II 14-16, ad II 14-16,
inflation of citta
cittonnatatva, *sems-kheṅs-pa*
PSP 4, p 68
influence
paribhāvayati, (*yoṅs-su-*)*bsgos-pa*
KSP 19, 20, 21, 22, 32, 38, 40
informs
vijñāpayati, *rnam-par-rig-byed*
KSP 11, 12
inherent nature
dharmatā, *chos-ñid*
PSP 5, p 73
initial cause
nidāna, *gži*
MVB IV 9a, ad IV 9a, ad V 31
initial mental application
vitarka, *rtog-pa*
PSP 4, p 66, definition, p 70, note 14; *TK* 14
innate lack of duration

āśaya, bsam-pa
KSP 2

intentness
abhiniveśa, mṅon-par-žen-pa
MVB ad III 6b, ad III 8c

interdependence
pāratantrya, gžan-(gyi-)dbaṅ-ñid
MVB III 19, ad III 19

interdependent
paratantra, gžan-(gyi-)dhaṅ
TK 21, 22; *MVB* I 5, ad I 5, ad III 3a, ad III 3b, ad III 4, ad III 5, ad III 6, ad III 7a, ad III 7b-8a, cf. ad III 8b, ad III 9b-10a, cf. ad III 10b, ad III 13a, ad III 14a, ad V 22; *TSN* 1, 2, 12, 15, 17, 20, 21, 24, 28

interference
vyavakiraṇa, ḥdres-pa
MVB ad II 11

internal
adhyātmika, naṅ
PSP 5, p 74; *MVB* ad I 17, ad III 18a, ad V 11, ad V 12

interrupted
chinna, chad-pa
KSP 21, 23

interval
kha, go-ḥbyed-pa
PSP 4, p 73

intimacy
paricaya, ḥdris-par-bya-ba
MVB ad V 29-30

intuitively realizing
sākṣātkṛti, mṅon-sum-(du-)bya(-ba)
MVB III 9b-10a, ad III 9b-10a

invariable concomitance
avinābhāva, med-na-mi-ḥbyuṅ-ba
VV 4, 5, 10, 16, 20

investigate
vicar, (rnam-par-)dpyad-pa; vyavacar, saṁpradhṛ, nirdhṛ
VV 1; *KSP* 2, 11, 15; *VV* ad 14, ad 15

investigation
(pra)vicaya, rab-tu-rnam-par-ḥdyed-pa

MVB IV 6, ad IV 6, ad IV 8b

pratyavekṣā, so-sor-rtog-pa

MVB ad V 23-26

invisible

asanidarśana, bstan-du-med-pa

PSP, p 66, p 74

irreversible stage

avinivartanīya-bhūmi, phyir-mi-ldog-paḥi sa

MVB ad V 29-30

is destroyed

naśyate, ḥjig-par-byed

KSP 8, 11

is found

vidyate, yod-pa

MVB I 1, ad I 1

is not logical

na yujyate, rigs-pa-ma-ḥgyur-ba

KSP 29; *VK* ad 2, ad 4c, ad 5, 14a, ad 14a; *MVB* ad V 22

isn't really to be found

na vidyate, ma yod-pa

TK 20

is situated

avatiṣṭhati, gnas-pa

KSP 4; *TK* 26, 27

is observed

dṛśyate, mthoṅ-ba

VV 10, 20

J

Jains

Tīrthika, Mu-stegs-su-stegs-can

MVB V 23, ad V 23

judgment

prajñānana, śes-rab

PSP 4, p 68-69

justification

hetu, gtan-tshigs

VV 4, 6, 7, 11, 12, 13, 14, 15, 16, 17, 20, 23

K

know
jñā, *jānāti*, *śes-pa*
VK ad 10a, ad 20b
knowable
jñeya, *śes-bya* (see also "obstruction to the knowable", "thing to be known", "to be known")
TSN 36
knowledge
jñāna, *ye-śes*
VK 21a, ad 21a, ad 21b, ad 22b; *TK* 29;
MVB ad I 15, ad I 17, ad II 12-13, ad III 4, ad III 11, III 13b, ad III 13b, III 22a, ad III 22a, ad V 3, ad V 18b-c, ad V 19, ad V 20, ad V 21, ad V 22, ad V 23-26, ad V 27b-28a, V, ending verse.
VV 10
knowledge free from discriminations
nirvikalpaka-jñāna, *rnam-par-mi-rtog-paḥi-ye-śes*
MVB ad V 3, ad V 22, ad V 23-26
knowledge of everything that can be known in all its various aspects
sarvākārasarvajñeya jñāna, *śes-bya-thams-cad-kyi-rnam-pa-thams-cad-la-mkhyen-pa*
VK ad 22b.
known, completely known
parijñāta, *yoṅs(-su)-śes*
MVB IV 2, ad IV 2

L

lack of an own-being
asvabhāvatā, *ṅo-bo-ñid-med-pa*
MVB ad V 23-26
lack of arising
anutpāda, *ḥdyuṅ-ba-med-pa*
MVB ad V 23-26
lack of attachment
visaṁyoga, *bral-bar-bya-ba*
MVB ad IV 12b

lack of birth
ajāti, skye-ba-med-pa
MVB ad V 23-26
lack of calm
nirvyupaśama, rnam-par-ma-ži-ba
PSP 4, p 69
lack of compassion
akṛpatā, akāruṇyā, sñiṅ-rje-med-pa
MVB II 4-8, ad II 10a
lack of complete use of sense-fields
anāyatana, skye-mched-min
MVB II 4-8, ad II 10a
lack of confidence
anadhimukti, ma-mos, mi-mos-pa
MVB II 4-8, ad II 10a
lack of confusion
amoha, gti-mug-med-pa
PSP 4, p 66; definition, p 67;
MVB IV 1 (*avimoha, mi-rmoṅs*), ad IV 1(*asaṁmoha, rmoṅs-pa-med-pa*), ad II 9, ad II 10a, ad V 22(*abhrānti, ḥkhrul-pa-med-pa*)
lack of dealing with
asamudāhāra, no Tib.
MVB ad II 14-16
lack of detriment
ahīnatā, ḥgrib-pa-med-pa
MVB ad V 22
lack of discrimination
avikalpanatā, rnam-par-mi-rtog-pa-ñid
MVB ad V 22
lack of distractedness
avikṣiptatā, rnam-par-mi-gYeṅ-ba
MVB V 11, ad V 11, cf. ad V 12
lack of diversity
anānātva, tha-dad-pa-med-pa
MVB II 14-16, ad II 14-16
lack of division
abheda, tha-dad-pa-med-pa
MVB II 14-16, ad II 14-16
lack of dread of blame

anapatrāpya, khrel-med-pa
PSP 4, p 66; definition, 4, p 69; *TK* 13
lack of engagement in meditation
samādhyaparikarmitā, samādher aparikarmitva, tiṅ-ḥdzin-sbyaṅs-pa-ma-byas-pa, tiṅ-ṅe-ḥdzin-yoṅs-su-sbyar-ba-ma-byas-pa
MVB II 4-8, ad II 10a
lack of excellence
aviśiṣṭatā, khyad-par-du-ḥphags-pa-med-pa-ñid
MVB ad V 22
lack of exhaustion
aparyādāna, yoṅs-su-gtugs-par-mi-ḥgyur-ba
MVB ad V 3
lack of faith
aśraddhā, ma-dad-pa
PSP 4, p 66; definition, 4, p 69; *TK* 13; *MVB* ad II 2-3a, ad II 4-8, ad II 10a, ad IV 7a
lack of familiarity
asaṁstava, ma-ḥdris
MVB V 14
lack of fear
atrāsitā, mi-dṅaṅ-ba
MVB V 13, ad V 22
lack of greed
alobha, ma-chags-pa
PSP 4, p 66, definition, 4, p 67; *KSP* 27, 29; *TK* 11
lack of hostility
adveṣa, ži-sdaṅ-med-pa
PSP 4, p 66; definition, 4, p 67
lack of a justification
ahetu, gtan-tshigs-med-pa
VV 11
lack of knowledge
ajñāna, mi-śes-pa
PSP, 4, p 68
lack of loss
asaṁmoṣa, brjed-par-mi-gyur
MVB IV 5b, ad IV 5b, IV 6, ad IV 6
lack of maturation of insight
prajñā 'vipākatva, prajñā'paripakvatā,

śes-rab-ma-smin, śes-rab-yoṅs-su-ma-smin-pa

MVB II 4-8, ad II 10a

lack of means (to rouse oneself from inactivity)

aprayoga, sbyor-ba-med-pa

MVB II 4-8, ad II 10a

lack of mental attention

amanasikāra, yid-la-mi-byed-pa

MVB II 4, ad II 10a

lack of motivating factors

asaṁskāra, anabhisaṁskāra ḥdu-byed-med, mṅon-par-ḥdu-mi-byed

MVB IV 4, ad IV 4

lack of obstructions

anāvṛti, anāvaraṇa, sgrip-pa-med (-pa)

MVB II 9, ad II 10a

lack of planting

aropaṇa, mi-skyed-pa

MVB II 11, ad II 11

lack of pride

anunatti, kheṅs-pa-med-pa

MVB V 12b-15a, ad V 22

lack of recognition

asaṁprajanya, śes-bžin-ma-yin-pa

PSP 4, p 66; definition, 4, p 70; *TK* 14.

lack of repose

aśama, ma-ži, ži-ma-byed

MVB V 10b, ad V 10b

lack of reverence for the good Dharma

saddharme gaurava, dam-(paḥi-)chos(-la)-ched-cher-mi-ḥdzin-pa

MVB II 4-8, ad II 10a

lack of reversal

aviparyāsa, phyin-ci-ma-log-pa

MVB III 11, V, 11, ad V 11, V 18b, ad V 18 b-c, V 19, ad V 19, V 20, ad V 20, V 21, ad V 21, V 22, ad V 22, V 11-15a, V 14, V 15, ad V 15, V 16, ad V 16, V 17, ad V 17, ad V 31

lack of a self

anātmatā, bdag-med-pa-ñid

MVB, ad III 4

lack of selfishness
amātsarya, amatsaritva, ser-sna-med-pa
MVB II 9, ad II 10a
lack of separation
avisaṁyoga, ma-bral-ba
MVB III 8c, ad III 8c
lack of shame
āhrīkya, ṅo-tsha-med-pa
PSP 4, p 66; definition, p 69; *TK* 13
lack of skill
akauśala, mi mkhas
MVB II 11, ad II 11
lack of transformation
nirvikāra, ḥgyur-med
MVB III 11b, ad III 11b
lack of trouble
akṛcchratva, tshegs-med-pa
MVB V 3, ad V 3
lack of trust
apratyayitā, yid-mi-ches-pa
PSP 4, p 69
lasting
nitya, rtag-pa
KSP 40; *PSP* 4, p 95
learner
śaikṣa, slob-pa
MVB ad IV 11b-12a, ad IV 13-14, ad IV 15, ad IV 18
length
dīrghatva, riṅ-po
KSP 2
liable to be connected with afflictions
sāsrava, zag-pa-daṅ-bcas-pa
PSP 5, p 74; *KSP*, note 43; *MVB* ad IV 1
liberation
mukti, grol-ba
PSP 4, p 69; *TK* 30; *MVB* I 4b, II 17, ad II 17
liberated
mukta, grol-ba
MVB I 21, ad I 21, III 15-16a, ad III 15-16a
liberate

vimocayati, grol-ba
MVB ad V 6
liberating
vimocana, grol-bar-byed, rnam-par-grol-bar-byed-pa
MVB II 13, ad II 12-13, ad III 22b, V 6
life-course
gati, ḥgro-ba
KSP 34, 46, 50, verse.
life-force
jīvitendriya, srog-gi-dbaṅ-po
PSP 4, p 71; *KSP* 34; *VK* ad 19; *MVB* ad V 23-26 (*jīvasa, srog*)
life-stream
saṁtāna, rgyud (see also "series of moment-events")
MVB ad IV 12b
lightness
laghutva, yaṅ-ba-ñid
PSP 1, p 66
limb
aṅga, yan-lag
MVB IV 8b, ad IV 8b, ad IV 9a, IV 9b-10a, ad IV 9b-10a
limbs of enlightenment
bodhyaṅga, byaṅ-chub-kyi-yan-lag
MVB ad II 11, ad III 19, ad IV 8a, IV 8b, ad IV 8b
limbs of the Path
margāṅga, lam-gyi-yan-lag
MVB ad II 11, ad IV 9a, IV 9b-10a, ad IV 9b-10a
limited
prādeśika, ñi-tshe-ba
MVB II 1, ad II 1, ad II 17
linguistic habits
uccāraṇatā, brjod-pa
MVB ad V 13-14
liquidity
snehatva, gśer-ba-nid
PSP 1, p 65
listening
śruta, thos-pa
MVB V 7, ad V 7, ad V 8b
locus

deśa, yul
KSP 4, 6, 7, 9, 10, 11, 12, 13, 46
VK ad 12a, 12b, ad 12b, ad 14b
logical, logically
yukta, yuktam, rigs-pa
KSP 4, 7, 8c, 21, 29; *VK* 2, ad 14, ad 15
logical fitness
yukti, rigs-pa
MVB I 22c
logical pervasion
vyāpti, khyab-pa
VV, Introduction, pp 42-43, 16
long
dīrgha, riṅ-po
KSP 2, 3, 4, 5, 22.
longing
abhilāṣa, ḥdod-pa
MVB ad IV 5a
longing for enjoyment
bhoga-sakti, spyod-la-chags-pa
MVB II 4-8, ad II 10a
loss of mindfulness
muṣitasmṛtitā, brjed-ṅas-pa
PSP 4, p 66; definition, p 70; *VK* 19 ("loss of memory", *smṛti-lopa*), *TK* 13.
love of self
ātma-sneha, bdag-la-chags-pa
PSP 5, p 72; *TK* 6
loving kindness
maitrī, byams-pa
PSP, 4, p 67; *MVB*, ad IV 8b
luminousness
prabhāsvaratā, ḥod-gsal-ba
MVB I 22b, ad V 22

M

magical creation
māyā, sgyu-ma
MVB V 15b-18a, ad V 17, ad V 22; *TSN* 27

magical show
māyā, sgyu-ma
TSN 34
magician
māyākāra, sgyu-ma-mkhan
MVB ad V 23-26
magnanimity
audārya, rgya-che-ba
MVB V 3, ad V 3
main
agra, dam-pa
KSP 5
maintained
abhīṣṭa, mṅon-par-ḥdod-do
VV 2, 3
makes something stop
sthāpayati, gnas-byed-pa
TK 27
male organ
puruṣendriya, phoḥi dbaṅ-po
MVB ad III 20a
malice
upanāha, khon-du-ḥdzin-pa
PSP 4, p 66; definition, 4, p 69; *TK* 12.
maliciousness
pradāsa, ḥtshig-pa
PSP 4, p 66; definition 4, p 69; *TK* 12
manas
yid
PSP 5, p 71-72; *KSP* 2, 23, 45, 47, 49, 50; *VK* ad 7; *TK* 5; *MVB* ad I 3, ad III 23, ad V 18b-c, ad V 23-26.
manifest action
vijñapti(-karma), rnam-par-rig-byed(paḥi las)
PSP 1, p 65; *KSP* 2, 5, 6, 11, 12, 13, 14, 49, note 3.
mastery
adhigama, khoṅ-du-chud-pa
MVB ad V 27b-28a
material elements (see also "great elements"), bhūta, ḥbyṅu-ba
VK ad 5, 6, ad 6, ad 7
materiality

rūpa, gzugs
PSP 1, 5; *KSP* 8, 28; *MVB* ad III 16, ad III 17a, ad V 23-26
materiality derived from the great elements
bhautika-rūpa, (Ḥbyuṅ-ba-las-)rgyun-byas-paḥi-gzugs
PSP 1, p 65; *KSP* 43, 44.
maturation
vipāka, rnam-smin
TSN 9, 8 (maturational *vaipākika*); *TK* 1, 2.
meaning
artha, don
MVB ad II 13, ad V 8, ad V V 9, V 12 b-15 a, ad I 1, I 12, ad I 14; *KSP* 48
meaningfulness
sārthakatva, don-yod-pa-ñid
MVB ad V 13-14
meaninglessness
nirarthakatva, don-med-pa-ñid
MVB ad V 13-14
means of cognition
pramāṇa, tshad-pa
See *VV* 9, 16, 10; *VK* ad 15: *MVB* ad III 12 b
means of evidence
liṅga, rtags
VV 10
meditating
bhāvanā, sgom-pa
MVB ad II 11, ad V 7, ad V 8 a, V 9, ad V 9
meditation
dhyāna, bsam-gtan
MVB ad II 12-13, ad IV 112, V 5, ad V 6.
meditational concentration
samādhi, tiṅ-ṅe-ḥdzin
PSP 4, p 66; definition, p 67; *TK* 10; *MVB* II 11, ad II 11, ad IV 3, ad IV 5 a, ad IV 8 b, ad IV 9a, ad V 12.
meditational concentration on the treasury of the sky
gagana-gañja-samādhi, nam-mkhaḥ-mdzod-kyi-tiṅ-ṅe-ḥdzin
MVB ad V 3, note 57
meditational object

upacāra, ḥdogs, btags-pa
KSP 23, 34; *TK* 1
method of non-apprehension
anupalambha-yoga, mi-dmigs-paḥi tshul
MVB ad IV 12 b
middle path
madhyamā pratipad, dbu-maḥi lam
MVB I 2, ad I 2, ad V 23-26, ad V 31 a, ad V 31 b
mirror-reality
ādarśa-tattva, me-loṅ-lta-buḥi-de-kho-na
MVB ad III 22 b
mischievous exuberance
mada, rgags-pa
PSP 4, p 66; definition, 4, p 69; *TK* 13
moment
kṣaṇa, skad-cig
KSP 10, 14, 19, 32
momentary
kṣaṇika, skad-cig-pa
KSP 8 (*KST*), *VK* ad 16 b
more palpable states causing suffering
duḥkhana, sdug-bsṅal
MVB I 10-11 a, ad I 10-11 a
motivational impulse
abhisaṁskāra, mṅon-par-ḥdu-byed-pa
KSP 45
motivate
abhisaṁskaroti, mṅon-par-ḥdu-byed-pa
KSP 50
motivating dispositions, motivating factors
saṁskāra, ḥdu-byed
PSP 1, p 65; defined 4, pp 66-70;
KSP 24, 27, 37;*MVB* ad I 10-11a, ad I 11 b, ad II 11 ad III 16 b, IV 3, ad IV 3, ad IV 5 b (*abhisaṁskāra*), ad V 23-26 (*abhisaṁskāra*)
motive
abhisandhi, dgoṅs-pa
MVB ad III 22b
movement, motion
gati, ḥgro-ba

KSP 6, 9, 10, 11
muddle-headedness
līna-cittatā, *sems-žum-par(-gyur-pa)*
MVB II 4-8, ad II 10 a
mundane-and-supermundane
laukika-lokottara
ḥjig-rten-pa daṅ ḥjig-rten-las-ḥdas-pa
MVB ad V 27 b-28 a
mundane complete clearing
laukikaviśuddhi, *ḥjig-rten-paḥi-rnam-par-dag-pa*
MVB ad III 20 a
mutually
mithas, *phan-tshun*
VK 18 a, ad 18 a

N

naming
nāma, *miṅ*
MVB III 13 a, ad III 13 a, ad III 22 b
name
nāma, *miṅ*
MVB ad V 13-14, V 18b-c, ad V 18 b-c, ad V 27 b-28 a
narrow
pratanu, *chuṅ-ṅu*
MVB ad II 17
nature
prakṛti, *raṅ-bžin* (see also "emptiness of nature")
MVB ad I 19 a I 22 b, II 4-8, ad II 10a ("natural"), ad II 6, III 7a, ad III 7a, ad III 7 b-8 a, ad III 9 a, ad V 11, V 21, ad V 21, ad V 22, ad V 23-26, ad V 31; *KSP* 16-17
Nirvāṇa which has no basis
apratiṣṭhita-nirvāṇa, *mi-gnas-paḥi mya-ṅan-las-ḥdas-pa*
MVB, ad II 1, ad IV 12, ad IV 12 b
Nirvāṇa which has no remainder
nirupadhiśeṣa-nirvāṇa, *phuṅ-po-lhag-ma-med-paḥi mya-ṅan-las-ḥdas-pa*
(meaning a Nirvāṇa freed from any remnant of the personality-aggregates), *MVB*, ad I 18, ad I 18 d
noble

MVB ad V 19, ad V 31
non-deficiency
avaikalya, ma-tshar-(ba-)med-(pa)
MVB V 29-30, ad V 29-30
non-denial
anapavāda, skur-pa-ḥdebs-pa-med-pa
MVB III 18 b, ad III 18 b
non-different
abhinna, gžan-ma-yin (V), *dbyer-med, tha-mi-dad* (N)
TSN 19,19, 20, 21
non-discontinuity
anuccheda, rgyun-mi-ḥchad-pa
VK ad 8
non-distractedness
avikṣepa, mi-gYeṅ-ba
MVB V 29-30, ad V 29-30, ad V 31
non-duality
advayatva, gñis-po-med-pa(V), *gñis-med-ñid* (N)
TSN 4, 13, 16, 19
non-dual
advaya, gñis-med
TSN 26
non-eternality
anityatva, mi-rtag-pa-ñid
VV 2, 3, 4, 14, 16, cf. 18, cf. 23, 24
non-evolving
apravṛtti, mi-ḥjug
MVB V 18b-c
non-existence
nāstitva, asatva, med-pa, med-pa-ñid
VK ad 2, ad 15; *KSP* 15; *MVB* I 2, ad I 2, V 16, ad V 16, ad V 17, V 22; *TSN* 3, 14, 4, 20
non-existence as it appears
tathāvidyamānatā, de-ltar-ni-yod-pa-ma-yin
MVB V 15 b-19 a
non-existent
asat, med
VK 1, ad 3 c, ad 4 c; *MVB* ad I 3, ad I 5, ad I 6, ad I 11, III 3 b, ad III 3 b, III 5, ad III 5, ad III 7 a, ad V 22
TSN 4, 5, 18, 20, 21, 24, 29

non-forgetting
avismaraṇa, ma-brjed-pa
PSP 4, p 67
non-gliding
avisāra, mi-ḥphro-ba
MVB IV 6, ad IV 6, V 12b, ad V 17
non-grasping
niṣparigrahatā, yoṅs-su-ḥdzin-pa-med-pa
MVB II 14-16, ad II 14-16
non-harming
ahiṁsā, mi-tshe-ba
PSP 4, p 66; definition, 4, p 67-68; *TK* 11
non-informing
avijñāpaka, rnam-par-rig-par-mi-byed-pa
KSP 12
non-meditative state without cognitions
āsaṁjñika, ḥdu-śes-med-pa
PSP 4, p 71; *KSP* 21, 23
non-loss see "lack of loss"
non-otherness
ananyathā, gžan-med, gžan-ma-yin-pa
MVB I 15, ad I 15
non-reversal (see also "lack of reversal", "unreversed", "absence of reversals")
aviparyāsa, phyin-ci-ma-log-pa
MVB I 15, ad I 15, III 1-2, ad III 1-2, ad III 4, ad III 11
non-restraint
asaṁvara, sdom-pa-ma-yin-pa
KSP 14
non-restriction
aniyama, mi-ṅes-par-ḥgyur-ba
VK 2, ad 2, 3 b, ad 3 b, ad 3 c
non-returner
anāgāmin, mi-ḥoṅ-ba
KSP 34
non-stable
asthira, brtan-pa-ma-yin
PSP 4, p 70
non-superimposition
asamāropaṇa, sgro-ḥdugs-pa-med-pa

MVB III 18 b, ad III 18 b

non-utterance

anukti, ma-brjod-pa

VV II, 12, 17

nose

ghrāṇa, sna

PSP 1, p 65; 5, p 72

not-really

atattvataḥ, kho-na-ma-yin

MVB III 3b, ad III 3 b

not remaining tranquil

apraśrabdhi, rgyun-mi-gcod-pa

MVB V 29-30, ad V 29-30

nothing whatever

akiṁcana, ci-yaṅ-med-pa

KSP 28, 34

O

object-of-consciousness

ālambana, dmigs-pa

KSP 2, 5, 11, 29, 28, 31, 36, 37, 47

TK 5, 28; *MVB* ad III 22 b, IV 2, ad IV 2, ad IV 18, ad V 22

object apprehended

grāhya, gzuṅ-ba

VK ad 10 c, ad 21 b; *MVB* ad I 1, ad I 2, ad I 3, ad I 5, ad I 6, III 4, ad III 4, ad III 9 a, III 17 b, ad III 17 b, ad V 15, ad V 16, ad V 17, V 24, ad V 23-26

object (*of sense or understanding*)

artha, don

VV 1, 2, 3, 4, 5, 6, 8, 9, 10, 11, 12, 14, 15, 16, 20

KSP 19

VK 1, 2, ad 2, ad 3 a, ad 3 c, ad 10 c, ad 12 b, ad 16 a, 16 b, ad 16 b, ad 17 a, ad 17 b, ad 17 c, ad 18 a, ad 18 b, 21 a, ad 21 a, ad 21 b

MVB I 3, ad I 3, ad I 5, ad I 6, ad I 7 a, ad I 7 b, I 8, ad I 8, III 11 a, ad III 11 a, ad III 16 b, ad III 18 a, ad III 23, V 12-15 a, V 15-18 a, ad V 15, ad V 17, 23-26

TSN 5, 14, 31, 35, 36

object-of-sense

viṣaya, yul
VV 9; *PSP*, p 65 and throughout; *KSP* 49;
VK ad 10 c, 11, ad 11, ad 14, ad 15, 16 a, ad 16 b, ad 17 b, ad 17 c; *TK* 2, 8; *MVB* ad III 13 a, V 12, ad V 12, ad V 31

objection
codya, brgal-ba
MVB, ad V 22

observation
darśana, ltos-pa
VV 10; *KSP* 23 (*mthoṅ*) *MVB* ad V 15

obsession
adhyavāsana, lhag-par-žen-pa
MVB ad II 2-3 a

obstructed but indeterminate
nirvṛtāvyākṛta, bsgribs-la-luṅ-du-bstan-pa
KSP, note 43; *TK* 6

obstruction
āvaraṇa, sgrib-pa
KSP, note 43; *MVB* I 12, ad I 12, ad I 10-11 a, II 1, ad II 1, II 1 b, ad II 1 b, ad II 2 a, ad II 2 b-3 a, II 3, ad II 3, ad II 4-8, II 9, ad II 9, II 10 a, ad II 10 a, II 10 b, ad II 10b, ad II 11, II 12, ad II 12-13, II 14-16 ("obstructing", *āvṛti*), ad II 14-16, II 17, ad II 17, ad III 8, ad IV 17, ad V 29-30, ad V 31

obstructions consisting simply of afflictions
kleśāvaraṇa, ñon-moṅs-paḥi-sgrib-pa
MVB ad II 1, II 17, ad II 1 b, ad II 17, ad V 31

obstructions of the knowable
jñeyāvaraṇa, śes-byaḥi-sgrib-pa
MVB ad II 1, II 17, ad II 17, ad III 12 a, ad V 31

occur in every citta
sarvatraga, kun-tu-ḥgro-ba
PSP 4, p 66; *TK* 9 (enumerated 3)

of good effect
anuśaṁsa, phan-yon
MVB IV 8 b, ad IV 8 b, IV 13-14, ad IV 13-14

offense
avadya, kha-na-ma-tho-ba
PSP 4, p 67, p 69; *VK* ad 18 b, ad 20a, 20 b, ad 20 b

olfactory consciousness
ghrāṇa-vijñāna, snaḥi-rnam-par-śes-pa
PSP 5, p 73, p 74
one-pointedness
ekāgratā, rce-gcig-ñid
PSP 4, p 93
oneness
ekatva, gcig
MVB III 15-16 a, ad III 15-16 a
one's own realization
svādhigama, raṅ-gi rdogs-pa
MVB ad IV 9 b-10 a
origination (of suffering)
samudaya, kun-ḥdyuṅ-ba
MVB ad III 7 b-8 a, ad III 8 c, ad III 21, ad IV 1
otherness of own-being
svabhāvānyatva, ṅo-bo-ñid-gžan-du-ḥgyur-ba
MVB ad I 16 c
own-characteristic
svalakṣaṇa, raṅ-gi-mtshan-ñid
PSP 5, pp 73-74; *KSP* 15; *MVB* ad I 2, ad I 4b, III 7 b, ad III 7 b, V 18 b-c, ad V 18 b-c, V 18 d, ad V 31
own-being
svabhāva, ṅo-bo-ñid, raṅ-bžin
VK, ad 10 c; *TK* 20, 21, 23, 24; *MVB* ad I 4, ad I 5, III 3 a, III 3b, ad III 3b, ad III 4, ad III 5, ad III 6, ad III 12 a, ad III 12 c, ad III 13 a, ad III 13 b, ad III 15-16 a, IV 8 b, ad IV 8 b, IV 9 a, ad IV 9 a, ad V 22
TSN 1, 3, 10, 11, 13, 14, 15, 16, 18, 19, 20, 21, 22, 23, 26, 28, 31
own-nature
prakṛti or *svarūpa ? raṅ-bžin*
KSP 11

P

parallel positive example
sapakṣa, mthun-paḥi-phyogs
VV 5
pāramitā

oha-rol(-tu)-phyin-pa

MVB II 10b, ad II 11, ad II 12-13, ad II 17, ad V 1 a, ad V 3, V 4, ad V 4, V 5, ad V 5, ad V 6, ad V 26 b, ad V 27 b-28 a, ad V 29-30.

part

avayava, cha-śas

VK ad 11, 13, ad 13

KSP 2(*aṅga, yan-lag*), 3

particular knowledges (*pratisaṁvid, so-so-yang-dag-par-rig-pa*) which are : knowledge of dharma, knowledge of meanings, knowledge of language, and presence of mind

MVB ad II 12-14

past

atīta, ḥdas-pa

KSP 15, 16-17, 22; *MVB* ad III 17, ad III 20

path

mārga, lam

TK 7; *MVB* II 2-3 a, ad II 2-3 a, ad II 10 a, ad III 9 a, III 9 b-10 a, ad III 9 b-10 a, ad III 11 a, ad III 21, ad IV 1, ad IV 8 b, IV 9 b-10 a, ad IV 10 b, ad IV 11 a, ad IV 16, ad IV 18, ad V 23-26, ad V 27 b-28 a, ad V 29-30, ad V 31.

paths of action

karma-patha, las-kyi-lam

KSP 42, 46, 49

Path of Cultivation

bhāvanāmārga, bsgom-paḥi-lam

MVB, Introduction, pp 314-318; ad II 10 a, ad II 11, ad IV 9 b-10 a, ad V 27 b-28a

Path of (Initial) Application

prayoga-mārga, sbyor-baḥi-lam

MVB ad IV 15, ad IV 18; Introduction, pp. 308-310

Path of Seeing

darśana-mārga, mthoṅ-baḥi-lam

MVB, Introduction, pp. 310-313; ad II, 10 a, ad II 11, ad IV 8 b, ad IV 18, ad V 27 b-28 a

peace

śānti, ži-ba

MVB III 9 a, ad III 9 a

perceived

gṛhīta, gṛhyate, ḥdzin-ba, bzuṅ-ba, gzuṅ-ba, zin-pa
KSP 5, 8; *TSN* 11

perception
vijñapti, rnam-par-rig-byed
VK ad 1, 1, 2, ad 3 c, ad 10 b, ad 10 c, ad 11, ad 15, 17 a, ad 17 a, ad 17 b, ad 17 c, 18a, ad 18 a, ad 18 b, 19, ad 19, ad 20 a, ad 20 b, ad 21 b, 22 a
TK 2, 3, 17, 25, 26, 27;
MVB I 3, ad I 3, ad I 6, ad II 10 a, ad III 13 b, III 14 c, IV 10 b, ad V 23-26

perish
vipraṇaśyate, chad-zur-hgyur
KSP 15

perpetuation
āvedha, ḥphen-pa
KSP 34

persistence
āyatatva, yun-riṅ
MVB V 3, ad V 3

personality
pudgala, gaṅ-zag (see also "selflessness of personality")
VK 10 a, ad 10 a; *MVB* I 20, ad I 20, III 4, ad III 4, ad III 6, IV 6("person"), ad IV 6 ("Person"), V 22 ("person"). ad V 22 ("person"), V 23, ad V 23-26

pervading
vyāpi, khyab-pa
KSP 3, 34
MVB II 1, ad II 1, ad II 17

pervasive power
vyāpana, khyab-pa
MVB ad IV 18

planting
ropaṇa, ḥdebs-pa
MVB I 10-11 a, ad I 10-11 a

pleasant
svādu, žim-pa
PSP 1, p 65

pleasure
sukha, bde-ba
PSP 2, p 66 (definition); *VK* ad 5; *TK* 30 ("bliss")

possession
pariṣkāra, yo-byad
MVB ad II 2-3 a
potency
vaśitva, dbaṅ
MVB II 9, ad II 10 a, II 14-16 (*vaśitā*), ad II 14-16
potency in absence of discriminations
nirvikalpa-vaśitā, rnam-par-mi-rtog-la-dbaṅ-ba
MVB ad II 14-16
potency in action
karma-vaśitā, las-la-dbaṅ-ba
MVB ad II 14-16
potency in knowledge
jñāna-vaśitā, ye-śes-la-dbaṅ-ba
MVB ad II 14-16
potency in total clearing of the Buddha-field
kṣetra-pariśuddhi-vaśitā; ẓin-yoṅs-su-dag-pa-la-dbaṅ-ba
MVB ad II 14-16
power
vibhutva, dbaṅ-byed-pa
MVB ad II 10 a, IV 11 a (*vaibhutva*), ad IV 11 a
vittatva, dbyaṅ-ḥbyor
MVB V 3, ad V 3
power
bala, stobs
MVB ad I 19 b, ad II 10 a, ad II 11, ad II 12-13, ad IV 6, ad IV 7 a, ad IV 17, V 5, ad V 6, ad IV 7 b, ad IV 8 a, IV 8 a, IV 11 a, ad IV 11 a, IV 17, ad IV 17
powerful
balavat, stobs-daṅ-ldan-pa
MVB ad IV 6
practise
samudācāra, kun-tu-spyod-pa, kun-tu-ḥbyuṅ-ba
VK ad 18 a; *MVB* ad II 2-3, ad II 14-16, III 13, ad III 19, ad V 12
practise
pratipatti, sgrub-pa
MVB II 4-8, ad II 10 a, ad III 10 b, III 11 a, ad III 11 a, ad III 13 b, ad III 14 a, III 21 ("activity"), ad III 21, V 1 a, ad V 1 a, V 1b, V 2, ad V 2, V 3, ad V 3, ad V 4, ad V 23-25, V 26 b, ad V 26 b, ad V 29-30, ad V 31

vyāpṛti (lit : "Something which is to be fulfilled"), *byed-pa*
MVB ad V 23-25

prāpti
thob-pa
PSP 4, p 70

precise
sūkṣma, žib-pa
PSP 4, p 70

preparation
sambhāra, tshogs
MVB II 4-8, ad II 10 a

preparatory cause
nimitta, rgyu
MVB III 21, ad III 21, III 22 b, ad 22 b, ad IV 11 a

present
pratyutpanna, da-ltar-ḥbyuṅ-ba
MVB ad III 20, ad IV 17, ad V 23-26

preserverence
pradhāra, rab-tu-ḥdzin-pa
MVB V 27 b-28 a, ad V 27 b-28 a, ad V 31 (*ādhāra*)

pride
māna, ṅa-rgyal
PSP 4, p 66; definition, 4, p 68; *TK* 12

pride of thinking "I am"
asmi-māna, ṇaḥo-sñam-paḥi ṅa-rgyal
PSP 4, p 68; *MVB* ad II 2-3 a, ad V 12

pride, greater
mahā-māna, che-baḥi ṅa-rgyal
PSP 4, p 68

pride of self
ātma-māna, bdag-tu ṅa-rgyal
PSP 5, p 72; *TK* 6

pride of thinking deficiency
ūna-māna, chuṅ-zad sñam-paḥi ṅa-rgyal
PSP 4, p 68

pride that is more than pride
mānātimāna, ṅa-rgyal-las kyaṅ ṅa-rgyal
PSP 4, p 68

profound

gaṁbhīra, zab-pa (N), *zab-mo* (V)
TSN 1
profundity
gaṁbhīratā, zab-ñid (N), *zab-pa* (V)
TSN 10
progression
saṁkrānti, ḥpho-ba
KSP 6, 7, 8, 9, 10, 11
projected
ākṣipta, ḥphaṅs-pa
PSP 4, p 71; *KSP* 14, 15, 16-17, 27, 28; *MVB* ad I 10-11 a
prosperity
sampatti, phun-sum(-*tshogs*)
MVB ad V 3
pseudo-justification
hetu-sama, gtan-tshigs-ltar-snaṅ-ba
VV 7, cf. *Nyāya-kośa*, p 1073
pseudo-justification through a direct apprehension (*irrelevant to the inference*)
upalabdhi-sama, dmigs-pa-mtshuṅs-pa
VV 12, 16, cf. *Nyāya-kośa*, p 172
psychic mastery
vibhutva, phan-sum-tshogs-ḥbyor-ba-ñid
TSN 37, 38
psychic power
ṛddhi, rdzu-ḥphrul
VK, ad 19
psychophysical complex
nāmarūpa, miṅ daṅ gzugs
KSP 37; *MVB* ad I 10-11 a, ad 11 b
(*being*) *pulled along*
ākarṣaṇa, sdud-pa
MVB ad I 11 b
unity (*śuddhi, viśuddhi, rham-par-dag-pa*)
PSP 4, *p* 69 (cf. also "clarity")
purpose
prayojana, dgos
KSP 2, 41
putting to rest
praśama, śamana, ži-(*bar*)*byed-pa, rab-tu-ži-ba*

MVB III 22 b, ad III 22 b, V 25, ad V 23-26

R

range

viṣaya, *yul*

VK ad 22 a; *MVB* III 1-2, ad III 1-2

range of events

vastu, *dṅos-po* (this is the probable real meaning of this term in Abhidharma, cf. *Dhammasaṅgaṇi* 585)

PSP 4, p 67; *TK* 20; *MVB* ad III 12 a, ad III 12 b

reality

tattva, *kho-na*

MVB I 1 a, ad I 1a, ad I 13 c, ad I 22 c, II 2 a, ad II 2 a, ad II 17, III 1-2, ad III 3, III 4, ad III 4, III 5, ad III 5, ad III 6, III 7 a, III 7 b, ad III 7 b, ad III 9 a, ad III 9 b-10 a, ad III 11, ad III 12, III 12 b, ad III 12 b, III 13 b, ad III 13 b, III 14 a, ad III 14 a, ad III 14 b, ad III 15, ad III 16, ad III 23; *TSN* 31 (*de-ñid* V)

reality of settlement into perceptions

saṁniveśa-tattva, *gnas-paḥi de-kho-na*

MVB ad III 13 b, III 14 b, ad III 14 b

reality-limit

bhūta-koṭi, *yaṅ-dag-paḥi mthaḥ*

MVB I 14, ad I 15

reality which is seen

dṛṣya-tattva, *snaṅ-baḥi de-kho-na*

MVB ad III 22 b

realization

sākṣātkriyā, *mṅon-du-byas-pa* (V), *mṅon-sum-bya-ba*(N)

TSN 32

realm of desires

kāmāvacara, *ḥdod-pa-na spyod-pa*

PSP 4, p 68, p 74, note 12; *KSP* 14, 28; *MVB* ad I 8 a

realm of simple images

rūpāvacara, *gzugs-kyi spyod-pa*

PSP 5, p 74; *KSP* 14; *MVB* ad I 8 b

re-birth

punar-bhava, *yaṅ-srid-pa* (see also "being again")

KSP 33

reasoning
yukti, rigs
KSP 28
reasoning of conclusive substantiation
upapatti-sādhana-yukti, ḥthad-pas sgrub-paḥi rigs-pa
MVB ad III 12 b
rebuttal
parihāra, lan
KSP 22, 25; *MVB* ad V 22
reduction
see "spurious reply based on reduction"
reflecting, reflection
cintā, bsams-pa
MVB ad V 7, V 7, ad V 8 a, V 9 (*cintanā*), ad V 9, ad V 28
refutation
vivartana, ldogs-pa
VV 14
regret
kaukṛtya, ḥgyod-pa
PSP 4, p 66; definition, 4, p 70; *TK* 14
reject
apakṛṣ, bsal, sel
VV 9; *MVB* ad I 18 (*avakṛ*)
rejoicing
anumodana, rjes-su-yi-raṅ-ba
MVB ad V 3
rejoinder
pratihāra, lan
VV 11
related to artistic activity
śailpasthānika, bzoḥi gnas-pa
KSP 27
related to bodily postures
airyāpathika, spyod-lam-pa
KSP 27, 29
related to magical creations
nairmāṇika, sprul-pa
KSP 27
released

utsṛṣṭa, bor
KSP 15
relishing
āsvādanā, ro-myoṅ-ba
MVB V 12, ad V 12
remain
tiṣṭhati, ḥdug-pa
KSP 34
remaining in a tranquil state
praśaṭhatva, rnal-du-ḥdug-pa
PSP 4, p 67; *MVB* V 28, ad V 28
remember
smṛ, dran
VV 10; *VK* ad 16 b
remembering
smaraṇa, dran-pa
VK ad 16b, 17b
repeatedly
abhīkṣṇaṁ, rgyun-du
MVB V 7
residue
anuśaya, bag-la-ñal
KSP 34; *TK* 26
resistance
pratigha, thogs-pa
PSP 1, p 65; 5, p 74
resolve
praṇidhāna, smon-lam
MVB ad II 12-13, V 5, ad V 6
resort to, have recourse to
prapadyate, sgrub-par-byed
MVB ad I 17, ad I 19 b
respect for gain
lābhe gurutā, rñed-la gdu
MVB II 4-8
rest
upaśānti, ñe-bar-ži-bar-bya-ba
MVB ad I 22 c, ad IV 5
restraining (flaws)
niyāma, skyon-med-pa

MVB, ad V 29-30

restraint

saṁvara, sdom-pa

KSP 14, 49

restriction

niyama, ṅes(-par-ḥgyur-ba)

VK 2, ad 2, 3 a, ad 3 a, ad 4 c

result

phala, ḥbras-bu

VV 10; *PSP* 4, p 93; *KSP* 15; *VK* ad 18 a, 18 b; *MVB* ad II 12-13, III 18, ad III 18, IV 5 a, ad IV 5 a, IV 7 b, ad IV 7 b

TSN 6

result of retribution

vipākaja, rnam-par-smin-pa-las-skyes-pa

KSP 27, 28

resultant afflictions-together

phala-saṁkleśa, ḥbras-buḥi kun-nas-ñon-moṅs-pa

MVB ad I 11

resumption, resuming its course

ḥjug-pa-sñed-pa

KSP 32

retake its course

pratisandadhāti, mtshams-ḥbyor

KSP 22, 28

retribution

vipāka, rnam-par-smin-pa (see also "maturation")

VK ad 3 c, ad 4c; *TK* 2, 19; *MVB* ad I 10-11 a

KSP 33, 34, 47

retributory cause

vipāka-hetu, rnam-par-smin-paḥi rgyu

KSP 2

retributory consciousness

vipāka-vijñāna, rnam-par-smin-paḥi rnam-par-śes-pa

KSP 27, 28, 30, 32, 33, 34, 38

reverencing

pūjana, mchod-pa

MVB ad V 9, V 9

reversal

viparyāsa, phyin-ci-log-pa

MVB II, II 10, ad II 10, IV 11, 12, ad IV 11, 12, V end, I 15, ad I 15, ad I 11 b, ad V 13-14, V 19, ad V 19, V 20, ad V 20, V 21, ad V 21, V 22, ad V 22

reversed

viparīta, phyin-ci-log

VV 11, 12, 13, 14, 15, 16, 17, 18, 23

MVB I 1, ad I 1, III 3, ad III 3

revolution at the basis

āśraya-parāvṛtti, gnas yoṅs-su-gyur-ba

TK 29

right action

samyak-karmānta, yaṅ-dag-paḥi las-kyi mthaḥ

MVB ad IV 10b

right advice

samyag-avavāda, yaṅ-dag-paḥi gdams-ṅag

MVB ad V 6

right concentration

samyak-samādhi, yan-dag-paḥi tiṅ-ṅe-ḥdzin

MVB ad IV 9 b-10 a, ad IV 11 a

right effort

samyag-vyāyāma, yaṅ-dag-paḥi rtsol-ba

MVB ad IV 9 b-10 a, ad IV 11 a

right exertions

samyak-prahāṇa, yaṅ-dag-par spoṅ-ba

MVB ad II 11, ad IV 1, cf. ad IV 2

right intention

samyak-saṁkalpa, yaṅ-dag-paḥi rtog-pa

MVB ad IV 9 b-10 a

right knowledge

samyak-jñāna, yaṅ-dag-pahi śes

MVB III 13 b, ad III 13 b

right livelihood

samyag-ājīva, yaṅ-dag-paḥi ḥtshe-ba

MVB ad IV 10 b

right mindfulness

samyak-smṛti, yaṅ-dag-paḥi dran-pa

MVB ad IV 9 b-10 a, ad IV 11 a

right recognition

samyag-avabodhi, yaṅ-dag-par-rtogs-pa

PSP 4, p 67

right speech
samyag-vāc, yaṅ-dag-paḥi ṅag
MVB ad IV 9 b-10 a
right views
samyag-dṛṣṭi, yaṅ-dag-paḥi lta-ba
MVB ad IV 9 b-10 a
rightness
samyaktva, yaṅ-dag-pa-ñid
MVB V 26, ad V 23-26
ripen
pac, smin
KSP 15, verse; 16-17
root-consciousness
mūla-vijñāna, rtsa-baḥi rnam-par-śes-pa
KSP 35
TK 15
TSN 9, 29, 30
root of the beneficial
kuśala-mūla, dge-baḥi rtsa-ba
PSP 4, p 66; *KSP* 27; *MVB* ad II 10 a, ad IV 6, ad IV 17, ad V 29-30

S

saint
arhat, dgra-mchogs-pa
PSP 5, p 72
saintly state
arhatva, dgra-mchogs-ñid
TK 5, 7
salty
lavaṇa, lan-tshwa
PSP, 1, p 65
same
tad eva, de-ñid
KSP 11
sameness of self and others
ātma-para-samatā, bdag daṅ gźan mñam-pa-ñid
MVB, ad II 14-16, ad V 3

sameness of views
darśana-tulyatā, lta-ba-Mthun-pa
MVB ad III 12 a

Saṁsāra
ḥkhor-ba
PSP 5, p 72; *KSP* 37; *MVB* I 18 c, ad I 18 c, ad II 1, ad III 22 a, ad V 22, ad V 29-30

satisfaction with little, being satisfied by little
saṁlekha, yo-byad-bsñuṅs-pa
MVB II 2-3 a, ad II 2-3 a, IV 10 b, ad IV 10 b

scope
gocara, sbyor-yul
PSP, 5, p 74; *KSP* 29; *VK* ad 10 c (*viṣaya*), 21 b, ad 21b, 22a, ad 22 a, 22 b, ad 22 b; *MVB* ad III 1-2, ad III 12 b, III 12 c, ad V 31

scope of clearing
viśuddhi-gocara, rnam-dag-gi sbyor-yul
MVB ad III 12 b, III 12 c, ad III 12 c

scope of the exalted
ārya-gocara, ḥphags-paḥi sbyor-yul
MVB I 15, ad I 15

scriptural authority
āgama, luṅ
KSP 40; *VK*, ad 7

secondary affliction
upakleśa, ñe-baḥi ñon-moṅs-pa
PSP 4, p 66; *TK* 9, 12; *MVB* ad I 21, IV 11 a

seed
bīja, sa-bon
PSP, Introduction, pp 61-62, 4, p 70
KSP 15, 16-17, 23, 30, 31, 32, 33, 37, 39
VK ad 9; *TK* 2, 18; *MVB* III 17 b, ad III 17 b, ad III 22 b, *TSN* 7

seeing without an object
vaiyarthya-darśana, don-med-bžin-du mthoṅ (V), *bdag-med-mthoṅ-ba* (N N N)
TSN 35

seer
ṛṣi, draṅ-sroṅ
VK ad 19, 20 a, ad 20 a, ad 20 b

self
ātma, bdag
PSP 5, p 67; *KSP* 32, 37, 40; *VK* ad 8, 10 c, ad 10 c, ad 21 b, *TK* 1; *MVB* I 3, ad II 13, ad II 14, III 1-2, ad III 1-2, III 15, ad III 16, ad III 18, ad IV 1, ad V 3, ad V 25-26

self-being
ātma-bhāva, lus
MVB ad I 10-11 a

selfishness
mātsarya, ser-sna
PSP 4, p 66; definition 4, p 69; *TK* 12; *MVB* ad II 2-3 a

selflessness
nairātmya, bdag-med-pa-ñid
PSP 5, p 73; *MVB* III 7 b-8 a, ad III 7 b-8 a

selflessness of events
dharma-nairātmya, chos-kyi bdag-med-pa-ñid
VK 10 b, ad 10 b, ad 10 c

selflessness of personality
pudgala-nairātmya, gaṅ-zag-gi bdag-med-pa-ñid
VK 10 a, ad 10 a

semblance
ākāra, rnam-pa
MVB ad V 15, ad V 16

sense-faculty
indriya, dbaṅ-po
KSP 43; *MVB* ad I 3

sense-field
āyatana, skye-mched
PSP 5, p 72, p 73, p 74, p 75
KSP 2, 3, 6, 11, 12, 14
VK ad 7, 8 ad 8, 9, ad 9, ad 10 a, ad 10 c, ad 11
MVB ad I 10-11 a, ad I, 11 b, ad I 17, II 4-8, ad II 10 a, ad III 1-2, ad III 16, ad III 18 a

sense-object
viṣaya, yul, see "object of sense"

sense of "I"
KSP 49.
ahaṁkṛti, raṅ-ḥdzin
MVB V 12, ad V 12

sense of "mine"
mama, ṅa-yir
sense-organ
indriya, dbaṅ-po
PSP, 1, p 65; *KSP* 24
sensory domain
dhātu, khams
PSP, 5, pp 72, 73, 74, 75
MVB ad III 1-2, ad III 16 b, ad III 17 b, V 8 a, ad V 8 a
sentient being
sattva, sems-can
PSP 4, p 68; *VK* ad 8, ad 20 a, ad 20 b; *MVB* I 3, ad I 3, I 18 b, ad I 18 b, ad I 21, ad II 10 a, II 12, ad II 12, ad II 14-16, ad V 3, ad V 6, ad V 22, ad V 29-30, V, concluding verse; *KSP* 38
sentient materiality
rūpa-prasāda, gzugs-dad-po
PSP 1, p 65
separation
viccheda
VK ad 15
separate
vicchinna
VK 15, ad 15
separated
viyukta, bral-ba.
KSP 24
separate
pṛthak, so-so
KSP 23
separately
ekaika, re-re-la
KSP 3, 38
separateness
pṛthaktva, tha-dad-pa
MVB ad I 13, ad III 15 b, V 23
separation
vaidhurya, mi-ldan-pa
MVB II 4-8, ad II 10 a
serenity

prasāda, dad-pa
PSP 4, p 67
serial propagation
santānikôtkarṣa, rgyun-chags-pa
PSP 4, p 71
series of momentary events, moment-series
santāna, rgyud
PSP 4, p 71; 5, p 71; p 72
KSP 8, 15, 16-17, 18, 20, 21, 22, 23, 32, 34, 38, 39, 40, 46
VK ad 2, ad 17 c, ad 19 (*santati*)
MVB ad I 3 ("life-stream"), II 14, ad II 14, ad IV 12 b ("life-stream")
setting into agitation
calana, gYo-bar-byed-pa
KSP 46
set things going
avatārayati, ḥdzud
MVB, ad V 6
several
aneka, maṅ-po
VK ad 11, ad 14 c, 15, ad 15
severalness
anekatva, maṅ-po-ñid
VK ad 15; *MVB* III 17 a, ad III 17 a
severance
samuccheda, yoṅs-su-chad-pa (V), *chad-byed-pa* (N)
TSN 23
severed
chinna, chad-pa
PSP 5, p 72; *MVB*, ad V 13-14(*vicchinna*)
shame
lajjā, ḥdzem-pa
PSP 4, p 67, p 69
sharp
kaṭuka, tsha-ba
PSP 1, p 65
short
hrasva, chuṅ-ṅu
KSP 2, 3, 4
showing enlightenment forth

bodhi-sandarśana, byaṅ-chub-kun-tu-ston-pa
MVB ad V 29-30
sign
nimitta, mtshan ma
KSP 29; *PSP* 3, *MVB* ad I 15, IV 5 a, ad IV 5 a, ad V 11, ad V 12, ad V 31, ad II 14-16
signless
animitta, mtsham-ma-med-pa
KSP 28, 29; *MVB* I 14, ad I 15, ad V 23-26
TSN 32 (*gñis-su-med-pa* V, *mtshan-ma* N)
simultaneity
samakālatva, mñam-paḥi dus, dus-mñam-pa-ñid
MVB V 26, ad V 23-26
simultaneously
yaugapadyena, cig-car-du
KSP 38
yugapat, cig-car (V), *dus-gcig-tu* (N)
TSN 31
simultaneous
yugapat, (*lhan-*) *cig-car*
VK 15, ad 15; *VK* 31, 34
simultaneous arising
samotpatti, mñam-du-ḥbyuṅ-ba
MVB III 19, ad III 19
simultaneously arising
saha-jāta, lhan-cig-skyes-pa
KSP 25
simultaneous conjunction
yugapad-yoga, lhan-cig-gi ḥgrel-ba
VK 12 a, ad 12 a
single
ekāki, gcig-pu
KSP 3, 23, 40
eka, gcig
VK 11, ad 11, ad 14 b
singleness
ekatva, gcig-pu
VK 14 a, ad 14 a
singleness
ekatva, gcig-pu

VK 14 a, ad 14 a

singly

pṛthak, pratyeka, so-sor

KSP 2, *VK* ad 11

situation

avasthā, gnas-skabs

PSP 4, p 70; *KSP* 15, 24; *MVB* I 1a, ad I 1a, ad I 16a, ad I 22 c, IV, ad IV 13 a, IV 13-14, ad IV 13-14, ad IV 15, IV 16, ad IV 16, ad IV 18; *VK* ad 4 c, ad 17 c, ad 20 b

skill in means

upāya-kauśalya, thabs-la mkhas-pa

MVB ad II 12-13, III 1-2 (*kauśalya* only), ad III 1-2, ad III 14 b, ad III 15-16 a, ad III 22 b (*kauśalya* only), V 5, ad V 6

slackness

laya, byiṅ-ba

MVB IV 4, ad IV 4, IV 5 b, ad IV 5 b, ad IV 11 a, V 12, ad V 12

sloth

kausīdya, le-lo

PSP, 4, p 66, 70; definition 4, p 69; *TK* 13; *MVB* ad I 22 c, ("inactivity"), II 4-8, ad II 10 a, II 11, ad II 11, IV 4, ad IV 4

smells

gandha, dri

PSP 1, p 65; 5, p 72, p 73, p 74, p 75; *KSP* 12

softness

ślakṣṇatva, ḥjam-pa-ñid

PSP 1, p 66

solidity

kaṭhinatva sre-ba-ñid

PSP 1, p 65

someone first standing on a path

gotra-stha, rigs-la-gnas-pa

MVB ad IV 13-14

something that is to be feared

trāsya, skrag-(par) bya (=ba)

MVB V 25 ad V 23-26

something to be abandoned

praheya, spaṅ-bar-bya-ba

MVB ad V 23-26

something which is to be brought to rest
(pra) śāmya, ži-bya-, ži-bar-bya-ba
MVB V 25, ad V 23-26
sounds
śabda, sgra
PSP 1, p 65; 5, p 72, p 73, p 74, p 75; *KSP* 8, *MVB* ad III 12 a
sounds of speech
śabda, sgra
VV 4, 5, 6, 7, 8, 14, 15, 16, 17, 18, 20, 23, 24
sour
amla, skyur-ba
PSP, 1, p 65
space
ākāśa, nam-mkhaḥ
PSP 4, p 73 (definition); *MVB* I 16 c, ad V 21, ad V 22, ad V 23-26
special
viśeṣa, khyad-par, bye-brag
KSP 3, 4, 7, 8, 10, 11, 12, 15, 20, 25, 31, 32, 40, 43, 49
VK ad 9, ad 17 c, ad 18 a, 19, ad 19, ad 20 a
MVB I 8 b, ad I 8 b, ad IV 5 a, ad IV 13-14
special Buddha-events
āveṇika-buddha-dharma, ma-ḥdres-paḥi saṅs-rgyas-kyi chos
MVB ad I 19 a
special attainment
prāpti-viśeṣa, ḥthob-pa-khyad-par-can
MVB ad II 17
special differentiating characteristic
viśeṣa, khyad-par
KSP 7, 8, 25, 31, 37, 40
special states
viśeṣa-gati, khyad-par-du-ḥgro-ba
MVB ad II 17
specific mention
nirdeśana, ṅes-par-ston-pa
VV 5 (also "*nirdiś*" "specifically mention")
speech
vāk, ṅag
KSP 2, 48; *VK* ad 18 b

anutpatti-sama, ma-skyes-pa-mtshuṅs-pa
VV 22, 23
spurious argument based on unwarranted overextension of principles
atiprasaṅga-sama, thal-bar-ḥgyur-ba-mtshuṅs-pa
VV 19, 20
spurious argument based on various alternatives
vikalpa-sama, rnam-par-rtog-paḥi-mtshuṅs-pa
VV 12, 13
spurious reply
jātyuttara, ldag-chod
VV 17
stability
sthiti, ḥdug-pa
KSP 40
stable
sthita, sthayin, gnas
KSP 10
stable
dṛḍha, brtan-pa
PSP 4, p 70
stage-of-nothing-whatever
ākiñcanyāyatana, ci-yaṅ-med-paḥi-skye-mched
PSP 4, p 71
square
varga, lham-pa
KSP 4, note 12
stage
bhūmi, sa
KSP 28; *MVB* II 10 b, II 14-16, ad II 14-16, ad II 17, ad IV 13-14, ad IV 18, ad V 3, ad V 8 a, ad V 27 b-28 a
stage where confidence is cultivated
adhimukti-caryā-bhūmi, mos-paḥi spyod-paḥi sa
MVB, Introduction, pp 308-310; ad IV 4; ad V 3
state
sthāna, gnas
TK 3; *MVB* ad III 1-2, III 19, ad III 19
state-of-arising-immediately-upon-an-effort
prayatnānantarīyakatva, brtsal-ma-thag-tu-byuṅ-ba-ñid
VV 4, 14, 16, 23
state of becoming accumulated

citatva, bsags
TSN 7
state of confusion
bhrāntatva, ḥkhrul-pa
MVB ad III 3 b
state of continuance
sthititā, gnas-pa-ñid
PSP 5, p 72
state of developing
vṛttitva, ḥjug-paḥi dbaṅ (N), *ḥjug-pa* (V)
TSN 2
state of direct perception
pratyakṣatva, mṅon-sum-ñid
VK 16 b, ad 16 b
state of events of non-duality
advaya-dharmatā, gñis-med-chos (V), *gñis-med-chos-ñid* (N)
TSN 4
state of having objects
arthavatītva, don-daṅ-ldan-pa
VK, ad 10 c
state of inferability
anumeyatva, rjes-su-dpag-par-bya-ba-ñid
VV 2, 3
state of knowing
saṁprajanya, śes-bžin
MVB ad IV 5 a, ad IV 5 b
state of no obstructions
nirāvaraṇatā, sgrib-pa-med-pa
MVB V 29-30, ad V 29-30, ad V 31
state of non-otherness
ananyathātva, gžan-du-ḥgyur-med (V)
gžan-du-mi-ḥgyur-ba-ñid (N)
TSN 3
state-of-not-being-found
avidyamānatā, med-pa-(ñid)
TSN 3
state of own-being
svābhāvikatva, ṅo-bo-ñid
MVB ad I 19 a
state of rest

śānti, ži-ba
MVB IV 5 b
state of their being contradictory views in relation to the same moment
viruddhādhīkāraṇatva, mi-mthun-blo-yid-dbaṅ-sgyur (V)
gžen-po-blo-ni-sgyur (N)
TSN 35
state without citta
acittaka, sems-med
TK 16
statement
vacana, brjod-pa
VV 2, 3
steadiness
sthiti, gnas
MVB IV 3, ad IV 3
steady concentration, one in steady concentration
yogitva, rnal-ḥbyor-can
MVB III 15-16 a, ad III 15-16 a
steady flow
niṣyanda, rgyu-mthun (cf. also "yet higher aim which flows from that", "fruition which flows from that")
MVB II 14, ad II 14, ad IV 17, ad V 3
sticking to
śleṣa, ḥdre-ba
MVB ad IV 18
store-consciousness
ālaya-vijñāna, kun-gži-rnam-par-śes-pa
PSP 5, p 71-72; *TK* 2; *MVB* ad I 9, ad III 22 b; *TSN* 6
KSP 33, 37, 39, 40
stream see "series"
Suchness
tathatā, de-bžin-ñid
PSP 4, p 73 (definition); *TK* 25; *MVB* I 14, ad I 15, ad III 8, ad III 9 a, ad III 11 a, ad III 13 b, ad III 22 b, ad V 27 b-28 a; *TSN* 30
subject apprehendor
grāhaka, ādzin-pa
VK ad 10c, ad 21b; *MVB* ad I 1, ad I 2, ad I 3, ad I 5, ad I 6, III 4, ad III 4, ad III 9a, III 17b, ad III 17b, ad V 15, ad V 16, ad V 17, V 24, ad V 23-26

subject to
adhīna, rag-lus-pa
KSP 40; *TSN* 2 (*dbaṅ*)
subordinated
anubaddha, rjes-su-ḥbraṅ-ba
KSP 14
subsequent discursive thought
vicāra, dpyod-pa
PSP 4, p 66; definition, p 70; note 14; *TK* 14
substratum
āśraya, rten
KSP 37, 40; *MVB* III 15-16 a, ad V 22
subtle
sūkṣma, phra-ba
MVB III 1-2, ad III 1-2, ad III 9 b-10 a, III 10 b, ad III 22 b
success in aims
artha-siddhi, don-(rnams-) ḥgrub-pa
MVB V 8 a, ad V 8 a
suffering
duḥkha, sdug-bsnal
PSP 2 (definition); *KSP* 47; *VK* ad 4; *MVB* ad I 13 b, I 10, ad I 10-11 a, ad III 4, III 6, ad III 6, ad III 7 b-8 a, III 8 b, ad III 8 b, ad III 19, III 21, ad IV 1, ad V 23-26
suffering coming from the basic characteristics of the world
lakṣaṇa-duḥkhatā, mtshan-ñid-kyis-sdug-bsṅal-ñid
MVB ad III 7 b-8 a
suffering state
duḥkhatā, sdug-bsṅal-ñid
MVB ad IV 1
suggestion and investigation
uddeśa, bstan-pa
MVB ad IV 18
summits of existence
bhāvāgra, srid-paḥi-rtse-mo
PSP 4, p 70, note 19; *KSP* 28, 29, 34
summits
mūrdhānas, rtse-mo
MVB, Introduction, p 309; ad IV 8 a
superimposition
samāropa, sgro-ḥdogs-pa

MVB ad I 20, III 4, ad III 4, III 18b, ad III 18 b, V 23, ad V 23-26

superior

adhika, ḥphel

MVB II 14-16, ad II 14-16, ad V 22

super-knowledge

abhijñā, mṅon-par-śes-pa

MVB ad IV 11a, ad IV 13-14

supermundane

lokottara, ḥjig-rten-las-ḥdas

TK 7, 29

supermundane complete clearing

lokottara-viśuddhi, hjig-rten-las-ḥdas-paḥi-rnam-par-dag pa

MVB ad III 20 a

supermundane knowledge free from discriminations

lokottara-nirvikalpa-jñāna, ḥjig-rten-las-ḥdas-pa-rnam-par-mi-rtog-paḥi-ye-śes

VK ad 17 c

supernormal faculties

ṛddhi, rdzu-ḥphrul

MVB ad V 6

support

ādhāra, gži

MVB ad II 10 a, ad V 31; *KSP* 33

support

ālambana, dmigs

MVB V la, ad V l a, ad V 27 a, V 27 b-28 a, ad V 27-28 a

suppression

nirghātana, bcom-pa

KSP 49

supremacy

ānuttarya, bla (-na)-med-(pa-) ñid

MVB I l a, ad II 17, V, V l a, ad V l a, ad V 31

supreme perfect enlightenment

anuttara-samyak-sambodhi, yaṅ-dag-par-rdzogs-paḥi byaṅ-chub

MVB ad II 10 a

susceptibility to harm

dauṣṭhulya, gnas-ṅan-len

PSP 4, p 67; *TK* 29; *MVB* II 4-8, ad II 10 a, II 11, ad II 11, IV 1, ad IV 1, ad IV 9 a, ad V 11, ad V 12

sustaining
dhṛti, rten
MVB ad II 10 a
sustension
dhāraṇā, ḥdzin-pa
MVB V 27 b-28 a, ad V 27 b-28 a
sweet
madhura, mṅar-ba
PSP 1, p 65
syllable
akṣara, vyañjana, yi-ge
PSP 4, p 71; *KSP* 48
synonym
paryāya, rnam-graṅs
PSP 4, p 71; *MVB* ad I 8a, ad I 11, I 12, ad I 13b, I 14, ad I 14, ad I 22 c

T

tactile consciousness
kāya-vijñāna, lus-kyi-rnam-par-śes-pa
PSP 5, p 73-74; *MVB* ad III 22 b
tactile sensations
spraṣṭavya, reg-bya
PSP 1, p 65, p 66; 5, 73-75; 5, p 73-74; *KSP* 12, 23; *VK* ad 9
taking of life
prāṇātipāta, srog-gcod-pa
KSP 46; *VK* ad 18b
taking of what has not been given
adinnādāna, mi-byin-par-len-pa
KSP 46
taking part in an organism
nikāya-sabhāga, ris-mthun-pa
PSP 4, p 71 (definition), *VK* ad 19 (*sabhāga*); *KSP* 34
talk
jalpa, rtog-pa
MVB V 15 b-16 a, ad V 16
tastes
rasa, ro
PSP 1, p 65; 5, p 72-75; *VK* ad 16 b

termination

paryanta, mthaḥ-ma

MVB ad V 22

that accepted by right reasoning

yukti-prasiddha, rigs-paḥi-grags-pa

MVB ad III 11b, III 12 b

that accepted by the world at large

loka-prasiddha, ḥjig-rten-gyi-grags-pa

MVB ad III 11 b, III 12 a, ad III 12 a

that of which one has become conscious

cintya, bsams-pa

PSP 4, p 67

that which appears

yat khyāti, gaṅ snaṅ

TSN 2, 3, 4

that which can be known

jñeya, śes (-par-)=bya

MVB ad V 22

that which has arisen from not having understood

asaṁvedita-bhūta, rigs-pa-ma-yin-pas--bskyed-pa

PSP 3

thesis

pratijñā, dam-bcaḥ

VV 2

thirst

pipāsā, skom-pa

PSP 1, p 66; *KSP* 23

this-only

tanmātra, de ñid

TK 27

those which arise specifically

(*vi*)*niyatāḥ, ṅes-pa*

TK 9, 10

those who act with attachment (*hostility, or confusion*)

lit. "those who act with attachment, etc.", the "etc." being the other roots of the unbeneficial; *rāgādicarita, ḥdod-chags-a-sogs-paḥi-spyod-pa*

MVB ad II 1

those who make everything alike

samabhāgacarita, cha-mtshuṅs-par-spyod-pa

MVB ad II 1

three realms of existence

traidhātuka, khams-gsum-pa

VK ad 1

throw off

utsṛj, ḥdor-ba

MVB ad I 18 d

thrown forth

ākṣipta, ḥdebs

MVB ad I 11 b

thrust

āvedha, ḥphen-pa

KSP 11

tongue

jihvā, lce

PSP 1, p 65; 5, p 72-75

topic

pakṣa, phyogs

VV 1, 14

tormented

āghāta, kun-nas-mnan

PSP 4, p 68

torpor

middha, gñed

PSP 4, p 66; definition, p 70; *VK* 18 b; *TK* 14, 16

total tranquility

pratipraśrabdha, lhun-gyis-grub-pa

PSP 4, p 67

totally

ekāntena, gcig-tu

MVB ad I 2

totally clear

śubha-kṛtsna, dge-rgyas

PSP 4, p 70

training

śikṣā, bslab-pa

KSP 42

tranquility

praśrabdhi, śin-tu-spyaṅs-pa

PSP 4, p 66; definition, p 67; *TK* 11; *MVB* ad IV 4, ad IV 5 a,

IV 5 b, ad IV 5 b, ad IV 8 b, ad IV 9 a, V 27 b-28 a, ad V 27 b-28 a

transcended

atikrānta, ḥdaḥ-bar-byed

KSP 28

transformation

pariṇāma, (yoṅs-su-)ḥgyur-ba

KSP 2, 8, 5, 20, 32, 40; *VK* 6, ad 6, ad 7, ad 9, ad 17 c; *TK* 1, 8, 17, 18

transform

pariṇam

VK ad 5; *MVB* ad II 10 a ("evolve") ad II 14-16

transformation undergone with great enlightenment

mahā-bodhi-pariṇāmanā, byaṅ-chub-chen-por-yoṅs-su-bsṅos-pa

MVB ad V 3, ad V 6

transmutation

vivartana, ldog-pa

KSP 8 c; *PSP* 5, p 100

Truths

satya, bden-pa

MVB ad III 1-2, ad III 7 b-8 a, ad III 8 b, ad II 2-3 a, ad III 9 a, ad III 9 b-10 a, ad III 21, IV 1, ad IV 1, ad IV 5 a

U

ultimate (truth)

paramārtha, dam-paḥi don

TK 25; *MVB* I 14 (*paramārthatā*), ad I 15, ad I 16 d, ad I 17, ad III 9 b-10 a, ad III 10 b, III 10 c, ad III 10 c, III 11 a, ad III 11 a, V 4, ad V 4, V 18 d

unable

aśakya, mi-nus-pa

KSP 15

unappropriated

anupātta, zin-pa-ma-yin-pa

PSP 1, p 65; 5, p 75

unbeneficial

akuśala, mi-dge-ba

PSP 5, p 74;

PSP 5, p 71; *KSP* 36

uneven

viśāta, phya-le-ma-yin-pa

KSP 4

unfailing ascertainment and advice

nirdeśa, bśad-pa

MVB ad IV 18

unfulfilment

aprapūrṇatā, rab-tu-ma-rdzogs

MVB II 4-8, ad II 10c (*aparipūrṇa*)

ungraspable

alabhya, dmigs-med

TSN 26 (*brjod-med* N)

unity

eka(*tva*), *gcig*(*-pu*)

VK, ad 11, 15, ad 15

universal characteristic

sāmānya-lakṣaṇa, spyiḥi mtshan-ñid

MVB V 19, ad V 19

unliable to be connected with afflictions (see also "without distress")

anāsrava, zag-pa-daṅ-mi-ldan-pa

PSP 5, p 74; *KSP* 34, note 43; *TK* 30

unmanifest action

avijñapti(*-karma*), *rnam-par-rig-byed-ma-yin-pa* (*ḥi las*)

PSP 1, p 65; definition, 1, p 65; *KSP* 2, 14, note 3

unobstructed-indeterminate

anāvṛtāvyākṛta, ma-bsgribs-la-luṅ-du-ma-bstan-pa

KSP 26, 27; *TK* 4

unreal

asamyak, yaṅ-dag-ma-yin-pa

VV 11

unreversed

aviparīta, aviparyasta, phyin-ci-ma-log-pa

MVB ad I 1, ad III 3 ("unreversedness", *aparītatva, phyin-ci-ma-log-pa-ñid*), IV 11 b-12 a, ad IV 11 b-12 a

V

Vain assertion

āropa, sgro-btags-pa
VV 16
Vajra-words
vajra-padāni, rdo-rjeḥi tshig
MVB ad V 22
variation
nānātva, tha-dad-pa
KSP 10
variety
vicitratā, sna-tshogs
PSP 5, p 71
various
citra, sna-tshogs
TSN 7
Vehicle
yāna, theg-pa
MVB I 12, ad I 12, ad II 1, ad III 1-2, III 22, ad III 22, ad III 23, ad IV 18, V, ad V 1, ad V 7 b-8 a, ad V 9, ad V 29-30, ad V 31
verbal act
vāk-karma, ṅag-gi las
KSP 1, 2, 15, 18, 21, 40, 41, 42, 48
views
dṛṣṭi, lta-ba
PSP 4, p 66; definition, 4, pp 68-69; *KSP* 24; *TK* 12; *MVB* ad II 2-3 a, ad II 11, ad III 6 b, ad V 23-26
view of a self in the body
satkāya-dṛṣṭi, ḥjigs-tshogs-la lta-ba
PSP 4, p 68; *MVB* II 2-3 a, ad II 2-3 a
view of self
ātma-dṛṣṭi, bdag-tu lta-ba
PSP 5, p 72; *TK* 6; *MVB* III 1-2, ad III 14 b, III 15-16 a, ad III 16 b, ad V 23-26
views regarding the permanence or impermanence of the elements constituting personality
antagrāhadṛṣṭi, mthar-ḥd-in-par-lta-ba
PSP 4, p 68
vigor
vīrya, brtson-ḥgrus
MVB IV 2, ad IV 2, ad IV 3, ad IV 7 b, ad IV 8 b, V 5, ad V 6

PSP 4, p. 66; definition, 4, p 67; *TK* 11
visible
rūpa, gzugs
PSP 1, p 65; 5, p 71, 72, 73, 74, 75.
KSP 2, 6, 11, 13
VK ad 2, ad 5, 6, ad 7, 8, ad 8, ad 9, ad 10 b, ad 10 c, ad 11, ad 14 c, ad 15, ad 16 b, ad 17 b
MVB ad I 3, ad II 10 a, ad III 12 a, ad III 17 b, ad III 20 a, ad V 18 b
visual consciousness
cakṣur-vijñāna, mig-gi-rnam-par-śes-pa
PSP 5, p 73-75; *MVB* ad II 10 a
volition
cetanā, sems-pa
PSP 4, p 66; definition, 4, p 67
KSP 2, 20, 25, 27, 28, 37, 40, 43, 46, 47, 48, 49
TK 3; *MVB* ad I 9, ad IV 5 a, ad IV 5 b, ad V 23-26
volition which decides
niścaya-cetanā, ṅes-paḥi sems-pa
KSP 46
volition which prepares
gati-cetanā, ḥgro-baḥi sems-pa
KSP 46
volition which sets into agitation
kiraṇa-cetanā, gYo-bar-byed-paḥi sems-pa
KSP 46

W

was
bhūta, yaṅ-dag-pa
MVB ad V 23-26
was not
abhūta, yaṅ-dag-ma-yin-pa
VK ad 17b, ad 17 c; *MVB* ad I 7 b, ad V 23-26
water-element
ab-dhātu, chuḥi khams
PSP 1
wearying distress and agitation
parikhedita, yoṅs-su-skyo-ba

MVB II 4-8, ad II 10 a

welfare

śubha, dge-ba

MVB II 3, ad II 4-8, II 9, ad II 9, ad II 10a, ad II 17, ad V 23-26, (*hita, phan-par-bya-ba*): I 18 b, ad I 18 b

what has been heard

(particularly "what one has heard of religious discourses", though not exclusively that)

śruta, thos-pa

MVB II 4-8, ad II 10a, ad II 12-13, ad II 14-16, cf. V 7b-8a, ad V 8 b, ad V 9, ad V 27 b-28 a

whatever fits (into place), whatever has dimensionality

eka-deśa, ci yaṅ ruṅ ste

PSP 1

whatever is felt

yat kiñcid veditavyam, gaṅ-gi tshor yaṅ ruṅ

PSP

which relate to experience

aupabhogika, ñe-bar-spyod-can

MVB I 9, ad I 9

which rest upon the material organs

rūpīndriyāśrita, dbaṅ-po-gzugs-can-la gnas-pa

KSP 23

wind-element

vāyu-dhātu, rluṅ-gi khams

PSP 1; *KSP* 11, 12, 46

without distress

(see also "unliable to be connected with afflictions")

anāsrava, zag-pa-med-pa

PSP 5, p 74; *KSP*, note 43; *TK* 30

word

pāda, tshig

PSP 4, p 70, 71; *KSP* 2, 48

words used in religious practise

udbhāvanā, brjod

MVB III 10 b, ad III 10 b

working against

pratibhāvitatva, rab-tu-phye-ba

MVB ad II 11

worldly supermundane subsequently attained seeing

laukika-lokottara-pṛṣṭhalabdha (*darśana*), *ḥjig-rten-pa-ḥjig-rten-las-ḥdas-paḥi-rjes-lab-thob-pa-*
(*lta-ba*)
MVB ad IV 9 b-10 a

wrongness
mithyātva, *log-pa-ñid*
MVB V 26, ad V 23-26

Y

yet higher aim which flows from that
niṣyandâgrârtha, *rgyu-mthun-pa-don-gyi-mchog*
MVB II 14-16, ad II 14-16

you and others are really the same
(see also "sameness of self and others")
ātma-para-samatā, *bdag daṅ gžan mñam-pa-ñid*
MVB II 14-16, ad V 3

Z

zest
chanda, *ḥdun-pa*
PSP 4, p 66; definition, 4, p 67; *TK* 10
MVB ad II 11, ad IV 4, ad IV 5 a, IV 6, ad IV 6

अथ विंशिकावृत्तिः

(1) महायाने त्रैधातुकं विज्ञप्तिमात्रं व्यवस्थाप्यते। चित्तमात्रं भो जिनपुत्रा यदुत त्रैधातुकमिति सूत्रात्। चित्तं मनो विज्ञानं विज्ञप्तिश्चेति पर्यायाः। चित्तमत्र ससंप्रयोगमभिप्रेतं। मात्रमित्यर्थप्रतिषेधार्थं।

विज्ञप्तिमात्रमेवेदमसदर्थावभासनात् ।
यद्वत् तैमिरिकस्यासत्केशोण्ड्रकादिदर्शनं ॥१॥

अत्र चोद्यते।

न देशकालनियमः संतानानियमो न च ।
न च कृत्यक्रिया युक्ता विज्ञप्तिर्यदि नार्थतः ॥२॥

किमुक्तं भवति। यदि विना रूपाद्यर्थेन रूपादिविज्ञप्तिरुत्पद्यते न रूपाद्यर्थात्। कस्मात् क्वचिद्देश उत्पद्यते न सर्वत्र। तत्रैव च देशे कदाचिदुत्पद्यते न सर्वदा। तद्देशकालप्रतिष्ठितानां सर्वेषां संतान उत्पद्यते न केवलमेकस्य। यथा तैमिरिकाणां संताने केशाद्याभासो नान्येषां। कस्माद्यत्तैमिरिकैः केशभ्रमरादि दृश्यते तेन केशादिक्रिया न क्रियते न च तदन्यैर्न क्रियते। यदन्नपानवस्त्रविषायुधादि स्वप्ने दृश्यते तेनान्नादिक्रिया न क्रियते न च तदन्यैर्न क्रियते। गन्धर्वनगरेणासत्त्वान् नगरक्रिया न क्रियते न च तदन्यैर्न क्रियते। तस्मादसद् यदभावनाभासने देशकाल-

[2a] नियमः संतानानियमः कृत्यक्रिया च न युज्यते॥ न खलु न युज्यते यस्मात्।

देशादिनियमः सिद्धः स्वप्नवत्

स्वप्न इव स्वप्नवत्। कथं तावत्। स्वप्ने विनाप्यर्थेन क्वचिदेव देशे किंचिद् भ्रमरारामस्त्रीपुरुषादिकं दृश्यते न सर्वत्र। तत्रैव च देशे कदाचिद्दृश्यते न सर्वकालमिति सिद्धो विनाप्यर्थेन देशकालनियमः।

प्रेतवत्पुनः।

(1) La première page manque au manuscrit; j'ai tenté de la restituer en sanscrit, pour la commodité des lecteurs indiens, en m'aidant des traductions en tibétain et en chinois. (S. Lévi)

संतानानियमः

सिद्ध इति वर्तते प्रेतानामिव प्रेतवत् कथं सिद्धः समं।

सर्वैः पूयनद्यादिदर्शने ॥३॥

पूयपूर्णा नदी पूयनदी। घृतघटवत्। तुल्यकर्मविपाकावस्था हि प्रेताः सर्वेऽपि पूयपूर्णां नदीं पश्यन्ति नैक एव। यथा पूयपूर्णामेवं मूत्रपुरीषादिपूर्णां दण्डासिधरैश्च पुरुषैरधिष्ठितामित्यादिग्रहणेन। एवं संतानानियमो विज्ञप्तीनामसत्यप्यर्थे सिद्धः।

स्वप्नोपघातवत्कृत्यक्रिया

सिद्धेति वेदितव्यं। यथा स्वप्ने द्वयसमापत्तिमन्तरेण शुक्रविसर्गलक्षणः स्वप्नोपघातः। एवं तावदन्यान्यैर्दृष्टान्तैर्देशकालनियमादिचतुष्टयं सिद्धं।

नरकवत्पुनः।

सर्वं

सिद्धमिति वेदितव्यं। नरकेष्विव नरकवत्। कथं सिद्धं।

नरकपालादिदर्शने तैश्च बाधने ॥४॥

यथा हि नरकेषु नारकाणां नरकपालादिदर्शनं देशकालनियमेन सिद्धं श्ववायसायसपर्वताद्यागमनगमन[2b] दर्शनं चेत्यादिग्रहणेन सर्वेषां च नैकस्यैव तैश्च तद्बाधनं सिद्धमसत्स्वपि नरकपालादिषु समानस्वकर्मविपाकाधिपत्यात्। तथान्यत्रापि सर्वमेतद्देशकालनियमादिचतुष्टयं सिद्धमिति वेदितव्यं॥ किं पुनः कारणं नरकपालास्ते च श्वानो वायसाश्च सत्वा नेष्यन्ते। अयोगात्। न हि ते नारका युज्यन्ते। तथैव तद्दुःखाप्रतिसंवेदनात्। परस्परं यातयतामिमे नारका इमे नरकपाला इति व्यवस्था न स्यात्। तुल्याकृतिप्रमाणबलानां च परस्परं यातयतां न तथा भयं स्यात्। दाहदुःखं च प्रदीप्तायामयोमय्यां भूमावसहमानाः कथं तत्र परान्यातयेयुः। अनारकाणां वां नरके कुतः संभवः। कथं तावत्तिरश्चां स्वर्गसंभवः। एवं नरकेषु तिर्यक्प्रेतविशेषाणां नरकपालादीनां संभवः स्यात्।

तिरश्चां संभवः स्वर्गे यथा च नरके तथा।
न प्रेतानां यतस्तज्जं दुःखं नानुभवन्ति ते ॥५॥

ये हि तिर्यञ्चः स्वर्गे संभवन्ति ते तद्भाजनलोकसुखसंवर्तनीयेन कर्मणा तत्र

संभूतास्तज्जं सुखंप्रत्य नुभवन्ति। न चैवं नरकपालादयो नारकं दुःखं प्रत्यनुभवन्ति। तस्मान्न तिरश्चां संभवो युक्तो नापि प्रेतानां। तेषां तर्हि नारकाणां कर्मभिस्तत्र भूतविशेषाः संभवन्ति वर्णाकृतिप्रमाणबलविशिष्टा ये नरक [3a] पालादिसंज्ञां प्रतिलभन्ते। तथा च परिणमन्ति यद्विविधां हस्तविक्षेपादिक्रियां कुर्वन्तो दृश्यन्ते भयोत्पादनार्थं। यथा मेषाकृतयः पर्वता आगच्छन्तो गच्छन्तो ऽयःशाल्मलीवने च कण्टका अधोमुखीभवन्त ऊर्द्ध्वमुखीभवन्तश्चेति। न ते न संभवन्त्येव।

यदि तत्कर्मभिस्तत्र भूतानां संभवस्तथा।
इष्यते परिणामश्च किं विज्ञानस्य नेष्यते ॥६॥

विज्ञानस्यैव तत्कर्मभिस्तथा परिणामः कस्मान्नेष्यते किं पुनर्भूतानि कल्प्यन्ते। अपि च।

कर्मणो वासनान्यत्र फलमन्यत्र कल्प्यते।
तत्रैव नेष्यते यत्र वासना किं नु कारणं ॥७॥

येन हि कर्मणा नारकाणां तत्र तादृशो भूतानां संभवः कल्प्यते परिणामश्च तस्य कर्मणो वासना तेषां विज्ञानसंतानसंनिविष्टा नान्यत्र। यत्रैव च वासना तत्रैव तस्याः फलं तादृशो विज्ञानपरिणामः किं नेष्यते। यत्र वासना नास्ति तत्र तस्याः फलं कल्प्यत इति किमत्र कारणं॥ आगमः कारणं। यदि विज्ञानमेवरूपादि प्रतिभासं स्यान्न रूपादिको ऽर्थस्तदा रूपाद्यायतनास्तित्वं भगवता नोक्तं स्यात्। अकारणमेतद्यस्मात्।

रूपाद्यायतनास्तित्वं तद्विनेयजनं प्रति।
अभिप्रायवशादुक्तमुपपादुकसत्ववत् ॥८॥

यथास्ति सत्व उपपादुक इत्युक्तं भगवता। अभिप्रायवशाच्चित्तसंतत्यनुच्छेदमा[3b] यत्यामभिप्रेत्य।

नास्तीह सत्व आत्मा वा धर्मास्त्वेते सहेतुकाः

इति वचनात्। एवं रूपाद्यायतनास्तित्वमप्युक्तं भगवता तद्देशनाविनेयजनमधिकृत्येत्याभिप्रायिकं तद्वचनं॥ को ऽत्राभिप्रायः।

यतः स्वबीजाद्विज्ञप्तिर्यदाभासा प्रवर्तते।
द्विविधायतनत्वेन ते तस्या मुनिरब्रवीत् ॥९॥

किमुक्तं भवति। रूपप्रतिभासा विज्ञप्तिर्यतः स्वबीजात्परिणामविशेषप्राप्तादुत्पद्यते तच्च बीजं यत्प्रतिभासा च सा ते तस्या विज्ञप्तेश्चक्षूरूपायतनत्वेन यथाक्रमं भगवानब्रवीत्। एवं यावत् स्प्रष्टव्यप्रतिभासा विज्ञप्तिर्यतः स्वबीजात्परिणामविशेषप्राप्तादुत्पद्यते। तच्च बीजं यत्प्रतिभासा च सा ते तस्या कायस्प्रष्टव्यायतनत्वेन यथाक्रमं भगवानब्रवीदित्ययमभिप्रायः ॥ एवं पुनरभिप्रायवशेन देशयित्वा को गुणः।

तथा पुद्गलनैरात्म्यप्रवेशो हि

तथा हि देश्यमाने पुद्गलनैरात्म्यं प्रविशन्ति। द्वयाद्विज्ञानषट्कंप्र वर्तते। न तु कश्चिदेको द्रष्टास्ति न यावन्मन्तेत्येवं विदित्वा ये पुद्गलनैरात्म्यदेशनाविनेयास्ते पुद्गलनैरात्म्यं प्रविशन्ति।

अन्यथा पुनः।

देशना धर्मनैरात्म्यप्रवेशः

अन्यथेति विज्ञप्तिमात्रदेशना कथं धर्मनैरात्म्यप्रवेशः। विज्ञप्तिमात्रमिदं रूपादिधर्मप्रतिभासमुत्पद्यते न तु रूपादिलक्षणो धर्मः कोऽप्यस्ती[4a] ति विदित्वा। यदि तर्हि सर्वथा धर्मो नास्ति तदपि विज्ञप्तिमात्रं नास्तीति कथं तर्हि व्यवस्थाप्यते। न खलु सर्वथा धर्मो नास्तीत्येवं धर्मनैरात्म्यप्रवेशो भवति। अपि तु।

कल्पितात्मना ॥१०॥

यो बालैर्धर्माणां स्वभावो ग्राह्यग्राहकादिः परिकल्पितस्तेन कल्पितेनात्मना तेषां नैरात्म्यं न त्वनभिलाप्येनात्मना यो बुद्धानां विषय इति। एवं विज्ञप्तिमात्रस्यापि विज्ञप्त्यन्तरपरिकल्पितेनात्मना नैरात्म्यप्रवेशात् विज्ञप्तिमात्रव्यवस्थापनया सर्वधर्माणां नैरात्म्यप्रवेशो भवति न तु तदस्तित्वापवादात्। इतरथा हि विज्ञप्तेरपि विज्ञप्त्यन्तरमर्थः स्यादिति विज्ञप्तिमात्रत्वं न सिध्येतार्थवतीत्वाद्विज्ञप्तीनां ॥ कथं पुनरिदं प्रत्येतव्यमनेनाभिप्रायेण भगवता रूपाद्यायतनास्तित्वमुक्तं न पुनः सन्त्येव तानि यानि रूपादिविज्ञप्तीनां प्रत्येकं विषयीभवन्तीति। यस्मात्।

न तदेकं न चानेकं विषयः परमाणुशः।
न च ते संहता यस्मात्परमाणुर्न सिध्यति ॥११॥

इति। किमुक्तं भवति। यत्तद्रूपादिकमायतनं रूपादिविज्ञप्तीनां प्रत्येकं विषयः स्यात्तदेकं वा स्याद्यथावयविरूपं कल्प्यते वैशेषिकैः। अनेकं वा परमाणुशः। संहता

वा त एव परमाणवः। न तावदेकं विषयो भवत्यवयवेभ्योऽन्यस्यावयविरूपस्य क्वचिदप्यग्रहणात्। नाप्यनेकं[4b] परमाणूनां प्रत्येकमग्रहणात्। नापि ते संहता विषयीभवन्ति। यस्मात्परमाणुरेकं द्रव्यं न सिध्यति॥ कथं न सिध्यति। यस्मात्।

षट्केन युगपद्योगात्परमाणोः षडंशता।

षड्भ्यो दिग्भ्यः षड्भिः परमाणुभिर्युगपद्योगे सति परमाणोः षडंशता प्राप्नोति। एकस्य यो देशस्तत्रान्यस्यासंभवात्।

षण्णां समानदेशत्वात्पिण्डः स्यादणुमात्रकः॥१२॥

अथ य एवैकस्य परमाणोर्देशः स एव षण्णां। तेन सर्वेषां समानदेशत्वात्सर्वः पिण्डः परमाणुमात्रः स्यात्परस्परव्यतिरेकादिति न कश्चित्पिण्डो दृश्यः स्यात्॥ नैव हि परमाणवः संयुज्यन्ते निरवयवत्वात्। मा भूदेष दोषप्रसङ्गः। संहतास्तु परस्परं संयुज्यन्त इति काश्मीरवैभाषिकास्त इदं प्रष्टव्याः। यः परमाणूनां संघातो न स तेभ्योऽर्थान्तरमिति।

परमाणोरसंयोगे तत्संघातेऽस्ति कस्य सः।

संयोग इति वर्तते।

न चानवयवत्वेन तत्संयोगाद् न सिध्यति॥१३॥

अथ संघाता अप्यन्योन्यं न संयुज्यन्ते। न तर्हि परमाणूनां निरवयवत्वात्संयोगो न सिध्यतीति वक्तव्यं। सावयवस्यापि हि संघातस्य संयोगानभ्युपगमात्। तस्मात्परमाणुरेकं द्रव्यं न सिध्यति। यदि च परमाणोः संयोग इष्यते यदि वा नेष्यते।

दिग्भागभेदो यस्यास्ति तस्यैकत्वं न युज्यते।

अन्यो हि परमाणोः पूर्वदिग्भागो[5a] यावदधोदिग्भाग इति दिग्भागभेदे सति कथं तदात्मकस्य परमाणोरेकत्वं योक्ष्यते।

छायावृती कथं वा

यद्येकैकस्य परमाणोर्दिग्भागभेदो न स्यादादित्योदये कथमन्यत्र छाया भवत्यन्यत्रातपः। न हि तस्यान्यः प्रदेशोऽस्ति यत्रातपो न स्यात्। आवरणं च कथं भवति परमाणोः परमाण्वन्तरेण यदि दिग्भागभेदो नेष्यते। न हि कश्चिदपि परमाणोः

परभागोऽस्ति यत्रागमनादन्येनान्यस्य प्रतिघातः स्यात्। असति च प्रतिघाते सर्वेषां समानदेशत्वात्सर्वः संघातः परमाणुमात्रः स्यादित्युक्तं। किमेवं नेष्यते पिण्डस्य ते च्छायावृती न परमाणोरिति। किं खलु परमाणुभ्योऽन्यः पिण्ड इष्यते यस्य ते स्यातां। नेत्याह।

अन्यो न पिण्डश्चेन्न तस्य ते ॥१४॥

यदि नान्यः परमाणुभ्यः पिण्ड इष्यते न ते तस्येति सिद्धं भवति। संनिवेशपरिकल्प एषः। परमाणुः संघात इति वा। किमनया चिन्तया। लक्षणं तु रूपादि यदि न प्रतिषिध्यते। किं पुनस्तेषां लक्षणं चक्षुरादिविषयत्वं नीलादित्वं च। तदेवेदं संप्रधार्यते। यत्तच्चक्षुरादीनां विषयो नीलपीतादिकमिष्यते किं तदेकं द्रव्यमथ वा तदनेकमिति। किं चातः। अनेकत्वे दोष उक्तः।

एकत्वे न क्रमेणेतिर्युगपन्न ग्रहाग्रहौ।
विच्छिन्नानेकवृत्तिश्च सूक्ष्मानीक्षा च नो भवेत् ॥१५॥

यदि यावदविच्छिन्नं नानेकं[5b] चक्षुषो विषयस्तदेकं द्रव्यं कल्प्यते पृथिव्यां क्रमेणेतिर्न स्याद्गमनमित्यर्थः। सकृत्पादक्षेपेण सर्वस्य गतत्वात्। अर्वाग्भागस्य च ग्रहणं परभागस्य चाग्रहणं युगपन्न स्यात्। **न हि तस्यैव तदिदानीं ग्रहणं चाग्रहणं च** युक्तम्। विच्छिन्नस्य चानेकस्य हस्त्यश्वादिकस्यानेकत्र वृत्तिर्न स्याद्यत्रैव ह्येकं तत्रैवापरमिति कथं तयोर्विच्छेद इष्यते। कथं वा तदेकं यत्प्राप्तं च ताभ्यां न च प्राप्तमन्तराले तच्छून्यग्रहणात्। सूक्ष्माणां चौदकजन्तूनां स्थूलैः समानरूपाणामनीक्षणं न स्यात्।

यदि लक्षणभेदादेव द्रव्यान्तरत्वं कल्प्यते नान्यथा। तस्मादवश्यं परमाणुशो भेदः कल्पयितव्यः। स चैको न सिध्यति। तस्यासिद्धौ रूपादीनां चक्षुरादिविषयत्वमसिद्धमिति सिद्धं विज्ञप्तिमात्रं भवतीति। प्रमाणवशादस्तित्वं नास्तित्वं वा निर्धार्यते सर्वेषां च प्रमाणानां प्रत्यक्षं प्रमाणं गरिष्ठमित्यसत्यर्थे कथमियं बुद्धिर्भवति प्रत्यक्षमिति।

प्रत्यक्षबुद्धिः स्वप्नादौ यथा

विनाप्यर्थेनेति पूर्वमेव ज्ञापितं।

स च यदा तदा।

न सोऽर्थो दृश्यते तस्य प्रत्यक्षत्वं कथं मतं ॥१६॥

यदा च सा प्रत्यक्षबुद्धिर्भवतोदं मे प्रत्यक्षमिति तदा न सोऽर्थो दृश्यते मनोविज्ञानेनैव परिच्छेदाच्चक्षुर्विज्ञानस्य च तदा निरुद्धत्वादिति । कथं तस्य प्रत्यक्षत्वमिष्टं। विशेषेण तु क्षणिकस्य विषय[6a] स्य **तदिदानीं** निरुद्धमेव तद्रूपं रसादिकं वा। नाननुभूतं मनोविज्ञानेन स्मर्यत इत्यवश्यमर्थानुभवेन भवितव्यं तच्च दर्शनमित्येवं तद्विषयस्य रूपादेः प्रत्यक्षत्वं मतं। असिद्धमिदमनुभूतस्यार्थस्य स्मरणं भवतीति। यस्मात्।

उक्तं यथा तदाभासा विज्ञप्तिः

विनाप्यर्थेन यथार्थाभासा चक्षुर्विज्ञानादिका विज्ञप्तिरुत्पद्यते तथोक्तम्।

स्मरणं ततः ।

ततो हि विज्ञप्तेः स्मृतिसंप्रयुक्ता तत्प्रतिभासैव रूपादिविकल्पिका मनोविज्ञप्तिरुत्पद्यत इति न स्मृत्युत्पादादर्थानुभवः सिध्यति। यदि यथा स्वप्ने विज्ञप्तिरभूतार्थविषया तथा जाग्रतोऽपि स्यात्तथैव तदभावं लोकः स्वयमवगच्छेत्। न चैवं भवति। तस्मान्न स्वप्न इवार्थोपलब्धिः सर्वा निरर्थिका। इदमज्ञापकं। यस्मात्।

स्वप्नदृग्विषयाभावं नाप्रबुद्धो ऽवगच्छति ॥१७॥

एवं वितथविकल्पाभ्यासवासनानिद्रया प्रसुप्तो लोकः स्वप्न इवाभूतमर्थं पश्यन्न प्रबुद्धस्तदभावं यथावन्नावगच्छति। यदा तु तत्प्रतिपक्षलोकोत्तरनिर्विकल्पज्ञानलाभात्प्रबुद्धो भवति तदा तत्पृष्ठलब्धशुद्धलौकिकज्ञानसंमुखीभावाद्विषयाभावं यथावदवगच्छतीति समानमेतत्॥ यदि स्वसंतानपरिणामविशेषादेव सत्वानामर्थप्रतिभासा विज्ञप्तय उत्पद्यन्ते नार्थविशे[6b] षात्। तदा य एष पापकल्याणमित्रसंपर्कात्सदसद्धर्मश्रवणाच्च विज्ञप्तिनियमः सत्त्वानां स कथं सिध्यति असति सदसत्संपर्के तद्देशनायां च।

अन्योन्याधिपतित्वेन विज्ञप्तिनियमो मिथः।

सर्वेषां हि सत्त्वानामन्योन्यविज्ञप्त्याधिपत्येन मिथो विज्ञप्तेर्नियमो भवति यथायोगं। मिथ इति परस्परतः। अतः संतानान्तरविज्ञप्तिविशेषात्संतानान्तरे विज्ञप्तिविशेष उत्पद्यते नार्थविशेषात्। यदि यथा स्वप्ने निरर्थिका विज्ञप्तिरेवं जाग्रतो ऽपि स्यात्कस्मात्कुशलाकुशलसमुदाचारे सुप्तासुप्तयोस्तुल्यं फलमिष्टानिष्टमायत्यां न भवति। यस्मात्।

मिद्धेनोपहतं चित्तं स्वप्ने तेनासमं फलं ॥१८॥

इदमत्र कारणं न त्वर्थसद्भावः ॥ यदि विज्ञप्तिमात्रमेवेदं न कस्यचित्कायो ऽस्ति न वाक्। कथमुपक्रम्यमाणानामौरभ्रिकादिभिरुरभ्रादीनां मरणं भवति। अतत्कृते वा तन्मरणे कथमौरभ्रिकादीनां प्राणातिपातावद्येन योगो भवति।

मरणं परविज्ञप्तिविशेषाद्विक्रिया यथा।
स्मृतिलोपादिकान्येषां पिशाचादिमनोवशात् ॥१९॥

यथा हि पिशाचादिमनोवशादन्येषां स्मृतिलोपस्वप्नदर्शनभूतग्रहावेशविकारा भवन्ति। ऋद्धिवन्मनोवशाच्च। यथा सारणस्यार्यमहाकात्यायनाधिष्ठानात्स्वप्नदर्शनं। आरण्यकर्षिमनःप्रदोषाच्च वेमचित्र[7a] पराजयः। तथा परविज्ञप्तिविशेषाधिपत्यात्परेषां जीवितेन्द्रियविरोधिनी काचिद्विक्रियोत्पद्यते यया सभागसंततिविच्छेदाख्यं मरणं भवतीति वेदितव्यं ॥

कथं वा दण्डकारण्यशून्यत्वमृषिकोपतः।

यदि परविज्ञप्तिविशेषाधिपत्यात्सत्वानां मरणं नेष्यते। मनोदण्डस्य हि महासावद्यत्वं साधयता भगवतोपालिर्गृहपतिः पृष्टः। कच्चित्ते गृहपते श्रुतं केन तानि दण्डकारण्यानि मातङ्गारण्यानि कलिङ्गारण्यानि शून्यानि मेध्यीभूतानि। तेनोक्तं। श्रुतं मे भो गौतम ऋषीणां मनःप्रदोषेणेति।

मनोदण्डो महावद्यः कथं वा तेन सिध्यति ॥२०॥

यद्येवं कल्प्यते। तदभिप्रसन्नैरमानुषैस्तद्वासिनः सत्त्वा उत्सादिता न त्वृषीणां मनःप्रदोषान्मृता इत्येवं सति कथं तेन कर्मणा मनोदण्डः कायवाग्दण्डाभ्यां महावद्यतमः सिद्धो भवति। तन्मनःप्रदोषमात्रेण तावतां सत्त्वानां मरणात्सिध्यति ॥ यदि विज्ञप्तिमात्रमेवेदं परचित्तविदः किं परचित्तं जानन्त्यथ न। किंचातः। यदि न जानन्ति कथं परचित्तविदो भवन्ति। अथ जानन्ति।

परचित्तविदां ज्ञानमयथार्थं कथं यथा।
स्वचित्तज्ञानं

तदपि कथमयथार्थं।

अज्ञानाद्यथा बुद्धस्य गोचरः ॥२१॥

यथा तन्निरभिलाप्येनात्मना[7b] बुद्धानां गोचरः। तथा तदज्ञानात्तदुभयं न

यथार्थं वितथप्रतिभासतया ग्राह्यग्राहकविकल्पस्याप्रहीणत्वात्। अनन्तविनिश्चय-प्रभेदगाधगाम्भीर्यायां विज्ञप्तिमात्रतायां।

विज्ञप्तिमात्रतासिद्धिः स्वशक्तिसदृशी मया।
कृतेयं सर्वथा सा तु न चिन्त्या

सर्वप्रकारा तु सा मादृशैश्चिन्तयितुं न शक्यते। तर्काविषयत्वात्। कस्य पुनः सा सर्वथा गोचर इत्याह।

बुद्धगोचरः ॥२२॥

बुद्धानां हि सा भगवतां सर्वप्रकारं गोचरः सर्वाकारसर्वज्ञेयज्ञानाविघातादिति॥

विंशतिका विज्ञप्तिमात्रतासिद्धिः।
कृतिरियमाचार्यवसुबन्धोः।

अथ त्रिंशिकाविज्ञप्तिकारिकाः

आत्मधर्मोपचारो हि विविधो यः प्रवर्तते।
विज्ञानपरिणामेऽसौ परिणामः स च त्रिधा ॥१॥
विपाको मननाख्यश्च विज्ञप्तिर्विषयस्य च।
तत्रालयाख्यं विज्ञानं विपाकः सर्वबीजकम् ॥२॥
असंविदितकोपादिस्थानविज्ञप्तिकं च तत्।
सदा स्पर्शमनस्कारवित्संज्ञाचेतनान्वितम् ॥३॥
उपेक्षा वेदना तत्रानिवृताव्याकृतं च तत्।
तथा स्पर्शादयस्तच्च वर्तते स्रोतसौघवत् ॥४॥
तस्य व्यावृतिरर्हत्वे तदाश्रित्य प्रवर्तते।
तदालम्बं मनोनाम विज्ञानं मननात्मकम् ॥५॥
क्लेशैश्चतुर्भिः सहितं निवृताव्याकृतैः सदा।
आत्मदृष्ट्यात्ममोहात्ममानात्मस्नेहसंज्ञितैः ॥६॥
यत्रजस्तन्मयैरन्यैः स्पर्शाद्यैश्चार्हतो न तत्।
न निरोधसमापत्तौ मार्गे लोकोत्तरे न च ॥७॥
द्वितीयः परिणामोऽयं तृतीयः षड्विधस्य या।
विषयस्योपलब्धिः सा कुशलाकुशलाद्वया ॥८॥
सर्वत्रगैर्विनियतैः कुशलैश्चैतसैरसौ।
संप्रयुक्ता तथा क्लेशैरुपक्लेशैस्त्रिवेदना ॥९॥
आद्याः स्पर्शादयश्छन्दाधिमोक्षस्मृतयः सह।
समाधिधीभ्यां नियताः श्रद्धाथ ह्रीरपत्रपा ॥१०॥
अलोभादि त्रयं वीर्यं प्रश्रब्धिः साप्रमादिका।
अहिंसा कुशलाः क्लेशा रागप्रतिघमूढयः ॥११॥
मानदृग्विचिकित्साश्च क्रोधोपनहने पुनः।
म्रक्षः प्रदाश ईर्ष्याथ मात्सर्यं सह मायया ॥१२॥
शाठ्यं मदोऽविहिंसाह्रीरत्रपा स्त्यानमुद्धवः।
आश्रद्धमथ कौसीद्यं प्रमादो मुषिता स्मृतिः ॥१३॥
विक्षेपोऽसंप्रजन्यं च कौकृत्यं मिद्धमेव च।
वितर्कश्च विचारश्चेत्युपक्लेशा द्वये द्विधा ॥१४॥
पञ्चानां मूलविज्ञाने यथाप्रत्ययमुद्भवः।
विज्ञानानां सह न वा तरङ्गाणां यथा जले ॥१५॥

मनोविज्ञानसंभूतिः सर्वदासंज्ञिकादृते ।
समापत्तिद्वयान्मिद्धान्मूर्छनादप्यचित्तकात् ॥१६॥
विज्ञानपरिणामोऽयं विकल्पो यद्विकल्प्यते ।
तेन तन्नास्ति तेनेदं सर्वं विज्ञप्तिमात्रकम् ॥१७॥
सर्वबीजं हि विज्ञानं परिणामस्तथा तथा ।
यात्यन्योन्यवशाद् येन विकल्पः स स जायते ॥१८॥
कर्मणो वासना ग्राहद्वयवासनया सह ।
क्षीणे पूर्वविपाकेऽन्यद्विपाकं जनयन्ति तत् ॥१६॥
येन येन विकल्पेन यद्यद् वस्तु विकल्प्यते ।
परिकल्पित एवासौ स्वभावो न स विद्यते ॥२०॥
परतन्त्रस्वभावस्तु विकल्पः प्रत्ययोद्भवः ।
निष्पन्नस्तस्य पूर्वेण सदा रहितता तु या ॥२१॥
अत एव स नैवान्यो नानन्यः परतन्त्रतः ।
अनित्यतादिवद् वाच्यो नादृष्टेऽस्मिन् स दृश्यते ॥२२।
त्रिविधस्य स्वभावस्य त्रिविधां निःस्वभावताम् ।
संधाय सर्वधर्माणां देशिता निःस्वभावता ॥२३॥
प्रथमो लक्षणेनैव निःस्वभावोऽपरः पुनः ।
न स्वयंभाव एतस्येत्यपरा निःस्वभावता ॥ २४ ॥
धर्माणां परमार्थश्च स यतस्तथतापि सः ।
सर्वकालं तथाभावात् सैव विज्ञप्तिमात्रता ॥ २५ ॥
यावद्विज्ञप्तिमात्रत्वे विज्ञानं नावतिष्ठति ।
ग्राहद्वयस्यानुशयस्तावन्न विनिवर्तते ॥ २६ ॥
विज्ञप्तिमात्रमेवेदमित्यपि ह्युपलम्भतः ।
स्थापयन्नग्रतः किंचित् तन्मात्रे नावतिष्ठते ॥ २७ ॥
यदालम्बनं विज्ञानं नैवोपलभते तदा ।
स्थितं विज्ञानमात्रत्वे ग्राह्याभावे तदग्रहात् ॥ २८ ॥
अचित्तोऽनुपलम्भोऽसौ ज्ञानं लोकोत्तरं च तत् ।
आश्रयस्य परावृत्तिर्द्विधा दौष्ठुल्यहानितः ॥ २६ ॥
स एवानास्रवो धातुरचिन्त्यः कुशलो ध्रुवः ।
सुखो विमुक्तिकायोऽसौ धर्माख्योऽयं महामुनेः ॥ ३० ॥

त्रिंशिकाविज्ञप्तिकारिकाः समाप्ताः ॥
कृतिरियमाचार्यवसुबन्धोः ।

मध्यान्तविभागभाष्यम्

लक्षणपरिच्छेदः प्रथमः

[1b] ओं नमो बुद्धाय

शास्त्रस्यास्य प्रणेतारमभ्यर्ह्य सुगतात्मजम् ।
वक्तारं चास्मदादिभ्यो यतिष्येऽर्थविवेचने ॥

१. शास्त्रशरीरम्

तत्रादितः शास्त्रशरीरं व्यवस्थाप्यते—

लक्षणं ह्यावृतिस्तत्त्वं प्रतिपक्षस्य भावना ।
तत्रावस्था फलप्राप्तिर्यानानुत्तर्यमेव च ॥१॥

इत्येते सप्तार्थाश्चास्मिन् शास्त्र उपदिश्यन्ते । यदुत लक्षणमावरणं तत्त्वं प्रतिपक्षस्य भावना तस्यामेव च प्रतिपक्षभावनायामवस्था फलप्राप्तिर्यानानुत्तर्यं च सप्तमोऽर्थः ॥

२. शून्यतालक्षणम्

तत्र लक्षणमारभ्याह—

अभूतपरिकल्पोऽस्ति द्वयं तत्र न विद्यते ।
शून्यता विद्यते त्वत्र तस्यामपि स विद्यते ॥१॥

तत्राभूतपरिकल्पो ग्राह्यग्राहकविकल्पः । द्वयं ग्राह्यं ग्राहकं च । शून्यता तस्याभूतपरिकल्पस्य ग्राह्यग्राहकभावेन विरहितता । तस्यामपि स विद्यत इत्यभूतपरिकल्पः । एवं यद्यत्र नास्ति तत्तेन शून्यमिति यथाभूतं समनुपश्यति । यत्पुनरत्रावशिष्टं भवति तत्सदिहास्तीति यथाभूतं प्रजानातीत्यविपरीतं शून्यतालक्षणमुद्भावितं भवति ॥

न शून्यं नापि चाशून्यं तस्मात् सर्वं विधीयते ।
सत्त्वादसत्त्वात् सत्त्वाच्च मध्यमाप्रतिपच्च सा ॥२॥

न शून्यं शून्यतया चाभूतपरिकल्पेन वा न वा शून्यद्वयेन ग्राह्येण ग्राहकेण च, "सर्वं सं[2ª]स्कृतं चाभूतपरिकल्पाख्यमसंस्कृतं च शून्यताख्यं" विधीयते निर्दिश्यते। सत्त्वादभूतपरिकल्पस्य, असत्त्वाद्द्वयस्य, सत्त्वाच्च शून्यताया अभूतपरिकल्पे, तस्यां चाभूतपरिकल्पस्य, सा च मध्यमाप्रतिपद् यत् सर्वं नैकान्तेन शून्यं नैकान्तेनाशून्यम्। एवमयं पाठः प्रज्ञापारमितादिष्वनुलोमितो भवति—सर्वमिदं न शून्यं नापि चाशून्यमिति ॥

एवमभूतपरिकल्पस्य सल्लक्षणमसल्लक्षणं च ख्यापयित्वा स्वलक्षणं ख्यापयति—

अर्थसत्त्वात्मविज्ञप्तिप्रतिभासं प्रजायते।
विज्ञानं नास्ति चास्यार्थस्तदभावात्तदप्यसत् ॥३॥

तत्रार्थप्रतिभासं यद्रूपादिभावेन प्रतिभासते। सत्त्वप्रतिभासं यत्पञ्चेन्द्रियत्वेन स्वपरसन्तानयोः। आत्मप्रतिभासं क्लिष्टं मन आत्ममोहादिसंप्रयोगात्। विज्ञप्तिप्रतिभासं षड्विज्ञानानि। नास्ति चास्यार्थ इत्यर्थसत्त्वप्रतिभासस्यानाकारत्वात्, आत्मविज्ञप्तिप्रतिभासस्य च वितथप्रतिभासत्वात्। तदभावात्तदप्यसदिति यत्तद्ग्राह्यं रूपादि पञ्चेन्द्रियं मनः षड्विज्ञानसंज्ञकं चतुर्विधं, तस्य ग्राह्यस्यार्थस्याभावात् तदपि ग्राहकं विज्ञानमसत् ॥

अभूतपरिकल्पत्वं सिद्धमस्य भवत्यतः।
न तथा सर्वथा[2ᵇ]भावात्

यस्मान्न तथाऽस्य भावो यथा प्रतिभास उत्पद्यते। न च सर्वथाऽभावो भ्रान्तिमात्रस्योत्पादात् ॥

किमर्थं पुनस्तस्याभाव एव नेष्यते। यस्मात्—

तत्क्षयान्मुक्तिरिष्यते ॥४॥

अन्यथा न बन्धो न मोक्षः प्रसिध्येदिति संक्लेशव्यवदानापवाददोषः स्यात् ॥

एवमभूतपरिकल्पस्य स्वलक्षणं ख्यापयित्वा संग्रहलक्षणं ख्यापयति, अभूतपरिकल्पमात्रे सति यथा त्रयाणां स्वभावानां संग्रहो भवति—

कल्पितः परतन्त्रश्च परिनिष्पन्न एव च।
अर्थादभूतकल्पाच्च द्वयाभावाच्च देशितः ॥५॥

अर्थः परिकल्पितः स्वभावः। अभूतपरिकल्पः परतन्त्रः स्वभावः। ग्राह्यग्राहकाभावः परिनिष्पन्नः स्वभावः ॥

इदानीं तस्मिन्नेवाभूतपरिकल्पेऽसल्लक्षणानुप्रवेशोपायलक्षणं परिदीपयति—

उपलब्धिं समाश्रित्य नोपलब्धिः प्रजायते ।
नोपलब्धिं समाश्रित्य नोपलब्धिः प्रजायते ॥६॥

विज्ञप्तिमात्रोपलब्धिं निश्रित्यार्थानुपलब्धिर्जायते । अर्थानुपलब्धिं निश्रित्य विज्ञप्तिमात्रस्याप्यनुपलब्धिर्जायते। एवमसल्लक्षणं ग्राह्यग्राहकयोः प्रविशति ॥

उपलब्धेस्ततः सिद्धा नोपलब्धिस्वभावता ।

उपलभ्यार्थाभावे उपलब्ध्ययोगात् ॥

तस्माच्च समता ज्ञेया नो[3a]पलम्भोपलम्भयोः ॥७॥

उपलब्धेरुपलब्धित्वेनासिद्धत्वात् अभूतार्थप्रतिभासतया तूपलब्धिरित्युच्यतेऽनुपलब्धिस्वभावापि सती ॥

तस्यैवेदानीमभूतपरिकल्पस्य प्रभेदलक्षणं ख्यापयति—

अभूतपरिकल्पश्च चित्तचैत्तास्त्रिधातुकाः ।

कामरूपारूप्यावचरभेदेन ॥

पर्यायलक्षणं च ख्यापयति—

तत्रार्थदृष्टिर्विज्ञानं तद्विशेषे तु चैतसाः ॥८॥

तत्रार्थमात्रे दृष्टिर्विज्ञानम् । अर्थविशेषे दृष्टिश्चैतसा वेदनादयः ॥

प्रवृत्तिलक्षणं च ख्यापयति—

एकं प्रत्ययविज्ञानं द्वितीयं चौपभोगिकम् ।
उपभोगपरिच्छेदप्रेरकास्तत्र चैतसाः ॥९॥

आलयविज्ञानमन्येषां विज्ञानानां प्रत्ययत्वात्प्रत्ययविज्ञानम् । तत्प्रत्ययं प्रवृत्तिविज्ञानमौपभोगिकम् । उपभोगो वेदना । परिच्छेदः संज्ञा । प्रेरकाः संस्कारा विज्ञानस्य चेतनामनस्कारादयः ॥

संक्लेशलक्षणं ख्यापयति—

छादनाद्रोपणाच्चैव नयनात्संपरिग्रहात् ।
पूरणात् त्रिपरिच्छेदादुपभोगाच्च कर्षणात् ॥१०॥
निबन्धनादाभिमख्याद् दुःखनात् क्लिश्यते जगत् ।

तत्र छादनादविद्यया यथाभूतदर्शनविबन्धनात् । रोपणात् संस्कारैर्विज्ञाने कर्मवासनायाः प्रतिष्ठापनात् । नयनाद् विज्ञानेनोप[3b]पत्तिस्थानसंप्रापणात् । संपरिग्रहान्नामरूपेणात्मभावस्य । पूरणात् षडायतनेन । त्रिपरिच्छेदात् स्पर्शेन । उपभोगाद्वेदनया । कर्षणात् तृष्णया कर्माक्षिप्तस्य पुनर्भवस्य निबन्धनादुपादानैर्विज्ञानस्योत्पत्त्यनुकूलेषु कामादिषु । आभिमुख्याद् भवेन कृतस्य कर्मणः पुनर्भवे विपाकदानायाभिमुखीकरणात् । दुःखनाज्जात्या जरामरणेन च, परिक्लिश्यते जगत् ॥

सोऽयम्—

त्रेधा द्वेधा च संक्लेशः सप्तधाऽभूतकल्पनात् ॥११॥

त्रेधा संक्लेशः क्लेशसंक्लेशः कर्मसंक्लेशो जन्मसंक्लेशश्च । तत्र क्लेशसंक्लेशोऽविद्यातृष्णोपादानानि । कर्मसंक्लेशः संस्कारा भवश्च । जन्मसंक्लेशः शेषाण्यङ्गानि । द्वेधा संक्लेशो हेतुसंक्लेशः फलसंक्लेशश्च । तत्र हेतुसंक्लेशः क्लेशकर्मस्वभावैरङ्गैः । फलसंक्लेशश्च शेषैः । सप्तधा संक्लेशः सप्तविधो हेतुः, विपर्यासहेतुराक्षेपहेतुरुपनयहेतुः परिग्रहहेतुरुपभोगहेतुराकर्षणहेतुरुद्वेगहेतुश्च । तत्र विपर्यासहेतुरविद्या । आक्षेपहेतुः संस्काराः । उपनयहेतुर्विज्ञानम् । परिग्रहहेतुर्नामरूपषडायतने । उपभोगहेतुः स्पर्शवेदने । आकर्षणहेतुस्तृष्णोपादानभवाः । [4a]उद्वेगहेतुर्जातिजरामरणानि । सर्वश्चैष संक्लेशोऽभूतपरिकल्पात्प्रवर्तत इति । पिण्डार्थः पुनरभूतपरिकल्पस्य नवविधं लक्षणं परिदीपितं भवति । सल्लक्षणमसल्लक्षणं स्वलक्षणं संग्रहलक्षणमसल्लक्षणानुप्रवेशोपायलक्षणं प्रभेदलक्षणं पर्यायलक्षणं प्रवृत्तिलक्षणं संक्लेशलक्षणं च ॥

एवमभूतपरिकल्पं ख्यापयित्वा यथा शून्यता विज्ञेया तन्निर्दिशति—

लक्षणं चाथ पर्यायस्तदर्थो भेद एव च ।
साधनं चेति विज्ञेयं शून्यतायाः समासतः ॥१२॥

कथं लक्षणं विज्ञेयम्—

द्वयाभावो ह्यभावस्य भावः शून्यस्य लक्षणम् ।

द्वय [स्य] ग्राह्यग्राहकस्याभावः । तस्य चाभावस्य भावः । शून्यताया लक्षणमित्यभावस्वभावलक्षणत्वं शून्यतायाः परिदीपितं भवति ॥

यश्चासौ तदभावस्वभावः सः—

न भावो नापि वाभावः

कथं न भावो यस्माद्द्वयस्याभावः। कथं नाभावो यस्माद्द्वयाभावस्य भावः। एतच्च शून्यताया लक्षणम् ॥

तस्मादभूतपरिकल्पात्—

न पृथक्त्वैकलक्षणम् ॥१३॥

पृथक्त्वे सति धर्मादन्या धर्मतेति न युज्यते, अनित्यतादुःखतावत्। एकत्वे सति विशुद्ध्यालम्बनं ज्ञानं न स्यात् सामान्यलक्षणं च। एतेन तत्त्वान्यत्वविनिर्मुक्तं लक्षणं परिदीपितं भव[4b]ति ॥

३. शून्यताव्यवस्थानम्

कथं पर्यायो विज्ञेयः—

तथता भूतकोटिश्चानिमित्तं परमार्थता।
धर्मधातुश्च पर्यायाः शून्यतायाः समासतः ॥१४॥

कथं पर्यायार्थो विज्ञेयः—

अनन्यथाविपर्यासतन्निरोधार्यगोचरैः।
हेतुत्वाच्चार्यधर्माणां पर्यायार्थो यथाक्रमम् ॥१५॥

अनन्यथार्थेन तथता नित्यं तथैवेति कृत्वा। अविपर्यासार्थेन भूतकोटिर्विपर्यासावस्तुत्वात्। निमित्तनिरोधार्थेनानिमित्तं सर्वनिमित्ताभावात्। आर्यज्ञानगोचरत्वात्परमार्थः परमज्ञानविषयत्वात्। आर्यधर्महेतुत्वाद् धर्मधातुरार्यधर्माणां तदालम्बनप्रभवत्वात्। हेत्वर्थो ह्यत्र धात्वर्थः ॥

कथं शून्यतायाः प्रभेदो ज्ञेयः—

संक्लिष्टा च विशुद्धा च

इत्यस्याः प्रभेदः ॥

कस्यामवस्थायां संक्लिष्टा, कस्यां विशुद्धा—

समला निर्मला च सा।

यदा सह मलेन वर्तते तदा संक्लिष्टा। यदा प्रहीणमला तदा विशुद्धा ॥

यदि समला भूत्वा निर्मला भवति, कथं विकारधर्मिणीत्वादनित्या न भवति। यस्मादस्याः—

अब्धातुकनकाकाशशुद्धिवच्छुद्धिरिष्यते ॥१६॥

आगन्तुकमलापगमान्न तु तस्याः स्वभावान्यता।

अयमपरः प्रभेदः। षोडशविधा शून्यता। अध्यात्मशून्यता, बहिर्द्धाशून्यता, अध्यात्मबहिर्द्धाशून्यता, महाशून्यता, शून्यताशून्यता, परमार्थशून्यता, संस्कृतशून्यता, असंस्कृतशून्यता, अत्यन्तशून्यता, अनवराग्रशून्यता, अनवकारशून्यता, प्रकृतिशून्यता, लक्षणशून्यता, सर्वधर्मशून्यता, अभावशून्यता, अभावस्वभावशून्यता। सैषा समासतो वेदितव्या।

भोक्तृभोजनतद्देहप्रतिष्ठावस्तुशून्यता।
तच्च येन यथा दृष्टं यदर्थं तस्य शून्यता ॥१७॥

तत्र भोक्तृशून्यता आध्यात्मिकान्यायतनान्यारभ्य। भोजनशून्यता बाह्यानि। तद्देहस्तयोर्भोक्तृभोजनयोर्यदधिष्ठानं शरीरं तस्य शून्यताध्यात्मबहिर्द्धाशून्यतेत्युच्यते। प्रतिष्ठावस्तु भाजनलोकस्तस्य विस्तीर्णत्वाच्छून्यता महाशून्यतेत्युच्यते। तच्चाध्यात्मिकायतनादि येन शून्यं दृष्टं शून्यताज्ञानेन तस्य शून्यता शून्यताशून्यता। यथा च दृष्टं परमार्थाकारेण तस्य शून्यता परमार्थशून्यता। यदर्थं च बोधिसत्त्वः प्रपद्यते तस्य च शून्यता ॥
किमर्थं च प्र(प)द्यते—

शुभद्वयस्य प्राप्त्यर्थं

कुशलस्य संस्कृतस्यासंस्कृतस्य च ॥

सदा सत्त्वहिताय च।

अत्यन्तसत्त्वहितार्थम् ॥

संसारात्यजनार्थं च

अनवराग्रस्य हि संसार[5b]स्य शून्यतामपश्यन् खिन्नः संसारं परित्यजेत् ।।

कुशलस्याक्षयाय च ।।१८।।

निरुपधिशेषनिर्वाणेऽपि यन्नावकिरति नोत्सृजति तस्य शून्यतानवकारशून्यतेत्युच्यते ।।

गोत्रस्य च विशुद्ध्यर्थं

गोत्रं हि प्रकृतिः स्वाभाविकत्वात् ।।

लक्षणव्यञ्जनाप्तये ।

महापुरुषलक्षणानां सानुव्यञ्जनानां प्राप्तये ।।

शुद्धये बु[द्ध]धर्माणां बोधिसत्त्वः प्रपद्यते ।।१९।।

बलवैशारद्यावेणिकादीनाम् । एवं तावच्चतुर्दशानां शून्यतानां व्यवस्थानं वेदितव्यम् ।।

का पुनरत्र शून्यता—

पुद्गलस्याथ धर्माणामभावः शून्यतात्र हि ।
तदभावस्य सद्भावस्तस्मिन् सा शून्यतापरा ।।२०।।

पुद्गलधर्माभावश्च शून्यता । तदभावस्य च सद्भावः । तस्मिन् यथोक्ते भोक्त्रादौ नान्या शून्यतेति शून्यतालक्षणख्यापनार्थं द्विविधामन्ते शून्यतां व्यवस्थापयति—अभावशून्यतामभावस्वभावशून्यतां च, पुद्गलधर्मसमारोपस्य तच्छून्यतापवादस्य च परिहारार्थं यथाक्रमम् । एवं शून्यतायाः प्रभेदो विज्ञेयः ।।

कथं साधनं विज्ञेयम्—

संक्लिष्टा चेद्भवेन्नासौ मुक्ताः स्युः सर्वदेहिनः ।
विशुद्धा चेद्भवेन्नासौ व्यायामो निष्फलो भवेत् ।।२१।।

यदि धर्माणां शून्यता आगन्तुकैरुपक्लेशैरनुत्पन्नेऽपि प्रतिपक्षे न संक्लिष्टा भवेत् संक्लेशाभावादयत्नत एव मुक्ताः सर्वसत्त्वा भवेयुः। अथोत्पन्नेऽपि प्रतिपक्षे न शुद्धा भवेत्, मोक्षार्थमारम्भो निष्फलो भवेत् ॥

एवं च कृत्वा—

[6a] न क्लिष्टा नापि चाक्लिष्टा शुद्धाशुद्धा न चैव सा।

कथं न क्लिष्टा नापि चाशुद्धा, प्रकृत्यैव—

प्रभास्वरत्वाच्चित्तस्य

कथं नाक्लिष्टा न शुद्धा—

क्लेशस्यागन्तुकत्वतः ॥२२॥

एवं शून्यताया उद्दिष्टः प्रभेदः साधितो भवति ॥

४. शून्यतापिण्डार्थः

तत्र शून्यतायाः पिण्डार्थो लक्षणतो व्यवस्थानतश्च वेदितव्यः। तत्र लक्षणतः, अभावलक्षणतो भावलक्षणतश्च। भावलक्षणं पुनर्भावा [भा] वविनिर्मुक्तलक्षणतश्च तत्त्वान्यत्वविनिर्मुक्तलक्षणतश्च। व्यवस्थानं पुनः पर्यायादिव्यवस्थानतो वेदितव्यम्। तत्रैतया चतुष्प्रकारदेशनया शून्यतायाः स्वलक्षणं कर्मलक्षणं संक्लेशव्यवदानलक्षणं युक्तिलक्षणं चोद्भावितं भवति—

विकल्पत्रासकौसीद्यविचिकित्सोपशान्तये ॥

॥ मध्यान्तविभागभाष्ये लक्षणपरिच्छेदः प्रथमः ॥

आवरणपरिच्छेदो द्वितीयः

आवरणमधिकृत्याह—

व्यापिप्रादेशिकोद्रिक्तं समादानविवर्जनम् ।
द्वयावरणमाख्यातम्

तत्र व्यापि क्लेशज्ञेयावरणं बोधिसत्त्वगोत्रकाणां साकल्यात् । प्रादेशिकं क्लेशावरणं श्रावकादिगोत्रकाणाम् । उद्रिक्तं तेषामेव रागादिचरितानाम् । समं समभागचरितानाम् । संसारादानत्यागावरणं बोधिसत्त्वगोत्रकाणामप्रतिष्ठितनिर्वाणावरणादित्ये[त]द्यथायोगमुभयेषा[6b]मावर[ण]माख्यातं बोधिसत्त्वगोत्रकाणां श्रावकादिगोत्रकाणां च ॥

पुनर्—

नवधा क्लेशलक्षणम् ॥१॥

संयोजनान्यावरणम्

नव संयोजनानि क्लेशावरणम् ॥
कस्यैतस्यावरणम्—

उद्वेगसमुपेक्षयोः ।

तत्त्वदृष्टेश्च

अनुनयसंयोजनं संवेगस्यावरणम् । प्रतिघसंयोजनमुपेक्षायाः । तेन हि प्रतिकूलमपि प्रतिघवस्तूपेक्षितुं न शक्नोति । शेषाणि तत्त्वदर्शनस्यावरणम् ॥
कथं कृत्वा ? तानि हि यथाक्रमम्—

सत्कायदृष्टेस्तद्वस्तुनोऽपि च ॥२॥

निरोधमार्गरत्नेषु लाभसत्कार एव च ।
संलेखस्य परिज्ञाने

संयोजनान्यवरणं भवन्ति। मानसंयोजनं हि सत्कायदृष्टिपरिज्ञाने भवत्यावरणम्, अभिसमयकाले सान्तरव्यन्तरास्मिमानसमुदाचारवशेन तदप्रहाणात्। अविद्यासंयोजनं सत्कायदृष्टिवस्तुपरिज्ञाने, तेनोपादानस्कन्धापरिज्ञानात्। दृष्टिसंयोजनं निरोधसत्यपरिज्ञाने, सत्कायान्तग्राहदृष्टि[भ्यां त]दुत्त्रासात् मिथ्यादृष्टचा चापवादात्। परामर्शसंयोजनं मार्गसत्यपरिज्ञाने, अन्यथाग्रशुद्धिपरामर्शनात्। विचिकित्सासंयोजनं रत्नत्रयपरिज्ञाने, तद्गुणानभिश्रद्धानात्। ईर्ष्यासंयोजनं लाभस-[7a]त्कारपरिज्ञाने तद्दोषादर्शनात्। मात्सर्यसंयोजनं संलेखपरिज्ञाने परिष्काराध्यवसानात्॥

शुभादौ दशधापरम् ॥३॥

अपरं पुन[रा]वरणं दशविधे शुभादौ वेदितव्यम्। किं तदावरणम्, के च शुभादय :—

अप्रयोगोऽनायतनेऽयोगविहितश्च यः।
नोत्पत्तिरमनस्कारः सम्भारस्याप्रपूर्णता ॥४॥

गोत्रमित्रस्य वैधुर्यं चित्तस्य परिखेदिता।
प्रतिपत्तेश्च वैधुर्यं कुदुष्टजनवासता ॥५॥

दौष्ठुल्यमवशिष्टत्वं त्रयात्प्रज्ञाविपक्वता ।
प्रकृत्या चैव दौष्ठुल्यं कौसीद्यं च प्रमादिता ॥६॥

सक्तिर्भवे च भोगे च लीनचित्तत्वमेव च।
अश्रद्धानधिमुक्तिश्च यथारुतविचारणम् ॥७॥

सद्धर्मेऽगौरवं लाभे गुरुताकृपता तथा ।
श्रुतव्यसनमल्पत्वं समाध्यपरिकर्मिता ॥८॥

एतदावरणम् ॥

के शुभादयः—

शुभं बोधिः समादानं धीमत्ताभ्रान्त्यनावृती।
नत्यत्रासोऽमत्सरित्वं वशित्वं च शुभादयः ॥९॥

एषां शुभादीनां कस्य कत्यावरणानि ज्ञेयानीत्याह—

त्रीणि त्रीणि च एतेषां ज्ञेयान्यावरणानि हि ।

कुशलस्य त्रीण्यावरणानि—अप्रयो[गो]ऽनायतनप्रयोगोऽयोनिशः प्रयोगश्च । बोधेस्त्रीणि कुशलस्यानुत्पत्तिर[7b]मनसिकरणम् अपरिपूर्णसम्भारता च । समादानं बोधिचित्तोत्पादः । तस्य त्रीणि—गोत्रवैधुर्यं कल्याणमित्रवैधुर्यं परिखेदचित्तता च । धीमत्त्वं बोधिसत्त्वता । तस्याः प्रज्ञाने त्रीण्यावरणानि—प्रतिपत्तिवैधुर्यं कुजनवासो दुष्टजनवासश्च । तत्र कुजनो मूर्खजनः, दुष्टजनः प्रतिहतः । अभ्रान्तेस्त्रीणि—विपर्यासदौष्ठुल्यं क्लेशाद्यावरणत्रयादन्यतमावशिष्टता विमुक्तिपरिपाचिन्याः प्रज्ञाया अपरिपक्वता च । आवरणप्रहाणमनावरणम् । तस्य त्रीणि—सहजदौष्ठुल्यं कौसीद्यं प्रमादश्च । परिणतेस्त्रीणि यैरन्यत्र चित्तं परिणमयति नानुत्तरस्यां सम्यक्संबोधौ—भवसक्तिर्भोगसक्तिर्लीनचित्तता च । अत्रासस्य त्रीणि—असम्भावना पुद्गलेऽ[न]धिमुक्तिर्धर्मे यथारुतविचारणार्थे । अमात्सर्यस्य त्रीणि—सद्धर्मेऽगौरवं, लाभसत्कारपूजायां गौरवम्, सत्त्वेष्वकारुण्यं च । वशित्वस्य त्रीणि, यैर्विभुत्वं न लभते—श्रुतव्यसनं धर्मव्य[सन]संवर्तनीयकर्मप्रसवनात्, अल्पश्रुत्वं, समाधेरपरिकर्मितत्वं च ॥

तत्पुनरेतदावरणं शुभादौ यत्रार्थे दश कारणानि तदर्थाधिकारेण वेदितव्यम् । दश[8a] कारणानि—उत्पत्तिकारणं तद्यथा चक्षुरादयश्चक्षुर्विज्ञानस्य । स्थितिकारणं तद्यथा चत्वार आहाराः सत्त्वानाम् । धृतिकारणं यद्यस्याधारभूतं तद्यथा भाजनलोकः सत्त्वलोकस्य । अभिव्यक्तिकारणं तद्यथा आलोको रूपस्य । विकारकारणं तद्यथा अग्न्यादयः पाक्यादीनाम् । विश्लेषकारणं तद्यथा दात्रादयश्छेद्यादीनाम् । परिणतिकारणं तद्यथा सुवर्णकारादयः सुवर्णादीनां कटकादिभावेन परिणतौ । संप्रत्ययकारणं तद्यथा धूमादयोऽग्न्यादीनाम् । संप्रत्यायनकारणं तद्यथा हेतुः प्रतिज्ञायाः । प्राप्तिकारणं तद्यथा मार्गादयो निर्वाणादीनाम् । एवमुत्पत्त्यावरणं शुभे द्रष्टव्यं तस्योत्पादनीयत्वात् । स्थित्यावरणं बोधौ तस्या अकोप्यत्वात् । धृत्यावरणं समादाने बोधिचित्तस्याधारभूतत्वात् । अभिव्यक्त्यावरणं धीमत्त्वे तस्य प्रकाशनीयत्वात् । विकारावरणमभ्रान्तौ [त]स्या भ्रान्तिपरिवृत्तित्वेन विकारत्वात् । विश्लेषावर[ण]मनावरणे तस्यावरणविसंयोगत्वात् । परिणत्यावरणं नतौ तस्या बोधौ चित्तपरिणतिलक्षणत्वात् । संप्रत्ययावरणमत्रासेऽसंप्रत्ययेन त्रसनात् । संप्रत्यायनावरणममत्सरित्वे धर्मामत्सरित्वेन परसं[8b]प्रत्यायनात् । प्राप्त्यावरणं वशित्वे तस्य विभुत्वप्राप्तिलक्षणत्वात् ॥

कारणं दशधोत्पत्तौ स्थितौ धृत्यां प्रकाशने ।
विकारविश्लेषनतिप्रत्ययप्रापणाप्तिषु ॥
चक्षुराहारभूदीपवह्न्यादिस्तदुदाहृतिः ।
दात्रशिल्पज्ञताधूमहेतुमार्गादयोऽपरे ॥

बोधिं प्राप्तुकामेनादित एव तावत् कुशलमूलमुत्पादयितव्यम्। ततः कुशलमूलबलाधानेन बोधिः प्राप्तव्या। तस्याः पुनः कुशलमूलोत्पत्तेर्बोधिचित्तं प्रतिष्ठा। तस्य बोधिचित्तस्य बोधिसत्त्व आश्रयः। तेन पुनरुत्पादितबोधिचित्तेन कुशलमूलबलाधानं प्राप्तेन बोधिसत्त्वेन विपर्यासं प्रहाय अविपर्यास उत्पादयितव्यः। ततो दर्शनमार्गे अविपर्यस्ते भावनामार्गे सर्वावरणानि प्रहातव्यानि। प्रहीणावरणेन पुनस्त्रीणि कुशलमूलानि अनुत्तरायां सम्यक्सम्बोधौ परिणामयितव्यानि। ततः परिणामनाबलाधानेन गम्भीरोदारधर्मदेशनासु नोत्त्रसितव्यम्। तथानुत्त्रस्तेन शासनधर्मेषु गुणदर्शिना परेषां ते धर्मा विस्तरेण संप्रकाशयितव्याः। ततः स बोधिसत्त्व एवं विचित्रगुणबलाधानप्राप्तः क्षिप्रमनुत्तरां सम्यक्संबोधिमनुप्राप्तवान्सर्वधर्मवशिताम् अनुप्राप्नोत्येषोऽनुक्रमः शुभादीनां॥

४. तत्त्वप्रवेशाद्यावरणम्

पक्ष्यपारमिताभूमिष्वन्यदावरणं पुनः ॥१०॥

बोधिपक्ष्येषु तावत्—

वस्त्वकौशलकौसीद्यं समाधेर्द्वयहीनता।
अरोपणाथ दौर्बल्यं दृष्टिदौष्ठुल्यदुष्टता ॥११॥

स्मृत्युपस्थानेषु वस्त्वकौशलमावरणम्। सम्यक्प्रहाणेषु कौसीद्यम्। ऋद्धिपादेषु समाधेर्द्वयहीनता अपारिपूर्या छन्दवीर्यचित्तमीमांसानामन्यतमवैकल्यात्, भावनया च प्रहाणसंस्कारवैकल्यात्। इन्द्रियेषु मोक्षभागीयानामरोपणम्। बलेषु तेषामेवेन्द्रियाणां दौर्बल्यं विपक्षव्यवकिरणात्। बोध्यङ्गेषु दृष्टिदोषस्तेषां दर्शनमार्गप्रभावितत्वात्। मार्गाङ्गेषु दौष्ठुल्यदोषस्तेषां भावनामार्गप्रभावितत्वात्॥

पारमितास्वावरणम्—

ऐश्वर्यस्याथ सुगतेः सत्त्वात्यागस्य चावृतिः।
हानिवृद्ध्योश्च दोषाणां गुणानामवतारणे ॥१२॥
विमोचनेऽक्षयत्वे च नैरन्तर्ये शुभस्य च।
नियतीकरणे धर्मसंभोगपरिपाचने ॥१३॥

अत्र दशानां पारमितानां यस्याः पारमिताया यत्फलं तदावरणेन तस्या आवरणमुद्भावितं भवति। तत्र दानपारमिताया ऐश्वर्याधिपत्यावरणमावरणम्। शीलपारमिताया सुगत्यावरणम्। क्षान्तिपारमितायाः सत्त्वा[9b]परित्यागावरणम्।

वीर्यपारमिताया दोषगुणहानिवृद्ध्यावरणम्। ध्यानपारमिताया विनेयावतारणावरणम्। प्रज्ञापारमिताया विमोचनावरणम्। उपायकौशल्यपारमिताया दानाद्यक्षयत्वावरणम्, बोधिपरिणामनया तदक्षयत्वात्। प्रणिधानपारमिताया: सर्वजन्मसु कुशलनैरन्तर्यप्रवृत्त्यावरणम्, प्रणिधानवशेन तदनुकूलोपपत्तिपरिग्रहात्। बलपारमिताया: तस्यैव कुशलस्य नियतीकरणावरणं प्रतिसंख्यानभावनाबलाभ्यां विपक्षानभिभवात्। ज्ञानपारमिताया आत्मपरयोर्धर्मसम्भोगपरिपाचनावरणमावरणमयथावत् श्रुतार्थावबोधात्॥

भूमिषु पुनर्यथाक्रमम्——

सर्वत्रगार्थे अग्रार्थे निष्यन्दाग्रार्थ एव च।
निष्परिग्रहतार्थे च सन्तानाभेद एव च॥१४॥

निःसंक्लेशविशुद्ध्यर्थे अनानात्वार्थ एव च।
अहीनानधिकार्थे च चतुर्द्धा वशिताश्रये॥१५॥

धर्मधातावविद्येयं ह्यक्लिष्टा दशधावृतिः।
दशभूमिविपक्षेण प्रतिपक्षास्तु भूमयः॥१६॥

धर्मधातौ दशविधे सर्वत्रगाद्यर्थे यदक्लिष्टमज्ञानं तद्दशसु बोधिभूमिष्वावरणं यथाक्रमं तद्विपक्षत्वात्। यदुत सर्वत्रगार्थे प्रथमया हि भूम्या धर्मधातोः सर्वत्रगार्थं प्रतिविध्यति येनात्मपर[स]मतां प्रतिलभते। [10ᵃ] द्वितीययाग्रार्थं येनास्यैवं भवति तस्मात्तर्ह्यस्माभिः समानेऽभिनिर्हारे सर्वाकारपरिशोधनाभिनिर्हार एव योगः करणीय इति। तृतीयया तन्निष्यन्दाग्रार्थम्, येन धर्मधातुनिष्यन्दस्य श्रुतस्याग्रतां विदित्वा तदर्थं त्रिसाहस्रमहासाहस्रप्रमाणायामप्यग्निखदायामात्मानं प्रक्षिपेत्। चतुर्थ्या निष्परिग्रहतार्थम्, तथा हि धर्मतृष्णापि व्यावर्तते। पञ्चम्या सन्तानाभेदार्थं दशभिश्चित्ताशयविशुद्धिसमताभिः। षष्ठ्या निःसंक्लेशविशुद्ध्यर्थं प्रतीत्यसमुत्पादे नास्ति स कश्चिद्धर्मो यः संक्लिश्यते वा विशुध्यते वेति प्रतिवेधात्। सप्तम्या अनानात्वार्थं निर्निमित्ततया सूत्रादिधर्मनिमित्तनानात्वासमुदाचारात्। अष्टम्या अहीनानधिकर्थमनुत्पत्तिकधर्मक्षान्तिलाभात् संक्लेशे व्यवदाने वा कस्यचिद् धर्मस्य हानिवृद्ध्यदर्शनात्। चतुर्धा वशिता——निर्विकल्पवशिता क्षेत्रपरिशुद्धिवशिता ज्ञानवशिता कर्मवशिता च। तत्र प्रथमद्वितीयवशिताश्रयत्वं धर्मधाताष्टम्यैव भूम्या प्रतिविध्यति। ज्ञानवशिताश्रयत्वं नवम्यां प्रतिसंविल्लाभात्। कर्मवशिताश्रयत्वं दशम्यां यथेच्छं निर्माणैः सत्त्वार्थकर[10ᵇ]णत्वम्[1]।

समासेन पुनः—

क्लेशावरणमाख्यातं ज्ञेयावरणमेव च ।
सर्वाण्यावरणानीह यत्क्षयान्मुक्तिरिष्यते ॥१७॥

अस्य हि द्विविधस्यावरणस्य क्षयात् सर्वावरणेभ्यो मुक्तिरिष्यते ॥

आव[र]णानां पिण्डार्थः । महदावरणं यद्व्यापि । प्रतन्वावरणं यत् प्रादेशिकम् । प्रयोगावरणं यदुद्रिक्तम् । प्राप्त्यावरणं यत्समम् । प्राप्तिविशेषावरणं यदादानविवर्जने । सम्यक्प्रयोगावरणं यन्नवधा क्लेशावरणम् । हेत्वावरणं यच्छुभादौ दशविधहेतुत्वाधिकारात् । तत्त्वप्रवेशावरणं यद्बोधिपक्ष्येषु । शुभानुत्तर्यावरणं यत् पारमितासु । तद्विशेषगत्यावरणं यद्भूमिषु । संग्रहावरणं यत् समासतो द्विविधम् ॥

॥ मध्यान्तविभागे आवरणपरिच्छेदो द्वितीयः ॥

तत्त्वपरिच्छेदस्तृतीयः

तत्त्वमधिकृत्याह—

मूललक्षणतत्त्वमविपर्यासलक्षणम् ।
फलहेतुमयं तत्त्वं सूक्ष्मौदारिकमेव च ॥१॥

प्रसिद्धं शुद्धिविषयं संग्राह्यं भेदलक्षणम् ।
कौशल्यतत्त्वं दशधा ह्यात्मदृष्टिविपक्षतः ॥२॥

इत्येतद्दशविधं तत्त्वं यदुत मूलतत्त्वं लक्षणतत्त्वमविपर्यासतत्त्वं फलहेतुतत्त्वमौदारिकसूक्ष्मतत्त्वं प्रसिद्धतत्त्वं विशुद्धिगोचरतत्त्वं संग्रहतत्त्वं प्रभेदतत्त्वं कौ[11a]-शल्यतत्त्वं च। तत्पुनर्दशविधं दशविधात्मग्राहप्रतिपक्षेण वेदि[त]व्यम् । तद्यथा स्कन्धकौशल्यं धातुकौशल्यमायतनकौशल्यं प्रतीत्यसमुत्पादकौशल्यं स्थानास्थानकौशल्यमिन्द्रियकौशल्यं अध्वकौशल्यं सत्यकौशल्यं यानकौशल्यं संस्कृतासंस्कृतकौशल्यं च ॥

तत्र मूलतत्त्वम्—

स्वभा[व]स्त्रिविधः

परिकल्पितः परतन्त्रः परिनिष्पन्नश्च, तत्रान्यतत्त्वव्यवस्थापनात् ॥

किमत्र स्वभावत्रये तत्त्वमिष्यते—

असच्च नित्यं सच्चाप्यतत्त्वतः ।
सदसत्तत्त्वतश्चेति स्वभावत्रयमिष्यते ॥३॥

परिकल्पितलक्षणं नित्यमसदित्येतत् परिकल्पितस्वभावे तत्त्वमविपरीतत्वात् । परतन्त्रलक्षणं सच्च न च तत्त्वतो भ्रान्तत्वादित्येतत्परतन्त्रस्वभावे तत्त्वम् । परिनिष्पन्नलक्षणं सदसत्तत्त्वतश्चेत्येतत् परिनिष्पन्नस्वभावे तत्त्वम् ॥

लक्षणतत्त्वं कतमत्—

समारोपापवादस्य धर्मपुद्गलयोरिह ।
ग्राह्यग्राहकयोश्चापि भावाभावे च दर्शनम् ॥४॥

यज्ज्ञानान्न प्रवर्त्तेत तद्धि तत्त्वस्य लक्षणम् ।

पुद्गलधर्मयोः समारोपापवाददर्शनं यस्य ज्ञानान्न प्रवर्तते तत्परिकल्पितस्वभावे तत्त्वलक्षणम्। ग्राह्यग्राहकयोः समारोपापवाददर्शनं यस्य ज्ञानान्न प्रवर्तते तत्परत[11b]न्त्रस्वभावे तत्त्वलक्षणम्। भावाभावे समारोपापवाददर्शनं यस्य ज्ञानान्न प्रवर्तते तत्परिनिष्पन्नस्वभावे तत्त्वलक्षणम्। एतन्मूलतत्त्वे लक्षणमविपरीतं लक्षणतत्त्वमित्युच्यते ॥

अविपर्यासतत्त्वं नित्यादिविपर्यासप्रतिपक्षेणानित्यदुःखशून्यानात्मता। मूलतत्त्वे यथाक्रमं कथं च तत्रानित्यतादिता वेदितव्या——

असदर्थो ह्यनित्यार्थ उत्पादव्ययलक्षणः ॥५॥

समलामलभावेन मूलतत्त्वे यथाक्रमम्।

त्रयो हि स्वभावा मूलतत्त्वम्। तेषु यथाक्रममसदर्थो ह्यनित्यत्वार्थ उत्पादव्ययार्थः समला[मल]भावश्च ॥

दुःखमादानलक्ष्माख्यं सम्बन्धेनापरं मतम् ॥६॥

मूलतत्त्वे यथाक्रमं दुःखमुपादानतः पुद्गलधर्माभिनिवेशोपादानात्, लक्षणतस्त्रिदुःखतालक्षणत्वात्, संबन्धतश्च दुःखसम्बन्धात्, तत्रैव मूलतत्त्वे यथाक्रमं वेदितव्यम् ॥

अभावश्चाप्यतद्भावः प्रकृतिः शून्यता मता।

परिकल्पितलक्षणं न केनचित्प्रकारेणास्तीत्यभाव एवास्य शून्यता। परतन्त्रलक्षणं तथा नास्ति यथा परिकल्प्यते, न तु सर्वथा नास्तीति तस्यातद्भावः शून्यता। परिनिष्पन्नलक्षणं शून्यतास्वभावमेवेति प्रकृतिरेवास्य शून्यता ॥

अलक्षणं च नैरात्म्यं तद्विलक्षणमे[12a]व च ॥७॥

स्वलक्षणं च निर्दिष्टं

परिकल्पितस्य स्वभावस्य लक्षणमेव नास्तीत्यलक्षणमेवास्य नैरात्म्यम्। परतन्त्रस्यास्ति लक्षणं न तु यथा परिकल्प्यत इति [त]द्विलक्षणमस्य लक्षणं नैरात्म्यम्। परिनिष्पन्नस्तु स्वभावो नैरात्म्यमेवेति प्रकृतिरेवास्य नैरात्म्यमिति। त्रिविधे मूलतत्त्वे त्रिविधानित्यता परिदीपिता——असदर्थानित्यता उत्पादभङ्गानित्यता समलनिर्मलानित्यता च। त्रिविधा दुःखता——उपादानदुःखता लक्षणदुःखता सम्बन्धदुःखता च। त्रिविधा शून्यता——अभावशून्यता अतद्भावशून्यता[स्वभावशून्यता]

च। त्रिविधं नैरात्म्यम्—अलक्षणनैरात्म्यं विलक्षणनैरात्म्यं स्वलक्ष णनैरात्म्यं च ॥

फलहेतुमयं तत्त्वं तत्रैव मूलतत्त्वे दुःखसमुदयनिरोधमार्गसत्यत्वम्। कथं त्रिविधं मूलतत्त्वं दुःखादिसत्यत्वं, यतस्तदनित्यादिलक्षणम्—

दुःखसत्यमतो मतम्।

त्रिविधेन समुदयार्थेन समुदयसत्यम्। त्रिविधः समुदयार्थः—

वासनाथ समुत्थानमविसंयोग एव च ॥८॥

वासनासमुदयः परिकल्पितस्वभावाभिनिवेशवासना। समुत्थानसमुदयः कर्मक्लेशाः अविसंयोगसमुदयः तथताया आवरणाविसंयोगः ॥

त्रिविधेन निरोधेन निरोधसत्यम्। त्रिवि[12b]धो निरोध :—

स्वभावद्वयनोत्पत्तिर्मलशान्तिद्वयं मतम्।

स्वभावानुत्पत्ति[ग्राह्य]ग्राहकयोरनुत्पत्तिर्मलशान्तिद्वयं च प्रतिसंख्यानिरोध-स्तथताख्यः इत्येष त्रिविधो निरोधो यदुत स्वभावनिरोधो द्वयनिरोधः प्रकृति-निरोधश्च ॥

मार्गसत्यं त्रिविधे मूलतत्त्वे कथं व्यवस्थाप्यते—

परिज्ञायां प्रहाणे च प्राप्तिसाक्षात्कृतावपि ॥९॥

मार्गसत्यं समाख्यातं

परिकल्पितस्य परिज्ञाने, परतन्त्रस्य परिज्ञाने प्रहाणे च, परिनिष्पन्नस्य परिज्ञाने प्राप्तिसाक्षात्करणे च। एवमत्र परिज्ञानप्रहाणसाक्षात्क्रियायां मार्गसत्यव्यवस्थानं वेदितव्यम् ॥

औदारिकसूक्ष्मतत्त्वं पुनः संवृतिपरमार्थसत्यम्। तन्मूलतत्त्वे कथं वेदितव्यम्—

प्रज्ञप्तिप्रतिपत्तितः।

तथोद्भावनयोदारं

त्रिविधा हि संवृतिः—प्रज्ञप्तिसंवृतिः प्रतिपत्तिसंवृतिरुद्भावनासंवृतिश्च। तया संवृतिसत्यत्वं मूलतत्त्वे यथाक्रमं वेदितव्यम् ॥

परमार्थं तु एकतः ॥१०॥

परमार्थसत्यमेकस्मात्परिनिष्पन्नादेव स्वभावाद्वेदितव्यम् ॥

स पुनः कथं परमार्थः—

अर्थप्राप्तिप्रपत्त्या हि परमार्थस्त्रिधा मतः।

अर्थपरमार्थस्तथता परमस्य ज्ञानस्यार्थ इति कृत्वा। प्राप्तिपरमार्थो निर्वाणं परमोऽर्थ इति कृत्वा। प्रतिपत्तिपरमार्थो [13a] मार्गः परमोऽस्यार्थ इति कृत्वा ॥

कथमसंस्कृतं च संस्कृतं च परिनिष्पन्नः स्वभाव उच्यते—

निर्विकाराविपर्यासपरिनिष्पत्तितो द्वयम् ॥११॥

असंस्कृतमविकारपरिनिष्पत्त्या परिनिष्पन्नम्। संस्कृतं मार्गसत्यसंगृहीतमविपर्यासपरिनिष्पत्त्या पुनर्ज्ञेयवस्तुन्यविपर्यासात् ॥

प्रसिद्धतत्त्वं मूलतत्त्वे कथं व्यवस्थाप्यते? द्विविधं हि प्रसिद्धतत्त्वं—लोकप्रसिद्धं युक्तिप्रसिद्धं च। तत्र—

लोकप्रसिद्धमेकस्मात्

परिकल्पितस्वभावात्। यस्मिन् वस्तुनि संकेतसंस्तवानुप्रविष्टया बुद्धया सर्वेषां लौकिकानां दर्शनतुल्यता भवति पृथिव्येवेयं नाग्नीरूपमेवेदं न शब्द इत्येवमादि ॥

त्रयाद्युक्तिप्रसिद्धकम्।

यत् सतां युक्तार्थपण्डितानां तार्किकाणां प्रमाणत्रयं निश्रित्योपपत्तिसाधनयुक्त्या प्रसिद्धं वस्तु ॥

विशुद्धिगोचरतत्त्वं द्विविधं क्लेशावरणविशुद्धिज्ञानगोचरं ज्ञेयावरणविशुद्धिज्ञानगोचरं च। तदेतत्—

विशुद्धिगोचरं द्वेधा एकस्मादेव कीर्तितम् ॥१२॥

परिनिष्पन्नादेव स्वभावात्। न ह्यन्यस्वभावो विशुद्धिज्ञानद्वयगोचरो भवति ॥

कथं त्रिविधे मूलतत्त्वे संग्रहतत्त्वं वेदितव्यम्—

निमित्तस्य विकल्पस्य नाम्नश्च द्वयसंग्रहः।

यथायोगं पञ्चवस्तून्यारभ्य निमित्तविकल्पयोः परतन्त्रेण सं[13b]ग्रहः। नाम्नः परिकल्पितेन ॥

सम्यग्ज्ञानसतत्त्वस्य एकेनैव च संग्रहः ॥१३॥

तथतासम्यग्ज्ञानयोः परिनिष्पन्नेन स्वभावेन संग्रहः ॥

प्रभेदतत्त्वं मूलतत्त्वे कथं वेदितव्यम्? सप्तविधं प्रभेदतत्त्वम्—प्रवृत्तितत्त्वं लक्षणतत्त्वं विज्ञप्तितत्त्वं सन्निवेशतत्त्वं मिथ्याप्रतिपत्तितत्त्वं विशुद्धितत्त्वं सम्यक्प्रतिपत्तितत्त्वं च। तत्र प्रवृत्तितत्त्वादि त्रिविधं। अनवराग्रेष्येति संसारः तथताचित्तसंक्लेशात्सत्त्वाः संक्लिष्यन्त इति सर्वे दुःखादिसत्यं च यथासंख्यं। सन्धिनिर्मोचनसूत्रे सप्तविधा तथता निर्दिष्टा। तत्र—

प्रवृत्तितत्त्वं द्विविधं

मूलतत्त्वं वेदितव्यम्। परिकल्पितपरतन्त्रलक्षणम्। यथा प्रवृत्तितत्त्वं तथा—

सन्निवेशः कुपन्नता।

सन्निवेशमिथ्याप्रतिपत्तितत्त्वे अपि तथैव द्विविधं मूलतत्त्वम्।

एकं लक्षणविज्ञप्तिशुद्धिसम्यक्प्रपन्नता ॥१४॥

लक्षणतत्त्वादीनि चत्वार्येकं मूलतत्त्वं परिनिष्पन्नलक्षणम् ॥

कौशल्यतत्त्वं दर्शनप्रतिपक्षेणेत्युक्तम्। कथमेषु स्कन्धादिषु दशविधमात्मदर्शनम्–

एकहेतुत्वभोक्तृत्वकर्तृत्ववशवर्तने।
आधिपत्यार्थनित्यत्वे क्लेशशुद्धाश्रयेऽपि च ॥१५॥

योगित्वामुक्तमुक्तत्वे ह्यात्मदर्शनमेषु हि।

एष दशविध आत्मसद्ग्राहः स्कन्धादिषु प्रवर्तते। यस्य प्रति[14a]पक्षेण दशविधं कौशल्यं यदुतैकत्वग्राहो हेतुत्वग्राहो भोक्तृत्वग्राहः कर्तृत्वग्राहः स्वतन्त्र[त्व]ग्राह अधिपतित्वग्राहो नित्यत्वग्राहः संक्लिष्टव्यवदानत्वग्राहो योगित्वग्राहोऽमुक्तमुक्तत्वग्राहश्च। कथमिदं दशविधं कौशल्यतत्त्वं मूलतत्त्वेऽन्तर्भवति, यतस्त्रिषु स्वभावेषु ते स्कन्धादयः अन्तर्भूताः ॥

कथमन्तर्भूताः—

परिकल्पविकल्पार्थधर्मतार्थेन तेषु ते ॥१६॥

त्रिविधं रूपम्। परिकल्पितं रूपं यो रूपस्य परिकलिपतः स्वभावः। विकल्पितं

रूपं यो रूपस्य परतन्त्रः स्वभावस्तत्र हि रूपविकल्पः क्रियते। धर्मतारूपं यो रूपस्य परिनिष्पन्नः स्वभावः। यथा रूपमेवं वेदनादयः स्कन्धा धात्वायतनादयश्च योज्याः। एवं त्रिषु स्वभावेषु स्कन्धादीनामन्तर्भावाद्दशविधं कौशल्यतत्त्वं मूलतत्त्व एव द्रष्टव्यम्। उक्तमिदं यथा दशविधात्मदर्शनप्रतिपक्षेण स्कन्धादिकौशल्यम् ॥

स्कन्धाद्यर्थस्तु नोक्तः। स इदानीमुच्यते—

अनेकत्वाभिसंक्षेपपरिच्छेदार्थ आदितः।

आदितस्तावत् स्कन्धाः। ते त्रिविधेनार्थेन वेदितव्याः। अनेकत्वार्थेन यत्किञ्चिद्रूपमतीतानागतप्रत्युत्पन्नमिति विस्तरः। अभिसंक्षेपार्थेन तत्सर्वमैकध्यमभिसंक्षिप्येति। परिच्छेदार्थेन [14b] च रूपादिलक्षणस्य पृथक्त्वव्यवस्थानात्। राश्यर्थो हि स्कन्धा[र्थः]। एवं च लोके राश्यर्थो दृष्ट इति ॥

ग्राहकग्राह्यतद्ग्राहबीजार्थश्चापरो मतः ॥१७॥

कतमोऽपरः। धातुः। तत्र ग्राहकबीजार्थश्चक्षुर्धात्वादयः। ग्राह्यबीजार्थो रूपधात्वादयः। तद्ग्राहबीजार्थश्चक्षुर्विज्ञानधात्वादयः ॥

वेदितार्थपरिच्छेदभोगाय द्वारतोऽपरम्।

किमपरम्। आयतनम्। तत्र वेदितोपभोगाय द्वारार्थेन षडाध्यात्मिकान्यायतनानि। अर्थपरिच्छेदोपभोगाय द्वारार्थेन षड् बाह्यानि ॥

(घ) प्रतीत्यसमुत्पादार्थः

प्रतीत्यसमुत्पादार्थः—

पुनर्हेतुफलायासानारोपानपवादतः ॥१८॥

हेतुफलक्रियाणामसमारोपानपवादार्थः प्रतीत्यसमुत्पादार्थः। तत्र हेतुसमारोपः संस्कारादीनां विष[म]हेतुकल्पनात्। हेत्वपवादो निर्हेतुकत्वकल्पनात्। फलसमारोपः [सात्म]कानां संस्कारादीनामविद्यादिप्रत्ययप्रवृत्तिकल्पनात्। फलापवादो न सन्त्यविद्यादिप्रत्ययाः संस्कारादय इति कल्पनात्। क्रियासमारोपोऽविद्यादीनां संस्काराद्युत्पत्तौ व्यापारकल्पनात्। क्रियापवादो निःसामर्थ्यकल्पनात्। तदभावादसमारोपानपवादो वेदितव्यः ॥

अनिष्टेष्टविशुद्धीनां समोत्पत्त्याधिपत्ययोः।
सम्प्राप्तिसमुदाचा[15a]रपारतन्त्र्यार्थतोऽपरम् ॥१९॥

स्थानास्थानं सप्तविधपारतन्त्र्यार्थेन वेदितव्यम्। तत्रानिष्टे पारतन्त्र्यं दुश्चरितेनानिच्छतोऽपि दुर्गतिगमनात्। इष्टे पारतन्त्र्यं सुचरितेन सुगतिगमनात्। विशुद्धौ पारतन्त्र्यं पञ्च निवरणान्यप्रहाय यावत् सप्त बोध्यङ्गान्यभावयित्वा दुःखस्यान्ताकरणात्। समोत्पत्तौ पारतन्त्र्यं द्वयोरपूर्वाचरमयोस्तथागतयोश्चक्रवर्तिनोश्चैकस्मिन् लोकधातावनुत्पादात्। आधिपत्ये पारतन्त्र्यं स्त्रियाश्चक्रवर्तित्वाद्यकरणात्। सम्प्राप्तौ पारतन्त्र्यं स्त्रियाः प्रत्येकानुत्तरबोध्यनभिसंबोधात्। समुदाचारे पारतन्त्र्यं दृष्टिसम्पन्नस्य वधाद्युपक्रमासमुदाचारात् पृथग्जनस्य च समुदाचारात्। विस्तरेण बहुधातुकसूत्रानुसारादनुगन्तव्यम्॥

इन्द्रियं पुनर्द्वाविंशतिविधम्—

ग्रहणस्थानसन्धानभोगशुद्धिद्वयार्थतः।

ग्रहणार्थेन यावद् विशुद्धिद्वयार्थेन तेषु तदाधिपत्यात्। रूपादिविषयग्रहणे हि चक्षुरादीनां षण्णामाधिपत्यम्। स्थाने जीवितेन्द्रियस्य तदाधिपत्येनामरणात्। कुलसन्धाने स्त्रीपुरुषेन्द्रिययोरपत्यप्रसवाधिपत्यात्। उपभोग वेदनेन्द्रियाणां कुशलाकुशलकर्मफलोपभोगात्। लौकिकविशुद्धौ श्रद्धा[15b]दीनां लोकोत्तरविशुद्धौ अनाज्ञातमाज्ञास्यामीन्द्रियादीनाम्॥

फलहेतूपयोगाच्च नोपयोगात्तथापरम्॥२०॥

किमपरम्। अध्वत्रयम्। यथायोगं फलहेतूपयोगार्थेनातीतोऽध्वा फलहेत्वनुपयोगार्थेनानागतोऽध्वा हेतूपयोगफलानुपयोगार्थेन प्रत्युत्पन्नोऽध्वा वेदितव्यः॥

वेदनासनिमित्तार्थतन्निमित्तप्रपत्तितः।
तच्छमप्रतिपक्षार्थयोगादपरमिष्यते॥२१॥

किमपरम्। सत्यचतुष्टयम्। तत्र दुःखसत्यं वेदनासनिमित्तार्थेन यत्किञ्चिद्वेदितमिदमत्र दुःखस्येति कृत्वा। वेदनानिमित्तं पुनर्वेदनास्थानीया धर्मा वेदितव्याः। तन्निमित्तप्रतिपत्तितः समुदयसत्यम्। दुःखसत्यनिमित्तं या प्रतिपत्तिः। तयोः शमार्थेन निरोधसत्यम्। प्रतिपक्षार्थेन मार्गसत्यम्॥

गुणदोषाविकल्पेन ज्ञानेन परतः स्वयम्।
निर्याणादपरं ज्ञेयं

यानत्रयं यथायोगम्। तत्र निर्वाणसंसारयोर्गुणदोषज्ञानेन परतःश्रुत्वा निर्याणार्थेन

श्रावकयानम्। तेनैव स्वयमश्रुत्वा परतो निर्याणार्थेन प्रत्येकबुद्धयानम्। अविकल्पेन ज्ञानेन स्वयं निर्याणार्थेन महायानं वेदितव्यम् ॥

सप्रज्ञप्तिसहेतुकात् ॥२२॥

[16a] **निमित्तात्प्रशमात्सार्थात् पश्चिमं समुदाहृतम् ॥२३॥**

संस्कृतासंस्कृतम्। तत्र प्रज्ञप्तिर्नामकायादयः। हेतुर्बीजसंगृहीतमालयविज्ञानम्। निमित्तं प्रतिष्ठादेहभोगसंगृहीतं प्रवृत्तिविज्ञानसंगृहीताश्च मनउद्ग्रहविकल्पाः। एतत् सप्रज्ञप्तिसहेतुकं निमित्तं ससम्प्रयोगं संस्कृतं वेदितव्यम्। तत्र मनो यन्नित्यं मन्यनाकारम्। उद्ग्रहः पञ्चविज्ञानकायाः। विकल्पो मनोविज्ञानं तस्य विकल्पकत्वात्। असंस्कृतं पुनः प्रशमश्च निरोधः प्रशमार्थश्च। तत्र प्रशमो निरोधो मार्गश्च यच्च प्रशमो येन चेति कृत्वा। प्रशमार्थस्तथता प्रशमस्यार्थ इति कृत्वा। तथताया मार्गालम्बनत्वात्। मार्गस्य प्रशमत्वं तेन प्रशमनात्। इत्येतेनार्थेन स्कन्धादिषु ज्ञानं स्कन्धादिकौशल्यं वेदितव्यम् ॥

तत्त्वस्य पिण्डार्थः। समासतो द्विविधं तत्त्वम्—आदर्शतत्त्वं दृश्यतत्त्वं च। तत्रादर्शतत्त्वं मूलतत्त्वम्। तत्र शेषाणां दर्शनात्। दृश्यतत्त्वं नवधा—निरभिमानदृश्यतत्त्वमविपर्यासदृश्यतत्त्वं श्रावकयाननिर्याणदृश्यतत्त्वं महायाननिर्याणदृश्यतत्त्वमौदारिकेन परिपाचनात् सूक्ष्मेण च विमोचनात्, परवादिनिग्रहदृश्यतत्त्वं दृष्टान्तसन्निश्रयेण यु[16b]क्त्या निग्रहात्, महायानाभिद्योतनदृश्यतत्त्वं सर्वाकारज्ञेयप्रवेशदृश्यतत्त्वमवितथ[तथ]ताभिद्योत[न]दृश्यतत्त्वमात्मग्राह्यवस्तुसर्वाभिसन्धिप्रवेशदृश्यतत्त्वं च ॥

॥ मध्यान्तविभागशास्त्रे तत्त्वपरिच्छेदस्तृतीयः ॥

प्रतिपक्षभावनावस्थाफलपरिच्छेदश्चतुर्थः

प्रतिपक्षभावना बोधिपक्ष्यभावना। सेदानीं वक्तव्या ॥

तत्र तावदादौ—

दौष्ठुल्यात्तर्षहेतुत्वाद्वस्तुत्वादविमोहतः।
चतुःसत्यावताराय स्मृत्युपस्थानभावना ॥१॥

कायेन हि दौष्ठुल्यं प्रभाव्यते। तत्परीक्षया दुःखसत्यमवतरति, तस्य सदौष्ठुल्यसंस्कारलक्षणत्वात्। दौष्ठुल्यं हि संस्कारदुःखता, तया सर्वं सास्रवं वस्त्वार्या दुःखतः पश्यन्तीति। तृष्णाहेतुर्वेदना, तत्परीक्षया समुदयसत्यमवतरति। आत्माभिनिवेशवस्तु चित्तम्, तत्परीक्षया निरोधसत्यमवतरति, आत्मोच्छेदभयापगमात्। धर्मपरीक्षया सांक्लेशिकवैयवदानिकधर्मासम्मोहान्मार्गसत्यमवतरति। अत आदौ चतुःसत्यावताराय स्मृत्युपस्थानभावना व्यवस्थाप्यते ॥

ततः सम्यक्प्रहाणभावना। यस्मात्—

परिज्ञाते विपक्षे च प्रतिपक्षे च सर्वथा।
तदपायाय वीर्यं हि चतुर्धा संप्रवर्तते ॥२॥

स्मृत्यु[17a]पस्थानभावनया विपक्षे प्रतिपक्षे च सर्वप्रकारं परिज्ञाते विपक्षापगमाय प्रतिपक्षोपगमाय च वीर्यं चतुर्धा संप्रवर्तते। उत्पन्नानां पापकानामकुशलानां धर्माणां प्रहाणायेति विस्तरः ॥

कर्मण्यता स्थितेस्तत्र सर्वार्थानां समृद्धये।
पञ्चदोषप्रहाणाष्टसंस्कारभावनान्वया ॥३॥

तस्यां तदपायाय वीर्यभावनायां चित्तस्थितेः कर्मण्यता चत्वार ऋद्धिपादाः सर्वार्थसमृद्धि[हे]तुत्वात्। स्थितिरत्र चित्तस्थितिः समाधिर्वेदितव्यः। अतः सम्यक्प्रहाणानन्तरमृद्धिपादाः। सा पुनः कर्मण्यता पञ्चदोषप्रहाणायाष्टसंस्कारभावनान्वया वेदितव्या ॥

कतमे पञ्च दोषा इत्याह—

कौसीद्यमववादस्य संमोषो लय उद्धतः ।
असंस्कारोऽथ संस्कारः पञ्च [दो]षा इमे मताः ॥४॥

तत्र लयौद्धत्यमेको दोषः क्रियते । अनभिसंस्कारो लयौद्धत्यप्रशमनकाले दोषः । अभिसंस्कारः प्रशान्तौ ॥ एषां प्रहाणाय कथमष्टौ प्रहाणसंस्कारा व्यवस्थाप्यन्ते । चत्वारः कौसीद्यप्रहाणाय च्छन्दव्यायामश्रद्धाप्रस्रब्धयः । ते पुनर्यथाक्रमं वेदितव्याः—

आश्र[17b]योऽथाश्रितस्तस्य निमित्तं फलमेव च ।

आश्रयश्छन्दो[व्या]यामस्य । आश्रितो व्यायामः । तस्याश्रयस्य च्छन्दस्य निमित्तं श्रद्धा, सम्प्रत्यये सत्यभिलाषात् । तस्याश्रितस्य व्यायामस्य फलं प्रस्रब्धिरारब्धवीर्यस्य समाधिविशेषाधिगमात् । शेषाश्चत्वारः प्रहाणसंस्काराः स्मृतिसंप्रजन्यचेतनोपेक्षाश्चतुर्णां दोषाणां यथासंख्यं प्रतिपक्षाः । ते पुनः स्मृत्यादयो वेदितव्या यथाक्रमम्—

आलम्बने असंमोषो लयौद्धत्यानुबुद्धचना ॥५॥

तदपायाभिसंस्कारः शान्तौ प्रशठवाहिता ।

स्मृतिरालम्बनेऽसंप्रमोषः । संप्रजन्यं स्मृत्यसम्प्रमोषे सति लयौद्धत्यावबोधः । अनुबुद्धच तदपगमायाभिसंस्कारश्चेतना । तस्य लयौद्धत्यस्योपशान्तौ सत्यां प्रशठवाहिता चित्तस्योपेक्षा ॥

ऋद्धिपादानामनन्तरं पञ्चेन्द्रियाणि श्रद्धादीनि । तेषां कथं व्यवस्थानम्—

रोपिते मोक्षभागीये छन्दयोगाधिपत्यतः ॥६॥

आलम्बने असंमोषाविसारविचयस्य च ।

आधिपत्यत इति वर्तते । ऋद्धिपादैः कर्मण्यचित्तस्यारोपिते मोक्षभागीये कुशलमूले छन्दाधिपत्यतः प्रयोगाधिपत्यतः । आलम्बनासम्प्र[18a]मोषाधिपत्यतः अविसाराधिपत्यतः प्रविचयाधिपत्यतश्च यथाक्रमं पञ्च श्रद्धादीनीन्द्रियानि वेदितव्यानि ॥

तान्येव श्रद्धादीनि बलवन्ति बलानीत्युच्यन्ते । तेषां पुनर्बलवत्त्वं—

विपक्षस्य लेखाद्

यदा तान्याश्रद्धयादिभिर्विपक्षैर्न व्यवकीर्यन्ते । कस्मात् श्रद्धादीनां पूर्वोत्तरनिर्देश :—

यस्मात्पूर्व[स्य] फलमुत्तरम् ॥७॥

श्रद्दधानो हि हेतुफले वीर्यमारभते। आरब्धवीर्यस्य स्मृतिरुपतिष्ठते। उपस्थितस्मृतेश्चित्तं समाधीयते । समाहितचित्तो यथाभूतं प्रजानाति । अवरोपितमोक्षभागीयस्येन्द्रियाण्युक्तानि ॥

अथ निर्वेधभागीयानि किमिन्द्रियावस्थायां वेदितव्यानि आहोस्विद् बलावस्थायाम्—

द्वौ द्वौ निर्वेधभागीयाविन्द्रियाणि बलानि च।

उष्मगतं मूर्द्धानश्चेन्द्रियाणि । क्षान्तयो लौकिकाश्चाग्रधर्मा बलानि॥

बलानन्तरं बोध्यङ्गानि । तेषां कथं व्यवस्थानम्—

आश्रयाङ्गं स्वभावाङ्गं निर्याणाङ्गं तृतीयकम् ॥८॥

चतुर्थमनुशंसाङ्गं निःक्लेशाङ्गं त्रिधा मतम्।

दर्शनमार्गे बोधावङ्गानि बोध्यङ्गानि। तत्र बोधेराश्रयाङ्गं स्मृतिः। स्वभावाङ्गं धर्म[18b]विचयः। निर्याणाङ्गं वीर्यम्। अनुशंसाङ्गं प्रीतिः। असंक्लेशाङ्गं त्रिधा प्रस्रब्धिसमाध्युपेक्षाः। किमर्थं पुनरसंक्लेशाङ्गं त्रिधा देशितम्—

निदानेनाश्रयेणेह स्वभावेन च देशितम् ॥९॥

असंक्लेशस्य निदानं प्रस्रब्धिदौष्ठुल्यहेतुत्वात् संक्लेशस्य, तस्याश्च तत्प्रतिपक्षत्वात्। आश्रयः समाधिः। स्वभाव उपेक्षा॥

बोध्यङ्गानन्तरं मार्गाङ्गाणि । तेषां कथं व्यवस्थानम्—

परिच्छेदोऽथ सम्प्राप्तिः परसम्भावना त्रिधा।
विपक्षप्रतिपक्षश्च मार्गस्याङ्गं तदष्टधा॥१०॥

भावनामार्गेऽस्य परिच्छेदाङ्गं सम्यग्दृष्टिः लौकिकी लोकोत्तरपृष्ठलब्धा यया स्वाधिगमं परिच्छिनत्ति। परसंप्रापणाङ्गं सम्यक्संकल्पः सम्यग्वाक्च ससमुत्थानया वाचा तत्प्रापणात्। परसम्भावनाङ्गं त्रिधा सम्यग्वाक्कर्मान्ताजीवाः। तैर्हि यथाक्रमम्—

दृष्टौ शीलेऽथ संलेखे परविज्ञप्तिरिष्यते।

तस्य सम्यग्वाचा कथासांकथ्यविनिश्चयेन प्रज्ञायां सम्भावना भवति । सम्यक्कर्मान्तेन शीलेऽकृत्याकरणात् । सम्यगाजीवेन संलेखे, धर्मेण मात्रया च चीवराद्यन्वेषणात् । विपक्षप्रतिपक्षाङ्गं त्रिधैव सम्यग्व्यायामस्मृतिसमा[19a]धयः । एषां हि यथाक्रमम्—

क्लेशोपक्लेशवैभुत्वविपक्षप्रतिपक्षता ॥११॥

त्रिविधो हि विपक्षः । क्लेशो भावनाहेयः । उपक्लेशो लयौद्धत्यम् । विभुत्वविपक्षश्च वैशेषिकगुणाभिनिर्हारविबन्धः । तत्र प्रथमस्य [स]म्यग्व्यायामः प्रतिपक्षस्तेन मार्गभावनात् । द्वितीयस्य सम्यक्स्मृतिः शमथादिनिमित्तेषु सूपस्थितस्मृतेर्लयौद्धत्याभावात् । तृतीयस्य सम्यक्समाधिर्ध्यानसन्निश्रयेणाभिज्ञादिगुणाभिनिर्हारात् ॥

सैषा प्रतिपक्षभावना समासेन त्रिविधा वेदितव्या—

अनुकूला विपर्यस्ता सानुबन्धाविपर्यया ।
अविपर्यस्ता विपर्यासाननुबन्धा च भावना ॥१२॥

विपर्यस्तापि अविपर्यासानुकूला, अविपर्यस्ता विपर्यासानुबन्धा, अविपर्यस्ता विपर्या[स]निरनुबन्धा च यथाक्रमं पृथग्जनशैक्ष्याशैक्ष्यावस्थासु ॥

बोधिसत्त्वानां तु—

आलम्बन[मन]स्कारप्राप्तितस्तद्विशिष्टता ।

श्रावकप्रत्येकबुद्धानां हि स्वसान्तानिकाः कायादय आलम्बनम् । बोधिसत्त्वानां स्वपरसान्तानिकाः । श्रावकप्रत्येकबुद्धा अनित्यादिभिराकारैः कायादीन् मनसि कुर्वन्ति । बोधिसत्त्वास्त्वनुपलम्भयोगेन । **श्रावकप्रत्येकबुद्धाः स्मृत्युपस्थानादी-[19b]नि भावयन्ति यावदेव कायादीनां विसंयोगाय, बोधिसत्त्वा नं विसंयोगाय नाविसंयोगाय यावदेवाप्रतिष्ठतनिर्वाणाय** । उक्ता प्रतिपक्षभावना ॥

२. अवस्था

तत्रावस्था कतमा—

हेत्ववस्थावताराख्या प्रयोगफलसंज्ञिता ॥१३॥

कार्याकार्यविशिष्टा च उत्तरानुतरा च सा ।
अधिमुक्तौ प्रवेशे च निर्याणे व्याकृतावपि ॥१४॥

कथिकत्वाभिषेके च सम्प्राप्तावनुशंसने ।
कृत्यानुष्ठा[न] उद्दिष्टा

तत्र हेत्ववस्था या गोत्रस्थस्य पुद्गलस्यावतारावस्था उत्पादितबोधिचित्तस्य । प्रयोगावस्था चित्तोत्पादादूर्ध्वमप्राप्ते फले । फलावस्था प्राप्ते । सकरणीयावस्था शैक्षस्य । अकरणीयावस्था अशैक्षस्य । विशेषावस्थाभिज्ञादिगुणविशेषसमन्वा(ग)-तस्य । उत्तरावस्था श्रावकादिभ्यो भूमिप्रविष्टस्य बोधिसत्त्वस्य । अनुत्तरावस्था बुद्धस्य, तत ऊर्ध्वमवस्थाभावात् । अधिमुक्त्यवस्था बोधिसत्त्वानां सर्वस्यामधि-मुक्तिचर्याभूमौ । प्रवेशावस्था प्रथमायां भूमौ । निर्याणावस्था तदुत्तरासु षड्भूमिषु । व्याकरणावस्था अष्टम्यां भूमौ । कथिकत्वावस्था नवम्याम् । अभिषेकावस्था दशम्याम् । प्रप्त्यवस्था बुद्धा[20a]नां धर्मकायः । अनुशंसावस्था सांभोगिकः कायः । कृत्यानुष्ठानावस्था निर्माणकायः । सर्वाप्येषा बहुविधावस्थाभिसमस्य वेदितव्या ॥

धर्मधातौ त्रिधा पुनः ॥१५॥

अशुद्धा[शुद्ध]शुद्धा च विशुद्धा च यथार्हतः ।

तत्राशुद्धावस्था हेत्ववस्थामुपादाय या[व]त् प्रयोगात् । अशुद्धशुद्धावस्था शैक्ष्याणाम् । विशुद्धावस्था अशैक्ष्याणाम् ॥

पुद्गलानामवस्थानं यथायोगमतो मतम् ॥१६॥

अतोऽवस्थाप्रभेदाद् यथायोगं पुद्गलानां व्यवस्थानं वेदितव्यम् । अयं गोत्र-स्थोऽयमवतीर्ण इत्येवमादि । उक्तावस्था ॥

फलप्राप्तिः कतमा—

भाजनत्वं विपाकाख्यं बलं तस्याधिपत्यतः ।
रुचिर्वृद्धिर्विशुद्धिश्च फलमेतद्यथाक्रमम् ॥१७॥

भाजनत्वं यः कुशलानुकूलो विपाकः । बलं या भाजनत्वाधिपत्यात् कुशलस्याधि-मात्रता । रुचिर्या पूर्वाभ्यासात् कुशले रुचिः । वृद्धिर्या प्रत्युत्पन्ने कुशलधर्माभ्यासात् कुशलमूलपरिपुष्टिः । विशुद्धिर्यदावरणप्रहाणम् । एतद् यथाक्रमं फलं पञ्चविधं वेदितव्यम् । विपाकफलमधिपतिफलं निष्यन्दफलं पुरुषकारफलं विसंयोगफलं च ॥

उत्तरोत्तरमाद्यं च तदभ्यासात्समाप्तिः।
आनुकूल्याद्विपक्षाच्च विसंयोगाद्विशेषतः ॥१८॥
उत्तरानु[20b]त्तरत्वाच्च फलमन्यत्समासतः ।

उत्तरोत्तरफलं गोत्राच्चित्तोत्पाद इत्येवमादि परंपरया वेदितव्यम् । आदिफलं प्रथमलोकोत्तरधर्मप्रतिलम्भः । अभ्यासफलं तस्मात्परेण शैक्ष्यावस्थायाम् । समाप्तिफलम् अशैक्ष्या धर्माः । आनुकूल्यफलमुपनिषद्भावेनोत्तरोत्तरफलमेव वेदितव्यम् । विपक्षफलं प्रहाणमार्गो यदेवादिफलं प्रतिपक्षोऽभिमतः । विसंयोगफलं निरोधसाक्षात्क्रिया । अभ्यासफलं समाप्तिफलं च क्लेशविसंयोगः शैक्ष्याशैक्ष्याणां यथाक्रमम् । विशेषफलमभिज्ञादिको गुणविशेषः । उत्तरफलं बोधिसत्त्वभूमयस्तदन्ययानोत्तरत्वात् । अनुत्तरफलं बुद्धभूमिः । एतानि चत्वारि अभ्याससमाप्तिफलप्रभेद एव । एतदन्यत्फलं समासनिर्देशतः । व्यासतस्त्वपरिमाणम् ॥

४. प्रतिपक्षभावनापिण्डार्थः

तत्र प्रतिपक्षभावनायाः पिण्डार्थः—व्युत्पत्तिभावना, निर्लेखभावना, परिकर्मभावना, उत्तरोत्तरं समारम्भभावना, श्लिष्टभावना दर्शनमार्गश्लेषात्, प्रविष्टभावना, उत्कृष्टभावना, आदिभावना, मध्यभावना, पर्यवसानभावना च, सोत्तरा भावना, निरुत्तरा च भावना या आलम्बनमनस्कारप्राप्तिविशिष्टा ॥

५. अवस्थापिण्डार्थः

अवस्थानां [21a] पिण्डार्थः । भव्यतावस्था गोत्रस्थस्य । आरम्भावस्था यावत् प्रयोगात् । अशुद्धावस्था, अशुद्धशुद्धावस्था, विशुद्धावस्था, सालङ्कारावस्था, व्याप्त्यवस्था दशभूमिव्यापनात्, अनुत्तरावस्था च ॥

६. फलपिण्डार्थः

फलानां पिण्डार्थः । संग्रहतस्तद्विशेषतः पूर्वाभ्यासत उत्तरोत्तरनिर्हारत उद्देशतो निर्देशतश्च । तत्र संग्रहतः पञ्च फलानि । तद्विशेषतः शेषाणि । पूर्वाभ्यासतो विपाकफलम् । उत्तरोत्तरनिर्हारतस्तदन्यानि चत्वारि । उद्देशत उत्तरोत्तरफलादीनि चत्वारि । निर्देशत आनुकूल्यफलादीनि षट् तेषामेव चतुर्णां निर्देशात् ॥

॥ मध्यान्तविभागे प्रतिपक्षभावनावस्थाफलपरिच्छेदश्चतुर्थः ॥

आनुत्तर्यपरिच्छेदः पञ्चमः

१. त्रिविधमानुत्तर्यम

यानानुत्तर्यमिदानीं वक्तव्यम् । तदुच्यते—

आनुत्तर्यं प्रपत्तौ हि पुनरालम्बने मतम् ।
समुदागम उद्दिष्टं

त्रिविधमानुत्तर्यं महायाने येनैतदनुत्तरं यानं, प्रतिपत्त्यानुत्तर्यमालम्बनानुत्तर्यं समुदागमानुत्तर्यं च ॥

२. प्रतिपत्त्यानुत्तर्यम

तत्र प्रतिपत्त्यानुत्तर्यं दशपारमिताप्रतिपत्तितो वेदितव्यम् ॥

प्रतिपत्तिस्तु षड्विधा ॥१॥

अत्र पारमितासु—

परमार्थमनस्कारे अनुधर्मान्तिवर्जने ।
विशिष्टा चाविशिष्टा च

इत्येषा षड्विधा प्रतिपत्तिर्यदु[21b]त परमा प्रतिपत्तिर्मनस्कारप्रतिपत्तिरनुधर्मप्रतिपत्तिरन्तद्वयवर्जिता प्रतिपत्तिर्विशिष्टप्रतिपत्तिरविशिष्टप्रतिपत्तिः ॥

२ (क). परमा प्रतिपत्तिः

ततः—

परमा द्वादशात्मिका ॥२॥

औदार्यमायतत्वं च अधिकारोऽक्षयात्मता ।
नैरन्तर्यमकृच्छ्रत्वं वितत्वं च परिग्रहः ॥३॥
आरम्भप्राप्तिनिष्यन्दनिष्पत्तिः परमा मता ।

इत्येषा द्वादशविधा परमता । यदुतौदार्यपरमता आयतत्वपरमता अधिकार-

परमता अक्षयत्वपरमता नैरन्तर्यपरमता अकृच्छ्रत्वपरमता वितत्त्वपरमता परिग्रहपरमता आरम्भपरमता प्रतिलम्भपरमता निष्यन्दपरमता निष्पत्तिपरमता च । तत्रौदार्यपरमता सर्वलौकिकसम्पत्त्यनर्थित्वेनोत्कृष्टतया वेदितव्या । आयतत्वपरमता त्रिकल्पासंख्येयपरिभावनात् । अधिकारपरमता सर्वसत्त्वार्थक्रियाधिकारात् । अक्षयत्वपरमता महाबोधिपरिणामनयात्यन्तमपर्यादानात् । नैरन्तर्यपरमतात्मपरसमताधिमोक्षात् सर्वसत्त्वदानादिभिः पारमितापरिपूरणात् । अकृच्छ्रत्वपरमता अनुमोदनामात्रेण परदानादीनां पारमितापरिपूरणात् । वितत्त्वपरमता[22a] गगनगञ्जसमाध्यादिभिर्दानादिपरिपूरणात् । परिग्रहपरमता निर्विकल्पज्ञानपरिगृहीतत्वात् । आरम्भपरमताधिमुक्तिचर्याभूमावधिमात्रायां क्षान्तौ । प्रतिलम्भपरमता प्रथमायां भूमौ । निष्यन्दपरमता तदन्यास्वष्टासु भूमिषु । निष्पत्तिपरमता दशम्यां भूमौ ताथागत्यां च बोधिसत्त्वनिष्पत्त्या बुद्धनिष्पत्त्या च ॥

ततश्च परमार्थेन दश पारमिता मताः ॥४॥

यत एषा द्वादशविधा परमता एतासु संविद्यते ततः परमा इत्यनेनार्थेन दश पारमिताः ॥

कतमा दशेत्येकेषां तन्नामव्युत्पादनार्थमुच्यते—

दानं शीलं क्षमा वीर्यं ध्यानं प्रज्ञा उपायता ।
प्रणिधानं बलं ज्ञानमेताः पारमिता दश ॥५॥

इति । किमासां प्रत्येकं कर्म—

अनुग्रहोऽविघातश्च कर्म तस्य च मर्षणा ।
गुणवृद्धिश्च सामर्थ्यम् अवतारविमोचने ॥६॥
अक्षयत्वं सदावृत्तिर्नियते भोगपाचने ।

इत्येतदासां कर्म यथाक्रमम् । दानेन हि बो[धि]सत्त्वः सत्त्वाननुगृह्णाति । शीलेनोपघातं परेषां न करोति । क्षान्त्या परैः कृतमुपघातं मर्षयति । वीर्येण गुणान् वर्धयति । ध्यानेनद्धर्यादिभिरावर्ज्यावतारयति । प्रज्ञया सम्यगववाददानाद् विमोचयति उपायकौ[22b] शल्यपारमितय महाबोधिपरिणामनाद्दानादीनक्षयान् करोति । प्रणिधानपारमितयानुकूलोपपत्तिपरिग्रहात् सर्वजन्मसु बुद्धोत्पादारागणतो दानादिषु

सदा प्रवर्तते। बलपारमितया प्रतिसंख्यानभावनाबलाभ्यां नियतं दानादिषु प्रवर्तते । विपक्षानभिभवात् । ज्ञानपारमितया यथारुतधर्मसंमोहापगमाद्दानाद्याधिपतेयधर्मसम्भोगं च प्रत्यनुभवति सत्त्वांश्च परिपाचयति । उक्ता परमा प्रतिपत्तिः ॥

२ (ख). मनस्कारप्रतिपत्तिः

मनसिकारप्रतिपत्तिः कतमा—

यथाप्रज्ञप्तितो धर्मे महायानमनस्क्रिया ॥७॥
बोधिसत्त्वस्य सततं प्रज्ञया त्रिप्रकारया ।

दानादीन्यधिकृत्य यथाप्रज्ञप्तानां सूत्रादिधर्माणां महायाने मनसिकरणमभीक्ष्णं श्रुतचिन्ताभावनामय्या प्रज्ञया मनसिकारप्रतिपत्तिः । सा त्रिप्रकारया प्रज्ञया मनसिक्रिया कं गुणमावहति—

धातुपुष्ट्यै प्रवेशाय चार्थसिद्ध्यै भवत्यसौ ॥८॥

तत्र श्रुतमय्या प्रज्ञया मनसिकुर्वतो धातुपुष्टिर्भवति। चिन्तामय्या तस्य श्रुतस्यार्थं भावेन प्रविशति । भावनामय्यार्थसिद्धिं प्राप्नोति, भूमिप्रवेशपरिशोधनात् ॥

संयुक्ता धर्मचरितैः सा ज्ञेया दशभिः [23a] पुनः ।

सा पुनर्मनसिकारप्रतिपत्तिर्दशभिर्धर्मचरितैः परिगृहीता वेदितव्या । कतमद् दशधा धर्मचरितम्—

लेखनं पूजना दानं श्रवणं वाचनोद्ग्रहः ॥९॥
प्रकाशनाथ स्वाध्यायश्चिन्तना भावना च तत् ।

महायानस्य लेखनं, पूजनं, परेभ्यो दानं, परेण वाच्यमानस्य श्रवणं, स्वयं च वाचनम्, उद्ग्रहणं, परेभ्यः प्रकाशनं ग्रन्थस्यार्थस्य वा स्वाध्यायनं, चिन्तनं भावनं च ॥

अमेयपुण्यस्कन्धं हि चरितं तद्दशात्मकम् ॥१०॥

कस्मान्महायान एव धर्मचरितमत्यन्तं महाफलं देश्यते, सूत्रेषु न पुनः श्रावकयाने । द्वाभ्यां कारणाभ्याम्—

विशेषादक्षयत्वाच्च

कथं विशेषात् कथमक्षयत्वात्—

परानुग्रहतोऽशमात् ।

परानुग्रहवृत्तित्वाद्विशिष्टत्वं परिनिर्वाणेऽप्यशमान्न अनुपरमादक्षयत्वं वेदितव्यम् । उक्ता मनसिकारप्रतिपत्तिः ॥

२ (ग). अनुधर्मप्रतिपत्तिः

अनुधर्मप्रतिपत्तिः कतमा—

अविक्षिप्ताविपर्यासपरिणतानुधार्मिकी ॥११॥

इत्येषा द्विविधानुधर्मप्रतिपत्तिर्यदुताविक्षिप्ता चाविपर्यासपरिणता च ॥

(अ) अविक्षिप्तपरिणता

तत्र षड्विधविक्षेपाभावादविक्षिप्ता । तत्र षड्विधो विक्षेपः—प्रकृतिविक्षेपो [23b]बहिर्धाविक्षेपः अध्यात्मविक्षेपो निमित्तविक्षेपो दौष्ठुल्यविक्षेपो मनसिकारविक्षेपश्च । स एष किंलक्षणो वेदितव्य इत्यत आह—

व्युत्थानं विषये सारस्तथास्वादलयोद्धतः ।
सम्भावनाभिसन्धिश्च मनस्कारोऽप्यहंकृतिः ॥१२॥
हीनचित्तं च विक्षेपः परिच्छेदे हि धीमता ।

"इत्येवंलक्षणः षड्विधो विक्षेपोत्पादस्तत्र सहेतुः परिज्ञेयः । तत्र व्युत्थानं समाधितः पञ्चभिर्विज्ञानकायैः प्रकृतिविक्षेपः । विषये विसारो बहिर्धाविक्षेपः । समाधेरास्वादना लयौद्धत्यं चाध्यात्मविक्षेपः । सम्भावनाभिसन्धिर्निमित्तविक्षेपः, तन्निमित्तं कृत्वा प्रयोगात् । साहंकारमनस्कारता दौष्ठुल्यविक्षेपो, दौष्ठुल्यवशेनास्मिमानसमुदाचारात् । हीनचित्तत्वं मनसिकारविक्षेपो, हीनयानमनसिकारसमुदाचारात् ॥

(आ) अविपर्यासपरिणता

तत्राविपर्यासो दशविधे वस्तुनि वेदितव्यः । यदुत—

व्यञ्जनार्थमनस्कारे विसारे लक्षणद्वये ॥१३॥
दौष्ठुल्यशुद्धावागन्तुकत्वेऽत्रासे अनुन्नतौ ।

तत्र—

संयोगात्संस्तवाच्चैव वियोगादप्यसंस्तवात् ॥१४॥
अर्थसत्त्वमसत्त्वं च व्यञ्जने सोऽविपर्ययः ।

संयोगे सति व्यञ्जनानामव्यञ्जनानमविच्छन्नोविच्छिन्नोच्चारणतयास्य चेदं नामेति संस्तवात् सार्थकत्वम्, विपर्ययान्निरर्थकत्वमिति यदेवंदर्शनं सोऽविपर्यासो व्यञ्जने वेदितव्यः ॥

तत्कथमर्थेऽविपर्यासः—

द्वयेन प्रतिभासत्वं तथा चाविद्यमानता ॥१५॥
अर्थे स चाविपर्यासः सदसत्त्वेन वर्जितः ।

द्वयेन ग्राह्यग्राहकत्वेन प्रतिभासते तदाकारोत्पत्तितः । तथा च न विद्यते यथा प्रतिभासत इति । अर्थे यद् दर्शनं स तत्राविपर्यासः । अर्थस्य सत्त्वेन वर्जितो ग्राह्यग्राहकाभावात् । असत्त्वेन वर्जितस्तत्प्रतिभासभ्रान्तिसद्भावात् ॥

तञ्जल्पभावितो जल्पमनस्कारस्तदाश्रयः ॥१६॥
मनस्कारेऽविपर्यासो द्वयप्रख्यानका(र)णे ।

ग्राह्यग्राहकजल्पपरिभावितो जल्पमनस्कारस्तस्य ग्राह्यग्राहकविकल्पस्याश्रयो भवतीत्ययं मनस्कारेऽविपर्यासः । कतमस्मिन् मनस्कारे । ग्राह्यग्राहकसंप्रख्यानकारणे । स ह्यसौ जल्पमनस्कारोऽभिलापसंज्ञापरिभावितत्वाद् ग्राह्यग्राहकविकल्पाश्रयो वेदितव्यः ॥

मायादिवदसत्त्वं च सत्त्वं चार्थस्य तन्मतम् ॥१७॥
सोऽविसारेऽविपर्यासो भावाभावाविसारतः ।

यत्तदर्थस्यासत्त्वं सत्त्वं चानन्तरमुक्तं [24b] तन्मायादिवन्मतम् । एषा माया न हस्त्यादिभावेनास्ति, न च नैवास्ति, तद्भ्रान्तिमात्रास्तित्वात्, एवमर्थोऽपि न चास्ति यथा संप्रख्याति ग्राह्यग्राहकत्वेन, न च नैवास्ति तद्भ्रान्तिमात्रास्तित्वात् । आदिशब्देन मरीचिस्वप्नोदकचन्द्रादयो दृष्टान्ता यथायोगं वेदितव्या इति यन्मायाद्युपमार्थे दर्शनादविसारं चेतसः पश्यति सोऽविसारेऽविपर्यासस्तेन भावाभावयोश्चित्तस्याविसरणात् ॥

सर्वस्य नाममात्रत्वं सर्वकल्पाप्रवृत्तये ॥१८॥
स्वलक्षणेऽविपर्यासः

सर्वमिदं नाममात्रं यदिदं चक्षूरूपं यावन्मनोधर्मा इति यज्ज्ञानं सर्वविकल्पानां प्रतिपक्षेण । अयं स्वलक्षणेऽविपर्यासः । कतमस्मिन् स्वलक्षणे—

परमार्थे स्वलक्षणे ।

संवृत्यां तु नेदं नाममात्रमिति गृह्यते ॥

धर्मधातुविनिर्मुक्तो यस्माद्धर्मो न विद्यते ॥१९॥
सामान्यलक्षणं तस्मात् स च तत्राविपर्ययः ।

न हि धर्मनैरात्म्येन विना कश्चिद्धर्मो विद्यते तस्माद् धर्मधातुः सर्वधर्माणां सामान्यं लक्षणमिति यदेवं ज्ञानम्, अयं सामान्यलक्षणेऽविपर्यासः ॥

विपर्यस्तमनस्काराविहानिपरिहानिता ॥२०॥
तदशुद्धिर्विशुद्धिश्च स च तत्राविपर्ययः ।

विपर्यस्तमनस्काराप्रहाणं तस्य धर्मधातोरविशुद्धिस्तत्प्रहाणं विशुद्धिरिति यदेवं ज्ञानम्, अयमविशुद्धौ विशुद्धौ चाविपर्यासो यथाक्रमम् ॥

धर्मधातोर्विशुद्धत्वात्प्रकृत्या व्योमवत्पुनः ॥२१॥
द्वयस्यागन्तुकत्वं हि स च तत्रा[25a]विपर्ययः ।

धर्मधातोः पुनराकाशवत् प्रकृतिविशुद्धत्वाद् द्वयमप्येतदागन्तुकमविशुद्धि[विशुद्धि]श्च पश्चादिति यदेवं ज्ञानम्, अयमागन्तुकत्वेऽविपर्यासः ॥

संक्लेशश्च विशुद्धिश्च धर्मपुद्गलयोर्न हि ॥२२॥
असत्त्वात्त्रासतामानौ नातः सोऽत्राविपर्ययः ।

न हि पुद्गलस्य संक्लेशो न विशुद्धिर्नापि धर्मस्य, यस्मान्न पुद्गलोऽस्ति न धर्मः। यतश्च न कस्यचित् कर्मसंक्लेशो न व्यवदानम्, अतो न संक्लेशपक्षे कस्यचिद्धानिर्न व्यवदानपक्षे कस्यचिद्विशेषो यतस्त्रासो वा स्यादुन्नतिर्वेत्ययमत्रासेऽनुन्नतौ चाविपर्यासः ॥

दश वज्रपदानि

एते च दशाविपर्यासा दशसु वज्रपदेषु यथाक्रमं योजयितव्याः । दश वज्रपदानि—सदसत्ताऽविपर्यास आश्रयो मायोपमता अविकल्पनता प्रकृतिप्रभास्वरता संक्लेशो व्यवदानमाकाशोपमता अहीनता विशिष्टता च ॥

वज्रपदानां शरीरव्यवस्थानं स्वभावत आलम्बनतोऽविकल्पनतश्चोद्यपरिहारतश्च । तत्र स्वभावतस्त्रयः स्वभावाः परिनिष्पन्नपरिकल्पितपर[त]न्त्राख्या आद्यैस्त्रिभिः पदैर्यथाक्रमम् । आलम्बनतस्त एव । अविकल्पनतो येन न विकल्पयति निर्वि[25b]कल्पेन ज्ञानेन यच्च न विकल्पयति प्रकृतिप्रभास्वरताम् । तदनेन ज्ञेयज्ञानव्यवस्थानं यथाक्रमं वेदितव्यं यदुत त्रिभिः स्वभावैरविकल्पनतया च । चोद्यपरिहारतः शिष्टानि पदानि । तत्रेदं चोद्यम्—यद्येते परिकल्पितपरतन्त्रलक्षणा धर्मा न संविद्यन्ते, कथमुपलभ्यन्ते । अथ संविद्यन्ते धर्माणां प्रकृतिप्रभास्वरता न युज्यते । तन्मायोपमतया परिहरति—यथा मायाकृतं न विद्यते उपलभ्यते च । यदि प्रकृतिप्रभास्वरता धर्माणां तत्कथं पूर्वं संक्लेशः पश्चाद् व्यवदानम् । अस्य परिहारः—संक्लेशव्यवदानमाकाशोपमतया वेदितव्यम् । यथाकाशं प्रकृतिपरिशुद्धं संक्लिश्यते व्यवदायते चेति । यद्यप्रमेयबुद्धोत्पादे सति अप्रमेयाणां सत्त्वानां क्लेशोपशमः तत्कथं न संसारसमुच्छेदो न निर्वाणवृद्धिर्भवति । तस्याहीनाविशिष्टतया परिहारः । अप्रमेयत्वात् सत्त्वधातोर्व्यवदानपक्षस्य च ।

द्वितीयं शरीरव्यवस्थानम्—

यत्र या च यतो भ्रान्ति[रभ्रान्ति]र्या च यत्र च ।
भ्रान्त्यभ्रान्तिफले चैव पर्यन्तश्च तयोरिति ॥
सदसत्ताविपर्यास आश्रयो माययोपमा ।
अकल्पना प्रकृत्या च भास्वरत्वं सदैव हि ॥
[26a]संक्लेशो व्यवदानं च आकाशोपमता तथा ।
अहीनानधिकत्वं च दश वज्रपदानि हि ॥

उक्तानुधर्मप्रतिपत्तिः ॥

२ (घ). अन्तद्वयवर्जनप्रतिपत्तिः

अन्तद्वयवर्जने प्रतिपत्तिः कतमा या रत्नकूटे मध्यमा प्रतिपत्तिरुपदिष्टा । कस्यान्तस्य वर्जनायासौ वेदितव्या—

पृथक्त्वैकत्वमन्तश्च तीर्थ्यश्रावकयोरपि ॥२३॥

समारोपापवादान्तो द्विधा पुद्गलधर्मयोः ।
विपक्षप्रतिपक्षान्त(:) शाश्वतोच्छेदसंज्ञितः ॥२४॥

ग्राह्यग्राहकसंक्लेशव्यवदाने द्विधा त्रिधा ।
विकल्पद्वयतान्त(त्व)त्स च सप्तविधो मतः ॥२५॥

भावाभावे प्रशाम्येऽथ शमनेत्रास्यतद्भये ।
ग्राह्यग्राहकसम्यक्त्वमिथ्यात्वे व्यापृतौ न च ॥२६॥
अजन्मसमकालत्वे सविकल्पा द्वयान्तता ।

तत्र रूपादिभ्यः पृथक्त्वमात्मन इत्यन्तः । एकत्वमित्यन्तः । तत्परिवर्जनार्थं मध्यमा प्रतिपत् । यया नात्मप्रत्यवेक्षा यावन्न मानवप्रत्यवेक्षा । आत्मदर्शने हि जीवस्तच्छरीरं अन्यो जीवोऽन्यच्छरीरमिति भवति दर्शनम् ।

नित्यं रूपमिति तीर्थिकान्तः । अनित्यमिति श्रावकान्तः । तत्परिवर्जनार्थं मध्यमा प्रतिपत् या रूपादीनां न नित्यप्रत्यवेक्षा नानित्यप्रत्यवेक्षा ।

आत्मेति पुद्गलसमारोपान्तो नै[26b]रात्म्यमित्यपवादान्तः प्रज्ञप्तिसतो अप्यपवादात् । तत्परिवर्जनार्थं मध्यमा प्रतिपत् यदात्मनैरात्म्ययोर्मध्यं निर्विकल्पं ज्ञानम् ।

भूतं चित्तमिति धर्मसमारोपान्तः । अभूतमित्यपवादान्तः । तत्परिवर्जनार्थं मध्यमा प्रतिपद् यत्र न चित्तं न चेतना न मनो न विज्ञानम् ।

अकुशलादयो धर्माः संक्लेश इति विपक्षान्तः । कुशलादयो व्यवदानमिति [प्रति]-पक्षान्तः । तत्परिवर्जनार्थं मध्यमा प्रतिपद् योऽस्यान्तद्वयस्यानुपगमोऽनुदाहारो अप्रव्याहारः ।

अस्तीति शाश्वतान्तस्तयोरेव पुद्गलधर्मयोर्नास्तीत्युच्छेदान्तः । तत्परिवर्जनार्थं मध्यमा प्रतिपद्यदनयोर्द्वयोरन्तयोर्मध्यम् ।

अविद्या ग्राह्या ग्राहिका चेत्यन्तः । एवं विद्या संस्काराश्चासंस्कृतं च तत्प्रतिपक्षो यावज्जरामरणं ग्राह्यं ग्राहकं चेत्यन्तस्तन्निरोधो ग्राह्यो ग्राहको वेत्यन्तो येन मार्गेण तन्निरुध्यते । एवं ग्राह्यग्राहकान्तो द्विधा कृष्णशुक्लपक्षभेदेन । तत्परिवर्जनार्थं मध्यमा प्रतिपद् विद्या चाविद्या चाद्वयमेतदिति विस्तरेण विद्याविद्यादीनां ग्राह्यग्राहकत्वाभावात् ।

त्रिविधः संक्लेशः—क्लेशसंक्लेशः [27a] कर्मसंक्लेशो जन्मसंक्लेशश्च । तत्र क्लेशसंक्लेशस्त्रिविधः— दृष्टिः रागद्वेषमोहनिमित्तं पुनर्भवप्रणिधानं च, यस्य प्रतिपक्षो ज्ञानशून्यता ज्ञानानिमित्तं ज्ञानाप्रणिहितं च । कर्मसंक्लेशः शुभाशुभकर्माभिसंस्कारो यस्य प्रतिपक्षो ज्ञानानभिसंस्कारः । जन्मसंक्लेशः पुनर्भवजातिर्जातस्य चित्तचैत्तानां प्रतिक्षणोत्पादः पुनर्भवप्रबन्धश्च यस्य प्रतिपक्षो ज्ञानाजातिर्ज्ञानानुत्पादो ज्ञानास्वभावता च । एतस्य त्रिविधस्य संक्लेशस्यापगमो व्यवदानम् । तत्र ज्ञानशून्यतादिभिर्ज्ञेयशून्यतादयो धर्मा एतेन त्रिविधेन संक्लेशेन यथायोगं यावन्न शून्यतादयः क्रियन्ते प्रकृत्यैव शून्यतादयो धर्मधातोः प्रकृत्यसंक्लिष्टत्वात् । तेन यदि धर्मधातुः संक्लिश्यते वा विशुध्यते वेति कल्प[य]त्ययमन्तः प्रकृत्यसंक्लिष्टस्य संक्लेशविशुद्धयभावात् । एतस्यान्तस्य परिवर्जनार्थं मध्यमा प्रतिपद् यन्न शून्यतया धर्मान् शून्यान् करोति, अपि तु धर्मा एव शून्या इत्येवमादि ॥

अपरः सप्तविधो विकल्पद्वयान्तस्तद्यथा—भावेऽपि विकल्पोऽन्तोऽभावेऽपि पुद्गलोऽस्ति यस्य वि[27b]नाशाय शून्यता नैरात्म्यमपि वा नास्तीति कल्पनात् । तदेतस्य विकल्पद्वयान्तस्य परिवर्जनार्थमियं मध्यमा प्रतिपत्—न खलु पुद्गलविनाशाय शून्यता अपि तु शून्यतैव शून्या । पूर्वान्तशून्यता अपरान्तशून्यता प्रत्युत्पन्नशून्यता इत्येवमादि विस्तरः ॥

शाम्येऽपि विकल्पोऽन्तः शमनेऽपि विकल्पोऽन्तः प्रहेयप्रहाणकल्पनया शून्यतायास्त्रसनात् । एतस्य विकल्पद्वयान्तस्य परिवर्जनार्थमाकाशदृष्टान्तः ॥

त्रास्येऽपि विकल्पोऽन्तस्ततश्च त्रास्याद्भयेऽपि, परिकल्पितरूपादित्रसनाद् दुःखभीरुतया । एतस्य विकल्पद्वयान्तस्य परिवर्जनार्थं चित्रकरदृष्टान्तः । पूर्वको दृष्टान्तः श्रावकानारभ्य, अयं तु बोधिसत्त्वान् ॥

ग्राह्येऽपि विकल्पोऽन्तो ग्राहकेऽपि । एतस्य विकल्पद्वयान्तस्य परिवर्जनार्थं मायाकारदृष्टान्तः । विज्ञप्तिमात्रज्ञानकृतं ह्यर्थाभावज्ञानम् । तच्चार्थाभावज्ञानं तदेव विज्ञप्तिमात्रज्ञानं निवर्तयति, अर्थाभावे विज्ञप्त्यसंभवादिति तत्र साधर्म्यम् ॥

सम्यक्त्वेऽपि विकल्पोऽन्तो मिथ्यात्वेऽपि, भूतप्रत्यवेक्षां सम्यक्त्वेन कल्पयतो मिथ्यात्वेन वा । एतस्यान्तद्वयस्य परिवर्जनार्थं काष्ठद्वयाग्निदृष्टान्तः । यथा[28a] काष्ठद्वयादनग्निलक्षणादग्निर्जायते, जातश्च तदेव काष्ठद्वयं दहति । एवमसम्यक्त्व-

लक्षणाया यथाभूतप्रत्यवेक्षायाः सम्यक्त्वलक्षणमार्यं प्रज्ञेन्द्रियं जायते । जातं च तामेव भूतप्रत्यवेक्षां विभावयति । इत्येतदत्र साधर्म्यम् । न चासम्यक्त्वलक्षणाऽपि भूतप्रत्यवेक्षा मिथ्यात्वलक्षणा सम्यक्त्वानुकूल्यात् ॥

व्यापृतावपि विकल्पोऽन्तोऽव्यापृतावपि ज्ञानस्य बुद्धिपूर्वां क्रियां निःसामर्थ्यं वा कल्पयतः । एतस्य विकल्पद्वयान्तस्य परिवर्जनार्थं तैलप्रद्योतदृष्टान्तः ॥

अजन्मत्वेऽपि विकल्पोऽन्तः समकालत्वेऽपि, यदि प्रतिपक्षस्यानुत्पत्तिं वा कल्पयति संक्लेशस्यैव वा दीर्घकालत्वम् । एतस्य विकल्पद्वयान्तस्य परिवर्जनार्थं द्वितीयस्तैलप्रद्योतदृष्टान्तः । उक्ताऽन्तद्वयपरिवर्जने प्रतिपत्तिः ॥

२ (ङ–च) विशिष्टाविशिष्टप्रतिपत्तिः

विशिष्टा चाविशिष्टा च प्रतिपत्तिः कतमा—

विशिष्टा चाविशिष्टा च ज्ञेया दशसु भूमिषु ॥२७॥

यस्यां भूमौ या पारमितातिरिक्ततरा सा तत्र विशिष्टा । सर्वासु च सर्वत्र समुदागच्छतीत्यविशिष्टा । उक्तं प्रतिपत्त्यानुत्तर्यम् ॥

३. आलम्बनानुत्तर्यम्

आलम्बनानुत्तर्यं कतमत्—

व्यवस्थानं ततो धातुः साध्यसाधनधारणा ।
अवधार[28b]प्रधारा च प्रतिवेधः प्रतानता ॥२८॥

प्रगमः प्रसठत्वं च प्रकर्षालम्बनं मतम् ।

इत्येतद्द्वादशविधमालम्बनम् यदुत धर्मप्रज्ञप्तिव्यवस्थानालम्बनं धर्मधात्वालम्बालम्बनं साध्यालम्बनं साधनालम्बनं धारणालम्बनमवधारणालम्बनं प्रधारणालम्बनं प्रतिवेधालम्बनं प्रतानतालम्बनं प्रगमालम्बनं प्रसठतालम्बनं प्रकर्षालम्बनं च । तत्र प्रथमं पारमितादयो धर्मा व्यवस्थाप्यन्ते । द्वितीयं तथता । तृतीयचतुर्थे त एव यथाक्रमं धर्मधातुप्रतिवेधेन पारमितादिधर्माधिगमात् । पञ्चमं श्रुतमयज्ञानालम्बनम् । षष्ठं चिन्तामयस्यावगम्य धारणात् । सप्तमं भावनामयस्य प्रत्यात्मं धारणात् । [8]अष्टमं प्रथमायां भूमौ दर्शनमार्गस्य । नवमं भावनामार्गस्य

यावत्सप्तम्यां भूमौ । दशमं तत्रैव लौकिकलोकोत्तरस्य मार्गस्य प्रकारशो धर्माधिगमात् । एकादशमष्टम्यां भूमौ द्वादशं नवम्यादिभूमित्रये । तदेव हि प्रथमद्वयं तस्यां तस्यामवस्थायां तत्तदालम्बनं नाम लभते उक्तमालम्बनम् ॥

४. समुदागमानुत्तर्यम्

समुदागमः कतमः—

अवैकल्याप्रतिक्षेपोऽविक्षेपश्च [29a] **प्रपूरणा ॥२९॥**
समुत्पादनिरूढिश्च कर्मण्यत्वाप्रतिष्ठता ।
निरावरणता तस्याप्रस्रब्धिः समुदागमः ॥३०॥

इत्येष दशविधः समुदागमः । तत्र प्रत्ययावैकल्यं गोत्रसमुदागमः । महायानाप्रतिक्षेपो अधिमुक्तिसमुदागमः । हीनयानाविक्षेपश्चित्तोत्पादसमुदागमः । पारमितापरिपूरणा प्रतिपत्तिसमुदागमः । आर्यमार्गोत्पादो नियामावक्रान्तिसमुदागमः । कुशलमूलनिरूढित्वं दीर्घकालपरिचयात्सत्त्वपरिपाकसमुदागमः । चित्तकर्मण्यत्वं क्षेत्रपरिशुद्धिसमुदागमः । संसारनिर्वाणाप्रतिष्ठता अविनिवर्तनीयभूमिव्याकरणलाभसमुदागमः संसारनिर्वाणाभ्यामविनिवर्तनात् । निरावरणता बुद्धभूमिसमुदागमः । तदप्रस्रब्धिर्बोधिसन्दर्शनसमुदागमः । इत्येतत्

शास्त्रं मध्यविभागं हि

मध्यमा प्रतिपत्प्रकाशनान्मध्यान्तविभागमप्येतन्मध्यस्यान्तयोश्च प्रकाशनात् । अस्य परिवर्जितस्य मध्यस्य वा[1]

गूढः सारार्थमेव च ।

तर्कस्यागोचरत्वात् परवादिभिरभेद्यत्वाच्च यथाक्रमम् ।

महार्थं चैव

स्वपराधिकारात् ।

सर्वार्थम्

यानत्रयाधिकारात् ।

सर्वानर्थप्रणो[29b]दनम् ॥३१॥

क्लेशज्ञेयावरणप्रहाणावाहनात् ॥

५. आनुत्तर्यपिण्डार्थः

आनुत्तर्यपिण्डार्थः । समासतस्त्रिविधमानुत्तर्यम्—प्रतिपत्तिः प्रतिपत्त्याधारः प्रति[पत्ति]फलं चैव । सा च प्रतिपत्तिर्यादृशी परमा येन च

यथाप्रज्ञप्तितो धर्मे महायानमनस्क्रिया

इत्येवमादिना यथा येन प्रकारेण विक्षेपपरिणता च शमथभावनया अविपर्यासपरिणता च विपश्यनाभावनया, यदर्थं च मध्यमया प्रतिपदा निर्याणार्थं यत्र च दशसु भूमिषु विशिष्टा चाविशिष्टा च ॥

६. अविपर्यासपिण्डार्थः

अविपर्यासानां पिण्डार्थः। व्यञ्जनाऽविपर्यासेन शमथमेव निमित्तं प्रतिविध्यति। अर्थाविपर्यासेन विपश्यनानिमित्तं प्रतिविध्यति । मनस्काराविपर्यासेन विपर्यासनिदानं परिवर्जयति। अविसाराविपर्यासेन तन्निमित्तमुद्गृहीतं करोति । स्वलक्षणाविपर्यासेन तत्प्रतिपक्षेणाविकल्पं मार्गं भावयति । सामान्यलक्षणाविपर्यासेन व्यवदानप्रकृतिं प्रतिविध्यति । अशुद्धिमनस्काराविपर्यासेन तदावरणानावरणप्रहीणतां प्रजानाति। तदागन्तुकत्वाविपर्यासेन संक्लेशव्यवदानं यथाभूतं प्रजानाति। अत्रासानुन्नत्यविपर्यासेन निरावरणो निर्याति ॥

॥ आ[30a] नुत्तर्यपरिच्छेदः पञ्चमः ॥
॥ समाप्तो मध्यान्तविभागः ॥

व्याख्यामिमामुपनिबध्य यदस्ति पुण्यं
पुण्योदयाय महते जगतस्तदस्तु।
ज्ञानोदयाय च यतोऽभ्युदयं महान्तं
बोधित्रयं च न चिराज्जगदश्नुवीत ॥

इति मध्यान्तविभागकारिकाभाष्यं समाप्तम् ॥
॥ कृतिराचार्यभदन्तवसुबन्धोः ॥

त्रिस्वभावनिर्देशः

कल्पितः परतन्त्रश्च परिनिष्पन्न एव च।
त्रयः स्वभावा धीराणां गंभीरं ज्ञेयमिष्यते ॥१॥
यत्ख्याति परतन्त्रोऽसौ यथा ख्याति स कल्पितः।
प्रत्ययाधीनवृत्तित्वात् कल्पनमात्रभावतः ॥२॥
तस्य ख्यातुर्यथाख्यानं या सदाविद्यमानता।
ज्ञेयः स परिनिष्पन्नः स्वभावोऽनन्यथात्वतः ॥३॥
तत्र किं ख्यात्यसत्कल्पः कथं ख्याति द्वयात्मना।
तस्य का नास्तिता तेन या तत्राद्वयधर्मता ॥४॥
असत्कल्पोऽत्र कश्चित्तं यतस्तत्कल्प्यते यथा।
यथा च कल्पयत्यर्थं तथात्यन्तं न विद्यते ॥५॥
तद्धेतुफलभावेन चित्तं द्विविधमिष्यते।
यदालयाख्यविज्ञानं प्रवृत्याख्यं च सप्तधा ॥६॥
संक्लेशवासनाबीजैश् चितत्वाच्चित्तमुच्यते।
चित्तमाद्यं द्वितीयं तु चित्राकारप्रवृत्तितः ॥७॥
समासतोऽभूतकल्पः स चैष त्रिविधो मतः।
वैपाकिकस्तथा नैमित्तिकोऽन्यः प्रातिभासिकः ॥८॥
प्रथमो मूलविज्ञानं तद्विपाकात्मकं यतः।
अन्यः प्रवृत्तिविज्ञानं दृश्यदृग्वित्तिवृत्तिनः ॥९॥
सदसत्त्वाद् द्वयैकत्वात् संक्लेशव्यवदानयोः।
लक्षणाभेदतश्चेष्टा स्वभावानां गंभीरता ॥१०॥
सत्त्वेन गृह्यते यस्मादत्यन्ताभाव एव च।
स्वभावः कल्पितस्तेन सदसल्लक्षणो मतः ॥११॥
विद्यते भ्रान्तिभावेन यथाख्यानं न विद्यते।
परतन्त्रो यतस्तेन सदसल्लक्षणो मतः ॥१२॥
अद्वयत्वेन यच्चास्ति द्वयस्याभाव एव च।
स्वभावस्तेन निष्पन्नः सदसल्लक्षणो मतः ॥१३॥
द्वैविध्यात्कल्पितार्थस्य तदसत्त्वैकभावतः।
स्वभावः कल्पितो बालैर्द्वयैकत्वात्मको मतः ॥१४॥
प्रख्यानाद् द्वयभावेन भ्रान्तिमात्रैकभावतः।
स्वभावः परतन्त्राख्यो द्वयैकत्वात्मको मतः ॥१५॥

द्वयभावस्वभावत्वादद्वयैकस्वभावतः ।
स्वभावः परिनिष्पन्नो द्वयैकत्वात्मको मतः ॥१६॥
कल्पितः परतन्त्रश्च ज्ञेयं संक्लेशलक्षणम् ।
परिनिष्पन्न इष्टस्तु व्यवदानस्य लक्षणम् ॥१७॥
असद्द्वयस्वभावत्वात्तदभावस्वभावतः ।
स्वभावात्कल्पिताज्ज्ञेयो निष्पन्नोऽभिन्नलक्षणः ॥१८॥
अद्वयत्वस्वभावत्वाद्द्वयाभावस्वभावतः ।
निष्पन्नात्कल्पितश्चैव विज्ञेयोऽभिन्नलक्षणः ॥१९॥
यथाख्यानमसद्भावात्तथासत्त्वस्वभावतः ।
स्वभावात्परतन्त्राख्यान्निष्पन्नोऽभिन्नलक्षणः ॥२०॥
असद्द्वयस्वभावत्वाद्यथाख्यानास्वभावतः ।
निष्पन्नात्परतन्त्रोऽपि विज्ञेयोऽभिन्नलक्षणः ॥२१॥
क्रमभेदः स्वभावानां व्यवहाराधिकारतः ।
तत्प्रवेशाधिकाराच्च व्युत्पत्त्यर्थं विधीयते ॥२२॥
कल्पितो व्यवहारात्मा व्यवहारात्मकोऽपरः ।
व्यवहारसमुच्छेदः स्वभावश्चान्य इष्यते ॥२३॥
द्वयाभावात्मकः पूर्वं परतन्त्रः प्रविश्यते ।
ततः प्रविश्यते तत्र कल्पमात्रमसद्द्वयम् ॥२४॥
ततो द्वयाभावभावो निष्पन्नोऽत्र प्रविश्यते ।
तथा ह्यसावेव तदा अस्ति नास्तीति चोच्यते ॥२५॥
त्रयोऽप्येते स्वभावा हि अद्वयालम्ब्यलक्षणाः ।
अभावाद् अतथाभावात् तदभावस्वभावतः ॥२६॥
मायाकृतं मन्त्रवशात्ख्याति हस्त्यात्मना यथा ।
आकारमात्रं तत्रास्ति हस्ती नास्ति तु सर्वथा ॥२७॥
स्वभावः कल्पितो हस्ती परतन्त्रस्तदाकृतिः ।
यस्तत्र हस्त्यभावो ऽसौ परिनिष्पन्न दृष्यते ॥२८॥
असत्कल्पस्तथा ख्याति मूलचित्ताद्द्वयात्मना ।
द्वयमत्यन्ततो नास्ति तत्रास्त्याकृतिमात्रकम् ॥२९॥
मन्त्रवन्मूलविज्ञानं काष्ठवत्तथता मता ।
हस्त्याकारवदेष्टव्यो विकल्पो हस्तिवद्द्वयम् ॥३०॥
अथतत्त्वप्रतिवेधे युगपल्लक्षणत्रये ।
परिज्ञा च प्रहाणं च प्राप्तिश्चेष्टा यथाक्रमम् ॥३१॥
परिज्ञानुपलम्भोऽत्र हानिरख्यानमिष्यते ।
उपलम्भोऽनिमित्तस्तु प्राप्तिः साक्षात्क्रियापि च ॥३२॥

द्वयस्यानुपलम्भेन द्वयाकारो विगच्छति ।
विगमात्तस्य निष्पन्नो द्वयाभावोऽधिगम्यते ॥३३॥
हस्तिनोऽनुपलम्भश्च विगमश्च तदाकृतेः ।
उपलम्भश्च काष्ठस्य मायायां युगपद्यथा ॥३४॥
विरुद्धधीकारणत्वाद् बुद्धेर्वैयर्थ्यदर्शनात् ।
ज्ञानत्रयानुवृत्तेश्च मोक्षापत्तेरयत्नतः ॥३५॥
चित्तमात्रोपलम्भेन ज्ञेयार्थानुपलम्भता ।
ज्ञेयार्थानुपलम्भेन स्याच्चित्तानुपलम्भता ॥३६॥
द्वयोरनुपलम्भेन धर्मधातूपलम्भता ।
धर्मधातूपलम्भेन स्याद्विभुत्वोपलम्भता ॥३७॥
उपलब्धविभुत्वश्च स्वपरार्थप्रसिद्धितः ।
प्राप्नोत्यनुत्तरां बोधिं धीमान्कायत्रयात्मिकाम् ॥३८॥

BIBLIOGRAPHY

[Abbreviations :

tr. translation
S. Sanskrit
T. Tibetan
C. Chinese
E. English
F. French
G. German]

Abhidharmadīpa, ed. Padmanabh S. Jaini, K. P. Jayaswal Research Institute, Patna, 1959.

Ācārāṅga-sūtra (E. tr. Hermann Jacobi), Sacred Books of the East, XXII, Motilal Banarsidass, Delhi.

Aiyaswami Sastri, N., "On the *Pañcavastukavibhāṣā* of Dharmatrāta", *Brahmavidyā* 20, 1956, 234-246.

Aiyyangar, Krishnaswamy, "The Hun Problem in Indian History (and the date of Kālidāsa)," *Indian Antiquary*, 1919, 69.

Akṣayamati-nirdeśa-sūtra, T. tr., Peking/Tokyo T. Tripiṭaka, volume 34, pp. 35-74.

Aṅguttara-Nikāya, (ed. E. Hardy, Richard Morris), Luzac & Co., London, 1898, 1955.

Anuruddha, *Abhidhammaṭṭhasaṅgaha*, E. tr. S.Z. Aung, *Compendium of Philosophy*, Luzac & Company, London, 1910, 1956.

Apte, Vaman Shivaram, *Sanskrit-English Dictionary*, ed. and enlarged P. K. Gode and C. G. Karve, Prasad Prakashan, Poona, 1958 (Motilal Banarsidass Rept).

Āryabhaṭa. *Āryabhaṭīya*, ed. H. Kern, with Parameśvara's *Bhaṭadīpikā*, Leiden, 1874.

Asaṅga,

Abhidharmasamuccaya

ed. Prahlad Pradhan, Santiniketan, 1950.

T. tr., Peking/Tokyo T. Tripiṭaka, volume 112, pp. 4 ff.

Bodhisattvabhūmi
ed. Nalinaksha Dutt, K. P. Jayaswal Research Institute, Patna, 1966.
ed. Unrai Wogihara, Tokyo, 1930-1936.
Mahāyānasaṁgraha, ed., F. tr., E. Lamotte, Muséon, Louvain, 1938.
Vajracchedikā-prajñā-pāramitā-sūtra-śāstra-kārikā, ed. G. Tucci, *Minor Buddhist Texts*, volume I, IsMeo, Rome, 1956.
Aṣṭasāhasrikā-prajñā-pāramitā-sūtra
ed. P.L. Vaidya, Mithila Institute, Darbhanga, 1960.
E. tr., E. Conze, Calcutta Oriental Series, 1958.
Aśvaghoṣa,
Mahāyānaśraddhotpāda (attrib), E. tr. *Awakening of the Mahayana Faith*, Hikeda, Columbia U. Press, N. Y.
Paramārthabodhicittabhāvanākramavarṇasaṁgraha, T. tr., Padmakaravarma, Rin-chen-bzaṅ-po, Peking/Tokyo T. Tripiṭaka, volume 102, p. 19.
Saṁvṛtibodhicittabhāvanopadeśavarṇasaṁgraha, T. tr. Dharmatāśīla, Yes-śes-sde, Peking/Tokyo T. Tripiṭaka, volume 102, pp. 18-19.
Sūtrālaṅkāra (attrib) : see Kumāralāta, *Kalpanamaṇḍatikā*.

Bhattacharyya, Benoytosh, *An Introduction to Buddhist Esoterism*,. Motilal Banarsidass Rept, 1980.
Bhattacharya, J.V., "The Evolution of Vijñānavāda", *Indian Historical Quarterly*, X, 1934, 1-11.
Bhāvaviveka,
Karatalaratna, F. tr. Louis de la Vallée Poussin, *Mélanges Chinois et Bouddhiques* II, 1933
Madhyamakahṛdaya, T. tr. in Peking/Tokyo T. Tripiṭaka, volume 96
Nikāyabhedavibhaṅgavyākhyā, F. tr. A. Bareau, *Journal Asiatique*, 1956, 167-173.
Bareau, André,
Les sectes bouddhiques du Petit Véhicule, École Française d'Extrême-Orient, Saigon, 1955.
"Les sectes bouddhiques du Petit Véhicule et leur Abhidharma-Piṭaka," *BEFEO* v. 44, 11ff.

Bṛhad-āraṇyaka-Upaniṣad, see *Upaniṣads*

Buddhaghosa,

Aṭṭhasālinī, E. tr., Maung Tin, *The Expositor*, Oxford U. Press, London, 1920.

Manorathapūraṇī, ed. Max Walleser, Oxford U. Press, London, 1924.

Papañcasūdanī, ed. J.H. Woods, D. Kosambi, Pali Text Society, London, 1928.

Sārathappakāsinī, Bangkok, 1919

Sumaṅgalavilāsinī, Bangkok, 1920

Visuddhimagga, ed. Henry Clarke Warren, Harvard U. Press, Cambridge, Mass., 1950.

Bu-ston, *Chos-'byung*, E. tr. E. Obermiller, Suzuki Research Foundation Re-print Series No. 1, Tokyo, 1961.

Candrakīrti, *Prasannapadā*, ed. La Vallée Poussin, 1932.

Caraka, *Saṁhitā*, ed. Rajeśvaradatta Śāstrī, Chowkhamba Vidya Bhavan, Benares, 1961.

Daśabalasrīmitra, *Saṁskṛtāsaṁskṛtaviniścaya*, T. tr., Peking/Tokyo T. Tripiṭaka, volume 140, pp 4-109.

Daśabhūmika-sūtra, ed. P.L. Vaidya, Mithila Institute, Darbhanga, 1967.

Das, Sarat Candra, *Tibetan-English Dictionary*, 1902, Motilal Banarsidass Rept., 1970.

Dasgupta, Shashibhushan, *An Introduction to Tantric Buddhism*, U. of Calcutta, 1950.

Obscure Religious Cults, U. of Calcutta, 1946.

Dasgupta, Surendranath, "The Philosophy of Vasubandhu in the *Viṁśatikā* and *Triṁśikā*", *Indian Historical Quarterly*, IV, 1928, 34 ff.

Dayal, Har, *The Bodhisattva Doctrine*, Motilal Banarsidass Rept., 1978.

Demiéville, Paul, *Le Concile de Lhasa*, Imprimerie Nationale de France, Paris, 1952.

"Le *Yogācārabhūmi* de Saṅgharakṣa", *BEFEO* XLIV/

"Les origines des sectes bouddhiques d'après Paramārtha", *Mélanges Chinois et Bouddhiques*, I, pp. 1 ff.

Devaśarman, *Vijñānakāya*, F. tr. Louis de la Vallée Poussin), *Études Asiatiques*, 1925, 343 ff.

Dhammapada, ed., E. tr., S. Radhakrishnan, Oxford U. Press, London, 1950.

Dhammasaṅgaṇi (ed. E. Müller), London, 1885.
E. tr. Carolyn Rhys-Davids, *A Buddhist Manual of Psychological Ethics*, London, 1900.

Dharmakīrti,
Nyāyabindu, ed. Candraśekhara Śāstrī, Chowkhamba Sanskrit Series, Kashi series No. 22, Benares, 1954.
Pramāṇavārttika, I. ed. Raniero Gnoli, IsMeo. Rome, 1960.

Dharmapāla, *Ālambanaparīkṣābhāṣya*, re-tr. into S., N. Aiyaswami Sastri, Adyar Library, Adyar, 1942.

Dharmaśrī, *Abhidharmasāra*, C. tr., Taishō no. 1550.

Dharmatrāta the Sarvāstivādin, *Pañcavastukavibhāṣā*, C. tr., Taishō no. 1555.
Saṁyuktābhidharmasāra, C. tr., Saṅghavarman, Taishō no. 1552.

Dhātukathā, ed. Jagadish Kashyap, Nālandā Devanāgarī Pāli Granthamālā, Nālandā, 1960.

Dīgha-Nikāya, ed. T.W. Rhys-Davids, Pali Text Society, Oxford U. Press, London, 1938, 1949.

Dignāga,
Ālambanaparīkṣā, re-tr. into S., N. Aiyaswami Sastri, Adyar, 1942.
Marmapradīpa, T. tr., Peking/Tokyo T. Tripiṭaka volume 118 pp. 275-331.
Pramāṇasamuccaya, I, "On Perception", ed., E. tr., Masaaki Hattori, Harvard Oriental Series no. 47, Cambridge, Mass., 1968.

Divyāvadāna, ed. P.L. Vaidya, Mithila Institute, Darbhanga, 1959.

Dutt, Nalinaksha, *Aspects of Mahāyāna Buddhism and its Relation to Hīnayāna*, Luzac, London, 1930
"Doctrines of the Sarvāstivādins", *Indian Historical Quarterly*, 14, 1937, 114-120, 799-812.
"Pratisaṅkhyānirodha and apratisaṅkhyānirodha", *HIQ* 33, 1937, 156 ff.

Fa-hsien, *Travels*, E. tr. H.A. Giles, Cambridge U. Press, 1923.

Falk, Maryla, *Nāmarūpa and dharmarūpa*, U. of Calcutta Press, 1943.

Fleet, J., "The Kali-yuga Era of B.C. 3102", *JRAS* 1911, 480 ff.

Frauwallner, Erich, "Abhidharma-Studien : Pañcaskandhaka und Pañcavastuka", *WZKSOA* II, 1958.
"Amalavijñānam und Ālayavijñānam", *Beiträge zur indischen Philosophie und Altertumskunde*, pp. 148-159.
On the Date of the Buddhist Master of the Law Vasubandhu, IsMeo, Rome, 1951.
"Zu den Fragmenten buddhistischer Logiker im *Nyāyavārttikam*", *WZKM*, 40, 1933, 281-307.
"vasubandhus *Vādavidhiḥ*", *WZKSOA* I, 1957, 104 ff.

Freud, Sigmund, *Basic Writings*, Modern Library, New York, 1938.

Gautama Akṣapāda, *Nyāya-sūtras*, ed. Ganganatha Jha and Dhundhiraja Shastri Nyāyopādhyāya, Chowkhamba Sanskrit Series, Benares, 1925.

Gaganagañja-paripṛcchā-sūtra, T. tr., Vijayaśīla, Śilendrabodhi, Yes-śes-sde, Peking/Tokyo T. Tripiṭaka, volume 33, pp. 1-36.

Ghoṣaka, *Abhidharmāmṛta*, re-tr. into S. by Shanti Bhikshu Shastri, Viśvabharati, Santiniketan, 1953

Gokhale, V.V., "The *Pañcaskandha* of Vasubandhu and its commentary by Sthiramati", *Annals of the Bhandarkar Oriental Research Society*, XVII, no. 3.
"What is avijñapti-rūpa ?", *New Indian Antiquary*, 1, 1938-39, 69-73.

Govindagupta (Bālāditya), Basarh seals, *ASR* 1903-4.

Guenther, Herbert, *Philosophy and Psychology of the Abhidharma*, Motilal Banarsidass, 1978.

Guhyasamāja-Tantra, ed. S. Bagchi. Mithila Institute, Darbhanga, 1965.

dGe-bśes-chos-kyi-grags-pa, Peking, 1957.

Haribhadra, *Abhisamayālaṅkārāloka*, ed. P. L. Vaidya, Mithila Institute, Darbhanga, 1960.

Harivarman, *Satyasiddhiśāstra*, C. tr., Taishō 1646; F. tr. excerpts, La Vallée Poussin, *Mélanges Chinois et Bouddhiques*, 5, 1936.

History and Culture of the Indian People, Bharatiya Vidya Bhavan, gen. ed., R. C. Majumdar, Volume III "The Classical Age", Bombay, 1960.

Hṛdaya-prajñā-pāramitā-sūtra, ed. E. Conze, *JRAS* 1948, pp 34 ff.

Hsüan-tsang, *Records of the Western Kingdoms*, E. tr. Samuel Beal, Trübner & Co., London, 1906.
Vijñaptimātratāsiddhi, F. tr. La Vallée Poussin, Geunther, Paris, 1928.
Ingalls, Daniel H. H., *Materials for the Study of Navya-Nyāya Logic*, Harvard Oriental Series, 1951.
Īśvarakṛṣṇa, *Sāṅkhya-kārikās*, ed. Radhanath Phukan, Mukhyopadhyay, Calcutta, 1960.
Itivuttaka, ed. Ernst Windisch, publ. for Pali Text Society by G. Cumberledge, London, 1948.
Jaini, Padmanabh S., "On the Theory of the two Vasubandhus", *BSOAS*, 21, 1958, 48-53.
"Origin and development of the theory of viprayukta-saṁskāras", *BSOAS* 22, 1959, 531 ff
"The Sautrāntika Theory of Bīja", *BSOAS* 22, 1959, 236 ff
"The Vaibhāṣika Theory of Words", *BSOAS* 22, 1959, 95 ff.
Jäschke, H.A., *Tibetan-English Dictionary*, Motilal Banarsidass, Delhi, 1976.
Jātakas, ed. Faustböll, Pali Text Society, 1960.
Jñānaprasthāna, C. tr. Taishō 1543-44; first two chapters re-tr. to S. by Śānti Bhikṣu Śāstri, Visva Bharati, Santiniketan, 1955.
Jung, C.G., *Collected Works*, Pantheon Books, New York, 1953-60.
Kālidāsa,
Mālavikāgnimitra, Nirnaya Sagar Press, Bombay, 1959.
Meghadūta, ed. Franklin Edgerton, Ann Arbor, 1964.
Śākuntalam, Nirnaya Sagar Press, Bombay, 1958.
Kaṇāda, *Vaiśeṣika-sūtras*, ed., E. tr., A. Gough, Benares, 1873.
Karmaprajñapti-śāstra, T. tr., Peking/Tokyo T. Tripiṭaka, volume 115, pp. 85-114.
Kaṭha-Upaniṣad : see *Upaniṣads*
Kathāvatthu, ed. Jagadish Kashyap, Nalanda Devanagari Pali Granthamala, Nalanda, 1960.
Kumāralāta, *Kalpanamaṇḍatikā*, ed. G. Lüders, Kgl. Preussische Turfan-Expeditionen, kleinere S.-texte, Heft 2, 1926.
Kauśika-prajñā-pāramitā-sūtra, ed. P.L. Vaidya, in *Mahāyāna-sūtra saṁgraha*, Mithila Institute, Darbhanga, 1961.

Kāśyapa-parivarta-sūtra, ed. Baron A. von Staël-Holstein, Commercial Press, Shanghai, 1926.

Kundakunda, *Pañcāstikāya-samayasāra*, ed. A. Chakravarti-nayanar, Kumar Devendra Prasada, Central Jaina Publishing House, Arrah, 1920.

La Vallée Poussin, Louis de,

Analyse du Prajñapti-śāstra, Memoires de l'Académie Royale de Belgique, 2- série, tome VI.

"Buddhica", *HJAS*, 1938, 137 ff.

"Controverse Vaibhāṣika-Sautrāntika sur l'existence et causalité d'un acte passé", *EA* 1925, 343 ff.

"Devānāmpriya", *Bulletin de l'Académie de Bruxelles*, 1925, 35 ff.

"Dogmatique bouddhique", *JA* 1902, 237-306; 1903, 358 ff.

La Morale Bouddhique, Paris, 1927.

"Notes sur l'ālayavijñāna", *Mélanges Chinois et Bouddiques*, 3, 1934, pp. 145-168.

"Notes sur le moment ou kṣaṇa des Bouddhistes", *RO* VIII, 1931-32, 1 ff.

"The two nirvāṇadhātus according to the *Vibhāṣā*", Ac. de Belgique, Oct, 1929.

"Vasubandhu l'Ancien", *Bulletin de l'Académie Royale de Belgique*, 16, 1930, 15-39.

Lamotte, Etienne,

"La critique d'authenticité dans le Bouddhisme", *India Antiqua*, Brill, Leiden, 1947, 213 ff.

"La critique d'interpretation dans le Bouddhisme", *Annuaire de l'Institut de philologie et d'histoire orientales et slaves*, Université Libre de Bruxelles, IX, 1949, 341-361.

Laṅkāvatāra-sūtra, ed. P. L. Vaidya, Mithila Institute, Darbhanga, 1960.

Law, Bimala Churn, *Buddhaghosa*, Bombay Branch Royal Asiatic Soc., 1946.

Le Manh That, "Đũa vào việc kháo cú'u triêt Vasubandhu", typescript

Lévi, Sylvain, "Devānāmpriya", *JA* 1891, 549.

Matériaux pour l'étude du systemè Vijñaptimātra", Bibliothèque de l'École des Hautes Études, fasc. 260, Librairie Honoré Champion, Paris, 1932.

Lin Li-kuang, *L'Aide Memoire de la Vraie Loi*, Paris, 1946.

Luk, Charles, *Ch'an and zen Teachings*, first Series, Shanbhala, Berkeley, 1970.

Mādhavācārya, *Sarvadarśanasaṁgraha*, E. tr. E. B. Cowell and A. Gough, London, 1914.

Mahābhārata, Gita Press, Gorakhpur.

Maitreyanātha,

Abhisamayālaṅkāra, ed. P.L. Vaidya, in *S Aṣṭasāhasrikā* q.v., E. tr. E. Conze, IsMeo, F Rome, 1954.

Mahāyānasūtrālaṅkāra, ed. S. Bagchi., Mithila Institute, Darbhanga, 1970.

Madhyāntavibhāga, ed. G. Nagao, Suzuki Research Found., Tokyo, 1962.

Majjhima-Nikāya, ed. R. Chalmers, Pali Text Society, London, 1951.

Majumdar, R.C. & Altekar, A.S., *Vākāṭaka-Gupta Age*, Motilal Banarsidass, Delhi, 1967.

Mallavādin, *Dvādaśāraṇyacakra*, ed. Muni Jambuvijaya, Śrī Ātmānand Jaina Granthamālā, No. 92, Bharnagar, 1966.

Masuda, J., "Origins and doctrines of Early Buddhist Schools", *Asia Major*, II, 1925, 60 ff.

Matthews, *Chinese-English Dictionary*, Harvard U. Press, 1952.

McGovern, William, *A Manual of Buddhist Philosophy*, Kegan Paul, Trench, Trübner & Co., London, 1923.

Mishra, Umesha, *The Conception of Matter in Nyāya-Vaiśeṣika*, Allahabad, 1936.

Nāgārjuna,

Mahāyānaviṁśikā, ed. G. Tucci, Minor Buddhist Texts, I, Rome, 1956.

Mūla-madhyamaka-kārikā, ed. P. L. Vaidya, Mithila Inst., Darbhanga, 1960.

Ratnāvalī (sections only in T), E. tr. Kyo Kanda, Madison, 1966.

Vigrahavyāvartanī, ed. E. H. Johnston, A. Kunst, *Mélanges Chinois et Bouddhiques*, 10, 1951, pp. 99 ff.

Nagao, Gadjin,

"Idealistic School of Buddhism preserved in Tibet", *IBK*, 1953, 75-84.

Index to the Mahāyānasūtrālaṅkāra, Nippon Gakujutsu Shinkō-kai, Tokyo, 1958.

"What Remains in Śūnyatā", in *Mahāyāna Buddhist Meditation*, ed. M. Kiyota, U. of Hawaii Press, Honolulu, 1978.

Nagatomi, Masatoshi, "Arthakriyā", *Brahmavidyā*, 31, 1967, 52-73.

Nettipakaraṇa, ed. E. Hardy, Pali Text Society, London, 1902.

Nyanatiloka, *Guide through the Abhidhamma-Piṭaka*, Colombo, 1957.

Nyāya-kośa, compiled Bhīmācārya Jhalakikar, Bombay S. Series, Chowkhamba, Benares, 1901.

Pañcaviṁśati-sāhasrikā-prajñā-pāramitā-sūtra, ed. N. Dutt, London, 1934.

Paramārtha, *Life of Vasubandhu*, E. tr. J. Takakusu, *T'oung-Pao*, 5, 1904, 269-296.

Parameśvara, *Bhaṭadīpikā*, ed. H. Kern, Leiden, 1874.

Pathak, J., "Kumāragupta the patron of Vasubandhu", *J. Bombay Branch RAS*, 1910, 105; *IA* 40, 1911, 170-171.

Péri, Noel, "A propos de la date de Vasubandhu", *BEFEO* XI, 1911, 355 ff.

Potter, Karl, "Astitva jñeyatva abhidheyatva", *Beiträge zur Geistesgeschichte Indiens, Festschrift für E. G Frauwallner*, ed. G. Oberhammer, Vienna, 1968.

"Introduction to Nyāya-Vaiśeṣika", typescript.

Presuppositions of India's Philosophies, Prentice Hall, 1963.

Pāṇini, *Aṣṭādhyāyī*, ed. Śriśa Candra Vasu, Motilal Banarsidass, 1962.

Patañjali, *Yoga-sūtras*, Dehātī Pustak Bhandar, Delhi, 1961-62.

Paṭṭhāna, ed. Carolyn Rhys-Davids, Pali Text Soc., H. Frowde, London, 1906.

Prajñākaramati, *Bodhicaryāvatarāpañjikā*, ed. P.L. Vaidya, Mithila Institute, Darbhanga, 1959.

Praśastapāda, *Padārthadharmasaṁgraha*, ed. Durgadhar Jha Sharma, Varanasi Saṁskṛta Viśvavidyālaya. Varanasi, 1963.

Praśastapādabhāṣyaṭīkāsaṁgraha, Chowkhamba S. Series, Benares, 1916.

Praśna-Upaniṣad : see *Upaniṣads*

Przyluski, Jean, "Bouddhisme et Upanishad", *BEFEO* 1932.

"Dārṣṭāntika, Sautrāntika, et Sarvāstivādin," *IHQ* 16, 1940, 246 ff.

"Sautrāntika et Dārṣṭāntika", *RO* VIII, 1932, 14 ff.

Rangasvami Sarasvati, "Vasubandhu or Subandhu ?", *IA* 1924, 8-12, 177.

Ratnakīrti, *Kṣaṇabhaṅgasiddhi*, ed. Anantlal Thakur, in *Ratnakīrtinibandhāvalī*, K.P. Jayaswal Research Inst., Patna, 1953.

Ray, Niharranjan, *Theravāda Buddhism in Burma*, U. of Calcutta Press, 1946.

Rhys-Davids, Carolyn,

The Birth of Indian Psychology and its Development in Buddhism, Luzac, London, 1936.

Buddhist Manual of Psychological Ethics: see *Dhammasaṅgaṇi*,

Buddhist Psychology, Quest Series, London, 1914.

Robinson, Richard, "Classical Indian Axiomatic", *Philosophy East and West*, XVII, 1967, 145 ff.

Sakurabe, H., "*Abhidharmāvatāra* by an unidentified author", Nava Nālandā Mahāvihāra Research Inst., II, 1965, 363 ff.

Saletore, R.N., *Life in the Gupta Age*, Popular Book Depot, Bombay, 1943.

Saṁmitīyanikāyaśāstra, C. tr., Taishō 1649, E. tr. Viśva-Bharati Annals 6, 155 ff.

Samyutta-Nikāya, ed. Leon Feer, Pali Text Soc., London, 1884-1904

Sandhinirmocana-sūtra, ed. F. tr. E. Lamotte, Louvain, 1935.

Sanghabhadra, *Abhidharmanyāyānusāra*

chapts. 1, 32, tr. La Vallée Poussin, *BEFEO* XXX, 259-298.

chapts 50-51, tr. Vallée, *MCB* V, pp. 23 ff.

Sankalia, Hasmukh, *The University of Nālandā*, B. C. Paul & Co., Madras, 1934.

Śaṅkarācārya, *Brahma-sūtra-bhāṣya*, ed. S.K. Belvalkar, Poona, 1931

Śāntarakṣita, *Tattvasaṁgraha*, Gaekwad's Oriental Series, Baroda, 1957.

Śāntideva, *Bodhicaryāvatāra*, ed. P.L. Vaidya, Mithila Inst., Darbhanga, 1959.

Śikṣāsamuccaya, ed. P.L. Vaidya, Mithila Inst., Darbhanga, 1960.
Samādhi-rāja-sūtra, ed. P.L. Vaidya, Mithila Inst., Darbhanga, 1961
Saraha, *Doha-kośa*, ed. Shahidullah.
Sarathcandra, "The Abhidhamma Psychology of Perception and the Yogācāra Theory of Mind", *U. of Ceylon Review*, 1956, 49-57.
Sasaki, Genjun, *A Study of Abhidharma Philosophy*, Tokyo U., 1958.
Śatapatha-Brāhmaṇa, E. tr. Julius Eggeling, Sacred Books of the East, volumes 12, 24, 41, 43, 44, Motilal Banarsidass, Delhi.
Śatasāhasrikā-prajñā-pāramitā-sūtra (first part only), ed. Prtaapacandra Ghoṣa, Royal Asiatic Society, Calcutta, 1902.
Schmidthausen, Lambert, "Sautrāntika-Voraussetzungen in *Viṁśatikā* und *Triṁśikā*", *WZKSOA* XI, 1967, 109 ff.
Schubring, Walter, *The Doctrine of the Jainas*, Motilal Banarsidass, 1962.
Shastri, Dharmendra Nath, *Critique of Indian Realism : A study of the Conflict between the Nyāya-Vaiśeṣika and the Buddhist Dignāga School*, Agra U. Press, Motilal Banarsidass, 1964.
Śrīdhara, *Nyāyakandalī*, ed. Durgadhar Jha Sharma, Varanasi Saṁskṛta Viśvavidyālaya, Varanasi, 1963.
Stcherbatsky, The *Buddhist Logic*, Dover re-print, 1962.
"Drei Richtungen in der Philosophie des Buddhismus", *RO* X, 1934, 1 ff.
The Central Conception of Buddhism, Motilal Banarsidass, Delhi, 1978.
"The dharmas of the Buddhists and the guṇas of the Sāṅkhyas", *IHQ* 10, 1934, 237 ff.
Sthiramati,
Madhyāntavibhāgaṭikā
ed. Susumu Yamaguchi, Librairie Hajinkahu, Nagoya, 1934.
ed. R. Pandeya, Motilal Banarsidass, Delhi, 1971.
Triṁśikāvijñaptibhāṣya
ed. S. Lévi, Bibliothèque de l'École des Hautes Études, Librairie Honoré Champion, Paris, 1932.

Subandhu, *Vāsavadattā*, Chowkhamba S. Series, 1935.
Sumatiśīla, *Karmasiddhiṭīkā*, T. tr., Peking/Tokyo T. Tripiṭaka volume 114, pp. 203-223.
Sūtrakṛtāṅga, E. tr. Hermann Jacobi, *Jaina Sūtras*, Sacred Books of the East 45, Motilal Banarsidass, Delhi.
Sutta-Nipāta, ed. Bhikṣu Dharmaratna, Benares, 1960.
Suvarṇaprabhāsa-sūtra, S. text ed. S. Bagchi, Mithila Inst., Darbhaga, 1967. I-tsing's C. tr. tr. to G. by J. Nobel, Leiden, 1958.
Suvikrānta-vikrāmi-paripṛcchā-prajñā-pāramitā-sūtra, ed. P.L. Vaidya, *Mahāyāna-sūtra-saṁgraha*, Mithila Inst., Darbhanga, 1961.
Suzuki, D.T., *Index to the Laṅkāvatāra-sūtra*, S. Buddh. Texts Publ. Soc., Kyoto, 1934.
Studies in the Laṅkāvatāra-sūtra, G. Routledge & Son, London, 1930.
Zen Buddhism, Doubleday Anchor, New York, 1956.
Svalpākṣara-prajñā-pāramitā-sūtra, ed. P.L. Vaidya, Mithila Inst., Darbhanga, 1961.
Takakusu, J., "A Study of Paramārtha's Life of Vasubandhu and the date of Vasubandhu", *JRAS* 1905, 33-53.
"On the Abhidharma Literature of the Sarvāstivādins", *JPTS* 10 1905, 67 ff.
"The date of Vasubandhu", *ISCRL*, 78-83.
Tāranātha, *Geschichte des Buddhismus in Indien*, G.tr., Anton Schiefner, re-print Suzuki Research Foundation, Tokyo.
Tarthang Tulku, *Crystal Mirror* V, Dharma Press, Emeryville, Cal, 1977
Tatia, "Sarvāstivāda", Nava Nālandā Mahāvihāra Research Inst. II, 1960.
Tucci, Giuseppe, "Buddhist Logic before Dignāga", *JRAS* 1929, 151-88, corrections 870-1.
Uddyotakara, *Nyāyavārttika*, Kashi S. Series 33, Benares, 1916.
Umāsvāmī *Tattvārthasūtra*, ed.tr. Sarat, Chandra Ghosal, Kumar Devendra Prasada, Central Jaina Publishing House, Arrah, 1920.
Upaniṣads, ed. E. tr., S. Radhakrishnan, *The Principal Upaniṣads*, Allen and Unwin, London, 1953.
Vajracchedikā-prajñā-pāramitā-sūtra, ed. P.L. Vaidya, in *Mahāyāna-sūtra-saṁgraha*, Mithila Inst., Darbhanga, 1961.

Vāmana, *Kāvyālaṅkārasūtravṛtti*, ed. Viśveśvara Siddhāntaśiromaṇi, Hindi Anusandhān Pariṣad, Delhi, 1954.

Vasubandhu,

Abhidharmakośa

ed. Prahlad Pradhan, K.P. Jayaswal Research Inst., Patna, 1967.

T. tr., Peking/Tokyo T. Tripiṭaka, volume 115.

F. tr. La Vallée Poussin, Geunther, Paris, 1924.

Akṣayamati-nirdeśa-ṭīkā

T. tr., Peking/Tokyo T. Tripiṭaka, volume 104.

Daśabhūmivyākhyāna

T. tr. Mañjuśrīgandha, Yes-śes-sde, Peking/Tokyo T. Tripiṭaka, volume 104, pp 54-136.

Karmasiddhiprakaraṇa

T. tr. Viśuddhisiṁha, Devendrarakṣita,d Pal-brtsegs, Peking/Tokyo T. Tripiṭaka, vol. 113, pp. 295 ff.

F. tr. from the C. tr. of Hsüan-tsang, Taishō 1608-9, in *Mélanges Chinois et Bouddhiques*, E. Lamotte, 4, 1936, pp 151 ff.

Madhyāntavibhāga-bhāṣya

ed. G. Nagao, Suzuki Research Foundation, Tokyo, 1964.

ed. Nathmal Tatia, Anantalal Thakur, K. P. Jayaswal Research Inst., Patna, 1967.

T. tr., Śīlendrabodhi, Yes-śes-sde, Peking/Tokyo T. Tripiṭaka, volume 112, pp. 121-133.

Mahāyānasaṁgraha-bhāṣya

T. tr., Peking/Tokyo T. Tripiṭaka, vol. 112, pp. 272-307.

Mahāyānasūtrālaṅkāra-bhāṣya

ed. S. Bagchi, Mithila Inst., Darbhanga, 1970.

Pañcakāmaguṇopalambhanirdeśa

T. tr. Dharmaśrībhadra, Rin-chen-bzaṅ-po, Peking/Tokyo T. Tripiṭaka, volume 29, pp. 234 ff.

Pañcaskandhakaprakaraṇa

T. tr. Jinamitra, Śīlendrabodhi, Dānaśīla, Yes-śes-sde, Peking/Tokyo T. Tripiṭaka, vol. 113, pp 231-239.

Pratītyasamutpādādivibhaṅganirdeśa

S. fragments ed. G. Tucci, *JRAS* 1930, 611 ff.

T. tr. Surendrakarabhadra, Peking/Tokyo T. Tripiṭaka vol. 104, pp 277-306.

Śīlaparikathā

ed. A. Basu, *IHQ* VII, 1931, 28-33.

Sukhāvativyūhopadeśa

C. tr., Bodhiruci, Taishō 1514, tr. to E. by M. Kiyota, in *Mahāyāna Buddhist Meditation*, U. Press of Hawaii, Honolulu, 1978, pp. 249-290.

Triṁśikā-kārikā

ed. S. Lévi), Bibliothéque de l'École des Hautes Études, Librairie Honoré Champion, Paris, 1925, volume 241-245.

T. tr., Jinamitra, Śīlendrabodhi, Yes-śes-sde, Peking/Tokyo T. Tripiṭaka, vol. 113, pp 232-234.

Trisvabhāvanirdeśa

ed. La Vallée Poussin, Mélanges Chinois et Bouddhiques, II, 1932-33, pp 147-161.

Vādavidhi, ed. G. tr., E. Frauwallner, *WZKSOA* I 1957, 104 ff

Viṁśatikā and *Viṁśatikā-vṛtti*

ed. S. Lévi, Bibliothéque de l'École des Hautes Études, Librairie Honoré Champion, Paris, 1925, volume 241-245.

T. tr., Jinamitra, Śīlendrabodhi, Dānaśīla(kārikās only), Yes-śes-sde, Peking/Tokyo T. Tripiṭaka, v. 113, pp 234 ff.

Vyākhyāyukti

T. tr., Viśuddhisimha, Śākyadharma, Devendrarakṣita, Peking/Tokyo T. Tripiṭaka, vol. 113, pp 241-291.

Vasumitra, Bhadanta,

Pañcavastuka, C. tr., Taishō 1556.

Vasumitra the Ancient,

Dhātukāya, C. tr, Taishō 1540.

Prakaraṇapāda, C. tr, Taishō 1541, 1542.

Sangītiśāstra, C. tr., Taishō 1549.

Vasumitra the Commentator,

Samayabhedoparacanacakra, F. tr., A. Bareau, *JA* 1954, 229 ff.

Vātsyāyana,
Nyāya-bhāṣya, ed. Ganganatha Jha, Dhundhiraja Shastri, Chowkhamba S. Series, Benares, 1925.

Vibhaṅga, ed. Jagadish Kashyap, Nālandā Devanāgarī Pāli Granthamālā, 1960.

Vibhāṣā
selections, F. tr, La Vallée Poussin, Mélanges Chinois et Bouddhiques I, II
chapter 31-34, F. tr., La Vallée Poussin, *BEFEO* 1930, pp. 1-28.
chapter 75 " " ", 1931, 17 ff, 248 ff.
chapter 76, " ", *Mélanges* 5, pp 7 ff.

Vimalakīrti-nirdeśa-sūtra, E. tr. Charles Luk, Shambhala, Berkeley, 1972.

Vyāsa, *Yoga-sūtra-bhāṣya*, see Patañjali

Wayman, Alex, *Analysis of the Śrāvaka-Bhūmi Ms*, U. of California Publications in Classical Philology, VII, 1961, Berkeley.
"The rules of debate according to Asanga", *JAOS* LXXVIII, 1958, 29-40.

Yamada, Kyodo, "On the idea of avijñapti-rūpa", *IBK* 10, 1962, 51 ff.

Yamaguchi, Susumu, *Seshin no jōgorōn*, Toyko, 1951.

Yamaka, ed. Carolyn Rhys-Davids, Pali Text Soc., H. Frowde, London, 1911-1913.

Yaśomitra, *Abhidharmakośavyākhyā* ("*Sphuṭārtha*"), chapters I-III, ed. Narendra Nath Law, Luzac, London, 1949.

gZhon-nu-dpal, Yid-bzang-rtse, *Blue Annals*, E. tr. G. Roerich, Royal Asiatic Socety of Bengal, 1949.

INDEX OF PROPER NAMES

14, travels to Kashmir 15, studies with Kashmirian masters 15-16, returns to Puruṣapura 16, composition of *Kośa* 17-18, and *Kośa-bhaṣya* 17, *Pudgala-pratiṣedha-prakaraṇa* 18, journey to Śākala 18, moves to Ayodhyā 18, early estimate of Asaṅga 19, conversion to Mahāyāna 19-20, composition of *Akṣayamati-nirdeśa-ṭīkā* 19, composition of *Daśabhūmika-vyākhyāna* 19, fondness for *Prajñā-pāramitā sūtras* 19-20, *Commentary on Saddharmapuṇḍarīka* studied by Kumārajīva 20, debate with Sāṅkhyas 20-21, helps build monasteries, schools, hospitals, and rest-houses 21, 22, 23, meditative activity 21, 22, tutors the crown prince and the Empress 21, 22, helps quench great fire at Rājagṛha 22, helps stop epidemic in Janāntapura 22, pupils 2, 20, 27, composition of *Twenty* and *Thirty Verses* 20, wanders again 22, challenged to debate by Saṅghabhadra 22, estimate of Saṅghabhadra 22-23, last journeys 23-24, composition of *Teaching of the Three Own-Beings* 23, death 23, character 24, as a logician 31-37, insistence of statement of invariable concomitance 32, 39, definition of logical pervasion 32, 38-39, criteria for inference-schema 32-33, 34-36, 38-39, reduction of spurious argument types 33, 39, 41-47, definition of direct perception 40, definition of inference 40-41, his *Vāda-vidhi* (*Method for Argumentation*) 31-47, his *Pañcaskandhaka-prakaraṇa* (*Discussion of the Five Aggregates*) 51-75, approach to Abhidharma 57-58, criticizes Mahīśāsaka categories 58-59, 78, 79, 82, succinctness of definitions 58, new use of term "*manas*" 61, metaphor of "seed" 61-62, store-consciousness 61-62, 71-72, 80, 89, 111-117, 183-189, definitions of psychological terms 63-64, 65-75, on mental application, discursive thought, and discrimination 77-81, and problem of psychic continuity 85-90, distinction between condition - as - object - of - consciousness and truly generative condition 48, 87, arguments against Vaibhāṣikas 86-90, 93-96, 102-116, 138-139, arguments against Ārya-Sāmmitīyas 90, 96-100, discussion of theory of Bhadanta Vasumitra on subtle consciousness 107-111, arguments against existence of past and future 102-105, arguments against idea of motion 96-100, arguments against a self 115-116, 156, reduction of action with retributional effect to volition 116-120, arguments against configuration 93-96, 129-133, arguments against unmanifest action 102-103, 118, arguments against Vaibhāṣika concept of "dravya" 124-125, critique of atomism 125, 167-170, critique of Vaiśeṣika composite whole 129-131, geometry 95, 129-134, investigation of combustion 97, 135-136, on causes of two contradictory results not being one 136, on homogeneous causes 136, on retribution of action 105-120, 139-140, 142, on directly antecedent conditions 143, ethical categories 146-149, his *Karma-siddhi-prakaraṇa* (*Discussion for the Demonstration of Action*) 93-120, arguments for store-consciousness in *Mahāyānasaṅgraha - bhāṣya* 150, on Buddhist Canon 1, 4, 115, 151-154, on Jain ethics 90, 118, 156, on perception-only 159, 161-167, 170-175, 183-189, on "illusion" 159-167, 209, 261-263, 266-268, 275-276, 279, 284-285, his *Viṃśatikā-kārikā* (*Twenty Verses*) 161-178, his *Triṃśikā-Kārikā* (*Thirty Verses*) 178-189, Śūnyavāda 194, 211-213, 216-222, 261-269, therapeutic techniques 194, 195-197, 198-209, three own-beings 188, 194-195, 231-240, 275, 289-297, his *Madhyānta-vibhāga-bhāṣya* (*Commentary on the Separation of the Middle from Extremes*) 211-273, on obstructions 222-231, on aggregates 64-75, 159, 280-281, on causes 225-227, on dependent origination 241, on various categories used in skill in means 232-245, on three times 243, on Truths 244, on Vehicles 244-245, on compounded and uncompounded 245, on techniques of meditation 246-250, 251-252, on limbs of enlightenment 249, on limbs of path 250-252, on stages of Path 252-256, on highest form of Mahāyāna practise 256-258, on pāramitās 258-259, on "extremes" and avoidance 261-269, on full realization 271, difference from technique of Nāgārjuna 193-195, 273-274, his *Mahāyānasūtrālaṅkāra-bhāṣya* (selection from) 285, his

GENERAL INDEX

aggregates constituting "personality", 52, 57-63, 65ff, 124, 240
canonicity of various Buddhist texts, 115, 155
dependent origination, 61, 241-242, 275
Emptiness, 3, 4(note 12), 18-19, 75, 82 (note 37), 87, 124, 184, 194, 196, 209, 211, 212, 214, 217-222, 262, 263, 264, 270, 275, 289-296
Four Noble Truths, 232, 244, 246
"insanity", outlooks towards, 15, 54-56, 63-64
invariable concomitance, defined: 32, 34, 35, 36, 40
meditation, 21, 22, 55, 56, 63, 76, 77, 194, 246-252
mental troubles, outlook towards, 15, 54-56, 63-64, 195-196
multiple realities, 15, 87, 123-124, 159-160, 161-167, 183-189, 231-246
Noble Eightfold Path, 250, 251
Path, Mahāyāna Buddhist, 194, 197-209, 222-231, 246-262, 269, 270-271, 285-6
perception-only, 159-175, 187, 189
revolution at the basis, defined, 3, 190 (note 14)
"seed", defined, 61, 140, 159, 188
stages of a Bodhisattva, 206-209, 229-230
store-consciousness (*ālaya-vijñāna*), 61-62, 71-72, 80, 89-90, 111-116, 183ff
theory of the two Vasubandhus, 2, 5, 6, 7, 10
three own-beings (*tri-svabhāva*), 87, 184, 188-189, 194-195, 213, 232-240, 289-297
Vasubandhu,
appraisal of Asaṅga's works, initial, 18
appraisal of Saṅghabhadra, 23
as an Abhidharmika, 2, 15-18, 185
as a logician, 31-48
as a Mahāyāna Abhidharmika, 58-127
as a Mahāyānist, 19-24, 157-297, esp. 193-297
at Kauśāmbī, 22
at Sialkot, 18, 22, 23
birth and birth-place, 11
converted to Mahāyāna, 18-19
date, 7-10, 24-26
death, 23
debate with Sāṅkhyas, 20-21
enters Buddhist order, 14
founds hospitals and schools, 21, 24
last journeys, 23
Jainas (relations to) 90, 117, 266
Mâdhyamikas (relations to), 2, 3, 124, 185, 193-196, 289
meditation and, 21, 22, 55, 56, 63, 76, 194, 246-252
Mīmāṁsakas (relations to), 34, 41-47
moves to Ayodhyā, 18
Nyāya-Vaiśeṣikas (relations to), 33, 37, 94, 116, 117, 128-130, 167-168, 171
parentage, 11
place in Buddhist lineages, 1
political and social activism and, 21-22
Prajñā-pāramitā-sūtras (relations to), 2, 19, 212
range of interests, 1
reactions of Vaibhāṣikas towards, 17, 87-89
relations with Candragupta II and family, 8, 21, 22
Sāmmitīyas (relations to), 90, 96-100
specifically Yogācāra ideas of, 157-190, 289-297
studies in Kashmir, 15-16
types of works written by, 1
writes *Kośa*, 17
writes *Twenty* and *Thirty Verses*, 22
Yogācāra, meaning of term, 3, 194

Corrections

p. 24, note 2. Le Manh That, "Đủa Vaò việc khao cú'u triêt Vasubandhu"

p. 463, line 11 from bottom.

अशुद्धिशुद्धिमनस्काराविपर्यासेन